T0367051

DUMBARTON OAKS
MEDIEVAL LIBRARY

Jan M. Ziolkowski, General Editor

LIVES AND MIRACLES

GREGORY OF TOURS

DOML 39

Lives and Miracles

Gregory of Tours

Edited and Translated by

GISELLE DE NIE

DUMBARTON OAKS
MEDIEVAL LIBRARY

HARVARD UNIVERSITY PRESS
CAMBRIDGE, MASSACHUSETTS
LONDON, ENGLAND
2015

Printed in the United States of America

Library of Congress Cataloging-in-Publication Data
Gregory, Bishop of Tours, Saint, 538–594.
[Works. Selections]
Lives and miracles / Gregory of Tours ; edited and translated by Giselle de Nie.
pages cm.—(Dumbarton Oaks medieval library ; 39)
Latin text on the versos, English translation on the rectos.
Includes bibliographical references and index.
ISBN 978-0-674-08845-0 (alk. paper)
1. Christian saints—France—Biography—Early works to 1800. 2. Fathers of the church—Early works to 1800. 3. Miracles—Early works to 1800. 4. Church history—Primitive and early church, ca. 30–600—Sources. I. Nie, Giselle de. II. Gregory, Bishop of Tours, Saint, 538–594. Liber vitae Patrum. III. Gregory, Bishop of Tours, Saint, 538–594. Liber vitae Patrum. English. IV. Title.
BX4659.F8G665 2015
270.2092′2—dc23
[B] 2015008336

Contents

Introduction

After the Frankish kings had conquered all of Roman Gaul, Georgius Florentius was born in what is now Clermont-Ferrand in 538/39 as the second son of a Gallo-Roman family of senatorial rank.[1] He lost his father before he was ten, was placed in the household of his father's brother Gallus, then bishop of the city (525–551), and was educated by his archdeacon Avitus, later bishop. Gregory completed his clerical training with his maternal great-uncle Bishop Nicetius of Lyon (552–573). In 573 Bishop Eufronius of Tours, his mother's cousin, died while King Chilperic (561–584) was threatening to incorporate the city into his subkingdom of Neustria. King Sigebert (561–575)—in whose subkingdom Austrasia Tours then lay—hurriedly had our author, who happened to be at his court, consecrated as bishop of that city as an ally in what would prove to be the ongoing fratricidal conflict of the royal brothers.

It may have been at that time that our author adopted the name Gregorius (Gregory), after his maternal great-grandfather, Bishop Gregory of Langres (506/7–539/40). During Gregory's twenty-one years in Tours, he functioned as one of the most important prelates of the Frankish kingdom. And although his city suffered sieges in nineteen of those years, he found time to write a history of the world up to and including his own time—the *Histories*—recording both current political events and manifestations of what he believed were divine interventions guiding them.[2] It is the only large-scale extant historical source for this period and not infrequently records Gregory's own role in the events.

As further evidence of what he believed was divine governance in his disorderly world, Gregory recorded many miracles and a number of saints' lives.[3] His seven books of miracles consist of one on the miracles of his original patron saint Julian of Brioude (near Clermont), four on the miracles of his city's patron saint Martin of Tours, one on those of the Gallic martyrs, and one on those of the Gallic confessors (those who suffered, but did not die for their faith). Besides that, he wrote one book containing a series of biographies of Gallic saints, in which he included those of the abovementioned episcopal relatives, as well as those of certain holy men living around Clermont or Tours. One conspicuous quality of his style makes his stories about saints and sinners lively reading even today: the insertion of direct discourse in events that he can have heard about only from others. Clearly his own inventions, they make the situations come alive. In addition to these literary works, he made a list of the liturgical offices to be performed at Tours and the times at which they were to be performed as determined according to the positions of the stars, as well as a commentary on the psalms, of which only the chapter titles survive; it indicates that he was well acquainted with the contemporary practice of allegorical exegesis.[4] He died in 593/94.

After having been neglected and disparaged for centuries by secular historians, Gregory's books of miracles began to excite academic interest in the twentieth century as documents of microhistory and sixth-century daily life, perhaps beginning with Dill's *Roman Society* in 1926; but this trend received its decisive impetus from Peter Brown's socio-historical studies in the seventies and eighties.[5] Today, with an increased interest in the spiritual *imaginaire* of Late Antiquity, scholars have welcomed the information Gregory's stories provide about the contemporary religious mentality and the then persisting oral culture.[6] To elucidate some of the unfamiliar associations and assumptions in his stories, a brief overview follows that presents some key elements of Gregory's worldview that will be encountered: first, the centrality of Christ's passion, death, and resurrection as the model for the true life, a life that rejected worldly life and that of the body; then, the understanding of biblical events, images, and persons as perennial "figures" or "types" of God's ongoing relations with mankind, especially as manifested in contemporary saints and their miracles; and finally, underlying all this, a sacramental view of the visible world. Subsequently, the content of each of the three texts will be briefly summarized, and in conclusion, some considerations about the rendering and translation of Gregory's text will be given.

The Rejection of the World and the Body as Imitation of Christ's Passion

Perhaps the strangest feature for modern readers is the rejection of the world and the body that permeates all the stories. In a seminal study, Peter Brown has set out the Platonist-influenced philosophical foundations implicit in the late-antique rejection of the body and its sexuality.[7] For

Plato and his followers, the only real reality was the unchangeable one of the spirit; material phenomena were constantly changing and uncertain. This heavily influenced the tradition of the New Testamental, especially Pauline, view that the true reality was God's invisible kingdom, in which one could fully participate only in the afterlife. Christ's passion was the model for the Christian martyrs, and as soon as the state-sponsored persecutions stopped after the year 306, those who still wished to pursue a heroic life in the spirit took to the Syrian and Anatolian highlands or the Egyptian desert to mortify their bodies there. Especially in Gregory's *Life of the Fathers (VP),* we see that his model for the holy life was greatly influenced by the asceticism of these so-called Desert Fathers. Their self-torture—especially the avoidance of sleep (based on a literal interpretation of Psalm 1:2 and the fear of a demonic invasion) and water (as a possible vehicle of demonic forces)—now strikes us as harsh. It was their way, however, of disciplining their spirits and even emptying their hearts and minds of all but the contemplation of God, so that they might eventually be found pure enough to merit admission to the heavenly kingdom. For the notion of spiritual "purity"—interpreted as total severance from the body and its needs and drives—had become an ecclesiastical concern.

In the later fourth century, the ascetic heroes of the desert were increasingly admired. In a world where church and state had become intertwined, the Roman Church decided that celibacy would be appropriate to distinguish those who served God in the world (and to prevent them from favoring their family's interests). This policy looked to the rules governing priestly abstention in the book of Leviticus—there always for limited periods of time, however. And so the notion of "pollution" entered the Church's thinking and was also applied to other activities deemed inappropriate to the sacred, such as working on the holy day of the Lord (Sunday), or not showing appropriate respect for the holy. Holy and evil power were experienced everywhere; they had to be constantly respected or guarded against by ritual gestures and practices, such as the sign of the cross and unceasing prayer. For admitting evil powers could result in crimes or the antics of possession. Violations of the sacred tended to be punished by what Gregory qualifies as divine "vengeance," another Old Testament notion, this one also resembling contemporary Germanic practices.

Thinking about the World and History through Images in the Bible

In the third century, the Alexandrian philosopher-exegete Origen had expanded the New Testament's pointing to Christ's fulfillment of Old Testament prophecies about the coming of a savior of the Jewish people into an exegetical method; it regarded all sayings and events in the Bible as images, or "figures," of invisible divine truths.[8] The deeper truth, then, was not what could be read in the text or be seen in its events, but what could be imagined: starting from the literal and the visible and regarding these "with the eyes of faith."[9] It was this approach that enabled Gregory to make sense too of the jumble of past and current events of his own time; he saw the rewards of the good and the punishments of the bad as all guided by a God who, as in the Old Testament, could from time to time be persuaded to grant a request by a particularly holy person.

Contemporary saints and their miracles—when designated as *virtutes,* here translated as "powerful deeds" or "deeds of power" (and in English translations of the Greek New Testament as "mighty works"[10])—are prominent in the *Histories* and the main subject of Gregory's hagiographical works. Although the cult of martyrs and saints first developed freely in the fourth century after the end of the persecutions,[11] Gregory understands them as carrying on the tradition of the Old Testament prophets and the New Testament apostles.[12] The "power" manifested is always that of God or Christ, present through the intercession or mediation of the saint, alive or already in heaven, through request, evocation in prayer, and/or direct or indirect physical contact with him or her, or with relics.

The basis for the expectation of miracles is Jesus's saying in the gospel that all that is asked for in faith will be given.[13] Along with the Bible, the first biography of a Western ascetic bishop, Sulpicius Severus's *Life of Saint Martin,* about Bishop Martin of Tours (373–397), set the pattern for Gregory's expectations about the holy. For Martin had shown how miracles could still be asked for and granted in present times. But whereas the saint is there said to have been, above all, forgiving about personal insults, we see in Paulinus of Périgueux's later *Life of Saint Martin,* a verse rendition of Sulpicius's stories composed sixty years after Martin's death, that disrespect for the dead saint's memory could then lead to merciless punishment.[14] Gregory's stories about Bishop Quintianus, however, show that in a living person, too, access to divine power could be used to punish those who disregarded what he considered to be his rightful prerogatives.[15] Gregory's evident grim satisfaction with these divine punishments—in contrast to the gospels' injunction to love one's enemies[16]—seems to show that the unarmed Church needed such sanctions to hold its own in an insufficiently ordered society, in which armed noblemen and public authorities often acted as they wished.

Gregory's stories about marvelous happenings, however, often associated with natural phenomena or animals, have been scrutinized for traces of magic.[17] Thus Valerie Flint recognizes a spring with originally magical associations in what Gregory, in his *Glory of the Martyrs (GM)* 23, presents as a divine miracle around a baptismal spring in Spain,[18] and regards many miracle stories as rescued magic, deemed necessary for survival in a hostile, spirit-filled environment. Modern studies have accordingly shown that, in practice, religion and "magic" (its very definition is controversial) cannot always be securely distinguished: religious practices too often include some kind of (indirect) manipulation.[19] Margarete Weidemann gives a list of pagan elements in Gregory's writings.[20] In addition to overtly pagan phenomena, such as temple worship, divination, and wizardry, these include lightly Christianized practices in the books translated here, such as the use of relics as amulets (almost everywhere), interpreting unusual natural phenomena as prodigies and signs (as in *VP* 6.6.3), and demons appearing as, or in, animals (*VP* 11.1.5, 16.3.6, 17.3.7).

František Graus distinguishes folktale motifs from magic and pagan elements.[21] His meticulous study of folk motifs in Merovingian hagiography shows, however, that in this period hagiography was a clerical phenomenon that, occasionally, purposely adapted folk stories or motifs—but also biblical and literary traditions, which could well be similar—to serve its own purposes.[22] In Gregory's miracle books, these could be natural phenomena acting in unusual and opportune ways, such as the healing spring in *The Miracles of the Martyr Julian (VJ)* 3 (there associated with the washing of the martyr's head), or an animal (a dove leading someone to rescue captured villagers in *VJ* 7, which he justifies by a similar incident in antique Christian historiography). The hermit Friardus's making a dry tree trunk come to life, blossom, and produce fruit (*VP* 10.3) would be recognized by the biblically educated as having a precedent in Aaron's rod in Numbers 17:8, although Gregory does not refer to it. As for spiritual phenomena, the noonday demon is mentioned in Psalms 90:6 [91:6], and the devil as a snake and a large serpent (*VP* 11.1) occurs in Genesis 3 and Revelation 12:3. Finding a treasure (as in *VP* 1.3) could be a folk motif, as could footprints in a stone (*The Miracles of Bishop Martin* [*VsM*] 4.31), as well as the light-giving weapons (*VsM* 1.14), and a water mill swallowed by the earth (*VP* 18.2).[23] But, Graus warns, a motif in Gregory's stories may have more than one source, and similarity does not necessarily mean derivation.[24] Furthermore, Gregory always attempts to name and date his events and frequently mentions witnesses and informants. However, when, as in the story of the guiding dove, a phrase like "they say," *ut aiunt* (*VJ* 7.2), or an equivalent occurs, it is likely that he is recording an anonymous oral tradition and, if it is of non-Christian origin, assimilating it to the context at hand. For he always keeps his biblical perspective firmly in mind.

A Sacramental View of Reality

All this points to one of the most important differences between our worldview and Gregory's. Ours is based on a scientific model originating in the eighteenth century that may or may not coexist uncomfortably with a very different religious outlook. Gregory's, however, did not strictly separate interior from "outside" realities, nor natural from "supernatural" powers. Although he did have a notion of the usual workings of nature, he believed that these had been instituted by God at Creation and continued to be permeated with spiritual powers, good and evil, everywhere.[25] As for "interior" and "exterior" reality, we see in his stories that thinking or saying the name of Christ or a saint was experienced as actually making him invisibly present; even written words about Christ or a saint made him present, for the word was regarded as spiritually connected to its referent. Similarly, when bad things are done by human beings, Gregory often implies or explicitly states that the real agent was an evil spiritual being; sometimes the human vessel actually carrying it out is not mentioned at all. And the same applies to physical and mental afflictions. What for us are invisible bacteria, viruses, and biochemical reactions that require physical antidotes, for him were invisible evil spiritual entities, sometimes also designated as "humors." To distinguish his personalized designations of these evil forces—for instance, as "the Enemy"—from possible human agents, they have been capitalized where necessary in the translation. Rather than by ordinary medical remedies, these entities could best be expelled by spiritual means, such as prayer for heavenly help and some kind of physical contact with what was regarded as the holy that would transmit its inherent healing power. Thus Gregory not infrequently refers to particles of a saint's remains or to objects that have (indirectly) been in touch with these, as *pignora*—literally, pledges, sureties, or tokens—of Christ's power channeled through him; these have been uniformly translated as "relics." In short,

Gregory had a sacramental view that merged spiritual and material phenomena: what he "saw with the eyes of faith" was for him the real truth. This meant that visions, apparitions, and dreams too were regarded as legitimate messages from the invisible realm.

Gregory's habit of understanding biblical and historical events as affective-spiritual realities, figures of spiritual truths that are not easily expressed in words, carried over into his approach and understanding of the world around him. Although he had to use words, the underlying interactive images that he was involuntarily and concurrently imagining could sometimes wordlessly connect the events he was describing. This was analogical and associative thinking, a wakeful kind of dreaming rather than syntactical and logical thinking. For him, his mental images are spiritual realities. Thus, for instance, he understood a holy man's dead body not to have decayed because, during his life, he had not been "corrupted" by lust. Other, unexpressed, associations are more difficult to discover, but they are there. They give his prose some of the qualities of poetry.[26]

The Life of the Fathers

Gregory's biographies of Gallic saints stand in the tradition of Rufinus's fourth-century *Historia monachorum,* which (there designated as *Vitae patrum*) Gregory says he gave to the hermit Leobard to allow him to learn how to order his life.[27] It consists of very short biographies and anecdotal descriptions of the ascetic lifestyle of those living in the desert. Gregory's other model, Sulpicius Severus's *Life of Saint Martin,* written around 400, is much longer and resembles classical Roman biography and historiography. It describes Martin as a new kind of ascetic, now not in the desert but in the world, caring for its needs with his miracles. Gregory differentiates himself from both when he begins his series of spiritual biographies by saying in his general prologue that what he wants to describe is not the individual lives as such but the kind of life that all saints share. Nevertheless, his anecdotal style and attention to concrete details of daily life resemble those in Rufinus's stories. Concurrently with our author, his namesake Pope Gregory I was composing his *Dialogues* about the lifestyle and miracles of contemporary Italian saints, wanting to show that, notwithstanding the many current disasters—wars, plundering, natural calamities, epidemics—God had not forgotten about contemporary men and women.[28] The stories were intended as a continuation of the Bible in the present time. Only the second book of Pope Gregory's work gives something like a biography; it recounts the miracles of the abbot Benedict of Nursia, whose monastic rule was to become dominant in the West.

All the persons described by our Gregory lived in the Frankish kingdom, some near his birth city of Clermont (chapters 2–6, 9, 11–14), in his mother's Burgundy (1, 7, 8, 18), or in and around his episcopal city Tours (9, 15–16, 19–20). He must have heard from friends or family about those who lived before his time (2–5, 7, 14); others he had known himself as members of his family (6, 8). Some he visited with his spiritual father Avitus (11), others he heard about from friends and colleagues (9, 10, 12, 13, 17, 18), and still others he encountered in his role of spiritual supervisor in Tours (15, 16, 19, 20).

His saints are often propertied—they founded monasteries presumably on their own lands—but there are also simple freeholders (a herder and a farmer: 9–10, 16, 20), a descendant of a foreign prisoner of war (15), a beggar (13), and a slave (5). Two come from afar: from North Africa and Persia (3, 4). And their lifestyles differ. Some believe in physical self-torture, others are more given to spiritual exercises. And his saints can be hermits, abbots, or bishops. Because of the many needy people, there are even hermits who often care for those around them, performing healing miracles. One imagines that Gregory let these stories be read to his clergy at mealtimes for their edification, and perhaps gave copies to some of his episcopal friends.

One might ask whether Gregory's singular *Life*—instead of the more usual *Lives*—perhaps points to a view that denies individuality to these saints as well as to everyone else. He specifies, however, that the "life" he is talking about is that of the body. But, like Rufinus, what he really wants to show is, as he says, the underlying unity of the various forms of the holy life of these saints—as hermit, abbot, and bishop—that, as evidenced by their miracles, all led to God. Central in all these forms was the choice of God as opposed to all that is worldly, material, and physical. Sometimes it included self-torture as penance for supposed sins, and often, but not always, solitude (so that angels could approach), but not without compassion, when necessary, for the needy. The aim of detachment and purification is fundamental; it consists of a complete emptying of the heart and mind through prayer, psalm singing, and meditation, so that God or Christ could live there as in a temple or tabernacle to direct every thought and act. The conscious aim, then, was not, as in our age, the realization of one's own perceived potentialities, but a sharing in the common life and joy of all the saints and angels in the worship of God that would be perfect only after death in heaven. All the constructive things the saints did in this world—administering bishoprics, founding monasteries, healing the sick, ransoming captives, building bridges over dangerous rivers—were still directed toward this one ultimate goal. Following Church tradition, Gregory understood the participation in this joy to be the true and ultimate goal and ultimate identity of each and every human being.

The Miracles of the Martyr Julian

As we saw, *virtutes* originally meant and could still mean "virtues," but Gregory tended to use the word in the sense of "mighty works" or deeds of power, the equivalent of our "miracles." Similarly, *sanctus* in this period usually meant "holy" in a general sense; hence, the substantive "saint" has been avoided where possible. Gregory uses *beatus* interchangeably with *sanctus;* the former has consistently been translated as "blessed."

The collection begins with a short account of Julian's martyrdom, perhaps based on an earlier source,[29] and then tells how Gregory became a client of the saint through his family. The stories that follow relate post mortem miracles effected by the saint's relics. The tradition of this kind of miracle was set for the West by Bishop Ambrose of Milan in 386, when he explained the sudden healing of a blind man who touched the cloth covering the body of a dead martyr as a renewal of the miracles in the apostolic period, when touching Paul's clothing had had the same effect.[30] After that, the first collection of stories about miracles at and around a shrine was written around 424 to 428 in Uzalis, a town about seventy miles from what is now Tunis, commissioned by its bishop Evodius, a friend of Augustine.[31] There is no evidence that Gregory was acquainted with this collection. Perhaps, however, he knew indirectly about its miracles through Book 22 of Augustine's *City of God*.[32] Although Gregory nowhere mentions Augustine, recent studies have found evidence that he was acquainted with at least some of his ideas.[33] The next surviving shrine-based collection in the West was that of the sixth book of Paulinus of Périgueux's *Life of Saint Martin,* which Gregory knew very well and paraphrases in *VsM* 1.

In addition to the touching of relics, Gregory emphasizes the existence of an unshakeable faith as the condition for a miracle to be granted. In a number of his stories, the effect of envisioning an image of a smiling, powerful saint imparting health resembles that of a life-enhancing symbol in modern visualization therapies, triggering the body's autonomous systems to conform to its vitalizing pattern.[34] That there was also a strong social component of reintegration into the community in Gregory's stories of healing miracles has been effectively demonstrated by Peter Brown and Raymond Van Dam;[35] the latter also traces the development of Saint Julian's cult in Gaul and Gregory's personal involvement in it.[36]

The Miracles of Bishop Martin

Van Dam likewise gives a compelling account, not only of the rise of the cult of Saint Martin in Gaul and of how the saint's image changed with the changing needs of his clients, but also of Gregory's personal relationship with Martin before and during his episcopate, by establishing a timeline for his stories about this saint.[37] For by combining evidence from Gregory's other works, especially the *Histories,* he can date a number of them; his findings, noted as such in the present translation, are here gratefully acknowledged. Gregory's first book of Martin's miracles mentions stories that had already been recorded by Sulpicius Severus and gives summaries of later stories of the dead saint's miracles collected by Bishop Perpetuus of Tours (458/59–490/91) and versified by Paulinus of Périgueux (mistakenly identified by Gregory as Paulinus of Nola), as well as of stories told by Gregory's friend, the poet and priest Venantius Fortunatus. The miracles in Books 2, 3, and 4 happened, as our author indicates, after his arrival in Tours. A few miracles, however, ended up in the *Glory of the Confessors.*[38]

The Prologues

The themes that Gregory emphasizes in the prologues to these works offer something close to his own assessment of what he especially wanted to tell his readers and listeners. In *The Life of the Fathers,* it was the saints' different ways of imitating what they understood to have been the life and passion of Christ as examples for Christian living, and in the miracle books, the need for everyone to access the Savior's unlimited compassion for human suffering through the saints' proven effective intercession. To take them in the order in which they appear: in *The Life of the Fathers,* pointing to the parable of the talents, he begins by mentioning the effective management of one's potential in the monastic life to "yield" the profit of eternal life (chapter 1). Next, he points to Jesus's and the Apostle Paul's words about self-mortification as the way to become one with the crucified Christ as "seeds of the eternal life," and claims that living according to these makes the saints already "glow [. . .] with the light of the resurrection" (2). Then he says that a solid faith, resulting in life as a "new man," will gladly accept exile, like the Patriarch Abraham (3). An injunction to avoid carnal concerns and to live the life of the spirit follows (4).

Then comes, first, the example of a humble person whom God lifts up because of his holy life (5), and, second, two nobles who reject the privileges of their class and devote their life to God alone in humility and self-mortification (6 and 7), thereby achieving a heavenly reward. That saints are not self-made men is made clear when Gregory mentions as a matter of course that the saints' holy lives were predestined by God (8). After a humble assessment of his own contribution as a writer of miracle stories to God's temple as "goats' hairs," but hoping that these stories may inspire their readers with the same zeal for the heavenly life as the saints (9), he returns to a related theme: the need to constantly seek God's help in everything and to attribute all one's holy actions to God (10).

Readers are told that heavenly discipline teaches wisdom, which, in turn, teaches one how to love God (12), and that serving God in contrition and unremitting meditation on the divine word while living a life of solitude and extreme poverty is the way to access the eternal joy and peace of Paradise (11, 12, and 13). The virtue of the generosity of forgiveness is then highlighted (14), as well as the ability to overcome an intrusion of pride or vanity about one's spiritual prowess (15). The reader is then again urged to look to the saints as teachers of the eternal life and to request divine help in imitating their actions (16). To prove the veracity of his stories about a saint he could not have known, Gregory next brings forward his friend Abbot Aredius of Limoges as a miracle worker, and therefore as a trustworthy narrator (17). Subsequently, the saints are again said to teach by example (18). But a woman too, although she belongs to what he calls "the weaker sex," can be such a model by following holy precepts and leaving her home and country behind (19.prol.). Immediately thereafter, however, she is said to learn heavenly wisdom through seeing Martin's miracles and learn how to access Paradise from "the priestly fount" (preaching)—perhaps because she could not read and meditate upon the divine word, as the male saints are said to have done.

The collection closes with another admonition to those who may have strayed from their singleness of purpose, or might stray in the future: how, with others' advice and sufficient effort, such errancy could be remedied (20). The stories show that these exceptional people went against their family, class, and other odds to pursue sometimes controversial ways of life. In accordance with his belief in predestination, Gregory describes their choices as inspired by God. Sometimes, however, seeing or hearing about miracles happening at a saint's tomb also plays a role in making the decision (16.1.2, 19.prol.4, 20.2.2). Perhaps through what I sense to be his belief—following that of the Apostle Paul in Thessalonians 2:13, that Christ as the divine Word inheres in all faithfully spoken words about divine things[39]—Gregory evidently hoped that his stories might play a role in this process of inspiration.

The prologue to Julian's miracles stresses the martyr's reliability in granting requests, as he will be heard by the Lord because of his holy life. Gregory asserts that seeing Martin's miracles strengthens faith because, continuing Christ's work long ago, they prove that such things actually happened (*VsM* prol.1). After humbly hoping that his stories may provide a more eloquent writer with rich material (prol.2), Gregory praises Christ as the true Physician and tells his readers exactly how heartfelt contrition and prayer to Martin as intercessor at his tomb, while also touching it, achieves spiritual as well as physical healing (prol.3). In the last prologue, he urges everyone to honor the saint of his choice, so as to receive advantages from him, notably including his (albeit indirect) remission of their sins (often referred to elsewhere), in the future life as well as the present one (prol.4). With this perhaps controversial statement by Gregory, later himself sainted, I happily let him have the last word about one of his deepest convictions.

Various translations of Gregory's writings are available. The French translation accompanying Bordier's editions of 1856, 1860, and 1862 was lightly revised by Pierre Sicard, volumes 3–5.[40] *The Life of the Fathers* was translated into English by Edward James;[41] it contains an extensive historical introduction, maps, family trees of Gregory and of the Merovingian kings, as well as a note on the manuscript tradition. The stories of the martyr Julian's miracles and those of Bishop Martin of Tours have been translated by Raymond Van Dam,[42] with a very helpful book-length introduction showing how they illustrate Gregory's experience in the Gaul of his times, as well as a note on the dates of Gregory's writings and on editions of his works.

The present edition and translation aim to combine a readable Latin text, with normalized spelling, with an English translation that stays as close as possible to the author's train of thought. For further historical information, the reader is directed to the above-mentioned translations with their comments, and to the literature in the bibliography. The use in my notes of some of Krusch's, James', and Van Dam's information on people, places, and events is gratefully acknowledged; their individual contributions have been acknowledged in situ. Where identifiable, place-names have been given in their modern equivalents.

The biblical references in all of Gregory's texts are to the Revised Standard Version. Gregory often seems to quote from memory, and his renderings not infrequently differ from the Vulgate, because he may have used other, older Latin versions. All the translations are my own.

The structure of Gregory's sentences and the composition of his narrative can be problematic. His writing has been described as similar to the paratactic style—"and then, and then"—of the Bible, which would match what he says about having been educated only in the Bible and ecclesiastical authors (*VP* 2.prol.). In addition, Sulpicius Severus's artful imitation of the "humble" style in his canonical early fifth-century stories about Saint Martin will have been influential. With the exception of Venantius Fortunatus's conventionally simple saints' lives, other literary sources of Gregory's time exhibit a rather baroquely ornate style. Gregory's prologues attempt a more elaborate style, with longer sentences than the stories, the latter being more "conversational." After repeated apologies for his unadorned "rustic" narrative style, such as those in the *VsM* and *VP* 2 prologues, Gregory eventually realized that it served his community better than a more intricate one. Thus he writes in *VsM* 2.19, "To us, versed as we are in church dogma, it seems that the stories that pertain to the church's edification should avoid wordiness and be woven into a brief and simple speech."[43]

But that is not all. Gregory's narrative sentences often fail to follow more general syntactic conventions: he creates run-on sentences, changes the verb tense or person, or even the subject, halfway through, and adduces ostensibly unrelated material without explanation. In the prologue to the *Glory of the Confessors,* Gregory recognized this, recording how he had been criticized for his insufficiently refined style, for not distinguishing between masculine, feminine, and neuter nouns, and for mixing up ablatives and accusatives. Gregory's response was that he was nonetheless providing material for the poets to work with. Because of this, there has been a long debate about his supposedly "muddled" thinking and how it reflects perhaps not only his lack of classical literary training but also the near-anarchy of his time.[44] Yet what he tells us, however, in the *Histories* about his deft diplomacy and handling of perilous situations in no way suggests a muddled or naive individual. One might thus wonder whether he sometimes dictated his sentences in a conversational manner to a stenographer. This could account for the fact that many of them resemble spoken language—and the stream of consciousness—with its pauses, ellipses, associations, additions, changes of direction, and afterthoughts. Gregory's alternations between "I" and "we" for himself, sometimes in the same sentence, could also be part of the oral situation (in the translation these changes have usually been reproduced). If the stenographer-notary simply noted down what he heard, and Gregory did not or could not edit the result thoroughly afterward, the result could have been the surviving text.

As I attempted to show in my *Views from a Many-Windowed Tower* (1987), there is an additional possibility, which does not exclude the above: that part of what appears to be disjointed discourse is determined by associative leaps in Gregory's thinking from one biblical image that he perceived as underlying events to another, a mental habit of assigning meaning, which he had acquired through the allegorical exegesis of biblical texts. In my translation of his lively descriptions of past events, his sometimes-changing verb tenses will usually be rendered as in the original (assuming that he used the present tense for vividness), but sentences will conform to modern syntactic conventions. At the same time, the translation attempts to preserve as much as possible the conversational tone and the dynamics of the images inherent in Gregory's vocabulary; these have also been preserved as far as possible. It is hoped that the first part of this Introduction, with its references to the relevant literature, as well as the Notes to the Translations will supply the information necessary to understand the most important unstated—and for many not immediately familiar—presuppositions that shaped his perception of his world, now almost 1,500 years ago.

It is a great pleasure, finally, to thank the editors Danuta Shanzer, Jan Ziolkowski, Roger Wright, and Michael Winterbottom, and their assistants Julian Yolles, Angela

Kinney, and Raquel Begleiter, for their unremitting, generous help and attentive care in answering questions and solving problems, great and small. Warm thanks too are due to the Netherlands-based Centre for Patristic Research for their generous technical support in the final phase of the preparation of these volumes.

Notes

1 Wood, *Gregory of Tours,* gives a concise summary of Gregory's life; the fullest account is that of Pietri, *Tours,* 246–334.

2 The most recent edition is that of Krusch and Levison.

3 Edited and translated by Bordier, *Les livres des miracles,* SHF 88, 103, and 114; and Krusch, MGH SSrM 1.2, 451–820.

4 Edited by Bordier, SHF 125 (1864), 8–27, and 114, 402–10, respectively, and Krusch, MGH SSrM 1.2, 854–72 and 873–77. Some scholars have credited him with the authorship of the *Miraculi sancti Andreae apostoli,* purporting to be the rendition of a Syrian's translation from a Syrian source (ed. M. Bonnet, Krusch, SSrM 1.2, 371–96), and the *Passio sanctorum martyrum septem dormientium apud Ephesum* (ed. Krusch, ibid. 397–403).

5 Especially his "Relics and Social Status" and *Cult of the Saints.* See on the reception of Gregory's writings, De Nie, *Views,* 1–22, and more specifically on that of his miracle books, Shanzer, "So Many Saints." An exhaustive catalog of all the information in Gregory's writings has been made in Weidemann, *Kulturgeschichte.*

6 De Nie, *Views,* and various articles in *Word, Image and Experience;* as interfaces with an oral culture: Giselle de Nie, "Text, Symbol and 'Oral Culture' in the Sixth-Century Church: The Miracle Story," *Mediävistik* 9 (1997): 115–33. Reprinted in De Nie, *Word, Image and Experience,* XVI.

7 Brown, *Body and Society.*

8 See Pépin, *La tradition de l'allégorie.*

9 As for instance Augustine, *Sermo* 274, *PL* 38: 1252D: "oculi fidei."

10 Matthew 7:22.

11 See on this Brown, *Cult.*

12 Heinzelmann, *Gregor von Tours,* shows how this view also permeated the *Histories.*

13 Mark 11:24.

14 Paulinus, *Vita M* 6 records a number of them.

15 *VP* 4.1–3.

16 Matthew 5:44.

17 Valerie I. J. Flint, *The Rise of Magic in Early Medieval Europe* (Oxford, 1991).

18 Flint, *Magic,* 268.

19 As in David E. Aune, "Magic in Early Christianity," in *Aufstieg und Niedergang der römischen Welt,* vol. 2.23.2, ed. Wolfgang Haase (Berlin, 1980), 1507–57.

20 *Kulturgeschichte,* 157–61; christianized elements, almost all from the *Historiae:* 159–61. On natural prodigies and nature in Gregory, see De Nie, *Views,* 27–69 and 71–132.

21 *Volk, Herrscher und Heiliger im Reich der Merowinger. Studien zur Hagiographie der Merowingerzeit* (Prague, 1965). On Gregory: 217–20. To my knowledge, there is no exhaustive study of folk and other motifs in Gregory's writings. For an exhaustive list of folk motifs in general, see Stith Thompson, *Motif-Index of Folk Literature.* Rev. ed., 6 vols. (Copenhagen, 1956).

22 Graus, *Volk,* 280.

23 Ibid., 226–27, 218, 256, 229, respectively.

24 Ibid., 214.

25 See on this view in Martin, Stancliffe, *St. Martin,* 215–27.

26 See on Gregory's affinity for and interest in poetry, Shanzer, "Gregory of Tours and Poetry."

27 *VP* 20.3.2. The "Vita[e] patrum" must be Tyrannius Rufinus, *Historia monachorum sive de vita sanctorum patrum* (ed. E. Schulz-Flügel, Berlin, 1990). Gregory's prologue, however, shows similarities to that of Palladius's *Historia lausiaca* (ed. A. Wellhausen, Berlin, 2003), which has briefer and more anecdotal vignettes.

28 Gregory the Great. *Dialogues,* ed. Adalbert de Vogüé, trans. Paul Antin. SC 260, 265 (Paris, 1978–1980).

29 *Vita patrum Iurensium,* ed. François Martine, in *Vie des pères du Jura.* SC 142 (Paris, 1968).

30 Ambrose, *Epistola* 77(22).9.

31 *Miraculi sancti Stephani.*

32 Augustine, *De civitate Dei.*

33 Heinzelmann, *Gregor von Tours,* about the ordering of history and society, and De Nie, "The Language in Miracle," about the working of the divine Word.

34 As in Achterberg, *Imagery.*

35 Brown, "Relics and Social Status"; and Van Dam, *Saints,* 82–115.

36 Van Dam, *Saints,* 41–49.

37 Van Dam, "Images," 13–28, and *Saints,* 50–81.

38 *GC* 5 and 6 (compare Van Dam, *Saints,* 199).

39 Explained in my "The Language in Miracle."

40 Paleo, 2003.

41 TTH 1, (1985) 1991.

42 Princeton, 1993.

43 "Nobis in ecclesiastico dogmate versantibus videtur ut historia quae ad aedificationem ecclesiae pertinet, postposita verbositate, brevi ac simplici sermone texatur."

44 De Nie, *Views,* 8–22.

THE LIFE OF THE FATHERS

Prologus

Statueram quidem illa tantum scribere, quae ad sepulcra beatissimorum martyrum confessorumque divinitus gesta sunt; sed quoniam quaedam de his nuper reperi quos beatae conversationis meritum evexit ad caelum, quorumque vitae tramitem certis relationibus cognitum ecclesiam aedificare putavi, dicere aliqua ex illis opportunitate cogente non differo; quia sanctorum vita non modo eorum pandit propositum, verum etiam auditorum animos incitat ad profectum.

2 Et quaeritur a quibusdam utrum "vitam" sanctorum, an "vitas" dicere debeamus. Agellius autem et complures alii philosophorum "vitas" dicere voluerunt. Nam Plinius auctor in tertio artis grammaticae libro ait: "Vitas antiqui cuiuscumque nostrum dixerunt; sed grammatici pluralem non putaverunt habere vitam." Unde manifestum est melius dici vitam patrum quam vitas; quia cum sit diversitas meritorum virtutumque, una tamen omnes vita corporis alit in mundo.

3 Et scripsi, fateor, in inferiore confessorum libro aliqua de quorumdam vita, quae in corpore operati sunt breviora: idcirco quia cum de Dei virtute ingentia censeantur, parva

Prologue

I had decided to write only about events that happened through divine intervention at the tombs of the most blessed martyrs and confessors. But because I recently found out certain facts about those who were raised up to heaven by the merit of their blessed way of life, and thought that their life's journeys, known through reliable testimonies, would edify the Church, I am compelled by this opportunity not to delay saying something about them. For the life of the saints not only reveals their aim, but also stimulates the hearts of listeners to attempt to improve their souls.

And someone might ask me whether we should speak of 2
the "life" or of the "lives" of the saints. Aulus Gellius and a number of other philosophers wished to speak of "lives." But Pliny, in the third book of his *The Art of Grammar,* says: "The ancients spoke of the 'lives' of each of us; but the grammarians did not think that the word 'life' has a plural." Therefore it is clearly better to speak of the "life" of the fathers rather than of their "lives," for although their merits and powerful deeds are diverse, in this world all are nourished by one and the same life of the body.

I admit that I wrote several brief accounts of what some 3
of them did while in their earthly bodies in my book about the confessors that follows, and therefore, although they are considered great things since they participate in God's power, they are nonetheless rendered smaller in my

4 tamen redduntur in scriptis. Prolixiora quoque in hoc, quod vita sanctorum vocitare voluimus libro, imperiti idiotaeque praesumimus propalare, orantes Dominum, ut dignetur dare verbum in ore nostro, qui ora mutorum ad usus pristinos saepius reseravit, ut auditoribus lectoribusque salutaria et sanctis patribus digna labia mea referant, et quae in sanctis praecipit scribi, reputet ea suis in laudibus declamari.

I

De Lupicino atque Romano abbatibus

Prologus

Series evangelicae admonet disciplinae, ut dominicae largitionis pecunia nummulariis fenerata, cum digno multiplicationis fructu dispensante Domino restauretur; nec altis de fossa foveis recondatur ad detrimentum, sed rationabili dispensatione porrecta, aeternae vitae crescat ad lucrum; ut incipiens retributionis Dominus quae commodavit inquirere, cum usuris receptis fenerationis suae duplici satisfactione talentis, dicat: "Euge, serve bone, quia super pauca

writings. In this present book which I wish to call *The Life of* 4
Holy Men, though inexperienced and uneducated, I intend to speak about these matters at greater length, and pray to the Lord who often opened the mouths of the dumb to their former use that he may deign to grant words to my mouth, so that my lips may speak words to listeners and readers that will be salutary and worthy of these fathers; and that he may regard what he orders to be written in honor of the saints as proclaimed in his praise.

I

About the holy abbots Romanus and Lupicinus

Prologue

The gospel's injunction, as handed down, admonishes us that the money which our Lord gave us should be loaned out at an interest to merchants so that, with the Lord's help, it may deservedly and fruitfully multiply, and not remain uselessly hidden in deep pits covered with earth, but distributed by reasonable management to make it grow and yield the profit of eternal life. Thus, when the Lord comes to ask for the return of what he has lent and receives the interest on his loan of the talents as a double yield, he may say: "Well done, good servant. Because you were faithful in

fuisti fidelis, super multa te constituam: intra in gaudium domini tui" [Matthew 25:21].

2 Praedestinatorum est enim ista cum Dei ope perficere, qui ab ipsis cunabulorum vagitibus, ut saepe de multis legitur, Dominum scire meruerunt, cognitoque eo, numquam ab eius praeceptionibus recesserunt, neque post baptismi sacramentum niveam illam pollentemque regenerationis stolam impudicis actibus polluerunt.

3 Qui merito sequuntur Agnum quocumque ierit, quos ipsius agni candor egregius liliis decoris nullo temptationis aestu marcentibus coronavit. His denique sertis, dextera inclytae dominationis extenta, inchoantes provocat, vincentes adiuvat, victores adornat, quos nominis sui titulo praesignatos de terrenis gemitibus elevans, in caelorum evehit gaudia gloriosos.

4 De quorum niveo electionis numero et illos esse non ambigo, qui Iurensis eremi opaca lustrantes, non modo se Dei templum efficere meruerunt, verum etiam in multis mentibus Spiritus sancti gratiae tabernacula paraverunt: id est Lupicinus Romanusque, germanus eius.

1. Igitur Lupicinus ab exordio aetatis suae Deum toto requirens corde, litteris institutus, cum ad legitimam transiisset aetatem, genitore cogente, cum animi non praeberet consensum, sponsali vinculo nectitur. Romanus vero adhuc adolescentior, et ipse ad Dei opus animum extendere

a few things, I shall give you power over many. Enter into the joy of your Lord."

We read concerning many that it is the predestined who 2
achieve this with God's help. They are the ones who from their first cries in the cradle deserved to know the Lord and, knowing him, never deviated from his precepts nor polluted their snowy-white-gleaming, powerful robes of regeneration after their baptism with shameful acts.

They were worthy to follow the Lamb wherever he might 3
go, and were crowned by the Lamb's whiteness, more brilliant than that of beautiful lilies unmarred by the heat of any temptation. In the end, they are garlanded by the right hand of the Sublime Power that encourages beginners, aids those who are winning, crowns the victorious, lifts up from this world of sighs the ones who are marked in advance with his name, and carries these glorious ones with joy into the heavens.

I do not doubt that to that snow-white number of the 4
elect also belong those who illuminated the dark wilderness of the Jura mountains; not only did each merit to make himself into a temple of God, but they also built a tabernacle for the grace of the Holy Spirit in many hearts: I speak of Lupicinus and his brother Romanus.

1. From the beginning of his life Lupicinus sought God with his whole heart; after he had been educated in letters and reached the age of legal majority, his father forced him, even though he was unwilling, to be bound by the shackles of marriage. As for Romanus, since he was the younger one and also wished to devote his soul to the service of God, he

2 cupiens, nuptias refutavit. Parentibus vero relinquentibus saeculum, hi communi consensu eremum petunt, et accedentes simul inter illa Iurensis deserti secreta, quae inter Burgundiam Alemanniamque sita, Aventicae adiacent civitati, tabernacula figunt; prostratique solo Dominum diebus singulis cum psallentii modulamine deprecantur, victum de radicibus quaerentes herbarum.

3 Sed quoniam livor illius qui de caelo delapsus est semper insidias humano generi consuevit intendere, contra hos Dei servos armatur, hosque per ministros suos a coepto itinere nititur revocare. Nam lapidibus urgere eos daemones per dies singulos non desinebant, et quotiescumque genua ad orandum Dominum deflexissent, statim imber lapidum super eosdem iacentibus daemoniis deruebat, ita ut saepe vulnerati immensis dolorum cruciatibus torquerentur.

4 Interea aetas adhuc immatura coepit iniurias quotidiani hostis metuere, nec passa diutius sufferre dolores, relinquens eremum, ad propria redire deliberat. Sed quid invidia
5 non cogat Inimici? Verum ubi, relinquentes hoc habitaculum quod expetierant, ad villas manentium sunt regressi, domum cuiusdam pauperis ingrediuntur. Percunctatur autem mulier de quo itinere milites Christi venirent. Respondent non sine confusione se reliquisse eremum, et quae eos causa a coepto distulerit opere, per ordinem pandunt.

6 At illa ait: "Oportuerat vos, o viri Dei, contra insidias diaboli viriliter dimicare, nec formidare eius inimicitias, qui

refused marriage. When their parents had left this world, 2
they sought the desert with a common purpose, entered the
depths of the wilderness of the Jura that lies between Bur-
gundia and Alemannia, and made their dwellings in a region
adjoining the territory of the city of Avenches; prostrated
upon the ground, they prayed to the Lord every day with
psalm-melodies, and sought their nourishment from the
roots of plants.

But because the Envious one who fell from the sky has 3
always been accustomed to lay snares for the human race, he
moved to attack these servants of God and, through his assistants, attempted to turn them back from the journey they
had begun. For every single day, demons did not cease harassing them with stones; every time they bent their knees
to pray to the Lord a shower of stones thrown by the demons at once fell upon them, so that they were often
wounded and endured excruciating torments.

Because they were still young, they began to fear the daily 4
attacks of the Enemy; unable to suffer these torments any
longer, they decided to abandon their solitary way of life and
return home. What can the Enemy's envy not make us do?
When they had left the dwelling that they had sought and 5
gone back to the houses of those who had stayed behind,
they entered the home of a poor woman. She asked these
soldiers of Christ from what journey they were returning.
They replied, not without embarrassment, that they had
left their solitary way of life, and told her the story of what
had caused them to give up their undertaking.

And she said: "You men of God ought to have fought 6
manfully against the devil's tricks, and not been afraid of his

saepius ab amicis Dei superatus occubuit. Aemulus est enim sanctitati, dum metuit ne unde ille perfidiabilis corruit ge-
7 nus humanum fide nobilitatum ascendat." At illi compuncti corde, et seorsum discreti a muliere, dixerunt: "Vae nobis, quia peccavimus in Deum dimittendo propositum nostrum. Ecce nunc a muliere arguimur pro ignavia! Et qualis nobis in posterum erit vita, si ea, unde aestu Inimici expulsi fuimus, non repetamus?"

2. Tunc armati vexillo crucis, sumptis in manu bacillis, regressi sunt ad eremum. Quibus venientibus, iterum eos insidiae daemonis lapidibus coeperunt urgere; sed persistentes in oratione, obtinuerunt a Domini misericordia ut, remota temptatione, liberi ad illum divini cultus famulatum expeditique perseverarent.

2 His denique in oratione vacantibus, coeperunt ad eos turbae fratrum hinc et inde confluere et audire verbum praedicationis ab eis. Cumque iam beati eremitae populis, ut diximus, publicati fuissent, fecerunt sibi monasterium, quod Condatiscone vocitari voluerunt, in quo, succisis silvis et in plana redactis, de laboribus manuum propriarum victum quaerebant.

3 Tantusque fervor de Dei amore proximos locorum ascenderat, ut congregata ad officium Dei multitudo simul habitare non posset, feceruntque iterum aliud monasterium, in quo felicis alvearis examen instituerunt. Sed et his deinceps cum Dei adiutorio ampliatis, tertium intra Alemanniae ter-
4 minum monasterium locaverunt. Ibantque vicissim hi duo

hostilities, for he has often been overcome by the friends of God. He is envious of sanctity for he fears that the human race, which his perfidy caused to fall, will rise again ennobled through its faith." Struck by the pangs of conscience, 7
they pulled away from the woman and said: "Woe to us, for we sinned against God in abandoning our way of life. Look, now we are being accused of weakness by a woman! And what will be our life from now on if we do not return to the places from which we were expelled by the rage of the Enemy?"

2. Then they picked up their sticks and, armed with the banner of the cross, returned to the wilderness. Upon their arrival, the demons' treachery again began harassing them with stones; but they persisted in prayer and obtained from the compassionate Lord that the attack be diverted, so that they might freely and without impediment persevere in their service of divine worship.

When they had now devoted themselves entirely to 2
prayer, crowds of brothers began to come from all directions to listen to their preaching. And when the blessed hermits, as we said, became known to the people around them, they built themselves a monastery which they called Condat; after the forest had been cleared and made into a level field, they procured food there by the labor of their hands.

And because the fervor of their love of God was so great 3
among those living near them, the multitude assembled for the worship of God could not live together in the same place, and they built another monastery in which they placed a swarm from the blessed hive. After they had with God's help expanded still more, they established a third monastery in the territory of Alemannia. And these two 4

patres, requirentes filios, quos divinis imbuerant disciplinis, praedicantes in singulis monasteriis ea quae ad institutionem animae pertinebant. Lupicinus tamen abbatis super eos obtinuit monarchiam.

5 Erat autem valde sobrius et a cibo potuque abstinens, ita
ut plerumque tertia die reficeretur. Cum autem eum, sicut
corporis humani deposcit necessitas, sitis arriperet, vas cum
aqua exhiberi faciebat, in qua manus immersas diutius retinebat. Mirum dictu, ita absorbebat caro eius aquam appo-
sitam ut putares eam per os eius assumi, et sic ardor sitis
6 exstinguebatur. Erat enim severus valde in districtione fratrum, nec quemquam non modo perverse agere, verum
etiam nec loqui sinebat; mulierum quoque vel colloquia, vel
occursus, valde vitabat. Romanus ita erat simplex, ut nihil
de his penitus ad animum duceret sed omnibus, tam viris
quam mulieribus, aequaliter flagitatam benedictionem Divinitatis nomine invocato tribueret.

3. Lupicinus igitur Abba cum minus haberet unde tantam sustineret congregationem, revelavit ei Deus locum in eremo in quo antiquitus thesauri reconditi fuerant. Ad quem locum accedens solus, aurum argentumque, quantum levare poterat, monasterio inferebat, et exinde, coempto cibo, reficiebat fratrum multitudines quos ad Dei officium congregaverat. Sicque faciebat per singulos annos. Nulli tamen fratrum patefecit locum quod ei Dominus dignatus est revelare.

2 Factum est autem ut quodam tempore visitaret fratres quos in illis Alemanniae regionibus diximus congregatos.

fathers went in turn to see the spiritual sons whom they had imbued with divine teachings, preaching in each monastery about the instruction of souls. Lupicinus, however, obtained the exclusive power of abbot over them.

He was extremely sober and abstemious with regard to 5
food and drink so that he often took food only every third
day. When, in accordance with the need of the human body,
thirst overcame him, he had a jar with water brought and
immersed his hands in it for a long time. Amazingly, his flesh
absorbed the water around it so that one would think it was
being taken in by his mouth, and in this way his parching
thirst was extinguished. He was very severe, too, in disci- 6
plining the brothers, not permitting anyone either to act
wickedly or even to speak in such a way; and he carefully
avoided not only speaking with women but even meeting
them. Romanus was so simple a soul that none of these
temptations reached his soul but, after invoking the divine
name, gave equally to all men and women the blessing they
asked for.

3. When Abbot Lupicinus did not have enough resources to sustain such a large community, God revealed to him a place in the wilderness in which a treasure had been buried in ancient times. He went to this place by himself and brought to the monastery as much gold and silver as he could carry; buying food with this, he fed the many brothers he had gathered for the worship of God. And he did this every year. However, he did not reveal the place that the Lord had deigned to show him to any of the brothers.

It happened one day that he was visiting the brothers 2
whom, we said, he had gathered in the region of Alemannia.

Et accedens meridie, cum adhuc fratres in agro essent, ingressus est domum in qua cibi coquebantur ad reficiendum.
Viditque diversorum ferculorum apparatum magnum, pis-
ciumque multitudine aggregatam, dixitque in corde suo:
"Non est dignum ut monachi, quorum vita solitaria est, tam
3 ineptis utantur sumptibus." Et statim iussit praeparari aeneum magnum. Cumque locatus super ignem fervere coepisset, posuit in eo cunctos simul quos paraverant cibos,
tam pisces quam olera sive legumina, vel quidquid ad come-
dendum monachis destinatum fuerat, dixitque: "De his pul-
tibus nunc reficiantur fratres. Nam non deliciis vacent, quae
eos a divino impediant opere."

4 Quod illi cognoscentes, valde moleste tulerunt. Tunc
duodecim viri, habito consilio, iracundia inflammati, reliquerunt locum et abierunt per deserta vagantes, et ea quae
erant saeculi delectabilia inquirentes. Revelatumque est statim per visum Romano, nec ei voluit divina miseratio rem
actam occultare. Regresso quoque abbate ad monasterium,
dicit: "Si sic futurum erat, ut ad dispersionem fratrum
5 abires, utinam nec accessisses ad eos." Cui ille: "Noli," inquit, "moleste ferre, frater dilectissime, quae acta sunt. Nam
scias purgatam esse aream Domini, et triticum tantum reconditum in horreo, paleas autem eiectas esse foras." Et ille:
"Utinam nullus abscessisset ex his! Sed nunc indica, quaeso,
mihi quanti exinde abierunt." Qui respondit: "Duodecim
viri cothurnosi atque elati, in quibus Deus non habitat."

Arriving at noon, while the brothers were still in the field,
he entered the building in which the food was being cooked
for the meal. When he saw a large array of different dishes
as well as a large number of fish he said in his heart: "It is not
right that monks, who lead the solitary life, should enjoy
such unsuitable extravagances." And he immediately or- 3
dered a large cauldron to be brought. When it had begun to
heat up on the fire, he put in it all the dishes that had been
prepared, fish as well as vegetables and beans, with whatever
had been prepared for the monks to eat, saying: "Let the
monks now be nourished by this stew. For they should not
abandon themselves to the sort of delicacies that might distract them from divine worship."

When the monks found out about this, they were ex- 4
tremely angry. And twelve men, having taken counsel with
each other, left the place in a flaming rage to wander about
in the wilderness, seeking the pleasures of the world. This
was at once revealed to Romanus in a vision, for the compassionate Lord did not want to hide from him what had happened. When the abbot returned to the monastery at Condat, he said to him: "If this is to happen in the future, that
you go to the brothers to disperse them, I would rather that
you had not gone to them!" And the abbot said to him: 5
"Dearest brother, don't be vexed about what has happened.
For know that the threshing floor of the Lord has been
purged, and only wheat has been stored in the granary, the
chaff has been thrown away." And Romanus answered: "I
wish none of these men had left! But now tell me, I beg you,
how many have gone away from there." Lupicinus replied:
"Twelve proud and arrogant men, in whom God does not

6 Tunc Romanus cum lacrimis ait: "Credo in illo divinae miserationis respectu, quia nec illos separabit a thesauro suo, sed congregabit eos et lucri eos faciet, pro quibus pati dignatus est." Et facta pro his oratione, obtinuit ut reverterentur ad gratiam omnipotentis Dei.

7 Dominus autem compungi fecit corda eorum. Et agentes paenitentiam pro excessu suo, congregaverunt singuli congregationes suas, et fecerunt sibi monasteria, quae usque hodie in Dei laudibus perseverant. Romanus autem persistebat in simplicitate et operibus bonis, visitans infirmos et salvans eos oratione sua.

4. Factum est autem quodam tempore, dum iter ageret ad visitandos fratres, ut, occupante crepusculo, ad hospitiolum diverteret leprosorum. Erant autem novem viri. Susceptusque ab eis, statim plenus caritate Dei iussit aquam calidam fieri atque omnium pedes manu propria lavit; lectulumque spatiosum fieri praecepit, ut omnes in uno stratu requiescerent, non abhorrens luridae maculam leprae.

2 Quod cum factum fuisset, obdormientibus leprosis, hic inter decantationes psalmorum vigilans, extendit manum suam et tetigit latus infirmi unius, statimque mundatus est. Tactuque salubri interim tangens alium, et ipse protinus est mundatus. Cumque se sensissent redditos sanitati, tetigit unusquisque proximum suum, ut scilicet expergefacti ro-
3 garent sanctum pro emundatione sua. Sed cum tacti ab invicem fuissent, et ipsi mundati sunt. Mane autem facto aspiciens omnes nitente cute effulgere, gratias agens Deo,

dwell." Then Romanus said, with tears: "I believe when I 6
consider God's compassionate attitude that he will not separate these men from his treasure, but will gather them up
and win back those for whom he deigned to suffer." And
by praying for them he obtained that they returned to the
grace of almighty God.

For the Lord pierced their hearts with remorse. Doing 7
penance for their departure, they gathered their own communities and founded monasteries that up to today persevere in God's praises. Romanus himself persisted in his simplicity and good works, visiting the sick and healing them
with his prayers.

4. It happened once that when he was on his way to visit the brothers that, as dusk was falling, he turned aside to stay at a hut of lepers. There were nine men. When he had been received by them he at once, full of the love of God, ordered water to be heated and washed everyone's feet with his own hands; and, not being afraid of the blemish of pale leprosy, he commanded a spacious bed to be made so that all should sleep in it together.

When this had been done and the lepers slept he stayed 2
awake, and while singing psalms, he stretched out his hand
and touched the side of one of the sick men, who was instantly cleansed. When he touched another with his healing touch, that man too was at once cleansed. When
these felt themselves to have been made healthy, each
touched his neighbor, so that when awake they all might
ask the saint to cleanse them. But when they had all been 3
touched by one another they were already cleansed.
When morning came, the blessed Romanus saw all of
them shine with a glowing skin and gave thanks to God.

et vale dicens ac singulorum oscula libans, abscessit, mandans eis ut semper ea quae Dei erant et retinerent pectore et operibus exercerent.

5. Lupicinus autem iam senex factus accessit ad Chilpericum regem, qui tunc Burgundiae praeerat; audierat enim eum habitare apud urbem Ianubam. Cuius cum ingressus est portam, tremuit cathedra regis, qui ea hora ad convivium residebat. Exterritusque ait suis: "Terrae motus factus est!"
2 Responderunt qui aderant nihil se sensisse commotionis. Et
ille: "Occurrite quantocius ad portam, ne forte aliquis adver-
sari cupiens regno nostro adsit, quasi nociturus nobis! Non
3 enim sine causa haec sella contremuit." Qui protinus concurrentes, offenderunt senem in veste pellicia, et dixerunt
regi de eo, qui ait: "Ite, adducite eum in conspectu meo, ut
intelligam cuius ordinis homo sit." Et statim adductus, stetit
coram rege sicut quondam Iacob coram Pharaone. Cui ille
ait: "Quis es, vel unde venis? Aut quod est opus tuum? Vel
quid necessitatis eges ut venias ad nos? Edicito."

4 Cui ille: "Pater sum," inquit, "dominicarum ovium, quas
cum Dominus spiritalibus cibis iugi administratione refi-
ciat, corporalia eis interdum alimenta deficiunt. Ideo petimus potentiam vestram ut ad victus vestitusque necessaria
aliquid tribuatis." Rex vero haec audiens ait: "Accipite agros
vineasque, de quibus possitis vivere ac necessitates vestras
5 explere." Qui respondit: "Agros et vineas non accipiemus,
sed si placet potestati vestrae, aliquid de fructibus delegate;
quia non decet monachos facultatibus mundanis extolli, sed
in humilitate cordis Dei regnum iustitiamque eius exqui-
rere."

Bidding farewell to each with a kiss, he departed, instructing them always to remember God's injunctions in their hearts and to carry them out in their deeds.

5. When Lupicinus had already become an old man he
went to see King Chilperic, who then ruled Burgundy and
who, he had heard, was living in the city of Geneva. As he
entered the gate, the seat of the king, who at that hour was
sitting at a meal, trembled. Terrified, the king said to his
companions: "There was an earthquake!" Those present re- 2
plied that they had not felt any movement. And he said:
"Run as fast as you can to the gate, in case there is someone
who is hostile to our kingdom and wishes to harm us. For
this seat did not tremble without cause." Rushing there at 3
once, they ran into an old man clothed in animal skins, and
reported back to the king about him; and he said: "Go, bring
him into my sight, that I may know what kind of man he is."
Led there at once, he stood before the king as Jacob had
once stood before the Pharaoh. The king asked: "Who are
you and where do you come from? And what is your business? Why do you need to come to us? Speak!"

Lupicinus said to him: "I am the father of the Lord's 4
sheep whom the Lord continuously refreshes by giving
them spiritual food, but who lack bodily nourishment.
Therefore we implore Your Majesty to grant us some of the
food and clothing we need." Hearing this, the king said: "Accept, then, fields and vineyards from which you will be able
to live and meet your needs." Lupicinus answered: "We will 5
not accept fields and vineyards, but, if it pleases Your Majesty, send us some of their produce; for it is not fitting for
monks to be exalted by worldly resources; they should seek
the kingdom of God and his justice with humble heart."

6 At rex, cum audisset haec verba, dedit eis praeceptionem ut annis singulis trecentos modios tritici eiusdemque mensurae numero vinum accipiant, et centum aureos ad comparanda fratrum indumenta. Quod usque nunc a fisci ditionibus capere referuntur.

6. Post haec autem, cum senes perfectaeque essent aetatis, Lupicinus abbas scilicet et Romanus frater eius, ait Lupicinus germano suo: "Dic," inquit, "mihi, in quali monasterio
2 vis tibi parari sepulcrum, ut simul quiescamus?" Qui ait: "Non potest fieri ut ego in monasterio sepulcrum habeam, a quo mulierum accessus arcetur. Nosti enim quod mihi indigno et non merenti Dominus Deus meus gratiam tribuit curationum, multique per impositionem manus meae ac virtutem crucis dominicae a diversis languoribus sunt erepti. Erit autem concursus ad tumulum meum, si ab hac luce migravero. Ideoque rogo, ut eminus a monasterio requiescam."

3 Pro hac vero causa, cum obiisset in decem milibus a monasterio in monte parvulo sepultus est. Super cuius deinceps sepulcrum magnum templum aedificatum est, in quod ingens frequentia populi diebus singulis accurrit. Multae enim virtutes ibi in Dei nomine nunc ostenduntur, nam et caeci ibi lumen et surdi auditum, et paralytici gressum plerumque recipiunt.

4 Lupicinus autem Abbas obiens, intra monasterii basilicam est sepultus. Reliquitque Domino pecuniae creditae multiplicata talenta, id est beatas monachorum congregationes in eius laude devotas.

When the king heard these words, he ordered them to be 6
granted three hundred pecks of wheat and the same measure of wine each year, as well as a hundred gold coins to buy the brothers' clothing. They are said still to receive this annually from the administration of the royal domains, even up to present times.

6. After this, when they were old and had reached the end of their years, I mean Lupicinus and his brother Romanus, Lupicinus said to his brother: "Tell me," he said, "in which monastery do you want to prepare a tomb, so that we may
rest together?" Romanus replied: "It is not possible for me 2
to have my tomb in the monastery, because it does not allow women to enter. As you know, the Lord God has granted me, unworthy and undeserving, the grace of healing, and many have been rescued from various illnesses by the laying on of my hands and the power of the holy cross. There will be a crowd at my tomb when I have departed from the light of this life. Therefore I ask that I may rest at a distance from the monastery."

For this reason, when he died he was buried on a small 3
hill ten miles from the monastery. After that a great church was built over it to which large crowds of people came every day. Many acts of power are now manifested there in God's name, for often the blind receive light, the deaf their hearing, and paralytics their ability to walk.

When Abbot Lupicinus died, he was buried in the basil- 4
ica of the monastery. He left the Lord a multiplication of the talents lent to him: that is, communities of blessed monks devoted to his praise.

2

De sancto Illidio episcopo

Prologus

Inter reliqua vitae perpetuae semina quae caelestis Sator ex illo divinitatis fonte mentis incultae arvum vel irrigavit institutione, vel dogmate fecundavit, ait: "Omnis qui non accipit crucem suam et sequitur me, non est me dignus"
2 [Matthew 10:38]. Et alibi: "Nisi granum frumenti cadens in terram mortuum fuerit, ipsum solum manet; si autem mortuum fuerit, multum fructum affert. Qui amat animam suam in hoc mundo, perdet eam; et qui odit animam suam in hoc mundo, in vitam aeternam custodit eam" [John 12:24–25]. Sed et ille nihilominus "vas electionis" [Acts 9:15] beatus Paulus apostolus dicit: "Semper mortificationem Christi in corpore vestro circumferentes, ut et vita Iesu manifestetur in corpore vestro mortali" [2 Corinthians 4:10].

3 Ergo confessores Christi, quos tempus persecutionis ad martyrium non lacessivit, ipsi sibi persecutores effecti, modo ut digni Deo haberentur, diversas abstinentiae cruces adhibuerunt. Et ut, mortificatis membris, soli illi viverent de quo idem apostolus dixit: "Iam non vivo ego, vivit autem
4 in me Christus" [Galatians 2:20]. Aspiciebant enim per illos mentis internae oculos Dominum caelorum descendisse ad terras, non abiectum ad humilitatem, sed humiliatum misericorditer ad mundi redemptionem; aspiciebant pendentem

2

About the holy bishop Illidius

Prologue

Among the seeds of eternal life which the heavenly
Sower has sowed in the field of barren minds, watered from
the fount of his divinity with his precepts, and made fertile
with his teaching, he said: "He who does not take up his
cross and follow me is not worthy of me." And elsewhere: 2
"Unless a grain of wheat falls upon the earth and dies, it
remains alone; but if it dies, it bears much fruit. Whoever
loves his soul in this world shall lose it, and whoever hates
his soul in this world, will keep it in eternal life." And that
"chosen vessel," the blessed apostle Paul, speaks of "always
carrying Christ's dying in your body so that Jesus's life may
also be manifested in your mortal body."

Therefore the confessors of Christ who had not been 3
driven to martyrdom by the time of persecution became
their own persecutors, afflicting themselves with the crosses
of various abstinences so as to become worthy of God. And
they mortified their bodies so that they might live according to the Him of whom the apostle said: "It is no longer I
who live, but Christ who lives in me." For with the eyes of 4
their inner mind they kept seeing the Lord of the heavens
descending to the earth, not abased in humility but compassionately humbled for the redemption of the world; they

in patibulo, non Dei gloriam, sed assumpti corporis hostiam
mundam, de qua Ioannes paulo ante praedixerat: "Ecce
Agnus Dei, ecce qui tollit peccata huius mundi" [John 1:29].

5 Habebant in se et clavorum affixionem, cum a timore
eius confixi atque a iudiciis divinis exterriti, nihil indignum
eius omnipotentiae in corporis sui habitatione gerebant
iuxta illud quod psalmo centesimo decimo octavo scriptum
est: "Confige timore tuo carnes meas; a iudiciis enim tuis ti-
6 mui" [Psalms 119:120]. Fulgebat in his et illud resurrectionis
lumen insigne quo angelus refulsit, dum revolvit lapidem
monumenti de quo Marci decimo sexto: "Et introeuntes in
monumentum, viderunt iuvenem sedentem in dextris, coopertum stola candida, et obstupuerunt" [Mark 16:5]. Quo
et Iesus splenduit sub illa ostiorum obseratorum inclusione,
cum improvisus in medio apostolici senatus astitit comitatu, quo idem Dominus eosdem verbis vitae imbuens cae-
lesti est evectus in arce.

7 Inter quos et beatus confessor Illidius ita haec omnia in
cordis sui tabernaculo collocavit, ut et ipse quoque templum
sancti Spiritus effici mereretur. De cuius vita aliqua scripturus, veniam peto a legentibus. Non enim me artis grammaticae studium imbuit, neque auctorum saecularium polita lec-
tio erudivit, sed tantum beati patris Aviti Arverni pontificis
8 studium ad ecclesiastica sollicitavit scripta. Si mihi non ad
iudicium contingerent quae ipso praedicante audivi, vel cogente relegi, quia ea nequeo observare; qui me post Davidici

saw hanging on the cross, not the glory of God but the pure
offering of the body he had taken on, about which John the
Baptist had prophesied a little earlier: "Behold the Lamb of
God, behold the one who takes away the sins of this world!"

Pierced by fear of him and terrified by the divine judg- 5
ments, they also had driven into them the nails of the Crucifixion when they tolerated nothing unworthy of his omnipotence in the dwelling of their bodies, according to what is
written in the hundred-eighteenth psalm: "Transfix my flesh
with fear of you, for I fear your judgments." And in them 6
glowed the precious light of the resurrection with which the
angel shone when he removed the stone from the tomb, as
Mark's sixteenth chapter says: "And entering the tomb, they
saw a young man sitting on the right side, dressed in a white
robe, and they were amazed." With this light Jesus too
blazed as he entered unexpectedly through closed doors
into the gathering of the apostles, and again when, having
imbued them with life-giving words, this same Lord was
taken up into heaven.

Among these holy men was also the blessed confes- 7
sor Illidius, who cherished all these sayings so securely
in the tabernacle of his heart that he too deserved to be
made into a temple of the Holy Spirit. As I begin to write
about his life, I beg my readers' indulgence. For the study
of grammar has not saturated me, nor did the reading of
polished secular authors refine me, but the blessed father Avitus, bishop of Clermont, persuaded me to study
only ecclesiastical writings. Even if what I heard him 8
preach about and what he made me read did not inform
my judgment, because I am unable to carry them out in
my life, he was the one who guided me from David's

carminis cannas, ad illa evangelicae praedicationis dicta, atque apostolicae virtutis historias epistolasque perduxit.

9 De quo ea tantum capere potui ut cognoscerem Iesum Christum filium Dei ad salutem mundi venisse atque amicos eius qui, accepta cruce austerae observantiae, Sponsum secuti sunt, dignis obsequiis honorare. Qua de re crudae rusticitatis temeritatem ostendens, quae de beato cognovi Illidio, illo quo possum proferam stylo.

1. Sanctus igitur Illidius cum perfectae vitae sanctitate polleret ac diversarum in se gratiarum charismata, largiente Domino, congessisset, illud quod adhuc sanctitatis culmini deerat, Deo inspirante ac populo eligente promeruit, ut sacerdos Arvernae ecclesiae, et dominicarum ovium pastor eligeretur. Cuius sanctitatis fama dum per diversos gratiarum evehitur ascensus, non solum ipsos Arverni territorii terminos, verum etiam vicinarum urbium fines adivit.

2 Unde factum est ut haec gloria Treverici imperatoris aures attingeret, cuius filia cum a spiritu immundo correpta graviter vexaretur, et non inveniretur a quo posset erui, beatum Illidium fama detexit. Et dicto citius ab imperatore directi pueri, sanctum senem in antedicta repertum urbe, potestati regiae celeriter repraesentant. At ille, venerabiliter exceptum, de exitu infelicis conqueritur filiae.

poetic songs to the sayings of the gospels' preaching and the histories and letters describing the apostles' holy power.

From these I was able to learn only that I knew Jesus Christ to be the Son of God who was sent for the salvation of the world, and to honor with worthy homage his friends who took up the cross of austere observance and followed the Bridegroom. Having therefore displayed the boldness of my crude rusticity, I shall now write as best I can about what I have come to know about the blessed Illidius. 9

1. When the holy Illidius was strong in the sanctity of his perfect life and had accumulated in himself the gifts of various graces granted by the Lord, he deserved to receive the one thing that had up to then been lacking to the consummation of his sanctity: that, by God's inspiration and the people's choice, he be elected the bishop of the church of Clermont and shepherd of the Lord's sheep. The renown of his holiness, which had risen through various steps of graces, not only extended to the boundaries of the territory of Clermont but even crossed into those of nearby cities.

Hence it happened that this glory reached the ears of the emperor at Trier, whose daughter had been seized by an unclean spirit and was being sorely harassed; he had not been able to find anyone to cure her until he found out about the blessed Illidius's fame. Faster than a word can be uttered, the emperor sent messengers who found the holy old man in the aforementioned city [Clermont] and quickly brought him to the mighty presence of the emperor. After he had received the holy man with great respect, he bewailed his daughter's dire condition. 2

3 Ille vero confisus in Domino, in oratione prosternitur, nocteque cum sacris hymnis canticisque spiritalibus ducta, immissis in os puellae digitis, nequam spiritum a corpore abegit obsessae. Quod miraculum imperator cernens, immensos auri argentique cumulos sancto offert sacerdoti. Quod ille exsecrans ac refutans, hoc obtinuit ut Arverna civitas, quae tributa in specie triticea ac vinaria dependebat, in auro dissolveret, quia cum gravi labore penui inferebantur imperiali.

4 Sanctus vero, ut aiunt, impleto vitae praesentis tempore, in ipso itineris curriculo migravit ad Christum, a suisque delatus, in urbe sua sepultus est.

2. Et forsitan, ut plerumque homines murmurare soliti sunt, quispiam garrulatur, dicens: "Non potest hic haberi in-
2 ter sanctos pro unius tantum operatione miraculi." Nam si perpenditur illud quod Dominus ait in evangelio: "Multi," inquit, "dicunt mihi in illa die: 'Domine, Domine, nonne in nomine tuo daemonia eiecimus virtutesque multas fecimus?' Et respondebo eis, dicens quia 'non novi vos'" [Matthew 7:22–23], profecto intelliget quod magis proficit ad laudem virtus egressa de tumulo, quam ea quae quisquam vivens gessit in mundo. Quia illa labem habere potuerunt per assidua mundanae occupationis impedimenta, haec vero
3 omni labe ad liquidum caruerunt. Ergo quia illa, ut credimus, quae sanctus Illidius ante hoc tempus operatus est, oblivioni data sunt nec ad nostram notitiam pervenerunt, ea quae propriis inspeximus oculis, expertique sumus, vel quae a fidelibus agnita cognovimus, declaramus.

Illidius trusted in the Lord and prostrated himself in 3
prayer; after having spent the night singing sacred hymns
and spiritual songs, he put his fingers in the girl's mouth and
drove the evil spirit out of her tormented body. When the
emperor saw this miracle, he offered the bishop great heaps
of gold and silver. He, however, cursed and refused this, and
obtained the concession that the city of Clermont, which
paid its taxes in wheat and wine, would from then on pay
them in gold, because the commodities could only with difficulty be transported to the imperial depot.

The saint, they say, having fulfilled the time of his present 4
life, migrated to Christ during that journey, was brought to
his city by his retinue and buried there.

2. And since people often complain, perhaps someone
will speak idly and say: "This man cannot be counted among
the saints for performing only one miracle." But if one con- 2
siders what the Lord said in the gospel: "Many will say to me
on that day: 'Lord, Lord, did we not expel demons in your
name and perform many deeds of power?' And I shall answer them, saying 'I did not know you,'" he will truly understand that a powerful deed that emanates from a tomb is
more praiseworthy than one performed by someone living
in this world. For the latter can be tainted by continuing and
impeding worldly concerns, whereas the former are clearly
free of all blemish. Therefore since, as we believe, those 3
deeds of power which the holy Illidius performed before
that time have been forgotten and have not come to our
knowledge, we will relate what we have seen with our own
eyes, what we have experienced, and what we have learned
that trustworthy people have seen.

4 Tempore quo Gallus Episcopus Arvernam regebat ecclesiam, horum scriptor in adolescentia degens graviter aegrotabat, et ab eo plerumque dilectione unica visitabatur, eo quod patruus eius esset. Erat enim valetudo cum nimia stomachi pituita ac febre valida. Interea advenit parvulo desiderium et, credo, inspirante Deo, ut ad beati Illidii basilicam deportaretur. Illatusque manibus puerorum ad eius tumulum, fusa oratione cum lacrimis, leviorem se sensit esse quam cum venerat.

5 Reversusque ad domum, iterum a febre corripitur. Quadam vero die cum gravius agere coepisset, eumque febris asperior solito aggravaret, et utrum evaderet dubia sub sorte iaceret, accedens genitrix eius, ait ad eum: “Maestum hodie, dulcis nate, sum habitura diem, cum te talis attinet febris.” Et ille: “Nihil,” inquit, “prorsus, obsecro, contristeris, sed ad sepulcrum me remitte beati Illidii pontificis. Credo enim, et fides mea est, quod virtus eius, et tibi laetitiam et mihi tribuet sospitatem.”

6 Tunc, sancti deportatus ad tumulum, orationem ad Dominum fudit, spondens prostratus sponte, si eum obtentu
antistitis sui Dominus ab hoc contagio liberaret, clericum se
futurum, nec prorsus moraretur, si deprecatio obtineret effectum. Haec effatus, sensit protinus discedere febrem, vo-
7 catoque puero, domum se reportari deposcit. Cumque in
recubitu, ubi tunc epulabantur, fuisset illatus, erumpente a
naribus sanguinis copia, febris simul cruorque defluxit, quod
meritis beati confessoris praestitum habetur probatum.

CHAPTER 2

When Bishop Gallus governed the church of Clermont 4
the writer of these words, then a boy, became seriously ill
and was frequently visited by him with singular affection because he was his uncle. It was an illness with a great deal of
phlegm in the stomach and a high fever. While this was happening, a desire came to the boy, as I believe inspired by
God, to be carried to the basilica of the blessed Illidius. And
when he had been carried by servants to the saint's tomb
and had poured forth a prayer with tears, he felt less oppressed than he had when he had arrived.

After his return home, he was again seized by fever. On a 5
certain day, when he began to feel worse because the fever
afflicted him more severely than usual and it seemed doubt-
ful whether he would ever recover, his mother came to him
and said: "Today will be a sad day for me, dearest son, since
such a fever is gripping you." And he said: "Do not be sad, I
beg you, but send me back to the tomb of the blessed bishop
Illidius. For I believe and trust that his power will give joy to
you and health to me."

When he had been carried to the holy man's tomb he 6
poured forth a prayer to the Lord while lying prostrate, and
vowed of his own free will that if, through the bishop's intercession, the Lord would deliver him from this illness, he
would at once become a cleric when his prayer had been answered. As soon as he had said this he felt the fever instantly
recede, called for a servant, and asked to be carried home.
When he had been carried into the dining room, where a 7
meal was then being served, a large amount of blood burst
forth from his nose; the fever flowed out together with the
blood, and this proves that the cure was effected by the
merits of the blessed confessor.

8 Sed et nuper Venerandi comitis servus, cum in diuturna caecitate resideret, celebratis vigiliis, sanus abscessit.

3. De reliquiis vero eius haec ipse praefatus scriptor, ut actum est, propria contemplatione prospexit. Dedicaverat igitur oratorium infra domum ecclesiasticam urbis Turonicae in primo sacerdotii sui anno, in quo cum reliquorum sanctorum pignoribus huius antistitis reliquias collocavit.

2 Post multos vero dedicationis dies admonitus est ab abbate ut reliquias quas in altari ipso locaverat visitaret, ne ab umore novi aedificii umectatae, aliquid in his putredinis insideret. Quas cum requirens reperisset infectas, ablatas ex altari contra ignem siccare coepit. Verum ubi ligaturas illas singillatim composuit, ventum est ad reliquias beati Illidii
3 episcopi. Denique tenens easdem contra ignem, filum quo ligatae erant, quia erat valde prolixum, super ardentes decidit pruna, et tamquam aeneum aut ferreum ab ardore ignis incanduit. Illo quoque parvi pendente quid filum fieret, tantum sanctae reliquiae siccarentur, aestimans autem eum iam in favillam fuisse resolutum, comperit adhuc integrum et incorruptum, quippe quod vinculum et ligamen paulo ante fuisset huius gloriosi pontificis. Haec videns attonitus, valde beati antistitis virtutem admiratur. Qui non grandi metu unde haec abstulerat referens, gloriam eius omnibus revelavit. Filum autem illud erat ex lana.

4. Puer erat parvulus quasi mensium decem, qui ut res veritatis edocuit, ipsius beati abnepos habebatur, gravissimi incommodi accessu afficiebatur. Flebat autem illius genetrix

Recently, too, a servant of Count Venerandus who had 8
been blind for a long time went home healthy after he had celebrated vigils near the saint's tomb.

3. What happened with his relics the aforesaid writer saw with his own eyes. In the first year of his episcopate, he dedicated a chapel in the bishop's house of the city of Tours and placed relics of Illidius in it, along with those of other saints.

Many days after the dedication he was warned by the ab- 2
bot to check the relics which he had placed in the altar to see whether they might have been made damp by the humidity of the new building and become moldy. He inspected them and found them affected, and took them from the altar and began to dry them out near a fire. When he had arranged their bundles one by one near the fire, he came to
the relics of the blessed bishop Illidius. While these were 3
held close to the fire, the thread that bound them, because it was very long, fell upon the burning coals and began to glow like copper or iron in the heat of the fire. Not caring what happened to the thread as long as the holy relics dried out, and assuming that it had disintegrated into ashes, afterward he nevertheless found it whole and unharmed because, a little earlier, it had been the bond and connection for this glorious bishop's remains. Looking at this in astonishment, he marvels at the power of the blessed bishop. And bringing them back with great awe to the place from which he had taken them, he revealed the bishop's glory to everyone. For that thread was made of wool.

4. A little boy of about ten months, who was rightly considered the blessed man's great-great-grandson, was afflicted by an attack of a dangerous illness. His mother wept both

non minus obitum parvuli, quam quod non fuerat adhuc divino delibutus sacramento. Denique consilio habito, beati confessoris adiit tumulum, exponit in pavimento aegrotum, qui nihil aliter quam solo spiritu palpitabat, atque in vigiliis obsecrationibusque coram sepulcro antistitis excubat.

2 Cumque plausum ales ille lucis nuntius, repercussis alis, altius protulisset, puer qui valde exanimis proiectus fuerat, convaluit. Et gaudia cordis risu praecedente patefaciens, aperto divinitus ore, evocat matrem, dicens: "Accede huc!" At illa cum tremore et gaudio accedens, quae numquam adhuc filii vocem audierat, stupens: "Quid vis," inquit, "dulcissime nate?" Qui ait: "Curre quantocius, atque aquarum mihi
3 pocula defer." At illa persistens immobilis usque ad adventum lucis in oratione, gratias agens sancto antistiti, subolemque devovens; abscessit ad domum, porrectaque aqua, hausit infans. Atque ab omni infirmitas nexu absolutus, ad plenum convaluit. Deinde ad pristinos infantiae vagitus rediens, loqui ultra non potuit, nisi cum ad illam aetatis seriem, in qua infantium lingua ad loquendum laxari solet, educatus accessit.

4 Sed nec illud silere arbitror quod quodam tempore, quo clibanus ad coquendas calces basilicae ipsius succenderetur, actum est. Iugum igitur quod os fornacis validissime confirmabat, dormientibus cum ipso loci abbate qui aderant, est effractum. Quo facto, astitit presbytero repente per visum quasi sacerdos dicens: "Festina velociter et excita dormientes ne eos futurae ruinae casus anticipet! Iam enim paratum

for fear of his imminent demise and because he had not yet been anointed by the divine sacrament of baptism. After taking counsel, she went to the tomb of the blessed confessor and laid the sick boy, who was only just still breathing, on the pavement; she herself lay before the bishop's tomb keeping vigils and praying for help.

Then, when the bird announcing dawn had beat its wings 2
and expressed louder plaudits, the boy who had been lying unconscious recovered. As he showed the joy in his heart with a laugh, his mouth was opened in a divine manner and he called out to his mother, saying: "Come here!" And she, who had up to then never heard her son speak, came in joy and trembling and said in astonishment: "What do you want, dearest son?" He said: "Go quickly and bring me a cup
of water." But she remained motionless in prayer until the 3
light had come, thanking the holy bishop and dedicating her son to him; then she went home and gave the infant water, which he drank. Freed from every bond of the illness, he recovered completely. After this he returned to the babblings of infancy and was no longer able to speak until he had been educated and reached the age at which children's tongues are usually loosened for speaking.

But I do not think I should be silent about what hap- 4
pened once when a furnace had been lit to bake limestone for the church. While the abbot in charge of the place and those who were there had fallen asleep, the lintel that held the door of the furnace in place began to crack. As soon as this happened, someone who seemed to be a bishop stood before the priest in a dream vision and said: "Hurry and wake up the sleepers so that the furnace does not collapse on top of them! For the lintel which supports the whole pile

est iugum, quod totam molem lapidum sustinet, cum ipso
5 igne corruere!" Ille vero expergefactus, amotis ab ore fornacis omnibus, cecidit ab utraque parte acervus lapidum
aggregatus, nullum de astantibus laedens, quod non sine
antistitis intercessione praestitum reor. Tunc presbyter memoratus, oratione facta ad sepulcrum sancti, reparatis iugis
lapidibusque relatis, in clibano opus coeptum, antistite opitulante, peregit.

6 Huius confessoris beatum corpus ab antiquis in crypta sepultum fuit. Sed quia artum erat aedificium ac difficilem habebat ingressum, sanctus Avitus pontifex urbis, constructa in circuitu miri operis apsida, beatos inquisivit artus, reperitque in capsa tabulis formata ligneis. Quos assumens, involvit dignis linteis et iuxta morem sarcophago clausit; oppletamque cryptam altius collocavit.

7 In hoc loco et meritis et nomine Iustus requiescit, qui fuisse huius glorioso pontificis fertur archidiaconus.

5. Multa quidem et alia de hoc sancto miracula sunt relata, quae scribere longum putavi, haec aestimans fidei perfectae sufficere quae dicta sunt, quia cui pauca non sufficiunt, plura non proderunt. Nam ad huius tumulum caeci illuminantur, daemones effugantur, surdi auditum et claudi recipiunt gressum, praestante Domino nostro Iesu Christo, qui credentibus repromisit a se petita sine ambiguitate largiri.

of stones is on the point of collapsing, together with the
fire!" When the priest had woken up and made everyone 5
move away from the door of the furnace, the heap of stones fell from both sides, and hurt none of those present; this, I think, could not have happened without the bishop's intercession. Then the aforesaid priest, after he had prayed at the tomb of the holy man, had the lintel repaired and the stones replaced and so, with the help of the bishop, he finished the work begun in the furnace.

The blessed body of this confessor had from ancient 6
times been buried in a crypt. But because it was a narrow building with an inaccessible entrance, the holy Avitus, bishop of the city, built a beautiful apse around it, looked for the blessed body, and found it in a coffin made of wooden planks. He took the body, wrapped it in a shroud worthy of it, and placed it in a stone sarcophagus, as is customary. And after he had filled up the crypt, he put the sarcophagus in a higher place.

In this place Justus, just in merit as well as in name, 7
also rests; he is said to have been this glorious bishop's archdeacon.

5. Many other miracles have been reported of this saint which I thought would amount to too much writing, judging that what has been said suffices for perfect faith; for more miracles will not convince or satisfy those for whom a few miracles are insufficient. Thus at his tomb, the blind are given light, demons are put to flight, the deaf receive their hearing, and the lame their ability to walk: all brought about by our Lord Jesus Christ, who promised those who believe that what they asked for from him would certainly be granted them.

3

De sancto Abraham abbate

Prologus

Nulli catholicorum esse occultum reor quod Dominus ait in evangelio: "Amen dico vobis, si habueritis fidem integram et non haesitaveris, si dixeritis huic monti 'Transfer te,' et transfert se" [Matthew 21:21]; et "Omnia quaecumque petieritis in nomine meo, credite quia accipieritis et venient vobis" [Mark 11:24]. Ergo non erit dubium quin sancti obtinere possint a Domino quod petierint, quia in eo fidei fundamine positi, nullis haesitationum fluctibus vacillantur.

2 Pro qua fide non solum infra patriae terminum propriae, dum caelestem vitam agere cupiunt, exsules facti sunt, sed etiam transmarina ac peregrina petierunt loca, ut ei cui se devoverant plus placerent, sicut nunc beatus Abraham abba qui, post multas temptationes saeculi, fines est territorii ingressus Arverni.

3 Qui non immerito Abrahae illi comparatur seni pro magnitudine fidei, cui quondam dixerat Deus: "Exi de terra tua et de cognatione tua, et vade in terram quam monstravero tibi" [Genesis 12:1]. Reliquit autem hic non solum terram propriam, sed etiam illam veteris hominis actionem, et induit novum hominem, qui secundum Deum formatus est in
4 iustitia, sanctitate, et veritate. Ideoque cum se perfectum

3

About the holy abbot Abraham

Prologue

I do not think there is any catholic who does not know that in the gospel the Lord says: "Truly I say to you, if you have faith and never doubt and say to this mountain 'Take yourself up,' it will take itself up"; and: "All, whatever it may be, that you ask for in my name, believe that you will receive it, and it will come to you." There is no doubt, therefore, that holy men can obtain what they ask for from the Lord because their faith is securely founded and they are not driven back and forth by waves of hesitation.

On account of this faith and because they wished to lead 2
the heavenly life, they became exiles not only within the boundaries of their own countries but even sought foreign lands overseas so that they might better please the One to whom they had devoted themselves; in this way, after many trials in this world, the blessed abbot Abraham entered the territory of Clermont.

On account of his great faith he is not undeservedly com- 3
pared to that ancient Abraham to whom God said: "Go out from your country and your kindred, and go into the land which I shall show you." For this man left not only his own country but also the life of the old man and put on the new man, who is fashioned according to God in justice, sanctity,
and truth. And therefore when he saw himself to be perfect 4

in Dei ope cerneret, non fuit dubius in fide petere quod per vitam sanctam confisus est obtinere, per quem opifex caeli, maris, ac terrae, parva quidem numero, sed admiranda miracula operari dignatus est.

1. Igitur Abraham iste super Euphratis fluvii litus exortus est, ubi, in Dei opere proficiens, ad visitandos eremitas adire Aegypti solitudines concupivit. Quod iter dum tereret, a paganis comprehensus et multis pro Christi nomine affectus verberibus, in vincula conicitur; in quibus per quinque annos exsultans, angelo solvente, laxatur.

2 Occidentalem quoque plagam visitare cupiens, Arvernis advenit, ibique ad basilicam sancti Cyrici monasterium collocavit. Erat enim mirae virtutis, fugator daemonum illuminatorque caecorum, aliorum quoque morborum potentissimus medicator.

3 Igitur cum festivitas supradictae basilicae advenisset, praepositum vocat, ut vasa vino plena ad reficiendum populum, qui solemnitate aderat in atrio, ex more componeret. Causatur monachus, dicens: "Ecce episcopum cum duce et civibus invitatum habes, et vix nobis supersunt quattuor vini
4 amphorae. Unde omnia ista complebis?" Et ille: "Aperite mihi," inquit, "penum." Quo aperto, ingressus est. Et dans orationem, quasi novus Elias, elevatis ad caelum manibus,

in the service of God he did not hesitate to seek what he was confident he could obtain through a holy life; for through him, the maker of the sky, the sea, and the earth deigned to work miracles which deserve admiration, though they be few in number.

1. This Abraham, then, was born on the shore of the river Euphrates, and when he had found himself to be proficient in the service of God, wished to go to the deserts of Egypt to visit the hermits. While he was exhausting himself with the journey, he was captured by pagans, tortured with repeated beatings for the name of Christ, and put in chains; he rejoiced at this for five years, and then an angel released him and he was freed.

Wishing to visit the West, he came to Clermont and there 2
founded a monastery near the basilica of the holy Cyricus. He had marvelous power, put demons to flight, gave light to the blind, and cured other illnesses too as a very potent healer.

Thus when the feast of the above-mentioned ba- 3
silica came around, he called the prior to prepare a vessel filled with wine as usual in the forecourt of the church to refresh the people present for the solemnity. The monk excused himself, saying: "Look, you have invited the bishop, the duke, and the citizens, and we have less than thirty-four gallons of wine left. Where will you get
enough to fill all these pitchers?" And Abraham said: 4
"Open the cellar for me." When it was opened, he went in. And praying as a new Elijah, raising his hands to heaven,

infusis fletu luminibus, ait: "Ne deficiat, quaeso, Domine, de hoc vasculo vinum, donec cunctis ministretur in abundantia." Et irruente in se Spiritu sancto, ait: "Haec dicit Dominus: 'Non deficiet vinum de vase, sed omnibus petentibus affatim tribuetur, et abundabit.'"

5 Verumtamen ad verbum et hilaritatem dispensationis illius cuncto populo in abundantia ministratum est, et superfuit. Sed quia strenuitas praepositi prius mensuraverat vasculum quinquagenarium, et repererat quattuor palmorum mensuram, cernens quae acta fuerant, in crastino iterum mensurans, tantum reperit in vase, quantum in eo praecedente reliquerat die.

6 Ex hoc sancti virtus in populis declarata est, in quo monasterio plenus dierum obiit, ibique cum honore sepultus
est. Erat enim eo tempore sanctus Sidonius episcopus et
Victorius dux, qui super septem civitates principatum, Eu-
7 richo Gothorum rege indulgente, susceperat. Huius vero
sancti epitaphium beatus Sidonius scripsit, in quo aliqua de
his quae locutus sum est praefatus. Ad huius enim beati
Abrahae sepulcrum plerumque frigoritici decubantes medicinae caelestis praesidio sublevantur.

his eyes filled with tears, he said: "Let there be no lack of wine in this vessel, I beg you, Lord, until all have been given in abundance." Then, as the Holy Spirit rushed into him, he said: "Thus says the Lord: 'Wine will not lack in this vessel, and enough will be given to all those who ask for it, and there shall be some left.'"

And according to his word it was served in abundance to 5
all the people, who drank it with joy, and there was some left. But the conscientious prior had previously measured the vessel, which could hold fifty measures, and found that the wine stood four hands high. When he saw what had happened, he measured the wine again the next morning and found the same amount as on the previous day.

After this event had made his holy power manifest to the 6
people, the holy man died at an advanced age in this monastery and was buried there with honor. At that time the holy Sidonius was bishop, and Victorius was duke: he had received the governance of seven cities from Euric, the king of
the Goths. The blessed Sidonius wrote the epitaph for this 7
saint, and in it some of the things I related are mentioned. Frequently, the fever-stricken who sleep at the tomb of this blessed Abraham are relieved of their illness by the succor of heavenly healing.

4

De sancto Quintiano episcopo

Prologus

Omnis qui se terrenae materiae corpus ferre cognoscit, cogitare debet, ne in his devolvatur quae terrena et carnis huius amica esse noscuntur. Quia iuxta apostolum Paulum manifesta sunt opera carnis plena immunditia et iniquitate, pollutumque et foetidum hominem qui ea sectatus fuerit reddunt, atque ad extremum fletibus deputant sempiternis. Fructus autem spiritus est omne quod in Deo pollet ac nitet, quod in hoc saeculo, mortificata carne, animam exsultare facit, in futuro autem gaudiis donat aeternis.

2 Unde nos qui nunc sumus in corpore positi, aspicere debemus quae operatus est Deus in sanctis suis, in quibus, tamquam in splendidum candidumque ac levigatum meritis tabernaculum, diversisque virtutum floribus adornatum, residens, extensa dexterae maiestate, dignatus est per eos miseratione propria perficere quae petiissent, sicut nunc per beatum Quintianum, de quo sermo futurus est, mentis nobilis generositate fulgidum iustitiae opus plerumque complevit.

3 Ergo non nos more pecorum carnis sectatio ad terrena submergat ac deprimat, sed potius sanctorum exemplis illecti, prudenter intelligentes quae Dei sunt, spiritalis nos

4

About the holy bishop Quintianus

Prologue

Every man who knows that he bears a body of earth should take care not to become involved in matters that are known to be earthly and sweet to the flesh. For according to the apostle Paul the works of the flesh are manifestly full of impurity and wickedness, rendering the man who indulges in them polluted and rotten, and at the end of his life send him off to eternal weeping. The fruit of the spirit, however, is what is powerful and shines in God; the flesh having been mortified, it is what makes the soul exult in this world and gives eternal joy in the future one.

Therefore we who are now placed in bodies should look 2
at what God has accomplished through his saints, in whom he dwells as if in a splendid tabernacle, white and smooth through their merits and adorned with the flowers of various virtues; and through whom he deigns, in his compassion, to extend his right hand to do through them what they request, as now with blessed Quintianus, noble of mind and shining in generosity, through whom God often fulfilled the works of his justice and of whom we are now about to speak.

Therefore let not the striving like beasts after fleshly 3
things pull us down and bind us to earthly affairs but, rather, persuaded by the examples of the saints wisely to understand the things of God, let spiritual works lift us up to

opera ad caelestia ac sempiterna sustollat; neque in nobis mens, ab impudicis actionibus victa, luxuriet, sed aeternitatis pro meritis vindicans solium, victrix sapientia regnet.

1. Igitur beatissimus Quintianus, Afer natione, et ut quidam volunt, nepos Fausti Episcopi, qui genitricem suam suscitasse perhibetur, sanctitate praeditus, virtutum dote fulgidus, caritatis igniculo fervidus, castitatis flore praecipuus, ad episcopatum Rutenae ecclesiae eligitur, expetitur, ordinatur.

2 In quo episcopatu ampliatis adhuc virtutibus, cum in Dei semper operibus cresceret, auctam beati Amantii antistitis basilicam, sanctum corpus in antea transtulit. Sed non fuit sancto acceptabile hoc opus. Unde factum est ut per visum apparens diceret ei: "Quia ausu temerario artus in pace quiescentes visus es amovisse, ecce ego removebo te ab hac urbe, et eris exsul in regione altera. Verumtamen non priva-
3 beris ab honore quo frueris." Non post multum vero tempus, orto inter cives et episcopum scandalo, Gothos, qui tunc in antedicta urbe morabantur, suspicio attigit quod se vellet episcopus Francorum ditionibus subdere; consilioque accepto, cogitaverunt eum perfodere gladio. Quod cum viro sancto nuntiatum fuisset, de nocte consurgens, cum fidelissimis ministris suis ab urbe illa egrediens, Arvernis advenit.

4 Ibique a sancto Eufrasio episcopo, qui Aprunculo quondam antistiti successerat, receptus est, largitisque ei tam

heavenly and eternal things; let not our mind run riot, overcome by shameful acts, but let wisdom reign victorious there, laying claim to our future dwelling in eternity through her merits.

1. The most blessed Quintianus was an African and, as some have it, the nephew of Bishop Faustus who is said to have raised his own mother from the dead; he was endowed with holiness, resplendent with the gift of virtues, glowing with the spark of charity, and distinguished in the flower of his chastity when he was elected, sought for, and ordained bishop of the church of Rodez.

While his virtues increased because he kept growing in 2
the works of God, he enlarged the basilica of the blessed bishop Amantius and moved his holy body into it. But this deed was not acceptable to the holy man. Hence it happened that Amantius appeared to Bishop Quintianus in a vision and said to him: "Because you appear to have thoughtlessly moved my body, which was resting in peace, I shall remove you from this city and you will be an exile in another region. But I shall not deprive you of the honor you enjoy."
Not much later, a dispute arose between the citizens and 3
the bishop, and a suspicion reached the Goths who then lived in Rodez that the bishop wished to subjugate himself to the domination of the Franks; having taken counsel among themselves, they planned to run him through with a sword. When this was announced to the holy man, he rose at night and left Rodez for Clermont with his most faithful servants.

There he was received by the holy bishop Eufrasius, who 4
had succeeded the former bishop Aprunculus, and he was

domibus quam agris et vineis; vel ille, vel qui Lugdunensi urbi praeerat, summa cum diligentia excolebant. Erat enim iam senex et verus Dei cultor.

5 Decedente autem ab hoc mundo sancto Eufrasio, Apollinaris, tribus mensibus sacerdotio subministrato, migravit. Cum autem haec Theoderico regi nuntiata fuissent, iussit inibi sanctum Quintianum constitui, et omnem ei potestatem tradi ecclesiae, dicens: "Hic ob nostri amoris zelum ab urbe sua eiectus est."

6 Denique cum sanctus Quintianus in antedicta urbe potiretur episcopatu, Proculus quidam, ex aerario presbyter ordinatus, multas ei iniurias intulit, omnemque potestatem illi
de rebus ecclesiae auferens, vix ei quotidianum satis tenuem
victum ministrari praecepit. Sed per eius orationem a civibus correptus prudentioribus, restituta omni potestate, se
7 ab eius removit insidiis. Antedictus tamen sacerdos non immemor iniuriae, sicut quondam Paulus apostolus de Alexan-
dro, ita et hic de Proculo decantabat, dicens: "Proculus aerarius multa mala mihi fecit. Reddat illi Dominus secundum
opera sua." Quod in posterum ei evenisse manifestum est.

2. Erat enim vir beatus in oratione assiduus, et in tantum amator populi sui, ut adveniente Theoderico, ac vallante cum exercitu urbem, sanctus Dei muros eius per noctem

given houses with fields and vineyards; and Eufrasius, as well as the <bishop> who led the city of Lyons, treated him with the greatest respect, for he was already an elderly man and a true servant of God.

When the holy Eufrasius had departed from this world, 5
Apollinaris held the episcopacy for three months and then left this world. When these events had been announced to King Theodoric, he ordered the holy Quintianus to be established there, and all the power of the church to be given to him, saying: "This man was thrown out of his city on account of his fervent love for us."

When the holy Quintianus had at last acquired the epis- 6
copacy in Clermont a certain Proculus, an employee of the royal treasury who had been ordained priest, did his best to harm him, taking away his power over ecclesiastical resources and ordering him to be given scarcely enough for his daily sustenance. But through Quintianus's prayer to God for help, Proculus was rebuked by the more prudent citizens, all power was given back to the holy man Quintianus,
and he was safe from the priest's attacks. Quintianus, how- 7
ever, had not forgotten the injury, for as formerly the apostle Paul had spoken of Alexander, so also did he keep chanting a saying about Proculus: "The treasurer Proculus has done many evil things to me. May the Lord reward him according to his works." And it is clear that this indeed later happened to him.

2. The blessed man was assiduous in prayer and cared so much for his people that when Theoderic came and besieged the city with his army, the holy man of God walked

psallendo circuiret, et ut regioni vel populo Dominus velociter succurrere dignaretur, afflictus in ieiuniis atque vigiliis instanter orabat.

2 Porro Theodericus rex cum cogitaret etiam muros urbis
evertere, mollivit eum misericordia Domini, et oratio sacerdotis sui, quem in exsilium retrudere cogitabat. Nam nocte
pavore perterritus de stratu suo exsilit, ac solus per viam
publicam fugere nititur. Perdiderat enim sensum, nesciens
quid ageret. Quod animadvertentes sui, eumque retinere
conantes, vix potuerunt, cohortantes ut se signo salutari
3 muniret. Tunc Hilpingus dux eius, accedens propius ad regem, ait: "Audi, gloriosissime rex, consilium parvitatis meae.
Ecce muri civitatis istius fortissimi sunt, eamque pro-
pugnacula ingentia vallant. Quod ut plenius magnificentia
vestra cognoscat, de sanctis quorum basilicae muros urbis
ambiunt haec loquor, sed antistes loci illius magnus apud
Deum habetur. Noli facere quod cogitas; noli episcopo iniu-
4 riam inferre aut urbem evertere." Cuius consilium rex clementer accipiens, praeceptum posuit ne ullus ab octavo urbis miliario laederetur. Quod obtentu sacerdotus praestitum
nullus ambigat.

5 Tunc et Proculus ille presbyter, inruptis Lovolautrensis castri muris, ab ingredientibus hostibus ante ipsum altare gladiorum ictibus in frusta discerptus est, reddiditque illi Dominus, sicut sacerdos cantare consueverat, secundum opera sua.

around the walls at night, singing psalms and, humbling himself in fasts and vigils; he prayed ceaselessly that the Lord might quickly deign to rescue the region and the people.

Therefore, just when King Theoderic was planning to 2
raze the city's walls, his heart was softened by the Lord's mercy and by the prayer of his bishop, whom the king had been planning to send into exile. For one night he was seized by a terrible fright, leaped out of his bed and, all alone, attempted to flee down the public road. He had lost his mind and did not know what he was doing. Having seen this, his companions tried with great difficulty to restrain him and urged him to protect himself with the saving sign of the
cross. Then Hilpingus, their duke, came up to the king and 3
said: "Most glorious king, hear the advice of My Insignificance. You can see that the walls of this city are very strong and that they are additionally protected by mighty fortifications. That Your Magnificence may understand more precisely, I speak of the saints whose churches surround the walls of this city, but also of the bishop of this place, who is held in great esteem by God. Therefore do not carry out what you have in mind; do not harm the bishop or destroy
the city." The king received his advice favorably and gave 4
an order that no one should be hurt within eight miles of the city. Let no one doubt that this happened through the bishop's intercession.

Then, too, when the castle of Vollore was taken, the 5
priest Proculus, while standing in front of the altar itself, was hacked to pieces by the blows from the swords of the invaders, and so did the Lord reward him according to his works, as the bishop used to chant.

3. Post peractam igitur stragem cladis Arvernae, Hortensius, unus ex senatoribus, comitatum urbis illius agens, quendam de parentibus sancti, id est Honoratum nomine, in urbis platea nequiter retineri iussit. Quod celeriter beato viro nuntiatum est. At ille per amicos suos coepit rogare ut eum, data audientia, absolvi iuberet. Quod ille nullatenus praestitit.

2 Tunc beatus senex deferri se in plateam qua ille tenebatur iubet; allatus autem rogabat milites ut eum dimitterent. Illi vero timentes, oboedire ausi non sunt pontifici. Et sacerdos: "Ad domum," inquit, "Hortensii me velociter deportate." Erat enim senes valde et propriis pedibus abire non poterat.
3 Deferentes autem eum in domum Hortensii ministri eius, excutiens in eam pulverem calciamenti sui, ait: "Maledicta sit domus haec, et maledicti habitatores eius in sempiternum, fiatque deserta, et non sit qui inhabitet in ea!" Et dicit omnis populus: "Amen." Et adiecit: "Quaeso, Domine, numquam de hac generatione provehatur quisquam ad episcopale sacerdotium, qui episcopum non obaudit."

4 Egresso autem ex ea sacerdote, protinus omnes familiae quae in domum illam erant a febre corripiuntur, et parumper ingemiscentes spiritum exhalabant. Quod cum iam tertia die ageretur, videns Hortensius sibi nihil de suis servientibus reservari, timens ne etiam et ipse pariter interiret, ad sanctum virum maestus ingreditur, proiectusque ad pedes
5 eius, cum lacrimis veniam rogat. Quam ille benignissime indulgens, benedictam aquam domui transmisit, illaque per

3. After the slaughter and destruction of the territory of
Clermont, Hortensius, one of the senators who held the office of count of the city, ordered one of the saint's relatives
named Honoratus unjustly to be seized on the city's street.
It was quickly announced to the blessed man. And he began to ask the count, through his friends, for the man to be
granted an audience and released. But he did not manage to
achieve this.

Then the blessed old man ordered himself to be borne to 2
the street where Honoratus was being held and when he had
arrived there asked the soldiers to let his relative go. Because they were afraid, however, they did not dare to obey
the bishop. Then the bishop said: "Carry me as quickly as
possible to Hortensius's house." For he was very old and
could not go there on his own feet. When his servants had 3
carried him to Hortensius's house, he shook the dust off his
shoes and said: "Let this house be cursed and all its inhabitants be accursed forever, and let it be deserted so that no
one will inhabit it!" And all the people said: "Amen." Then
he added: "I beg, Lord, that no one from this family, which
did not obey its bishop, ever be elevated to the episcopate."

When the bishop had left the house, all the members of 4
the household present in that house were at once seized by a
fever and breathed out their spirits after groaning a short
while. When this had gone on for three days, Hortensius realized that none of his servants would be left and, fearing
that he himself might also die, went in great distress to see
the holy man, threw himself at his feet and, with tears, requested forgiveness. When the bishop had kindly granted 5
him this, he sent blessed water to the house; and when it had
been sprinkled on the walls, a great deed of holy power ap-

parietes respersa, omnis aegritudo protinus est depulsa, magnaque ibi virtus apparuit. Nam et qui incurrerant sanati sunt, et qui sani erant ultra non incurrerunt.

4. In ecclesiasticis vero scripturis eruditus est habitus hic sacerdos, sed et in eleemosynis magnificus fuit. Nam cum pauperem quempiam clamare cerneret, aiebat: "Succurrite, quaeso, succurrite, et pauperi victus necessaria ministrate! Ignari enim estis, o desides, et forsitan ipse est qui se per evangelicae lectionis seriem reficiendum in pauperibus minimis esse mandavit."

2 Eiciebat autem et daemonia se confitentia. In monasterio autem Cambidobrensi veniens, cum inergumenum quendam reperisset atrocius debacchantem, misit presbyteros ut ei manus imponerent. Sed cum eorum exorcizatione larva non fuisset expulsa, sanctus Dei comminus appropinquans et immissis in os eius digitis, personam reddit absolutam. Multa et alia miracula vir beatus operatus est, ut oratione facta, saepius quae petisset ad Dominum obtinebat.

3 Porro in Arverno quodam tempore cum magna siccitas consumeret arva, et arentibus herbis nulla penitus iumentis pabula remanerent, et sanctus Dei rogationes illas, quae ante Ascensionem dominicam aguntur devotissime celebra-
4 ret. Die tertia, cum iam portae civitatis appropinquarent, suggerunt ei ut ipse antiphonam dignaretur imponere, dicentes: "Si tu, beate pontifex, devote antiphonam imposueris, confidimus de sanctitate tua, quod protinus nobis Dominus pluviam dignabitur benigna pietate largiri." At ille,

peared: all of the illness was expelled at once. For not only did those who had incurred it recover, those who were still healthy did not subsequently incur it.

4. This bishop is said to have been learned in ecclesiastical writings but also magnificent in almsgiving. For whenever he saw some poor man crying aloud, he said: "Hurry, hurry, and give the poor man the food he needs! For you are ignorant—lazy ones!—and perhaps this man is the one who, in the gospel, commanded himself to be fed in the poorest man!"

He also drove out demons that identified themselves as 2
such to him. When he came to the monastery of Cambidobrum, and found there a certain demoniac raving violently, he sent his priests to lay hands upon him. But when the demon was not expelled by the priests' exorcism, the holy man of God came closer, put his fingers in the man's mouth and so released him. The blessed man performed many other miracles as well for, when he prayed, he often obtained what he requested from the Lord.

Thus when at a certain time a severe drought had dried 3
up the fields in the territory of Clermont and, because of the desiccated grass, almost no food was left for the cattle, the holy man of God most devoutly celebrated the Rogations which are customarily held before the Lord's ascen-
sion. On the third day, when the procession was approach- 4
ing the city gate, people suggested to the bishop that he should start intoning the antiphon they were to sing, saying: "If you, blessed bishop, devoutly intone the antiphon, we believe that because of your holiness the Lord in his benevolent care will at once deign to grant us rain." And he,

prostratus super cilicium suum in ipsa platea, diutissime cum fletu oravit.

5 Exsurgens autem antiphonam quam petebant, ut virtus fuit, imposuit. Verba autem eius ex illa Salomonicae orationis edita haec erant: "Si clauso caelo pluviae non fuerint propter peccata populi, et conversi deprecati fuerint faciem tuam, exaudi, Domine, et dimitte peccata populi tui et da pluviam terrae, quam dedisti populo tuo ad possidendum" [2 Chronicles 6:26–27].

6 Cumque psallere devotissime coepissent, penetravit excelsae potentiae aures humilis oratio confessoris, et ecce contenebratum est caelum ac nubibus obtectus. Et priusquam portam urbis attingerent, descendit pluvia vehemens super universam terram illam, ita ut omnes mirarentur ac dicerent ad preces hoc beati viri fuisse largitum.

5. Senuit autem sacerdos Dei, et in tantum aetate provec-
tus est ut sputum oris in terram proicere non valeret, sed
adhibitum labiis truclionem, in eum salivas oris exponeret.
Non caligavit oculus eius, nec immutatum est cor a viis Dei;
non seposuit vultum pauperis, nec metuit personam potentis. Sed una eademque ei fuit in omnibus sancta libertas, ut
ita susciperet penulam pauperis, ac si veneraretur togam in-
2 cliti senatoris. Obiit autem perfectus in sanctitate, et sepultus est in basilica sancti Stephani ad laevam altaris, ad cuius
nunc tumulum plerumque quartanorum febris, melancholia
compressa, restinguitur.

prostrating himself upon his hair shirt in the middle of the road, prayed for a long time with tears.

Then he arose and, to the extent his strength allowed 5
him, intoned the antiphon they had asked for. Its words, taken from Solomon's prayer, were these: "If heaven is closed and there are no rains because of the sins of the people, and they pray turned toward your face, hear them, Lord, and forgive the sins of your people and give rains to the land which you gave to your people to possess."

When they began to sing devoutly, the prayer of the con- 6
fessor reached the ears of the lofty power, and behold! the sky darkened and became covered with clouds. And before they reached the city gate, a heavy rain fell down upon that whole region, so that all were astonished and said that it had been granted because of the prayer of the blessed man.

5. The bishop of God, however, became old and was so advanced in age that he no longer had the strength to spit on the ground; he had to have a bowl next to his lips to catch his saliva. His eyes did not cloud over, however, nor did his heart stray from the ways of God; he did not turn away from the face of a poor man, nor did he fear a powerful one. But he had one and the same free manner with all, so that he received the mantle of the poor man as though he were venerating the toga of an illustrious senator. He died perfect in 2
holiness and was buried in the basilica of the holy Stephen on the left side of the altar, and today quartan fever is often extinguished and melancholy is driven out at his tomb.

5

De sancto Portiano abbate

Prologus

Quanta omnipotens Deus suo dicatis nomine indulgeat, quantaque eisdem pro fideli servitio benignitatis ope compenset! Magna quidem se pollicetur redditurum in caelo, sed quae accepturi sunt plerumque hoc declarat in saeculo. Nam saepius de servis liberos, de liberis efficit gloriosos, iuxta illud Psalmographi dictum: "Suscitans a terra inopem, et de stercore erigens pauperem, ut collocet eum cum prin-
2 cipibus populi sui" [Psalms 113:7–8]. De hoc et Anna, uxor Helcanae, ait: "Saturati prius pro pane se locaverunt, et famelici saturati sunt" [1 Samuel 2:5]. Ex hoc et ipsa Redemptoris nostri genetrix virgo Maria dicebat: "Deposuit potentes de sede, et exaltavit humiles" [Luke 1:52]. Sic et ipse Dominus in evangelio ait: "Erunt primi novissimi, et novissimi primi" [Matthew 20:16].

3 Micet ergo amore suo divina misericordia super inopes, ut de parvis magnos statuat ac de infimis Unigeniti sui faciat cohaeredes. Praefecit enim de hac mundana egestate in caelo, quo scandere non potuit terrenum imperium, ut accedat illuc rusticus, quo accedere non meruit purpuratus.

4 Sic nunc de beato Portiano abbate, quem non modo de onere mundani servitii eruit, verum etiam magnis virtutibus

5

About the holy abbot Portianus

Prologue

How much does almighty God give to those dedicated to his name, and how much does his generosity reward them for their faithful service! Great things does he promise them in heaven, but often he also tells them what they shall receive in this life. For frequently he frees those who were slaves and makes glorious those who are free, according to the saying of the psalmist: "He raises the poor from the dust, and the needy from the dung heap, to cause them to sit
with the princes of his people." Of this Hannah too, the 2
wife of Helkanah, said: "Those who were full have hired themselves out for bread, and those who were hungry are full." About this the Virgin Mary, mother of our Redeemer, also said: "He has put down the mighty from their thrones and exalted the humble." Likewise the Lord himself said in the gospel: "The last will be first, and the first last."

Therefore God's compassion shines with his love upon 3
the poor, so that he makes the humble great and raises up the lowest to be coheirs with his Only Son. For he has lifted up the world's lowest to heaven where the earthly empire cannot ascend, so that the peasant enters where the purple-robed emperor was unworthy to go.

This is true of the blessed abbot Portianus, whom he not 4
only released from the burden of earthly servitude but also

sublimavit, atque post mundum et pressuras saeculi in requie aeterna constituit, locavitque eum inter angelorum choros, de quibus expulsus est dominus ille terrenus.

1. Beatissimus igitur Portianus ab ineunte aetate Deum quaerere caeli semper, etiam inter terrena servitia, conabatur. Hic enim servus fertur fuisse cuiusdam barbari, isque cum plerumque ad monasterium confugeret, ut eum domino suo abbas redderet excusatum. Ad extremum fugiens, dominus eius de vestigio sequitur, et abbatem calumniari coepit, reputans quod ipse eum seduceret ne sibi suus fa-
2 mulus deserviret. Cumque de consuetudine ut eum redderet calumniando abbatem insisteret, dicit abbas Portiano: "Quid vis ut faciam?" Et ille: "Redde," inquit, "me excusatum." Cumque excusatus redditus fuisset, et dominus eius reducere eum domum vellet, ita caecatus est ut nihil penitus
3 posset agnoscere. Cernens autem se gravibus doloribus affici, abbatem vocat, dicens: "Supplica, quaeso, pro me Dominum, et accipe hunc servum ad eius cultum. Forsitan pro-
4 merebor recipere lumen amissum." Tunc abbas, vocatum beatum, ait: "Impone, quaeso, manus tuas super oculos eius." Cumque ille refutaret, tandem abbatis devictus precibus, super oculos domini sui signum beatae crucis imposuit. Statimque, disrupta caligine et sedato dolore, pristinae redditus est sanitati.

5 At vero exin beatus Portianus clericus factus tanto virtutis cumulo est praelatus, ut, decedente abbate, ipse succederet. Qui fertur aestivo tempore, cum ardor solis vi caloris

ennobled with great deeds of power, established in eternal rest after this world and its tribulations, and placed with the choirs of angels from which the Ruler of this world is excluded.

1. Notwithstanding his earthly status as a slave, then, the most blessed Portianus attempted from his earliest childhood to seek the Lord of heaven. He is said to have been the slave of a certain barbarian, and often to have fled to a monastery so that its abbot had to give him back to his master after having been pardoned by him. The last time he fled, his master followed his tracks and began to accuse the abbot falsely of enticing Portianus not to serve him any longer.
When his master was slandering the abbot as usual and 2
pressing him to return Portianus, the abbot said to the latter: "What do you want me to do?" And he said: "Give me back, pardoned." When he had been given back to his master and that man wished to take him home, he became so
blinded that he could see almost nothing. Afflicted with se- 3
vere pain, he called the abbot and said: "Implore the Lord for me, I beg you, and accept this slave for his service. Maybe then I shall deserve to recover the light I have lost."
The abbot thereupon called the blessed man and said: "I beg 4
you, put your hands on his eyes." He at first refused but was finally persuaded by the abbot's pleading and made the sign of the cross over the eyes of his master. At once, the darkness dissipated, the pain was soothed, and he was restored to his original health.

Eventually the blessed Portianus became a cleric, and dis- 5
played so much virtue that when the abbot died he succeeded him. It is said of him that in summertime, when the

sui cuncta consumeret, et etiam corpora quae robustiora
potu ciboque erant, ab aestu defatigaret, hic, ieiuniis post
perditum omnem ab ore umorem, salem aestuans rumina-
bat, ex quo iterum assumpto liquore arentes gengivas pa-
6 rumper inficeret. Quae res, quamquam palatum aridum
umectaret, tamen maius tormentum addita corporis siti
praestabat. Sal enim, ut nulli occulitur, magis ardorem sitis
concitat quam exstinguit, sed hic, tribuente Domino, arce-
batur ab eo.

2. His diebus Theodericus ingressus Arvernum terminum, omnia exterminabat, cuncta devastabat. Cumque in
Arthonensis vici pratis castra metasset, antedictus senex ad
2 occursum eius properat quasi pro populo rogaturus. Ingressusque castra mane, rege adhuc in tentoriis dormiente, Sigivaldi papilionem, qui tunc primus cum eo habebatur, aggressus est. Et dum de hac captivitate conqueritur, Sigivaldus
ut, ablutis manibus, merum dignaretur accipere, deprecatur,
dicens: "Magnum mihi hodie gaudium commodumque divina pietas praestat, si infra tentorii mei saepta, facta orati-
3 one, potum dignaris accipere." Audierat enim famam sanctitatis eius, idcirco et honorem ei pro Dei reverentia
impendebat. Quod ille diversis modis excusans, asserebat
hoc non posse fieri, quia, inquit, nec hora debita esset, nec
regi dignum praebuisset occursum, et quod his omnibus
potius erat, necdum adhuc Domino psalmorum decanta-
4 tionem debitam exsolvisset. Sed, his sepositis, vi eum com-
pulit, allatumque vasculum quo potio tenebatur, rogat ut
eum sanctus imposita prius manu sanctificaret. Qui, elevata

blazing sun consumes all things with the force of its heat and even bodies strengthened by food and drink are exhausted, this man, having lost all the saliva from his mouth through fasting, chewed salt when he was hot and moistened his dry gums with the moisture it produced. Although 6
he moistened his palate, it caused a greater torment for his body by increasing his thirst. For as everyone knows salt excites rather than extinguishes thirst. But God's grace prevented this from happening to him.

2. In these days, Theodoric came into the territory of Clermont, exterminating and destroying everything. When he had set up camp in the meadows around the village of Artonne, the aforesaid old man Portianus hurried to meet
him in order to plead for the people. He entered the camp 2
early in the morning while the king was still asleep in his tent and came to the tent of Sigivald, who was then first in the king's favor. And while Portianus was complaining to him about the conquest, Sigivald asked him to wash his hands and to deign to drink unmixed wine with him, saying: "The divine Goodness will give me great joy and well-being today if you would deign to say a prayer and accept a drink
in my tent." For he had heard men speaking of his sanctity, 3
and therefore honored him out of reverence for God. But Portianus protested with various excuses, saying that he could not do this for, he said, it was not yet the appropriate time of day, he had not yet paid his respects to the king, and, more important than all this, he had not yet fulfilled
his obligation to sing the psalms. But Sigivald thrust these 4
protests aside and forced him to acquiesce; a vessel with wine was brought, and he asked the holy man to bless it by the imposition of his hand. When Portianus had raised his

dextera, cum signum crucis imposuisset, vasculum scinditur
medium, ac vinum quod infra tenebatur cum immenso ser-
5 pente terrae diffunditur. Quod cernentes qui aderant, metu
exterriti ad pedes beati viri decidunt, lambunt vestigia, osculantur et plantas. Mirantur omnes virtutem senis, mirantur et se ab iniqui anguis viru divinitus fuisse salvatos. Ad istud miraculum concurrit omnis exercitus, vallat multitudo
omnis beatum virum, cupiens eius fimbrias manu tangere,
etsi osculo honorare non potuit.

6 Et rex exsilit de stratu suo, accurritque ad beati confessoris adventum, illoque tacente, cunctos quos repetebat capti-
vos absolvit, et reliquos deinceps, ut voluit, sic recepit. Du-
plex ibi beneficium Domino cooperante largitus, et illos a
morte eruit, et hos a iugo captivitatis exemit. Vere, ut credo
et fides mea est, quia constat ab hoc periculo salvatos quasi
suscitatos a mortuis.

3. Nec hoc praeterire volui quod eum diabolus diversis
machinis conatus illudere, cum videret se nihil posse nocere,
visibilibus illum praeliis est aggressus. Nam nocte quadam
dum se sopori dedisset, subito expergefactus vidit cellulam
suam quasi incendio concremari. Exsurgensque perterritus
2 ostium petiit. Quod cum reserare nequiret, in oratione
prosternitur, ac signum salutare coram se et circum se faciens, protinus phantasia flammarum quae apparuerat evanuit, cognovitque hoc diaboli fuisse fallaciam.

right hand and made the sign of the cross over it, the vessel broke in half and the wine it contained spilled on the ground together with a huge snake. Seeing this, those present were 5
terrified; they fell at the saint's feet and kissed them. All admired the old man's holy power, and were amazed that they had been divinely saved from the poison of the wicked serpent. Everyone in the army rushed up to see this miracle and the whole multitude surrounded the blessed man, wishing to touch the fringe of his robe with their hands, although they were not allowed to honor it by kissing it.

The king too leaped up from his bed and ran to meet the 6
blessed confessor, and before the saint could say anything, he released all the captives whom the holy man had been hoping to liberate; subsequently the saint received the others he wished. With God's help the holy man gave a double benefit there in that he rescued the former from death and redeemed the latter from the yoke of captivity. In truth, I believe and am confident that those who were rescued from this danger were as though raised from the dead.

3. I do not wish to pass over how the devil, when he had tried to fool Portianus using various illusions and had seen that he could not hurt him, attacked him with battles he could see. For on a certain night when the saint was sleeping, he was suddenly awakened and saw that his cell seemed to be on fire. Jumping up terrified, he tried to find the door.
When he was unable to open it, he prostrated himself in 2
prayer, and after he made the saving sign of the cross upon himself and around himself the phantom flames at once vanished, and he realized that it had been a trick of the devil.

3 Idque statim revelatum est beato Protasio, qui tunc apud Cambidobrense monasterium habebatur reclusus. Qui cum summa festinatione monachum ex cellula sua ad fratrem dirigens, hortatus est, dicens: "Oportet te, dilectissime frater, insidiis diaboli resistere viriliter, et nihil de illius dolositate pavescere, sed omnia quae intulerit oratione assidua, ac signo crucis e contra opposito evincere, quia talibus semper temptationibus servos Dei nititur expugnare."

4 Senuit autem vir beatus, et impleto boni operis cursu, migravit ad Dominum, cuius nunc tumulus saepius divinis glorificatur virtutibus. Haec tantum de sancto viro cognovimus, non diiudicantes alios qui maiora de eo cognoverunt, si voluerint aliqua in eius laudem conscribere.

6

De sancto Gallo episcopo

Prologus

Nobilitatis mundanae fastigium semper inhiat cupiditatibus, gaudet honoribus, inflatur occursibus, litibus forum pulsat, rapinis pascitur, calumniis delectatur, rubiginosa auri talenta desiderat. Et dum parva possedere videtur, ut

This was immediately revealed to the blessed Protasius, who was at that time a recluse at the monastery of Cambidobrum. He hastily sent a monk from his cell to his brother Portianus, to tell him: "You ought to resist the devil's wiles manfully, dearest brother, and not fear his deviousness, but all that he does to you you should overcome with assiduous prayer and by opposing it with the sign of the cross, for he always tries to attack the servants of God with such trials." 3

The blessed man became old, however, and, having completed the course of his good works, he went to the Lord; his tomb is now often glorified by divine deeds of power. This is all we know about this holy man; we will not pass adverse judgment on others who know more about him if they wish to write something in his praise. 4

6

About the holy bishop Gallus

Prologue

Those of the noblest rank in this world always follow their desires, enjoy being honored, take pride in social contacts, pursue litigation in the courts, feed on plunder, delight in slander, and crave ruddy-gold talents. When they seem to possess a little, they are all the more inflamed to

agglomeret plurima magis accenditur, ingeritque ei congeries auri sitim arduam possidendi, sicut Prudentius ait:

"Auri namque fames procedit maior ab auro."

2 Unde fit ut dum gaudet pompis saeculi et vanis honoribus oblectari, nihil ei de mansuris dignitatibus in memoriam revocetur, nec respicit ad ea quae non videntur, dummodo illa quibus satiari animum putat, importune possideat.

3 Sed sunt qui se de his nexibus, tamquam aves de muscipulis evolantes et ad altiora tendentes, mentis alacriores ingenio absolverunt, ac relictis exosisque terrenis facultatibus, totis se viribus ad illa quae sunt caelestia aptaverunt. Sicut sanctus Gallus, incola Arvernae urbis, quem a Dei cultu abstrahere non potuit nec splendor generis, nec celsitudo sena-
4 torii ordinis, nec opulentia facultatis. Quem separare a Dei amore non potuit nec dilectio patris, non matris blanditiae, non amor nutricum, non obsecundatio baiulorum. Sed his omnibus pro nihilo ductis, et tamquam stercora exosis, Dei se dilectioni, Dei se officio vovens, monasteriali se districtioni subegit.

5 Sciebat enim iuvenilis fervor flammas non aliter posse devincere, nisi censurae canonicae et disciplinae severissimae subderetur. Sciebat enim se ab humilitate saeculi ad altiora sublevaturum, et per patientiam tolerationis ad illa excelsi apicis gloriam evecturum, quod postea probavit eventus.

gather more, and a heap of gold induces in them a fierce thirst to possess: as Prudentius said,

"With the amassing of gold the thirst for gold increases."

2 Thus it happens that while they enjoy being pleased by the pomp and empty honors of the world, they do not remember to think of dignities that remain and do not pay attention to what is not seen, since they unjustly possess things which they think will satisfy their longings.

3 But there are those who, through a greater intelligence, have released themselves from these bonds, like birds who fly out of their snares up to the sky: leaving their detested earthly possessions behind, they apply themselves with all their strength to heavenly things. Such a one was Gallus, an inhabitant of the city of Clermont, who could not be diverted from the service of God by the splendor of his lineage, the distinction of his senatorial rank, or the opulence
4 of his resources. He could not be separated from his love of God either by his father's love, his mother's tenderness, his nurse's care, or the compliance of his servants. Holding all these for nothing and detesting them as though they were dung, he pledged himself to God's love and God's service and subjected himself to monastic discipline.

5 For he knew that the flames of youthful fervor could not be overcome except by subjugating them to canonical supervision and the most severe discipline. And he knew that he would lift himself from the baseness of the world to higher things, and that through the patience of humility he would be conveyed aloft to the highest pinnacle of glory, which subsequent events proved to be the case.

1. Sanctus denique Gallus ab adolescentia sua devotus Deo esse coepit, diligensque ex tota anima Dominum, et ea quae Deo dilecta esse noverat diligebat. Pater eius nomine Georgius, mater vero Leocadia a stirpe Vectii Epagati descendens, quem Lugduni passum Eusebii testatur Historia, qui ita de primoribus senatoribus fuerunt ut in Galliis nihil inveniatur esse generosius atque nobilius.

2 Cumque ei pater cuiusdam senatoris filiam quarere vellet, ille assumpto secum uno puerulo monasterium Cromonense expetiit, sexto situm ab Arverna urbe miliario, suppliciter abbatem exorans ut sibi comam capitis tondere dignaretur. At ille videns prudentiam atque elegantiam pueri, nomen inquirit, interrogat genus et patriam. Ille vero Gallum se vocitari pronunciat, civem Arvernum, Georgii filium senato-
3 ris. Quem abbas ut cognovit de prima progenie esse progenitum, ait: "Bene desideras, fili, sed primum oportet haec in patris tui deferri notitiam. Et si hoc ille voluerit, faciam quae deposcis." Denique abbas pro hac causa nuntios mittit ad patrem, interrogantes quid de puero observari iuberet.

4 At ille parumper contristatus, ait: "Primogenitus," inquit, "erat mihi, et ideo eum volui copulare. Sed si eum Dominus ad suum dignatur ascire servitium, illius magis quam nostra voluntas fiat." Et adiecit: "Quidquid vobis infans, Deo inspirante, suggesserit, adimplete."

2. Tunc abbas ista nuntiis referentibus discens, puerum clericum fecit. Erat autem egregiae castitatis, et tamquam

CHAPTER 6

1. The holy Gallus, then, began to be devoted to God from his youth, loving the Lord with his whole heart, and loving the things which he knew delighted God. His father was named Georgius, and his mother Leocadia was descended from the family of Vectius Epagatus, whom Eusebius's *History* mentions as having died a martyr's death in Lyons; and they belonged to leading senatorial families, so much so that no one more noble or magnanimous could be found in Gaul.

When his father wished him to seek the daughter of a 2
certain senator in marriage, he took with him one servant
and went to the monastery of Cournon, situated six miles
from the city of Clermont, and humbly asked the abbot to
shave the hair off his head. But seeing the prudence and the
elegant appearance of the boy, he asked his name and inquired about his family and country. He said his name was
Gallus, that he was a citizen of Clermont, and the son of
senator Georgius. When the abbot found out that he came 3
from the first family of the city, he said: "Your desire is good,
son, but first it should be made known to your father. And if
he wishes this, I shall do what you ask." Then the abbot sent
messengers to the boy's father on account of this matter, in-
quiring what he commanded to be done about the boy.

And, a bit saddened, he said: "He was my firstborn, and 4
therefore I wanted him to marry. But if God deigns to take him into his service, let his will be done rather than mine." And he added: "Whatever the God-inspired child tells you, do it!"

2. When the abbot learned this from the messengers, he made the boy a cleric. For he was perfectly chaste and, as

senior, nihil perverse appetens, iocis se etiam iuvenilibus cohibebat. Habens mirae dulcedinis vocem cum modulatione suavi, lectioni incumbens assidue, delectans ieiuniis, et abs-
2 tinens se multum a cibis. Quem cum beatus Quintianus episcopus ad idem monasterium veniens cantantem audisset, non eum permisit ultra illuc retineri, sed secum ad civitatem adduxit, et ut caelestis pater in dulcedine spiritali nu-
3 trivit. Cumque, defuncto patre, vox eius magis ac magis die adveniente componeretur, atque idem in populis maximum haberet amorem, nuntiaverunt haec Theoderico regi, quem dicto citius arcessitum tanta dilectione excoluit, ut eum proprio filio plus amaret. A regina autem eius simili amore diligebatur, non solum pro honestate vocis, sed etiam pro castimonia corporis.

4 Nam tunc Theodericus rex ex civibus Arvernis clericos multos abduxit, quos Trevericae ecclesiae ad reddendum famulatum Domino iussit assistere. Beatum vero Gallum a se nequaquam passus est separari. Unde factum est ut eunte
5 rege in Agrippinam urbem, et ipse abiret simul. Erat autem ibi fanum quoddam diversis ornamentis refertum, in quo barbaries proxima libamina exhibens, usque advomitum cibo potuque replebatur. Ibi et simulacra ut deum adorans, membra secundum quod unumquemque dolor attigisset, sculpebat in ligno.

6 Quod ubi sanctus Gallus audivit, statim illuc cum uno tantum clerico properat, accensoque igne, cum nullus ex stultis paganis adesset, ad fanum applicat ac succendit. At

though he were an older man, did not desire anything perverse but refrained even from youthful jocularity. He had a beautiful voice and could modulate it wonderfully; devoting himself assiduously to reading, he also delighted in fasting and often abstained from food. When the blessed bishop 2
Quintianus once came to the monastery and heard him singing, he did not allow him to stay there any longer but took him along to the city and raised him as a heavenly father in spiritual sweetness. When Gallus's father died, his 3
voice had become more beautiful day by day, and he was much loved by the people. They announced this to King Theoderic and no sooner was it said than it was done: Theoderic sought him out and cherished him with more affection than he did his own son. The queen too cherished him equally not only for his lovely voice but also for the chastity of his body.

At that time King Theoderic took many clerics from the 4
citizens of Clermont and commanded them to serve the Lord in the church of Trier. And he never let himself be separated from the blessed Gallus. Thus it happened that when the king went to Cologne, Gallus went with him. In Trier 5
there was a pagan shrine adorned with various ornaments where the barbarians offered liquid sacrifices and gorged themselves with food and wine until they vomited. They worshipped idols there as God, and when some part of their body had been in pain, they sculpted it out of wood [as an offering of gratitude].

When the holy Gallus heard about this, he at once rushed 6
to the place with only one cleric, and after lighting a torch while none of the foolish pagans were present, he put it to

illi videntes fumum delubri ad caelum usque conscendere, auctorem incendii quaerunt, inventumque evaginatis gladiis prosequuntur. Ille vero in fugam versus, aulae se regiae
7 condidit. Verum postquam rex quae acta fuerunt, paganis minantibus, recognovit, blandis eos sermonibus lenivit et sic eorum furorem improbum mitigavit. Referre enim saepe erat solitus vir beatus haec cum lacrimis, et dicebat: "Vae mihi qui non perstiti ut in hac causa finirer!" Fungebatur eo tempore diaconatus officio.

3. Denique cum beatus Quintianus episcopus ab hoc saeculo, iubente Domino, transisset, sanctus Gallus apud urbem Arvernam eo tempore morabatur. Cives autem Arverni ad domum Impetrati presbyteri eiusdem avunculi convenerunt, conquerentes de obitu sacerdotis, et qui in eius locum deberet substitui requirentes. Quod diutissime pertractantes, regressus est unusquisque ad semetipsum.

2 Post quorum discessum, sanctus Gallus vocavit unum ex clericis, et irruente in se Spiritu sancto, ait: "Quid hi mussitant? Quid cursitant? Quid retractant? Vacuum est," inquit, "opus eorum, ego ero episcopus! Mihi Dominus hunc honorem largiri dignabitur! Tu vero, cum me redire de praesentia regis audieris, accipe equum decessoris mei stratum, et egrediens te in obviam exhibe mihi. Quod si audire despexeris,
3 cave ne te in posterum paeniteat." Cumque haec loqueretur, super lectulum decumbebat. Tunc iratus contra eum clericus, cum multa exprobaret, elisum super spondam lecti latus eius laesit, turbidusque discessit.

the shrine and set it on fire. Seeing the smoke of their shrine rising to the sky, however, they looked for the author of the blaze, and when they had found him pursued him with
drawn swords. He fled and hid in the royal palace. When the 7
belligerent pagans told the king what had happened, he mollified them with blandishments and in this way appeased their wicked fury. The blessed man, however, would often talk about this with tears, saying: "Woe to me for not persisting, so that I might have ended my life for this cause!" At that time he served in the office of deacon.

3. Later, at the time that the blessed Quintianus left this world at the command of the Lord, the holy Gallus was staying in the city of Clermont. The citizens of Clermont came together at the house of the priest Impetratus, his uncle, mourning the bishop's passing and looking for someone to take his place. After discussing the matter for a very long time, each went back to his own house.

After their departure the holy Gallus called one of the 2
clerics, and as the Holy Spirit inspired him, said: "Why do these men find fault? Why do they run back and forth? What is there to discuss? Their efforts are in vain, for I shall be bishop! The Lord will deign to grant me this honor. As for you, when you hear that I have returned from my audience with the king, take my predecessor's horse, saddle it, come out to meet me and offer it to me. And if you disdain
to obey me, take care not to repent of it later!" While he 3
spoke in this manner, he was resting on his couch. Then the cleric became very angry with him; he shouted insults, shoved him against the side of the couch so that he hurt his side, and left in a rage.

4 Quo discedente, ait Impetratus presbyter ad beatum Gallum: "Audi, fili, consilium meum. Noli penitus retardare, sed vade ad regem et nuntia ei quae hic contigerint. Et si ei inspirat Dominus ut tibi hoc sacerdotium largiatur, magnas Deo referemus gratias. Sin aliud, vel ei qui ordinatus fuerit commendaberis."

5 Ille vero abiens, quae de beato Quintiano contigerant regi nuntiavit. Tunc etiam et Aprunculus Treverorum Episcopus transiit. Congregatique clerici civitatis illius ad Theodericum regem, sanctum Gallum petebant episcopum. Quibus ille ait: "Abscedite et alium requirite. Gallum enim diaconum alibi habeo destinatum." Tunc eligentes sanctum Nicetium episcopum acceperunt.

6 Arverni vero clerici cum consensu insipientium facto et multis muneribus, ad regem venerunt. Iam tunc germen illud iniquum coeperat fructificare, ut sacerdotium aut venderetur a regibus, aut compararetur a clericis. Tunc hi audiunt a rege quod sanctum Gallum habituri essent episcopum.

7 Quem presbyterum ordinatum iussit rex ut, datis de publico expensis, cives invitarentur ad epulum, et laetarentur ob honorem Galli futuri episcopi. Quod ita factum est. Nam referre erat solitus non amplius donasse se pro episcopatu quam unum triantem coquo qui servivit ad prandium. Post haec rex, datis ad solatium eius duobus episcopis, Arvernis eum direxit.

8 Clericus vero ille qui super spondam lecti latus eius illiserat, Viventius nomine, ad occursum pontificis secundum verbum illius properat, non sine magno pudore et se, simulque equum quem iusserat, repraesentat. Ingressis utrisque

When he had left, the priest Impetratus said to the 4
blessed Gallus: "Listen to my advice, my son. Don't delay,
but go to the king and tell him what has happened here. And
if the Lord inspires him to grant you this bishopric, we will
give great thanks to God. If not, you will be commended to
the one who will be ordained."

He left and announced the death of the blessed Quintia- 5
nus to the king. At that time Bishop Aprunculus of Trier also
left this world. The clergy of this city came to the king and
asked for the holy Gallus to become their bishop. The king
said to them: "Go and look for another one. I have destined
the deacon Gallus for another place." Then they elected and
received the holy Nicetius as their bishop.

The clergy from Clermont then came to the king with 6
their agreement among fools and many gifts. Already then
the seed of that evil practice began to sprout in which the
episcopal office is either sold by kings or bought by clerics.
Then these people heard from the king that they were to
have the holy Gallus as their bishop.

When the priest Gallus had been ordained, the king or- 7
dered that the citizens be invited to a meal at public expense
and that all should rejoice at the honor of their future bishop
Gallus. And so it happened. For he used to relate that, in exchange for the bishopric, he had not given more than one
third of a solidus to the cook who prepared the lunch. After
this the king gave him two bishops as traveling companions
and sent him to Clermont.

The cleric, named Viventius, who had hurt Gallus's side 8
against the bed, hurried to meet the bishop as Gallus had
told him to and presented himself, not without great embarrassment, together with the horse as he had ordered. When

in balneum, dolorem lateris, quem ab impulsu superbiae eius clerici incurrerat, clementer improperat, magnam ex hoc ei ingerens verecundiam, non cum ira, sed tantum ioco spiritali delectatus.

9 Igitur exinde cum multo psallentio in civitatem suscipitur, et in sua ecclesia episcopus ordinatur.

4. Iam vero assumpto episcopatu, tanta humilitate tantaque caritate cum omnibus usus est, ut ab omnibus dilige-
retur. Patientiam vero ultra hominum morem habens, ita ut,
si dici fas est, Moysi compararetur ad diversas iniurias susti-
2 nendas. Unde factum est ut a presbytero suo in convivio percussus in capite, ita se quietum reddiderit, ut nec sermonem
quidem asperum respondisset. Sed omnia quae ei accide-
bant patienter ferens, in Dei hoc arbitrio, a quo se petebat
enutriri, iactabat.

3 Nam et Evodius quidam ex senatoribus presbyter, cum in convivio ecclesiae eum multis calumniis atque conviciis lacessisset, consurgens sacerdos loca basilicarum sanctarum circuibat. Tamen cum hoc Evodio fuisset perlatum, post eum cursu veloci dirigens, et se ante pedes eius in ipsa platea prosternens, veniam petiit, deprecans ut eum oratio eius cum omnipotente iudice non fuscaret.

4 At ille benigne eum colligens, cuncta quae locutus fuerat clementer indulsit, eum arguens ne haec ultra contra
sacerdotes Domini auderet appetere, quia ipsa episcopatum numquam promereretur accipere. Quod postea pro-
5 bavit eventus. Nam cum in Gabalitano ad episcopatum iam
electus, iam in cathedra positus, iam cuncta parata essent
ut benediceretur episcopus, ita subito contra eum omnis

they had both entered the baths, the blessed man gently reproached him for the pain in his side which he had suffered
through the cleric's pride, thereby causing him great shame
because the blessed man did not reprove him in anger but
spoke of it with a smile, as a kind of spiritual joke.

Then he was received into the city with a great deal of 9
psalm singing and consecrated bishop in his church.

4. When he had succeeded to the episcopate, he conducted himself toward everyone with such great humility
and affection that he was loved by all. He had more than human patience so that, if one may say so, he might be compared to Moses in his tolerance of injuries. Thus it happened 2
that when he had been struck on the head by a priest during a meal, he kept silent and did not respond with a bitter word. He tolerated everything that was done to him pa-
tiently, leaving the matter to the will of God, by whom he
wished to be guided.

So too when Evodius, a priest of senatorial rank, pro- 3
voked him with many calumnies and insults during a meal
with the clerics, the bishop rose and went to walk around
the saints' basilicas. When this was told to Evodius, he
quickly went after him and prostrated himself on the street
before his feet, begging forgiveness and imploring him not
to condemn him in his prayers to the almighty Judge.

And he kindly raised him and generously forgave all that 4
had been said, urging him however not to presume to attack
bishops of the Lord in this way again, for he himself would
never deserve to receive a bishopric. And later events confirmed this. For when Evodius had been elected bishop in 5
Javols and was already sitting on the throne, everything being ready for his consecration as bishop, suddenly the whole

populus consurrexit, ut vix vivus posset evadere. Qui postea presbyter transiit.

5. Apud Aurelianensem autem urbem, incriminato ab iniquis Episcopo Marco et in exsilium truso, magnus episcoporum conventus est aggregatus, Childebertho rege iubente. In qua synodo cognoscentes beati episcopi hoc esse vacuum quod contra eum fuerat mussitatum, eum civitati et cathedrae suae restituunt.

2 Denique tunc in servitio sancti Galli Valentinianus diaconus, qui nunc presbyter habetur atque vocalis, abiit. Cumque episcopo alio missas dicente, diaconus ille propter iactantiam potius quam pro Dei timore cantare vellet, a sancto
Gallo prohibebatur, dicente sibi: "Sine," inquit, "fili.
Quando, Domino iubente, nos celebraverimus solemnia,
tunc et tu canere debes. Nunc eius clerici concinant qui
3 consecrat missas." At ille et tunc se posse pronuntiat. Cui
sacerdos: "Fac ut libet, nam quod volueris non explebis." Ille
quoque negligens mandatum pontificis abiit, at tam defor-
4 miter cecinit, ut ab omnibus irrideretur. Adveniente autem
alia dominica, dicente saepe dicto pontifice missas, iussit
eum abire : "Nunc," inquit, "in nomine Domini quod volueris explicabis." Quod cum fecisset, in tantum vox eius praeclara facta est ut a omnibus laudaretur. O beatum virum, cui
talis gratia concessa est, ut sicut animae, ita et cum eo voces
hominum sub eius potestate consisterent, quas et cum voluit cantu prohibuit et cantare permisit!

6. Praestitit autem Deus et alia miracula magna per illum. Nam cum Iulianus defensor, presbyter deinceps, dulcissimae voluntatis homo, a quartano typo correptus graviter

populace rose up against him so that he narrowly escaped with his life. He died later as a priest.

5. In the city of Orléans, a large group of bishops gathered at the command of King Childebert because Bishop Marcus of Orléans had been accused by wicked men and sent into exile. In this synod the blessed bishops found the complaints against him to be groundless, and they reinstated him in his city and on his throne.

Then the deacon Valentinianus, at that time in holy Gal- 2
lus's service and now priest and cantor, had gone with him. While another bishop was saying mass and the deacon, more out of pride than out of reverence for God, wished to sing, he was forbidden to do so by holy Gallus, who said: "Stop, my son. When we celebrate mass, by God's command, then you should sing. Now let the clergy of the one
who celebrates this mass sing." But the deacon said that he 3
could sing then too. The bishop said to him: "Do as you like, but you won't be able to do what you wish." Disregarding the bishop's order, the deacon left his seat and thereupon sang so awkwardly that he was laughed at by everyone.
When another Sunday came, and bishop Gallus was saying 4
mass, he commanded the deacon to leave his seat, saying: "Now, in the name of the Lord, you will carry out what you wish." And when he did this, his voice was so pure and clear that all praised him. O blessed man, to whom so great a grace was given that, as with souls, men's voices were so completely in his power that he could forbid as well as permit them to sing!

6. God also worked other great miracles through him. For when Julian, formerly the church's advocate, now a priest and a most kind man, was gravely tormented by the

cruciaretur, lectulum sancti sacerdotis expetiit. In quo decubans, a lectuaria ipse coopertus, paululum obdormiens, ita sanatus est ut nec confractus postea ab hac infirmitate fuisset.

2 Cum autem Arverna civitas maximo incendio cremaretur et hoc sanctus comperisset, ingressus ecclesiam, diutissime Dominum ante sanctum altare cum lacrimis exoravit; surgensque, evangelia comprehensa, apertaque in obviam se igni obtulit. Qua contra parata, protinus ad aspectum eius ita omne incendium est exstinctum ut nec favillae quidem in eo igneae remansissent.

3 Sub eius autem tempore magno terrae motu Arverna civitas est concussa, sed cur hoc acciderit ignoramus. Hoc tamen scimus, quod nullum ex populo laesit.

4 Cum autem lues illa, quam inguinariam vocant, per diversas regiones desaeviret et maxime tunc Arelatensem provinciam depopularet, sanctus Gallus non tantum pro se quantum pro populo suo trepidus erat. Cumque die noctuque
Dominum deprecaretur ut vivens plebem suam vastari non
cerneret, per visum noctis apparuit ei angelus Domini, qui
tam caesariem quam vestem in similitudinem nivis candi-
5 dam efferebat. Et ait ad eum: “Bene enim te, O sacerdos,
prospectat divina pietas pro populo tuo supplicantem. Ideoque ne timeas, exaudita est enim oratio tua. Et ecce eris cum
populo tuo ab hac infirmitate liberatus; nullusque te vivente
in regione ista ab hac strage deperibit. Nunc autem noli metuere. Post octo vero annos time.” Unde manifestum fuit,
transactis his annis eum a saeculo discessisse.

quartan fever, he sought the holy bishop's bed. After he had lain down on it under the covers and slept for a little while, he recovered so completely that he was thereafter never again racked by this illness.

When a great fire consumed the city of Clermont, and 2
this holy man learned about it, he went into the church and for a very long time prayed to the Lord with tears before the altar; then he arose, took the gospel and carried it, opened, toward the fire. Its appearance instantly extinguished the blaze so completely that not one glowing ember remained.

About this time Clermont was shaken by a great earth- 3
quake, but why this happened we do not know. We do know, however, that none of the people were hurt.

And when the plague which they call "inguinal" came and 4
ravaged various regions, depopulating the province of Arles above all, the holy Gallus feared not so much for himself as for his people. While he prayed to the Lord day and night that he might not live to see his people destroyed, there appeared to him in a dream an angel of the Lord whose hair as
well as his robe shone white as snow. And the angel said to 5
him: "Divine piety looks kindly upon you, O bishop, on account of your supplication for your people. Therefore do not fear, for your prayer has been heard. You and your people will indeed be rescued from this illness; while you are alive no one in this region will perish from its devastation. So don't be afraid at this time. After eight years, however, do be afraid." From this it was evident that he would leave this world after these years had passed.

6 Expergefactus autem, et Deo gratias pro hac consolatione agens, quod per caelestem nuntium confortari dignatus est, rogationes illas instituit, ut media Quadragesima psallendo ad basilicam beati Iuliani martyris itinere pedestri venirent. Sunt autem in hoc itinere quasi stadia trecenta sexaginta.

7 Cum autem regiones illas, ut diximus, lues illa consumeret, ad civitatem Arvernam, sancti Galli intercedente oratione, non attigit. Unde ego non parvam censeo gratiam eius qui hoc meruit, ut pastor positus oves suas devorari, defendente Domino, non videret.

7. Sed veniamus ad illud tempus cum eum Dominus de hoc mundo iussit assumi. Cum gravatus incommodo decubaret, ita febris interna omnia membra eius depavit ut capil-
2 los et barbam simul amitteret. Sciens autem se, revelante Domino, post triduum migraturum, convocat populum et omnibus, confracto pane, communionem sancta ac pia voluntate largitur. Adveniente autem die tertia, quae erat dominica dies, quae civibus Arvernis immanem intulit luctum, albescente iam caelo, interrogat quid in ecclesia psallerent.
3 Dixerunt benedictionem eos psallere. At ille, psalmo quinquagesimo et benedictione decantata et alleluiatico cum capitello expleto, consummavit matutinos. Quo perfuncto officio, ait: "Vale dicimus vobis, fratres." Et haec dicens, extensis membris, spiritum caelo intentum praemisit ad Dominum.

4 Transit autem aetatis suae anno sexagesimo quinto, episcopatus vero sui septimo et vigesimo anno. Exinde ablutus

When he woke up and had given thanks to God for this 6
consolation and for His having deigned to comfort him with a heavenly messenger, he instituted the prayers and processions called Rogations in the middle of Lent, when people go on foot to the basilica of the blessed Julian in Brioude. This is a journey of about forty miles.

And when that illness ravaged other regions, as we said, it 7
did not reach the city of Clermont because of holy Gallus's intercessory prayer. Hence I regard his grace as by no means small since he as their shepherd merited not to see his sheep being devoured, for they were protected by the Lord.

7. But let us come to the time that the Lord commanded him to be taken from this world. As he lay afflicted by an illness, the fever so consumed his internal organs that he lost
his hair as well as his beard. Knowing through a revelation 2
of the Lord that he would pass away on the third day, he called together the people, broke the bread, and gave communion to all with holy and pious intention. When the third day came, which was the Sunday that caused the citizens of Clermont immense grief, and dawn was already lightening the sky, he asked what was being sung in the church. They
told him that they were singing the benediction. And he fin- 3
ished the Matins by singing the fiftieth psalm, the benediction, and the alleluia. When he had completed the office he said: "I say 'Farewell' to you, brothers." After he had said this, he stretched out his body and sent his spirit, reaching out toward heaven, ahead to the Lord.

He passed in the sixty-fifth year of his life, the twenty- 4
seventh of his episcopate. After he had been washed and

atque vestitus in ecclesiam defertur, donec comprovinciales ad eum sepeliendum convenirent.

5 Magnum enim ibi miraculum ostensum populis fuit,
quod sanctus Dei, attracto dextro pede in feretro, se in aliud
latus, quod erat versus altare, contulit. Dum haec agerentur,
rogationes illae, quae quotannis ubique in Paschate fiunt,
6 celebrantur. Iacuit autem in ecclesia triduo, assiduo instante
psallentio cum magna frequentia populi. Episcopis autem
quarta die advenientibus, eum de ecclesia levaverunt, et
portantes in sancti Laurentii basilicam, ibi sepeliunt.

7 Iam vero in exsequiis eius quantus planctus, quanti populi adfuere, enarrari vix potest: mulieres cum lugubribus indumentis tanquam si viros perdidissent, similiter et viri, obtecto capite ut in exsequiis uxorum facere mos est, ipsi quoque Iudaei accensis lampadibus plangendo prosequebantur.

8 Omnes praeterea populi una voce dicebant: "Vae nobis, qui post hanc diem numquam similem merebimur habere pontificem." Et quia, ut diximus, provinciales longe distabant nec celerius venire potuerunt, ut mos rusticorum habetur, glebam super beatum corpus posuere fideles, quo ab aestu non intumesceret.

9 Quem caespitem post eius exsequias mulier quaedam et vere, ut ego diligenter inquisivi, virgo purissima et devota Deo, Meratina nomine, ab aliis eiectum collegit, in horto suo posuit, et infusa saepius aqua, Domino incrementum dante, vivere fecit. De quo caespite infirmi non solum auferentes atque bibentes herbam sanabantur, verum etiam

dressed, he was carried into the church to rest there until
the bishops of his province came to bury him.

A great miracle was shown there to the people when the 5
holy man of God on the bier drew up his right foot and
turned on his other side to face the altar. When this took
place, the Rogations which are held annually after Easter
were being celebrated. He lay for three days in the church 6
while psalms were continuously sung and great crowds of
people came. When the bishops came on the fourth day,
they took him from the church, carried him to the basilica
of holy Lawrence, and buried him there.

How loud a wailing and how many people attended his 7
funeral can scarcely be told: the women wore mourning as
though their husbands had died, likewise the men covered
their heads as is the custom at the funeral of a wife, and even
the Jews followed the procession, wailing and carrying
lighted lamps.

All the people cried with one voice: "Woe to us, we who, 8
after this day, will never deserve a bishop like him!" And because, as we said, the bishops of his province were far away
and could not come more quickly, the faithful put earth over
his blessed body, as is the custom of country people, so that
it not be swollen by the heat.

After his funeral a woman named Meratina who, in truth, 9
as I diligently inquired, was a most pure virgin and devoted
to God, collected the earth which had been thrown away by
the others and placed it in her garden; frequently watering
it, she made it come alive with plants, for the Lord made
them grow. Not only the sick who took away and imbibed
some of these plants in a drink recovered, but also the

fidelis super eum oratio suffragium merebatur. Quae postea per incuriam, virgine migrante, deperiit.

10 Denique ad sepulcrum eius multae virtutes ostensae sunt. Nam quartanarii et diversis febribus aegroti, ut ad beatum tumulum fideliter attingunt, protinus hauriunt sanitatem.

11 Valentinianus igitur cantor, cuius supra meminimus, qui
nunc presbyter habetur, cum diaconatus fungeretur officio,
a typo quartano corripitur ac per multos dies magna defec-
12 tione laboravit. Factum est autem ut in die accessus huius
febris, loca sancta circuire disponeret orans. Veniensque ad
huius sancti sepulcrum, prostratus ait: "Memor esto mei,
beatissime ac sancte sacerdos! A te enim educatus, doctus ac
provocatus sum. Memor esto alumni proprii quem amore
13 unico dilexisti, et erue me ab hac qua detineor febre!" Haec
effatus, herbulas quae ad honorem sacerdotis tumulo re-
spersae fuerant a devotis colligit. Et quia virides erant, ori
applicat, dentibus decerpit, succumque earum deglutit.
Praeteriit enim dies illa, nec ab hac est pulsatus incommodo,
et deinceps ita sospitati est restitutus ut nec illas quas vulgo
fractiones vocant ultra perferret.

14 Hoc ab ipsius presbyteri ore ita gestum cognovi. Non enim ambigitur per illius potentiam prodire virtutes de tumulis servorum suorum, qui Lazarum vocavit ex monumento.

faithful who said a prayer over them merited to be heard. When the virgin had passed away, however, the plot was neglected and forgotten.

At his tomb many powerful deeds have been manifested. 10
For when the sick suffering from quartan and other fevers touch the blessed tomb full of faith, they soon drink in their health.

When the cantor Valentinianus, whom we mentioned 11
earlier and who is now a priest, served as deacon, he was seized by the quartan fever and was seriously debilitated for
many days. However, on the day that the fever was due to 12
return, he decided to walk around the tombs of the saints and pray there. And when he had come to the tomb of this holy man, he prostrated himself and prayed: "Remember me, most blessed and holy bishop! For it was you who raised me, taught me, and called me to my office. Now remember me, your foster son, whom you cherished with your special love, and rescue me from the fever that clutches me!"
After he had said this, he picked up some small plants which 13
had been strewn around the tomb by the faithful. Since they were still fresh, he put them in his mouth, chewed them, and swallowed their sap. That day passed without his being racked by that illness, and from that time onward he recovered so completely that he never again suffered those chills which are popularly called "breakings."

I learned that it happened thus from the lips of that same 14
priest. It cannot be doubted that it is through the power of the one who called forth Lazarus from his tomb that deeds of power are brought forth from the tombs of his servants.

7

De sancto Gregorio episcopo Lingonensi

Prologus

Egregiae sanctitatis viri, quos palma perfectae beatitudinis e terris editos evexit ad caelos, hi sunt quos aut non fictae caritatis vinculum ligat, aut eleemosynarum fructus ditat, aut flos castitatis adornat, aut martyrii agonizatio certa
2 coronat. In quibus ad inchoandum perfectae iustitiae opus illud fuit studium, ut in primis corpus sine macula praeparatum habitaculum Spiritui sancto praeberent et sic ad reliquarum virtutum excelsa contenderent. Atque ipsi sibi persecutores facti, dum in se sua perimebant vitia, tamquam martyres probati, peracto cursus agonis legitimi, trium-
3 pharent. Quod nullus sine Dei ope valebit perficere, nisi dominici adiutorii protegatur vel parma vel galea. Et quod egerit non sui, sed ad divini nominis gloriam deputet, iuxta illud Apostoli: "Qui gloriatur, in Domino glorietur" [1 Corinthians 1:31].

4 In hoc enim et beatus Gregorius omnem gloriam contulit, qui de excelsa senatorii ordinis potentia ad illam se humilitatem subdidit ut, omnibus saeculi curis abiectis, soli se Deo dicaret opere, quem in pectore retinebat.

7

About the holy Gregory, bishop of Langres

Prologue

Men of outstanding holiness whom the palm of perfect beatitude lifts up from the earth to heaven are those whom either a bond of unfeigned charity connects, the harvest of alms enriches, the flower of chastity adorns, or the certain
struggle of the martyr crowns. When they began to achieve 2
perfect justice their first concern was to offer a body without stain, ready to be a dwelling for the Holy Spirit, and from there to seek to acquire the heights of the remaining virtues. And so they made themselves their own persecutors when they killed vices in themselves and triumphed as martyrs by being tested in a similar fight. This no one will be 3
able to accomplish without God's aid, unless he is protected by the shield and helmet of the Lord's assistance. And what he does should not be attributed to his own glory but to that of the divine name: as the Apostle says: "Let him who glories, glory in God."

In this name the blessed Gregory too sought his entire 4
glory: by leaving behind the power of the highest senatorial order he subjected himself to humility so that, rejecting all cares of this world, he might dedicate himself only to the work of God whom he cherished in his heart.

1. Igitur sanctus Gregorius ex senatoribus primis, bene
litteris institutus, Augustodunensis civitatis comitatum am-
bivit. In comitatu autem positus regionem illa per quadraginta annos iustitia comitante correxit. Et tam severus atque districtus fuit in malefactoribus ut vix ei ullus reorum
2 posset evadere. Coniugem de genere senatorio habens Ar-
mentariam nomine, quam ad propagandam generationem
tantum dicitur cognovisse, de qua et filios, Domino largiente, suscepit. Aliam vero mulierem, ut iuvenilis assolet fervor, inardescere non contigit.

2. Post mortem autem uxoris, ad Dominum convertitur
et, electus a populo, Lingonicae urbi episcopus ordinatur.
Cui magna fuit abstinentia, sed ne iactantia putaretur, occulte sub triticeos panes alios tenues ex hordeo supponebat.
Triticeum frangens aliis erogabat, ipse vero clam hordeum,
2 nemine intelligente, praesumens. Similiter et de vino faciens, dum aquam ei pincerna porrigerent, ad dissimulan-
dum aquam desuper effundi iubebat, tale vitrum eligens
quod claritatem aquae obtegeret. Iam in ieiuniis, eleemosynis, orationibus et vigiliis tam efficax tamque devotus erat,
ut in medio mundi positus novus effulgeret eremita.

3 Nam cum apud Divionense castrum moraretur assidue,
et domus eius baptisterio adhaereret in quo multorum sanctorum reliquiae tenebantur, nocte de stratu suo, nullo
sentiente, consurgens, ad orationem, Deo tantum teste, per-
gebat. Ostio divinitus reserato, adtente psallebat in baptisterio.

CHAPTER 7

1. The holy Gregory, then, first among the senators and well educated in letters, desired the office of count of the city of Autun. When he had taken office he preserved just order in that region for forty years. And he was so severe and rigorous with malefactors that almost no criminals could escape him. He had a wife of senatorial rank named Armen- 2
taria whom he is said to have known only in order to have children, and the Lord gave him sons from her. Never, as often occurs in youthful fervor, did he become inflamed with passion for another woman.

2. After the death of his wife he turned to the Lord, was elected bishop by the people, and was consecrated bishop of the city of Langres. His abstinence was great, but lest he be thought to be vain he stealthily slipped slim barley loaves under the wheaten ones intended for others. Breaking the wheaten bread for others, he fed them while he himself, though no one noticed, secretly ate from the barley loaves.
He did something similar with wine: when the steward of- 2
fered him water, he ordered it to be poured into an opaque glass he had chosen to hide the pale color of the water already in it. In fasting, almsgiving, praying, and keeping vigils he was so assiduous and devout that, although placed in the middle of the world, he shone like a new kind of hermit.

He usually lived in the fort of Dijon and his house there 3
adjoined the baptistery which contained the relics of many saints; at night he left his bed without anyone noticing and went to pray there, with only God as his witness. The door opened in a divine manner, and in the baptistery he sang psalms from the depths of his heart.

4 Sed cum hoc multi temporis spatio ageret, tandem ab
uno diacono res cognita atque manifestata est. Idem cum
cognovisset haec agi, a longe ne eum vir beatus sentire posset, prosequabatur et quid ageret spectabat. Aiebat enim
diaconus, quod veniens sanctus Dei ad ostium baptisterii,
pulsans manu propria, ostium nemine comparente aperieba-
tur, illoque ingrediente diutissime silentium erat. Postea
psallentium tamquam multarum vocum per trium horarum
5 et fere amplius spatium audiebatur. Credo ego quod cum
magnorum sanctorum in eodem loco haberentur reliquiae,
ipsi se beato viro revelantes psallentium Domino in commune reddebant. Nam, impleto cursu, revertens ad lectulum, ita se caute super stratum ponebat, ut prorsus nemo
sentiret. Observatores vero ostium baptisterii obseratum
invenientes, clave sua solite aperiebant, commotoque signo,
sanctus Dei, sicut reliqui, novus ad officium dominicum
consurgebat.

6 Nam cum energumeni eum primo die episcopatus sui
confiterentur, rogabant eum presbyteri ut eos benedicere
dignaretur. Quod ille viriliter ne vanam incurreret gloriam
refugiebat, clamans indignum se ad manifestandas virtutes
7 dominicas esse ministrum. Sed tamen quia diutius hoc dissi-
mulare non potuit, adduci eos ad se iubens, sine ullo tactu,
facto tantum signo crucis e contra, verbo daemonia discedere imperabat. Quod illa protinus audientia corpora quae
sua nequitia devinxerant absolvabant.

After he had been doing this for a long time, it finally be- 4
came known and evident to one deacon. When this man had
found out that this was happening, he followed the blessed
man at a distance so that he would not notice it and watched
what he did. The deacon said that the holy man of God
came to the door of the baptistery, knocked on it with his
hand, and that the door opened of its own accord; and also
that when he had gone in, there was a long silence. After
that a singing as of many voices was heard for about three
hours or a bit more. I myself believe that since there were 5
relics in this place of many great saints, they revealed themselves to the blessed man and sang psalms together with him
for the Lord. When the office had been completed, he returned to his bed and carefully laid himself down in such a
manner that no one noticed. The custodians who came to
the baptistery the next morning found the door locked and
opened it with their key as usual, and when the bell had been
rung, the holy man of God rose anew with the others for the
Lord's office.

On the first day of his episcopate, when the possessed 6
were confessing their crimes to him, the priests asked him
to deign to bless them. Wishing to avoid vainglory, he strenuously avoided this, asserting that he was unworthy to be
the means of manifesting the Lord's powerful deeds. But no 7
longer able to hide his holy power, he at last ordered them to
be brought to him and, without touching them, only made
the sign of the cross before them, with a word commanding
the demons to depart. Upon hearing this, the demons at
once freed the bodies they had fettered with their wickedness.

8 Nam illo absente, multi de virga quam in manu solitus erat suspensos atque signatos energumenos expellebant. Nam et de stratu eius si quis aegrotus quidpiam abstulisset, erat praesens medicamentum.

9 Armentaria autem, neptis eius, cum graviter quodam tempore in adolescentia sua a quartano fatigaretur incommodo, ac medicorum studio plerumque fota, nullum posset sentire levamen, et ab ipso confessore beato saepius ut orationi insisteret hortatur, quadam die lectum eius expetiit, in quo posita ita febris cuncta restincta est, ut numquam hac deinceps aegrotaret.

3. Sanctus vero Gregorius cum per diem sanctam Epiphaniorum ad civitatem Lingonas ambulasset, a modica febre pulsatus, relicto saeculo migravit ad Christum. Cuius beata facies ita erat glorificata post transitum ut rosis similis cerneretur. Haec enim apparebat rubea, reliquum corpus tamquam candens lilium refulgebat, ut aestimares eum iam tunc ad futurae resurrectionis gloriam praeparatum.

2 Quod deferentes ad castrum Divionense ubi se iusserat tumulari, in campania illa quae a parte aquilonis habetur haud procul a castro aggravat. Gestatores non sustinentes feretrum, solo deposuerunt. Ibique parumper resumentes vires, et post paululum elevantes, ad intramuraneam ecclesiam eum detulerunt. Advenientibus autem quinta die episcopis, ab ecclesia ad basilicam beati Iohannis deferebatur.

3 Et ecce vincti carceris ad beatum corpus clamare coeperunt, dicentes: "Miserere nostri, piissime domine! Ut quos vivens in saeculo non absolvisti, vel defunctus caeleste

In his absence, many used the stick which he was accustomed to hold in his hand to expel demons from the possessed who were hanging in the air or bound by them. And if an ill person took anything from his bed, it healed him at once. 8

His granddaughter Armentaria suffered gravely from the quartan fever in her youth; since the repeated efforts of doctors had been unable to make her recover, she was often urged by the blessed confessor to devote herself to prayer; one day she went to lie in his bed and the fever was at once so completely extinguished that it subsequently never again made her ill. 9

3. When the holy Gregory went on foot on the holy day of Epiphany to the city of Langres, he was attacked by a mild fever and left the world to go to Christ. After his death, his blessed face was so glorified that it looked like roses. For it looked rosy-tinted and the rest of his body shone with the whiteness of lilies, so that one might think he was then already prepared for the glory of the future resurrection.

While they were carrying him to the fort of Dijon, where he had ordered himself to be buried, his body increased in weight in the countryside north of, and not far from, the fort. No longer being able to support the bier, the carriers put it on the ground. After a little while, when they had regained some strength there, they rose and carried him into the church inside the walls. On the fifth day he was carried by the bishops from the church to the basilica of the blessed John the Baptist. 2

And behold! the chained men in the prison began to shout to the blessed body, saying: "Have pity upon us, most pious lord! The ones whom you did not absolve in the world, 3

regnum possidis digneris absolvere. Visita nos, quaesumus, et miserere nostri!" Haec et alia illis clamantibus, aggravatum est corpus ita ut ipsum penitus sustinere non possent. Tunc ponentes feretrum super terram, virtutem beati antis-
4 titis praestolabantur. His ergo exspectantibus, subito reseratis carceris ostiis, trabes illa qua vinctorum pedes coarctabantur, repulsis obicibus, scinditur media; confractisque catenis, omnes pariter dissolvuntur et ad beatum corpus, nemine retinente, perveniunt. Dehinc elevantes feretrum gestatores, hii inter reliquos obsequuntur. Qui a iudice postea sine damno aliquo sunt dimissi.

4. Post haec beatus confessor multis se virtutibus declaravit. Aiebat enim quidam religiosus, caelos se apertos in die eius sepulturae vidisse. Nec enim ambigitur quin post actus angelicos sidereis sit coetibus aggregatus.

2 Vinctus quidam, per viam illam qua beatum corpus Lingonis est exhibitum, ad antedictum castrum adducebatur. Cumque milites cum equitibus praecedentes post terga traherent vinctum, ad locum ubi beati confessoris artus quieverant pervenerunt. Quem praetereuntes, vinctus, invocato nomine beati antistitis, petiit ut eum sua misericordia libe-
3 raret. Quo orante, laxati sunt laquei de manibus eius, et sentiens se solutum, quietum reddidit, coopertisque manibus, putabatur adhuc esse ligatus. Ingressi autem portam castri, cum ante atrium ecclesiae pervenissent, hic exsiliens, et

you ought to deign to absolve now that you are dead and possess the heavenly kingdom. Visit us, we implore you, and have pity on us!" As they were shouting these and other things, the body became so heavy that the bishops could no longer support it. They put the bier on the ground and waited hopefully for the arrival of the blessed bishop's holy
power. As they waited, the doors of the prison suddenly 4
opened, the stocks which held the prisoners' feet split down the middle and let go of its fastenings, and the chains broke; all the men were released at the same time and came up to the blessed body without anyone holding them back. When the carriers thereafter lifted the bier, the former prisoners joined the others in the procession. The judge later sent them home without any punishment.

4. After this, the blessed confessor manifested himself with many deeds of power. A certain religious man said that he had seen the heavens opened on the day of the holy man's burial. And after his angelic deeds there is no doubt about his admission into the society of the stars.

A certain prisoner was being led along the road on which 2
the blessed body had been taken from Langres to the aforesaid fort. The soldiers on horseback rode ahead, dragging the man in chains behind them, and came to the place where the blessed man's body had rested awhile. As they passed it, the prisoner invoked the name of the blessed bishop and
asked him to have mercy and liberate him. While he prayed 3
the bonds around his hands loosened, and feeling them loosened, he held his peace, keeping his hands covered, so that it looked as though he were still bound. When they had entered the gate of the fort, however, and had reached the

corrigiam ligaminis trahentium in ora proiciens, ecclesiam petiit, per quam cum auxilio omnipotentis Dei et obtentu beati pontificis liberatus est.

4 Admirabile autem est illud miraculum: qualiter beatum
corpus eius, cum post multa tempora transferretur, apparuit
gloriosum. Cum beatus pontifex in angulo basilicae fuisset
sepultus, et parvus esset locus ille, nec ibi populi sic possent
accedere ut devotio postulabat, sanctus Tetricus, filius et
successor eius, haec cernens et virtutes ibidem assidue operari prospiciens, ante altare basilicae fundamenta iecit, erec-
5 taque apsida, miro opere construxit et transvolvit. Qua
transvoluta disruptoque pariete, arcum aedificat. Quod
opus perfectum atque exornatum, in medio apsidae loculum
fodit. Quo corpus beati patris transferre volens, convocat
presbyteros et abbates ad illud officium, qui vigilantes ora-
bant, ut se beatus confessor ad hanc praeparatam habita-
tionem transferri permitteret. Mane autem facto, cum choris psallentium, apprehensum sarcophagum ante altare in
apsidam quam beatus episcopus aedificaverat, transtule-
runt.

6 Quod sepulcrum dum diligenter componunt, subito, et ut credo ad Dei iussum, opertorium sarcophagi motum est in una parte. Et ecce apparuit beata facies eius ita integra et illaesa ut putares eum non mortuum esse sed dormientem. Sed nec de ipso vestimento, quod cum eo positum fuit, aliquid ostensum est diminutum.

forecourt of the church, the man leaped up, hurled his bonds in the faces of those who had dragged him along, and ran into the church; and so he was freed with the aid of the almighty God and at the intercession of the blessed bishop.

Greatly to be admired is the next miracle: how when 4
much later his blessed body was moved it appeared to be glorified. The blessed bishop had been buried in a corner of the basilica in a place too small for the people to come as their devotion required; the holy Tetricus, his son and successor, seeing this and noticing that deeds of power were frequently performed there, laid foundations before the altar and built an apse, vaulting it with admirable workmanship. After the round wall had been raised, he broke down 5
the existing straight wall and made an arch. When the work was finished and decorated, he had a hole dug in the middle of the apse. Wishing to transfer the body of his blessed father there, he summoned the priests and abbots to this office and all held vigils and prayed that the blessed confessor would allow them to bring him to the dwelling place prepared for him. And when morning came, choirs sang psalms while they took up the sarcophagus and carried it in front of the altar into the apse which the blessed bishop Tetricus had built.

While they were carefully arranging the sarcophagus in 6
its new place, suddenly—I believe at God's command—its cover shifted slightly to one side. And behold! the holy man's blessed face appeared so undiminished and unimpaired that one would think him not dead but sleeping. Nor had the robe in which he had been buried deteriorated at all.

7 Unde non immerito apparuit gloriosum post transitum, cuius caro non fuit corrupta ludibrio. Magna est enim corporis et cordis integritas, quae et in praesenti saeculo praestat gratiam, et in futuro vitam largitur aeternam, de qua Paulus apostolus ait: "Pacem sequimini et sanctificationem, sine qua nemo videbit regnum Dei" [Hebrews 12:14].

5. Puella quaedam, die dominico cum suum caput componeret, pectine apprehenso, credo ob iniuriam diei sancti, in manibus eius adhaesit, ita ut affixi dentes tam in digitis
2 quam in palmis magnum ei dolorem inferrent. Quae cum basilicas sanctorum flens atque obsecrans circuiret, ad sepulcrum beati Gregorii antistitis in eius virtute confisa prosternitur. Cumque diutissime beati confessoris praesidium flagitasset, directa manus eius ad opus pristinum pectine decidente reducitur.

3 Sed et energumeni eum confitentes ad eius sepulcrum saepe purgantur. Nam plerumque vidimus post eius transitum, virgula, cuius supra meminimus, quam manu gerebat, per parietes ita eos affixos, ut putares illos validis atque acutissimis sudibus retineri.

6. Multa quidem et alia de eodem gesta cognovimus, sed ne fastidium incitarent, de pluribus pauca perstrinximus. Obiit autem episcopatus sui anno tricesimo tertio, aetate nonagenarius, qui se virtutibus manifestis saepius declaravit.

Thus it was entirely merited that he appeared to be glorified after his passing, for his flesh had not been corrupted by lust. Integrity of body and soul is thus a great thing; it achieves grace in the present life and grants eternal life in the future one as well, about which the apostle Paul said: "Strive for peace and holiness, without which no one will see the kingdom of God." 7

5. When a girl was combing her hair on a Sunday and picked up her comb—I believe it was because she disrespected the holy day—it stuck to her hands; its teeth became fixed in her fingers and palm and caused great pain.
Walking around the basilicas of the saints weeping and im- 2
ploring their help, she prostrated herself at the tomb of the blessed bishop Gregory, trusting in his holy power. After she had implored his help for a long time, the comb was released from her hand; the latter was straightened and restored to its original condition.

The possessed, too, often call upon him at his tomb and 3
are cleansed. For after his passing we often see them pinned to the walls by the stick which, as we mentioned earlier, he used to carry in his hand, so that one might think they were being held in place by strong and pointed stakes.

6. We know of many other deeds of this same holy man but, lest they become tiresome, we have recounted only a few of them. He died aged ninety in the thirty-third year of his episcopate and often presents himself through manifest deeds of power.

8

De sancto Nicetio Lugdunensi episcopo

Prologus

Praesentiae divinae bonum, quod plerumque regno suo provideat quos asciscat, ipsa saepius sacrae lectionis testantur oracula, sicut ad Hieremiam eximium vatem caelestis oris mystica deferuntur eloquia, dicentis: "Priusquam te formarem in utero novi te, et antequam exires de vulva sanctifi-
2 cavi te" [Jeremiah 1:5]. Et ipse Dominus utriusque conditor Testamenti, cum illos quos largitio hilaris agneo decoratos vellere suis locat a dextris, quid ait? "Venite, benedicti Patris mei, percipite praeparatum vobis regnum a constitutione mundi" [Matthew 25:34]. Sed et ille vas electionis, beatus Apostolus: "Quos," inquit, "praescivit et praedestinavit conformes fieri imaginis Filii sui" [Romans 8:29]. Nam et de Isaac, Iohanneque, qualiter nasceretur vel quid agerent, et nomen et opus praedixit et meritum.

3 Sic nunc et de beato Nicetio ipsa illa prisca miseratio pietatis, quae immerita ditat, non nata sanctificat, et omnia priusquam gignantur et disponit et ordinat, qualibus sacerdotalis gratiae infulis floreret in terris, prius genetrici voluit revelare. De cuius vita retinetur quidem exinde libellus nobiscum, nescio a quo compositus, qui multas quidem

8

About the holy bishop Nicetius of Lyons

Prologue

The goodness of the divine omnipresence, which often foresees whom it will admit to its kingdom, is frequently mentioned in the oracles of sacred scripture, as when the following mystic words of the heavenly mouth were communicated to the lofty seer Jeremiah: "Before I formed you in the womb I knew you, and before you were born I sanctified you." And when the Lord, the author of both Testa- 2
ments, places on his right side those whom he has adorned with the fleece of the Lamb as his joyful gift, what does he say? "Come, O blessed of my Father, inherit the kingdom made ready for you since the creation of the world." But the chosen vessel, the blessed apostle Paul, speaks of "Those whom he foreknew he also predestined to be conformed to the image of his Son." For he also foretold of Isaac and John the Baptist how they would be born and what they would do, as well as their names, works, and merits.

Thus now too, in the case of the blessed Nicetius, the an- 3
cient compassionate generosity that enriches the undeserving, sanctifies those not yet born, and arranges and orders all things before they are born, wished to reveal ahead of time to his mother the marks of priestly grace with which he would flourish on earth. We have a book about his life by an unknown author that publishes many of his deeds of power,

virtutes eius pandit, non tamen vel exordium nativitatis
conversionisque eius, vel seriem virtutum declarat ad liqui-
4 dum. Et licet nec nos omnes eius virtutes investigavimus,
quas per eum Dominus vel occulte operari est dignatus, vel
publice, tamen quae ad priorem auctorem non pervenerunt,
etsi rusticiori stylo pandere procuravimus.

1. Igitur Florentius quidam ex senatoribus, accepta Artemia coniuge, cum duos haberet liberos, ad episcopatum Ia-
nubensis urbis expetebatur et, re iam obtenta cum principe,
ad domum revertitur, coniugique quae egerat nuntiavit.
Quod illa audiens, respondit viro: "Desine, quaeso, dulcissime coniux ab hac causa, et ne quaesieris episcopatum urbis, quia ego ex conceptu a te sumpto episcopum gero in
2 utero." Requievit vir sapiens, audita uxore, rememorans illud quod vox divina quondam principi fidei nostrae Abrahae
beato praeceperat: "Omnia quaecumque dixerit tibi Sara,
audi vocem eius" [Genesis 21:12]. Denique impletis pariendi
diebus mulier enixa est puerum, quem quasi victorem futurum mundi, Nicetium in baptismo vocavit, eundemque
summa nutritum diligentia litteris ecclesiasticis mandavit
3 institui. Defuncto autem patre, hic cum genetrice iam clericus in domo paterna residens, cum reliquis famulis manu
propria laborabat, intelligens commotiones corporeas non
aliter nisi laboribus et aerumnis opprimi posse.

4 Quodam vero tempore, cum adhuc in domo ipsa degeret,
orta est ei pusula mala in facie, quod virus invalescens ac ex-
coquens fecit puerum desperatum. Sed mater eius iugiter

but does not tell the whole story of his birth, his conversion,
and the series of his powerful deeds. And although we too 4
will not investigate all his miracles—those which the Lord
performed through him either in private or in public—we
will nevertheless, be it in a more rustic manner, take on the
task of telling about those unknown to the earlier author.

1. A certain senator named Florentinus, who had taken
Artemia as his wife and had had two children by her, was
sought as bishop of the city of Geneva; the matter had already been agreed to by the king when Florentinus came
home to tell his wife what he had done. Hearing it, she answered her husband: "I beg you, do not go through with this,
dearest husband, and do not seek the episcopacy of this city,
for I carry in my womb a bishop I conceived from you." The 2
wise man listened to his wife and let the matter rest, remembering how the divine voice had once instructed blessed
Abraham, the founder of our faith: "Whatever Sarah will say
to you, do as she says." When the time for giving birth came
the woman was delivered of a boy whom, as though he were
the future victor over the world, she named Nicetius at his
baptism; she arranged for him to be raised with the greatest care and to be educated in the writings of the Church.
After his father died, he lived with his mother in the pater- 3
nal home, and, although already a cleric, worked with his
hands along with the rest of the household, understanding
that corporeal impulses can be stifled only by work and
hardship.

While he was still living at home an unpleasant sore once 4
appeared in his face, whose pus made the boy desperate as it
increased and boiled over. His mother kept invoking the

inter multa sanctorum nomina, beati Martini nomen pro
5 eius salute peculiarius invocabat. Cumque per biduum puer
iacuisset in lectulo clausis oculis et nullum verbum consolationis matri lamentanti proferret, sed potius ipsa genetrix
inter spem metumque titubans, iuxta ritum exsequiarum
necessaria funeris praepararet, secunda die ad vesperum
aperiens oculos, ait: "Quo ivit mater mea?" Quae statim ad-
6 veniens, ait: "Ecce adsum! Quid vis, fili?" Et ille: "Ne timeas,"
inquit, "mater. Beatus enim Martinus super me crucem
Christi faciens, surgere iussit incolumem." Haec effatus,
statim surrexit a lectulo. Geminavitque virtus divina miraculi huius gratiam, ut et Martini panderetur meritum, et hic
quia futurus erat pontifex, a contagio salvaretur. Testis enim
fuit huius causae visa cicatrix eius in facie.

2. Aetate quoque iam tricinaria presbyterii honore praeditus, nequaquam se a labore operis quod prius gessit abstinebat, sed semper manibus propriis operabatur cum famulis, ut Apostoli praecepta compleret, dicentis: "Laborate manibus, ut habeatis unde tribuere possitis necessitatem patientibus" [Ephesians 4:28].

2 Illud omnino studebat, ut omnes pueros qui in domo eius nascebantur, ut primum vagitum infantiae relinquentes loqui coepissent, statim litteras doceret ac psalmis imbueret, scilicet ut ingressi tale iungeretur psallentium, ut tam antiphonis quam meditationibus diversis, ut devotio flagitabat animi, posset implere.

3 Castitatem autem non modo hic diligenter erat custodiens, verum etiam custodiendi gratiam aliis iugiter praedicabat, et a polluto tactu et verbis obscenis ut desisterent

names of many saints, especially of the blessed Martin, for
his health. When the boy had lain in bed for two days, his 5
eyes closed, without a word of consolation for his lamenting
mother and she, wavering between hope and fear, was preparing what was needed for the funeral rite, he opened his
eyes on the evening of the second day and said: "Where has
my mother gone?" Coming to him at once, she said: "Here I
am! What do you want, my son?" And he said: "Don't be 6
afraid, mother. For the blessed Martin has made the sign of
Christ's cross over me and told me to arise in good health."
When he had said this, he at once got out of bed. And the
divine power doubled the grace of this miracle, so that not
only was Martin's merit made known but this boy, a future
bishop, was also saved from the illness. The scar that remained on his face attested this event.

2. At the age of thirty he was honored with the dignity of the priesthood, but he did not abstain from his previous work, always laboring with his hands along with the servants to fulfill the precept of the Apostle who had said: "Work with your hands, so that you may be able to give to those in need."

He was especially concerned that all the servant boys 2
born in the household, as soon as they had left behind their
childish babbling and had begun to speak, be taught to read
and to sing psalms, so that they could join others singing and
be able to participate in antiphons as well as in various med-
itations, as their spiritual devotions required.

As for chastity, not only did he diligently guard his own, 3
but kept preaching the grace of its maintenance to others,
teaching them to refrain from polluting by their touch and

4 edocebat. Nam recolo in adolescentia mea cum primum litterarum elementa coepissem agnoscere, et essem quasi oc-
tavi anni aevo, et ille indignum me lectulo locari iuberet, ac
paternae dilectionis dulcedine ulna susciperet, oram indumenti sui articulis arripiens, ita se colobio concludebat ut
5 numquam artus mei beata eius membra contingerent. In-
tuemini, quaeso, et advertite cautelam viri Dei! Quod si ab
infantuli artubus, in quo nulli adhuc esse poterant stimulae
concupiscentiae, nulla incitamenta luxuriae, ita se, ne ab
eius artubus tangeretur, abstinuit, qualiter de loco ubi suspi-
6 cio luxuriae esse potuit, ille refugit! Erat enim, ut diximus,
castus corpore, mundus corde, non in scurrilitate verba pro-
ferens, sed semper quae Dei sunt loquens. Et licet omnes
homines in illo caelestis caritatis vinculo diligeret, matri tamen ita erat subditus ut quasi unus ex famulis obaudiret.

3. Denique aegrotante Sacerdote Lugdunensi Antistite in
urbe Parisiaca, cum a Childeberto seniore magno amore di-
ligeretur, voluit rex usque ad eius lectulum proficisci, ac visitare infirmum. Quo veniente, ait episcopus: "Optime nosti,
O rex piissime, quod tibi in omnibus necessitatibus tuis fideliter servierim, ac quaecumque iniunxisti devote impleve-
rim. Nunc precor ut quia tempus resolutionis meae adest,
ne dimittas me ab hoc mundo cum dolore discedere, sed
2 unam petitionem quam supplico libenter indulge." Et ille:
"Pete," inquit, "quod volueris, obtinebis." "Rogo," ait, "ut
Nicetius presbyter, nepos meus, ecclesiae Lugdunensi

lascivious words. For I recall that in my youth, when I had 4
just begun to learn to read and was about eight years of age,
he told my unworthy self to get into bed with him. And as he
embraced me with the sweetness of a father's love, he drew
up his clothing around his limbs, and covered himself with
his tunic so that my body would nowhere touch his. Con- 5
sider this, I beg you, and notice the caution of the man of
God! If he kept his body from touching the body of a child,
in which there could be no stimulus to concupiscence or any
incitement to wantonness, how must he have fled from a
place where there could be a suspicion of lust! For, as we 6
said, he was chaste of body and pure in heart, not uttering
scurrilous words but speaking only of God. And although he
loved all men in the bond of heavenly charity, he was so subject to his mother that he obeyed her as though he were one
of her servants.

3. Later, when Bishop Sacerdos of Lyons became ill in
Paris, King Childebert the Elder, by whom he was much
loved, wished to come to his sickbed and visit him in his illness. When he had come, the bishop said: "You know very
well, O most pious king, that I have served you faithfully in
all you required, and that I have devoutly carried out whatever task you asked me to perform. I pray, now that the
time of my release is here: do not let me leave this world
with sadness, but willingly grant the one request which I
humbly ask for." And the king said: "Ask what you wish and 2
you shall obtain it." "I ask," he said, "that the priest Nicetius, my nephew, be given as bishop to the church of Lyons.

substituatur episcopus. Est enim, ut mei testimonii verba proferunt, amator castimoniae dilectorque ecclesiarum et in eleemosynis valde devotus, et quaecumque servos Dei decent, et operibus gerit et moribus." Respondit rex: "Fiat voluntas Dei."

3 Et sic pleno regis et populis suffragio episcopus Lugdunensis ordinatus fuit. Erat enim praecipuus concordiae ac pacis amator; et si laesus fuisset ab aliquo, statim aut remittebat per se, aut per alium insinuabat veniam deprecari. Nam vidi ego quodam tempore Basilium presbyterum missum ab eo ad Armentarium Comitem, qui Lugdunensem ur-
4 bem his diebus potestate iudiciaria gubernabat. Dixitque ad eum: "Pontifex noster causae huic, quae denuo impetitur, dato iudicio, terminum fecit, ideoque commonet ne eam iterare praesumas." Qui furore succensus respondit presbytero: "Vade et dic ei, quia multae sunt causae in eius con-
5 spectu positae, quae alterius iudicio finiendae sunt." Regressus presbyter, quae audivit simpliciter exposuit. Sanctus vero Nicetius, commotus contra eum, ait: "Vere, inquam, quia eulogias de manu mea non accipies, pro eo quod verba quae furor exegit meis auribus intulisti."

6 Erat autem convivio recumbens, ad cuius et ego laevam cum adhuc diaconatus fungerer officio propinquus accubueram. Dixitque mihi secretius: "Loquere presbyteris, ut deprecentur pro eo." Cumque locutus fuissem, non intelligentes voluntatem sancti, silebant. Quod ille cernens: "Tu," inquit, "surge et deprecare pro eo." At ego cum trepidatione consurgens osculatus sum sancta eius genua, orans pro

For he is, as the words of my testimony show, a lover of chastity, a benefactor of churches, and very devout in almsgiving, doing in his works and his way of life everything a servant of God should do." The king answered: "Let God's will be done."

And in this way, with the full consent of the king and the 3
people, he was consecrated bishop of Lyons. For he was an outstanding lover of concord and peace, and if he had been hurt by anyone he either forgave him at once or let someone else ask for his forgiveness. For once I saw him send the priest Basilius to Count Armentarius, who then governed
the city of Lyons with judicial powers. The priest said to Ar- 4
mentarius: "Our bishop has given his judgment and thereby settled the case which you are now opening again, and accordingly warns you not to presume to reopen it." Inflamed with fury, the count answered: "Go and tell him that there are many cases argued in his presence which will be settled
by someone else's decision!" When the priest returned, he 5
simply related what he had heard. The holy Nicetius then became angry with him and said: "Truly, you will not receive the sacrament from my hand, for you have brought words spoken in anger to my ears."

He was then reclining at a meal, and I, then functioning 6
as deacon, had reclined at his left side. He covertly said to me: "Talk to the priests so that they may plead for his forgiveness." When I spoke to them, however, they did not understand the holy man's wish, and remained silent. Seeing this, he said: "You stand up and plead for him." And so I stood up, trembling, kissed his holy knees, and pleaded for

7 presbytero. Quo indulgente, atque eulogias porrigente, ait: "Rogo, dilectissime fratres, ut verba inutilia quae ignave mussitantur, aures meas non verberent, quia non est dignum ut homines rationabiles irrationabilium hominum procacia verba suscipiant. Hoc tantum vos studere oportet, ut illi qui contra Ecclesiae utilitatem quaedam machinare cupiunt, vestris propositionibus confundantur. Irrationabilia enim non solum non admirari, sed nec audire desidero."

8 O beatum virum, qui omni intentione vitare cupiebat scandalum! Audiant autem haec illi, qui si offensi fuerint, ignoscere nolunt, sed totam in sua ultione convocantes urbem, etiam testes adhibere non metuunt, qui vocibus nefariis dicant: "Haec et haec audivimus de te hunc loquentem." Et ita fit ut pauperes Christi talibus accusationibus misericordia postposita opprimantur.

4. Quodam autem mane cum surrexisset ad matutinas, sanctus Nicetius, exspectatis duabus antiphonis, ingressus est in sacrarium, ubi dum resideret, diaconus responsorium
2 psalmum canere coepit. Et ille commotus, ait: "Sileat! Sileat! Nec praesumat canere iustitiae Inimicus!" Et dicto citius, obpilato ore, siluit. Iussitque eum vocari ad se sanctus, et ait: "Nonne praeceperam tibi ne ingrederis ecclesiam Dei? Et cur ausu temerario ingredi praesumpsisti? Aut cur vocem in canticis dominicis es ausus emittere?"

the priest. After granting him forgiveness and then giving 7
him the sacrament, he said: "I ask you, most beloved brothers, that useless words which are idly uttered not strike my ears, for it is not right for reasonable men to have to tolerate the brash words of unreasonable men. You ought to work to one end alone: that those who wish to scheme against the interest of the Church be confounded by your arguments. As for unreasonable arguments, not only do I not want to be confronted by them, I do not even wish to hear about them."

O blessed man, who with all his heart wished to avoid of- 8
fense! Let this be heard by those who, if offended, are unwilling to ignore the fact, but call together the whole city to support them, and are unafraid even to summon witnesses who with perverse voices say: "We have heard such and such being said about you by this person." And in this manner it happens that compassion is set aside, and Christ's poor are oppressed by such accusations.

4. On a certain morning, when the holy Nicetius arose to go to matins and he had waited while two antiphons were sung, he went into the sanctuary, and while he was sitting
there a deacon began to sing the refrain of the psalm. And 2
Nicetius became angry, saying: "Let him be quiet! Let him be quiet! Let the Enemy of justice not presume to sing!" And quicker than can be said, the deacon's throat was blocked, and he fell silent. The holy man then commanded the deacon to come to him and said: "Did I not order you not to enter the church of God? And why have you rashly dared to enter? And why do you dare to send forth your voice in the Lord's songs?"

3 Stupentibus autem omnibus qui aderant, et nihil mali de diacono noverant, exclamavit daemonium in eo, et se torqueri a sancto immensis cruciatibus confitetur. Ipse enim praesumpserat in ecclesia canere, cuius vocem ignorantibus populis sanctus agnovit, et ipsum verbis acerrimis, non diaconum, exsecravit. Tunc impositis sanctus diacono manibus, eiecto daemone, personam restituit integrae menti.

5. His et aliis signis declaratus in populis, episcopatus sui anno XXII, aetate sexagenaria, migravit ad Christum. Qui dum ferretur ad sepeliendum, caecus quidam se sub feretro flagitavit adduci, statimque ingressus, vultus diu lumine viduatus, reseratis oculis, adornatur. Nec distulit divina pietas beatos artus glorificare signis, cuius beatam animam cum choris angelicis suscipiebat in astris.

2 Post dies autem quos lex Romana sancivit, ut defuncti cuiuspiam voluntas publice relegatur, huius antistitis testamentum in foro delatum, turbis circumstantibus, a iudice reseratum recitatumque est. Presbyter quoque basilicae tumens felle, quod nihil loco illi in quo sepultus fuerat reliquisset, ait: "Aiebant semper plerique stolidum fuisse Nicetium. Nunc ad liquidum verum esse patet, cum nihil basilicae in qua tumulatus est delegavit!"

While all those who were present gasped in astonishment, for they had not known anything bad about the deacon, the demon in him cried out and confessed that he was being tormented with terrible tortures. For it was the demon who had presumed to sing in church, whose voice, unbeknownst to the people, the holy man had recognized; and it had been the demon, not the deacon, whom he had reproached with bitter words. When the holy man had placed his hands upon the deacon, the demon was expelled and the deacon was restored to his right mind. 3

5. After his sanctity had been manifested to the people through these and other signs, he went to Christ in the twenty-second year of his episcopate at the age of sixty. When he was being carried to his grave, a certain blind person begged to be led underneath his bier, and as soon as he had done this his eyes opened and his face, long deprived of light, was adorned with it. Thus divine piety did not refrain from glorifying with signs the blessed body whose blessed soul it was receiving in the stars with choirs of angels.

After the days had passed that are required by Roman law 2
before the will of a deceased person can be read in public, this bishop's testament was brought to the forum where it was opened and read aloud by the judge, surrounded by crowds. And the priest of the basilica was very angry because Nicetius had left nothing to the place where he was buried, saying: "Many used to say that Nicetius was insensitive. Now this turns out to be true, for he has left nothing to the basilica in which he is entombed!"

3 Sequenti autem nocte apparuit presbytero cum duobus episcopis, id est Iusto atque Eucherio, in veste fulgenti, dicens ad eos: "Hic presbyter, sanctissimi fratres, blasphemiis me obruit, dicens quia nihil facultatis scripserim templo huic quo requiesco. Et nescit quia quidquid pretiosius habui
4 ibidem reliqui, id est glaebam corporis mei!" At illi dixerunt: "Iniuste fecit ut detraheret servo Dei!" Conversusque sanctus ad presbyterum, pugnis palmisque guttur eius illisit, dicens: "Peccator conterende, desine stulte loqui!"

5 Expergefactus autem presbyter, tumefactis facibus, ita doloribus coarctatur, ut ipsas quoque salivas oris vix cum labore posset maximo deglutire. Unde factum est ut per dies quadraginta lectulo decubans graviter cruciaretur. Sed, invocato confessoris nomine, sanitati redditus, numquam ausus est ea verba quae prius praesumpserat garrulare.

6 Et quia novimus Priscum Episcopum huic sancto semper fuisse adversum, diacono cuidam huius casulam tribuit. Erat autem valida, eo quod et ipse vir Dei robusto fuisset corpore. Cappa autem huius indumenti ita dilatata erat atque consuta, ut solent in illis candidis fieri quae per Paschalia
7 festa sacerdotum humeris imponuntur. Ibatque diaconus cum hoc vestimento discurrens, ac parvipendens de cuius usibus remansisset, hoc habens in lectulo, hoc utens in foro, de cuius fimbriis, si credulitas certa fuisset, reddi potuit salus infirmis.

CHAPTER 8

In the night that followed, however, the bishop appeared 3
to the priest in a shining robe together with two other bishops, Justus and Eucherius, and said to them: "This priest, most holy fathers, buried me under blasphemies when he said that I left none of my resources to this temple in which I rest. And he does not realize that I left there my
most precious possession: the dust of my body!" And they 4
said: "He disparaged a servant of God and acted unjustly!" And turning to the priest, the holy man pounded his throat with his fists and palms, saying: "Sinner who deserves to be trodden underfoot, stop speaking such nonsense!"

When the priest woke up his jaws were swollen and he 5
was so tormented with pain that he could scarcely swallow his saliva. He thus lay in bed in severe torment for forty days. When finally he invoked the name of the confessor, he recovered and never again dared to babble the words that he had rashly spoken earlier.

Bishop Priscus, whom we know always to have been at 6
cross-purposes with this holy man, gave the bishop's cape to a certain deacon. It was wide because the man of God had been stout. The cape's hood too was capacious and sewn together, as was the custom, with the white bands that the
priests wear on their shoulders at Easter. The deacon went 7
about with this cape not caring who had worn it previously, using it on his bed and wearing in the forum a piece of clothing by whose threads, if accompanied by an unhesitating faith, the sick could have been cured.

8 Cui ait quidam: "O diacone, si scires virtutem Dei, et quis fuit cuius vestimento uteris, cautius te cum eo vivere oportebat." Cui ille: "Vere," inquit, "dico tibi, quia et hac casula tergo utor, et de capsa eius parte prolixiore decisa tegumen pedum aptabo." Fecit illico miser quod pollicitus est,
9 suscepturus protinus divini iudicii ultionem. Verum ubi deciso cucullo aptatis pedulis pedes operuit, extemplo arreptus a daemone ruit in pavimento. Erat enim solus in domo, nec erat qui succurreret misero. Cumque spumas cruentas ore proiecerit, extensis ad focum pedibus, pedes cum pedulibus ignis pariter devoravit. Hactenus de ultionibus.

6. Agiulfus quoque diaconus noster a Roma veniens, beata nobis sanctorum pignora deferebat. Hic causa orationis tantum locum quo sanctus quiescit adivit. Ingressus aedem, dum diversorum miraculorum opus illustre perpendit, vidit immensum catervatim populum ad eius sepulcrum, ac velut felicium examina apum ad consuetum alveare conflu-
2 ere. Et alios, presbytero qui aderat ministrante, particulas cerae pro benedictione sumere, alios parumper pulveris, nonnullos disruptas ab opertoria eius fimbrias capere, et abire ferentes in disparibus causis unam gratiam sanitatis.

3 Haec ille cernens, fide compunctus, lacrimans, ait: "Si marinorum me moles fluctuum sulcare tonsis actum mei sacerdotis devotio fecit, ut lustrata Orientalium martyrum sepulcra, aliquid de eisdem pignoris deferre deberem, cur non

Someone said to him: "O deacon, if you were acquainted 8
with God's power and knew who the person was whose
clothing you are using, you ought to treat it more cautiously." The priest replied: "Truly I say to you that I will use
this cape to cover my body and cut out a piece of the large
hood to cover my feet." He did what he had promised and
was about to experience the revenge of divine judgment. In 9
truth, when he had cut the hood in pieces and put the socks
he had made of it on his feet, he was at once seized by a demon and fell on the ground. Alone in the house, the unhappy
man could not be helped by anyone. While he vomited
bloody saliva from his mouth, his feet stuck to the hearth,
and its fire consumed them together with the socks. So
much about the bishop's vengeances.

6. Our deacon Agiulf, on his return from Rome brought
us back blessed relics of saints. Because he wished to pray
there, he went to the place where the holy man rests. When
he had entered the basilica and pondered the distinguished
register of miracles which had been enacted there, he saw a
great crowd of people at his tomb, streaming toward it as
happy bees do toward their familiar hive. And he saw some 2
take bits of candles from the ministering priest as a blessing,
others took bits of dust, and still others took threads pulled
out of the tomb cover–all taking away, in various guises, one
and the same healing grace.

Seeing this and deeply moved by their faith, he wept and 3
said: "If my bishop's devotion made me plow with oars
through the mass of waves to visit the tombs of Eastern
martyrs and take away some of their relics, why should I not

Gallicani mei confessoris pignora capiam, per quae mihi
4 meisque salus integra reparetur?" Et statim accedens, quasdam de herbulis quas devotio sacrum iecit in tumulum, manu linteo operta, sacerdote porrigente, suscepit, repositasque diligenter domum detulit. Sed statim fidem hominis miraculorum actio comprobavit. Nam discerptis de his foliis, frigoriticis cum aquae potu porrectis, protinus cum haustu salutem invexit; sed et multis deinceps. Quando autem nobis haec retulit, iam quattuor exinde sanos factos ab hac infirmitate narravit.

5 Iohannis autem presbyter noster, dum ab urbe Massiliensi cum commercio negotiationis suae rediret, ad huius sancti sepulcrum in oratione prosternitur. De qua consurgens, aspicit confractas compedes, disruptasque maculas catenarum, qua culpabilium vel astrinxerant colla vel suras attriverant, et admiratus est. Sed haec contemplatio non fuit vacua miraculis. Nam rediens ad nos presbyter, asserebat cum sacramento tres coram se ibi caecos fuisse lumini redditos, ac domum rediisse salvatos.

6 Nam apud Genabensem Galliarum urbem dum eius reliquiae cum honore psallentii portarentur, tantam ibi Dominus gratiam praestare dignatus est, ut suppliciter adorantes, et caeci visum, et claudi reciperent gressum. Nec dubitare poterat quispiam praesentem esse confessorem, cum videbant talia infirmis remediorum munera ministrari.

take some relics of my Gallic confessor through which full
health may be restored to me and my loved ones?" And at 4
once he went closer, accepted from a priest–with his hand covered with a cloth–some of the plants which devotion had thrown on the sacred tomb, wrapped them up carefully, and took them home. And immediately the miracles performed justified the man's faith. For when cutoff scraps of these leaves were administered to the fever-stricken in water, they recovered at the very instant that they drank it, and this happened to many more from then onward. At the time that he told us this, he said that already four people had been cured of this illness.

After our priest John had returned from the city of Mar- 5
seilles with the merchandise of his trade he prostrated himself in prayer at the tomb of the holy man. When he arose from there, he saw broken fetters and shattered links from chains that had constricted the necks and chafed the legs of the guilty, and he was astonished. But during this moment of contemplation, too, miracles continued to happen. For when he came back to us, the priest asserted with an oath that in his presence three blind men had been given back their sight and had returned home healed.

And when the holy man's relics were being carried with 6
psalm singing through the Gallic city of Geneva, the Lord deigned to manifest so much grace there that, after having humbly prostrated themselves, the blind received their sight back and the lame their ability to walk. No one could doubt that the confessor was present when they saw such gifts of healing granted to the sick.

7. Seditio etenim in quodam loco exorta, cum vulgo sae-
viente volantibus saxis ac facibus, furor arma non mediocri-
ter ministraret, unus elevato ensis acumine cum assultu
gravi virum perculit. Post dies autem paucos nactus ab inter-
2 empti germano, simili exitu trucidatur. Quod cum iudex loci
illius comperisset, vinctum virum in carcerem retrudi praecepit, dicens: "Dignus est leto hic scelestus occumbere, qui
voluntatis propriae arbitrio, nec exspectato iudice, ausus est
temere mortem fratris ulcisci."

3 In qua dum teneretur custodia, et multorum sanctorum
nominibus invocatis misericordiam precaretur, quasi ad
sanctum Dei proprie conversus, ait: "Audivi de te, sancte
Niceti, quod sis potens in opere misericordiae, ac pius in
compeditorum flentium absolutione. Deprecor nunc, ut me
illa supereminenti pietate visitare digneris, qua in reliquo-
4 rum absolutione vinctorum saepius claruisti!" Et post paululum obdormiens, apparuit ei vir beatus, dicens: "Quis es tu,
qui nomen Nicetii invocas? Aut unde nosti quis fuerit, quod
eum obsecrare non desinis?" At ille causam delicti ex ordine
reserans, adiecit: "Miserere, quaeso, mihi, si tu es vir Dei
quem invoco!" Cui sanctus ait: "Surge in nomine Christi, et
ambula liber. A nullo enim comprehenderis."

5 At ille in hac expergefactus voce, se absolutum, catenis
comminutis confractaque trabe, miratur. Nec moratus,

7. When a riot had begun in a certain place, the raging crowd let stones and torches fly, and their fury quickly led to the use of arms: one man lifted his naked sword and struck another dead with a fierce blow. A few days later he encountered the dead man's brother and was killed by him in a similar manner. When the judge of that place heard about this, 2
he ordered the killer to be chained and put in prison, saying: "This criminal deserves death because he followed his own will instead of waiting for the judge to decide and dared to avenge his brother's death."

While this man was in prison and was invoking the names 3
of many saints to pray for their compassion, he turned to the holy man of God as his personal protector and said: "I have heard, holy Nicetius, how powerful you are in acts of compassion, and how pious in breaking the fetters of those who weep. Now I pray that you will deign to visit me with the great piety with which you frequently shone in releasing other chained men!" And after he had fallen asleep for a 4
while, the blessed man appeared to him and said: "Who are you that you invoke Nicetius's name? And how do you know who he is while you keep entreating him?" After the man had explained the circumstances leading to his crime, he added: "Have pity on me, I beseech you, if you are the man of God whom I invoke!" The holy man then said to him: "Arise in Christ's name and walk away free. For you will not be seized by anyone."

Awoken by these words, he was amazed to find himself 5
released, his chains shattered, and the stocks enclosing his

nemine retinente, usque ad eius sepulcrum perrexit intrepidus. Tunc a iudice noxialis culpae damnatione concessa, laxatus abscessit ad propria.

8. Gratum est illud addi miraculis, quid accensus ad lectum eius fecerit cicindilis, quia ingentia sunt quae hic sanctus in caelis habitans operatur in terris. Igitur lectulus, in quo sanctus quiescere erat solitus, saepius miraculis adornatur illustribus. Quique, grandi studio ab Aetherio nunc episcopo fabricatus, devotissime adoratur non immerito, cum frigoritici saepius sub eo siti, compresso vapore ac frigore, salvantur; ceterique infirmi ibidem proiecti protinus sublevantur.

2 Palla etenim speciosa tegitur, lychni in ea iugiter accenduntur. Unus igitur ex his per quadraginta dies totidemque noctes, ut ipse aedituus asseruit, absque ullius fomenti adiutorio perduravit splendens. In quo nec papyrus addita, nec gutta olei stillantis adiecta, sed in ipsa qua primum statutus est compositione, permansit in luce praeclara.

3 Huius sancti reliquias Gallomagnus, Tricassinorum pontifex, devotus expetiit. Quae cum psallentio deducerentur, et caecorum oculi illuminati sunt earum virtute, et aliorum morborum genera meruerunt recipere medicinam.

4 Ad nos quoque facietergium, dependentibus villis intextum, quod sanctus super caput in die obitus sui habuit, est perlatum. Quod nos tamquam munus caeleste suscepimus. Factum est autem, ut post dies plurimos ad benedicendum ecclesiam in parochia Paternacensi urbis Toronicae invitaremur. Accessi, fateor, sacravi altare, decerpsi fila de linteo, locavi in templo; dictis missis, facta oratione, discessi.

feet broken. At once he walked fearlessly to the saint's tomb without anyone to restrain him. Thereafter he was relieved of his condemnation by the judge, and returned home a free man.

8. It is a pleasure to add to these miracles the one which this holy man performed with the lamps lit beside his bed, for though he lives in heaven, his achievements on earth are great. Thus the bed in which he used to sleep is often graced by brilliant miracles. It was made with great care by Aetherius, now bishop of the city, and is deservedly revered, for the fever-stricken are often healed when they lie under it and their heat and chills are subdued; other sick persons who are put there also are quickly relieved.

A beautiful cloth covers it and around it lamps burn con- 2
tinuously. One of these, as the custodian asserts, continued burning for forty days and nights without replenishment. Without a papyrus wick being added, or a drop of oil put in, it remained in its original state, shining brightly.

Bishop Gallomagnus of Troyes devoutly sought relics of 3
this saint. And when these were brought to him with psalm singing, the eyes of the blind were given light through their power; other kinds of illnesses, too, deserved to receive remedies.

A facecloth with a woven-in fringe was sent to us, which 4
the holy man had worn on his head on the day of his death. We received it as a heavenly gift. Several days later, however, we were invited to consecrate a church in the parish of Pernay in the city of Tours. I went there, I confess, and consecrated the altar, cut off a thread from the cloth and placed it in the temple; and after having said mass and prayed, I left.

5 Paucis deinde diebus interpositis, advenit ad nos ille qui
invitaverat, dicens: "Gaude in nomine Domini, sacerdos
Dei, de virtute beati Nicetii antistitis. Nam noveris quia
6 ostendit magnum miraculum in ecclesia quam sacrasti. Caecus enim erat in pago nostro diuturna caecitatis et caliginis
oculorum nocte detentus. Cui apparuit vir quidam per visum noctis, dicens: 'Si vis sanus fieri, prosternere in orationem coram basilicae sancti Nicetii altari, et recipies visum.'
Quod cum fecisset, disruptis tenebris, lumen ei virtus divina
patefecit."

7 Posui, fateor, de his pignoribus et in aliis basilicarum alta-
ribus, in quibus et energumeni sanctum confitentur, et fide-
8 lis oratio saepius promeretur effectum. Phronimii igitur
Agathensis Episcopi famulus epileptici morbi accessu fati-
gabatur, ita ut plerumque cadens ac spumans linguam suam
propriis dentibus laceraret. Et cum ei a medicis plurima
fierent, accidebat ut, paucis mensibus interpositis, non tangeretur a morbo; sed iterum in recidivum cruciatum ruens,
9 peius quam prius egerat perferebat. Dominus vero eius cum
vidisset tantas virtutes ad sepulcrum beati Nicetii fieri, dixit
ad eum: "Vade et prosternere coram sepulcro sancti, orans
ut te adiuvare dignetur." Qui cum iussa explesset, sanus regressus est, nec ultra eum hic attigit morbus. Septimus enim
erat annus ab incolumitate pueri, quando eum nobis episcopus praesentavit.

9. Quidam vero pauper, vivente sancto, litteras ab eo elicuit, manu eius subscriptas, qualiter sibi per devotorum

After a few days, the man who had invited us came to us 5
and said: "Rejoice in the name of the Lord, bishop of God,
on account of the blessed bishop Nicetius's holy power. For
know that he has manifested a great miracle in the church
which you consecrated. There was a blind man in our region 6
whose eyes had been imprisoned in a long night of blindness
and darkness. A man appeared to him in a dream vision who
said: 'If you wish to be made healthy, prostrate yourself in
prayer before the altar of the basilica of the holy Nicetius,
and you will receive your sight.' When he had done this, the
darkness was dispersed and divine power opened his eyes."

I confess that I also placed some of these relics on the al- 7
tars of other churches where the possessed confessed his
power, and the petition of a faithful prayer was often deservedly fulfilled. For a servant of Bishop Phronimius of Agde 8
had been so severely tormented by attacks of epilepsy that
he often fell and foaming at the mouth wounded his tongue
with his teeth. When several procedures had been tried out
on him by doctors, he was free from the illness for several
months; but when he relapsed into renewed torments, he
was worse off than before. When his master saw how many 9
acts of power were being performed at the blessed Nicetius's tomb, he said to him: "Go and prostrate yourself before the tomb of the holy man, and pray that he may deign
to come to your aid." When the servant had carried out this
command, he returned healed and was never again touched
by the illness. It was in the seventh year after the end of his
illness that the bishop presented him to us.

9. During the saint's lifetime, a poor man had received a letter from him, signed with his own signature, so that he could beg for alms at the homes of the devout. After the

domos eleemosynam flagitaret. Post cuius obitum, adhuc
cum ipsa circuiens epistola, non pauca ab eleemosynariis
2 pro sancti memoria capiebat. Desiderium enim erat omnibus, ut quisque vidisset subscriptionem sancti, aliquid praeberet egenti. Quod videns Burgundio, non honorans neque
venerans sanctum, observare pauperem coepit a longe. Vi-
densque eum silvas ingressum, irruit et abstulit ei sex aureos
3 cum epistola; collisumque calcibus reliquit exanimem. At
ille inter calces et reliqua verbera hanc vocem emisit: "Adiuro
te per Deum vivum et virtutem sancti Nicetii, ut vel epistolam eius mihi reddi facias, quia mihi ultra non erit vita si
eam perdidero!" Ille vero ea proiecta in terram abiit, quam
pauper colligens venit ad civitatem.

4 Erat enim ibi eodem tempore Phronimius episcopus,
cuius supra meminimus. Ad quem accedens pauper ille, ait:
"Ecce homo qui me graviter caesum exspoliavit, abstulitque
sex aureos, quos pro intuitu epistolae sancti Nicetii accepe-
5 ram." Episcopus autem narravit haec comiti. Iudex vero vocatum Burgundionem, percunctari coepit ab eo quid exinde
diceret. Negavit autem coram omnibus, dicens quia: "Numquam vidi hominem istum, neque res eius abstuli."

6 Episcopus autem, aspiciens epistolam, vidit subscriptionem sancti, et conversus ad Burgundionem, ait: "Ecce in
hac epistola subscriptio sancti Nicetii tenetur. Si es innocens, accede proprius, et iura tangens manu scripturam

bishop's death, he continued to make the rounds with that letter and received considerable sums from almsgivers who cherished the holy man's memory. For everyone wished to 2
see the saint's signature and accordingly gave something to the poor man. Having seen this, a certain Burgundian who did not honor or venerate the saint began to keep an eye on the poor man from a distance. And having seen him go into a forest, he attacked him and took away six gold coins as well as the letter; after kicking him until he was half dead, he left him there. But while he was being kicked and beaten, 3
the poor man shouted: "I beg you by the living God and the power of the holy Nicetius that you give me back the letter he gave me, for I cannot make a living if I lose it!" The Burgundian then indeed threw it on the ground before he left, and the poor man picked it up and went to the city of Agde.

At that time, Phronimius, whom we mentioned earlier, 4
was bishop there. The poor man came to him and said: "Look, there is a man who beat me seriously and robbed me; he took the six gold coins which I had received for letting people look at the holy Nicetius's signature." The bishop 5
told this to the count, this judge summoned the Burgundian, and began to ask him what he had to say about it. He denied the fact in the presence of all, saying: "I have never seen that man, nor have I taken away his possessions."

When the bishop looked at the letter however, and saw 6
the holy Nicetius's signature, he turned to the Burgundian and said: "Look, this letter contains the holy Nicetius's signature. If you are innocent, come here and swear to this with your hand on the signature which he wrote. For we

quam ipse depinxit. Credimus enim de virtute illius quia aut te hodie reddet ab hoc scelere comprobatum, aut certe abire
7 permittet innoxium." At ille nihil moratus, accedit ad manus episcopi, qui hanc epistolam extentam tenebat. Elevansque manus suas ut sacramentum daret, cecidit retrorsum supinus, et clausis oculis, spumas ab ore proiciens, quasi mortuus putabatur. Transeunte autem quasi duarum horarum spatio, aperuit oculos suos, dicens: "Vae mihi quia peccavi
8 auferendo res pauperis huius!" Et statim retulit per ordinem qualiter iniuriam intulerit homini illi. Tunc episcopus cum iudice obtenta culpa, ea tantum quae abstulerat inopi reddidit, et pro caede duos insuper solidos addidit, et sic uterque a iudicis conspectu discessit.

10. Quanti per hunc sanctum carcerali ergastulo revincti absoluti sint, quantorum compeditorum catenae sive compedes sint confractae, testis est hodie moles illa ferri, quae in basilica eius aspicitur, de supradictis suppliciis aggregata.

2 Nuper autem in conspectu Guntchramni Principis Syagrium Augustodunensem Episcopum regi referentem audivi, in una nocte in septem civitatibus carcerariis apparuisse beatum virum, eosque absolvisse ab ergastulo, et abire liberos permisisse. Sed nec iudices contra eos quidquam agere deinceps ausi sunt.

3 De cuius sepulcro si febricitans, si frigores habens, ac diversis morbis laborans, quid pulveris sumpserit ac dilutum acceperit, mox recipit sanitatem. Quod non dubium praestare eum qui ait sanctis suis: "Omnia quaecumque petieritis in nomine meo, credite quia accipietis, et venient vobis" [Mark 11:24].

believe in the power of Him who will today either convict you of this crime or, indeed, will permit you to leave as an
innocent man." And the Burgundian unhesitatingly came up 7
to bishop's hands which were holding out the letter. When he had raised his hands to swear the oath, he fell backward on his back, his eyes closed, froth came out of his mouth, and he seemed to be dead. After about two hours, he opened his eyes and said: "Woe to me, for I sinned when I took this
poor man's possessions away!" And at once he explained 8
how he had injured that man. When the bishop had established his guilt with the judge, the Burgundian gave the poor man as much as he had taken from him, adding two gold coins as compensation for the blows, and in this manner they both left the presence of the judge.

10. How many men chained in prison were released by this holy man and how many fetters or stocks were broken is shown today by the heap of such ironmongery, collected from the above-mentioned punishments, which may be seen in his basilica.

Recently, while in the presence of King Guntram, I heard 2
Bishop Syagrius of Autun telling the king that in one night the blessed man had appeared to prisoners in seven cities, liberated them from the prisons and allowed them to leave as free men. Even the judges did not dare to undertake anything against them afterward.

If anyone is fever-stricken or suffering chills or other dis- 3
eases takes some dust from his tomb and drinks it diluted in water, he soon recovers. This is without doubt done by the one who said to his saints: "Whatever you ask in my name, believe that you will receive it, and you will."

11. Igitur apud vicum Prisciniacensem urbis Turonicae ecclesia dudum constructa absque sanctorum pignoribus habebatur. Cumque incolae loci plerumque peterent ut eam
quorumpiam sanctorum cineribus sacraremus, de supradictis reliquiis sancto altari collocavimus; in qua ecclesia saepius virtus Domini per beatum manifestatur antistitem.
2 Nuperrimo autem tempore, mulieres quaedam vexatae a
daemonio, ex termino Biturigo venientes, tres numero, dum
ad basilicam sancti Martini deducerentur, hanc ecclesiam
sunt ingressae. Illico collisis in se palmis, dum sancti Nicetii
faterentur se virtutibus cruciari, proicientes ab ore nescio
quid purulentum cum sanguine, ab obsessis spiritibus protinus sunt mundatae.

3 Dado, unus ex his pagensibus, cum in hostilitate illa apud
Convenas acta est accessisset, et plerumque in periculis
mortis irrueret, vovit ut si domum reverteretur incolumis,
ad memoratam ecclesiam exornandam in honore sancti Ni-
4 cetii aliqua ex his quae acquisierit largiretur. Rediens igitur
duos calices argenteos detulit, vovitque iterum in itinere, ut
hos ecclesiae conferret, si ad propria sospes accederet. Ad
domum igitur accedens, unum tantummodo dedit, alium
fraudare procuravit, dans coopertorium Sarmaticum quo altare dominicum cum oblationibus tegeretur.

5 Apparuit autem viro vir beatus per somnium, dicens:
"Quousque dubitas, et votum implere dissimulas? Vade," inquit, "et calicem alterum quem vovisti redde ecclesiae, ne
pereas tu et domus tua. Coopertorium vero, quia rarum est,
non ponatur super munera altaris, quia non exinde ad plene

11. In the parish of Pressigny, in the diocese of Tours, a recently constructed church did not yet have any relics of the saints. And when the inhabitants of the place frequently requested that we consecrate the church with the remains of some saints, we placed some of the above-mentioned relics inside the holy altar; and the power of the Lord was thereafter often manifested in that church through the blessed
bishop. Very recently, certain women from the territory of 2
Bourges, three in number, who were being harassed by demons, were being led to the basilica of the holy Martin, when they entered this church. There, while they struck their hands one against another, they confessed that they were being tormented by the powers of the holy Nicetius, and vomiting from their mouths some kind of pus with blood, were soon cleansed of the spirits possessing them.

Dado, one of the country people who participated in the 3
expedition against Comminges, and who had several times been in danger of being killed, vowed that if he should return home unhurt he would give some of his booty to adorn
the church mentioned. On his way back, he took with him 4
two silver chalices and vowed again during his journey that he would give these to the church if he arrived home safely. But when he did reach his home, he gave only one and tried to defraud the church of the other one by substituting a Sarmatian cloth to cover the offerings on the Lord's altar.

The blessed man, however, appeared to him in a dream 5
and said: "How long will you hesitate and delay fulfilling your vow? Go and give the other chalice which you promised to the church, lest you and your house perish. For the cloth is thin and should not be placed on the offerings of the altar because it does not fully cover the mystery of the

tegitur mysterium corporis sanguinisque dominici." At ille, exterritus, nihil moratus, votum quod voverat velociter adimplevit.

6 Huius hominis frater ad vigilias dominici natalis advenit, monuitque presbyterum, dicens: "Vigilemus unanimiter ad ecclesiam Dei, atque exoremus devote beati Nicetii potentiam, ut eo obtinente huius anni curriculum cum pace ducamus." Quod presbyter audiens, gavisus iussit signum ad vigi-
7 lias commoveri. Quo commoto, adveniente presbytero cum clericis et reliquo populo, hic gulae inhians moras veniendi innectebat. Misitque saepius presbyter ad eum arcessendum. Quibus respondebat: "Paulisper sustinete, et venio." Quid plura? Transactis vigiliis, data luce, hic qui prius commonuerat, ad vigilias non accessit.

8 Presbyter vero, impleto officio, commotus contra hominem, ad metatum eius properat, quasi eum a communione suspenderet. At ille correptus febre, sicut vino ita divino exurebatur incendio. Nec mora, viso presbytero, datis voci-
9 bus cum lacrimis, supplicabat sibi paenitentiam tradi. Cumque eum presbyter increparet, dicens, "Merito a sancti Nicetii virtute exureris, ad cuius ecclesiam venire ad vigilias neglexisti," inter sermocinantium colloquia spiritum exhalavit. Facta quoque hora tertia, cum populus ad missarum solemnia conveniret, hic mortuus in ecclesiam est delatus. Quod virtute sancti antistitis actum nemo ambigere potest. Haec enim nobis ipse exposuit presbyter.

Lord's body and blood." He was terrified by this and no longer delayed, but immediately fulfilled his vow.

Dado's brother came to the vigils of the Lord's birth and 6
spoke to the priest, saying: "Let us keep the vigils together in the church of God, and pray devoutly to the blessed Nicetius's power so that his intercession may obtain that we live in peace this year." Upon hearing this, the priest rejoiced
and ordered the bell to be rung for the vigil. When this had 7
taken place, the priest came with the clerics and the rest of the people, while this man gulped down food and kept on giving excuses for delaying his coming. The priest sent messengers to him many times to call him. He kept replying to them: "Wait just a little, and I will come." Need I say more? When the vigils were finished and daybreak came, the man who had first said he would come had not shown up.

When the office had been completed, the priest was an- 8
gry with the man and hurried to this lodging, intending to suspend him from communion. But he found him seized by fever, burning not only with the heat of the wine but also with divine fire. When he saw the priest, he wept and cried
out, begging him to impose penance upon him. And while 9
the priest reproached him, saying, "Deservedly do you burn with the power of the holy Nicetius, to whose church you neglected to come to celebrate vigils," he breathed out his spirit during these words. At the third hour, when the people came together for the solemnity of mass, the dead man was carried into the church. No one will doubt that this occurred through the power of the holy bishop. The priest himself told us these things.

10 Plurima etenim de his vel proprie experti sumus, vel per fidelium relationem cognovimus, quae indicare longum putavimus.

12. Sed quoniam placuit libello clausulam dare, unum adhuc admirandum de libro vitae eius, quem supra a quodam scriptum praefati sumus, memorabo miraculum. De quo virtus procedens non reliquit inglorium, sed ad comprobandam virtutem dictorum patefecit esse plurimis gloriosum.

2 Diaconus enim Augustodunensis gravi oculorum caecitate turbatus, audivit haec quae glorificator sanctorum suorum Deus ad sancti tumulum exercebat. Dixitque suis: "Si eius adirem sepulcrum, aut aliquid de sanctis pignoribus sumerem, aut certe si pallium, quo sancti artus teguntur me-
3 rerer attingere, fierem sanus." Cumque haec et huiusmodi cum suis verba conferret, astitit repente clericus quidam, dicens: "Bene," inquit, "credis. Sed si de iisdem firmare mentem cupis virtutibus, en volumen chartaceum, quod de his habetur scriptum, ut facilius credas ea quae ad auditum tuarum aurium pervenerunt."

4 At ille, priusquam legere appeteret, inspirante divinae pietatis respectu, ait: "Credo quia potens est Deus egregia operari per famulos suos!" Et statim posuit volumen super
5 oculos suos. Extemplo autem, fugato dolore disruptaque caligine, usum videndi recipere meruit voluminis a virtute; et in tantum claritate positus est, ut ipse propriis oculis legens virtutum gesta cognosceret.

We know of many other miracles, either because we our- 10
selves experienced them or through accounts of reliable witnesses, but I think it would take too long to retail them.

12. However, since this book needs a closing story, I will commemorate one miracle concerning the book about his life which we mentioned earlier as the work of an unknown author. The divine power that went forth from it did not leave him without glory, but by proving the power of the words said about him revealed to many that he had been glorified.

A deacon of Autun who was afflicted with grievous blind- 2
ness heard about what God, the glorifier of his saints, performed at the holy man's tomb. He said to his companions: "If I go to his tomb or take a particle of his holy relics or certainly if I deserve to touch the cloth with which his body
is covered, I shall be made healthy." As he was uttering these 3
and similar words to his companions, suddenly a certain cleric stood before them; he said: "Your belief is sound. But if you wish to strengthen your faith in these acts of power even more, here is a papyrus roll with writings about these miracles, so that you may more easily believe what you have come to hear."

But before the deacon sought to read it, he was inspired 4
by the care of the divine piety to say: "I believe that God has the power to work outstanding things through his servants!"
And he immediately put the book upon his eyes. At once, 5
the pain fled, darkness dissipated, and he deserved to receive his sight from the power in the papyrus roll; and his eyes became so full of light that he learned about the powerful deeds that had been performed by reading about them with his own eyes.

6 Operatur haec autem unus atque idem Dominus, qui gloriatur in sanctis suis, atque ipsos illustribus miraculis editos efficit gloriosos. Ipsi gloria et imperium in saecula saeculorum. Amen.

9

De sancto Patroclo abbate

Prologus

Cum egregia Moysis vatis prudentia, ad conformandum divinae descensionis tabernaculum, iuxta ipsum oris dominici praeceptum, fabricare disponeret, atque ad hoc eundemque apparatum multa congerere iussus, non haberet cuncta in regestu promptuarii, quae ab ipso Domino ostensa fuerant in montis ardui summitate, iussit commoneri populum, ut offerret unusquisque pro viribus quiddam muneris
2 Deo, et hoc non ex necessitatibus sed sponte. Offerebant ergo donaria auri, argentique, aeris ac ferri metalla; gemmarum etiam micantium pulchritudines, ac fila byssi duplicati coccique bis torti; nonnulli pelles arietum rubricatas, pilosque caprarum. Sed cum haec omnia doctores ecclesiarum esse allegorica tradidissent, et in reliquis donariis gratiarum genera demonstrassent, in illis caprarum pilis laudationum verba comparaverunt.

These things are done by one and the same Lord, who is 6
glorified in his saints and renders them glorious by making brilliant miracles come forth. To him be the glory and the power, for ever and ever. Amen.

9

About the holy abbot Patroclus

Prologue

When the outstandingly prudent prophet Moses was preparing to build a tabernacle according to the Lord's instructions to be a fitting place for God to descend, he ordered many things to be collected for its construction because he did not possess everything that had been shown to him by the Lord on top of the lofty mountain; thus he ordered the people to be admonished that each should offer something according to his means as a gift to God, and this not because he was told to do so, but of his own free
will. Accordingly, they gave gifts of gold, silver, brass, and 2
iron; beautiful glowing gems, skeins of double-twisted linen and double-dyed scarlet cloths; and some brought rams' skins dyed red, and goat hairs. The tradition of the doctors of the Church, however, tells us that all these things are allegories signifying the various kinds of gifts of grace, and they interpreted goat hairs as signifying words of praise.

3 Ita nunc et nos steriles sensu, imperiti studio, squalentes in actu, etsi aurum argentumque vel gemmas filaque duplicata ac torta non offerrimus, saltem vel pilos caprarum, id est verba quae sanctorum atque amicorum Dei prodant miracula, in ecclesia sancta porrigimus, ut legentes eo incitentur studio quo sancti meruerunt scandere polum.

4 Ergo quia nobis de beati Patrocli vita nuper data relatio quaedam prodidit, non omittenda sed manifestanda curavi. Et licet sermone rustico, non tamen occuli arbitratus sum quae Deus gessit per famulum suum.

1. Igitur beatissimus Patroclus, Biturigi territorii incola, Aetherio patre progenitus, cum decem esset annorum pastor ovium destinatur; fratre Antonio tradito ad studia litterarum. Erant enim non quidem nobilitate sublimes, ingenui tamen.

2 Cumque quodam meridie hic a scholis, ille a grege commisso ad capiendum cibum paterno in hospitio convenissent, dixit Antonius fratri suo: "Discede longius, o rustice! Tuum est enim opus oves pascere, meum litteris exerceri; qua de re nobiliorem me ipsius officii cura facit, cum te huius custodiae servitus vilem reddat."

3 Quod ille audiens, et hanc increpationem quasi a Deo sibi transmissam putans, reliquit oves in campi planitie, et scholas puerorum nisu animi agili atque cursu velocissimo

Thus now we too, who are barren of mind, unskilled in studies, and filthy in deeds, even though we do not offer gold, silver, precious stones, double-twisted thread, or scarlet cloths, can at least offer goats' hairs, that is, bring into the holy Church words that proclaim the miracles of the saints and friends of God, so that their readers may be spurred on by the same zeal as the saints who deserved to rise to heaven. 3

Therefore, since a report of blessed Patroclus's life recently came to us, I took care not to leave it unmentioned but to publish it. And although it will be written in a rustic style, I have nevertheless decided that what God did through his servant should not be concealed. 4

1. The most blessed Patroclus, an inhabitant of the territory of Bourges, the son of Aetherius, was ten years old when he was given the task of herding sheep; his brother Antonius was sent to study letters. For, although they were not of the highest nobility, they were of free birth.

One day at noon when Antonius had come from school and Patroclus from the sheep entrusted to him, to take a meal in their paternal home, Antonius said to his brother: "Keep your distance from me, country boy! For it is your task to take care of sheep, mine to study letters; applying myself to these makes me nobler, whereas this menial task of herding makes you common." 2

When Patroclus heard this, he regarded it as a reproach from God; he left the sheep behind in the field and, with an agile effort of mind and the utmost speed, went to the 3

expetivit. Traditisque elementis, ac deinceps quae studio
puerili necessaria erant, ita celeriter, memoria opitulante,
imbutus est ut fratrem vel in scientia praecederet, vel alacri-
tate sensus, adiuvante divini numinis auxilio, anteiret.

4 Dehinc Nunnioni, qui quondam cum Childebertho Pari-
siorum rege magnus habebatur, ad exercendum commenda-
tus est. A quo cum summa amoris diligentia nutriretur, ita se
humilem atque subiectum omnibus praebebat, ut omnes
eum tamquam proprium parentem in summa bonitate dili-
gerent.

5 Regressus ad domum, patre defuncto, reperit matrem
suam adhuc superstitem. Cui illa ait: "Ecce genitor tuus, o
dulcissime nate, obiit. Ego vero absque solatio dego. Requi-
ram puellam pulchram ingenuamque, cui copulatus solatium praebeas maternae viduitati." At ille respondit: "Non
coniungor mundanae coniugi, sed quae concepit animus
6 cum Domini voluntate perficiam." Cui cum genetrix non intelligens quareret quid hoc esset, prodere noluit, sed abiit ad
Arcadium, Bituricae urbis episcopum, petiitque sibi comam
capitis tonderi, ascirique se in ordinem clericorum. Quod
episcopus, Domino volente, sine mora complevit.

7 Nec multo post diaconatus officium sumens, vacabat
ieiuniis, delectabatur vigiliis, exercebatur lectione, atque in
oratione assidua promptus effundebatur, ut nec ad convivium mensae canonicae cum reliquis accederet clericis.
8 Quod audiens archidiaconus, frendens contra eum, ait:

school for boys. When he had learned the basics and thereafter what was necessary for boys' instruction, he learned so quickly with the help of his excellent memory that, with the help of the divine Power, he surpassed his brother in knowledge and was quicker of mind than he.

Later he was commended for training to Nunnio, who 4
was then held in high esteem by Childebert, king of the Parisians. By this man he was raised with the greatest loving care and he conducted himself so humbly and deferentially toward all that everyone loved him dearly as though he were their own relative.

Upon his return home, he found that his father had died, 5
but that his mother was still alive. She said to him: "Look, dearest son, your father has died. And I live without any company. I shall find you a beautiful, freeborn girl to marry and therewith provide your widowed mother with some company." But he replied: "I shall not join myself to a bride of this world, but, if the Lord wills it, I shall carry out what I
have decided to do." When his mother, not understanding 6
what this might be, asked what it was, he would not tell her, but went to Arcadius, bishop of Bourges, and asked him to shave the hair off his head and admit him to the order of the clergy. This the bishop, following God's will, immediately did.

When not much later he accepted the office of deacon, 7
he so devoted himself to fasting, delighting in vigils, reading as much as he could, and continuously pouring forth assiduous prayers, that he did not always attend the canonical
meal with the other clerics. When the archdeacon heard 8

"Aut cum reliquis fratribus cibum sume, aut certe discede a nobis. Non enim rectum videtur ut dissimules cum his habere victum, cum quibus ecclesiasticum implere putaris officium."

2. Non est autem de his servus Dei commotus animo, qui
iam heremi sitiebat adire secretum. Sed egressus ab urbe
memorata, venit ad vicum Nereensem, ibique aedificato
oratorio, sancti Martini reliquiis consecrato, pueros erudire
2 coepit in studiis litterarum. Veniebant autem ad eum infirmi
et sanabantur, atque energumeni nomen eius confitentes
emundabantur. Nec ei erat solitudo ut voluerat, sed patefacta virtus publicum usquequaque reddebat. Tunc pro auspicio quiddam brevibus conscriptis posuit super altare, vigilans et orans tribus noctibus, ut quid ei Dominus agere iuberet, dignaretur manifestissime declarare.

3 Sed pietas divinae inclyta miseratio, quae eum praesciens eremitam esse decreverat, brevem illum accipere iubet, ut ad eremum properaret. Ille autem in cellula in qua degebat, congregatis virginibus, monasterium instituit puellarum, nihil de omni labore suo quod ibidem aggregaverat cum abscederet, sumens, nisi rastrum unum, unamque bipennem.

4 Ingressusque altas silvarum solitudines, venit ad locum qui dicitur Mediocantus. Ibique constructa cellula, in opere quod supra diximus Deo vacabat. Atque inibi cum multos energumenos, manu imposita, per signum crucis effugatis daemonibus, mente integra reddidisset, unus ad eum adductus est rabidus, qui rictibus patulis dentibusque

this he was very angry with him and said: "Either you eat with the other brothers, or you leave us. For it is not right that you refuse to eat with those with whom you think you share your ecclesiastical duties."

2. The servant of God was not angered by these words because he already thirsted to enter into the remote wilderness. He left the aforesaid city and came to the village of Néris, where he built a chapel which he consecrated with relics of the holy Martin and began to teach boys to write.
The sick also came to him and were healed, and the pos- 2
sessed confessed his name and were cleansed. So he did not enjoy the solitude he had sought, because the revelation of his holy power continuously made him a public figure. Thereupon he sought an oracle, putting a few written notes face down on the altar, and he kept vigils and prayed there for three days and three nights so that the Lord might deign to indicate very clearly what he commanded him to do.

The lofty compassion of divine piety, which foreknow- 3
ingly had decreed that he would be a hermit, commanded him to take the note that prompted him to hasten to the wilderness. After he had gathered some nuns, he established a monastery for women in the cell in which he had been living and left, taking nothing with him of all that he had collected through his labor there except one hoe and one ax.

When he had entered the deep solitudes of the forests, 4
he came to a place called Mediocantus. There he built a cell and served God in the way we described above. And there, when he had put the demons to flight through the sign of the cross and restored many possessed persons to their right mind, a rabid man was led to him whose open mouth showed

cruentis, quod attingere poterat dentibus propriis laniabat.
5 Pro quo per triduum in oratione prostratus, obtinuit ad illam divinae miserationis potentiam, ut, mitigato furore, leto obnoxius mundaretur: immissisque in os eius digitis, fugato feralis atrocitatis spiritu, personam restituit incolumitati.

6 Nullas enim ante eum vires habere poterat persuasionis iniquae praestigium. Nam sicut hos qui vexabantur emundabat, ita et quae immittebat occulte atrocia Auctor criminis, repellebat per crucis sacratissimae virtutem.

7 Nam Leubellae cuidam feminae, cum per luem illam inguinariam diabolus, Martinum mentitus, oblationes quibus quasi populus salvaretur nequiter obtulisset, haec ad sanctum delatae, non solum revelante Spiritu sancto evanuerunt, verumetiam ipse Incentor malorum sancto teterrimus apparens, quae nequiter gesserat est professus.

8 Transfigurat enim se saepe diabolus in angelum lucis, ut hac fraude decipiat innocentes. Sed cum ei multas intentaret insidias, ne hic ascenderet unde ille corruerat, immisit ei cogitationem, ut praetermisso eremo, ad saeculum reverti deberet. Sed hic sanctus cum virus grassari sensisset in pectore, in oratione prostratus petebat ut nihil aliud nisi quod
9 Deo esset placitum exerceret. Tunc apparuit ei angelus Domini per visum, dicens: “Si vis mundum videre, ecce columna, in quam ascendens contemplare omnia quae geruntur in eo.” Erat enim ante eum per ipsam visionem columna mirae celsitudinis collocata. In quam ascendens vidit

bloody teeth and who tore apart with them whatever he
could lay hold of. When the holy man had prayed for him 5
prostrate for three days, he obtained from the power of divine compassion that the man's fury be mitigated, and that
the one subject to death be purged; so when he stuck his fingers into the man's mouth, the spirit of wild savagery fled,
and he restored the man to health.

The phantoms of wicked delusions never had any power 6
over him. For just as he cleansed those who were harassed
by these, he also repelled with the power of the sacred cross
the wicked thoughts which the Author of evil stealthily put
in his mind.

During the time of the plague of the groin which we have 7
spoken about, the devil had appeared to a woman called
Leubella as a false Martin and had wickedly given her offerings which were supposed to save the people. When these
were shown to the holy man, not only did the Holy Spirit
make them vanish, but the hideous Instigator himself even
appeared to the holy man and confessed what he had wickedly done.

For the devil often transforms himself into an angel of 8
light to deceive the innocent by this ruse. And when he was
tempting Patroclus with many tricks, lest he should ascend
to the place from where he had fallen, he put the thought in
his head of leaving the wilderness and returning to the life of
this world. When the holy man felt the poison growing in
his heart, he prostrated himself in prayer and asked to do
only what would please God. Then an angel of the Lord ap- 9
peared to him in a vision and said: "If you wish to see the
world, here is a column. If you go up to the top you can see
everything that happens in it." And in the vision there appeared before him a wonderfully tall column. When he had

homicidia, furta, caedes, adulteria, fornicationes, et omnia prava quae geruntur in mundo.

10 Et descendens ait: "Ne, quaeso, Domine, revertar ad has
pravitates, quas dudum, te confessus, oblitus sum." Tunc ait
illi angelus qui cum eo loquebatur: "Desine ergo quarere
mundum, ne pereas cum eo. Sed potius vade in oratorium in
quo Dominum depreceris. Et quod ibi inveneris, hoc tibi
11 erit consolatio in peregrinatio tua." Ingressusque cellulam
oratorii, invenit tegulam fictilem, in qua signum crucis dominicae erat expressum. Agnoscensque munus divinum, intellexit sibi ad omnia mundanae persuasionis incitamenta hoc esse inexpugnabile munimentum.

3. Post haec aedificavit sanctus Patroclus monasterium Columbariense, in milibus quinque a cellula heremi in qua habitabat et, congregatis monachis, ut solitudinem libero potius fungeretur arbitrio, abbatem instituit qui gregi monasteriali praeesset.

2 Octavum enim et decimum in hoc heremi loco expleverat annum. Tum, congregatis fratribus, transitum suum annuntians, obiit in senectute bona, sanctitate praecipua. Qui aquis ablutus, feretroque impositus ferebatur ad monasterium suum, ubi se vivens sepeliri mandaverat. Tunc archipresbyter Nereensis vici, collecta clericorum cohorte, voluit
vi auferre glebam sancti corpusculi, videlicet ut ad vicum
3 suum unde egressus fuerat sepelitur. Sed cum furibundus
veniens vidisset a longe pallam quae tegebat artus sanctos eximio albere nitore, ita nutu Dei est metu perterritus, ut

gone up to its top, he saw murders, thefts, slaughter, adulteries, fornications, and all the perverse things that are done in the world.

And when he came down he said: "Lord, let me not re- 10
turn to the perversities which I had forgotten about since I
devoted myself to you." The angel with whom he was talking
then said: "So stop seeking the world, lest you perish with it.
Rather, go into the chapel where you pray to the Lord. And
what you will find there will be a consolation to you on your
journey." When he had gone into the chapel, he found a clay 11
tile engraved with the sign of the Lord's cross. Recognizing
it as a divine gift, he understood that the sign of the cross
was an invincible protection for him against all the temptations of worldly persuasions.

3. After this, the holy Patroclus built the monastery of Colombiers, five miles from the hermit's cell in which he lived; and when he had gathered the monks, he put an abbot in charge of the monastic flock in his stead, so that he could live in solitude as he pleased.

He lived for eighteen years in this lonely place. Then he 2
called together the brothers to announce his passing and
died in outstanding sanctity at a venerable age. After he had
been washed and placed on a bier, he was carried to his monastery where, during his lifetime, he had ordered himself to
be buried. The archpriest of the village of Néris, however,
mustered a troop of clerics and wanted to take away the dust
of the saint's body and bury it in his own village, from where
the saint had come. As he approached in a frenzy, he saw 3
from afar that the cloth covering the holy limbs was shining
with a brilliant light, and through God's will he was so

omni velocitate revocaret ab animo quod male conceperat levitatis arbitrio. Coniunctusque psallentio in exsequiis sancti progressus, tumulavit eum cum reliquis qui aderant fratribus, in ipso Columbariensi monasterio.

4 Ad cuius sanctum sepulcrum Prudentia caeca cum alia
Lemovicina puella, similiter lumine viduata, ut sepulcrum
sanctum in oratione osculatae sunt, lumen recipere meruerunt. Maxonidius autem post quintum caecitatis suae an-
5 num, hunc tumulum sanctum adiit, lumenque recepit. Energumeni vero Lupus, Theodulfus, Rucco, Scopilia, Nectariola,
et Tachildis ad hunc sancti tumulum sunt mundati. Sed et
puellae duae de Lemovicino venientes, oleo quod ipse sanctus benedixit perunctae, a nequitia qua obsidebantur mundatae sunt. Et quotidie ibidem ad corroborandam fidem
gentium operatur Dominus, qui perpetualiter glorificat
sanctos suos.

10

De sancto Friardo recluso

Prologus

Multi variique sunt gradus per quos ad caelorum regna conscenditur, de quibus, ut opinor, et David dicit quia: "Ascensus in corde disposuit" [Psalms 84:5]. Accipiuntur

terrified by this that he at once went back on the bad decision he had so hastily taken. Joining the procession singing at the saint's funeral, he together with the other brothers who were present, buried him in the monastery of Colombiers.

At his holy tomb the blind Prudentia and another girl 4
from Limoges, also lacking the light of her eyes, merited to receive light when they kissed the holy tomb during prayer. Maxonidius came to the holy tomb after five years of blindness and received his sight. The possessed persons Lupus, 5
Theodulf, Rucco, Scopilia, Nectariola, and Tachildis were cleansed at the tomb of this saint. When they had been anointed with the oil which the saint had blessed, two girls coming from Limoges were also cleansed of the wickedness by which they had been infested. And every day the Lord who perpetually glorifies his saints works there to strengthen the faith of the people.

10

About the holy recluse Friardus

Prologue

The steps by which one ascends to the kingdom of heaven are many and diverse, and I believe that it was about these that David said: "He placed steps in the heart." These steps

ergo hi gradus diversorum operum ad cultum divinum pro-
fectus, et nullus in his gressum figere potest, nisi fuerit, sicut
2 saepe testati sumus, Dei adiutorio provocatus. Sic enim
Psalmographus in illo mediae profectionis gradu loquitur,
dicens: "Nisi Dominus aedificaverit domum, in vanum labo-
rant qui aedificant eam" [Psalms 127:1]. Quod adiutorium,
non modo martyres, verum etiam et illi quos sacrae vitae ro-
boravit auctoritas, iugiter inquirentes, ad hoc sitis desiderii
3 spiritalis promebat alacres pervenerunt. Nam si ad martyrium mens accensa est, huius adiutorii opem poposcit martyr ut vinceret; si ieiunii observantiam adhibere studuit, ut
ab eo confortaretur afflictus est; si castitati artus reservare
voluit impollutos, ut ab illo muniretur oravit; si post igno-
rantiam paenitendo converti desideravit, ut ab eo nihilominus sublevarentur cum lacrimis flagitavit; et si quid operis
boni exercere eorum quispiam meditatus est, ut ab hoc
adiutorio iuvaretur expetiit.

4 Per hos ergo scalae huius ascensus tam difficiles, tamque
excelsos, tam arduos, cum sint diversi, ad unum tamen Dominum per huius adiutorii opem conscenditur. Idcirco semper ille poscendus, ille quaerendus, ille invocandus erit, ut
quod de bono mens concipit, adiutorio suo ipse perficiat, de
quo et nobis sine fine oportet dicere: "Adiutorium nostrum
in nomine Domini, qui fecit caelum et terram" [Psalms
5 124:8]. Sicut et ille beatissimus, de quo nunc nobis futurus
est sermo, qui inter diversas vel temptationes vel cruces saeculi, semper huius adiutorii munimen expetiit.

consisting of diverse works are understood to be the ones that make one progress in the service of God, and, as we have often borne witness, no one can tread upon them unless called to do so by God's help. For the author of the 2
psalms speaks of the step in the middle of the journey when he says: "Unless the Lord shall have built a house, those that build it work in vain." God's help was sought continuously not only by the martyrs, but also by those known to have led holy lives, and with it they quickly reached what their spiritual thirst deserved. For if a martyr's mind was aflame with 3
the desire for martyrdom, he asked for this support to win the contest; if a holy man sought to adhere to his fast, he mortified himself so as to be strengthened by it; if he wished to keep his body unpolluted, he prayed to be protected by it; if after sinning through ignorance he desired to convert through penitence, he implored it with tears to lift him up; and if he considered doing some good work, he sought to be aided by this help.

It is by the steps of this ladder, so difficult and so high, as 4
arduous as they are diverse, that one ascends to the one Lord with his help. Therefore his help must always be requested, sought, and invoked, so that whatever good the mind conceives, it may carry it out with his help; about this we should also continuously say: "Our help is in the name of
the Lord, who made heaven and earth." Thus, too, did that 5
most blessed man act about whom we will now speak, who constantly sought the protection of this aid in the various trials and afflictions of this world.

1. Fuit igitur apud insulam Vindunittam urbis Namneticae vir egregiae sanctitatis, Friardus nomine, reclusus, de cuius vita parumper ad aedificationem ecclesiae dicere delectat animum, quia ignoro si ab aliquo sit scripta.

2 Hic ab infantia sua semper Deo devotus fuit atque pudicus. Factus autem vir, semper in Dei laudibus, semper in oratione, semper in vigiliis degebat. Victus necessaria propriis manibus exigebat a terra. Et si in opera inter reliquos properaret, numquam ab oratione cessabat. Quod vicinis aut extraneis, ut mos rusticorum habet, ridiculum erat.

3 Quodam vero die, dum cum reliquis, in segetem culmis
incisis, manipulos colligaret, examen miserabilium atque
saevarum muscarum, quas vulgo vespas vocant, reperiunt.
Cumque acerrime messores, emissis aculeis lacerarent,
undique circumeuntes messem, locum illum in quo hae
4 adunatae erant transiliunt. Atque irridendo beatum Friar-
dum alloquuntur dolose, dicentes: "Veniat benedictus, veniat religiosus, qui orare non desinit, qui crucem auribus et
oculis semper imponit, qui viis itineris sui salutaria vexilla
praemittit. Ipse metat super examen, ipse eum sua oratione
mitescat."

5 Tunc quasi ad confusionem dominicae virtutis haec verba suscipiens, provolutus terrae orationem fudit ad Dominum. Et accedens, facto desuper signo crucis, ait: "Adiutorium nostrum in nomine Domini, qui fecit caelum et terram" [Psalms 124:8]. Ad hanc eius orationem confestim omnes vespae se infra antrum unde egressae fuerant abdiderunt.

CHAPTER 10

1. There was, in those days, on the island of Vindunitta in the territory of the city of Nantes, a man of great sanctity, a recluse named Friardus. I have decided to say something about his life to edify the Church, since I do not know if it has been written about by anyone else.

This man was devoted to God and chaste from his child- 2
hood. When he had become an adult, he was always praising God, always praying, always keeping vigils. The food he needed he derived from the earth by the work of his own hands. And if he encountered others during this work, he never ceased praying. As is the custom of country people, however, his neighbors as well as strangers found this conduct ridiculous.

One day when he was binding up sheaves of cut grain 3
with some other people, they came across a swarm of the wretched and savage insects they call wasps. Since they pricked the harvesters with their sharp stings and kept circling around the harvest, the other harvesters avoided the
place where the wasps gathered. And while laughing, they 4
craftily said to the blessed Friardus: "Let the blessed one come, let the religious one come, who doesn't stop praying, who constantly makes the sign of the cross over his ears and eyes, who sends the saving sign of the cross ahead of him on the paths of his journey. Let him harvest where the swarm is, let him pacify it with his prayer!"

The holy man took these words as slighting the Lord's 5
power, prostrated himself on the ground and poured forth a prayer to him. After rising, he made the sign of the cross over the wasps and said: "Our help is the name of the Lord who made heaven and earth." At this prayer, all the wasps at once went to hide themselves in the hole from which they

6 Ille vero ad spectaculum omnium messem desuper illaesus expetiit. Quod non sine miraculo irridentibus fuit, eo quod Dominus in se sperantem ad confusionem eorum sic dignatus fuerit roborare.

7 Denique post haec, cum in arborem pro quadam necessitate ascendisset, subito colliso sub pedibus ramo, ruere coepit. Cadensque deorsum per singulos quos percutiebat ramos, Christi beatissimum nomen invocabat, dicens: "Christe omnipotens, salva me!" Cumque pervenisset ad terram, nihil est nocitus, sed aiebat semper: "Adiutorium nostrum in nomine Domini, qui fecit caelum et terram."

2. His et aliis virtutibus animatus, coepit intra secreta cordis tacitus cogitare, dicens: "Si crux Christi et invocatio nominis eius, atque adiutorium postulatum ab eo, tantam potentiam habet ut aspera quaeque mundi devincat, periculosa obruat, temptationum atra depellat, et omnia quae sunt saeculi huius oblectamenta pro nihilo reputata fastidiat—quid mihi et mundo, nisi ut relictis omnibus quae eius sunt, in illius vacare solius debeam obsequiis, cuius nominis invocatione a periculis sum salvatus iniquis?"

2 Et egressus ab hospitiolo suo, oblitus parentes et patriam, eremum petiit, ne in saeculo habitanti impedimentum aliquod de oratione mundi sollicitudo conferret. Ipse quoque et abbas Sabaudus, qui quondam Regis Clotharii minister fuerat, paenitentiam accipientes, Vindunitensem Namnetici territorii insulam sunt aggressi; habebant autem secum
3 et Secundellum diaconem. Abbas vero, ablata de aratro Domini manu, ab insula discedens ad monasterium rediit; nec multo post, occultis de causis, gladio est peremptus.

had emerged. And while everyone watched, the saint un- 6
harmed bound up the sheaves in that place. This was a miracle intended for those who had laughed, because the Lord had deigned to vindicate the one who trusted in him in order to confound them.

Later, after this, when the saint climbed into a tree to 7
fetch something, a branch broke under his feet and he began to fall. As he fell from branch to branch, he kept invoking the name of the most blessed Christ, saying: "Almighty Christ, save me!" And when he reached the ground, he was completely unhurt; therefore he continued saying: "Our help is in the name of the Lord who made heaven and earth."

2. Inspired by these and other deeds of power, he began to ponder silently in the depths of his heart, and said to himself: "If Christ's cross, the invoking of his name, and the help consequently received from him has so much power that it overcomes any hardship in this world, destroys dangers, wards off dark temptations, and regards all the delights of the world as of no value—what, then, have I to do with this world except to abandon everything that belongs to it, to devote my services to him alone through invoking whose name I have been saved from wicked dangers?"

And he went out from his small house, forgot his family 2
and his homeland, and sought the wilderness, lest living in this world might cause worldly cares to be an impediment to his prayers. Together with Abbot Sabaudus, a former minister of King Clothar, he agreed to perform penance and went to the isle of Vindunitta in the territory of Nantes; they had
the deacon Secundellus with them. The abbot, however, 3
took his hands from the Lord's plow, left the island and returned to his monastery; not much later, he was killed by the

Sanctus vero Friardus cum Secundello diacono in supradicta
insula stetit immobilis. Habebat tamen uterque eorum propriam cellulam, sed procul a se positam.

4 Cumque strenue in oratione persisterent, nocte Secundello apparuit Temptator in specie Domini, dicens: "Ego
sum Christus, quem quotidie deprecaris. Iam enim sanctus
effectus es, et nomen tuum libro vitae cum reliquis sanctis
meis ascripsi. Egredere nunc ab hanc insula et vade, fac sani-
5 tates in populos." His et ille illectus deceptionibus discessit
ab insula, nec socio nuntiavit; tamen cum infirmis in nomine
Christi manus imponeret, sanabantur. Regressus autem post
multum tempus ad insulam, venit ad socium cum vana gloria, dicens: "Abii enim extra insulam, et virtutes multas in
6 populis feci." Cumque conterritus interrogaret quid hoc sibi
vellet, cuncta quae gesserat simpliciter pandit. At senior
obstupescens, suspiransque, et lacrimans, ait: "Vae nobis, in
quantum audio a Temptatore delusus es! Vade, age paenitentiam, ne ultra tibi praevaleant eius doli!" Quod ille intelligens et periisse se timens, cum fletu ad pedes eius prosterni-
7 tur, rogans ut pro se Dominum deprecaretur. Et ille: "Vade,"
inquit, "et pariter eius omnipotentiam pro salute animae
tuae poscamus. Non est enim difficilis Dominus se confiten-
tibus misereri, cum ipse per prophetam dicat: 'Nolo mortem peccatoris, sed ut convertatur et vivat'" [Ezekiel 33:11].

sword for unknown reasons. The holy Friardus and the deacon Secundellus, however, remained steadfastly on that island. Each had his own cell, and there was a great distance between them.

As they strenuously persisted in prayer, the Tempter ap- 4
peared one night to Secundellus in the shape of the Lord,
and said: "I am Christ to whom you pray every day. You have
already been made holy and I have written your name in the
Book of Life alongside the names of my other saints. Now
leave this island and go, heal the people." Seduced by these 5
deceitful words, Secundellus left the island without telling
his companion; when, however, he placed his hand upon the
sick in the name of Christ, they were healed. After a long
time, he returned to the island and came to his companion
full of vainglory, saying: "I have gone away from the island
and performed many deeds of power among the people."
When the terrified Friardus asked him what this meant, 6
Secundellus simply told him everything he had done. And
the older man was stunned; he sighed and wept, saying:
"Woe to us for, from what I hear, you have been deceived
by the Tempter! Go and do penance, lest his tricks deceive
you again!" Secundellus understood this and, fearing that he
might perish, prostrated himself weeping at his feet and
begged him to pray for him to the Lord. Friardus said: "Go, 7
and let us pray together to his Omnipotence for the salvation of your soul. It is easy for the Lord to take pity on those who confess, for as he said through the prophet: 'I do not desire the death of the sinner, but that he turn from his way and live.'"

8 Orantibus autem illis, advenit iterum Temptator in simili
specie ad Secundellum diaconum, dicens: "Nonne praeceperam tibi, eo quod oves meae morbidae essent et pastore in-
digerent, ut egredereris et visitares, atque opem sanitatis eis
9 tribueres?" Et ille: "In veritate enim comperi quod Seductor
sis, neque te Deum credo cuius te speciem mentiris habere.
Tamen si Christus es, crucem tuam quam reliquisti ipsam
ostende, et credam tibi." Cumque non ostenderet, diaconus
10 crucem Domini in os eius faciens, confusus evanuit. Rursumque ad eum veniens cum multitudine daemonum, tanta
eum caede mactavit, ut vix putaretur evadere. Et discedens,
nusquam comparuit. Idem postea diaconus in summa sanctitate perdurans, die debito defunctus est.

3. Beatus vero Friardus, cum magnis virtutibus effulgeret,
quadam vice effractum e vento ab arbore ramum, quem, ut
ferunt, ipse inseruerat collegit, compositumque baculum
sibi exinde, quem manu gereret, fecit. Post multum vero
tempus iam arefactam virgam in terra plantavit, infusaque
aqua saepius, baculus ille frondes emisit et poma, atque infra duos aut tres annos in magnam arboris proceritatem
2 distentus excrevit. Quod cum grande miraculum populis
cernentibus haberetur, et quotidie ad hanc visendam imma-
nis turba conflueret, et etiam ipsam remotionem insulae virtus prodita publicaret, sanctus Dei, ne vanae gloriae labe
subrueret, arborem, arrepta securi, succidit.

3 Rursusque sanctus alterius arboris ruinam cernens, quae
acta venti violentia floribus plena corruerat, misericordia
motus oravit, dicens: "Ne pereat, quaeso, Domine, huius
arbustae fructus, quae te iubente florum ornamenta

While they prayed, the Tempter again came to Secun- 8
dellus in the same appearance and said: "Didn't I command
you, because my sheep are ill and need a shepherd, to go visit
them and heal them?" Secundellus said: "I have recognized 9
the truth that you are the Tempter, and do not believe you to
be God, whose appearance you have falsely assumed. However, if you are Christ, show me that cross of yours which
you have left behind, and I shall believe you." When the apparition failed to show it, the deacon made the sign of the
cross before his face, so confounding him that he vanished.
When the Tempter thereafter came back to him with a mul- 10
titude of demons, he beat Secundellus so severely that he
scarcely escaped dying. Thereafter he left and never again
appeared. After this, the deacon continued in the utmost
sanctity and died on the day appointed for him.

3. The blessed Friardus, who shone with great virtues,
once made a walking stick out of a tree branch which, so
they say, he himself had grafted and which had been blown
down by the wind. After a long time, when it had completely
dried up, he put the stick in the earth; since he watered it
frequently, the stick sprouted leaves and apples and in two
or three years grew into a large tree. This was experienced as 2
a great miracle by the people coming to see it, and a great
crowd came to look at it every day, so that the deed of power
made the remote island known to all; the holy man of God
thereupon took an ax and cut the tree down, lest he suc-
cumb to the disgrace of vainglory.

Another time, when the holy man saw another tree full 3
of blossoms that had been blown down by the violence of
the wind, he was moved by pity and prayed: "I implore you,
Lord, let not the fruit of this tree, which produced flowers

produxit. Sed potius a te incrementum reparationis indul-
4 tum, fructuum adipisci mereatur effectum." Et haec dicens,
accepta secure, amputata arboris columna, super radices
quae adhuc haerebant, columnam ipsam in modum sudis fecit acutam, eamque terrae defixit. Mox ligatis sine radice radicibus, ad pristinum restituta statum, flores qui aruerant
viruerunt; ipso quoque anno haec arbor fructus cultori suo
restituit.

5 Credo ego de misericordia Dei, quod miraculum praesens exegit loqui, quia obtinere potuit hic oratione sua vitam mortuis a Domino impertiri, qui obtinuit arbores aridas in rediviva viriditate frondescere.

4. Idem cum plerumque transitum suum fratribus praediceret, quadam die tactus a febre, dicit suis: "Ite ad Felicem
Episcopum, et nuntiate ei discessum meum, dicentes: 'Frater tuus Friardus dixit: "Ecce, consummato cursu vitae
huius, de hoc mundo absolvor. Et ut sis certior de hoc verbo,
die dominica transitum accipio, et vado ad requiem quam
mihi promisit rex aeternus Deus. Veni, obsecro, et videam te
2 prius quam obeam."'" Cumque ille occasione nescio qua detinetur, mandatum misit, dicens: "Rogo, si fieri potest, ut
me modicum sustineas, donec, moris actionum dissolutis,
ad te usque perveniam." Revertentibus vero nuntiis et ista
dicentibus, cum iam lectulo decubaret, ait: "Surgamus ergo
et sustineamus fratrem nostrum."

3 O virum sanctitate ineffabilem! Qui quamquam festinaret dissolvi et cum Christo esse, non tamen oblitus caritatem, obtinuit apud Dominum adhuc esse in mundo, ut fratrem cerneret spiritali intuitu. Sed nec illum infimi reor fuisse meriti, cuius adventu Dominus huius sancti dilatare

as an ornament at your command, perish; rather, let it be restored through you so that it deserves to grow and produce
fruit." Saying this, he took an ax, cut off the trunk from 4
those roots which remained on it, sharpened it into a point,
and put it in the earth. Soon, it formed roots although planted without roots, was restored to its former appearance, and its flowers, which had withered, grew fresh again. And that same year the tree gave fruit to its cultivator.

I believe that the Lord's compassion, of which this mira- 5
cle speaks, would have made it possible for this holy man to obtain life for the dead through his prayers to the Lord, since he obtained renewed green foliage for withered trees.

4. After he had often foretold his passing to his brothers, one day when he was afflicted with a fever, he said to his companions: "Go to Bishop Felix and announce my departure to him, saying: 'Your brother Friardus says: "Behold, I have completed the course of my life and will be released from this world. And so that you may be better informed about the message, I shall pass on this Sunday and go to the repose which God, the eternal king, has promised me.
Come, I implore you, and let me see you before I die."'" Be- 2
cause the bishop was detained for some unknown reason, he sent a message saying: "Please wait for me a little, if possible, until I am released from delays involving legal cases and come to you." When the messengers returned saying this, the holy man, already lying in his bed, said: "Let us rise therefore, and wait for our brother."

O man of ineffable holiness! Although he hastened to be 3
released and to join Christ, he did not forget charity and obtained permission from the Lord to remain in the world to see his brother in the spirit. And I regard as equal the merit of the one for whose arrival the Lord postponed the holy

dignatus est dies. De qua tarditate accepto nuntio, protinus quiescente febre sanus surrexit a lectulo.

4 Post multum vero tempus adveniente episcopo, a febre
corripitur, ingressumque ad se salutat et osculatur, dicens:
"Grandes mihi moras de itinere debito facis, O sancte sacerdos!" Quibus vigilantibus nocte, quae erat dominica, mane
5 facto tradidit spiritum. Quo emisso, mox omnis cellula ab
odore suavitatis repleta tota contremuit. Unde indubitatum
est angelicam ibidem adfuisse virtutem, quae sancti meritum signans cellulam divinis faceret aromatibus effragrare.
Cuius gloriosum corpus sacerdos ablutum recondit in tumulo, Christus animam suscepit in caelo, relinquens terrigenis exempla virtutum.

II

De sancto Caluppane reclauso

Prologus

Semper paupertas saeculi regiam reserat caeli, atque utentes se non modo praeparat polo, verum etiam glorificatos miraculis illustres esse declarat in mundo. Quo fit ut

man's death. For when Friardus had received word of the delay from the messenger, his fever at once abated and he arose healthy from his bed.

When, after a long time, the bishop came, the saint was 4
again seized by a fever, and after they had greeted and kissed
each other, he said: "You made me wait a long time with the
journey which I must take, O holy bishop!" After they had
kept vigils for the night, which was one before a Sunday, the
saint gave up his spirit at daybreak. When it had left him, 5
the whole cell trembled and was filled with a sweet fragrance. Hence it cannot be doubted that there was angelic power present, showing the saint's merit by making his cell fragrant with divine scents. After having let it be washed, the bishop buried Friardus's glorious body in a tomb and Christ received his soul in heaven, leaving the earth dwellers the example of his virtues.

II

About the holy recluse Caluppa

Prologue

Poverty in this world always opens up the kingdom of heaven, and not only prepares those who live in it for heaven but also declares them to be distinguished in the temporal world because they have been glorified by miracles. For the

dum illa ergastularis contritionis revinctio paradisi ianuam patefacit, anima angelicis choris inserta in requie sempi-
2 terna persultet. Sicut nunc de beato Caluppane reclauso, quod verum cognovimus prorsus silere nequimus.

1. Hic autem ab ineunte aetate semper religionis ecclesiasticae bonum quaesivit et reperit, et apud monasterium Meletense termini Arverni conversus, in magna humilitate
2 se fratribus praebuit. Erat enim summae abstinentiae, ita ut ab inedia nimium attritus, quotidianam cum reliquis fratribus operam explere nequiret. Unde, ut mos est monachorum, magnum ei improperium inferebant, dicente sibi praesertim praeposito: "Qui non deliberat laborare, indigne postulat manducare."

3 Dum autem hic assidue ureretur his exprobriationum verbis, vallem haud procul a monasterio conspicatur, de cuius medio lapis natura praebente consurgens, provehitur in excelsum quasi in quingentis aut eo amplius pedibus, nullam penitus habens cum reliquis montibus circumpositis
4 coniunctionem. Cuius vallis medium fluvius alluit, qui hunc montem placide contingens dilabitur. In huius ergo lapidis scissuram, quod priscis temporibus quondam propter transitum hostium receptaculum fuit, eremita sanctus ingreditur. Et exciso lapide, habitacula statuit in quae nunc per scalam valde difficilem scanditur. Locus etenim ille tam difficilis est ad incedendum, ut etiam feris bestiis illuc accedere sit laboris.

5 In hoc loco oratoriolum parvulum quodam modo fecit, cui oranti, ut ipse nobis cum lacrimis referre erat solitus, serpentes super caput eius saepius decidebant, et invol-

chains worn in the prison of contrition opened the gate to
Paradise, and when the soul is placed among the angelic
choirs, it dances with them in eternal peace. Thus now we 2
are unwilling to be silent any longer about what we know to
be true of the blessed hermit Caluppa.

1. From his earliest years he always sought and found the
excellence of the ecclesiastical religious life and, after entering the monastery of Méallat in the territory of Clermont,
conducted himself with great humility toward his brothers.
He was so abstemious in eating, however, that he grew weak 2
for lack of nourishment and was unable to carry out his daily
work with the other brethren. As monks will do, they harassed him considerably about this, especially the prior, who
said to him: "Whoever does not choose to work does not
deserve to ask for food."

While he was burning continuously under these reproaches, 3
he noticed a valley not far from the monastery, in the middle
of which a natural rock cliff rose fifty or more feet high, with
no connection at all to the other mountains around it. In 4
the middle of this valley a river flowed, gently bathing the
foot of this mountain. There was a cave in this rock where
people had hidden in former times to escape enemies, and
the holy hermit went into it. And excavating more of the
stone, he made a dwelling which, even today, is very difficult
to reach even with a ladder. The place is so difficult to access
that even wild animals have trouble doing so.

Here he somehow made a small chapel in which, as 5
he used to tell us tearfully, snakes often fell upon his head
while he prayed and caused him great fear by winding themselves around his neck. Because the devil has the appearance

ventes se circa collum eius, non minimum ei inferebant
horrorem. Sed quia diabolus ad speciem callidi serpentis habetur, non ambigitur eius hanc fuisse immissionis insidiam.
6 Nam cum ille ad haec perstaret immobilis, nec moveretur
minorum anguium ictibus, quadam die duo dracones immensae magnitudinis ad eum ingressi, astiterunt procul.
Quorum unus—ut arbitror, ipse Dux temptationis—vali-
dior altero erat, qui erecto pectore os suum contra os beati
quasi aliquid mussitaturus erexit.

7 At ille, timore perterritus, tamquam aeneus valde diriguit, nullumque penitus membrum movere potens, neque
manum elevare ut signum beatae crucis opponeret. Cumque
ambo diutissime in silentio constitissent, venit in mentem
sancto per spiritum, ut orationem dominicam, et labia mo-
8 vere non poterat, vel corde clamaret. Quam dum tacitus loquitur, coeperunt paulatim membra eius, quae Inimici fuerant arte revincta, dissolvi. Et sentiens se manum dexteram
habere iam liberam, ori signum beatae crucis imponit.

9 Rursusque conversus ad hydrum, pingit iterum crucem
Christi adversus eum, dicens: "Tune es ille, qui protoplas-
tum de paradisi habitaculo proiecisti? Qui germani dexteram parricidio cruentasti? Qui Pharaonem ut populum Dei
persequeretur armasti? Qui ad extremum ipsum Hebraeum
populum ut, invidia succendente, persequeretur Domi-
10 num, excitasti? Discede a servis Dei, a quibus saepius superatus discessisti confusus! Tu es enim in Cain proiectus, in
Esau supplantatus, in Goliath prostratus, in Iuda traditore
suspensus! Et in ipsa illa dominicae virtutis cruce cum
potestatibus et dominationibus tuis triumphatus atque
11 contritus es! Abde nunc, Dei Inimice, caput et humiliare
sub signaculo crucis divinae, quia non est tibi portio cum

of the wily snake, there is no doubt that this snare was his
doing. But since the saint remained in place, unmoved by 6
the small snakes' attacks, two enormous serpents came to him one day and stood a little distance away from him. One of these—as I believe, the chief Tempter himself—was larger than the other one and stood upright, face to face with the saint, as though he had something to say to him.

And Caluppa, terrified, froze as though he had turned to 7
bronze; he was unable to move his limbs and even to lift his hand to make the sign of the blessed cross against him. While they both stood for a long time in silence, it occurred to him at the inspiration of the Holy Spirit to say the Lord's
prayer in his heart, since he could not move his lips. As he 8
thus spoke silently, his limbs, which had been bound by the Enemy's art, slowly began to loosen. And when he felt that his right hand was free, he made the sign of the cross before his face.

Turning then to the great serpent, he made the sign of the 9
cross against it, and said: "Are you not the one who threw the first human beings out of their home in Paradise? Who stained the right hand of the brother with murder? Who armed the Pharaoh to pursue the people of God? Who, in the end, incited the Hebrew people to persecute the Lord
out of envy? Depart from the servants of God, who have 10
often defeated you, and from whom you have departed in confusion! For you were thrown out in Cain, supplanted in Esau, prostrated in Goliath, and hanged in the traitor Judas! And in the cross of the Lord's power itself you and your powers and dominations were conquered and destroyed!
Leave then, Enemy of God, and bow your head before the 11
sign of the divine cross, for you share nothing with the

servis Dei, quorum est haereditas regnum Christi!" Haec et huiuscemodi sancto dicente, crucemque per singula faciente, draco huius vexilli virtute confusus, vicissim se humilians terrae subditur.

12 Sed dum haec agerentur, ille alius circa pedes et tibias sancti in insidiis volvebatur. Cumque hunc ad pedes suos confusum sanctus eremita videret, orationem faciens eum abire iussit, dicens: "Vade retro, Satanas! [Mark 8:33] Nihil
13 mihi in nomine Christi mei poteris ultra nocere!" At ille usque ad limen cellulae egressus, sonum validum per inferiorem partem emisit, et tanto cellulam foetore replevit, ut nihil aliud quam diabolus crederetur. Nec ultra coram sancto aut serpens aut draco comparuit.

2. Erat enim assiduus in opere Dei, nec vacabat ad aliud, nisi aut legeret, aut oraret; etiam cum parumper cibi caperet, semper orabat. Sumebat interdum piscem de flumine, raro quidem, sed cum voluisset, opitulante Domino, confestim aderat. Cibum panis non aliunde sumebat, nisi qui de
2 monasterio mittebatur. Si quis devotorum panes detulisset aut vinum, id in cibos deputabatur egentium, illorum dumtaxat qui ab eo aut signum salutare suscipere, aut infirmitatum remedia sumere flagitabant. Scilicet ut quos per orationem saluti dabat, etiam cibi refectione foveret, illud Domini recolens, quod in evangelio de turbis quas a diversorum morborum contagio sanaverat dixit: "Dimittere eos ieiunos nolo, ne deficiant in via" [Matthew 15:32].

servants of God who inherit the kingdom of Christ!" As the holy man said these and similar things, making the sign of the cross with each utterance, the great serpent was confounded by the power of the sign of the cross and humbled himself by burrowing into the earth.

While this was happening, however, the other enormous 12
serpent was treacherously winding itself around the saint's feet and legs. And when the holy hermit saw it thus struck down at his feet, he prayed and ordered him to depart, saying: "Get behind me, Satan! In the name of Christ, you cannot hurt me anymore!" And the serpent went to the thresh- 13
old of the cell and emitted a loud sound from his lower parts, filling the cell with such a stench that he could not conceivably be anyone except the devil. After this, neither snakes nor great serpents appeared to the holy man.

2. For he was assiduous in serving God and did nothing except either read or pray; even while eating a morsel of food, he prayed constantly. Occasionally, he took a fish from the river and when he wished to do so the Lord provided it at once. He ate no bread except what was sent from the
monastery. When the devout brought him bread or wine, he 2
gave it to the needy to eat, that is, to those who begged to receive from him either the saving sign of the cross or a remedy for their illnesses. Thus he also nourished those to whom he gave back their health through his prayers, remembering what the Lord said in the gospel about the crowds that he had healed of various illnesses: "I am unwilling to send them away hungry, lest they faint on the way."

3 Sed nec illud beneficium occuli arbitror, quod ei in loco illo divina pietas est largita. Nam a profundo vallis illius, quasi per stadia decem aqua deferretur, oravit ad Dominum, ut ei in ipso cellulae suae habitaculo fontis venam ostenderet. Sed non defuit virtus illa caelestis, quae quondam sitientibus populis aquas produxit a silice. Statimque igitur ad huius orationem gutta laticis a caute prorumpens, coepit
4 solum stillis frequentibus irrigare. At ille, munus caeleste congaudens, concavum in lapide parvulum in modum cisternae faciens, tenentem quasi congia duo, lymphas divinitus sibi indultas suscipiebat, de quibus tantum ei ministrabatur per dies singulos, quantum pueroque sufficeret qui ei minister fuerat datus.

3. Accessimus autem et nos ad locum cum beato Avito episcopo, et omnia quae narravimus, quaedam ab ipso relata cognovimus, quaedam oculis propriis inspeximus. A memorato autem pontifice diaconatus ac presbyterii sortitus est gradum; multa populo diversis vexatis morbis remedia con-
2 tulit. Nulli tamen cellulam egressus se praebuit contemplandum, nisi tantum per fenestellam extendens manum salutare signaculum imponebat. Et si a quoquam visitatus fuisset, ad hanc accedens speculam orationem colloquiumque praebabat. Denique in hac religione cursum vitae consummans, aevi anno quinquagesimo, ut opinor, migravit ad Dominum.

I also do not want to conceal what the divine piety 3
granted to him here. Since water was carried to him from the bottom of the valley, a distance of about one and a quarter mile, he prayed to the Lord to make a spring appear in the cell in which he lived. And the heavenly power that once brought forth water from a rock for the thirsting people was at hand. For immediately after his prayer drops of water burst forth from the stone and dripping frequently began to
moisten the ground. And he, rejoicing at this divine gift, 4
made a small hole in the stone in the form of a cistern that could hold about one and a half gallons, collecting the water divinely granted him; of this as much was given to him each day as was sufficient for him and for the boy who had been given to him as a servant.

3. We too went to see him there with the blessed bishop Avitus, and what we have narrated, part of it we learned from his own mouth and part we saw with our own eyes. The holy man was ordained as a deacon and thereafter as a priest by bishop Avitus; he obtained many cures for people
afflicted with various illnesses. Never did he show himself 2
outside of his cell, however, only extending his hand through a window to make the saving sign of the cross. And if he was visited by anyone, he went up to this window to pray and speak. Having completed the course of his life in this devout manner, he passed on to the Lord, I believe, in his fiftieth year.

12

De sancto Aemiliano eremita et Brachione abbate

Prologus

Quantum disciplina caelestis se custodientibus praebeat, quantumque non custodita negligentibus irrogare debeat, per os psalmographi Spiritus sanctus pandit: "Apprehendite," inquit, "disciplinam ne quando irascatur Dominus et pereatis a via iusta" [Psalms 2:11–12]. De bonis autem Salomon ait: "Disciplina pacis erit super eum" [Isaiah 53:5].
2 Disciplina ergo haec timorem Domini facit, timor autem Domini initium sapientiae praebet, sapientia vero diligere Deum docet. Dilectio autem Dei hominem a terrenis sublevat, ad caelos evocat, paradiso locat, in quo felicium animae ex illius Vitis vitalis sumpto vini novi liquore epulantur in regno Dei.

3 Desiderare ergo oportebat homines huius Vitis haurire mysterium, ut accedere valerent ad illum tam iucundae habitationis amoenissimum locum. Quod si istae quas nunc cernimus vites, quae per traduces extensae, emissis palmitibus pampino intextae, dependentibus uvis, amoena nos contemplatione laetificant, dum non solum proferant copiam fructuum, verum etiam opportuno nos umbraculo

12

About the holy hermit Aemilianus and the holy abbot Brachio

Prologue

How much the heavenly discipline grants to those who observe it, and how much it should be imposed upon those who neglect to observe it, is made known by the Holy Spirit through the mouth of the author of the psalms: "Embrace discipline, lest the Lord become angry at some time, and you perish from the way of righteousness." About the righteous, however, Solomon said: "The discipline of peace shall
be upon him." For discipline creates fear of the Lord, the 2
fear of the Lord brings about the beginning of wisdom, and wisdom teaches how to love God. The love of God, however, lifts man from earthly affairs, calls him up to heaven, and places him in Paradise where the souls of the blessed, drinking new wine from the Vine of Life, feast in the kingdom of God.

Men should long to drink the mystery of this Vine so that 3
they may be able to enter the most pleasant place in that beautiful dwelling. The vines which we now see, extended over trellises and woven through with new shoots and tendrils and with hanging grapes, delight us with their pleasing appearance while they not only bring forth much fruit but

protegunt igniti solis ab aestu, quas scimus post assumptum fructum temporis legitimi deciduis foliis quasi aridas reddi.
4 Quanto magis illa desiderare debemus, quae nullo fine deficiunt, neque nullo temptationis aestu marcescunt ubi, spe praeterita, res ipsa quae sperabatur et tenetur et fruitur.

5 Haec multi desiderantes non modo facultates proprias reliquerunt, verum etiam deserta quaeque et inculta aggressi sunt, ut sitim huius desiderii solitariae ac solatio remotioris orationis lacrimarumque fluento restinguerent, sicut nunc beatus Aemilianus, novus nostris temporibus eremita, fecisse probatur.

1. Hic igitur, relictis parentibus ac facultate propria,
eremi deserta petivit et se intra secreta silvarum Ponti-
ciacensium Arverni territorii abdidit. In qua decisa silva
modicum deplanans campum, rastro ipsam effodiens humum, vitae eliciebat alimentum. Habebat et hortum parvulum, quem aqua superveniente rigabat, de quo olus ad refec-
2 tionem nulla impinguatum adipe praesumebat. Solatium
absque Dei adiutorio nullum habens, cohabitatores enim
bestiae avesque illi erant, quae ad eum quotidie tamquam ad
Dei famulum confluebant. Vacabat autem ieiuniis et orationi, nec eum ab hac causa ulla mundanae sollicitudinis oc-
casio impedire poterat, quia praeter Deum aliud nihil habebat.

2. Erat autem tunc temporis apud Arvernam urbem Sigivaldus, magna potentia praeditus, in cuius servitio erat adolescens quidam, nomine Brachio, quod in eorum lingua interpretatur "Ursi catulus." Hunc antedictus vir ad capessendam porcorum silvestrium venationem delegerat,

also protect us with their convenient shade from the heat of
the fiery sun; we know, however, that after their fruit has
been gathered in its season they will lose their leaves and, as
it were, dry up. How much more, therefore, should we de- 4
sire those whose freshness never ends, which do not wither
in the oppressive heat of any tribulation, in the place where,
hope now being a thing of the past, the very thing that was
hoped for is possessed and enjoyed.

Many desiring this not only gave up their properties but 5
even went into deserted and uncultivated places to slake
their thirst for this longed-for solitude and for the solace of
prayer remote from the world with the flow of tears, as now
the blessed Aemilianus, a new hermit in our times, has certainly done.

1. He, then, left his parents and properties, sought the
solitude of the wilderness and hid himself in the depths of
the forests of Pionsat in the territory of Clermont. When he
had felled trees there and made a level field, he turned the
earth with a hoe and drew his life's sustenance from it. He
had a small garden too, moistened by rainwater, from which
he took vegetables, eating them without fat. He had no 2
company except for God's help, for his fellow inhabitants
were the animals and birds that came to him every day, as
though to the servant of God. He devoted himself to fasts
and prayer, and no worldly care could distract him from this
because, except for God, he possessed nothing.

2. At that time Sigivald had great power and resided in the city of Clermont. He had in his service a young man named Brachio, which means "bear cub" in their language. Sigivald had delegated the hunting of boars in the forest to

ibatque cum ingenti molossorum turba, circuiens silvas, et si quid cepisset domino deferebat.

2 Quadam vero die, dum suem immensi corporis cum hac latrantium turba prosequeretur, sus intra saepta quae circa cellulam erant sancti ingreditur. Prosequens vero canum turba cum latratu, usque ad aditum accessit vestibuli, moxque in suis haesit vestigiis nec ingredi est permissa post
3 suem. Quod cernens Brachio, et caelitus haec evenisse admirans, ad cellulam sancti se confert, viditque suem ante ostium stantem nihil penitus formidantem. Consalutatus autem ac osculatus a sene, invitatur ad residendum.

4 Quibus consedentibus, ait senex: "Video te, fili dilectissime, in grandi elegantia compositum, et sequi ea quae magis detrimentum animae praeparant quam salutem. Relinque, quaeso, terrenum dominum et sequere Deum verum, caeli et terraeque factorem, cuius nutu omnia gubernantur, cuius imperio cuncta subduntur, cuius maiestate ipsa quam
5 cernis bestia astat intrepida. Non te tumidum faciat aut extollat potentia domini tui, quae nihil est. Sic enim ait Paulus apostolus: 'Qui gloriatur, in Domino glorietur' [1 Corinthians 1:31]. Et alibi: 'Si hominibus placerem, Christi servus non essem' [Galatians 1:10]. Subde te eius servitio qui ait: 'Venite ad me omnes qui laboratis et onerati estis, et ego re-
6 ficiam vos' [Matthew 11:28]. Ipse enim est Dominus, cuius onus leve est, cuius iugum suave est, cuius cultus et tribuit praesentia et vitam largitur aeternam. Sic enim ait: 'Si quis renuntiaverit omnibusque quae possidet, centuplum accipiet, et insuper vitam aeternam possidebit'" [Matthew 19:29].

him, and he went around the forest with a great pack of
dogs, bringing to his master whatever he caught.

One day when he was pursuing an enormous boar with 2
his pack of baying hounds, it entered the fence around the
saint's cell. The pursuing pack of hounds in full cry came up
to the gate and then suddenly stopped in their tracks, forbidden to follow the boar. When Brachio saw this and re- 3
vered it as an act of heaven, he went to the holy man's cell
and saw the boar standing fearless before the door. When he
had been greeted and kissed by the old man, he was invited
to sit down.

When they were seated, the old man said: "I see you at- 4
tired with the utmost elegance, most beloved son, and pursuing what is more to the detriment than to the health of
your soul. Leave your earthly master behind, I beg you, and
follow the true God, the maker of heaven and earth, according to whose will all is governed, whose command subdues
everything, and through whose majesty even the animal you
see stands unafraid. Don't let your master's power make you 5
proud or high and mighty, for it is nothing. For thus says the
apostle Paul: 'Let him who glories, glory in God.' And elsewhere: 'If I were pleasing men, I would not be the servant of
Christ.' Submit to the service of the one who said: 'Come to
me all who labor and are heavy laden, and I will give you
rest.' For he is the Lord whose burden is light, whose yoke is 6
gentle, and whose service improves the present life as well
as granting eternal life. For he said: 'If anyone renounces all
he possesses, he will receive a hundredfold, and will possess
eternal life as well.'"

7 Haec et his similia sene viriliter disserente, sus illaesus silvas petiit. Puerque discessit ab eo non sine grandi admiratione, quod aprum quem inchoaverat sequi ferum, in conspectu senis mansuetum astare videbat ut agnum. Plurima
igitur animo tractans, ac multa secum revolvens quid ageret
quidve faceret, utrum saeculum relinqueret an saeculo de-
8 serviret. Tandem compunctus a divina pietate et, credo,
sancti Aemiliani oratione, aditum quarere coepit occulte
qualiter clericus esse posset, quia publice propter terrenum
dominum non audebat. Tamen, cum esset adhuc laicus, in
nocte bis aut ter de stratu suo consurgens, terrae prostratus
orationem fundebat ad Dominum.

9 Nesciebat tamen quid caneret, quia litteras ignorabat. Videns autem saepius in oratorio litteras super iconicas apostolorum reliquorumque sanctorum esse conscriptas, exemplavit eas in codice. Cumque ad occursum domini sui clerici vel abbates assidue convenirent, hic ex iunioribus quem primum potuisset accersire, secretius interrogabat nomina literarum, et ob hoc eas intelligere coepit. Antea autem, inspirante Domino, et legit et scripsit, quam litterarum seriem cognovisset.

10 Exinde, mortuo Sigivaldo, ad antedictum senem properat, et cum eodem duos vel tres annos faciens, psalterium memoriae commendavit. Quem eius germanus plerumque interficere voluit, quod nollet matrimonio copulari. Dehinc monachi ad eos additi sunt.

3. Impletis autem beatus Aemilianus diebus vitae suae et circiter nonagenaria aetate, egrediens a corpore Brachionem reliquit haeredem. Hic, stabilito monasterio, obtinuit a

While the old man was vigorously saying these and similar things, the boar returned unhurt to the forest. And as the young man left him, he marveled at how the wild boar that he had begun to chase seemed to stand like a gentle lamb in the presence of the old man. Therefore he pondered to himself, considering what he should do, whether he should leave 7
the world or continue to serve it. At last pierced in the heart by the divine piety and, I believe, by the blessed Aemilianus's prayer, he secretly began to seek a way to become a cleric because he did not dare to do so publicly out of fear of his earthly master. Nevertheless, even though at the time still a layman, he rose two or three times at night from his bed, prostrated himself on the earth and poured forth a prayer to the Lord. 8

He did not know what to sing, however, because he had not learned to read. Having often seen letters written above the pictures of the apostles and other saints in chapels, he copied them in a book. And when clerics or abbots came for a meeting with his master, he would secretly ask the first junior cleric whom he could approach the names of the letters; from this he learned to understand them. Through the Lord's inspiration however, he read and wrote before he knew the order of the letters. 9

After this, when Sigivald had died, he hurried to the old man, spent two or three years with him, and learned the psalter by heart. His brother tried several times to kill him because he did not want to marry. Later, monks joined them. 10

3. When the blessed Aemilianus had completed the days of his life, at the age of about ninety, and had gone out of his body, he left Brachio as his heir. He established a monastery,

Ranichilde, Sigivaldi memorati filia, multa terrarum spatia, quae ad hoc monasterium dereliquit: erat enim saltus ex domo Vindiacensi. Hic vero de hoc egressus monasterio, Turonis venit, ibique aedificatis oratoriis, duo monasteria congregavit.

2 Quodam autem tempore advenientes homines peregrini reliquias sanctorum detulerunt secum, quas super altare basilicae sancti Martini Turonis locaverunt, quasi in crastinum
3 profecturi. Adfuit ei Brachio abba, qui vigilans in basilica, circa medium fere noctis vidit quasi globum ignis immensi de sanctis pignoribus emicare et usque at templi cameram cum lumine magno conscendere. Quod non est dubium aliquid fuisse divinum. Nulli tamen de astantibus aliis, nisi illi tantum, fuit ostensum.

4 Post haec autem regressus est Arvernum ad prius monasterium, in quo per quinque annos inhabitans, venit Turonis, stabilitisque abbatibus in monasteriis supradictis, Arvernum regressus est. Cumque ad priorem cellulam resideret, in monasterium Manatense, qui per incuriam abbatis intepuerat, ordinatur, ut scilicet eius studio congregatio ipsa canonice regeretur.

5 Erat enim castissimae conversationis, sed et alios strenue distringebat castam agere vitam. Qui erat suavis colloquio, et blandus affectu. In transgressoribus vero regulae ita severus habebatur, ut aliquoties putaretur esse crudelis. In ieiuniis vigiliisque et caritate perfectum reddiderat virum.

having obtained from Ranichild, Sigivald's daughter, large tracts of land which he left to the monastery: they were the pastures belonging to the villa of Vensat. After having departed from the monastery, he came to Tours, built several chapels there, and founded two monasteries.

Once strangers came, bearing relics of the saints with 2
them which they placed on the altar of the basilica of the holy Martin of Tours, intending to set off again the next
morning. Abbot Brachio was present there, keeping vigils in 3
the basilica when, around midnight, he saw what seemed to be a huge globe of fire shine out from the holy relics and rise glowing intensely to the ceiling of the church. There is no doubt that this was something divine. It was shown to none of the others present however, only to him.

After this he returned to his first monastery in Clermont. 4
Having lived there for five years, he came back to Tours, installed abbots in the monasteries mentioned earlier, and then returned to Clermont. While he was staying in his old cell, he reestablished order in the monastery of Menat, so that through his effort the congregation was governed according to the canons, for it had become lax through the abbot's lack of oversight.

He was extremely chaste in his way of life and strenu- 5
ously disciplined others too to live a chaste life. His conversation was pleasing and his manner affable. To those who broke the rule, in truth, he was so severe that he might sometimes have been regarded as cruel. Through fasts and vigils and charity, however, he became a perfect holy man.

6 Cumque tempus migrationis appropinquaret, vidit in
visu, sicut ipse beato Avito episcopo retulit, ductum se ad
aethera in praesentiam Domini, ibique cherubim ac seraphim extensis alis obumbrare maiestatem Domini, et Isaiam
prophetam, extenso volumine, verba quae vaticinaturus erat
intimare, turbam circumstantem angelorum in laudem Dei
7 sedentis super aethera voce magna clamare. Dumque hoc
attonitus spectaret, expergefactus, somniumque suum attente discutiens ut finem vitae suae, Domino revelante,
cognosceret, dicit abbati quem in priorem statuerat in monasterio: "Locus ille secus fluvium, in quo oratorium facere
computabam, iucundus est valde. Ideo rogo ut quod ego volui tu expleas, atque illuc ossa mea transferre non abnuas."

8 Quo migrante et in oratorio prioris cellulae sepulto, cum
abbas iniunctum cuperet opus explere, nutu Dei et calces
coctos antiquitus, et fundamentum in ea mensura quam ipse
9 ponere cogitabat, nactus est. Perfecto aedificio, detexit abbatis sepulcrum. Quo patefacto, reperit corpusculum illae-
sum, ut putaretur ante diem alterum fuisse defunctum. Et
sic cum gaudio, prosequente caterva monachorum quam
ipse edocuerat, in locum illum post duos annos translatus
est.

When the time of his passing approached, as he himself 6
told the blessed bishop Avitus, he saw himself in a vision being lifted to heaven into the presence of the Lord; he saw
cherubim and seraphim there with outspread wings over-
shadowing the majesty of the Lord and the prophet Isaiah
with an open book roll, speaking the words which he would
prophesy, while the crowd of angels standing around loudly
acclaimed the praise of God, sitting above the heavens. As 7
he watched this in amazement, he woke up, and examining
his dream closely and realizing that the Lord had revealed
the imminence of his death, he said to the abbot whom he
had put in charge of the first monastery: "That place near
the river where I had planned to build a chapel is very pleasant. Therefore I ask you to carry out my wish, and not to refuse to move my bones to that place."

When he had passed away and had been buried in the 8
chapel of his old cell the abbot, wanting to carry out the
work which had been commanded, found through the will
of God in the designated place bricks baked in olden times
and a foundation of the dimensions which the holy man
himself had had in mind. When the building was completed, 9
the abbot uncovered the tomb. When he had opened it, he
found the body intact, so that one might think the holy man
had died the day before. And thus after two years he was joyfully carried into that place, followed by the crowd of the
monks whom he himself had trained.

13

De sancto Lupicino reclauso

Prologus

Athletae Christi atque triumphatores mundi vitae istius fugitivae iacturam facere cupientes, pertendere ad illam vitam voluerunt, quae in exsultatione perpetua manet, quae nullo gemitu obstrepit, nec quoquam fine concluditur, cuius lumen numquam exstinguetur, cuius serenitas nulla obscuritate nubis obtegitur. Ideoque semper praesentium dolorum contumelias pro nihilo habuerunt, scientes se in paucis
2 vexatos, in multis bene disponendos. Et ob hoc quisquis ille est, qui in isto agone contendit, metu non terretur, poena non solvitur, dolore non frangitur, ut tantum illa aeternae iucunditatis amoenitate cum electis Dei perfrui mereatur. Sicut multos fecisse novimus de sanctis viris, quorum nunc vita tractatur aut legitur.

1. Igitur Lupicinus quidam magnae sanctitatis, fortissimusque in operibus Dei, qui primum eleemosynam per domos devotorum deposcens, quae acquirere potuisset sibi
2 similibus erogabat. Ad extremum iam mediam habens aetatem, vicum Berberensem, qui nunc Lipidiaco dicitur, parietes antiquos reperit, ibique reclusus ab omnium se hominibus aspectibus inhibebat. Ac per modicam fenestellam

13

About the holy recluse Lupicinus

Prologue

The athletes of Christ and conquerors of this world wanted to abandon this present temporary life to arrive at that life in which one abides in perpetual exultation, in which there is no sighing, which has no end, whose light will never be extinguished, and whose clear sky will never be obscured by the darkness of a cloud. Therefore they always regard present tribulations as nothing, knowing that while
vexed by few things they will be rewarded in many. There- 2
fore whoever engages in this struggle fears no terror, does not give up because of troubles, and is not broken by pain, if only he may deserve the enjoyment of eternal happiness with the chosen ones of God. We know that this has been achieved by many of the holy men whose life is now written about or read.

1. A certain Lupicinus, of great sanctity and most powerful in the service of God, first begged alms from the houses of the devout and shared what he could get with those like
him. When middle-aged, he found ancient walls in the vil- 2
lage of Bèbre, which is now called Lipidiacum, and he shut himself up in them, withdrawing from the sight of men. And through a window he accepted small quantities of bread and

parumper panis vel aquae accipiens, quod ei aliquoties, cum esset valde exiguum, usque ad diem tertium perdurabat.

3 Aqua enim per canalem parvulum inferebatur, fenestella
vero velo operiebatur; utriusque tamen rei aditus ita obtectus erat, ut nullus beatum eius vultum posset advertere. Et
dum ibidem die noctuque in Dei laude psalmorum modulis
delectatur, tormentum sibi quod corpusculum plus gravaret
adhibuit, non immemor illius Apostoli dicti, quia: "Non
sunt condignae passiones huius temporis ad futuram glo-
4 riam quae revelabitur in nobis" [Romans 8:18]. Lapidem
namque grandem, quem duo homines vix levare poterant,
cervici impositum tota die, dum Deo caneret, per cellulam
deportabat. Nocte autem ad additamentum iniuriae, in
virga quam manu gerebat, duas defixerat sudes, desuper acu-
mina parans, quae ad mentum suum ne somnum caperet
supponebat.

5 Denique ad extremum vitae tempus, corrupto pectore a pondere saxi, sanguinem per os ejicere coepit; quem per parietes praesentes proiciens spuebat. Sed et plerumque fidelibus viris nocte ad cellulam clam appropinquantibus, quasi vox multi psallentii resonabat. Et multos infirmos, et praesertim ab accessionibus frigoriticis vel pusulis malis oppressos, tactu tantum vel signo salutari imposito, sanitati restituebat.

2. Cum autem iam senio inclinatus esset, vocavit ministrum suum, dicens: "Praeterito tempore occulendi, manifestandi tempus advenit. Scito ergo me post triduum ab hoc saeculo liberandum. Voca nunc fideles, quosque fratres et filios, quibus sum vale dicturus, ut veniant ad nos visitandum."

water which, even though the amounts were very small indeed, sometimes lasted him until the third day.

Water came to him through a small channel, and the little 3
window was covered with a curtain; both apertures were covered, so that no one could see his blessed face. And while he took pleasure there day and night in the melodies of psalms praising God, he tortured his body more, remembering the saying of the Apostle that: "The sufferings of the present time are not worthy of comparison with the glory
that will be revealed in us." Thus he put a large stone which 4
two men could scarcely lift on his neck the whole day, carrying it around in his cell while he sang to God. At night, to add to his suffering, he attached two thorns to the top of the stick he carried in his hand and placed it under his chin, so that he would not fall asleep.

At the end of his life he began to spit blood from his 5
mouth onto the walls because his chest had been bruised by the weight of the stone. But devout people who secretly approached his cell at night often heard the sound of what seemed to be many voices singing psalms. And he healed many who were sick, especially those oppressed by recurring fevers and abscesses, merely by touching them or making the saving sign of the cross over them.

2. When he had already become bent over with age, he called his servant and said: "The time of hiding is over, now it is time to show myself. Know therefore that I shall be released from this world in three days. Call the faithful now, all the brothers and sons to whom I will say goodbye, so that they may come and see us."

2 Illucescente autem die tertia, confluentibus fratribus, ostium quod clausum erat aperuit, atque ingredientibus, cunctis quid aderant consalutatis deosculatisque, orationem fudit ad Dominum, dicens: "Gratias tibi ago, Domine Iesu Christe, qui me salvari iussisti ab huius mundi impedimentis, et ita me fovere dignatus es in hoc saeculo, ut nihil suum
3 in me Auctor criminis inveniret." Et conversus ad plebem, ait: "Magnificate, quaeso, dilectissimi, Dominum mecum et 'exaltemus nomen eius in commune' [Psalms 34:3], qui me erectum de stercore, erutum de tenebrarum opere, amicorum suorum fecit esse consortem; qui misit angelum suum ad me accersendum ab hac mundana statione, et pollicitus est me in requiem sempiternam perducere, ut collega amicis eius effectus, mererer regno eius ascribi."

4 O beatum virum qui ita consolari meruit in hoc corpore, ut prius cognosceret quod erat fruiturus in caelo quam migraret a saeculo, meruitque hic obtinere apud divinam potentiam quod David saepius decantabat: "Notum fac mihi, Domine, finem meum, et numerum dierum meorum, ut sciam quid desit mihi" [Psalms 39:4]. Dehinc humo incumbens, spiritum caelo intentum praemisit ad Dominum.
5 Tunc omnes in fletu prostrati, alii plantas osculantur, alii fimbrias vestimenti diripiunt, alii de pariete beatum sanguinem qui ab eius fuerat ore proiectus, inter se certantes excudunt. Miserum se quisque dicebat, si immunis ab eius pignoribus discessisset.

6 Testis est hodieque et ipse paries, qui tot fossulis patet, quot ab ore beati confessoris sputus emeruit. Testis est ipse

CHAPTER 13

At daybreak on the third day, when the brothers had 2
come together, he opened the door which had been closed,
and when all who were there had entered, greeted, and
kissed him, he poured forth a prayer to the Lord, saying: "I
give thanks to you, Lord Jesus Christ, who ordered me to be
saved from the hindrances of this world, and who deigned to
nurture me in this life so that the Author of crime will find
nothing of his in me." And turning to the people he said: 3
"Magnify the Lord with me, I beg you, most beloved, and
'let us exalt his name together,' who has raised me from the
dung, snatched me from the works of darkness, and made
me the companion of his friends; who has sent his angel
to take me from this worldly place and promised to lead
me into eternal repose, so that, having been made the companion of his friends, I may merit to be admitted to his
kingdom."

O blessed man who deserved to be consoled in this body, 4
so that before he passed from this world he knew what he
would enjoy in heaven, and who was found worthy to obtain
from the divine power what David often sang: "Lord, let me
know my end and the number of my days so that I may know
how frail I am." After this he lay down on the ground and
sent his spirit to the Lord. Everyone thereupon prostrated 5
themselves on the ground weeping; some kissed his feet,
others pulled threads from his clothes, still others competed
among themselves and scraped the blessed blood from the
walls that had spittle on them. Anyone who left without
some of his relics counted himself unfortunate.

Today that wall is still a testimony to him, showing many 6
small scratches where it had merited to receive the saliva of
the blessed man's mouth. Another testimony is the channel

canalis de quo vir beatus aquam sumpsit ad usus, de quo fideliter osculantes hauriunt sanitatem. Nam vidi ego multos, qui evulsos a pariete sacrati oris sputos, in diversis infirmitatibus positi meruerunt accipere medicinam.

3. Denique hoc, ut diximus, defuncto, adfuit quaedam matrona, quae ablutum dignis induit vestimentis. Et cum eum ad vicum Transalicensem inferre vellet, restitit ei populus pagi Lipidiacensis, dicens: "Nostrum hunc solum fovit, nobis corporis eius glaeba debetur." Matrona autem respondebat ad haec: "Si aliqua de victus eius exprobratis necessitate, saepius ei ego et triticum misi et hordeum, quod
2 vel ille sumeret, vel aliis ministraret." At illi dicebant: "Nostri generis homo effectus est, nostri fluminis aquas hausit, nostra eum terra caelo transmisit. Aequumque ergo est ut tu, de terra aliena veniens, rapias eum de manu nostra? Noveris enim quia non hoc sustinebit quisquam nostrum, sed hic sepelietur." Matrona respondit: "Si germen stirpis eius inquiritis, ex aliis hic regionibus adventavit; si aqua fluminis ingeritis: parum sitim eius mollierunt, quam potius e caelo manans fons ille restinxit."

3 Cumque haec et huiusmodi inter se verba proferrent, et Lipidiacenses effossa humo et deposito sarcophago eum sepelire niterentur, convocatis matrona solatiis, fugatis pagensibus, rapuit sanctum corpus, ac ferre coepit in feretro ad vicum Transaliacensem, dispositis in itinere psallentium turmis cum crucibus cereisque, atque odore fragrantis thymia-
4 matis. Quod illi cernentes, paenitentia moti, miserunt post matronam, dicentes: "Peccavimus resistendo tibi, profecto

from which the blessed man took water, and from which those who kiss it with faith obtain healing. For I saw many who, having scraped the saliva of his sacred mouth from the wall, deserved to receive healing from it when suffering from various illnesses.

3. When he had died, as we said, a certain lady came who washed his body and dressed it in suitable clothes. She wished to carry him to the village of Trézelle but the people of the region of Lipidiacum resisted her, saying: "Our soil nourished him, therefore the dust of his body is owed to us." The lady, however, responded to this: "If you make your case on his need for victuals, I too often sent him wheat and barley, which he either ate himself or gave to others." And they 2
said: "He is of our kindred, drank water from our river, and our earth sent him to heaven. Is it therefore just that you, coming from a foreign soil, snatch him from our hands? Know that none of our people will tolerate this; he shall be buried here." The lady answered: "If you inquire about the origin of his family: he came here from other regions. And if you emphasize the water of the river: it did less to quench his thirst than did the fountain sprinkling from the sky."

While they were bandying these and similar arguments 3
back and forth, and the inhabitants of Lipidiacum had dug a hole in the earth and placed the sarcophagus in it, attempting to bury it, the lady called together her retinue, put the country people to flight, seized the holy body, and began to let it be carried on a bier to the village of Trézelle; she arranged for throngs singing psalms, holding crosses and candles and wafting fragrant incense to be set along the route.
When the people saw this, they repented and sent a mes- 4
sage to the lady saying: "We have sinned in resisting you, for

enim cognoscimus in hoc esse Domini voluntatem. Nunc autem petimus ut non abiciamur ab huius funeris obsequiis, sed admittamur officiis eius." Illa quoque permittente ut sequerentur, coniunctus est uterque populus.

5 Et sic pariter usque ad Transaliacensem vicum venientes, celebratis missis, beatum corpus cum summo honore gaudioque sepelierunt. In quo vico saepius se beatissimus in virtutibus declaravit. Sed et Lipidiaco, ut supra praefati sumus, plerumque opus eius sanctum ostenditur. Uterque enim locus unius sancti praesidiis communitur.

6 Et fortassis quorundam incredibilium latratus de his conatur obstrepere, noverint a me visum Deodatum presbyterum, summam octogenarii aevi ferentem, qui mihi haec ut scripta sunt contulit, confirmans sacramento nihil se de his admixto mendacio enarrasse.

14

De sancto Martio abbate

Prologus

Magnum nobis divina pietas largitur augmentum cum delictis nostris fieri praecepit de remissione refugium, si ignoscamus negligentibus, si indulgeamus laedentibus, si odientibus nos e contrario commodum benedictionis impertiamur, dicente Domino Iesu Christo: "Diligite inimicos

we truly understand this to be the Lord's will. Now, however, we beg not to be excluded from this funeral ceremony, but admitted to his last rites." When she had allowed them to follow, the two groups of people merged.

5 And so they went together to the village of Trézelle, celebrated mass, and buried the blessed body with the greatest honor and joy. In this village the most blessed man often manifests himself in deeds of power. But in Lipidiacum too, as we said earlier, his holy work is often displayed. Each place is therefore protected by the help of one and the same saint.

6 And if perhaps some yapping skeptics attempt to object to this report, let them know that I met with the priest Deodatus, then aged eighty years, who told me these things as they are written here, confirming by an oath that there were no lies mixed into what he had narrated.

14

About the holy abbot Martius

Prologue

Divine goodness grants us a great benefit when it gives a refuge for the remission of our sins if we overlook others' negligence, if we forgive those who injure us, and if we extend a blessing to those who hate us; for as the Lord Jesus said: "Love your enemies, bless those who hate you,

vestros, benefacite his qui oderunt vos, et orate pro calumniantibus et persequentibus vos, ut sitis filii Patris vestri qui
2 in caelis est" [Matthew 5:44–45]. Ecce quam magnum thesaurum congregat contemptus irae, reconciliatio damnati, remissio iudicati. Filium te Dei Patris facit, cohaeredem Christi ascribit, caelestibus te regnis habitatorem statuit.

3 Unde manifestum est oblitterari delicta eius in caelo qui delinquenti beneficium veniae impertitur in saeculo. Sic enim dominici oris sententia prolata testatur: "Si," inquit, "dimiseritis hominibus peccata eorum, dimittet et Pater vester caelestis peccata vestra" [Matthew 6:14]. Cum vero supplices famulos docet orare, ait: "Dimitte nobis debita nostra, quemadmodum et nos dimittimus debitoribus nostris" [Matthew 6:12].

4 Hic igitur sanctus Martius beatus abbas sanctitate praeclarus, divinis eruditus studiis, huius sententiae bonum retinuit corde, ut libenter dimitteret delinquenti. Et non solum ignovit noxam, verum etiam munere praebuit gratiam, ne in aliquo vilem redderet culpati personam. Sed ante de conversatione eius pauca locuturi sumus, priusquam ad huius gratiae beneficium accedamus.

1. Igitur beatissimus Martius, Arvernae urbis abbas, eiusdem territorii fuisse incola fertur, et pueritia sua, religiosam vitam agens, totum se Dei operibus dedicavit. Erat enim parcus in cibis, largus in eleemosynis, promptus in vigiliis, in orationibus valde devotus, totus viribus luxuriam abstinentiae freno, ac parcitatis agone coercens, ne sibi aliquid subrepere posset.

and pray for those who slander and persecute you, so that
you may be sons of your Father who is in heaven." Behold, 2
then, what a great treasure is gathered by disdaining anger, reconciling oneself with one who has been condemned, and absolving one who has been judged. It makes you a son of God the Father, admits you as coheir with Christ, and establishes you as an inhabitant of the heavenly kingdoms.

It is clear that in heaven the sins of one who grants for- 3
giveness to the delinquent on earth are erased. For so the teaching of the mouth of the Lord testifies: "If you forgive men their sins, your heavenly Father will also forgive your sins." And when he taught his humble servants to pray, he said: "Forgive us our sins as we forgive those who sin against us."

The holy Martius, a blessed abbot of outstanding sanc- 4
tity, learned in divine studies, kept the good of this teaching in his heart so that he might more easily forgive sinners. And not only did he overlook bad deeds but even offered the grace of a gift, so as not to humiliate the person of the accused in some way. But we will first speak a little about his way of life before coming to the benefit of this grace.

1. The most blessed Martius, abbot of the city of Clermont, is said to have dwelled in this territory and to have lived a religious life from his childhood, dedicating himself completely to the service of God. For he was sparing with food, generous in almsgiving, assiduous in keeping vigils, devout in praying, and subdued lust with all his strength by the rein of abstinence and the contest of frugality so that it not steal a march upon him.

2 Non immerito Martius vocitatus, qui Marte triumphali pullulantes actionum mortalium cogitationes gladio Spiritus sancti in ipso emicationis exordio succidebat, non surdus auditor apostolicae exhortationis dicta commemorans: "Accingite vos armatura Dei et gladio Spiritus sancti, ut possitis ignita diaboli tela contemnere" [Ephesians 6:11, 17].

3 Cumque ad illam aetatis legitimae perfectionem venisset, et tanquam sidus egregium in hac urbe fulgeret, adhuc aliquid sibi deesse putans, haud procul ab ea secessit. Acceptoque sarculo, montem lapidem caedere coepit, in quo cellula sculpens, habitacula sibi parvula fecit, scilicet ut artius sobrietatis catena constrictus, facilius Deo omnipotenti precum thura laudationumque holocaustomata super cordis mundi altare proferret, recolens Dominum dixisse per evangelium: "Intra in cubiculum et, clauso ostio, ora Patrem tuum. Et Pater tuus, qui videt in absconso, reddet tibi" [Matthew 6:6].

4 Sciebat enim et angelicae sibi visitationis consolationem
adfore, si se ab humanis aspectibus longius amovisset. In
hac ergo rupe cavati montis, habitationis necessaria praepa-
rabat, formans in antris ex ipso lapide scamnum, et sellulam
sive lectulum, in quo post laborem multum fessi corpusculi
5 requiem indulgeret. Sed erant haec immobilia, quia ex ipso
lapide incisa massae ipsi petrae inhaerebant. Nihil autem
super eam cum quiesceret sternebat, nisi tantum cum vestimento quo indutus erat decumbebat, nec alios habens ta-
petes, plumellas aut stragula, quibus haec operirentur, nisi
cum ipse desuper consedisset. Nihil enim habebat proprium

He was deservedly called Martius for like a victorious 2
Mars he struck down ever-sprouting thoughts of earthly matters right at the onset of the fight with the sword of the Holy Spirit; for he had hearkened unto and remembered the exhortatory words of the Apostle: "Put on the armor of God and the sword of the Holy Spirit, so that you may be able to quench the flaming darts of the devil."

When he had reached legal maturity and shone like a 3
great star in this city, he already sensed a lack within himself and withdrew a little distance from Clermont. With a hoe he cut out cells in the stone of a mountain and made small dwellings for himself so that, restrained by the chains of severe sobriety, he might more easily offer almighty God the incense of his prayers and the offerings of his praise on the altar of a pure heart—remembering what the Lord had said in the gospel: "Go into your room, shut the door, and pray to your Father. And your Father, who sees the hidden place, will reward you."

For he knew that the angels would stand by to comfort 4
him if he removed himself far from human sight. In this rock cave in the mountain he prepared what was necessary for living there, shaping in its caverns from the same stone a chair and a bench or bed on which he could allow his body
to rest when it was exhausted from his great labors. These 5
were unmovable because they were cut out of the same stone as the cave itself and remained attached to it. Nothing covered him when he rested except the clothes he wore, and while he slept he had nothing other than them to cover him, functioning as rug, featherbed, and mattress to lie upon. For he possessed nothing of his own except his service to

nisi Dei cultum, in quo indeficiens permanebat. Victum ei
interdum devotorum largitio ministrabat.

2. Denique et aeternus Dominus, qui iugiter glorificat
sanctos suos, coepit caeleste famuli meritum terrigenis declarare, vel qualis esset cultor suae divinitatis ostendere,
2 dum ei curationum gratiam dignatus est impertiri. Nam
daemones de obsessibus corporibus in nomine Iesu Christi
verbo fugabat, venenum malae pusulae crucis signaculo opprimebat, quartanis tertianisve febribus infuso benedicti
olei liquore pellebat, et multa alia beneficia populis, annuente Domino largitore bonorum omnium, tribuebat.

3 Ad tanti viri famam coeperunt quidam ad eum confluere,
gaudentes eius instrui disciplinis. Quid plura? Colligit viros,
format monachos, efficit ad opus Dei perfectos. Erat enim
magna patientia, tantamque adversus sustinendarum iniuri-
arum tela sumpserat bonitatem, ut putares eum lorica dulcedinis esse vallatum.

4 Erat autem monachis hortus, diversorum olerum copia
ingenti refertus, arborumque fructuum, et amoenus visibus
et fertilitate iucundus. Sub quarum arborum umbraculo
susurrantibus aurae sibilo foliis, beatus senex plerumque se-
5 debat. Quidam autem impudens et sine timore Dei, gulae
circumscriptus desiderio, effracta saepe horti, furtivo est
ingressus accessu, sicut Dominus exprobrat in evangelio,
quia: "Qui non intrat per ianuam, hic fur est et latro" [John
10:1]. Porro autem erat noctis tempus, nec enim poterant

God, in which he ceaselessly persisted. Food was given to him by the largesse of the devout.

2. After some time, the eternal Lord, who continuously glorifies his saints, began to declare the merit of his heavenly servant to those dwelling on earth, and to manifest the quality of the servant of his divinity, by granting him the
grace of healing. For the holy man put demons to flight from 2
the possessed by pronouncing the name of Jesus Christ, he overcame poisonous abscesses with the sign of the cross, he expelled quartan and tertian fevers by anointing with holy oil, and he gave many other benefits to the people with the help of the Lord, the giver of all good things.

The reputation of such a man caused people to begin to 3
come to him and to delight in being taught by him. Need I say more? He gathered men, made them into monks, and made them perfect for God's service. For he had great patience and wielded so great an affability against the darts of the offenses he sustained that one might think him protected by a corselet of kindness.

There was a garden for the monks, filled with a varied 4
abundance of vegetables and fruit trees; it was pleasant to look at and happily fertile. The blessed old man often used to sit in the shade of its trees while their leaves whispered in
the wind. Once, however, an impudent person without fear 5
of God and a slave to the desires of his palate, broke through the hedge and stealthily entered the garden; he did what the Lord condemned in the gospel: "Whoever does not enter by the door is a thief and a robber." Furthermore, it was at

haec nisi in nocte perpetrari, quia "Omnis qui male agit,
odit lucem" [John 3:20].

6 Hic vero, collectis oleribus, cepisque et aliis sive pomis,
oneratus fasce fraudis iniquae, ad aditum quo ingressus fuerat pergit. Sed nequaquam reperit ut egrederetur. Gravatur
onere, conscientia terretur, et inter labores ponderum alta
suspiria ducit; sustentatur interdum super columnas arbo-
7 rum. Circuit iterum iterumque omnem ambitionem horti,
et non modo ostium non reperit, verum etiam nec ipsum,
quem inter nocturnas tenebras patefecit, advertit ingressum. Torquetur enim duplici cruciatus dolore, ne aut tenea-
tur a monachis, aut a iudice capiatur. Inter has cogitationum
faces nox ei elongatur, iubar lucis non desideratae redditur.

8 Abbas vero in psallentio noctem ducit et, ut credo, revelante Deo, quae gerebantur agnoscit. Etenim, albescente
iam polo, vocat praepositum, dicens: "Accurre velocius ad
hortum, bos enim petulcus ingressus est in eum, sed nihil
laesit ex eo. Accede nunc et, impositis necessariis, dimitte
eum. Sic enim legitur: 'Bovi trituranti os non colligabis'" [1
9 Corinthians 9:9; Deuteronomy 25:4]. Praepositus quoque,
non intelligens quae narraret, abiit implere iussionem.
Quem cum vidisset homo appropinquantem, proiectis in
terram quam sumpserat, fugere coepit, ac inter spinas et ru-
bos caput immergit, et in modum porcorum aditum unde
egrederetur, ictu facili conatur aperire.

10 Quem monachus apprehendens, ait: "Ne timeas, fili, quia
senior noster misit me ut educam te ab hoc loco." Tunc
collectis monachus quae ille proiecerat, tam pomis quam

nighttime and these things can only be perpetrated during the night, since "Everyone who does evil hates the light."

When he had gathered vegetables, onions, garlic and ap- 6
ples, he went back to the place where he had entered, laden
with the burden of his wicked stealth. But he could not find
it and so could not leave the garden. Laden by the weight
of the vegetables, terrified by his conscience, and weighed
down by these difficulties, he heaved deep sighs and leaned
now and then against trunks of trees. And he walked again 7
around the whole circumference of the garden, not only not
finding the gate but not even the opening he had made in
the hedge in the darkness of night. And he was tormented
by a double anxiety: that he might be detained by the monks
or be put in prison by the judge. While he was occupied with
these burning thoughts, the night was coming to an end and
the morning star he did not want to see appeared.

The abbot, however, had spent the night singing psalms 8
and, as I believe, knew what had been happening through
divine revelation. When the sky was lightening he called the
prior and said: "Go quickly to the garden, for a wandering
ox has entered it but has not damaged anything. Go to him
now, give him what he needs, and let him go. For we read:
'You shall not muzzle an ox when it is treading grain.'" The 9
prior did not understand what he said, but left to carry out
the order. When the man saw him coming, he threw what he
had taken on the ground and began to flee, sticking his head
between the thorns and bushes, like a swine, trying to force
a way out by pushing hard.

The monk took hold of him and said: "Don't be afraid, 10
my son, for our lord has sent me to lead you out of this
place." Then gathering what the man had thrown on the

oleribus, imposuit humeris eius, et aperto ostio dimisit eum, dicens: "Vade in pace, et ne ultra repetas quae, ignavia comitante, gessisti."

3. Ipse quoque sacerdos, velut iubar veri luminis in orbe resplendens, infirmitatum morbida virtutum efficacia pellebat assidue.

2 Nivardus quidam diuturna febre detentus, dum aquas
aestuans ab ardore haurit assidue, ab hydrope intumuit, ita
ut tam venter quam stomachus in modum vesicae cerneretur
extensus. In desperatione ergo pro tali infirmitate positus,
deferri se ad sanctum beneficio plaustri deposcit. Denique
a lectulo elevatur, imponitur super vehiculum, atque
ad cellulam sancti Martii perducitur, deprecans humiliter ut
3 sibi sacerdos Dei manus imponeret. At ille, prostratus in
orationem coram Domino, conversus est ad infirmum, tactuque
blandissimo eius membra contrectans, eum in contemplatione
astantium reddidit sanum. Nam ita fertur tumor
omnis ante digitos eius aufugisse de corpore obsesso, ut
nullum in eo ulterius aegritudinis huius remaneret indicium.

4 Haec autem a mei genitoris relatione cognovi, eo quod ei
fuerit hic Nivardus in amicitiae coniunctione devinctus. Asserebat
autem idem vidisse se sanctum, his verbis: cum esset
adhuc puer, quasi annorum undecim, ab illo tertianarum accessu
febrium occupatur. Tunc amici, apprehensum puerum,
duxerunt eum ad virum Dei. Erat iam senex et proximus re-
5 solutionis diei, caligabantque oculi eius. Posita vero manu

ground, apples as well as vegetables, he put it on his shoulders, opened the gate, and sent him off, saying: "Go in peace
and do not hereafter repeat what you did in your weakness."

3. The priest himself, shining like a star of true light in the
world, constantly expelled the illnesses of the sick with his
unfailing deeds of power.

One Nivardus, who had long been in the grip of a fever 2
and burning with its fire, drank very frequently and swelled
up as if with dropsy, so that his belly as well as his stomach
visibly swelled like a bladder. Desperate at finding himself
so sick, he asked to be taken on a wagon to the holy man. He
was lifted from his bed, placed on the vehicle, and taken to
the cell of the holy Martius; there he humbly begged the
priest of God to lay his hand on him. And after he had pros- 3
trated himself in prayer in the presence of the Lord, the
holy man turned to the patient, stroked his body with a gentle touch and healed him right before those standing by. It is
said that all swelling fled from the possessed body at the approach of his fingers, so that no trace of this illness thereafter remained upon it.

These things I came to know through a story my father 4
told me, because Nivardus had been his friend. He said that
he himself had also seen the saint, in these words: when he
was still a boy, about ten years old, he was taken possession
of by onsets of tertian fever. Then friends took the boy and
led him to the man of God. He was already an old man, close
to the day of his release from the body, and his eyes had
grown dim. When he had placed his hand on the boy, he 5

super puerum, ait: "Quis est hic, vel cuius est filius?" Responderunt: "Famulus tuus est puer Florentius, Georgii quondam filius senatoris." Et ille: "Benedicat," inquit, "tibi Dominus Deus, fili mi, et sanare dignetur languores tuos." At osculans manus eius, et gratias agens abscessit sanus. Asserebat autem numquam deinceps se in omni vita sua ab hoc contagio fuisse pulsatum.

4. Ipse vero iam aetate nonagenarius, bono desudans certamine, consummato cursu vitae, servans in Deo fidem, ad illam coronam iustitiae quam in illa retributionis die redditurus est ei Dominus, commigravit. Dehinc cum summo honore ablutus, dignisque vestimentis indutus, intra oratorium monasterii est sepultus.

2 Quod autem beatus eius tumulus divinis virtutibus illustretur, ipsa quae astitit caterva poterit contestari, quae cum infirmos mittit ad tumulum, extemplo incolumes re-
3 mittit ad domum. Nam cum de diversis partibus confluentes, deferentesque morborum genera, inibi capiunt medicinam. Frigoriticorum tamen vibrantia tremore membra saepius ad soliditatem integram restaurantur, tribuente hoc Domino nostro Iesu Christo, qui glorificat illustribus miraculis sanctorum nunc tumulos, quondam mortuos reducens e tumulis. Ipsi gloria in saecula saeculorum. Amen.

said: "Who is this boy, and whose son is he?" They replied: "Your servant is the boy Florentius, son of the former senator Georgius." And he said: "May the Lord God bless you, my son, and deign to heal your illness." And kissing his hand, the boy left healthy, giving thanks. And he asserted that he had never from that time in his whole life been struck again by this disease.

4. When the holy man was aged ninety, having sweated in the good fight and reached the end of his life serving God in faith, he went to the crown of righteousness which the Lord will give him on the day of Judgment. When he had been washed with great honor, and clothed in worthy robes, he was buried in the chapel of the monastery.

The crowd that is always there can testify that his blessed 2
tomb is illuminated by divine deeds of power, since when
the sick are sent to his tomb, he at once sends them home
healed. For they come from various regions with their dif- 3
ferent illnesses and receive healing there. The fever-stricken, their bodies shaken by chills, are often restored to perfect health by the aid of our Lord Jesus Christ, who once led the dead forth from their tombs and now glorifies the tombs of the saints with shining miracles. Glory to him, for ever and ever. Amen.

15

De sancto Senoch abbate

Prologus

"Vanitas vanitantium," dicit Ecclesiastes, "omnia vanitas" [Ecclesiastes 1:2]. Verumne est ergo quod omnia quae
2 geruntur in mundo cuncta sint vanitas? Unde agitur, ut sancti Dei, quos nullus libidinum aestus exussit, nullus concupiscentiae exagitavit stimulus, quos nullum luxuriae caenum nec in ipsa, ut ita dicam, cogitatione temptavit, aestu Temptatoris elati, visi sunt sibi esse iustissimi, et ob hoc iactantiae cothurnosae perflati supercilio, saepius corruerunt. Factumque est ita, ut quos non valuit maiorum criminum gladius trucidare, levis vanitatis fumus addictus facile pessumdaret.

3 Sicut et ipse ille de quo nunc nobis sermo futurus est, cum multis virtutibus floruisset, paene in illo arrogantiae barathro obrutus occumberet, si eum non exhortatio fratrum fidelium attenta recuperasset.

1. Igitur beatus Senoch, genere Theifalus, Pictavi pagi, quem Theifaliam vocant, oriundus fuit, et conversus ad Dominum clericusque factus, monasterium sibi instituit. Reperit enim infra territorii Turonici terminum parietes antiquos, quos eruderans a ruinis, habitationes aptavit dignas.

15

About the holy abbot Senoch

Prologue

"Vanity of the vain ones," says the Preacher, "all is vanity." Is it true, then, of everything done in the world that all
of it is emptiness? For it happens that the saints of God, 2
who are not consumed by the heat of desires, nor agitated by any sting of concupiscence, nor tempted by any filthy lust even, so to speak, in their thoughts, can feel raised up through the Tempter's swelling tide to see themselves as very righteous; and puffed up by the arrogance of presumptuous vainglory on account of this, often fall to the ground. Thus it happens that men whom the sword of greater crimes cannot kill are easily brought low by the thin smoke of vanity.

Likewise the one of whom we are about to speak, while 3
blossoming with many virtues, became overwhelmed by vanity and would have fallen into that abyss of arrogance if the careful exhortation of faithful brothers had not brought him back.

1. The blessed Senoch, by birth a Theifal of the region in Poitiers called Theifalia, after he had turned to the Lord and been made a cleric, founded a monastery for himself. For in the territory of Tours he came upon ancient walls which he cleared of rubble and made into worthy dwellings.

2 Reperitque ibi oratorium, in quo ferebatur celebre nostrum orasse Martinum. Quod diligenti cura compositum, erecto altari, loculumque in eo ad recipiendas sanctorum reliquias praeparatum, ad benedicendum invitat episcopum. Adfuit tunc Euphronius beatus episcopus qui, consecrato altari, diaconatus eum honore donavit.

3 Celebratis igitur missis, cum capsulam reliquiarum in loculo cuperent collocare, exstitit capsa prolixior, nec recipi in loculum poterat. Tunc prostratus diaconus cum ipso sacerdote pronus ad orationem, lacrimas precibus mixtas effudit, obtinuitque petita. Mirum dictu, ita enim loculus divinitus amplificatus, capsulaque constricta est, ut in eum spatiosissime non sine admiratione reciperetur.

4 In hoc loco, collectis tribus monachis, Domino assidue
serviebat, et in primis arcto vitae tramite incedebat, ex-
iguosque cibos et tenues potiones sumens. Diebus autem
Quadragesimae sanctae addebatur augmentum abstinentiae
ciborum diminutione. Nam esus illi panis tantum hordea-
ceus erat et aqua, de utrisque elementis libras singulas per
5 dies singulos sumens. Rigorem vero hiemis sine ullo pedum
tegmine contentus, manibusque ac pedibus, sive et collo,
ferrea catena revinctus. Dehinc a fratrum contemplatione
demotus solitarie se reclusit in cellula, orans assidue, atque
in vigiliis et orationibus die noctuque sine ambiguitate perdurans.

6 Conferebat ei devotio fidelium plerumque pecuniam, sed non eam in abditis loculis, sed in pauperum marsupiis condebat, illud Domini eloquii oraculum saepe commemorans: "Nolite thesaurizare vobis thesaurum super terram, quia ubi fuerit thesaurus tuus, illic et cor tuum" [Matthew

He also found a chapel there in which our renowned Martin 2
is said to have prayed. Having restored it with great care and set up an altar with a small cavity prepared for the reception of saints' relics, he invited the bishop to come and bless it. The blessed bishop Eufronius then came, consecrated the altar, and granted him the honor of the diaconate.

When mass had been celebrated and they wished to place 3
the box with relics in the cavity, the box was too large and could not be fitted into it. The deacon then prostrated himself and prayed together with the bishop lying prone, pouring forth prayers mingled with tears, and obtained what he asked for. For, astonishing to say, that little space was divinely made larger and the box made smaller, in such a way that to the amazement of those present it could easily be fitted in.

Here he collected three monks and served the Lord de- 4
votedly; he entered upon the narrow path of life and took very little food and drink. During the holy days of Lent he increased his abstinence by diminishing his intake of food. For then he ate only barley bread and drank only water, one
pound per day of each. He fought the rigor of the winter 5
without any covering for his feet and fettered his hands, feet, and neck with iron chains. Then he removed himself from the sight of the brothers and confined himself alone in his cell, praying assiduously and continuing his vigils and prayers ceaselessly, day and night.

Out of devotion, the faithful often brought him money, 6
and it was not in hidden places but in the pouches of the poor that he placed it, often remembering the oracle of the Lord's saying: "Do not lay up for yourselves treasures on earth, for where your treasure is, there will your heart be

6:19, 21]. Dabat enim hic quae accipiebat pro Dei intuitu in diversis necessitatibus indigentium. Unde factum est ut in vita sua de his amplius quam ducentos a nexo servitutis debitique onere sublevaret.

2. Cum autem nos in Turonicum venissemus, egressus est de cellula, venitque ad inquirendos nos, salutatisque ac deosculatis regressus est iterum. Erat, ut diximus, valde abstinens, sanans infirmantum languores. Sed ut de abstinentia sanctitas, ita de sanctitate vanitas coepit obrepere. Nam egressus de cellula, iactantia cothurnosa ad requirendos visitandosque parentes in pago Pictavensi, cuius supra meminimus, abiit.

2 Regressusque, tumidus arrogantia sibi soli placere nitebatur. Sed obiurgatus a nobis, et accepta ratione quod superbi longe fiant a regno Dei, ita se purgatus iactantia humilem reddidit, ut nulla in eo penitus radix superbiae remansisset, ita ut profiteretur, dicens: "Vera nunc esse cognovi, quod Apostolus sacri oris contestatur eloquio: 'Qui gloriatur, in Domino glorietur'" [1 Corinthians 1:31].

3 Sed cum per eum Dominus super infirmos multas faceret virtutes, et ille ita se duxit includere ut numquam humanis aspectibus appareret, consilium suasimus ut non se perpetuo in hac conclusione constringeret, nisi in illis duntaxat diebus qui inter depositionem sancti Martini ac dominici Natalis solemnitatem habentur, vel in illis similiter quadraginta diebus quos ante Paschalia festa in summa duci
4 abstinentia Patrum sanxit auctoritas. Reliquis vero diebus

also." Therefore what he received for God's sake he dispensed to meet the various needs of the poor. And so it happened that during his life he redeemed more than two hundred people from the yoke of servitude or debt.

2. When we had arrived in Tours he came out of his cell to inquire after us, and after we had greeted and kissed one other he went back in again. He was, as we said, extremely abstemious, and healed the sick. But as his sanctity derived from his abstinence, it was from this very sanctity that vanity began to creep up on him. For he went away from his cell with a presumptuous arrogance to look for and visit his relatives in the region of Poitiers from which, as we said, he originated.

After his return, he was puffed up with pride and sought 2
only to please himself. When he had been reprimanded by us, however, and understood that the proud will be excluded from kingdom of God, he purged himself of arrogance; and he made himself so humble that absolutely no pride remained rooted in him, so much so that he admitted it, saying: "Now I know that it is true what the saying of the Apostle's holy mouth asserted 'Let whoever glories, glory in the Lord.'"

But since the Lord performed many deeds of power 3
upon the sick through him, and he thereupon secluded himself so strictly that he never came into the sight of men, we won him over with the advice not to stay in permanent seclusion; for the authority of the Fathers ordains precisely that only the days between the burial of the holy Martin and the solemnity on the birthday of the Lord, and similarly the forty days that precede the feast of Easter,
should be spent in the strictest abstinence. The other days 4

infirmorum gratia populis se praeberet. Audito enim consilio nostro, libenter quae dicta sunt accepit, implevitque sine ambiguitate.

3. Denique, quia de conversatione eius pauca prolocuti sumus, ad virtutes quas per illum medicabilis divinae potentiae dextera operari dignata est accedamus. Caecus quidam, Popusitus nomine, ad eum venit. Erat enim tunc beatus Senoch iam presbyter ordinatus. Qui dum aliquid alimenti postulat, tactis a sancti sacerdotis manu oculis, ut signum salutare meruit, protinus visum recepit.

2 Alius quoque Pictavensis puer huiuscemodo morbo laborans, audita confessoris huius opera, pro luminis perditi receptione precatur. Nec moratur ille, sed invocato Christi nomine, crucem oculis caeci imponit. Statimque defluente rivo sanguinis lux intravit, ac post viginti annorum curricula orbatae fronti geminorum siderum iubar inclaruit.

3 Duo pueri, membris omnibus debiles, et in modum sphaerae in rotunditate contracti, eius conspectibus sunt delati. Quibus impositis manibus, reintegratis artubus, unius horae momento utrumque reddidit absolutum, geminavitque deinde geminae virtutis beneficium.

4 Puer cum puella coram eo contractis manibus astiterunt. Erat autem tunc medium paschalis festum solemnitatis. Cumque pro suae directionis medela Dei famulo supplicarent, et ille pro ea quae ad ecclesiam convenerat populi

he should show himself to the people with the grace to heal the sick. He heeded our advice, willingly accepted what was said, and carried it out in all sincerity.

3. Since we have spoken a bit about his way of life, we come now to the deeds of power that the healing right hand of the Divine Power deigned to perform through him. A blind man named Popusitus came to him. This was when the blessed Senoch had already been ordained a priest. When the blind man was begging for food, the priest touched the man's eyes with his holy hand, and as he received the sign of the cross, he recovered his sight at once.

Another boy from the region of Poitiers was afflicted 2
with the same ailment, and when he had heard about the works of this confessor, he begged to receive his lost sight. Without hesitation, invoking Christ's name, the holy man made the sign of the cross over his blind eyes. At once a stream of blood flowed out, the light entered, and after twenty years the beacon of twin stars lit up a countenance that had been deprived of light.

Two boys who were debilitated in all their limbs and con- 3
tracted into round balls were carried into his presence. When he had placed his hands upon them their limbs were restored, and in the course of an hour he freed both of them, thereby doubling his good work with twinned deeds of power.

A boy and a girl stood before him with contracted hands. 4
It was at that time the middle of the solemnities for the feast of Easter. When they begged the servant of God to straighten them, he declined to do so on account of the crowd of people who had come to the church. He said he

frequentia haec agenda differet, indignum se clamitans per quem Deus infirmis praebere beneficia dignaretur, supplicantibus cunctis, manus eorum suis suscepit in manibus, quibus attrectatis, directis digitis, sanos abscedere iubet.

5 Sic et Benaia, hoc enim erat nomen mulieris, oculos deferens clausos, tactu salutaris dextrae benedicta, illuminata discessit.

6 Sed nec illud occuli puto, quod saepius eius oratio virus
serpentium exinanire obtinuit. Duo enim tumidi morsu hy-
dri eius pedibus prosternuntur, deprecantes ut virus quod
dens malae bestiae artubus moribundis iniecit, sua virtute
7 discuteret. At ille orationem fudit ad Dominum, dicens:
"Domine Iesu Christe, qui in principio cuncta mundi elementa creasti, et serpentem illum humanis dignitatibus ae-
mulum sub maledicto esse sanxisti, tu depelle ab his famulis
tuis veneni huius malum, ut non anguis de his, sed hi de
angue valeant triumphare." Haec autem cum dixisset, palpa-
vit omnem compagem corporis eorum. Statimque compresso tumore, virus mortiferum nocendi perdidit vires.

8 Dies dominicae resurrectionis advenerat, et homo quidam dum ad ecclesiam pergeret, vidit pecorum multitudinem suam segetem depascentem. Ingemuitque et ait: "Vae
mihi, quia annualis mei laboris opera ita deperit ut nihil
prorsus ex ea remaneat!" Et accepta secure, amputatis ramis,
aditum saepis claudere coepit. Confestimque contracta ma-
9 nus invita retinuit quod voluntarie comprehendit. Dolore
etiam instigante, ad sanctum confessorem maestus accessit,

was unworthy that God should deign to confer benefits
upon the sick through him; but because everyone kept on
imploring him to do it, he took their hands into his, stroked
them, straightened their fingers, and commanded them to
depart in health.

Likewise Benaia (this was the name of a woman whose 5
eyes were shut fast) was blessed by the touch of his saving
right hand and departed after having been granted light.

I must not conceal the fact that his prayers often caused 6
the poison of snakes to lose its strength. Two men swollen
with snakebites prostrated themselves at his feet, begging
that with his power he render harmless the venom that the
tooth of the evil creature had injected into their bodies,
which were likely to die from it. And he poured forth a 7
prayer to the Lord, saying: "Lord Jesus Christ, who in the
beginning created all the elements of the world and ordained that the snake, envious of the human dignity, should
be cursed, expel this evil poison from your servants, so that
the snake not triumph over them, but rather they over the
it." While saying this, he stroked their bodies all over. And
at once the swelling went down, and the venom lost its
deadly power.

Once, when the day of the Lord's resurrection had come 8
and a certain man was on his way to church, he saw a multitude of cattle feeding on his grain. Sighing, he said: "Woe to
me, for the result of my year's work is being so completely
destroyed that nothing at all will remain!" And he took an
ax, cut branches and began to close the opening in the
hedge. At once the hand which had taken up a branch volun-
tarily, involuntarily clenched it. Goaded by the pain, he went 9
in agony to the holy man, dragging behind him the branch

trahens post se ramum quem manu constrinxerat, narravitque omnia sicut gesta erant. Tunc ille oleo benedictione sanctificato manum manu perungens, abstracto ramo, sanitati restituit.

10 Sed et deinceps multos a serpentium morsu et a pusulae malignae veneno, signo crucis locato desuper, reddidit sospitati. Nonnullos autem obsessos daemonis saevi livore, ut manus imposuit, extemplo fugatis daemonibus, mentem energia turbatam ad integritatem intelligentiae reparavit.

11 Omnes enim quoscumque per eum a diversis infirmitatibus dextera divina salvavit, si inopes fuissent, ipse cibum vestitumque dispensatione hilari porrigebat. Tantaque ei cura de egentibus fuit, ut etiam pontes super alveos amnium diligenter instrueret, ne quis, inundantibus aquis, naufragia saeva lugeret.

4. In his ergo virtutibus clarus in populis declaratus, cum
esset annorum circiter quadraginta, modica pulsatus febre,
per triduum lectulo decubavit, nuntiatumque est mihi cum
transitus esset propinquus. At ego velocius illuc properans,
ad lectulum eius accessi, sed nihil ab eo collocutionis elicere
potui; erat enim valde defessus.Dehinc, interposito quasi
2 unius horae spatio, spiritum exhalavit. Congregataque est
ad eius exsequias multitudo illa redemptorum, quos supra
diximus, ab eo vel a iugo servitutis vel a diversis debitis absolutos, quos vel alebat cibo vel vestitu tegebat. Plangebant
enim dicentes: "Cui nos, pater sancte, relinquis?"

3 Post haec sepulturae locatus, saepius se manifestis virtutibus declaravit. Nam trigesimo ab eius obitu die, cum ad

which he had clenched in his hand, and told him everything just as it had happened. Then the holy man anointed the man's hand with oil sanctified by a blessing, extracted the branch, and restored his health.

After this, too, he healed many from snake bites and ab- 10
scesses by making the sign of the cross over them. When he put his hands upon a number of those possessed by the malice of savage demons, they were at once put to flight, and he restored these people's minds which were disturbed by the demons' workings to their full capacities.

And to all whom the divine right hand of God saved from 11
various illnesses through him, he cheerfully gave food and clothes if they were poor. His care for the needy was such that he even diligently built bridges for them over the riverbeds so that, if there were floods, no one would mourn unfortunate cases of drowning.

4. After he had shown himself to be illustrious among the people through these deeds of power, he was struck down by a moderate fever around the age of forty. When he had lain in bed for three days, it was announced to me that his passing was imminent. I quickly went there and came to his bedside, but could elicit no speech from him, for he was extremely weak. About an hour after this, he breathed out his
spirit. At his funeral a multitude gathered of those whom he 2
had redeemed from the yoke of servitude, as we said above, or from various debts, and those whom he had nourished with food and covered with clothes. They wailed loudly, saying: "To whose care do you leave us, holy father?"

After he had been placed in his tomb, he often mani- 3
fested himself through deeds of power. For on the thirtieth day after his death, when mass was being celebrated at his

eius tumulum missa celebraretur, Chaidulfus quidam contractus, dum stipem postulat, ad eius sepulturam accedit. Qui dum pallam superpositam osculis veneratur, dissolutis membrorum ligaturis, directus est. Sed et multa alia ibi gesta comperi, de quibus haec tantum memoriae habenda mandavi.

16

De sancto Venantio abbate

Prologus

Solitarium atque multiplex donum ecclesiis populisque terrigenis caelestis potentia praestat, cum largitur iugiter saeculo non modo peccatorum suffragatores, verum etiam vitae doctores aeternae. Quod unicum cernitur dum a maiestate divina tribuitur multiplex, quia cunctis qui expetere voluerint, affluenter indulgetur, iuxta illud: "Petite et accipietis," et reliqua [John 16:24].

2 Unde vigilanter incessanterque debet investigare mens humana sanctorum vitam, ut hoc provocato studio, accensa exemplo, ad ea semper extendatur quae Deo novit esse acceptabilia, ut ab ipso vel mereatur erui, vel possit audiri.

tomb, a lame beggar named Chaidulf, came to the holy man's tomb. While he was venerating the cloth covering it with kisses, the bonds constraining his limbs were loosened and he was straightened. I have learned about many other things that were done there too, but have entrusted only these to be set down in writing.

16

About the holy abbot Venantius

Prologue

The Heavenly Power provides a unique and manifold gift for earthly churches and peoples when it continuously gives us not only intercessors for our sins but also teachers of eternal life. What appears to be one gift is in fact a manifold one, since it is abundantly given by the Divine Majesty to all who have longed to seek it, according to the saying: "Seek and you shall receive," and so on.

The human mind should therefore attentively and un- 2
ceasingly investigate the life of the saints so that, stimulated by this zeal and set afire with this example, it will always reach out to what it knows to be pleasing to God, and may thereby deserve to be saved by him and to be heard by him.

3 Haec autem ab eius maiestate quarebant sancti percipere,
poscentes iugiter ut ipse insinuaret cordi, ipse perficeret in
opere, ipse loqueretur in ore, quo facilius purgata mens
cogitatione, eloquio, actione, cogitaret sancta, loqueretur
4 iusta, operaretur honesta. Unde factum est ut dum in his
quae Divinitati sunt placita famulabantur, obtinerent sibi
remitti peccati debitum, eruerentur a caeni sordentis contagio, caeleste pro meritis invitarentur ad regnum. Ponebant
etiam et praecessorum exempla ante oculos suos, et omnipotentem Dominum pro eorum affectibus collaudabant,
quorum, ut diximus, exempla sequi meditabantur.

5 Unde et nos in praeconio devoti Deo famuli Venantii Abbatis effari nitentes, Divinitati potius dona sua referimus,
quia dexteram eius manifestum est effecisse quod sanctos
constitit operasse, deprecantes ut aperiat os muti ad publi-
canda opera antistitis sui. Quia sicut esse nos recognoscimus
scientia tenues, ita novimus in conscientia peccatores.

1. Igitur sanctus Venantius Biturigi territorii incola fuit,
parentibus secundum saeculi dignitatem ingenuis atque ca-
tholicis. Qui dum esset iuvenili aetate florens, a parentibus
sponsali vinculo obligatur. Cumque ut aetati huic convenit,
amori se puellari praestaret affabilem, et cum poculis frequentibus etiam calciamenta deferret, contigit ut urbem
Turonicam, Domino inspirante, veniret. Erat tunc temporis
monasterium basilicae Martini propinquum, in quo Silvinus
2 abbas gregem Deo devotum regulari sceptro regebat. Ad

These things the saints sought to obtain from his Majesty, 3
continuously asking him to be in their hearts, act in their
works, and speak through their mouths, so that their minds,
pure in thought, speech, and deed, might more easily think
holy thoughts, speak righteous things, and act justly. Thus 4
since they served God in things that pleased him, they obtained the remission of their sins, their rescue from the polluting filth of lust and, for their merits, admission to the
heavenly kingdom. For they always kept the model of their
predecessors before their eyes and praised the Almighty
Lord out of love for those whose examples, as we said, they
desired to follow.

Therefore we too, seeking to praise the devout servant of 5
God, Abbot Venantius, are giving back to the Deity his own
gifts, because his right hand clearly brought about what he
enabled his saints to do; and we pray that he may open
the mouth of a mute man to publish the works of his prelate. For just as we recognize ourselves to be slight in knowledge, we likewise know in our consciences that we are
sinners.

1. The holy Venantius was an inhabitant of the territory
of Bourges, and as regards secular dignity his parents were of
free birth and catholic. When he was in the flower of youth,
his parents compelled him to take on the bonds of betrothal.
While, as is usual for his age group, he showed himself so-
licitous in his courtship of the girl, frequently bringing her
cups and even shoes, God inspired him to go to the city of
Tours. At that time there was a monastery close by the basilica of Martin where Abbot Silvinus governed the flock
dedicated to God with the scepter of monastic rule. The 2

hoc vir iste devotus accedens, virtutesque cernens beati Martini, ait intra se: "Ut conjicio, melius est servire impollutum Christo, quam per copulam nuptialem contagio involvi mundano. Relinquam sponsam territorii Biturigi, et annectar catholicae per fidem Ecclesiae, ut quae credo corde etiam opere merear effectui condonare."

3 Haec intra se volvens, advenit ad antedictum abbatem, provolutusque ad pedes eius, quid intimo corde gereret cum lacrimis patefecit. At ille gratias agens Deo pro fide pueri, et addita etiam praedicatione sacerdotali, iuvenem totondit et
4 gregi monasteriali ascivit. Ex hoc se in humilitate fratribus exhibens, caritatem cum omnibus diligens, in tanto sanctitatis apice evectus asseritur, ut ab omnibus tanquam parens proximus summo studio coleretur. Unde factum est ut, decendente abbate iam dicti monasterii, ipse in loco abbatis eligentibus fratribus substitueretur.

2. Denique quadam die dominica ad missarum celebranda solemnia invitatur, dixitque fratribus: "Iam enim oculi mei caligine obteguntur, nec possum libellum aspicere. Presbyter igitur haec alteri agenda mandate." Dicente igitur presbytero, ipse proximus astitit, ventumque est ut sanctum munus, iuxta morem catholicum, signo crucis superposito, benediceretur.

2 At ille intuitus, vidit quasi ad fenestram apsidae scalam positam, et quasi descendentem per eam virum senem, clericatus honore venerabilem, atque oblatum altario sacrifi-
3 cium dextera extensa benedicentem. Haec enim agebantur in basilica sancti Martini. Quod nullus videre meruit nisi

devout young man came to this monastery and when he saw the blessed Martin's deeds of power said to himself: "It seems to me that it is better to serve Christ unpolluted than to get involved in the contagion of the world through the bonds of matrimony. I shall give up my betrothed in the territory of Bourges and join the Catholic faith through my faith, so that I may practice what I believe in my heart."

Turning over these thoughts in his mind, he went to Ab- 3
bot Silvinus, threw himself at his feet, and revealed to him with tears what was in his heart of hearts. And Silvinus thanked God for the boy's faith and added to it through his priestly advice, shaved his head, and admitted him to the
monastic flock. After this, Venantius conducted himself 4
humbly toward the brothers, showed affection to all, and achieved at such a pinnacle of sanctity that he was loved by all as though he were their closest kinsman. Hence, when the abbot of the aforesaid monastery died, Venantius was elected by the brothers to take his place.

2. Much later, when he had been asked to celebrate mass on a Sunday, he said to the brothers: "My eyes are already covered with a mist and I cannot see the book. Let the priest therefore order someone else to do it." While the priest was saying this, he stood nearby, and the moment came when the holy sacrifice was to be blessed according to catholic practice with the sign of the cross.

And, looking, he saw a ladder placed as it were up to the 2
window of the apse and an old man, venerable in his clerical dress, seeming to descend it and then bless the sacrifice offered on the altar with his outstretched right hand. This 3
took place in the basilica of the holy Martin. No one else

ipse tantum. Reliqui vero cur non viderint, ignoramus. Ipse tamen deinceps fratribus retulit. Nec enim est dubium haec fideli famulo Dominum demonstrasse, cui etiam dignatus est arcanorum secreta caelestium revelare.

4 Nam idem dum de basilicis sanctorum die dominica expleta oratione reverteretur, super bacillum sustentatus in medio beati confessoris atrio, erectis auribus, oculisque ad caelum diutissime attentis, stetit immobilis. Deinde motus a loco, coepit dare gemitus ac suspiria longa producere.
5 Interrogatusque a suis quid hoc esset, aut, si aliquid divinum fuisset intuitus, enarraret, respondit: "Vae nobis inertibus et pigris! Ecce iam in caelo missarum solemnia expediuntur, et nos segnes nec inchoare coepimus huius mysterii sacramentum. Vere," inquit, "dico vobis, quod ego audivi voces angelorum in caelis, 'Sanctus, sanctus' in laude Domini proclamantes." Et dicto citius in monasterio missarum solemnia iussit expleri.

6 Sed nec illud praeteribo, quod quadam vice dum iuxta consuetudinem, ut supra diximus, de basilicis quas orationis gratia adierat repedaret, et in basilica ad missas dominicae orationis verba decantarentur, cum illi dixerunt: "Libera nos a malo" [Matthew 6:13], audivit e tumulo cuiusdam vocem dicentem similiter: "Libera nos a malo." Quod non sine perfectionis merito censetur ut haec meruisset audire.

7 Sed et ad Passivi presbyteri tumulum veniens, et qualitatem eius meriti et quantitatem refrigerii, ipso docente, cognovit.

was worthy to see it, only he. Why the others did not see it we do not know. Later, however, he told the brothers about it. And it cannot be doubted that the Lord showed this to his faithful servant and deigned to reveal to him heavenly mysteries.

For when the same abbot returned from his prayers in 4
the basilicas of the saints one Sunday, he stood still, leaning on his stick, in the middle of the confessor Martin's forecourt, pricked up his ears and directed his eyes for a long time at the sky. Finally he moved from that place and began
to groan and sigh deeply. When asked by his companions 5
why he did this, and, if he had seen anything divine, to tell them about it, he replied: "Woe to us sluggish, lazy people! Behold, in heaven the solemnity of mass is already being celebrated and we lazy ones have not even begun the rite of this mystery. In truth," he said, "I say to you: I heard the voices of angels in heaven proclaiming 'Holy, holy' in praise of the Lord." And faster than can be said he ordered a solemn mass to be carried out in the monastery.

I shall also not pass over what happened once when he 6
had walked back from the basilicas in which, as we said above, he used to go to pray; while the words of the Lord's prayer were being chanted during mass in the basilica of Martin, and they said: "Deliver us from evil," he heard someone's voice from one of the tombs likewise saying: "Deliver us from evil." It must be through his perfect merit that he deserved to hear this.

But when he came to the tomb of the priest Passivus, too, 7
he learned from him what the quality of his merit was, and the measure of his heavenly peace.

3. Et licet haec magna sint, ad illam tamen sanitatum gratiam, quam per eum Dominus infirmis protulit, libet accedere. Non enim ambigitur quod per eum, sicut supra diximus, operata sit dextera Dei, cui ista quae memoravimus tanta voluit revelare.

2 Puerulus enim quidam, Paulus nomine, crurum poplitumque gravi dolore vexatus, sanctum adiit prostratusque genibus eius, exorare coepit ut ei medicinam oratione sui a
3 Domini misericordia obtineat impertiri. Qui protinus oratione facta, cum oleo benedicto palpata membra infirmi, eum super lectulum suum requiescere fecit. Quo paululum quiescente, post unius horae curriculum surgere iubet. Qui consurgens, sanus matri suae sancti est manibus restitutus.

4 Faretri cuiusdam servus, infensus domino suo, huius sacerdotis oratorium expetivit. Sed ille, elatus superbia, absente beato viro, servum abstrahit, ceciditque. Sed mox a febre correptus, spiritum exhalavit.

5 Quartanarum, tertianarumque, vel reliquarum accessus febrium, oratione facta, saepius mitigavit; venenum malae pusulae, imposito salutari signo, restinxit; obsessos daemonibus, invocato Trinitatis nomine, emundavit.

6 Nam et ab ipsis daemonibus saepius impulsatus est, sed victor in certamine perstitit. Nam surgente eo quadam nocte de stratu suo ad reddendum officium, vidit duos arietes magnos suis foribus assistentes, quasi praestolantes adventum eius. Quo viso, furibundi ad eum cum impetu valido dirigunt. At ille signum crucis opponens, illis evanes-
7 centibus absque metu oratorium est ingressus. Alia nocte,

3. Although these are great things, I now wish to turn to the grace of healing which the Lord granted to the sick through him. For as we often said, it cannot be doubted that the right hand of God, who wished to reveal the many things we have commemorated, worked through him.

For a certain little boy named Paulus who was tormented 2
by severe pain in his shins and knees came to the holy man and, falling at his feet, began to beg him to obtain a cure
for him from the Lord's compassion through his prayer. The 3
holy man began praying at once, then applied blessed oil to the sick boy's limbs, and made him rest upon his own bed. The boy rested a little, and after an hour the saint ordered him to get up. When he had arisen, the saint gave him back healthy into his mother's hands.

The slave of a certain Faretrus was full of anger against 4
his master and sought protection in the oratory of this priest. But since the holy man was not there the master, filled with pride, dragged his slave out and killed him. Soon, however, he was seized by a fever and breathed out his spirit.

Venantius often subdued quartan, tertian, and other at- 5
tacks of fever through his prayer; poisonous abscesses he rendered innocuous by imposing the sign of the cross, and those possessed by demons he purged by invoking the name of the Trinity.

He himself too was often attacked by these demons, 6
but remained victorious in the fight. One night when he got up from his bed to say the office, he saw two large rams standing outside his door awaiting his arrival. When they saw him, they lunged at him furiously. But when he made the sign of the cross over them, they vanished and
he went into the chapel without fear. Another night, 7

regressus ab oratorio, invenit cellulam suam plenam daemoniis, dixitque eis: "Unde venitis?" "A Roma," aiunt, "hesterna die egressi, ad hunc locum accessimus." Quibus ille: "Abscedite," inquit, "detestabiles, et nolite accedere ad locum in quo nomen Domini invocatur!" Haec eo dicente, sicut fumus evanuerunt.

4. His et talibus virtutum magnarum gratia pollens, impleto vitae praesentis curriculo vitam percepturus aeternam, emicuit saeculo, cuius beatum sepulcrum miraculorum illustrium effectu plerumque redditur gloriosum.

2 Mascarpionis, servi ipsius monasterii, mentem iniquus daemon obsederat, qui per trium annorum curricula energumenus factus, ad sepulchrum beati viri debacchans, tandem eius est, ut credimus, oratione eiecto daemone, expurgatus, multos deinceps mente integra vivens annos.

3 Iuliani coniux quartanae febris accensu laborans, ut sepulcrum beati viri attigit, compresso ardore ac tremore corporali, sanata discessit. Simili sorte et Baudimundi uxor ab hac febre laborabat. Sed ubi ad lectulum sancti viri prostrata fudit orationem, mox incolumitati restituta convaluit.

4 Multa quidem et alia de eo audivimus, sed sufficere haec ad credulitatem catholicorum quae scripta sunt arbitramur.

when he had returned from the chapel, he found his cell full of demons, and said to them: "Where do you come from?" "We left Rome yesterday," they said, "and have come to this place." And he said to them: "Go away detestable ones, and don't enter a place where the name of the Lord is invoked!" As he said this, they vanished like smoke.

4. Shining with the grace of these and other such great deeds of power, he completed the course of his present life to receive life eternal, and the blessed tomb of the one who shone forth in the present life is often glorified by illustrious miracles.

A wicked demon had infested Mascarpio, a servant of 2
his monastery and possessed him for three years, raving in front of the blessed man's tomb until finally, as we believe at Venantius's prayer, the demon was expelled and he was cleansed, living thereafter for many years with his mind restored.

As soon as the wife of Julian, who was tormented by an 3
attack of quartan fever, touched the tomb of the blessed man, her physical heat and shaking were subdued, and she departed healed. In a similar manner Baudimund's wife too suffered from this fever. When she prostrated herself by the holy man's bed and poured forth a prayer, she soon recovered and her health was restored.

We have heard many other things about this holy man, 4
but regard that which has been written as sufficient to inspire faith among catholics.

17

De sancto Nicetio Treverorum episcopo

Prologus

Si fides dictis adhibetur, relatoribus sacrorum operum pro fidei merito fideliter arbitror esse credendum. Quia non omnia quae in scripturis leguntur obtutibus propriis cerni potuerunt, sed quaedam ipsius scripturae relatione firmata, quaedam aliorum auctorum testimonio comprobata, quae-
2 dam vero proprii intuitus auctoritate creduntur. Sed sunt, quod peius est, qui perverso sensu ut scripta non credunt, ita testificata reprehendunt, visa vero tamquam conficta fastidiunt. Non habentes illud in sua credulitate, quod Thomas apostolus gestabat in corde, dicens: "Nisi videro, non credam" [John 20:25]. "Beati" quidem "qui non viderunt, et crediderunt" [John 20:29]. Sed iste, ut vidit, statim credidit.

3 Nam, ut diximus, multi videntes non modo non credunt, sed et derident. Unde et ego aliqua de sancti Nicetii Treverici sacerdotis virtutibus, virilitate, magnanimitate, sanctitate scripturus, reprehendi ab aliquibus vereor, dicentibus mihi: "Tu cum sis iunior, quomodo seniorum gesta poteris scire? Qualiter ad te eorum facta venerunt? Nempe non aliud nisi conficta a te haec quae scripta sunt decernuntur."

17

About the holy bishop Nicetius of Trier

Prologue

If we are to believe things that are said, I think that we should faithfully believe those who tell us about sacred deeds done for the sake of faith. For not all the things that one reads in written works can be seen with one's own eyes; some of them are confirmed by the written account itself, others proven by the testimony of other authors, and still
others believed on eyewitness authority. Unfortunately 2
however, there are those who perversely refuse to believe what is written, find fault with others' testimonies, and even detect fraud in what they themselves have witnessed. Their belief does not even comprise what the apostle Thomas had in his heart when he said: "Unless I see, I shall not believe." "Blessed" indeed "are those who did not see and yet believed." But he, when he saw, at once believed.

Thus, as we said, many who see these things not only do 3
not believe them, but also make fun of them. Because of this, now that I am about to write about the powerful deeds, strength, generosity, and holiness of the holy bishop Nicetius of Trier, I fear that I shall be faulted by some saying to me: "Since you are younger, how can you know about the deeds of older men? How did the facts about them reach you? Surely, what you wrote must have been invented by

Qua de causa relatorem huius operis in medio ponere necesse est, ut hi qui veritati derogant confundantur.

4 Noverint igitur a beato Aredio abbate urbis Lemovicinae,
qui ab ipso Nicetio Antistite enutritus et clericatus ordinem
sortitus est, haec quae subiecta sunt me audisse. Quem in
hoc non credo fefellisse, cum per eum Deus eo tempore,
quando mihi ista retulit, et caecorum oculos illuminavit, et
paralyticis gressum praestitit, et energumenos, eiectis dae-
5 monibus, sanae mentis restituit. Nec credendum est eum
mendacii nube obumbrari posse quem Deus saepius ab im-
brium nube obtectum ita protexit, ut imbutis sociis, ipse
nulla stillarum cadentium infusione madesceret. Denique,
si de tali relator dubitatur, de beneficiis Dei diffiditur.

6 Aiebat ergo memoratus sacerdos de antedicto antistite: "Multa quidem, dulcissime frater, de sancto Nicetio bonorum virorum testimonio divulgata cognovi, sed plura meis oculis propriis inspexi, vel etiam ab eo, vix elicita, cognovi.

7 "Et cum mihi quaepiam de his quae per illum Deus operatus est explanaret, non cothurno iactantiae tumescebat, sed compunctus corde cum lacrimis aiebat: 'Ideo tibi haec, fili carissime, pandere videor, ut et tu cum summa conversans innocentia cordis similia mediteris. Non enim ad excelsa virtutum Dei contendere quis poterit, nisi "fuerit innocens manibus et mundo corde," sicut canna Davidici carminis canit'" [Psalms 24:4]. Haec ergo de eo praefatus, relator exorsus est.

you." For this reason it is necessary to take a good look at the narrator of this work, so that those who disparage its truth may be confounded.

Let them know, therefore, that I heard the things to be 4
related below from the blessed Aredius, abbot of the city of Limoges, who was raised by Bishop Nicetius himself and ordained a cleric by him. And I believe that he could not been untruthful about these matters, for at the time that he told them to me, it was through him that God gave light to the eyes of the blind, gave paralytics their ability to walk, and by expelling demons restored the possessed to their right
minds. One cannot believe that he was darkened by the 5
cloud of falsehood since God often protected him against rain clouds, so that while his companions were drenched, he was not moistened by any falling drops. Therefore, if one doubts such a witness, one doubts the beneficent deeds of God.

This abbot said about the aforesaid bishop: "There is 6
much that I have come to know about the holy Nicetius through the testimony of reliable men, dearest brother, but there is more that I saw with my own eyes and learned, though with difficulty, from him.

"And when he told me about something that God had 7
worked through him, he did not swell up with audacious pride but said with compunction in his heart and tears: 'I tell you this, dearest son, so that you too, living in the greatest innocence of heart, may consider doing similar things. For no one can rise to the heights of God's powerful deeds, unless he be "innocent in hands and pure in heart," as the flute of David's song chants.'" When the abbot had said this about him, he began his story.

1. Igitur sanctus Nicetius episcopus ab ipso ortus sui tempore clericus designatus est. Nam cum partu fuisset effusus, omne caput eius, ut est consuetudo nascentium infantum, a capillis nudum cernebatur. In circuitu vero modicorum pilorum ordo apparuit, ut putares ab eisdem coronam clerici fuisse signatam.

2 Exinde a studiosissimis enutritis parentibus, litteris institutus, abbati cuidam in monasterio commendatur. In quo loco ita se devotum Deo exhibuit ut migrante abbate ipse succederet. Iam vero assumpto abbatis officio, tantum se talemque ad instructionem atque districtionem fratrum exhibuit, ut non modo agere, verum etiam nulli liceret aliquid vel loqui perverse, dicens: "Cavenda est scurrilitas, dilectissimi, et omne verbum otiosum, ut sicut corpus omne purum exhibere debemus Deo, ita etiam et os non ad aliud aperire,
3 nisi ad laudem Dei. Quia tria sunt in quibus genus dilabitur humanum: aut enim cogitat, aut loquitur, aut agit. Ergo vos, dilectissimi, oportet vitare scurrilitatem, malitiam, et omne opus pessimum." Multa et alia exhortabatur fratres, ut eos dignos Domino exhiberet ac mundos.

4 Venerabatur autem eum et Rex Theodericus magno honore, eo quod saepius vitia eius nudaret ac crimina, [ut] castigatus, emendatior redderetur. Et ob hanc gratiam, decedente Trevericae urbis sacerdote, eum ad episcopatum iussit accersiri. Cumque dato consensu populi ac decreto regis ad ordinandum, a viris summo cum rege honore praeditis adducebatur.

5 Verumtamen cum propinqui ad urbem, cadente sole, fixis tentoriis mansionem pararent, illis confestim laxatis equitibus, per segetes pauperum dimiserunt. Quod cernens,

1. The holy bishop Nicetius was marked out for the clergy from the time of his birth. For when he was born, his whole head, as is usual with newborns, lacked hair. Around it, however, a ring of tiny hairs could be seen, so that one might think it already marked by the cleric's crown.

He was raised with the greatest care by his parents and 2
taught letters, and then he was commended to an abbot in a monastery. There he showed himself so devout to God that when the abbot passed away, he succeeded him. Already when he had assumed the office of abbot, he conducted himself in such a way as regards the instruction and discipline of the monks that he allowed no one not only to act but even to speak perversely, saying: "Watch out for scurrilous words, beloved, and all idle chatter, for just as we should keep our bodies pure for God so also should we not open our mouths for any reason other than to praise God. For 3
there are three ways in which humankind can fall into sin: in thinking, speaking, and acting. Therefore you, beloved, should avoid mockery, malice, and all evil works." In many other ways too he exhorted the brothers so as to present them to the Lord worthy and pure.

King Theoderic venerated him greatly because Nicetius 4
often pointed out his vices and crimes to him, so that once he had been reprimanded he might improve himself. On account of this grace, when the bishop of Trier died, the king ordered Nicetius to assume the episcopate. When the people's consent and the king's decree to ordain him had been given, he was led there by men high in the king's favor.

When they approached the city, however, and were set- 5
ting up their tents while the sun was setting, they let loose their horses to feed in the grain fields of the poor. Seeing

beatus Nicetius, misericordia motus, ait: "Expellite quantocius equos vestros a segete pauperis, alioquin removebo vos a communione mea!" At illi indignantes dixerunt: "Quaenam est haec causa quam loqueris? Adhuc enim episcopalem apicem non es adeptus, et iam excommunicationem mina-
6 ris?" Et ille: "Vere," inquit, "dico vobis quia destinavit rex ut me avulsum a monasterio huic oneri consecrari iuberet. Fiet quidem voluntas Dei, nam regis voluntas in omnibus malis, me obsistente, non adimplebitur." Tunc, cursu rapido abiens, eiecit equos a segete. Et sic cum admiratione hominum illorum ad urbem deductus est. Non enim honorabat personam potentis, sed Deum tantum in corde et operibus metuebat.

7 Impositus itaque in cathedra, dum lectionum series auscultaret, sensit nescio quid grave super cervicem suam. Cumque bis aut ter manum clam ad temptandum iniecisset, nullius rei causam invenire potuit, quae hoc pondus inferret. Divertensque caput ad dexteram et laevam, odoratus est odorem suavitatis. Intellexit quoque hoc onus esse sacerdotii ipsius dignitatem.

2. Assumpto vero episcopatu, tam terribilem se praebuit omnibus, si Dei mandata non servarent, ut imminere mortem proximam voce praeconis testaretur. Quibus de causis pauca loqui placet ad roborandam sacerdotum censuram, vel ad instructionem populi, sive etiam ad ipsorum regum praesentium emendationem.

this, the blessed Nicetius was moved with pity and said: "Drive your horses out of the poor men's fields as soon as possible or I shall remove you from my communion!" And they indignantly replied: "What are you talking about? You are not even ordained bishop and you are already threatening us with excommunication?" And he said: "In truth, I say 6
to you that the king has ordered me to be released from the monastery and to be consecrated for this onerous task. Let the Lord's will therefore be done, for the king's desires in all evil things will not be carried out but will be prevented by me." Then removing himself rapidly from the company, he drove the horses out of the grain field. And in this way he was admired by the men and led by them to the city. For he respected no powerful person and feared God alone in his heart and in his deeds.

When he had been placed on the bishop's seat, and was 7
listening to the readings, he felt something heavy upon his neck. Circumspectly touching it two or three times with his hand, he found nothing that could cause this pressure. When he turned his head to the right and to the left, however, he smelled a sweet fragrance and then understood that this burden was the dignity of the episcopate.

2. Once he had assumed the office of bishop he conducted himself in such an intimidating manner toward all that he announced, with the voice like that of a public crier, that if they did not observe God's laws, their death was imminent. This brings me to say something to defend bishops' right to censure, both for the people's instruction and even for the moral improvement of kings when they themselves are present.

2 Nam cum Theoderico decedente, Theodeberthus, filius eius, regnum ambiisset ac multa inique exerceret, et ab eodem plerumque corriperetur, quod vel ipse perpetraret, vel perpetrantes non argueret, advenit dies dominicus. Et ecce rex, cum his qui ab hoc sacerdote communioni abesse iussi fuerant, ecclesiam est ingressus.

3 Lectis igitur lectionibus quas canon sanxit antiquus, oblatis muneribus super altare Dei, ait sacerdos: "Non hic hodie missarum solemnia consummabuntur, nisi communione
4 privati prius abscedant." Haec rege renitente, subito exclamat unus de populo, arreptus a daemone, puer iuvenis, coepitque voce valida inter supplicia torturae suae et sancti viri virtutes et regis crimina confiteri. Dicebatque episcopum castum, regem adulterum, hunc timore Christi humilem, illum gloria regni superbum, istum sacerdotio impollutum a Deo in posterum praeferendum, hunc ab auctore sceleris sui velociter elidendum.

5 Cumque rex timore concussus peteret ut hic energumenus ab ecclesia eiceretur, dixit episcopus: "Prius illi qui te secuti sunt, id est incesti, homicidae, adulteri, ab hac ecclesia extrudantur, et hunc Deus silere iubebit." Et statim rex iussit omnes hos, qui sacerdotis sententia damnati fuerant,
6 egredi ab ecclesia. Quibus expulsis, iussit sacerdos daemoniacum foris extrahi. Sed cum, apprehensa columna, evelli a

CHAPTER 17

For when Theoderic had died, and Theodebert, his son, 2
was touring the kingdom and doing many unjust things, he
was often reproached by the bishop either for what he himself had done or for what he had failed to prevent others
from doing. And behold, on a Sunday the king entered the
church with the very men the bishop had barred from communion.

When the readings which the ancient canon prescribes 3
had been completed and the offerings had been placed on
the altar of God, the bishop said: "The celebration of mass
will not be completed today unless those barred from communion depart." And when the king refused to let this hap- 4
pen, one of the people, a young boy, was seized by a demon,
and amid his torments began to confess in a loud voice the
virtues of the bishop and the crimes of the king. He said
that the bishop was chaste and the king an adulterer, the
bishop humble through the fear of Christ and the king
proud in the glory of his kingship, that the bishop, because
of his office, would in the future be found to be without
stain by God, while the king would speedily be destroyed by
the Author of his crimes.

When the king, terrified, requested that the possessed 5
boy be thrown out of the church, the bishop said: "First let
those who have followed you, that is the incestuous, the
murderers, and the adulterers, be removed from this church.
Then God will silence this boy." And the king at once commanded all those who had been condemned by the bishop's
sentence to depart from the church. When they had been 6
expelled, the bishop ordered the possessed boy to be taken
out. But he had grabbed hold of a column, and when ten

decem viris non posset, sanctus Dei, sub vestimento suo propter iactantiam, faciens crucem Christi e contra, daemonem relaxari praecepit. Qui protinus corruens cum his qui eum trahere nitebantur, post paululum sanus erectus est.

7 Deinde post acta solemnia requisitus numquam reperiri potuit, nec ullus scivit unde venerit vel quo abierit. Coniciebatur tamen a plurimis eum a Deo missum, qui regis sacerdotisque opera non taceret. Unde factum est ut, sacerdote orante, rex mitior fieret, pastor, a Domino remunerandus, digne propheticum illud audiret, quia: "Qui reddiderit pretiosum de vili, tamquam os meum erit" [Jeremiah 15:19].

8 Quotidie autem praedicabat sacerdos populis, denudans crimina singulorum et pro remissione deprecans assidue confitentium. Unde adversus eum saepius odii virus exarsit,
9 quod tam veraciter multorum facinora publicaret. Nam plerumque se persecutoribus ultro obtulit, et gladio exserto cervicem praebuit, sed nocere eum Dominus non permisit. Voluit enim pro iustitia mori, si persecutor fuisset infestior; aiebat enim: "Libenter moriar pro iustitia!" Sed et Chlotarium Regem pro iniustis operibus saepius excommunicavit, exsiliumque eo minitante numquam est territus.

3. Quodam vero tempore, cum iam ad exsilium ductus, ab episcopis reliquis qui adulatores regis effecti fuerant removeretur, atque a suis omnibus derelictus, uni diacono qui adhuc perstabat in fide ait: "Quid tu nunc agis? Quare non sequeris fratres tuos, ut eas quo volueris sicut illi fecerunt?"

men could not pry him loose, the holy man of God, to avoid pride, made the sign of the cross upon him under his vestment and commanded the demon to release him. The boy fell to the ground at once along with those who had been trying to drag him away, but stood up a little later, healthy.

After the solemnities had been completed, he was sought 7
but could nowhere be found, nor did anyone know where he had come from or where he had gone. Thus many thought that he had been sent by God to reveal the deeds of the king and the bishop. And so it happened that the king was made gentler through the bishop's prayer, so that the pastor might be rewarded by the Lord and deservedly hear the prophecy: "Whoever makes something precious from the vile, shall be as my mouth."

Every day the bishop preached to the people, publicizing 8
the crimes of individuals and praying assiduously for the remission of the sins of those who confessed them. Because of this poisonous hate often rose up against him because he so
truthfully exposed the crimes of so many. Several times he 9
presented himself to his persecutors and offered his neck to the drawn sword, but the Lord did not allow him to be hurt. He wished to die for justice if the persecutor had been crueler; for he said: "Willingly would I die for justice!" Also he frequently excommunicated King Chlothar for unjust acts, yet was never afraid of his threats of exile.

3. Once, when he had already been conducted into exile and was being separated from the other bishops, who had become flatterers of the king, as well as abandoned by all his staff, he said to the one deacon who remained loyal to him: "What are you doing? Why don't you follow your brothers so that you can go where you wish, as they did?"

2 Qui ait: "Vivit Dominus Deus meus, quia usquequo spiritus meus infra hos artus contentus fuerit, numquam derelinquam te." Et ille: "Quia," inquit, "haec dixisti, dicam tibi quae Domino revelante cognovi. Cras enim in hac hora, et honorem recipiam et ecclesiae meae restituor. Hi autem qui me reliquerunt cum magno pudore ad me confugiunt."

3 Praestolabatur itaque diaconus rem promissam attonitus, quod postea est expertus. Illucescente autem die crastina, subito advenit legatus Sigiberti Regis cum litteris, nuntians Regem Clotharium esse defunctum, seque regnum debitum cum episcopi caritate debere percipere. Haec ille audiens, ad ecclesiam regressus, potestati restituitur, confusisque his a quibus derelictus fuerat, omnes in caritate recepit.

4 Iam vero quam fortis fuerit ad praedicandum, quam terribilis ad arguendum, quam constans ad sustinendum, quam prudens ad docendum, quis evolvere queat? Unus enim ei semper erat rigor in prosperis et adversis: nec minitantem timuit, nec a blandiente delusus est.

5 Nam vere, ut aiebat relator ille memoratus, parum fuit
quin iuxta Paulum apostolum non fuisset iniuriatus: "periculis fluminum, periculis latronum, periculis in civitate, peri-
6 culis in falsis fratribus" [2 Corinthians 11:26] et reliqua. Nam
quadam die dum Mosellam fluvium navigio transnataret, inter pilas pontis fluctuum actus impulsu, palmis tantum pilae adhaesit, pede continens navem, et sic ab intuentibus iam

And the deacon said: "As my Lord God lives, as long as my 2
spirit is contained in these mortal limbs, I shall never abandon you." And the bishop replied: "Because you have said this, I shall tell you what I have learned through the revelation of the Lord. Tomorrow at this time, I shall be given back my office and be reinstated in my church. The ones who abandoned me are coming back to me with great shame."

Amazed, the deacon awaited the promised event, which 3
he then experienced. For at daybreak the next day, a legate suddenly arrived with a letter from King Sigebert, announcing that King Clothar had died, that he was about to take over the kingdom, and that he wished for the bishop's friendship. When he heard this, the bishop went back to the church and was reinstated in his office; the ones who had left him were dismayed, but he received them again in charity.

How effective a preacher he was, how intimidating in ar- 4
guments, how constant in being true to himself, and how wise in his teaching, who can ever say enough about this? His strength was always the same, in prosperity and in adversity: he did not fear threats and was not fooled by blandishments.

For in truth, as the aforesaid speaker said, there was little 5
hardship which he had not experienced; as the apostle Paul
said: "the dangers of rivers, dangers of robbers, dangers in
the city, dangers of false brethren" and the rest. For once 6
when he was crossing the Moselle on a boat he was hurled by the waves between the piles of a bridge and clung to the pile with his hands alone while he held on to the boat with his feet, and thus was able to be rescued by onlookers even

ad demersionem paratus erutus est, quod non sine Temptatoris insidiis se pertulisse ferebat.

7 Sed et ipse Auctor criminis plerumque se obtutibus eius quasi nociturus ostendit. Denique dum quadam die iter ageret, descendens ab equo, inter vepres condensas ventris purgandi gratia est ingressus. Et ecce astitit ei umbra teterrima, statu procera, crassitudine valida, colore tetra, oculorum scintillantium immensitatem in modum tauri petulantis habebat, ore patulo quasi ad deglutiendum virum Dei parata. At illo faciente signum crucis e contra, in modum fumi ascendentis evanuit. Quod non ambigitur ipsum ei sceleris Principem fuisse monstratum.

4. In ieiuniis autem valde, ut diximus, fortis erat. Nam, ceteris reficientibus, saepe ipse, contecto capite a cucullo ne agnosceretur in publico, cum uno tantum puero sanctorum basilicas circuibat.

2 Sed et curationum gratia data est ei a Deo. Dum autem haec in illo, ut supra diximus, habitu sanctorum habitacula circuiret, ad templum sancti Maximini antistitis accessit, in cuius atrio post multas debacchationes tres energumeni pressi sopore quiescebant, cernensque eos somno deditos, fecit signum crucis e contra. Statimque expergefacti, elevantes in sublime voces, dato impetu ad vomitum, emundati sunt.

3 Cum autem lues inguinaria Trevericum populum in circuitu civitatis valde vastaret, et sacerdos Dei pro ovibus commissis Domini misericordiam imploraret assidue, factus est sonus de nocte magnus, tamquam tonitruum validum super pontem amnis, ita ut putaretur urbs ipsa dehiscere.

when he had resigned himself to drowning; he said that he had suffered this through the tricks of the Tempter.

But the Author of crime himself often appeared before 7
his eyes intending to harm him. Thus while traveling one day he descended from his horse to purge his bowels in some dense bushes. And behold, a most hideous shade appeared, tall and massive, black in color; it had huge flashing eyes like a fierce bull and its mouth was opened, ready to swallow the man of God. But when he made the sign of the cross against it, it vanished like rising smoke. No one can doubt that the Prince of crime himself had been shown to him.

4. He was most resolute in fasting, as we said. For while others were eating he would often make the rounds of the basilicas of the saints with just one servant boy, his head covered in a hood so as not to be recognized in public.

But the grace of healing was also given to him by God. 2
Once when he was walking around the saints' dwellings in the guise just mentioned, he came to the temple of the holy bishop Maximinus in whose forecourt three possessed persons were resting, oppressed by sleep after their many fits. And when he saw them asleep, he made the sign of the cross upon them. At once, they woke up, shrieked fiercely, vomited violently, and were cleansed.

And when the plague of the groin was severely afflicting 3
the people around the city of Trier, and the bishop of God was assiduously imploring the Lord's mercy for the sheep committed to his care, there was a loud noise one night, like an enormous thunderclap above the bridge over the river, so that one might think the city itself was falling apart.

4 Cumque omnis populus exterritus in lectulis resedisset, leti-
ferum sibi interitum opperiens, audita est in medio rumoris
vox una ceteris clarior, dicens: “Et quid hic, O socii, faciemus? Ad unam enim portam Eucharius Sacerdos observat,
ad aliam Maximinus excubabat, in medio versatur Nicetius.
Nihil hic ultra praevalere possumus, nisi sinamus hanc urbem eorum tuitioni.”

5 Hac voce audita, statim morbus quievit, nullusque ab eo
ultra defunctus est. Unde non ambigitur virtute memorati
antistitis fuisse defensam.

6 Invitatus autem quodam tempore sacerdos a rege, dicit
suis: “Quaerite nobis piscium multitudinem in abundan-
tiam, ut, euntes ad occursum regis, et nostrum expleatur
7 opus et amicis ministretur affatim.” Dixerunt ei: “Lapsus
noster, in quem pisces decidere soliti sunt, prorsus desertus
habetur. Sed et maceriae ipsae de locis suis amnis impetu
evulsae noscuntur. Non est qualiter iussio vestra adimplea-
tur, dum non est in promptu qualiter capiantur quae praeci-
pis.”

8 Et ille, haec audiens, ingressus in cellulam suam vocavit
puerum et ait: “Vade et dic coquorum praeposito ut exhi-
beat pisces ab amne.” Qui iussa referens, derisus est ab homine. Reversoque ait sacerdos: “Scio, quia locutus es ea quae
praecipi, sed audire noluerunt. Vade et dic eis ut eant.”
9 Cumque bis aut tertio hanc ordinationem dure susceperunt,
commoti tandem abierunt ad lapsum et, aspicientes, invenerunt eum ita refertum piscibus ut decem viri quae repere-
rant vix exhibere potuissent. Ostendebat enim ei virtus divina saepius quae ei opportuna erant.

As everyone sat up in bed terrified, trying to hide from a 4
deadly destruction, a voice was heard in the midst of the noise that was clearer than the others, saying: "What will we do here, companions? At one gate Bishop Eucharius is keeping watch, at the other Maximinus is stationed, and Nicetius holds the middle. We cannot accomplish anything here except leave this city to their protection."

When this voice had been heard, the illness at once 5
stopped and no one thereafter died of it. Hence it is clear that the city had been defended by the holy power of the bishop.

Sometime later, when the bishop had been invited by the 6
king, he said to his staff: "Go and find a large quantity of
fish, so that when we go to meet the king we may fulfill our
duty and give enough to our friends." They said to him: "Our 7
fish reservoir into which fish usually swim is completely empty. And even the fish traps are known to have been swept from their places by the force of the river. There is no way in which we can carry out your order, for there is nothing in storage from which to gather what you command."

When he heard this, he went into his cell; then he called 8
his servant and said: "Go and tell the head cook to collect
fish from the river." When the servant delivered this message, he was laughed at by the fellow. When he returned, the bishop said: "I know that you said what I instructed and
that they did not want to listen. Go again and tell them to
go." After the second or third command they became very 9
annoyed, but at last went in a rage to the fish reservoir; and when they looked at it, they found it to be so full of fish that ten men could hardly have carried away the contents. Thus divine power often provided him with what he needed.

5. Sed nec hoc silendum putavi, quod eidem de regibus Francorum a Domino fuit ostensum. Vidit enim in visu noctis turrem magnam, tanta celsitudine praeditam, ut polo propinqua suspiceretur, habentem fenestras multas, Dominumque stantem super cacumen eius et angelos Dei per spe-
2 culas illas positos. Unus autem ex eis tenebat librum magnum in manu, dicens: "Tantum temporis rex ille et ille victurus est in saeculo." Nominavitque omnes viritim, vel qui eo tempore erant, vel deinceps nati sunt, dixitque et qualitatem regni, et quantitatem vitae eorum. Sed post uniuscuiusque nomen semper "Amen" ceteri angeli respondebant. Sicque de his in posterum impletum est, sicut sanctus per praefatam revelationem annuntiavit.

3 Regressus autem a rege evectu navali, obdormivit. Et ecce commotus vento fluvius coepit fluctus in excelsa porrigere, ita ut putaretur navis ipsa demergi. Sacerdos autem, ut praefati sumus, dormiens somno nescio quo, ut plerumque dormientibus evenit, quasi ab aliquo oppressus est. Excitatus quoque a suis, fecit signum crucis super aqua, et cessavit
4 procella. Deinde suspirans crebrius, interrogatus a suis est quid vidisset. Qui ait: "Silere quidem decreveram, sed tamen dicam. Vidi enim me quasi per universum orbem retia ad capiendum extendere, et nullus erat adiutor meus, nisi tantum hic puer Aredius." Et merito eum Dominus retificem ostendere voluit, qui quotidie populos ad divinum officium capiebat.

5. I do not think I should be silent about what the Lord
showed him concerning the kings of the Franks. For he saw
in a dream vision a large tower, so high that it appeared to
approach heaven and with many windows; the Lord stood
on its summit and angels were placed at its windows. One of 2
these held a large book in his hand, saying: "For such a time
this and that king will live in the world." And he named each
one individually, saying what their times would be like, of
the ones alive in that time and of those who would be born
after it, and he described the quality of their reigns and how
long their lives would be. And after each name the other angels would respond by saying "Amen." And the things concerning these kings were later fulfilled, just as the holy man
had announced in the aforesaid revelation.

Once when returning from the king on a boat, the bishop 3
fell asleep. And behold, the wind began to raise the waves of
the river up so high that the ship seemed about to be swallowed by them. However, as we said, the bishop continued
in a kind of sleep that frequently happens to those slumber-
ing as though he were oppressed by something. Having at
last been awakened by his companions, he made the sign of
the cross over the water and the storm subsided. After this, 4
because he kept on sighing, he was asked by his companions
what he had seen during his sleep. He said: "I had decided
not to talk about it, but will tell you nevertheless. I saw myself as if I were spreading nets to capture the whole world,
and no one was helping me except this boy Aredius." And
deservedly did the Lord show him as a net maker because he
captured people daily at the divine office.

5 Venit autem ad eum homo quidam, caesariem barbamque prolixam efferens; prostratusque ad pedes eius ait: "Ego sum, domine, qui in maris periculo positus, tuo adiutorio sum salvatus." At ille, obiurgans hominem cur de eo laudationis huius proferret gloriam, ait: "Dic qualiter te Deus ab hac necessitate eripuit, nam virtus mea nullum iuvare potest."

6 Qui ait: "Nuperrimo tempore cum navem ascendens Ita-
liam peterem, multitudo paganorum mecum ingressa est,
inter quos et ego tantum solus eram inter illam rusticorum
multitudinem Christianus. Orta autem tempestate, coepi
invocare nomen Domini, atque ut me intercessio tua eripe-
7 ret flagitare. Pagani vero invocabant deos suos, et ille Iovem,
iste Mercurium proclamabat, alius Minervae, alius Veneris
auxilium flagitabat. Cumque iam in discrimine essemus, aio
ad eos: 'O viri, nolite hos deos invocare, non enim sunt dii
isti, sed daemones. Nam si vultis de praesenti interitu erui,
invocate sanctum Nicetium, ut ipse obtineat cum Domini
misericordia vos salvari.'

8 "Cumque una voce elevata in huiusmodi clamore dixissent: 'Deus Nicetii eripe nos,' protinus mare mitigatum est, ceciditque ventus, ac sole reducto, eo quo voluntas nostra fuit navis accessit. Ego autem vovi ne prius comam capitis tonderem quam tuis obtutibus praesentarer." Tunc iussu episcopi tonsuratus homo Arvernum adiit, unde se esse confessus est.

9 Innumera sunt enim, quae de hoc viro relata a memorato abbate cognovimus, sed finire libellum puto.

CHAPTER 17

Once a certain man came to him with long hair and a long 5
beard; prostrating himself at his feet, the man said: "My
lord, I am the man who was in danger at sea and was rescued
by your help." And the bishop reproved him and asked why
he gave him this glorious praise, saying: "Tell me how God
rescued you from this dire situation, for my own power cannot save anyone."

The man said: "Recently I boarded a boat going to Italy 6
with a multitude of pagans; among this crowd of rustics I
was the only Christian. When a storm arose, I began to call
upon the name of the Lord and beg for your intercession
to rescue me. The pagans, however, invoked their gods for 7
help, one calling upon Jove, another upon Mercury, still another upon the aid of Minerva, and one upon that of Venus.
And when we were in the greatest danger, I say to them: 'O
men, don't call upon these gods for they are not gods but demons. If you want to be rescued from this imminent death
call upon the holy Nicetius, that he may obtain your safety
through the Lord's compassion.'

"And while they were shouting this with one loud voice, 8
saying: 'God of Nicetius rescue us,' the sea at once calmed
down, the wind abated, the sun returned, and our ship arrived where we wished. I, however, vowed not to cut the
hair on my head until I had presented myself to your eyes."
Then, when his hair had been cut at the bishop's orders, he
returned to Clermont, from where he said he had come.

The stories which I heard about Nicetius from the afore- 9
said abbot cannot be counted, but I think I should finish
this book.

6. Cum autem propinquum transitus tempus migrationis suae cognovisset, fratribus retulit, dicens: "Vidi Paulum apostolum cum Ioanne Baptista invitantem me ad requiem sempiternam, atque exhibentem mihi coronam caelestibus margaritis ornatam, ac dicentibus mihi viris: 'Talibus enim
2 speciebus perfrueris in regno Dei.'" Haec quibusdam fidelibus referens, post paucos dies modica febre pulsatus spiritum praemisit ad Dominum; sepultusque est in basilica sancti Maximini antistitis. Cuius nunc tumulus plerumque divinis virtutibus illustratur.

18

De Urso et Leobatio abbatibus

Prologus

Legiferi vatis oraculum cum de principio principium fandi sumpsisset, et Dominum extendisse caelos dextera maiestatis fuisset effatus, ait: "Et fecit Deus duo luminaria magna et stellas, et posuit ea in firmamento caeli, ut praeessent diei ac nocti, et lucerent in firmamento caeli" [Genesis
2 1:16–18]. Sic nunc et in illo mentis humanae caelo, sicut priorum sanxit auctoritas, luminari magna dedit, Christum scilicet et Ecclesiam eius, quae luceant in tenebris ignorantiae et illuminent sensus humilitatis nostrae, sicut Ioannes

6. When he knew that the time of his passing was near, he spoke to his brothers and said: "I saw the apostle Paul with John the Baptist inviting me to eternal repose and showing me a crown adorned with heavenly pearls while saying to me: 'You will delight in such things in the kingdom of God.'"
Having told these things to certain of his loyal friends, he 2
was seized by a moderate fever a few days later, and sent his spirit ahead to the Lord; he was buried in the basilica of the holy bishop Maximinus, and his tomb is now frequently illumined by divine acts of power.

18

About the abbots Ursus and Leobatius

Prologue

When the oracle of Moses, the legislating prophet, began to speak of the beginning of beginnings, and told about the Lord spreading out the sky with his right hand, he said: "And the Lord made two great lights and stars, and placed them in the firmament of the sky, so that they might preside over day and night, and might shine in the firmament of the
sky." In the same way now, as the authority of our prede- 2
cessors ordains, he gave great lights in the sky of the human mind, that is Christ and his Church, so that they might shine in the darkness of ignorance and illuminate our

evangelista de ipso ait, quia hic est “lux mundi” [John 8:12], qui “illuminat omnem hominem venientem in hunc mundum” [John 1:9].

3 Posuit etiam in eo et stellas, patriarchas videlicet, pro-
phetas apostolosque, qui vel doctrinis nos erudiant, vel mirabilibus suis illuminent, sicut in evangelio ait, quia: “Vos
estis lux huius mundi” [Matthew 5:14]. Et: “Sic luceat lux
vestra coram hominibus ut videant opera vestra bona et glo-
4 rificent Patrum vestrum qui est in caelis” [Matthew 5:16]. Hi
enim apostoli merito pro tota accipiuntur Ecclesia, quae
non habens rugam aut maculam impolluta subsistit, sicut
Apostolus ait, quia: “Ipse sibi exhibuit Ecclesiam mundam,
non habentem maculam aut rugam, aut aliquid huiuscemodi” [Ephesians 5:27].

5 Ex horum ergo doctrina et usque ad nostra fuerunt tempora, qui in hoc saeculo quasi astrorum iubar, non solum meritorum radiantes luce, verum etiam dogmatum magnitudine coruscantes, orbem totum radio suae praedicationis illustraverunt, euntes per loca singula praedicando, ac monasteria ad divinum cultum locando, docendo homines a curis saecularibus abstinere et, relictis tenebris concupiscentiae, Deum verum sequi, per quem facta sunt omnia, sicut de Ursu Leobatioque abbatibus fidelium fratrum relatio signat.

1. Igitur Ursus abbas Cadurcinae urbis incola fuit, ab ineunte aetate religiosus et in Dei amore devotus. De quo egressus loco, Bituricum terminum est ingressus, fundatisque monasteriis apud Tausiriacum, Oniam, atque Pontiniacum; stabilitisque praepositis, sanctitate honorificis, dispensatione libratis, Turonicum territorium est ingressus et

humble human intelligence; for, as the evangelist John said
of him, he is the "light of the world" who "enlightens every
man that comes into this world."

For he placed there stars, that is patriarchs, prophets, and 3
apostles, who teach us with their doctrine or enlighten us
with their miracles; as Christ said in the gospel: "You are the
light of the world." And: "Let your light shine among men so
that they may see your good works and glorify your Father
who is in heaven." The apostles here addressed are deserv- 4
edly thought to represent the whole Church, which has no
wrinkle or stain and lives unpolluted; as the Apostle Paul
said: "He presented to himself a pure Church, without spot
or wrinkle, or any such thing."

Thanks to their doctrine there have been up to our times 5
those who shine in this world like stars, not only with the
light of their merits—they even shine through the greatness
of their doctrines, illuminating the whole world with the
ray of their preaching, traveling to and preaching in many
places, establishing monasteries for the divine service, and
teaching men to abstain from secular cares and leave the
darkness of concupiscence to follow the true God who
made all things. The following report by reliable brothers
about the abbots Ursus and Leobatius shows this.

1. The abbot Ursus was an inhabitant of the city of Cahors and from his childhood religious and devout in the love of God. He left that place, entered the territory of Berry, and founded monasteries in Toiselay, Heugnes, and Ponçin; when he had placed priors in them, venerable in sanctity, and provided them with books, he entered the territory of Tours and came to the place which an ancient author said

ad locum quem Senapariam vocitari priscus instituit auctor
2 accessit. Aedificatoque oratorio, monasterium stabilivit,
commissaque Leobatio praeposito summa regulae, monasterium aliud statuit, quod nunc Loccis vocant, situm scilicet
super fluvium Angerem in recessu montis, cui nunc castrum
3 supereminet, ipso nomine ut monasterium vocitatum. Ubi
adiuncta congregatione, statuit apud animum suum, ne ultra alium proficisceretur in locum, sed in eo cum omni congregatione manibus propriis operari, et victum a terra in sudore vultus exigere, illud fratribus inter reliqua praedicationum dona commendans quod Paulus apostolus ait: "Laborate manibus, ut habeas unde possis retribuere necessitatem patientibus" [Ephesians 4:28]. Et illud: "Quia qui non laborat, nec manducet" [2 Thessalonians 3:10].

4 Dedit autem ei Dominus et gratiam curationis, ita ut insufflatis energumenis, protinus daemonia eicerentur a corporibus obsessis. Sed et alias per eum Dominus dignatus est operari virtutes. Erat enim abstinens a cibis et potu, interdicens monachis sine cessatione avertere oculum et cogitatione ab omni luxuria.

2. Dum autem haec ageret, ac fratres molam manu vertentes triticum ad victus necessaria comminuerent, pro labore fratrum visum est ei molendinum in ipso Angeris fluvii alveo stabilire. Defixisque per flumen palis, aggregatis lapidum magnorum acervis, exclusas fecit atque aquam canale
collegit, cuius impetu fabricae rotam in magna volubilitate
2 vertere fecit. Hoc opere laborem monachorum relevans, atque uni fratrum delegans, opus necessarium implebatur.

should be called Sennevières. After building a chapel there, 2
he founded a monastery, and having installed Leobatius as prior to enforce the rule, he founded another monastery which is now called Loches on the river Indre, in a hollow in the mountain upon which the fort now stands which is
called by the same name as the monastery. After installing 3
a congregation there he decided in his heart not to go to yet another place but to work there with his hands together with this congregation to derive his nourishment from the earth by the sweat of his brow, commending to his brothers among other things the gifts of preaching which the apostle Paul gave, who said: "Work with your hands so that you may have something to give to those in need." And elsewhere: "If anyone does not work, let him not eat."

The Lord, however, gave him the grace of healing, so that 4
when he blew upon the possessed the demons were at once expelled from the bodies they had captured. And the Lord deigned to perform other deeds of power through him as well. For he was abstemious in eating and drinking and constantly urged his monks to avert their eyes and thoughts from all excess.

2. While he was living in this manner and the brothers were turning a millstone by hand to grind the grain necessary for their food, he conceived a plan to reduce their work by building a watermill in the riverbed of the Indre. Having driven piles along it and collected a great pile of stones to make a dam, he channeled the water so that the
force of the current made the wheel turn quickly. With 2
this construction he lightened the monks' work, and one monk was chosen to carry out the necessary operations.

Hanc enim fabricam Sichlarius quidem Gothus, qui magno cum Alarico Rege amore diligebatur, aemulus monasterio concupivit. Dixitque abbati: "Dona mihi hoc molendinum, ut sit sub ditione mea, et quod volueris repensabo."

3 Cui ille: "Cum grandi," inquit, "hoc labore paupertas nostra statuit, et nunc non possumus ipsum donare, ne fratres
mei fame pereant." Et ille: "Si vis," inquit, "ipsum bona voluntate tribuere, gratias ago. Sin aliud, vi ipsum auferam.
Aut certe faciam aliud, cuius exclusis aqua retrorsum con-
4 versa, rotam tuam vertere amplius non permittent." Abbas
respondit: "Non facies autem quod Deus non voluerit, nam
a nobis ipsum penitus non accipies." Tunc Sichlarius, fer-
vens felle, similem sub hoc fabricam adaptavit. Cumque
aqua retrorsum conversa sub huius operis rotam inundans
gurgitem fecisset, restitit prorsus, nec omnino potuit ut
consueverat.

5 Venitque custos eius ad abbatem, media ut ferunt nocte,
illo in oratorio cum fratribus vigilante, et ait: "Surge, abba,
deprecare attentius Dominum. Restitit enim rota molen-
dini ab inundatione canalis alieni, quem Sichlarius fecit." At
ille, haec audiens, misit confestim fratres singulos ad monasteria illa quae statuerat, dicens: "Prosternite vos in oratione, et non sit vobis opus aliud donec iterum ad vos diri-
6 gam." Sed et ipse non est egressus ab oratorio, deprecans

However, Sichlarius, a Goth who was held in high esteem by King Alaric, was envious of the monastery and wanted to have the mill. He said to the abbot: "Give me this mill so that it is mine, and I shall recompense you with what you wish."

The abbot replied: "Our poverty built this with great ef- 3
fort; we cannot give it away now lest my brothers die of hunger." And Sichlarius said: "If you are willing to give it to me of your own goodwill, I will thank you. But if not, I will take it from you by force. Or I will definitely build another one whose channeling barriers will push the water backward and
will prevent your wheel from turning." The abbot replied: 4
"You will not do what God does not wish, and you certainly will not receive the mill from us." Sichlarius then became enraged and built a similar mill below the monks' mill. And because of this the water rose up against the wheel of the monk's mill as a lake of standing water, their wheel could not turn at all as it had done before.

Its guard came to the abbot in the middle of the night, 5
they say, while he was in the chapel keeping vigil with the brothers, and said: "Arise, abbot, and pray devoutly to the Lord. For the wheel of our mill stands still on account of the flooding created by the new channel which Sichlarius has made." When he heard this, the abbot at once sent one brother apiece to the other monasteries which he had founded to tell them: "Prostrate yourselves in prayer and
don't do anything else until I send to you again." And he too 6

Dominum attente ac praestolans adventum eius misericordiae. Sic fecit per integros duos dies totidem noctes. Tertia iam illucescente die, accessit iterum monachus ille qui custos fuerat, nuntians rotam fabricae suae iuxta consuetudinem priorem in summa verti velocitate.

7 Egressusque abbas cum fratribus de oratorio, accedit ad litus, conspiciensque molendinum quod Sichlarius fecerat, non reperit. Accedens ad litus, et fundum alvei intuens, indi-
8 cium nullum de eo accepit. De quo non quidquam ligni, non lapidis, non ferri, vel ullius umquam genus indicii potuit ostendi, nisi quod conici potuit, ipso quo fabricatum fuerat loco, virtute divina dehiscens ab oculis humanum est ablatum. Tunc misit nuntios ad fratres, dicens: "Requiescite iam a labore, quia ultus est Deus iniuriam fratrum nostrorum."

3. His et talibus virtutibus praeditus, consummato cursu vitae, migravit ad Dominum. Ad cuius tumulum postea et energumeni sanati et caeci illuminati sunt. Post cuius obitum praepositi qui per monasteria erant, abbatum officium, episcopis largientibus, susceperunt. Sed et Leobatius apud Senaparium monasterium, quod infra territorium Turonicum erat, abbas instituitur, in summa sanctitate ac senectute perdurans, ibique et obiit ac sepultus est.

did not leave the chapel, but prayed devoutly to the Lord, awaiting the arrival of his compassion. This he did for two whole days and nights. When the third day dawned, the monk who had been the guard came to him and told him that the wheel of his mill was now turning as usual at great speed.

The abbot then left the chapel together with the broth- 7
ers and went to the riverbank to look for the mill which Sichlarius had built, but they could not find it. They went to the water's edge and looked into the riverbed, but saw no
trace of it. Since no trace of wood, stone, iron, or of any kind 8
at all could be found, they conjectured that the place on which the mill stood had been swallowed and removed from human sight by divine power. And then he sent messengers to the brothers, to tell them: "Now rest from your labor, for God has avenged the injury done our brethren."

3. Endowed with these and like powers, the abbot completed the course of his life and passed on to the Lord. At his tomb possessed persons were subsequently healed and blind persons given light. After his death the priors of the monasteries received the abbacy from the bishops. Leobatius too was made abbot of the monastery of Sennevières in the territory of Tours, and having continued in the greatest sanctity to a ripe old age, died and was buried there.

19

De Monegunde religiosa

Prologus

Insignia divinorum beneficiorum charismata, quae humano generi caelitus sunt indulta, nec sensu concipi, nec verbis effari, nec scripturis poterunt comprehendi. Cum ipse Salvator mundi ab illo rudis saeculi exordio patriarchis se praestat videri, prophetis annuntiari, ad extremum semper virginis intactaeque Mariae dignatur utero suscipi, et praepotens immortalisque Creator mortalis carnis patitur amictu vestiri, mortem pro hominis peccato mortui reparatione adire, victorque resurgere.

2 Qui nos gravium facinorum spiculis sauciatos, ac latronum insidiantium vulneribus affectos, infuso meri oleique liquore, ad stabulum medicinae caelestis, id est Ecclesiae sanctae, dogma perduxit.

3 Qui nos exemplis sanctorum vivere incessabili praeceptionis suae munere cohortatur, nobisque non modo viros, sed etiam ipsum inferiorem sexum, non segniter sed viriliter agonizantem, praebet exemplum, qui non solum viris legitime decertantibus, verum etiam feminis in his praeliis favo-
4 rabiliter desudantibus, siderea regna participat. Sicut nunc
beata Monegundis, quae relicto genitali solo, tamquam regina prudens quae audire sapientiam Salomonis adivit, ita haec beati Martini basilicam, ut eius miracula quotidianis

19

About the nun Monegund

Prologue

The extraordinary graces of divine benefits granted in a heavenly fashion to the human race cannot be grasped by the mind, or expressed in words, or captured in writing. For the Savior of the world who let himself be seen by the patriarchs in the beginning, when the world was still young and announced by the prophets, in the end deigned to be received by the womb of Mary, ever a virgin and pure, and thus the almighty and immortal Creator permitted himself to be clothed in a robe of mortal flesh, to die for the redemption of men dead through sin, and to rise again as the victor.

Pierced as we were by the javelins of our grave sins and 2
afflicted by the wounds of treacherous robbers, he anointed us with wine and oil and led us to the shelter of heavenly medicine, that is: the doctrine of the holy Church.

Exhorting us through the examples of the saints to live by 3
the continuous gift of his precepts, he gives us as models not only men but even the weaker sex, striving not feebly but manfully, and he admits to his starry kingdoms not only men fighting lawful combats but also women sweating success-
fully in these battles. So also now the blessed Monegund, 4
like the prudent queen who came to listen to Solomon's wisdom, left behind her native soil to seek the basilica of the blessed Martin to admire his miracles which were granted

indulta momentis miraretur, expetiit, hauriretque de fonte sacerdotali quod posset aditum nemoris paradisiaci recludere.

1. Igitur beatissima Monegundis, Carnotenae urbis indigena, parentum ad votum copulata coniugio, duas filias habuit, super quibus valde gavisa laetebatur, dicens quia: "Propagavit Deus generationem meam, ut mihi duae filiae
2 nascerentur." Sed hoc mundiale gaudium praevenit saeculi huius amaritudo, dum puellae modica febre pulsatae metam naturae debitam concluserunt. Ex hoc genetrix maesta deplorans, orbatamque se lugens, non diebus, non noctibus a fletu cessabat, quam non vir, non amicus, non ullus propinquorum poterat consolari.

3 Tandemque in se conversa, ait: "Si nullam consolationem de obitu filiarum capio, vereor ne ob hoc laedam Dominum meum Iesum Christum. Sed nunc haec lamenta reliquens, cum beato Iob consolata decantem: 'Dominus dedit, Dominus abstulit, quomodo Domino placuit ita factum est. Sit nomen Domini benedictum'" [Job 1:21].

4 Et haec dicens, exuta veste lugubri, iussit sibi cellulam parvulam praeparari, in qua unam tantummodo fenestellulam, per quam modicum lumen posset cernere, praecepit aptari. Ibique, contempto mundi ambitu, spreto viri consortio, soli Deo, in quo erat confisa, vacabat, fundens orationem pro suis populique delictis, habens puellulam unam cuius ei famulatu ministrabantur ea quae necessitas exige-
5 bat. Accipiebat etiam et farinam hordeaceam, infusosque

every day, and to drink from the priestly fount what might unlock for her the gate of the grove of Paradise.

1. The most blessed Monegund was born in the city of Chartres and joined in marriage at her parents' wish; she had two daughters with whom she was very happy, so that she used to say: "God has made me fertile so that two daughters might be born to me." But this worldly joy was followed 2
by the world's bitterness, because the girls were struck down by a moderate fever and ended their lives. This caused their sorrowing mother to grieve and to lament her loss, not ceasing to weep either day or night, and no one, neither her husband, a friend, or anyone close to her could console her.

At last coming to her senses, she said: "If I do not accept 3
any consolation for the death of my daughters, I fear I will offend my lord Jesus Christ. So I now leave these laments behind and console myself by chanting with the blessed Job: 'The Lord has given, and the Lord has taken away, as the Lord pleased, so it has happened. Blessed be the name of the Lord.'"

After she had said this, she took off her mourning and or- 4
dered a small cell to be prepared for her, in which she requested one tiny little window to be made through which some light could be seen. There, rejecting the surrounding world and the company of her husband, she devoted herself solely to God, in whom she put all her trust, pouring forth prayers for her own sins and for those of the people, and having only one little girl to serve her with what she needed.
For she received barley meal, to which she added water and 5

lymphis cineres, ac diligenter colans, ex ea aqua mixturam massae conficiebat, formatosque propriis manibus panes et ipsam coquens, post longa ieiunia reficiebatur. Reliquum domus suae cibum pauperibus dispensabat.

6 Factum est autem quodam die, ut memorata puella, quae ei consueverat famulari—et credo Inimici astu seducta, cui semper bonis iniurias irrogare mos est—se ab eius famulatu subtraheret, dicens: "Non potero ego cum hac domina permanere, quae in tali abstinentia commoratur, sed potius utar saeculo, ac cibum potumque in abundantia sumam."

7 Quintus autem iam fluxerat abscessionis eius dies, quo
haec religiosa neque farinam consuetam, neque aquam acceperat. Sed perstabat immobilis, et fixa manens in Christo, in
quo quisquam locatus nec venti turbine, nec fluctuum im-
pulsione dilabitur. Nec sibi illa de mortali cibo vitam, sed de
verbo Dei, sicut scriptum est, putabat inferri, commemorans illud Sapientiae verbum Salomoniacae proverbium,
quia: "Non necabit Dominus fame animam iusti" [Proverbs
8 10:3]. Et illud, quia: "Iustus ex fide vivit" [Romans 1:17]. Sed
quoniam corpus humanum absque esu terreno sustentari
nequit, prostrata in oratione, petiit ut qui manna populo
esurienti de caelo, lymphasque sitienti produxit e saxo, ipse
quoque alimentum quo parumper corpusculum fessum confortaretur, dignaretur indulgere.

9 Protinusque ad eius orationem, nix de caelo decidua humum operuit. Quod illa cum gratiarum actione cernens, educta manu per fenestram quod circa parietem erat ex ipsa nive collegit, de qua aquam exprimens panem solito formavit, quousque ad alios quinque dies victum corporeum ministravit.

ashes, carefully kneaded it, formed loaves of with her own hands, and baked them, and thus nourished herself after long fasts. What remained of her food she gave to the poor.

One day it happened, however, that the girl I mentioned, 6
who customarily served her—I believe she was seduced by the wiles of the Enemy, who always inflicts injuries upon the good—withdrew from her service, saying: "I cannot stay with a mistress who lives in such abstinence, but would rather live in the world where I will consume food and drink in abundance."

Five days passed after her departure and this religious 7
woman had received neither her usual flour nor water. But she remained immobile, fixed in Christ, knowing that whoever is grounded in him cannot collapse either through the force of a whirlwind or at the impact of a flood. Neither did she think of taking mortal food to sustain life but only, as is written, the word of God, remembering the proverb of Solomon's wisdom: "The Lord will not make the just man's soul perish from hunger." And also: "The just man lives through
faith." But since the human body cannot sustain itself with- 8
out earthly food, she prostrated herself in prayer, asking that he who brought forth manna from heaven for the hungry and water from a rock for the thirsty might deign to give her, too, some food to strengthen her exhausted body.

Immediately after her prayer, snow falling from heaven 9
covered the earth. Seeing this, she gave thanks and extended her hand through the window to collect some of this snow from around the walls of the cell; with the water from it she formed loaves of bread as she used to that provided her bodily nourishment for another five days.

10 Habebat enim contiguum cellulae parvulum viridiarium. In illud autem pro quadam relevatione prodire erat solita, in quod ingressa, dum intuens herbas loci ac deambulans, mulier quae triticum supra tectum suum siccandum posuerat, quasi de eminentiori loco, curis oppleta mundanis, importune prospexit, moxque, oculis clausis, lumine caruit.

11 Cognoscens autem reatum suum, ad eam accedit, remque ut gesta fuerat pandens. At illa, deiciens se in orationem, ait: "Vae mihi, quia pro parvitatis meae persona peccatrice aliorum clausi sunt oculi!" Et consummata oratione, imposuit manum mulieri. Confestim autem ut signum crucis expressit, mulier visum recepit.

12 Homo quidam ex pago illo, qui olim auditum perdiderat,
ad eius cellulam devotus advenit, pro quo deprecati sunt
parentes eius, ut ei manum haec benedicta dignaretur im-
13 ponere. Sed illa indignam se esse proclamans per quam
Christus haec operari dignetur, solo prostrata et quasi ipsa
dominicorum pedum vestigia lambens, humiliter pro eo
divinam clementiam supplicavit. Illaque adhuc solo decum-
bente, aures surdi apertae sunt, rediitque ad domum propriam, maerore ablato, cum gaudio.

2. His signis glorificata inter parentes, ne vanae gloriae lapsum incurreret, sancti Martini antistitis basilicam, relicto coniuge cum familia vel omni domo sua, fideliter expetivit.

2 Cumque iter coeptum carperet, venit ad vicum urbis Turonicae, cui nomen est Evena, in quo beati Medardi Suessionenci confesssoris reliquiae continentur, cuius et vigiliae ea

Around the cell she had a small garden where she used to 10
go for refreshment. Once when she had entered it and was walking around looking at the plants there, a woman filled with worldly thoughts who had been placing grain to dry on the roof of her nearby house, indiscreetly observed her from her lookout point; soon her eyes closed and she was blind.

Recognizing her transgression, she went to the blessed 11
Monegund and told her what she had done. And the blessed lady prostrated herself in prayer and said: "Woe to me that on account of my sinful, wretched person others' eyes are closed!" When she had completed her prayer, she placed her hands upon the woman. And immediately after she had made the sign of the cross, the woman received her sight.

A certain man from that region who had lost his hearing 12
once came devoutly to her cell, and his relatives begged the
blessed lady to deign to place her right hand upon him. But 13
she exclaimed that she was did not deserve for Christ to perform this through her. Nevertheless she prostrated herself on the ground and, as though kissing the Lord's feet, humbly implored divine mercy for him. While she was still lying on the ground, the deaf man's ears were opened and he, relieved of his distress, returned to his home with joy.

2. She was glorified among her relatives through these signs of holy power and because she wished to avoid falling into the trap of vainglory, she devoutly went to the holy bishop Martin's basilica, leaving behind her husband and family and her whole household.

When she had started on her journey, she came to the 2
village near the city of Tours which is called Esvres, in which are preserved the relics of the blessed confessor Medardus of Soissons, and whose vigils were being celebrated

nocte celebrabantur. In quibus illa attente excubans in oratione, hora debita cum reliquo populo ad missarum accessit
3 solemnia. Quae cum a sacerdotibus Dei celebrantur, advenit quaedam puella, pusulae malae veneno conflata, proceditque ad pedes eius, dicens: "Subveni mihi, quia mors inique vitam conatur eripere!" At illa, more solito in oratione prostrata, suggessit pro ea Deo, omnium creatori, erectaque signum crucis imposuit. Sicque, in quattuor partes vulnere excrepante, puellam, pure decurrente, mors importuna reliquit.

4 Post haec ad basilicam sancti Martini Monegundis beata pervenit. Ibique prostrata coram sepulcro, gratias agens quod tumulum sanctum oculis propriis contemplari meruerat, in cellula parva consistens, quotidie orationi ac ieiuniis vigiliisque vacabat.

5 Sed nec ille locus ab eius virtute fuit inglorius. Nam viduae cuiusdam filia manus contractas detulit, quae, ut exorata signum salutis imposuit, manibus suis digitos puellae contrectare coepit, extensis digitis nervisque directis, volas laxavit incolumes.

6 Dum autem haec agerentur, audita vir eius fama beatae, convocans amicos vicinosque suos, perrexit post eam ac reduxit ad propria, et eam in cellulam in qua prius habitaverat intromisit. At illa non cessabat ab opere quod consueverat, sed exercebatur ieiuniis obsecrationibusque, ut tandem locum in quo habitare desiderabat posset acquirere.

that night. After having attended these in devout prayer, she
came at the proper hour with the rest of the people to the
solemn mass. While this was being celebrated by the priests, 3
a girl came in who was swollen with an infected pustule; she
threw herself at the blessed lady's feet and said: "Help me,
for wicked death is trying to snatch my life from me!" And
Monegund prostrated herself in prayer as she usually did
and interceded for her with God, the Creator of all things;
when she rose, she made the sign of the cross over the girl.
And so the pustule burst, splitting into four parts, and savage death left the girl as the pus flowed out.

After this the blessed Monegund arrived at the basilica of 4
the holy Martin. And there she prostrated herself before his tomb, gave thanks that she had deserved to see his holy grave with her own eyes, and went to stay in a small cell, devoting herself to daily prayers, fasts, and vigils.

This place too was glorified by her holy power. For the 5
daughter of a certain widow had deformed hands, and, when asked to do so, the blessed Monegund made the sign of the cross over them and began to stroke her fingers with her hands; lengthening them and straightening the tendons, she freed the palms so that they became healthy.

While these things were happening, her husband heard 6
of the blessed lady's reputation, called together his friends and neighbors and came to bring her back; he took her home and returned her to the cell she had previously inhabited. There she did not stop doing what she usually did, but engaged in fasts and prayers that she might finally be able to gain the place in which she wished to live.

7 Inchoat iterum iter desideratum, implorans beati Martini auxilium, ut qui dederat desiderium tribueret et effectum perveniendi ad basilicam. Revertitur in cellula illa in qua prius fuerat commorata; in ea perstitit inconcussa, nec est amplius a viro suo quaesita.

8 Ibique paucas colligens monachas, cum fide integra et
oratione degebat, non sumens panem nisi hordeaceum, non
vinum nisi parumper in diebus festis, et hoc ipsum nimio la-
tice temperatum. Nullum habens stratum feni paleaeque
mollimen, nisi tantum illud quod intextis virgulis fieri solet,
quas vulgo mattas vocant, hoc superponens formulae, hoc
9 solo supersternens. Hoc erat quotidianum scamnum, hoc
culcitra, hoc plumella, hoc erat stragulum, hoc omnis lectuli
necessitudo, sic docens easdem facere quas secum ascivit.
Ibique in Dei laudibus degens, multis infirmis, oratione
facta, salutaria impertiebat medicamenta.

3. Mulier quaedam filiam suam exhibuit vulneribus plenam, et, ut quidam vocant, potae haec causa genuerat. Tunc illa, facta oratione, salivam ex ore suscipiens, vulnera saeva perunxit, puellamque reddidit sanam, opitulante eius virtute qui caeci nati oculos sputo formavit.

2 Puer vero incola loci maleficium in potione hausit, de
quo medificatus, ut asserunt, serpentes generati in intraneis
pueri magnum dolorem suis morsibus excitabant, ita ut
nulla quiescendi mora vel in modicum momentum indulge-
retur. Sed neque cibum aut potum capere poterat; et si post
3 diu aliquid accipiebat, protinus reiciebat. Qui adductus ad

Thus she again began the desired journey, imploring the 7
blessed Martin's help, so that he who had given her the desire to arrive at his basilica would help her to achieve it. And
when she had reached the basilica, she returned to the cell
in which she had dwelled before; from thence onward she
stood fast there, unshaken, and was no longer sought by her
husband.

Collecting a few nuns there, she passed her days full of 8
faith and in assiduous prayer, eating only barley bread,
drinking wine only on feast days, and that even mixed with a
great deal of water. She did not have a soft mattress of hay or
straw, but only what is usually made by weaving twigs, what
people call "mats," and placing these on a bench or strewing
them on the floor. This was her daily seat, her mattress, her 9
pillow, her blanket, all that she needed for her bed, and she
taught those who joined her to do likewise. Devoting herself to the praises of God, she administered healing remedies to many sick persons through her prayers.

3 A certain woman brought her daughter covered with sores and, as some say, she was born this way because her mother was a prostitute. Then the blessed Monegund prayed, took saliva from her mouth, and anointed the cruel wounds with it, thereby healing the girl with the help of the power of Him who, with spittle, created eyes for the man born blind.

A boy, an inhabitant of the place, had ingested a noxious 2
substance in a drink by which, they say, he was poisoned,
and snakes were generated in his intestines that caused him
so much pain when they bit him that he could not sleep even
for a moment. Nor had he been able to take food or drink; if,
after a long time, he did, he vomited it up at once. He was 3

beatam feminam, petiit se eius virtute mundari. Cumque illa reclamaret indignam se esse quae haec agere posset, implicata precatu parentum, ventrem pueri palpat et palma demulcet; sensitque ibi anguium venenatorum nequitiam latitare. Tunc accepto pampini viridis folio, saliva linivit,
4 fixitque super eum crucis beatae signaculum. Quod ponens super alvum iuvenculi, dolore paululum sedato, obdormivit in scamno, qui olim doloribus insistentibus caruerat somno. Post unius vero horae momentum consurgens, ad purgandem ventrem egressus, pestiferae generationis germen effudit; gratiasque referens ancillae Dei, sanus abscessit.

5 Alius vero puer paralysis aegritudine contractus, ante eam inter manus delatus est aliorum, deprecans a beata sanari. At illa in oratione prostrata, precem pro eo fudit ad Dominum. Consummata vero oratione consurgens, apprehensa manu pueri erexit eum, sospitemque abire permisit.

6 Mulier erat caeca, quae adducta ad eam, deprecata est ut ei manus imponeret. At illa respondit: "Quid vobis et mihi, homines Dei? Nonne sanctus Martinus hic habitat, qui quotidie illustrium virtutum opere refulget? Illuc accedite, ibi obsecramini, ut ipse vos visitare dignetur. Nam ego pecca-
7 trix, quid faciam?" Illa vero, in sua petitione perdurans, aiebat: "Deus per omnes timentes nomen suum quotidie opus exercet egregium. Ideoque supplex ad te confugio, cui praestita est divinitus gratia curationum." Tunc commota Dei famula, luminibus sepultis manus imposuit. Statimque,

led to the blessed lady and asked her to heal him by her holy
power. Although she exclaimed that she was unworthy to do
this, she was deeply moved by the prayers of his parents and
massaged the boy's stomach; pressing down upon it with her
hands, she felt that the evil of the venomous snakes lurked
there. Then she took a green vine leaf, moistened it with saliva, and placed it upon him with the sign of the cross. When 4
it had been laid on the boy's stomach, the pain abated
slightly and he fell asleep on a bench, whereas up to then he
had not been able to sleep for constant pain. Arising after
one hour, he went out to purge his bowels and let out the
offspring of a deadly race; then he gave thanks to God's
handmaiden and left in good health.

Another boy, who had been deformed by paralysis, was 5
brought to her carried by others, begging to be healed by
the blessed lady. She prostrated herself in prayer, pouring
forth a request for him to the Lord. When she had finished
her prayer, she took the boy's hand, raised him up, and allowed him to go home healthy.

A blind woman who was led to her begged her to lay her 6
hands on her. And she replied: "What business do you have
with me, men of God? Doesn't the holy Martin live here,
who shines every day with illustrious deeds of power? Go to
his tomb, and there beg that he may deign to visit you. For
what can I, a sinner, do?" The woman, however, persisted in 7
her request and said: "God performs outstanding works every day through those who fear his name. Therefore I come
as a suppliant to you, to whom the grace of healing has been
divinely granted." Moved by this, the handmaiden of God
then put her hands on the woman's eyes that were buried.

reseratis cataractis, mundum late patentem quae fuerat caeca prospexit.

8 Multis etiam energumenis ad eam ingressis, ut manus imposuit, fugato hoste nequam, sospitatem restituit. Nec morabantur ex his curari, quos ad se sancta permisisset accedere.

4. Iam autem tempus vocationis eius appropinquabat, et defessa corpore solvebatur. Quod cum viderent sanctimoniales quas secum habebat, flebant valde, dicentes: "Et cui nos, mater sancta, relinquis? Vel cui commendas filias, quas
2 in locum hunc pro Dei intuitu congregasti?" At illa, parumper lacrimans, ait: "Si pacem sanctificationemque sequamini, Deus erit protectio vestra. Habebetisque sanctum Martinum antistitem pastorem magnum. Nam et ego non discedam a vobis, sed invocato adero in medio caritatis vestrae."

3 At illae rogabant dicentes: "Venturi sunt multi infirmi ad nos, flagitantes benedictionem a te accipere, et quid faciemus cum te non viderent esse superstitem? Confusae enim eos foris emittemus, cum tuam faciem non contemplabimur. Rogamus autem ut, quia haec ab oculis nostris absconditur, saltem digneris oleum salemque benedicere, de quo possimus aegrotis benedictionem flagitantibus ministrare." Tunc illa, benedicto oleo ac sale, tradidit eis, quae suscipientes diligentissime servaverunt.

4 Sicque beatissima obiit in pace, et sepulta est in ipsa cellula, multis se in posterum virtutibus repraesentans. Nam de memorata benedictione multi post eius transitum aegroti incolumitatis beneficia sunt experti.

And at once the cataracts were parted, and she who had been blind saw the world spread out before her.

Many possessed persons also came to her, and when she 8
put her hands on them, the evil Enemy was put to flight and she restored their health. Those whom the saint allowed to come to her were all cured quickly.

4. The time approached, however, when she was to be summoned and when she would be released from her exhausted body. When the nuns who lived with her saw this they wept loudly, saying; "To whose care, holy mother, do you leave us? To whom do you entrust your daughters whom
you gathered here to contemplate God?" And she, shedding 2
a few tears, said: "If you strive after peace and holiness, God will be your protection. And you will have the holy bishop Martin as your great shepherd. I too, however, shall not abandon you, but when called upon I shall be in your dear company."

But they made a request, saying: "Many sick people will 3
come to us, begging to receive a blessing from you, and what shall we do when they see you are no longer here? We would be embarrassed to send them away when we no longer contemplate your countenance. Since your face will be hidden from our eyes, we ask that you deign at least to bless oil and salt with which we can minister to the sick who beg for a blessing." Then she blessed the oil and salt and gave them to them; they received and kept them with great care.

And thus the most blessed one died in peace and was bur- 4
ied in her own cell, manifesting herself thereafter through many deeds of power. For after her passing many sick persons experienced the benefit of health through the aforementioned blessing.

5 Bosonis denique diaconi pes unus a pusula mala conflaverat, ita ut gressum facere non valeret. Deportatusque ad eius tumulum, orationem fudit. Puellae vero accipientes ex oleo memorato, quod sancta reliquerat, posuerunt super pedem eius et, extemplo erumpente vulnere, defluente veneno, sanatus est.

6 Caecus quidam adductus ad eius tumulum in oratione
prosternitur. Irruente autem in eum sopore, obdormivit,
apparuitque ei beata dicens: "Indignam quidem me iudico
exaequari sanctis, sed tamen unius hic oculi recipies lumen.
Deinceps autem propera quantocius ad beati pedes Martini,
et prosternere in compunctione animi coram eo. Ipse enim
7 tibi restituet alterius oculi visionem." Expergefactus homo,
unius oculi recepto lumine, abiit quo iussio impulit imperantis. Ibique iterum obsecrans beati confessoris virtutem, depulsa caeci oculi nocte, videns abscessit.

8 Mutus etiam ad hunc beatae tumulum prostratus accubuit, qui in tantum fide compunctus est, ut rivis lacrimarum cellulae inficeret pavimentum. Qui consurgens absoluta lingua virtute divina regressus est.

9 Alius denique mutus veniens, et in oratione decumbens, corde tantum implorabat, et non voce solubili, beatae feminae auxilium. In cuius ore de memorata benedictione parte infusa, erumpente sanguine mixto cum pure, vocis officium meruit adipisci.

CHAPTER 19

One of deacon Boso's feet was swollen with pustules so 5
that he could not walk. When he had been carried to her
tomb, he poured forth a prayer. Then the nuns took some of
the above-mentioned oil that the saint had left behind and
put it on his foot, and the pustule at once erupted, the poison flowed out, and he was cured.

A certain blind man who had been led to her tomb pros- 6
trated himself in prayer. Drowsiness crept up on him, he fell
asleep, and the blessed lady appeared to him, saying: "I consider myself unworthy of equality with the saints, nevertheless you will receive the light of one eye here. After this,
however, hasten as fast as you can to the blessed feet of Martin and prostrate yourself in compunction before him. For
he will restore the sight of your other eye." When the man 7
woke up, one of his eyes had received light, and he went
where he had been commanded to go. There again when he
begged for the power of the blessed confessor, the dark
night of his blind eye was expelled, and he left able to see.

A mute man lay prostrated before the tomb of the blessed 8
lady, and he had so much compunction and faith that
streams of his tears moistened the floor of the cell. When he
arose and departed, his tongue was released by divine power.

Another mute man came and lay praying, imploring the 9
blessed lady's help with his heart alone, because he was unable to do so with his impaired voice. When some of the
aforesaid blessed oil had been poured into his mouth, blood
mixed with pus burst out, and he was worthy to regain the
use of his voice.

10 Frigoriticus quoque accedens ad hoc monumentum, ut pallam tegentem attigit, restincta contagionis febre, convaluit.

11 Contractus vero, Marcus nomine, manibus deportatus aliorum ad sepulcrum beatae, orationem diutissime fudit. Hora autem nona pedibus propriis stetit, domumque regressus est.

12 Leodinus puer cum in valetudinem gravem irruens quarto aegrotaret mense, et non solum gressum, verum etiam ciborum usum, insistente febre nimia, perdidisset, ad eius deportatus sepulcrum praemortuus, accepta salute surrexit e tumulo redivivus.

13 Quid de frigoriticis reliquis loquar, cum plerisque hoc fuit beneficium remedii, cum pallam tumuli eius sunt fideliter osculati? Quid etiam de energumenis, qui adducti ad cellulam beatae, cum limen sanctum fuerint ingressi, integrae menti restituuntur? Nec moratur larva egredi e corpore, cum sanctae huius senserit adesse virtutem, operante hoc Domino nostro Iesu Christo, qui timentibus nomen suum praemia largitur aeterna.

A fever-stricken man also came to the tomb, and when he touched the cloth covering it, the fever of the illness was extinguished, and he recovered. 10

A deformed man named Marcus was carried in the hands of others to the tomb of the blessed lady, and for a long time poured forth prayer. At the ninth hour he stood up on his own feet and returned home. 11

A boy called Leodinus had lapsed into a grave illness, was sick for four months and lost not only his ability to walk but also to take in food because of the continuous high fever; when he had been carried to her tomb in a state near to death, he received his health and arose at the tomb, restored to life. 12

What shall I say about the other fever-stricken ones for whom the remedy came when full of faith they kissed the cover of her tomb? What about the possessed who, when led to the blessed lady's cell, were restored to their right minds when they crossed the holy threshold? The demon hastened to leave the body when it sensed the presence of this holy lady's power through the working of our Lord Jesus Christ, who grants eternal rewards to those who fear his name. 13

20

De sancto Leobardo reclauso in Maiori Monasterio prope Turonum

Prologus

Ecclesia fidelis aedificatur quotiescumque sanctorum gesta devotissime replicantur. Et licet de his teneat maximum gaudium, quod hi qui ab initio aetatis religiosam vitam ducentes pervenire meruerunt perfectionis ad portum, tamen et de his, Domino iubente, laetatur, qui conversi a saeculo opus inchoatum valuerunt perducere, divina opitulante misericordia, ad effectum.

1. Igitur beatissimus Leobardus Arvernici territorii indigena fuit, genere quidem non senatorio, ingenuo tamen, qui ab initio Deum in pectore tenens, cum floreret natalibus, gloriosis meritis praefulgebat. Qui tempore debito cum reliquis pueris ad scholam missus, quaepiam de Psalmis memoriae commendavit, et nesciens se clericum esse futurum, iam ad dominicum parabatur innocens ministerium.

2 Sed cum ad legitimam pervenisset aetatem, cogentibus iuxta consuetudinem humanam parentibus ut arrham puellae, quasi uxorem accepturus, daret impellitur. Illo quoque

20

About the holy recluse Leobard in the monastery of Marmoutier near Tours

Prologue

The faithful Church is edified whenever the deeds of the saints are devoutly recounted. And although the greatest joy comes from those who have lived a religious life from their childhood and deserved to reach the port of perfection, at the Lord's command the Church also rejoices in those who turn away from the world and are able to carry on and complete the work they began with the help of the divine compassion.

1. The most blessed Leobard, who was born in the territory of Clermont to a family that although not senatorial was nevertheless of free birth, carried God in his heart from the beginning; and although he flourished through his parents' status, he also was distinguished by his own glorious merits. Sent to school at the appropriate age with other boys, he learned parts of the Psalms by heart, not knowing that he would be a cleric someday but unwittingly already preparing for the ministry of the Lord.

But when he reached the age of majority he was urged by 2
his parents, according to human custom, to offer a pledge to a girl to accept her as his wife. When he refused to do this,

respuente, ait pater: "Cur, dulcissime fili, voluntatem paternam respuis, nec te iungere vis connubio, ut semen excites nostro de genere saeculis sequentibus profuturum? Casso enim labore exercemur ad operandum si possessor deerit ad
3 fruendum. Quare implemus domum opibus, si de genere nostro non processerit qui utatur? Quid de mancipia dato pretio nostris ditionibus subiugamus, si rursum alienis debent dominationibus subiacere? Obedire debere filios voci parentum Scripturae testantur divinae. Et tu cum inoboediens esse parentibus probaris, vide ne te caelestibus eruere nequeas ab offensis!"

4 Haec patre loquente, licet haberet alium filium, facile tamen tali aetatulae persuasit voluntati propriae contraire. Denique, dato sponsae anulo, porrigit osculum, praebet calciamentum, celebrat sponsaliae diem festum. Interea genitor et genitrix mortis somno sopiti migraverunt a saeculo, vitae praesentis curriculo iam peracto.

5 Hic vero, cum germano tempore luctus expleto, oneratus donis nuptialibus, fratris pergit ad domum. Quem in tantum reperit vino madidum, ut nec cognosceret, nec reciperet propria in domo germanum. Ille vero, suspirans et lacrimans, secessit in partem, venitque ad tugurium in quo fenum fuerat aggregatum, ibique colligato praebens equiti pabulum, decubuit super fenum ad quiescendum.

6 Expergefactus autem media nocte, surgit de stratu suo, erectisque ad caelum manibus, gratias agere coepit omnipotenti Deo, quod esset, quod viveret, quod aleretur donis

his father said: "Why do you reject your father's wish, dearest son and why do you not want to unite yourself in marriage, so that you produce offspring to continue our family line in future times? For we work in vain if there be no
one to possess and enjoy the results. Why should we fill our 3
house with luxuries if they will not be used by anyone from our family? Why should we subject slaves, bought for a price, to our authority if they will have to submit to the rule of strangers? Scripture testifies that sons should obey the voice of their parents. And when you prove yourself disobedient to your parents, beware of being unable to escape heavenly punishments!"

Since his father spoke in this manner, although he had an- 4
other son, it was easy for him to persuade someone of that tender age to go against what his own heart's desire. Thus, in the end, Leobard gave the ring of engagement, offered the kiss and the gift of the shoe, and celebrated the feast of his betrothal. After this, his father and mother were overtaken by the sleep of death and passed on from this world, having completed the course of their present life.

When Leobard and his brother had completed their 5
mourning, he went to his brother's house laden with wedding gifts. But he found him so drunk with wine that he did not recognize Leobard and would not let his own brother into his house. Leobard, sighing and weeping, withdrew and came to a barn where hay had been stored; after tying up his horse and giving it food, he lay down on the hay to sleep.

In the middle of the night he awoke, arose from his 6
bed and, stretching his hands out to heaven, began to give thanks to God that he was, that he lived, that he was being

eius, et alia huiuscemodi prosecutus. Cum suspiria longa protraheret, atque lacrimis crebris genas ubertim rigaret, Deus omnipotens, qui illos quos praescivit et "praedestinavit conformes fieri imaginis Filii sui" [Romans 8:29], compunxit cor eius ut relicto saeculo manciparetur ad cultum divinum.

2. Tunc ille, quasi iam sacerdos custosque animae suae, praedicare sibi ipsi exorsus est, dicens: "Quid agis, anima? Quid in ambiguo suspensa teneris? Vanum est enim saeculum, vanae sunt concupiscentiae eius, vana gloria mundi, et ea quae in illo sunt 'omnia vanitas' [Ecclesiastes 1:2]. Melius est igitur relinquere eum et sequi Dominum, quam ad eius opera praebere consensum."

2 Haec effatus, cum diem terris reddere lux diurna coepisset, ascenso equite coepit ad hospitium suum reverti. Cumque per viam iam alacris pergeret, volvere intra se coepit quid ageret, quo abiret, dixitque: "Expetam Martini beati tumulum, unde procedit virtus alma super infirmos. Credo enim quod et mihi eius oratio iter reserabit ad Deum qui, deprecatus Dominum, mortuos reduxit a Tartaro."

3 Et sic viam carpens, oratione comite, sancti Martini basilicam est ingressus. Circa quam paucis diebus demoratus, transito amne, ad cellulam Maiori monasterio propinquam, de qua Alaricus quidam recesserat, devotus accesserat. Ibique se, propriis manibus membranas faciens, ad scribendum aptavit; ibi se, ut Scripturas sanctas intelligeret ac Davidici

nourished by his gifts, and continued in this vein for a long time. As he drew long sighs and wet his cheeks abundantly with frequent tears, almighty God, who foreknows those whom he has "predestined to be conformed to the image of his Son," reached into his heart by inspiring him to leave the world and join himself to the service of God.

2. Then, as though already a priest and the guardian of his soul, he began to preach to himself, saying: "What are you doing, my soul? Why do you hold yourself suspended in doubt? For the world is empty, empty are its desires, empty its glory, and 'all that is in it is empty.' Therefore it is better to leave it and follow the Lord than to consent to the works of the world."

When he had said this, and the light of day began to re- 2
turn to the earth, he mounted his horse and began to return to his home. And as he rode excitedly over the road, he began to turn over in his mind what he should do, where he should go, and he said: "I shall go to the tomb of the blessed Martin, from which life-giving power emanates over the sick. For I believe that the prayer of him who, after praying to the Lord, retrieved the dead from the underworld, will open my way to God."

And so he traveled, praying all the way, and entered the 3
holy Martin's basilica. Having stayed there for a few days, he crossed the river and devoutly came to the cell near the monastery of Marmoutier where a certain Alaric had lived. There he busied himself with writing and preparing the skins with his own hands; and, so that he might understand the holy Scriptures and the Psalms of David which he had

carminis psalmos, qui dudum excesserant memoriae, retine-
4 ret, exercuit. Sicque divinarum Scripturarum lectionibus
eruditus, cognovit verum esse quod ei Dominus prius inspi-
ravit in corde. Sed, ne haec cuiquam fabulosa videantur quae
retulimus, testor Deum quia ab ipsius benedicti Leobardi
haec ore cognovi.

5 At vero, interposito pauci temporis spatio, humilem se
tantumque praebuit ut honoraretur ab omnibus. Accepto
sarculo, cellulam in quam ingressus fuerat, incidens lapidem,
ampliavit. In qua cellula delectabatur ieiuniis, oratione,
psallentio, lectione; nec umquam a divinis officiis et oratione cessabat. Scribebat interdum, ut se a cogitationibus
noxiis discuteret.

3. Interea, ut se Temptator manifestaret Dei servis semper inimicum ac invidum, cum aliquis de illius monachulis
litem quendam cum vicinis habuisset, immisit ei cogita-
2 tionem, ut, relicta cellula illa, ad aliam transmigraret. Cumque ibi ad orationem solite devenissemus, dolum nobis veneni grassantis aperuit. Ego vero suspirans non minimo
dolore, increpare hominem coepi, asserens diaboli esse cal-
liditatem. Librosque ei et *Vitas Patrum* ac *Institutionem monachorum,* vel quales qui recluduntur esse debeant, vel cum
quali cautela monachos vivere oporteat, abscedens ab eo direxi.

3 Quibus relectis, non solum cogitationem pravam a se dis-
cussit, verum etiam tanto sensu acumine erudivit, ut miramur facundiam locutionis eius. Erat enim dulcis alloquio,
blandus hortatu, eratque ei sollicitudo pro populis, inquisi-
tio pro regibus, oratio assidua pro omnibus ecclesiasticis

long forgotten, he trained himself to memorize them. And 4
when he had in this way been taught through reading the divine Scriptures, he knew that what the Lord had earlier inspired in his heart was true. Lest anyone think that what we are telling is invented, I call God to witness that I learned this from the lips of the blessed Leobard himself.

And he conducted himself so humbly that, after a short 5
time, he was honored by all. He took a pickax and hewed out the stone to enlarge the cell in which he had come to live. In this cell he delighted in fasts, prayer, singing psalms, and reading; he never desisted from the divine office and prayer. From time to time he wrote, to repel harmful thoughts.

3. However, since the Tempter always shows himself hostile toward, and envious of, the servants of God, he used the occasion of a quarrel which one of Leobard's monks had with his neighbors to put the thought into his head to leave
that cell and go to another one. When we had come there 2
for our usual prayer, he revealed to us the deceit of the poison growing in his heart. Sighing with great sadness, I began to reproach the fellow, saying it was a trick of the devil. And when I had left, I sent him the books of *The Lives of the Fathers* and *The Monks' Institutions,* about how those in seclusion should conduct themselves, and about the caution with which monks ought to live.

When he had read these, not only did he repel the wicked 3
thoughts from his mind, but developed his understanding of these matters so acutely that the ease with which he spoke about them astonished us. For he was affable in speaking and kind in his advice, and he cared for the people, advised kings, and prayed assiduously for all the clerics who feared

Deum timentibus. Verumtamen non ille, ut quidam, dimissis capillorum flagellis aut barbarum demissione plaudebat, sed certo tempore capillum tondebat et barbam.

4 In qua cellula viginti et duos annos in hoc opere degens, tanta Domini gratia confortatus est, ut pusulis malis saliva oris sui perunctus, vim veneni saevientis opprimeret, frigoriticis vero per poculum vini charactere crucis beatae sanctificatum, frigorem accedentem aestumque restinxit, non immerito discutiens incommodas febres ab aliis, qui in se exstinxerat incentiva criminis noxialis.

5 Quodam autem tempore caecus ad eum veniens, ae-
rumnam doloris sui humiliter deplorabat, ac deposcebat ut
tactu dexterae suae sanctus lumina clausa palparet. Quod
ille diutissime renuens, tandem fletibus hominis victus, misericordia motus, cum per triduum pro eo orationem fudisset ad Dominum, quarta die imponens manum super oculos
eius, ait: "Domine omnipotens, Fili unigenite Dei Patris, qui
cum eo ac Spiritu sancto regnas in saecula, qui homini a nativitate caeco reddidisti lucem beati oris sputo, tu redde
huic famulo tuo luminis visum, ut cognoscat quia tu es Do-
6 minus omnipotens." Et haec dicens, ut crucem super oculos
caeci depinxit, mox, pulsis tenebris, lucem de praesenti restituit. Huius virtutis testimonio Eustachius abba astipula-
tor astitit.

4. Denique hic de labore lapidis submontani, quam assidue caedebat, confractus, ieiunii austeritate confectus, oratione indeficienti corroboratus, coepit paulatim corporis

God. And he was not, as some are, one who congratulated himself by letting his hair and beard grow long, but at certain times cut his hair and his beard.

He remained in this cell doing this for twenty-two years 4
and was rewarded with so much grace of the Lord that he overcame the force of savage poison when he anointed malignant pustules with saliva from his mouth, and extinguished the onset of heat and chills in the fever-stricken with a cup of wine sanctified by the sign of the cross; and not undeservedly did he expel incapacitating fevers from others, since he had extinguished urges to commit harmful crimes in himself.

A blind man once came to him, humbly complaining of 5
his adversity and pain and asking the saint to touch his eyes with his right hand. Although he kept on refusing to do it, he was in the end overcome by the man's weeping and moved by compassion, and when he had poured forth a prayer to the Lord for this man for three days, on the fourth he put his hand on his eyes and said: "Almighty Lord, Only Son of God the Father, who with him and with the Holy Spirit reigns forever, who gave light to the man born blind with the spittle of your blessed mouth, give this servant of yours the sight of his eyes, so that he may know that you are
the almighty Lord." Saying this, he made the sign of the 6
cross over the blind man's eyes, and at once the darkness was driven away, and light immediately returned. The testimony of this deed of power is backed up by Abbot Eustochius, who was present.

4. In the end, broken by his assiduous hewing of the stone in the cave and weakened by the austerity of his fasts, although strengthened by his unceasing prayers, he slowly

infirmitate destitui. Quadam autem die, dum nimium fessus haberetur, nos ad se vocari praecepit. Ad quem accedentes, postquam funeris sui necessitatem deflevit, eulogias a nobis
2 peccatoribus flagitavit. Quibus acceptis, hausto mero, ait: "Tempus meum iam impletur, iubente Domino, ut me ab huius corporis vinculis iubeat relaxari, sed adhuc paucis diebus erit spatium. Verumtamen ante diem sanctum Paschae vocandus ero."

3 O beatum virum, qui sic servivit Creatori omnium, ut suum obitum revelatione divina cognosceret! Erat enim mensis decimus quando haec est effatus. Duodecimo autem mense coepit iterum graviter aegrotare. Advenit dies dominica, vocat ministrum suum, et ait: "Praepara quiddam cibi quod accipiam, quia valde defessum me sentio." Illo quoque respondente: "Praesto est, domine," ait ad eum: "Egredere foras, et aspice si iam, celebratis solemnibus, populus de
4 missis egreditur." Hoc autem dicebat, non quod cibum capere vellet, sed ut transitus sui nullus testis adesset. Quo egrediente et revertente, cum ingressus fuisset cellulam, invenit virum Dei extensum corpore, clausis oculis spiritum exhalasse. Unde factum manifestum est eum ab angelis susceptum, qui hominem adesse noluit suum sacer heros ad transitum.

5 Haec cernens minister ille, elevavit vocem in fletu, sicque concurrentibus reliquis fratribus; ablutus ac vestimentis dignis indutus, in sepulcro quod ipse sibi in antedicta cellula sculpserat reconditus est, quem in consortio sanctorum ascitum nulli fidelium haberi reor incertum.

began to lose his life forces through the infirmity of his body. One day when he was extremely tired, he ordered us to be called to him. Having come to him, after he had mourned the fact that he would need a funeral, he begged us, sinners
that we were, to give him communion. Having received this 2
and drunk the wine, he said: "My time has now come: the Lord's command orders me to be released from the chains of this body, but there are still a few days left. I shall be called, however, on the day before holy Easter."

O blessed man who served the Creator of all things in 3
such a manner that he could know his own death through a divine revelation! For it was the tenth month when he said this. In the twelfth month he again began to become ill. When Sunday came, he called his servant and said: "Prepare some food for me to eat, for I feel very weak." And when the servant replied: "I am ready to serve you, master," he said to him: "Go outside, then, and see if the solemnities have already been celebrated and the people are coming out from
mass." He said this, however, not because he wanted to take 4
food but because he wished no one to witness his passing. The servant went out, and when he came back and entered the cell he found the man of God lying full length, his eyes closed, having breathed out his spirit. Hence it is clear that he was taken up by angels, for the holy hero did not want any man to be present at his passing.

Seeing this, the servant raised his voice in weeping, and 5
so the other brothers came running; when he had been washed and clothed in worthy robes, he was buried in the tomb which he himself had sculpted in the aforesaid cell, and that he was admitted to the company of the saints will not, I think, be doubted by any of the faithful.

THE MIRACLES OF THE MARTYR JULIAN

Prologus

Magnum in nobis quodammodo igniculum ad iustitiae suae adipiscendam semitam pietas divina succendit cum dicit: "Oculi Domini super iustos, et aures eius ad preces eorum" [Psalms 33:15], ostendens quod qui iustitiam ex toto corde dilexerit, cum deprecatus fuerit, audiatur a Domino. Utinam quisque nostrum, cum haec cantare coeperit, statim—spretis mundi scandalis, neglectis concupiscentiis vanis, derelictisque semitis pravis—iustitiae viam expeditus et sine impedimento saecularium actionum conaretur ir-
2 repere! Per hanc enim viam Abel iustus suscipitur, Enoch beatus assumitur, Noe reservatur, Abraham eligitur, Isaac benedicitur, Iacob dilatatur, Ioseph custoditur, Moyses sanctificatur, David praedestinatur, Salomon ditatur, tres pueri inter incendia rorulenta vaticinantur, Daniel inter innocuas bestias pascitur. Per hanc viam apostoli diriguntur,
3 martyres glorificantur. "Et qualiter?" inquis. Scilicet dum infirma curant, mortuos suscitant, praesentia contemnunt, futura desiderant, tortores despiciunt, poenas non sentiunt, ad caelestia regna contendunt; quod procul dubio virtute propria non obtinerent nisi, per viam iustitiae rectissime incedentes, a Domino audirentur.

Prologue

God's love somehow kindles in us a flame of desire to
enter upon the path of his justice when he says "The eyes
of the Lord are upon the just, and his ears inclined toward
their prayers," showing that whoever has loved righteousness with his whole heart will be heard by the Lord when he
prays. Would that each one of us, when beginning to sing
these words, would at once reject the world's stumbling
blocks, ignore vain desires, abandon depraved ways of life,
and be ready to strive to walk in the path of righteousness
free from the baggage of worldly concerns! For by following 2
this path Abel is acknowledged as just, the blessed Enoch is
taken up by God, Noah is saved, Abraham is chosen, Isaac
is blessed, Jacob becomes powerful, Joseph is protected,
Moses is sanctified, David is predestined, Solomon is made
rich, the three young men in the bedewing fire prophesy,
and Daniel is fed among predatory beasts that do not harm
him. By following this path the apostles too are guided, and
the blessed martyrs are glorified. "And how, then?" you ask. 3
By healing the sick, raising the dead, rejecting the present,
longing for the future, despising torturers and not feeling
their torments, while they hasten to reach the heavenly
kingdoms; doubtless, they would not have attained this by
their own strength unless, while advancing with the utmost
rectitude in the path of justice, they had been heard and acknowledged by the Lord.

I

De passione sancti Juliani martyris

Sic et inclutus martyr Iulianus, qui Viennensi ortus urbe Arvernis datus est martyr, ab hoc igne succensus, haec concupivit ac mente tota desideravit. Quia cum esset apud beatissimum Ferreolum iam tunc martyrii odore flagrabat. Qui relictis divitiis ac propinquis, tantum ob solius amorem martyrii Arvernum advenit. Sed nec hoc sine divino mandato peregit, cum tunc persecutio in Viennensi urbe ferveret. Legerat enim Dominum praedixisse: "Si vos persecuti fuerint in ista civitate, fugite in aliam" [Matthew 10:23].

2 Contulit ergo se hic in Arvernum territorium, non metu mortis, sed ut, relinquens propria, facilius perveniret ad palmam; metuebat enim ne ei parentes essent obvii, si inter eos hoc certamen iniisset, et perderet miles Christi coronam gloriae, si legitime non certasset. Igitur instante persecutione, ad Brivatensem vicum, in quo fanatici erroris neniae colebantur, advenit.

3 Et cum insequi adversarios nutu Dei sensisset, a vidua quadam se occuli deprecatur. Quem illa tegens, illico, martyre poscente, detexit; qui suis insecutoribus ita infit:

I

The suffering of the holy martyr Julian

So too the renowned martyr Julian, who though born in the city of Vienne, was granted to Clermont as a martyr, ablaze with this flame, fervently desired to attain these things, and longed for them with his whole heart. For already when he was staying with the most blessed Ferreolus he burned for the fragrance of martyrdom. He left his possessions and his relatives behind to come to Clermont for the love of martyrdom alone. Since, at that time, persecution also raged in the city of Vienne, he did not do this without divine sanction. For he had read the Lord's prediction: "If you are persecuted in one town, flee to another."

Therefore he went to the region of Clermont, not for fear 2
of death, but so that, leaving his homeland behind, he might more easily attain the victor's palm; for he feared that his relatives would try to prevent him if he entered this contest while among them, and that as a soldier of Christ he might lose the crown of glory if he had not fought properly. When the persecution had begun, therefore, he went to the village of Brioude, where mad, misguided pagan nonsense was being worshipped.

And when, at God's warning, he became aware that his 3
enemies were looking for him, he asked a certain widow to hide him. Although she was concealing him, she revealed him immediately at his own request; for he addressed his

"Nolo," inquit, "diutius commorari in hoc saeculo, quia sitio
4 tota animi aviditate iam Christum." At illi eductam vibranti dextera frameam, deciso capite, in tres, ut ita dicam, partes, gloriosus dividitur martyr. Nam caput Viennam defertur, artus Brivate reconduntur, felix anima a Christo conditore suscipitur. Senes quoque, qui sacrosanctum corpus mancipaverant sepulturae, ita redintegrati sunt ut in senectute summa positi tamquam iuvenes haberentur.

5 Caput quoque eius Ferreolus martyr accepit, completoque certamine, tam illius membra quam istius caput in unius tumuli receptaculo collocantur. Quod ne cuiquam fortassis videatur incredibilis esse narratio, quae audivi gesta fideliter prodam.

2

De revelatione capitis eius

Quodam autem tempore, dum ad occursum beati Nicetii antistitis usque Lugdunum processissem, libuit animo, non aliter nisi orationis causa, Viennam adire et praecipue sepulcrum visitare Ferreoli martyris gloriosi; insederat enim menti, propter antiquam dilectionem eorum, me sic esse

pursuers thus, saying: "I do not wish to linger in this world any longer, because I already thirst for Christ with the all my soul." And they, brandishing their unsheathed swords with 4
their right hands, cut off his head, dividing the glorious martyr, so to speak, into three parts. For his head was taken to Vienne, his body was laid to rest in Brioude, and his blessed soul was received by Christ, his Maker. And the elders, who consigned his sacred body to the grave, were so restored by this experience that, although they were very old, they could be taken for young men.

The martyr Ferreolus acquired his head, and when he had 5
completed his own contest of martyrdom, his body and Julian's head were placed together in the confines of one monument. Lest perhaps the following narration seem incredible to anyone, I shall make known his deeds exactly as I heard them.

2

About the revelation of his head

Once, when I was journeying to Lyons to meet the blessed Nicetius, I felt the desire to go to Vienne, to pray there and above all to visit the tomb of the glorious martyr Ferreolus; for, because of their ancient friendship, I had regarded myself as his foster son as much

2 eius alumnum ut Iuliani. Denique, oratione facta, erigo oculorum aciem ad tribunal, conspicioque in eo versiculos hoc modo conscriptos:

> "Heroas Christi geminos haec continet aula;
> Iulianum capite, corpore Ferreolum."

3 Cumque haec legens, aedituum consulerem, cur haec scripta sic fuerint, respondit: "Basilica sancti martyris Ferreoli super ipsum Rhodani litus ab antiquis fuerat collocata. Denique cum, impulsante violentia amnis, porticus, quae ab ea parte erat locata, corrueret, providus sacerdos, Mamertus nomine, qui tunc Viennensem regebat ecclesiam, ruinam futuram praeveniens, aliam basilicam eleganti opere et in ipsa mensura sagaci intentione construxit, illuc sancti martyris transferre cupiens corpus.

4 "Advenit autem ad hoc opus abbatum atque monachorum magnus numerus, vigilataque nocte, accepto sarculo, fodere coeperunt. Cumque in profundum descenderent, tria sepulcra reperiunt, ac confestim stupor mentes spectantium invadit: nec quisquam erat certus quisnam esset beati martyris tumulus.

5 "Igitur, cum starent omnes in hebetate mentis attoniti, inspirante, ut credo, Divinitate, unus ex circumstantibus exclamat, dicens: 'Antiquitus referri solitum erat, et celebri per populos sermone vulgatum, caput Iuliani martyris in sepulcro retineri martyris Ferreoli. Si opertorio amoto unusquisque consideretur, potest, quae sint membra Ferreoli martyris, protinus inveniri.'

as Julian's. When I had finished my prayer, I looked up at the raised platform and saw on it verses written as follows: 2

"This hall contains two heroes of Christ:
Julian, present through his head, and Ferreolus, through his body."

When I had read this, I asked the custodian why these things had been written, and he replied: "From ancient times, the church of the holy martyr Ferreolus had been located on the bank of the river Rhône. Later, when the forecourt situated there crumbled before the violent impetus of the water, the prudent Bishop Mamertus who then governed the church of Vienne anticipated the future collapse of the rest of the church and wisely built another church of equal size and elegant workmanship, to which he wished to transfer the body of the holy martyr. 3

"To carry this out, a large number of abbots and monks came, and after a night spent in vigils, they were given hoes and began to dig. When they had reached a certain depth, they found three sarcophagi, and immediately the onlookers froze: for no one knew which one belonged to the blessed martyr. 4

"Thus, while all stood around in speechless bewilderment, one of those present (as I believe, inspired by God) cried out saying: 'In ancient times, they used to say, and this celebrated saying has become common knowledge among the people, that the head of the martyr Julian was enclosed in the sarcophagus of the martyr Ferreolus. If the covers are removed and each one is inspected, it will be possible to discover at once which body is that of the martyr Ferreolus.' 5

6 "Haec audiens sacerdos, cunctos iubet in oratione prosterni. Qua impleta, procedit ad tumulos, detectosque duos, singulos in iis quiescentes invenit viros. Cumque aperuisset et tertium, invenit in eo virum iacentem illaeso corpore, integro vestimento, qui, deciso capite, caput amplexus aliud brachio retinebat. Erat enim ac si nuper sepultus, neque pallore faciei demutatus, neque capillorum decisione turpatus, neque ulla putredine resolutus, sed ita integer et illaesus ut putares eum adhuc sopore corporeo detineri.

7 "Tunc antistes, gaudio magno repletus, ait: 'Hoc esse cadaver Ferreoli, hoc esse caput Iuliani martyris, dubium non habetur.' Tunc cum magno psallentio, plaudente populo, in loco ubi nunc adoratur, Domino annuente, perducitur." Haec autem, ut ad sepulcrum martyris ab ipso aedituo cognovi, fideliter retuli.

8 Praebet tamen huic operi testimonium Sollius noster, ipsi Mamerto scribens his verbis: "Tibi soli concessa est in partibus orbis occidui martyris Ferreoli solida translatio, adiecto nostri capite Iuliani. Unde pro compensatione deposcimus ut nobis inde veniat pars patrocinii, quia vobis hinc rediit pars patroni."

"When the bishop had heard this, he commanded all present to prostrate themselves in prayer. When this was done, he went to the sarcophagi, opened up two of them, and found only a single man reposing in each of them. When he opened the third sarcophagus too, he found lying in it a man with an uncorrupted body and intact clothes, whose own head had been cut off, but who held another head cradled in his arm. It was as though he had been buried recently, not disfigured by a deathly pale face or disgraced by the loss of his hair, nor had his body decomposed or putrefied; it was so whole and undamaged that you might think he was still held fast in bodily sleep. 6

"At that moment, the bishop, overjoyed, said: 'That this is the corpse of Ferreolus and this the head of the martyr Julian cannot be doubted.' Thereupon, with God's approval, he was carried, with much psalm singing and clapping by the people, to the place where it is now venerated." I have related these things precisely as I learned about them from the custodian at the tomb of the martyr. 7

Our Sollius gives evidence supporting this account when he wrote the following words to that same Mamertus: "In the western part of the world, the translation of the whole body of the martyr Ferreolus, with the addition of the head of our Julian, has been granted to you alone. For this reason we beg that, as compensation, a portion of his patronage should come from your city to ours, for a part of our patron has been taken hence to you." 8

3

De virtute fontis, ubi caput eius ablutum est

In loco autem illo, quo beatus martyr percussus est, fons habetur splendidus, lenis, dulcibus aquis uberrimus, in quo et a persecutoribus caput amputatum ablutum est; de quibus aquis multae sanitates tribuuntur infirmis.

2 Nam saepe caecorum oculi ab his tacti illuminati sunt, tertianarum quartanarumque febrium ardore accensi, ut potati qui patiuntur fuerint, conquiescunt. Nam et si quis gravi laborans incommodo, inspirante martyre, desiderium habuerit hauriendi, protinus ut hauserit convalescit; et ita velociter exstinguitur vis febrium ceu si videas super immensum rogum, proiectis undis, incendia universa restingui.

3

About the power of the spring in which his head was washed

In the very place where the blessed martyr was beheaded there is a sparkling and gentle spring, overflowing with sweet water, in which his head was washed after his persecutors had severed it; many cures are granted to the sick by means of its water.

For often, when the blind have moistened their eyes with 2
it, they are given back their sight, and those burning with the heat of tertian and quartan fevers are relieved of their suffering when they have drunk from it. Thus whoever is suffering from a grave illness, and inspired by the martyr feels the desire to drink, recovers as soon as he has done so. In this way, the violence of the fever diminishes as quickly as if one were seeing all of the fire of a huge burning funeral pyre extinguished by waves of water thrown over it.

4

De senibus et matrona cuius vir carcere tenebatur

Post passionem vero beati martyris, ac fama praeeunte de senibus, qui, dum sanctos artus sepulturae mandarent, fortitudini pristinae fuerint restituti, multa ibi beneficia expetentes credentesque, indulgente martyre, consequuntur. De quibus pauca perstringenti deprecor veniam condonari, quod me minus vel idoneum vel peritum ad haec narranda cognosco, nec imbutum grammaticis artibus, nec litteris liberalibus eruditum; sed quid facio, quod impellit me amor patroni, ut nequeam silere?

2 Vinctus quidam a Hispaniis et carceri deditus, apud imperatorem Trevericum capitali diiudicatus sententia detinebatur. Quod coniux cognitum, dum tumulare viri membra festinat, ad Brivatensem vicum pervenit, repertosque viros, dum diversa studio intento rimaretur, cognoscit quid in eo loco vel de martyre, vel de senibus, fuerit gestum; fidelique insinuatione credens, ad sepulcrum beati martyris deliberat properare, ut causas suggerat, casus reseret, vel cunctum laborem sui doloris exponat. Asserentibus tum praeterea hominibus: "Absque dubio pollicemur, domina, tibi a

4

About the old men and the lady whose husband was in prison

After the blessed martyr's suffering and the dissemination of the report about the old men who were restored to their former strength when they committed the holy body to burial, many benefits followed those who sought them in the belief that they would be granted by the martyr. As I relate a few of these, I beg indulgence, for I know that I am not in the least qualified or experienced enough to tell about these things, for I have neither been instructed in the arts of grammar nor educated in literary culture; but what am I to do, since my love for my patron impels me so strongly that I cannot be silent?

Someone who had been brought fettered from Spain and 2
put in prison was sentenced to death by the emperor at Trier. When she learned of this, his wife hastened there to bury his body and came through the village of Brioude; she encountered some men, and while turning over various plans in her mind, found out what had happened in that place to the martyr and to the old men. Believing the accuracy of their account, she decided to hasten to the blessed martyr's tomb to present her case, explain her misfortune, and reveal the whole burden of her grief. For the men had also said: "There can be no doubt, noble lady, that the

martyre reddi laetitiam, qui senum quondam decrepitae aetatis membra rigentia antiquo vigori restituit."

3 Impletaque hac oratione, promittit ut, si sospitem reciperet coniugem, martyris sepulcrum, in quo posset spatio, caemento contegeret. Fide plena et de martyris pietate secura, Treveris est ingressa, inventumque virum gratia imperiali receptum, laeta regreditur; inquisitumque tempus, quo vir relaxatus esset e carcere, haec fuit absolutionis hora, qua illa martyris est auxilium imprecata. Dehinc pollicitationem quam promiserat cum immensis muneribus adimplevit.

5

De eo qui alium in basilica occidere voluit

Erat autem haud procul a cellula quam supra sepulcrum martyris haec matrona construxerat grande delubrum, ubi in columnam altissimam simulacrum Martis Mercuriique colebatur. Cumque delubri illius festa a gentilibus agerentur, ac mortui mortuis thura deferrent, medio e vulgo commoventur pueri duo in scandalum, nudatoque unus gladio,

martyr, who once restored their pristine vigor to limbs that were stiffened with debilitating age, will restore your joy."

When she had finished her prayer, she promised that, 3
if she were to secure her husband's return unharmed, she would cover the martyr's tomb with a spacious stone vault. Full of faith and trusting in the martyr's benevolence, she went to Trier, found her husband restored to the emperor's grace, and traveled back joyfully; and when she inquired at what time her husband had been released from prison, she found that the hour of his release was the same as that at which she had implored the help of the martyr. After this, she fulfilled her promise with great gifts.

5

About the man who wanted to kill another man in a church

Not far from the small chapel that this matron had built over the martyr's sarcophagus, there was a large shrine where a statue of Mars and Mercury, on a very high pillar, was worshipped. While the pagans were celebrating their festivals there, the dead offering incense to the dead, two young men were moved to fight in the middle of the crowd, and one of these, unsheathing his sword, wanted to kill the

alterum appetit trucidandum. At ille cernens, nihil veniae reservari, cum a diis suis non defensaretur, nostrae religionis custodiam, nostrae confessionis veniam, nostrae contagionis medelam, cellulam expetiit martyris gloriosi.

2 Tunc ille qui sequebatur, cum in assultu gladii eum non potuisset attingere, et hic super se ostium reserasset, atque ille, arreptum utrumque postem, ostium conaretur infringere; illico adhaerentes manus tabulis, dolore maximo quatiuntur, et tante afflictione miser torquetur, ut ubertim fluentes lacrimae, qualis esset dolor intrinsecus, extrinsecus nuntiarent. Interea, stupente vulgo, inclusus qui fuerat progreditur liber; parentes quoque illius qui virtute sancti retinebatur, cognoscentes martyris sepulturam, devotis multis muneribus pro filio exorabant.

6

De conversione incolarum

Factum est autem, dum haec agerentur, ut presbyter quidam via illa descenderet. Qui cum didicisset quae acta fuerant, pollicetur parentibus ut, si a gentilitate discederent,

other. The other man, realizing that no mercy was forthcoming because he would not be protected by his own gods, ran to seek the protection of our religion, the mercy of our confession, the remedy for our sinfulness, that is, the chapel of the glorious martyr.

When the pursuer realized that he could not strike the 2
man with his sword, and that he had barred the door behind him, he seized the doorposts on both sides and tried to break the door down; but as soon as he touched the planks with his hands, both were struck with an intense pain, and the unhappy man was tortured with such an affliction that his streaming tears made visible on the outside what he was suffering inside. Meanwhile, as the astonished crowd watched, the man who had shut himself in came out free; and the parents of the man who had been restrained by the saint's power, recognizing the power of the martyr's tomb, prayed devoutly for their son and offered many gifts.

6

About the conversion of the inhabitants

While these events were taking place, however, a priest happened to come down the road. When he learned what had occurred, he promised the young man's parents that, if

filium reciperent sanum. Ipse quoque sacerdos, sequenti nocte, videt per somnium simulacra illa quae a gentilibus colebantur numine divino comminui atque in pulverem redacta solo prosterni.

2 Quarta autem die, cum gentilitas vellet iterum diis exhibere libamina, maestus presbyter ad sepulcrum sancti prosternitur, et cum lacrimis exorat, ut tandem gentilitatem hanc, quae iacebat in tenebris, splendor divinae potentiae visitaret, et nec sineret ultra martyr beatus alumnos proprios ista caligine detineri, cum ille perennis claritatis gau-
3 dia possideret. Confestim ad eius orationem commoventur tonitrua, renident fulgura, descendit imber igne mixtus et grandine, turbantur omnia. Concurrit vulgus ad cellulam, prosternitur coram sacerdote omnis caterva gentilium, et, mixto cum lacrimis ululatu, cuncti Domini misericordiam deprecantur, pollicenturque sacerdoti, si grando recederet, ut martyrem patronum expeterent et ad Deum eius, relictis simulacrorum cultibus, integro de corde transirent.

4 Porro ille, fusa oratione, cuncta quae petiit meruit obtinere. Recedente autem tempestate, puer cum parentibus credens, ipsa die a doloribus liberatur; gentiles in Trinitatis nomine baptizati, statuas quas coluerant confringentes, in lacum vico amnique proximum proiecerunt. Ab eo enim tempore in loco illo et fides catholica et martyris virtus est amplius declarata.

they renounced their paganism, they would get their son back safe and sound. That same priest, too, saw a dream in the following night in which the statues that were being worshipped by the pagans were shattered by divine power, thrown down on the ground, and reduced to dust.

Three days later, when the pagans again wanted to pour 2
libations to their gods, the priest prostrated himself in grief at the tomb of the saint and prayed tearfully that the splendor of the divine power might finally visit the pagans who were lying in darkness, and that the blessed martyr no longer allow his foster children to be trapped in such darkness
while he himself enjoyed eternal light. At once, in response 3
to his prayer, peals of thunder shook the air, lightning flashed, rain mixed with hail and fire came down, and the whole place was thrown into confusion. The people ran to the cell, and the whole crowd of pagans prostrated itself before the priest; combining their wailing with tears, they all begged the Lord's compassion, and they promised the priest that if the hail went away they would seek the patronage of the martyr and wholeheartedly turn to his God by abandoning the worship of their statues.

Thereupon the priest prayed again and deservedly ob- 4
tained what he requested. When the storm had ceased, therefore, the young man and his parents professed their belief, and he was released from his suffering that very day; the pagans who had been baptized in the name of the Trinity destroyed the statues they had worshipped and threw them into the lake close to the village and the river. From that time onward, both the catholic faith and the power of the martyr were manifested more abundantly in that place.

7

Qualiter Hillidius populum ab hostilitate liberabat

Post haec venientes quidam de Burgundionibus ad Brivatensem vicum, eum cum armorum multitudine copiosa circumdant; captoque populo, direpto sacrosancto ministerio, ultra amnem transeunt, et viros gladio interficere, reliquum vulgus sorte dividere parant.

2 Tunc Hillidius, quidam a Vellavo veniens, et, ut aiunt, commonitione columbae alitis incitatus, super eos irruit. Hortatusque socios, ita hostes ad internecionem cecidit, ut, captivis laxatis, triumphans in laude martyris, amne transmisso, ad beatam cellulam tamquam novus Moyses cum omni populo canendo revertitur; nec minor, ut arbitror, exsultatio fuit ereptis, quam quondam Israhelitis dimersis fuit Aegyptiis.

3 Quod ne quis dubitet hanc beati martyris fuisse victoriam; sed insinuatio columbae aliquod mysterium fuisse creditur virtutis divinae. Nam, veniente Hillidio, haec in obviam venit; cum ille, ut assolet, aliquid demoraretur, haec in circuitu illius volitabat, illoque progrediente, ista praecedebat, et revertebatur in obviam, quasi accelerare deprecans iter. Dum haec agerentur, adveniens puer captivitatem

7

How Hillidius liberated the people from their enemies

After these events, some Burgundians came to the village of Brioude and surrounded it with a large multitude of armed men; when they had captured the people and seized the holy vessels of the church, they crossed the river and prepared to kill the men by the sword, dividing the rest of the people by lot to be carried off as slaves.

Then a certain Hillidius, coming from Velay and, as they 2
say, urged on by the portent warning of a dove in flight, fell upon them. Encouraging his companions to help him, he so thoroughly slaughtered the enemy that the captives were released, and, triumphantly proclaiming the praise of the martyr, he crossed the river with them and returned as a new Moses to the blessed shrine singing with all the people; the joy of the liberated, I think, was no less than that, formerly, of the Israelites when the Egyptians were drowned.

No one should doubt that this was a victory of the blessed 3
martyr; but the warning of the dove is believed to have been a kind of divine mystery. For it came to meet Hillidius on his way; when he stopped somewhere, as he was accustomed to do, it flew in circles above him, and when he went on, it flew ahead of him and turned back again, as though urging him to travel more quickly. As this was going on, a young man came and announced the people's captivity, and because of

annuntiat, et sic iste viam acceleravit. Sed et ipso pugnante, columba semper circa eum visa est decurrere.

4 Quod ne quis invideat confictum de columba et homini praestitum Christiano, cum Orosius consulem Romanum, id est Marcum Valerium, a corvo alite scribat adiutum.

8

De interitu eorum qui ministerium basilicae exportaverunt

Prostratis ergo ab Hillidio hostibus, quattuor ex his per fugam lapsi patenam et urceum, qui "anax" dicitur, in patriam deferunt, et divisam in tantis ut erant partibus patenam, urceum Regi Gundobado ob gratiam exhibent conqui-
2 rendam. Reliquum vero argentum reginae sagacitas reperit; cui additis multis muneribus, loco illi sancto restituit, fideliter insinuans regi, non oportere eum, ut gratiam martyris sancti propter argenti parvitatem amitteret.

this Hillidius accelerated his pace. But while he was fighting too, the dove was seen to keep on circling above his head.

Let no one doubt this story about the dove as a fabrication told about a Christian man, since Orosius wrote that a Roman consul, Marcus Valerius, had been assisted by a crow. 4

8

About the ruin of those who had carried off the vessels of the church

After these enemies had been defeated by Hillidius, four of them who had escaped carried off into their homeland a paten and an urn known by the name of "anax," and after dividing the paten into as many parts as there were persons, they offered the urn to King Gundobad to gain his favor.
But his wise queen discovered the rest of the silver; she re- 2
turned everything to the holy place with many additional gifts, for she believed, as she told the king, that it was unwise for him to lose the favor of the holy martyr on account of a small amount of silver.

9

De Fedamia paralytica

Pro quibus ac talibus virtutum ornamentis magna ibi basilica fabricata a fidelibus, virtutibus, ut praefati sumus, martyris beati refulget, in qua paralyticorum, claudorum, caecorum et aliorum morborum saepius petita remedia conquiruntur.

2 Fedamia quaedam mulier, paralysis umore constricta, cui nullum corporis membrum sine dolore vigebat, exhibita est, deferentibus propinquis, ad beatam basilicam, ut vel stipem a largientibus mereretur. Quae dum in porticu illa quae sanctae basilicae coniungitur, decubaret noctem dominicam, dum sacrosanctis vigiliis populi fides devota concelebrat, et illa quiescens lectulo paululum obdormisset, a viro quodam per visum correpta atque increpita est, dicente sibi, cur, reliquis excubias nocturnas Deo exhibentibus, illa deesset. Respondit, se ab omni membrorum parte debilem, nec penitus gressum agere posse.

3 Tunc quasi sustentata a viro qui loquebatur ei, et ad sepulcrum usque deducta, dum in sopore fundit orationem, visum est ei quasi multitudo catenarum ab eius membris solo decidere. A quo etiam sonitu expergefacta, sensit omnium artuum recepisse plenissimam sanitatem. Protinus surrexit

9

About the paralyzed woman Fedamia

A large church was built in Brioude by the faithful to commemorate these and other such famous deeds of power, in which, as we have said, the blessed martyr shone, and in which remedies for paralysis, lameness, blindness, and other illnesses were frequently sought and received.

A certain woman named Fedamia, constricted by a hu- 2
mor of paralysis and unable to move any part of her body without pain, was brought by her relatives and put on display at the blessed church, so that she might obtain alms from generous people. Once she lay resting in her bed in the forecourt adjoining the blessed church during the night preceding a Sunday, while the faithful devoutly celebrated the holy vigils; when she had fallen into a light sleep, she was rebuked and reproved by a man in a dream who asked her why she was not with the others who were offering their vigils to God. She replied that she was so feeble throughout her body that she was completely unable to walk.

Thereupon, she seemed to be lifted up by the man who 3
was talking to her, and led by him to the tomb; and when she offered her prayer there in her sleep, it seemed to her that a heap of chains fell from her body onto the floor. Awakened by this sound, she felt that she had received the fullest health in her whole body. Immediately she rose from her

a lectulo et, stupentibus cunctis, cum gratiarum actione vociferans, sanctam est ingressa basilicam.

4 Ferunt etiam quidam, solitam fuisse eam referre habitum viri qui eam fuerat allocutus. Dicebat eum statura esse procerum, veste nitidum, elegantia eximium, vultu hilarem, flava caesarie immixtis canis, incessu expeditum, voce liberum, allocutione blandissimum, candoremque cutis illius ultra lilii nitorem fulgere, ita ut de multis milibus hominum quae saepe vidisset, nullum similem conspicasset. Unde multis non absurde videtur, ei beatum martyrem apparuisse. Quae mulier post decem et octo annos sanata est.

10

De eo qui percussorem suum de basilica conabatur extrahere

Quidam, dum in seditione quam commoverat, oculum amississet, hominem qui ictum intulerat de basilica conabatur extrahere; quod dum agit, non modo amissi oculi non recipit lumen, verumetiam sentit alium, quem sanum habuerat, obcaecari. Porro, cum peccata sua confiteretur, dicens: “Merito mihi evenit iudicium sine misericordia, qui

bed and entered the holy church loudly proclaiming her thanks, astonishing everyone.

Some report that she used to describe the appearance of 4
the man who had spoken to her. She said that he was tall, dressed in white, and extremely elegant, that he had a smiling face, and blond hair streaked with gray, that his bearing was graceful, his voice melodious, and his conversation surpassingly kind, while the whiteness of his skin outshone that of lilies, so that among the many thousands of men whom she had often observed, she had seen no one like him. For this reason it did not seem improbable to many people that the blessed martyr had appeared to her. This woman was healed after eighteen years of illness.

10

About a man who tried to bring the man who had struck him out of the basilica

A man who, in a fight which he had started, lost the sight in one eye tried to bring the man who had given him the blow out from the church where he had taken refuge; while doing this, not only did he not recover his lost eyesight, but even noticed that the other eye, which had remained healthy, was turning blind. So when he confessed his sins, he said: "I have deserved this judgment without compassion,

2 non feci misericordiam." Prostratus coram sancto sepulcro, cum populo qui tunc ad festivitatem advenerat, indulgens laedenti, et visum recepit et gratiam. Sicque factum est, ut is qui sancti auxilium expetierat tutaretur, ille vero qui non credebat argueretur; et sic uterque laetus emendatusque discessit.

II

De contracto, qui die dominica boves iunxit

Alius quoque ausu temerario die dominica iungens boves, agrum sulcare coepit, apprehensa securi, ut aliquid emendaret in vomere, protinus contractis digitis manubrium in dextera eius adhaesit. Cumque prae dolore nimio cruciaretur, post duos annos veniens ad beati martyris basilicam, vigilias
2 fideliter celebravit. Statim in ipsa die dominica, reserata manus lignum, quod invitus tenebat, amisit; magnam inferens

for I myself did not forgive." After he had prostrated him- 2
self at the holy tomb together with the people who had then come to the saint's feast, and had pardoned the one who had injured him, he recovered both his eyesight and the saint's grace. And so it happened that he who had sought the saint's help was protected, while he who did not believe in this protection was censured; each thus departed happy and improved.

II

About a disabled man who had yoked his oxen on a Sunday

Another man dared impudently to yoke his oxen on a Sunday and began to plow his field; when he picked up an ax to fix something on his plowshare, his fingers immediately clenched, so that the handle stuck to his right hand. After he had suffered extreme pain for two years, he came to the church of the blessed martyr and faithfully celebrated the
vigil there. Immediately, on that very Sunday, his hand un- 2
clenched and let go of the wood which it had unwillingly

populo disciplinam, ut quod die dominica fuerat perpetratum ipsa die dominica purgaretur. At ille, magnificans gloriam martyris, recessit incolumis, nec ultra die resurrectionis dominicae quidnam ausus est operari.

12

De Anagildo muto et surdo vel caeco

Sic et Anagildus quidam, mutus, et surdus, et caecus, vel omnium membrorum compage debilitatus, ad limina sacrosancta proiectus est, scilicet ut, vel ab stipe pasceretur devotorum, qui victus alimoniam propriis manibus laborare non
2 poterat. Igitur, cum per annum integrum ante sanctam aedem decubasset, tandem visitatus a virtute beati martyris, ab omni infirmitate sanatus est.

held; this taught the people the great lesson that what had been wrongly done on a Sunday was forgiven on that same day. As for the man himself, he left safe and sound, praising the glory of the martyr, and thereafter never dared to do any work on the day of the Lord's resurrection.

12

About Anagild, who was mute, deaf, and blind

Likewise, a certain Anagild, mute, deaf, and blind, as well as debilitated in all the joints of his body, was placed at the sacred threshold of the basilica so that, unable to work with his own hands for a living, he might be nourished by the do-
nations of the devout. After he had lain in front of the holy 2
building for a whole year, he was at last visited by the power of the blessed martyr and healed of all his illnesses.

13

De his qui Theoderici Regis tempore basilicam irruperunt

Videtur mihi, ut, sicut sancti virtute curata morbida retexuntur, ita et infidelium pravitates oratione illius confutatae, ad emendationem aliorum, ne similia appetant, declarentur, quia utraque sancti gloria praestat, ut et hos sanitati reddat, ne amplius crucientur, et illos arguat, ne in futuro iudicio condemnentur.

2 Et quia nullum latere credo aliquid de hostilitate Theoderici Regis ac infirmitatibus Sigivaldi, quae ei in Arverno posito contigerunt, propter virtutem tamen beati martyris est diligentius exponendum, quo facilius fides dictis adhibeatur. Igitur, cum ad direptionem Arvernorum rex antedictus festinaret, et ingrediens terminum, vastationi cuncta subigeret, pars aliqua ab exercitu separata ad Brivatensem vicum infesta proripuit, fama vulgante, quod in basilica essent incolae cum multis thesauris adunati.

13

About those who broke into the basilica in the time of King Theoderic

It seems to me that, in the same way that illnesses cured by the saint's power have been related, the depravities of unbelievers overcome by his prayer should also be made known for the correction of others, lest they desire to do similar things. For through both of these the glory of the saint is manifested, restoring health to the former so that they suffer no longer, and censuring the latter lest they be condemned in the future Judgment.

And although I believe that there is no one who does not 2
know about King Theoderic's war, and about the illnesses that struck Sigivald when he was stationed in Clermont, a more detailed description is needed to make it easier to believe what has been related about the blessed martyr's power. When, therefore, the aforementioned King Theoderic was hastening to plunder Clermont and, while crossing its border, was devastating everything in his path, a part of his troops, separated from his army, hurried with deadly intent toward the village of Brioude; for the rumor had reached them that its inhabitants had all assembled in the basilica with their great wealth.

3 Cumque pervenissent ad locum, inveniunt multitudinem
promiscui sexus, obseratis ostiis, in templo ipso cum propriis facultatibus residere. Cumque intrare non possent,
unus effractam ceu fur in altario sancto fenestram vitream
ingreditur, quia qui non intrat per ianuam hic latro est. Dehinc, reseratis aedis illius valvis, exercitum intromittit. At
illi direptam cunctam pauperum supellectilem, cum ministris ipsius basilicae, reliquum quoque populum qui infra erat
eductum, foris diviserunt haud procul a vico.

4 Quae cum ad regem delata fuissent, comprehensos ex his
aliquos diversis mortibus condemnavit. Fugiens vero ille,
qui, irrupta aede, caput fuit huius sceleris, igne de caelo de-
lapso consumptus interiit. Super quem cum multi acervum
lapidum congregassent, a tonitruis et coruscationibus de-
5 tectus, terrena caruit sepultura. Qui vero de consentaneis
latentes regem in patria sunt regressi, correpti a daemone
diversis exitibus hanc vitam crudeliter finierunt. Haec audiens rex, omnia quae exinde sunt ablata reddidit. Praeceperat enim, ne in septimo a basilica miliario quis vim inferret.

When the soldiers came to the place, they indeed found a 3
multitude of men and women, staying in the sacred place
with their possessions after having barred the doors. Since
the soldiers could not enter, one of them broke the glass
windowpane near the sacred altar and entered through it
like a thief, for whoever does not enter by the door is a thief.
Then he unbarred the doors of the building and let the army
in. And after they had taken all the goods of the poor, they
divided the rest of the people who, together with the basilica's clergy, had been taken outside from the lower part of
the church to a little distance from the village to be led away
captive as slaves.

When these things had been reported to the king, he had 4
some of the soldiers seized and condemned to various forms
of execution. The one who had broken into the church and
was the initiator of this crime fled, and later died consumed
by fire from heaven. Even though many people had heaped a
pile of stones over his body, it was uncovered by thunder and
lightning, and he lacked a grave on earth. As for his compan- 5
ions who had returned to their homeland but hidden themselves from the king: they were seized by demons and ended
their days violently. When the king heard about this, he returned everything that had been taken. For he had commanded that there be no violence within seven miles of the
basilica.

14

De Sigivaldo pervasore

Tunc Sigivaldus cum rege praepotens cum omni familia sua in Arverna regione ex regis iussu migravit. Ubi, dum multorum res iniuste competeret, villam quandam, quam gloriosae memoriae Tetradius, episcopus Biturigensis, basilicae sancti Iuliani reliquerat, sub specie obumbratae commutationis, avidus pervasit; sed, mense tertio postquam aggressus est, correptus a febre et sine sensu effectus, declinavit caput ad lectulum.

2 Cuius uxor, dum de hoc exitu maesta penderet, a quodam sacerdote commonita est ut, eum si videre vellet incolumem, auferret a villa. At illa haec audiens, praeparatis carrucis compositoque plaustro, quo eum eveheret, mox ut praedium sunt egressi, protinus divina sunt pariter gratia munerati, nam iste sospitate, illa meruit ex huius incolumitate laetitiam.

3 Ferunt etiam in oratorium praedii illius sanctum Iulianum martyrem cum Tetradio Episcopo colloquentem cuidam religioso revelatum fuisse, promittentem se episcopo villam, quam pro animae suae remedio sibi reliquerat, recepturum. Sed et habitum beati martyris in eodem modo esse, ut quondam paralytica exposuerat, referebat.

14

About the land-grabber Sigivald

Then Sigivald, a most powerful man at the king's court, came at his command to reside in the region of Clermont with his whole retinue. There, while unjustly confiscating many people's possessions, he greedily seized, on the pretext of a dubious document of sale, a country estate which Bishop Tetradius of Bourges, of glorious memory, had left to the basilica of the holy Julian; but in the third month after he had gone to live in it he was seized by a fever, lapsed into unconsciousness, and was confined to his bed.

His wife, grieving about this, was advised by a certain 2
bishop to move him out of the house, if she wished to see him well again. Having listened to this, she arranged for carriages and brought together wagons with which to take him away, and as soon as they had left the estate, they were both immediately and equally rewarded by divine grace, for he deserved to recover his health, and she her joy at his recovery.

It is even said that the holy martyr Julian had been re- 3
vealed to a certain monk as speaking with Bishop Tetradius in the chapel of this estate, promising that he Julian would return to the bishop the country house which he had left to him for the good of his soul. He also said that the blessed martyr's appearance was the same as that formerly described by the paralyzed woman <Fedamia>.

15

De pastoris malitia

Pastor vero quidam, non strenuitate, sed nomine Ingenuus, dum in multis rebus contra basilicam sancti martyris iniuste ageret, ad hoc levitas eius, Inimico incrassante, convaluit, ut colonicas basilicae concupiscens, quae agro eius erant proximae, pervadere non timeret. Ad quem sacerdos loci, cum aliquos de clericis quasi legatos mitteret, ut, accepta ratione, quod male pervaserat, relaxaret, ille quasi contra iniquum hostem telis correptis, prosiluit, fugatisque sagittis clericis, res sancti in sua dominatione retinuit.

2 Factum est autem ut in proximo adveniret dies passionis martyris gloriosi ad quam ille, immemor pervasionis suae atque iniuriae quam intulerat clericis, ante quinque dies solemnitatis ad vicum Brivatensem advenit. Qui, cum in domo hospitalitatis suae convivio cum laetitia et exsultatione fungeretur, subito, coruscatione facta tonitruum sonuit; rursumque iterato iaculo igneo de caelis elapso, percussus est, nullo tamen de reliquis pereunte. Deinde ad exemplum omnium, tamquam rogus flammeus ardens, paulatim consume-
3 batur. Ad quod miraculum populus, qui ad beati festa conve-

15

About a shepherd's wickedness

A certain shepherd named Ingenuus, of free status in name alone and not in behavior, had acted unjustly to the detriment of the basilica of the holy martyr in many matters, and as the influence of the Enemy increased, his lack of respect became so pronounced that he coveted the tenant farms owned by the basilica which adjoined his field, and did not hesitate to take them into his possession. When the priest of the place sent him some of the clergy as messengers to persuade him to see reason and to let go of what he had wrongly seized, he took up his weapons and assaulted them as though they were a wicked enemy; and when the clergy had been put to flight with arrows, he retained the holy man's land.

It happened, however, that the day of the martyr's pas- 2
sion was approaching, and, forgetting his seizure of the land and the injuries he had inflicted upon the clergy, he went to the village of Brioude five days before the celebration. While he was merrily enjoying a meal in his lodging there, suddenly lightning flashed and a thunderclap sounded, and he was struck by the second flaming lance that fell from heaven; none of the others present, however, were hurt. Then, as an example to all, he was slowly consumed like a
blazing, flaming funeral pyre. The people who had come to- 3
gether for the saint's feast witnessed this miracle with

nerat, haec cernens cum admiratione, metuebat; satisque illi fuit ne de rebus sancti aliquid ultra contingeret. Quod ne fortuito actum quis putet, cernat inter multos innoxios unum interiisse sacrilegum.

16

De contumacia Becconis

Quid etiam ad Becconis Comitis confutandam superbiam beatus martyr sit operatus, evolvam. Hic, cum actiones ageret publicas et, elatus iactantia, multos contra iustitiam aggravaret, casu contigit ut dimissum accipitrem diu per diversa vagantem perderet; similiter, ut unus de servientibus basilicae sancti Iuliani accipitrem alium, dum per viam ambularet, quasi vagum invenit. Erat enim puer ille pincerna in domo basilicae.

2 Quod cum ad Becconem pervenisset, quod scilicet puer repertum teneret accipitrem, calumniari coepit ac dicere: "Meus ille erat," inquit, "et hic furto eum sustulit." Deinde, succendente avaritia, misit illum vinctum in carcere, delibe-
3 rans eum in sequenti patibulo condemnare. Tunc sacerdos maestus valde ad sepulcrum sancti properat, reseratisque

astonishment and were afraid; for them this was sufficient warning never to touch any of the holy man's possessions in the future. Lest anyone think that this happened by chance, let him notice that among many innocent people, only the impious one died.

16

About the insolence of Becco

Now I will relate what the blessed martyr did to confound the pride of Count Becco. This man, while he performed public functions and, elated by his vainglory, unjustly oppressed many people, happened to lose his hawk, which after its release had for a long time wandered away here and there; at the same time, one of the servants of the holy Julian's basilica, walking on the road, found another hawk that seemed to be lost. This young man was a cupbearer in the basilica's residence for the clergy.

When the report reached Becco that the boy had found 2
a hawk and was holding on to it, he began to accuse him falsely, saying: "That hawk was mine, and this man took it by theft." Thereupon, inflamed by greed, he chained the young man and put him in prison, planning to condemn him to the
gallows the next day. Then the priest, greatly distressed, has- 3
tened to the saint's tomb and, opening the collection boxes

cum gemitu capsis, apprehensis decem aureis, per fideles amicos Becconi obtulit. Quod ille pro nihilo respuens, cum iuramento asseruit numquam se puerum dimissurum, nisi exinde aureos triginta acciperet. Quod presbyter desuper sepulcro sancti accipiens, Becconi transmisit; quos acceptos, satiata auri cupiditate, puerum restauravit incolumem.

4 Sed Deus omnipotens, qui permanet ante solem, secundum bonitatis suae divitias humiliavit calumniatorem. Nam, ipsius anni transacto curriculo, veniens ad sancti festivitatem cum caterva satellitum, ingressus est limen sanctum. Procedente vero lectore, qui beatae passionis recenseret historiam, ut revolvit librum et in principio lectionis sancti Iuliani protulit nomen, confestim Becco voce nescio qua taeterrima ad terram corruit, cruenteque spumans, dare voces diversas coepit. Inde inter suorum manus sublatus, a
5 basilica domum reducitur. Nec fuit dubium pueris eius, haec ob iniuriam basilicaris famuli evenisse. Omnem quoque ornatum, quod super se tunc habuit, tam in auro quam in vestimentis, basilicae contulit, et multa deinceps munera misit, sed usque ad diem obitus sui sine sensu duravit.

with a sigh, took out ten gold coins and had them taken to Becco by trusted friends. He, however, rejecting them as worthless, asserted with an oath that he would never let the man go unless he received thirty more gold coins from there. The priest then took these from the box above the tomb and sent them to Becco; after having received them, his hunger for gold was satisfied and he gave the young man back unharmed.

But almighty God, who existed before the sun, humili- 4
ated the perverse man according to the riches of his goodness. For when that year had run its course, Becco came to the feast of the saint with all his retainers and went through the holy door of the basilica. When the lector, who was about to read the story of the saint's suffering, came forward, unrolled the scroll and, beginning the reading, pronounced the name of the holy Julian, Becco suddenly fell to the ground with an appalling cry, spat forth blood, and began to shout out unintelligible words. He was lifted up by the hands of his people and was taken out of the basilica to
his house. His servants had no doubt that this occurred on 5
account of his injuring the servant of the basilica. He gave all the valuables he then had with him to the basilica, gold as well as clothes, and thereafter sent many gifts, but until the day of his death he remained witless.

17

De diacono qui oves basilicae abstulit

Fuit etiam quidam diaconus, qui, relictam ecclesiam, fisco se publico iunxit, acceptaque a patronis potestate, tanta perpetrabat scelera, ut vix posset a vicinis circumpositis sustineri. Accidit autem quadam vice, ut saltus montenses, ubi ad aestivandum oves abierant, circumiret atque pascuaria quae fisco debebantur inquireret. Cumque diversos spoliaret iniuste, conspicit eminus greges, qui tunc sub nomine martyris tuebantur, ad quos levi cursu evolans, tamquam lupus rapax diripit arietes.

2 Conturbati atque exterriti pastores ovium dicunt ei: "Ne, quaesumus, contingas hos arietes, quia beati martyris Iuliani dominio subiugati sunt." Quibus ille haec irridens respondisse fertur: "Putasne, quia Iulianus comedit arietes?" Dehinc, ipsis verberibus affectis, quae voluit abstulit; ignorans miser, quod, qui de domibus sanctorum aliquid aufert, ipsis sanctis iniuriam facit, ipso sic Domino protestante: "Qui vos spernit, me spernit" [Luke 10:16], et: "Qui recipit iustum, mercedem iusti accipiet" [Matthew 10:41].

3 Contigit autem, ut post dies multos, non religione, sed casu conferente, ad vicum Brivatensem properaret, proiectusque humo ante sepulchrum, mox a febre corripitur, et

17

About the deacon who stole sheep belonging to the basilica

There was also a certain deacon who, having left the Church to join the public treasury, received power from his patrons and perpetrated so many crimes that his neighbors could scarcely tolerate him. It happened once that he was making the rounds of the mountainous meadows in which the sheep were pastured in the summer and collecting the pasture tax owed the public treasury. When he had exacted money unjustly from various people, he saw from afar herds which were then cared for in the name of the martyr and, rushing over to them, seized the rams like a hungry wolf.

The distressed and terrified shepherds said to him: 2
"Don't touch these rams, we beg you, for they are under the control of the blessed martyr Julian." It is said that, laughing, he gave them the following answer: "Do you think that Julian eats rams?" After this he whipped them and took what he wanted. The wretch did not know that whoever takes something away from saints' houses, injures the saints themselves, as is proclaimed by the Lord himself, when he said: "Whoever spurns you, spurns me," and: "Whoever receives the just, will receive the reward of the just."

Many days later, however, he was hastening to the village 3
of Brioude, not for pious reasons but by chance, and when he prostrated himself in front of the tomb was immediately

tanta vi caloris opprimitur, ut neque consurgere, neque puerum evocare posset. Famuli vero, cum vidissent eum extra solitum plus occumbere, accedentes: "Quid tu," inquiunt, "in tanta diuturnitate deprimeris? Non enim tibi tam longe mos erat orandi aut devotio." Ferebant autem de eo, quod, quandoquidem in ecclesia fuisset ingressus, parumper immurmurans, nec capite inclinato, regrediebatur.

4 Tunc, interpellantibus pueris, cum responsum reddere non valeret, ablatus manibus e loco, in cellam, quae erat proxima, lectulo collocatur. Igitur, invalescente febre, proclamat se miser incendi per martyrem, et, quod primo siluerat, admotis animae iudicii facibus, crimina confitetur, iactarique super se aquam, voce qua poterat, deprecabatur. Delatis quoque cum vasculo lymphis et in eum saepe deiectis, tamquam de fornace ita fumus egrediebatur e corpore.
5 Interea miseri artus, ceu combusti, in nigredinem convertuntur, unde tantus procedebat foetor, ut vix de astantibus possent aliqui tolerare. Innuens enim dehinc manu, indicat se esse leviorem; mox, illis recedentibus, hic spiritum exhalavit. De quo haud dubium est, qualem illic teneat locum, qui hinc cum tali discessit iudicio.

seized by a fever, and oppressed by such an intense heat that he was unable either to rise or to call his attendant. When his servants saw him lying there longer than usual, they came up to him and said: "Why are you humbling yourself for so long? It is not your custom to pray or show devotion for such a long time." For they used to say of him that whenever he had entered a church, he used to leave after a scarcely audible murmur and without bowing his head.

When he was unable to reply to his servants' questioning, 4
he was carried away from that place by their hands and put
on a bed in a nearby room. Then, as his fever increased, the
unhappy man cried out that he was being burned by the
martyr, and as the torches of divine judgment were applied to his soul, he confessed to the crime about which he
had up to then been silent, begging with whatever voice
he could manage that water be sprinkled over him. When
pitchers of water had been brought to him and splashed
over him many times, smoke began to come out his body as
though from a furnace. At the same time, the unhappy man's 5
body, as though it were in fact burning, began to turn black,
and emitted such a vile stench that some of those standing
around could hardly bear it. Thereafter he indicated with his
hand that he felt better; but as soon as they had left, he
breathed out his spirit. As a consequence, there is no doubt
about the kind of place occupied by one who departs from
here with such a judgment.

18

De eo qui caballum in vigilia sancti furatus est

Alius autem per vigiliam festivitatis equum alicuius, qui tunc forte ad eandem solemnitatem venerat, furto prehendit, ascensoque, velociter properat scilicet ut qui lumen perdiderat veritatis, non inveniretur a luce, et cuius pectus cupiditatis tenebrae obsederant, eius et furtivam fraudulentiam nox celaret. De talibus enim Dominus dicebat in evangelio: "Omnis qui male agit odit lucem" [John 3:20]. Albescente igitur caelo, dicebat: "Iam securus sum, nam triginta leugas a sancti basilica elongatus sum; iam secus propriam domum esse me credo."

2 Dum haec tacitus revolveret infra se, demotis ex axe tenebris, cognoscit se ipsi vico propinquum inter populos divagari; timensque, ne scelus suum patefieret publico, cum cautela grandi caballum in loco unde digressus fuerat reformavit. Sic miser virtute martyris tota nocte detentus in circuitu vici, et, ut ego credo, ab auctore qui eum obsederat est delusus, ut viam quam apprehendere voluit non valeret. O scelerata cupiditas, quid agis? Semper amatores tuos in confusione praecipitas.

18

About the man who stole a horse during the holy man's vigil

During the vigil before the saint's feast another man stole the horse of someone who had happened to come to the same celebration, mounted it, and rode away at a fast pace so that, having lost the light of truth, he might not be found out when the light of day returned; his heart having being clouded over by the darkness of greed, he hoped that the night would conceal the deceitfulness of his theft. About such men the Lord said in the gospel: "Everyone who does evil hates the light." And when the sky began to lighten, the thief said: "Now I am safe, for I am thirty leagues away from the holy church; I believe I am already close to my home."

While he silently rehearsed these thoughts to himself, 2
the darkness disappeared from the heavens and he saw that he was near the same village of Brioude and was wandering about among the people; fearing lest his crime become known to the public, he very cautiously hitched up the horse again in the place from where it had gone out. Thus the unhappy man had been detained in a circle around the village during the whole night by the power of the martyr and, as I believe, deluded by the agent who had taken possession of him so that he could not find the road he wanted. O wicked greed, what are you doing? You always throw your followers into confusion.

19

De eo qui propter triantem periuravit

Quidam alteri triantem praestiterat, quem, interpositis paucis diebus, recepit. Post annum vero, in atrio sancti, convento homine, rem suam, quasi non recepisset, sibi reddi deposcebat. At ille detestans asserebat, se reddidisse susceptum. Cumque diutissime altercarentur, ille qui reddiderat ait ad socium: "Usquequo uterque contendimus? Sub iudicio hoc omnipotentis Dei ponamus. Eamus ad tumulum martyris, et quod sub sacramenti interpositione dixeris discernat virtus sancta patroni."

2 At ille nec dubitans ingressusque sepulcrum, dum audacter elevat manus ut periuret, infeliciter miser inriguit. Haeret vox in gutture, lingua coartatur in fauce, vibrant labia vacua a sermone, ipsa quoque brachia, quae ad adiutorium frustrati sacramenti erexerat, prorsus retrahere non valebat. Ad haec vulgo admirante, publicato scelere, multitudo cuncta populi, una voce prorumpens, Domini misericordiam ac beati martyris auxilium deprecatur. Post quattuor vero aut eo amplius horas ad sensum regressus, quod iniuste repetebat publica confessione patefecit, et sic sanus abscessit.

19

About the man who committed perjury on account of a third of a solidus

A man who had lent another man a third <of a “solidus”> received it back from him a few days later. A year later however, he met the man who had borrowed it from him again in the forecourt of the saint’s basilica and, as if he had not yet received it, demanded that the coin be repaid to him. The other man asserted with an oath that he had returned what he had received. As they were altercating, the one who had repaid said to his companion: “How long will we keep arguing with each other? Let us subject this matter to the judgment of the omnipotent God. Let us go to the tomb of the martyr, and let the holy power of the patron judge what you will have said under oath.”

Unconcerned, the other approached the tomb, but when 2
he brazenly raised his hand to commit perjury, the unhappy man froze miserably. His voice stuck in his throat, his tongue shrunk in his jaw, his lips moved without speaking, and he was furthermore completely unable to lower his arms, which he had raised to lend support to his abortive oath. The crowd was astonished and, at the revelation of the crime, the whole multitude of the people burst out with one voice begging the mercy of the Lord and the aid of the blessed martyr. After four or more hours, when he had returned to his senses, he admitted his unjust demand in a public confession, and in this way left in good health.

20

De eo qui basilicam sanctam furto spoliavit

Saepe haec ille audierat qui basilicae sanctae violentiam intulit, sed iniquam mentem semel obsessam vitio bonitas mollire non potuit, Salomone obtestante: "In malevola anima non ingreditur sapientia" [Wisdom of Solomon 1:4]. Advenerat festivitas sancti, et ecce quidam e populo conspicatur ornamentis immensis beatam basilicam effulgere. Concupiscit iniqua mente, quod adipiscens non poterat occultare.

2 Igitur, discedente populo a basilica post gratiam vespertinam, hic se in angulo basilicae reprimens latitavit; ac, dato cunctis nocturna quiete silentio, vel operiente umbrosa caligine mundum, consurgit ab angulo, et nihil dubitans, utique quia satellite Satana impellebatur, super cancellum beati sepulcri cursu prosiliit rapido; detractamque a summo unam gemmis coruscantibus crucem, ad terram deiecit, collectisque velulis ac palliolis de circuitu parietum pendentibus, unum volucrum facit; imposuitque humeris ac, elevata cruce manu, locum unde discesserat repetit, ac, posita capiti sarcina, peccati sopore compressus, obdormivit.

20

About the man who plundered the holy basilica by thievery

These stories had often been heard by a man who violated the holy church, but a wicked mind, once it is possessed by vice, cannot be mollified by goodness, for as Solomon asserted: "Wisdom will not enter a malevolent soul." On the day of the saint's feast, behold, one of the people kept looking at the blessed basilica shining with many ornaments. His wicked mind longed to have what, once acquired, he could not conceal.

When the people had left the basilica after the evening 2
service of thanksgiving, therefore, this man hid himself in a corner; when silence had come in the quiet of the night and a dark mist covered the world, he rose from his corner; without hesitating, no doubt because he was being impelled by his companion Satan, he jumped quickly over the balustrade around the blessed tomb, pulled down a cross with sparkling gems from its top, and threw it on the ground; gathering the veils and drapes hanging on the surrounding walls, he made them into a single bundle; having put this on his shoulders and holding the cross in his hand, he returned to the place where he had been hiding, and then, overcome by the drowsiness of sin, he put the bundle under his head and fell asleep.

3 Media vero nocte, circumeuntes custodes sanctam basilicam, aspiciunt in angulo unam gemma crucis, tamquam iubar caeleste refulgere; obstupefacti accedunt comminus cum timore, admotoque cereo, inveniunt personam cum rebus furatis, quas auferre non potuerat, inibi decubare. Denique sub custodia eum illa nocte detentum, mane facto, cuncta quae fecerat patefecit, asserens se lassum obdormiisse, eo quod diutissime circumiens cum fasce basilicam, ostium unde egrederetur reperire non potuit.

21

De eo qui caballum in festivitate perdidit

Multa quidem et alia in praevaricatoribus ostendit, sed satis sint ista ad coercendam desidiam eorum. Nunc vero ad gaudia prosperitatum, qua larga pietate praestat populis, revertamur. Sed prius illud non arbitror postponendum quod expertum valde cognovimus, quid in rebus perditis apud hunc patronum fidelis deprecatio consequatur, ex quibus unum tantum commemorare studui.

At midnight, however, when the custodians were doing their rounds in the basilica, they saw in a corner one gem of the cross shining like a heavenly star; stunned, they fearfully came closer, and, holding a candle by it, they found the man sleeping there with the loot, which he had not been able to carry off. After he had been held in custody the whole night, when morning came, he confessed all he had done, saying that he had fallen asleep out of tiredness after walking for a very long time around the church with his bundle and not being able to find a door through which he could leave. 3

21

About a man who lost his horse during a feast

The martyr has manifested his power against wrongdoers in many other cases as well, but let this suffice to correct their lack of respect. We return, therefore, to the joys of the favors that he, in his great compassion, grants to the people. But, first, I think I should not omit what we ourselves know very well from our own experience, namely that when things are lost, a faithful prayer to this patron yields results. Of these events I have undertaken to commemorate only one.

2 Ad festivitatem beati martyris devotus pauper advenerat, laxatoque equite, sacram ingressus est aedem, ac vigiliis immobilis instans noctem cum ceteris orando deduxit. Illucescente vero caelo ad metatum regressus, caballum quem reliquerat non invenit, quaesitumque diutissime, nec signa
3 quidem qua in parte discessisset agnovit. Transacto igitur biduo, recurrit iterum per saltus, perscrutans locorum incolas, si forte aliquis aut teneret captum, aut capi vidisset ab aliquo. Nullum dehinc indicii genus reperiens, anxius atque maestus ad sepulcrum sancti regreditur, ibique causas doloris ac maeroris exponens aiebat: "Ad tua, sancte, limina veni, nihil aliud quam parvitatis meae vota deferre. Nihil iniuste abstuli, nihil gessi indignum tua solemnitate. Cur, inquam, perdidi rem meam? Rogo ut restituas amissum, ut necessarium reddas."

4 Haec fletu addito aiens, ut egressus est templum, conspicit eminus a quodam viro suum equitem retineri. Ad quem accedens, dum discutit unde sit aut unde venerit, aut ex quo tempore hunc habeat equum, didicit ipsa hora eum fuisse repertum qua ille beati martyris imploravit auxilium.

A poor, devout man had come to the feast and, having left 2
his horse outside, entered the holy building and spent the night immobile with the others praying during the vigils. When the sky began to lighten, he returned to his lodging but did not find the horse which he had left there, and after searching for a long time, did not even discover any tracks
indicating in which direction it had gone. Two days later, he 3
returned to the pastures and asked the inhabitants of nearby places if perhaps anyone held it captive or had seen it taken by anyone. When he did not find any indications of this kind, he returned anxious and sad to the tomb of the holy man and there made known the reasons for his grief and sorrow, saying: "I came to your threshold, holy man, bringing nothing other than the prayers of my humble self. I have not taken anything unjustly; I have done nothing unworthy of your solemnity. Why, I ask, did I lose my horse? I ask you to restore what is lost, so that you may provide for my need."

When he had said this with tears and came out of the 4
temple, he saw from afar his horse being held by a man. When he went toward him and asked where he was from or where he had come from, and from what time he had held the horse, he learned that it had been found at the very hour that he had implored the blessed martyr's help.

22

De caeco illuminato

Cum autem quidam ex eo loco per incursum diabolicum oculum perdidisset et ad hospitiolum suum viduatus lumine infeliciter resideret, ac manibus propriis nihil laborare praevalens spem ullam alimonii non haberet, apparuit ei vir in visu noctis, commonens ut ad beati basilicam ambularet, ibique, si devote suggerat, promittit auxilium inveniri. At ille nihil moratus, arrepto bacello, adminiculante puero, sanctum ingressus est locum.

2 Qui post completam orationem archipresbyterum qui tunc locum ipsum regebat, nomine Publianum, adivit, supplicans ut oculis caecis Christi crucem imponeret. Erat enim valde religiosus. Quod ille, dum iactantiam evadere cupit evitans, tenetur a caeco, nec omnino dimittitur, nisi
3 quae petebat adimpleret. Tunc ille prostratus ante sepulcrum diutissime martyris est suffragium deprecatus; deinde, admotam oculis caecis manum, protinus ut signum crucis imposuit, visum iste recepit.

4 Admiramini, quaeso, virtutem martyris cui, cum parum sit per se exercere miracula, nunc etiam per manus discipulorum, astipulante virtutis suae favore, publice operatur. Sed nec meritum discipuli fuit exiguum, cui haec praestita esse cernuntur.

22

How a blind man was given light

A man from this place lost his sight through a diabolic attack and, deprived of light and unable to work with his hands, lived unhappily in his little house with no hope of sustenance; then a man appeared to him in a dream vision, instructing him to go to the basilica of the blessed man and promising that, if he prayed devoutly, he would find help there. Losing no time, the man took his walking stick and, with a servant to guide him, he went to the sacred place.

After he had finished his prayer, he approached the arch- 2
priest, named Publianus, who was then governing the place, and asked him to make the sign of Christ's cross upon his blind eyes, for Publianus was very pious. When the archpriest refused because he wished to avoid pride, he was seized by the blind man, who would not let him go until he
agreed to do what had been asked. Then prostrating himself 3
before the tomb, Publianus prayed at length for the martyr's intercession; at last, after he had raised his hand to the blind eyes, the man received his sight at the very moment that the sign of the cross was applied.

Admire the power of the martyr, I beg you, who, while it 4
is a small thing for him to work miracles by himself, now also performs them publicly through the hands of his disciples, supported as they are by the favor of his power. But the merit of the disciple to whom this was seen to be granted was not small.

23

De pede Galli, postmodum episcopi, sanato

Erat enim tunc temporis apud urbem Arvernam patruus meus, Gallus episcopus, de quo non videtur omitti qualiter in adolescentia sua fuerit a sancti virtute iuvatus. Et quia saepius commemoravi quale excidium Arvernae regioni Rex Theodericus intulerit, cum neque maioribus neque minoribus natu aliquid de rebus propriis est relictum praeter terram vacuam quam secum barbari ferre non poterant.

2 His ergo temporibus gloriosae memoriae patruus meus, qui postea, ut dixi, sacerdotali fasce Arvernam rexit ecclesiam, pupillus erat, cuius facultates ita direptae sunt ab exercitu ut nihil prorsus remaneret in promptu. Ipse quoque cum uno tantum puerulo usque ad Brivatensem vicum, plerumque itinere pedestri, discurrebat.

3 Accidit autem quodam tempore dum hoc iter tereret ut, laxatis prae calore solis calciamentis, nuda incedens planta, sudem calcaret spineum, qui tunc fortassis incisus, adhuc terrae haerens, erecto acumine inter herbas virides latitabat. Qui defixus plantae et superegressus, effractusque deorsum extrahi nequibat. Igitur, defluente sanguinis rivo, cum gressum facere non valeret, beati martyris implorat auxilium;

23

How the foot of Gallus, who later became bishop, was healed

At that time my uncle Gallus was bishop of the city of Clermont, and the story of how, in his youth, he was helped by the power of the holy man should not be omitted. I have often recounted the kind of devastation that King Theoderic visited upon the region of Clermont, when neither the nobles nor the common people were left with any property except the empty land which the barbarians were unable to take with them.

In those days, my uncle of glorious memory, who later, as 2
I said, ruled the church of Clermont as bishop, was an orphan, whose properties had been so thoroughly plundered by the army that almost nothing was left in the barns. He used to go with only one servant boy to the village of Brioude, often on foot.

One day while he was on this journey he had taken off his 3
shoes because of the heat of the sun and was proceeding barefoot, when he stepped on the point of a thorny twig that, having perhaps been cut, had stuck to the ground and lain hidden in the green grass, its point alone projecting. This thorn pierced his foot, came out on the other side and, having been broken off, could not be pulled out. Since a stream of blood flowed from it and he was unable to walk, he called upon the aid of the blessed martyr. When the pain

paululumque dolore compresso, licet claudicando, iter quod coeperat expedivit.

4 Tertia vero nocte, computrescente vulnere, dolor maximus incitatur. Ille vero ad experta dudum praesidia confugiens sepulcro glorioso prosternitur, expletisque vigiliis, regressus ad lectulum, dum virtutem martyris praestolatur, somno incumbente deprimitur. Deinde consurgens, nullam doloris sentit iniuriam, aspectaque planta, pars sudis quae ingressa fuerat non videtur, evulsam tamen sentiebat a pede. Quod lignum diligenter inquirens in stratu suo reperit, admirans qualiter fuisset egressum.

5 Solitus namque erat in episcopatu suo locum vulneris ostendere, in quo magna adhuc fossa conspiciebatur, obtestans in hoc beati martyris fuisse virtutem.

24

De febre Petri fratris mei

Post multum vero tempus advenerat festivitas beati martyris, et pater meus cum omni domo sua ad huius solemnitatis gaudia properabat. Nobis vero iter agentibus, Petrus, frater meus senior, ab ardore febrium occupatur et tam graviter agit ut neque vigere neque cibum sumere posset. Totumque

had subsided a little, he continued the journey he had undertaken, limping.

Three nights later, the wound began to putrefy, and an ex- 4
treme pain afflicted him. Turning then to the help that he had recently experienced, he prostrated himself at the glorious tomb, finished his vigil, returned to his bed, and while waiting for the martyr's power to manifest itself, fell asleep. When he arose after this, he felt no painful injury and, inspecting his foot, did not see the part of the thorn that had entered it, but felt it to have been removed. When he looked for it carefully in his bed, he found it, and wondered how it had come out.

During his episcopate he used to show people the site of 5
this wound, where a large scar could still be seen, and asserted that in it a powerful deed of the blessed martyr had occurred.

24

About the fever of my brother Peter

A long time afterward, the date of the blessed martyr's feast came and my father with all his household went to the joyful solemnity. While we were traveling, Peter, my older brother, was seized by a high fever and suffered so acutely that he became very weak and could not take food. The

illud iter cum grandi agitur maerore, et discrimine res vertitur utrum convalescat aut pereat.

2 Denique cum isto labore pervenitur ad locum, ingredimur basilicam, adoramus sacrosancti martyris sepulturam. Prosternitur et aegrotus in pavimento, deprecans medelam a martyre glorioso. Post completam vero orationem ad metatum regressus, febris paululum conquievit. Veniente autem nocte, nobis ad vigiliis properantibus, rogat se et ille deferri, incumbensque ante sepulcrum, tota nocte martyris suffragium deprecatur.

3 Exactis deinde nocturnis excubiis, rogat ut de pulvere qui circa beatum erat tumulum collecto vel potui darent, vel collo suspenderent. Quo facto, ita omnis ardor febrium conquievit ut ipsa die et cibum caperet incolumis et ubi delectatio vertisset animum ambularet.

25

De mei capitis dolore

Sequenti vero festivitate, dum iterum cum magno gaudio ad sanctam properaremus basilicam, mihi caput a sole percussum graviter dolere coepit. Qui dolor accrescens febrem intrinsecus generabat, ita ut nec cibum me capere nec loqui

whole journey thereafter took place in great distress, and it was uncertain whether he would recover or die.

Having, in this state, at last reached our destination, we 2
entered the basilica and worshipped at the tomb of the most holy martyr. The sick man too prostrated himself upon the floor, praying for healing from the glorious martyr. When he had completed his prayer, he returned to our lodging and the fever quieted a bit. When night came and we were on our way to the vigils, he asked to be carried there as well, and prayed the whole night for the martyr's intercession while lying in front of the tomb.

After the nocturnal vigils had been carried out, he asked 3
to be given a drink containing dust that had been collected from around the blessed tomb, and that some of it be hung around his neck. When this had been done, all the heat of the fever subsided so quickly that on that same day he took food as a healthy man and walked wherever he pleased.

25

About my headache

At the next feast, while we were again going to the holy basilica with great joy, my head was struck by the sun and began to ache painfully. The increasing pain generated a fever inside me that did not permit me to take food or to

2 permitteret. Cumque per duos dies ab hoc dolore consumerer, die tertia ad basilicam sancti Ferreoli, cui fons ille de quo superius meminimus est contiguus, advenimus. Distat autem basilica a Brivatensi vico quasi stadiis decem. Cumque in loco illo venissemus, libuit animo ad fontem usque procedere, confidens de virtute martyris quod, si me exinde levis unda perfunderet, mox sanarer.

3 Adveniens vero orationem fundo, aquam haurio, os refrigero, caput infundo; statimque decedentibus lymphis, fugato dolore, sanus abscedo. Et usque ad sepulcrum martyris gloriosi laetus ingredior, admirans et gratias agens martyri, quod prius me virtute sua dignatus fuerit visitare quam ipsius mererer cernere sepulcrum.

26

De febricitante ad fontem sanato

Est enim ad hunc fontem, quia ibidem martyr percussus est, virtus eximia. Quidam a febre correptus, dum in extremis ageret, desiderium habet de aqua fontis haurire, ad
2 quam etiam se deportari fideliter exoravit. Qui a suis inter

talk. After I had been consumed by this pain for two days, 2
we arrived on the third at the basilica of the holy Ferreolus, whose spring, which I mentioned above, is nearby. This basilica is about one and a half miles from the village of Brioude. And when we arrived in that place I desired to go on to the spring, confident of the martyr's power, and trusting that if some of the water streaming from this spring poured over me, I would soon be healed.

Once I arrived there, I poured forth a prayer, drank some 3
water, refreshed my face, and immersed my head. And at the very moment the water descended upon me the pain fled, and I left healthy. Full of joy I approached the tomb of the glorious martyr, praising him and giving thanks to him that his power deigned to visit me before I deserved to behold his tomb.

26

How a man with a fever was healed at the spring

There is an extraordinary power in this spring, because the martyr was slain here. Someone who had been seized by a fever and was about to die wished to drink water from the
spring and, full of faith, asked to be carried there. When he 2

manus apprehensus et in loco depositus, protinus ut aquae haustum accepit et faciem caputque perfudit, recipere meruit sanitatem; et aliorum manibus inlatus, propriis gressibus est regressus. Fuit autem incola huius vici, sed excidit nomen eius.

27

De tonitruo in basilica facto cum coruscatione

Quadam autem die orta tempestas cum magno venti impetu super vicum Brivatensem rapide descendebat; micabant enim de nubibus fulgura ac tonitrua terribiliter voces dabant. Quatitur terra fragore et exuri a coruscatione pene omnia putabantur: sola erat exspectatio in virtute martyris
2 gloriosi. Nec mora, dato cum fulgore gravi sono tonitrui, iaculum igneum per aditum quo funis ille signi dependet ingreditur percussisque duabus columnis, frusta excussit. Inde repercutiens per fenestram quae super sanctum habetur tumulum est egressum, nullum tamen per beati custodiam de populo laesit.

3 O quam magnus circa alumnos proprios beati martyris amor! Columnas sustinuit percuti, non sinit phalangas;

had been taken up by others' hands and laid in this place, as soon as he drank the water and poured it over his face and head, he deservedly regained his health; although he had been borne there by the hands of others, he returned on his own two feet. He was an inhabitant of this village, but his name has been forgotten.

27

About the thunder and lightning that occurred in the basilica

One day a storm arose with mighty gusts of wind and descended swiftly upon the village of Brioude; lightning flashed from the clouds and the sound of the thunderclaps was terrifying. The ground shook with the crashes, and almost everything seemed to be on fire from the lightning: everyone's only hope was in the power of the glorious martyr.
The lightning was accompanied by heavy thunderclaps, and 2
soon a fiery bolt entered by the opening in which the bell rope hung and struck two columns, shattering them. Then because of the blessed man's protection it bounced back and left through the window above the holy tomb, injuring no one.

O how great is the love of the blessed martyr for his fos- 3
ter children! He allowed the columns to be struck, but not

confringi passus est vitream, non catervam; permisit super sepulcrum proprium praeterire coruscum, ne fieret multitudinis totius interitus. Igitur expulsum a basilica sancti martyris iaculum acervos faeni combussit, interfecit pecora, iumenta delevit.

4 Quod si haec fortuita quis putat, admiretur magis et stupeat incliti potentiam martyris, quod praeteriens ignis per medium populi neminem nocuit, sed ibi tantum explevit vota ubi se cognovit habere licentiam.

28

De eo qui prae multitudine populi ad sepulcrum non valebat accedere

Clericus autem quidam Aredii Lemovicini Abbatis ad festivitatem veniens, prae multitudine populi non modo ad sanctum tumulum accedere, verum etiam nec in ipsam basilicam potuit introire. Cumque maestus metatui se reddidis-
2 set, recubans in lectulo obdormivit. Protinus astitit ei vir in visu, dicens: "Quid tu," inquit, "sopore deprimeris? Vade celerius ad templum martyris et omnia invenies reserata."

the assembled people; the glass to be shattered, but not the crowd gathered there; he allowed the lightning to pass over his own tomb so that it did not destroy the whole multitude. After it had been expelled from the basilica of the holy martyr, the bolt of lightning consumed stacks of hay, killed cattle, and destroyed beasts of burden.

If anyone should regard these as chance occurrences, let 4
him instead be astonished at the power of the celebrated martyr, by whose agency the fire cutting through the middle of the crowd hurt no one, but accomplished its wishes only where it knew it had permission.

28

About the man who was unable to approach the tomb because of a great crowd

A cleric of Abbot Aredius of Limoges who had come to the feast could not approach the holy tomb because of the crowds of people; indeed, he could not even enter the basilica. Returning sadly to his lodging,
he went to bed and fell asleep. At once, a man stood be- 2
fore him in a dream vision, who said: "Why are you letting yourself be overcome by sleep? Go quickly to the temple of the martyr and you will find everything open."

At ille metu territus exsurgens, credulus dictioni, properat velociter experiri si vera essent quae sibi fuerant indicata.

3 Cumque venisset ad ostium, reperit, remotis undique populis, usque ad sanctum altare vel ipsum tumulum viam factam nullo obsistente. Et sic sine ulla impressione accedens, fusa oratione, cum gaudio est regressus. Quod ne quis dubitet, testor omnipotentem Deum, quia ipsius abbatis haec ore cognovi, apud cuius monachum gesta sunt.

29

De festivitate eius

Huius festivitatis tempus ignara plebs maesta pendebat, nesciens diem in quo martyr beatus deberet pro virtutis ac passionis gloria honorari. Et haec ignorantia usque ad beatum Germanum Autissiodorensem antistitem est protracta.

2 Factum est autem ut antedictus pontifex Brivatem adveniret, sciscitatusque ab incolis quo tempore huius sacra celebrarentur, se nescire respondent. Tunc ille: “Oremus,” inquit, “et fortassis nobis haec Domini potentia revelabit.”

3 Quod cum fecissent, mane orto, convocatisque senioribus

Awaking terrified, and believing the message, he hurried quickly to find out if what he had been told was true.

When he had come to the door he found that the crowd 3
had departed and there was no one obstructing his access to the holy altar and the tomb. And so he approached them without encountering any pressure from a crowd, poured forth his prayer, and left with joy. In case anyone doubts the story, I call almighty God to witness that I heard it from the mouth of the very abbot for whose monk these things were done.

29

About his feast

The people were sad and uncertain about the time of his feast, because they did not know on which day the blessed martyr should be honored for the glory of his power and his martyrdom. And this lack of knowledge persisted until the arrival of the blessed Germanus, bishop of Auxerre.

When the aforementioned bishop came to Brioude and 2
asked the inhabitants on what date the sacred solemnities of this martyr were celebrated, they replied that they did not know. Then he said: "Let us pray, and perhaps the power
of the Lord will reveal it to us." When they had done this, 3
and the morning had come, he called together the elders of

loci, ait quinto kalendarum mensis septimi celebrandam esse festivitatem. Ex hoc nunc devotus adveniens populus, vota praesuli reddens, refert et animae et corporis medicinam.

30

De energumenis

Energumeni vero, cum advenerint, plerumque evomunt in sanctum Dei convicia, cur sanctos alios ad sua convocet festa, ipsosque nominatim confitentes, eorum fatentur virtutes et merita. Aiunt enim: "Sufficiat tibi, Iuliane, nos propria virtute torquere! Ut quid reliquos provocas? Quid in-
2 vitas extraneos? Ecce Martinum Pannonicum inimicum iugiter nostrum, qui tres a nostris cavernis repulit mortuos. Adest Privatus ex Gabalis, qui oves suas barbaris, nostra
3 instigatione commotis, tradere noluit. Advenit Ferreolus collega tuus ex Viennensibus, qui nobis in te supplicium, incolis praesidium misit. Quid Symphorianum Aeduum, quid Saturninum vocas Tolosanum? Adgregasti concilium, ut nobis ingeras infernale tormentum!"

the place, and told them it should be celebrated on the fifth day before the Kalends of the seventh month. Since then the devout people who now come and pray to their leader at this time return with healed minds and bodies.

30

About the possessed

The possessed, when they come, often vomit forth insults to the holy man of God, asking why he invites other saints to his feasts, mentioning them by name, their powerful deeds, and their merits. Thus they say: "Let it be enough for you, Julian, to torment us with your own power! Why do you
call upon others? Why do you invite strangers? Behold here 2
the Pannonian Martin, our constant enemy, who expelled three dead persons from our caverns. Privatus of Javols is here, who was unwilling to hand over his flock to the barbarians, who had attacked at our instigation. Ferreolus, your 3
companion from Vienne, has come, who, because of you, has sent us tribulation, and the inhabitants protection. Why do you call Symphorianus of Autun? Why Saturninus of Toulouse? You have convened a council so as to inflict hellish torment upon us!"

4 Haec et his similia dicentibus, ita sanctos Dei humanis mentibus repraesentant ut nulli sit dubium eos inibi commorari. Multi tamen ab his infirmi curantur et sani recedunt.

31

De mansuetudine pecorum

Sed et illud est memoratu dignissimum quae sit mansuetudo pecorum in hac basilica votivorum: qualiter vituli petulantes, calcitrantes equi, grunnientes suillae, cum limen sanctum ingressi fuerint, conquiescunt. Nam vidimus saepe cothurnosos tauros, qui a quindecim aut eo amplius viris alligati funibus ducebantur, talem in hominibus impetum dare ut putares eos ipsos quoque dirumpere funes. Sed cum aedem sanctam ingressi sunt, ita quieverunt ut arbitreris eos tamquam agnos mansuetos haberi.

2 Vidimus et nunc per medias turmas multos ingredi, inclinato capite populos amoventes rostro, non cornibus, et tamquam tribunal adirent iudicis, aliquem sensum habere timoris: non calcem mittere, non aliquem cornu petere, non oculis torvis aspicere, sed in omni mansuetudine usque ad sanctum properantes altare, osculantesque, rursus in ipsa qua ingressi fuerant patientia repedare. Sic et reliquorum iumentorum petulantia, cum illuc accesserint, deposito

Saying these and similar things, they described the saints of God in such a way that no one doubted that they were indeed present there. And in fact many sick persons were cured by these saints and departed healthy. 4

31

About the gentleness of the animals

Also most worthy of remembrance is the gentle behavior of the animals offered as gifts in this basilica: how butting calves, recalcitrant horses, and grunting swine calmed down once they had crossed the threshold. For we have often seen fierce bulls, bound with ropes and brought by fifteen or more men, attacking the men in such a way that one would expect the ropes to break. But as soon as they had entered the holy building, they calmed down so completely that you might think they were gentle lambs.

Now too we see many beasts enter amid crowds, with 2
bowed head nudging the people with their muzzles instead of with their horns and, as though approaching a judicial tribunal, with a sense of awe: they do not kick, they do not attack with their horns, they do not glare fiercely, but proceed to the holy altar in all gentleness, and kiss it, before walking back with the same patience with which they had entered. In this way too does the restlessness of the remaining beasts

cuncto furore, mitescit ut ea in mansuetudine columbarum cum grandi admiratione conspicias.

3 De his vero quae votiva sunt nulli penitus quidpiam subtrahere licet; nullus, priusquam ad basilicam veniat, aut commutare praesumit aut emere. Nam qui fecerint saepius ultione divina graviter quatiuntur. Nam aut febris imminet, aut malum aliquod obrepit, aut damnum grave succedit, aut hoc quod abstulit morbus aufert. Difficile tamen sine praesenti ultione res praeterit.

32

De reliquiis eius in Campaniam translatis

De illis dixisse virtutibus sufficiat quae circa sanctam basilicam aut gesta sunt, aut geruntur. Nunc pauca de locis illis in quibus eius habentur reliquiae disserentes, finem huius libelli facere placet, devotione commonente.

2 Quidam apud Belgicae secundae provinciam, id est suburbano Remensis urbis, basilicam in honore beati martyris studiose construxit, cuius reliquias post perfectam fabricam expetiit fideliter ac devote. Quas acceptas, dum via cum

of burden quiet down when they enter here, so that, with great admiration, you see in them the gentleness of doves.

As for those animals which are offered to the church, no 3
one is allowed to take even one away; and let no one, before having come to the basilica, presume either to exchange or to sell them. For those who do this are often struck down by the divine vengeance. Thus either a fever comes upon them, some evil seizes them, a serious loss occurs, or an illness carries off the animal which had been taken. Rarely does such an event take place without a swift vengeance.

32

About his relics that were taken to the Countryside <of Reims>

Let it suffice to have spoken about those deeds of power which have occurred, and still occur in and near the holy basilica. Now our devotion moves us to end this book by talking about a few of the other places that have his relics.

Someone in the province of Belgica Secunda, on the out- 2
skirts of the city of Reims, built a basilica in honor of the blessed martyr with great care, and after the work had been completed went in faith and devotion to seek his relics.

psallendo regreditur, Remensem est ingressus Campaniam. Erat enim haud procul a via ager cuiusdam divitis campanensis, ad quem scindendum magna multitudo convenerat.

3 Igitur, appropinquante viatore cum his pignoribus, coepit quidam de aratoribus male torqueri et quasi in excessu mentis dicere: "En," inquit, "beatissimum Iulianum appropinquantem! Ecce virtutem eius! Ecce gloriam eius! Currite, viri, relinquite boves, dimittite aratra! Caterva omnis eat in obviam!"

4 Stupentes illi et quid narraret ignoti, dum hebetati admirantur tam voces quam dicta personae, protinus miser, relicto in arvis vomere, elidens se in terram verberansque palmas, in parte qua vir ille beati martyris veniebat cursu celeri rapitur, clamans: "Ut quid me, sancte, crucias? Ut quid me, gloriose martyr, incendis? Cur regionem tibi non debitam adgrederis? Cur habitacula nostra perlustras?"

5 Talia eo dicente, ad locum ubi iam sacerdos tabernaculum erexerat turbulentus advenit, prostratusque coram sancti reliquiis, diutissime humo incubuit. Tunc presbyter capsulam illam sanctam super eum ut posuit, illico erumpente ex ore eius sanguine, ab incursione diabolici erroris mundatus est. Deinceps virtutem sanctipraedicans, comes fuit huius itineris.

When he had received them and was returning on the road singing psalms, he came to the Countryside of Reims. Not far from the road, there was a field belonging to a wealthy local man where a large crowd had gathered to plow.

As the traveler with his relics was approaching, one of 3
the plowmen began to be sorely tormented and to shout, as though out of his mind: "Look! The most blessed Julian is approaching! Look at his power! Look at his glory! Hurry, men, leave your cattle, leave your plows! Let the whole crowd go to meet him!"

They stood astonished, not knowing what he was talking 4
about. While they wondered at his cries and words in their amazement, the unhappy man suddenly dropped his plowshare in the furrows, fell to the ground, and struck himself with his own hands. Then he hurried away at great speed in the direction of the man with the relics of the blessed martyr, shouting: "Why do you torment me, holy man? Why do you burn me, glorious martyr? Why do you come into a region where you have no ties? Why do you wander about among our homes?"

Saying such things, he came in great agitation to the place 5
where the priest had already set up his tent and, prostrating himself in front of the relics of the saint, he lay on the ground for a long time. Then, when the priest placed the holy casket upon him, blood immediately rushed forth from his mouth, and he was cleansed of the diabolical attack. After this, he praised the power of the holy man and accompanied the relics for the rest of their journey.

33

De reliquiis eius in Oriente exhibitis

Quid de eius reliquiis in Oriente fidelium fratrum relatio signat edicam. In quadam Orientis civitate, dum in ecclesia quidam a daemonio torqueretur, in navi beati martyris praedixit esse reliquias. Cumque navis portum fuisset adepta, hic ad eam saltuatim prosiliit, ac provolutus solo coram navi, erumpente ab ore et naribus tabe, persona purgata est.

2 Quae cum episcopo nuntiata fuissent, commovet populum cum accensis cereis ad portum usque procedere. Igitur nauclerus audiens flensque prae gaudio, in occursum episcopi properat, nihil se aliud asserens de beati sustulisse basilicam nisi parumper pulveris qui circa sanctum iacebat tumulum. Sed Deus omnipotens comprobans fidem viri,occuli virtutem martyris non permisit.

3 Dehinc episcopus sublatas reliquias usque ad sanctam ecclesiam cum magno honore deportat. Negotiator vero tanta cernens mirabilia basilicam in honore martyris aedificavit, in qua beatas reliquias collocans, multa deinceps ibi miracula vidit operari.

33

About his relics that were brought to the East

I shall now relate a story told to me by some reliable brothers about his relics in the East. In a certain eastern city, someone in the cathedral who was being tortured by a demon foretold that relics of the blessed martyr were coming in a ship. And when the ship had indeed reached the harbor, this man rushed forth with great leaps to greet it; when he had fallen to the ground before the ship, bloody matter streamed from his mouth and nose, and he was cleansed.

When these events had been announced to the bishop, 2
he invited the people to come to the harbor with lighted candles. When he heard about this, the ship's captain, weeping with joy, hurried to meet the bishop, but insisted that he had taken nothing from the blessed man's basilica except some of the dust that lay around the holy tomb. Almighty God, however, had confirmed the man's faith and did not allow the martyr's power to remain hidden.

After taking over the relics, the bishop carried them with 3
great honor from the harbor to the holy cathedral. As for the merchant, after seeing so many wonders, he built a basilica in honor of the martyr where he placed the blessed relics, and thereafter witnessed many miracles.

34

Qualiter Turonis in basilica eius reliquiae sunt locatae

Haec ego dudum expertus sum. Contigit ut post ordinationem meam Arvernos accederem, profectusque beati basilicam adivi. Expletaque festivitate, diruptis a palla quae sanctum tegit tumulum fimbriis, in his mihi praesidium ferre credens, impleta oratione discessi.

2 Apud Turonicam vero urbem monachi in honore ipsius martyris basilicam, qualem possibilitas eorum habuit, aedificaverunt, cupientes eam eius virtutibus consecrari. Audientes autem haec pignora a me fuisse delata, rogabant ut dedicata aedes iisdem augeretur exuviis.

3 At ego, apprehensam secretius capsam, ad basilicam beati Martini, incipiente nocte, propero. Referebat autem mihi vir fidelis, qui tunc eminus astabat, cum nos basilicam sumus ingressi, vidisse se pharum immensi luminis e caelo delapsam super beatam basilicam descendisse, et deinceps quasi intro ingressa fuisset. Cum enim nobis haec in crastinum a fidelibus relata fuissent, conicimus eam a virtute beati martyris processisse.

34

How his relics were deposited in the basilica in Tours

The following things I experienced recently. After my consecration, I happened to pass by Clermont and, continuing on my journey, arrived at the basilica of the blessed Julian. When his feast was over, I pulled out some threads from the cover that hung over the holy tomb, believing that these would offer me protection, and after I completed my prayer I departed.

At the city of Tours, some monks built, according to what 2
their means permitted, a basilica in honor of this martyr, and wished to consecrate it to his deeds of power. When they heard that these relics had been brought by me, they asked that the dedicated basilica be enriched by these spoils.

But I secretly took the casket and hurried at the begin- 3
ning of the night to the basilica of the blessed Martin. A trustworthy man who was standing some distance away told me that when we entered the church he had seen a globe of extremely bright light fall from the sky upon the blessed basilica and thereafter, as it were, enter it. When this was told to us the following day by the faithful, we surmised that it had been occasioned by the power of the blessed martyr.

4 Depositis ergo super altare sacrosanctis reliquiis, vigilata nocte, cum grandi psallentio ad antedictam deferebantur basilicam. Et ecce unus ex energumenis, manibus in se collisis, ore patulo, cruenta proiciens sputa, aiebat: "Ut quid te, Martine, Iuliano iunxisti? Quid eum in his provocas locis? Sat nobis erat praesentia tua supplicium, similem tui ad augenda tormenta vocasti! Cur haec agis? Quare nos cum Iuliano sic crucias?"

5 Haec et alia misero declamante, expletis missarum solemnitatibus, dum se ante sanctum altare diutissime collidit, profluente sanie ex ore eius, ab infestatione furoris diabolici liberatus est.

35

Quod vinum ea nocte crevit

Sed nec hoc silere puto quid in nocte illa, priusquam sanctae reliquiae ibidem collocarentur, sit gestum. Mona-
2 chus ipsius loci, dum de adventu solemnitatis gauderet et singulos quosque ad cellariolum basilicae promptissimus

After the holy relic had been deposited upon the altar, 4
and vigils had been celebrated during the night, the relics were carried with continuous psalm singing to the aforementioned basilica. And look what happened then! One of the possessed, striking himself with his hands and vomiting bloody spittle from his open mouth, cried out: "Martin! Why have you joined yourself to Julian? Why did you invite him to this place? Your presence was enough of a torment for us; now you have invited someone like yourself to increase the torture! Why do you do this? Why do you and Julian persecute us so?"

When the mass had been celebrated, the unhappy man, 5
shouting these and similar words as he kept beating himself in front of the holy altar, was liberated from the infestation of diabolical fury while bloody matter flowed from his mouth.

35

How the wine increased that night

But I think I should not be silent about what happened during the night before the holy relics were placed there.
The monk in charge of the place, joyful about the approach- 2
ing solemnity, urged those, whom he had hastened to invite to a small cellar in the basilica, to celebrate the vigil together

invitaret, hortans ut omnes in basilica fideliter vigilarent, extracto a vase vino, coepit eis causa devotionis cum gaudio propinare, dicens: "Magnum nobis patrocinium in beatum martyrem pietas divina largitur. Idcirco rogo caritatem vestram ut unanimiter vigiletis mecum. Cras enim sanctae eius reliquiae in hoc loco sunt collocandae."

3 Exacta quoque cum sacris hymnis modulisque caelestibus nocte, celebratis etiam missarum solemniis, festivitate ovans clericus coepit eos iterum, quos prius invitaverat, rogare ad refectionem, dicens: "Gratias vobis ago quod sic ad vigilandum immobiles perstitistis."

4 Sed nec martyr diu distulit bonam voluntatem virtutis suae gratia munerare. Nam ingressus promptuarium clericus reperit cupellam, quam pene mediam reliquerat, per superiorem aditum redundare, in tantum ut copia defluentis vini rivum per terram ad ostium usque deduceret. Quod ille admirans, posito deorsum vase, saepius extulit plenum; sed et de ipso, cum satis abundeque fuisset expensum, nihil prorsus defuit, sed usque in crastinum, mirantibus cunctis, semper stetit plenum.

5 Erat autem tertio kalendas mensis quinti. O admirabilis virtus martyris! Cum produxit de vase sine flore vindemiam: cum sit solitum ut collecta vina condantur in vascula, protulit dolium musta, in quo non uva, sed virtus sola defluxit! Turgescit vasculum a liquore, fructus non illatus est, sed creatus. Agit hoc ille Dominus ad glorificandum martyrem,

faithfully in the basilica. Drawing wine from a cask, he happily began to drink to their devotion, saying: "The divine goodness grants us powerful patronage through the blessed martyr. Therefore I ask your charity to keep wholeheartedly the vigil with me. For tomorrow his holy relics are to be installed here."

After having spent the night singing sacred hymns and 3
heavenly melodies, and after celebrating the solemnity of mass, the cleric, elated about the feast, again began to ask those whom he had previously invited to take a meal with him, saying: "I thank you for persisting in the vigils with such unremitting concentration."

And the martyr did not delay in rewarding this goodwill 4
with the grace of his power. For when the cleric entered the storeroom he found the small cask, which he had left barely half full, overflowing so vigorously through its opening at the top that the abundance of the overflowing wine made a rivulet to the door. Amazed at this, he placed a pitcher under the cask and filled it several times; but after enough and even more wine had been drawn, it never failed, and to everyone's astonishment the cask remained permanently full till the next day.

This happened, however, on the third day before the Ka- 5
lends of the fifth month. O astonishing power of the martyr! He brought forth a vintage from a cask although no vine had bloomed: whereas usually one collects the wine to be put into a vessel, the cask itself produced a new wine, in which not grapes but pure holy power flowed! The vessel brimmed over with the liquid, but the fruit was not brought to it: it was created there. The Lord did this to glorify his martyr,

qui implens uterum virginis sine semine permanere praestitit matrem in castitate.

6 Sed tamen hic novo Maius exuberat fructu, cum sine caudicibus Falerna porrigit ad bibendum. In aliis vineis vix adhuc erumpunt gemmae, in hoc vero vase vinum defluit. A virtute aequatur Maius Octobri cum nova porrigit pocula, et
plus habet quam ille, cum in promptu non ostenditur vinea
7 et in domo gignuntur falerna. Rudis etenim venit sine torculari vindemia, quae non in palmitibus, sed in occultis mysteriis est reperta; acervus acinorum non premitur ab arbore et vini defluunt undae; hauriuntur Falerna, cum in torculari non cernuntur impressa. Vitis ecce non aspicitur et pocula large complentur!

8 Sed quid inquam? Non enim deest fidelibus virtus illa caelestis. Nam qui quondam in nuptiis de aquis praestitit vina, nunc suis eadem large porrigit sine ullius elementi natura; et qui geminis piscibus quinque milia hominum satiavit, nunc bonae voluntati multiplicata restituit.

9 In ipsius enim ortus tempore angelica vox testata est, dicens: "Gloria in excelsis Deo et in terra pax hominibus bonae voluntatis" [Luke 2:14]. Sed iam ad sequentia virtutum opera veniamus.

just as he filled the womb of the Virgin without seed to let her become a mother while remaining chaste.

But this month of May abounded with a new fruit, offer- 6
ing a drink of Falernian wine that did not come from vines.
While for normal vines the blossoms had as yet barely appeared, wine already flowed from this cask. Through Julian's
power, May equals October because it offers a new kind of
drink, and it is superior to it, for no vineyard appears in the
storeroom, and wine is born in a house. Without a wine- 7
press, a fresh wine came into being, for it was found not in
vine shoots but in hidden mysteries; it was not from the vine
that the heap of grapes was pressed, yet wine flowed; Falernian wine was drunk that was not seen to have been pressed.
Behold, vines were not seen, yet cups were filled to the brim!

But why do I say this? For that heavenly power never fails 8
those who believe in it. So the one who once made wine
from water now extends to his believers a wine without the
nature of any of the elements <that constitute the earth>;
and the one who satisfied five thousand men with two fishes,
now renews this act many times for those of good will.

Thus at the time of his birth angels bore witness to him, 9
saying: "Glory to God in the highest and on earth peace to
men of good will." But let us now turn to his subsequent
works of power.

36

De contracto in eodem loco sanato

Serviens huius monasterii diu contractus infeliciter trahebatur. Adveniens autem ad ipsam sancti basilicam, vigilias celebrat. Quibus expletis, mane dum ad stratum suum regreditur, inter portantium manus resolutis sanatus est nervis.

37

De puella lippa

Puella quaedam lippis erat oculis et, nimio imbre lacrimarum profluente, paene caecata. Cuius pater, audita virtute martyris gloriosi, cum ea ad basilicam sanctam properat, celebratisque vigiliis, mane pauperibus qui ad matriculam il-
2 lam erant cibum potumque protulit. Epulantibus vero illis,

36

How a paralyzed man was healed here

A servant of this monastery whose tendons had been contracted for a long time was being carried around with difficulty. When he had come to the basilica of the holy man, he celebrated vigils there. After these were completed and he was returning to his bed in the morning, his tendons were released and he was healed while being carried by others' hands.

37

About a girl with bleary eyes

A girl had bleary eyes, and the excessive flow of her tears nearly blinded her. When her father heard of the glorious martyr's power, he hurried with her to the holy basilica, celebrated a vigil, and in the morning gave food and drink to
the poor who were on the poor roll there. While they were 2

subito puella capitis dolore se torqueri proclamat, et ut modico sopori indulgeatur implorat. Qua quiescente, cum convivae epulum explicarent, illa surrexit et ad sanctum se altare duci deposcit. Antequam solo prostrata fuisset et attente Domini misericordiam deprecaretur, restrictis lacrimis, purgatis lippitudine oculis, laeta surrexit. Tunc, patre gaudente, domi redditur sana.

38

De alio contracto

Alius quidam puerulus parvulus, cuius parentes haud procul ab ipsa basilica commanebant, in secundo ortus sui anno membris totis contractus, sine spe alicuius boni nutriebatur. Qui ita contractus erat ut genua ab eius ore penitus separari non possent.

2 Cuius parentes, cum ad sanctam basilicam vigilassent et proiectum infantulum coram sacrosanctis reliquiis dimisissent, post paululum reperiunt eum sedentem membris omnibus esse directum. Dehinc, fusa oratione, gaudentes ad domum suam regressi sunt.

eating, the girl suddenly cried out that she was being tormented by a headache and begged to be allowed to sleep a while. After she had slept and the guests had finished their meal, she arose and asked to be led to the holy altar. Before she had prostrated herself on the ground and prayed for the Lord's compassion, her tears were stopped, her eyes were cleansed of discharge, and she arose full of joy. Her elated father then took her home healthy.

38

About another paralyzed boy

A little boy, whose parents lived not far from the basilica, had become completely paralyzed at the age of two and was being raised without any hope of recovery. He was so deformed that his knees could hardly be separated from his chin.

After they had laid the child in front of the holy relics, his 2
parents kept vigils at the holy basilica. A bit later they found him sitting there with all his limbs straightened. Then they poured forth a prayer and returned with great joy to their home.

39

De periuris

Est etiam in Turonico vicus cui Gaudiaco nomen est, in quo beati martyris reliquiae continentur, qui cum magnis virtutibus crebro illustretur, in periuris tamen plerumque
2 agitata ultione. Nam cum ibidem quis, Inimico humani generis suadente, periuraverit, ita ultio divina prosequitur ut protinus aut in successione damni, aut in amissione proximi, aut in consumptione morbi manifesta patescat; non tamen causam remanere inultam martyr prorsus indulget, sed nec inibi tam ausu temerario periurat barbarorum cruda rustici-
3 tas. De quo negotio ista sufficiant, quia longum est singula quae de his acta sunt per ordinem memorare.

39

About perjurers

There is a village in the territory of Tours named Joué, in which relics of the blessed martyr are kept and which is frequently illumined by great acts of power, and in which vengeance is often exacted from perjurers. For when someone, 2
persuaded by the Enemy of the human race, perjures himself, divine vengeance follows in such a way that it is immediately manifest in a subsequent misfortune, the loss of a friend, or consumption by an illness; the martyr allows absolutely no perjury to remain unavenged, and even the barbarians, despite their crude boorishness and bold temerity, do not perjure themselves there. Let these words suffice about 3
this matter, for it is tedious to commemorate in sequence every single thing that was done regarding perjurers.

40

De reliquiis eius, quas Aredius presbyter sustulit

Cum autem ad me Aredius presbyter ex Lemovicino venisset, vir valde religiosus, cuius etiam in secundo virtutum beati Martini libro memini, dum sollicite vitam eius perscrutarer et actionem inquirere coepi quae ibidem beatissimus Iulianus in miraculis prodidisset; in honore enim beati martyris basilicam aedificavit, quam et eius reliquiis illustravit.

2 Sicut ergo est verecundissimus, diu cunctatus, tandem haec et valde invitus exposuit: "Quando," inquit, "primum beati Iuliani adivi basilicam, parumper cerae a sepulcro sustuli. Inde veniens ad fontem in quo beati martyris sanguis effusus est, abluta aquis facie, parvam ab his pro benedictione complevi ampullam. Testor omnipotentem Deum quia, antequam ad domum accederem, colore, spissitudine, atque odore in balsamum commutata est.

3 "Veniens vero sacerdos ad dedicandam aedem, cum haec exposuissem, nihil aliud pro reliquiis in sanctum altare condere voluit nisi vasculum cuius aqua in balsamum commutata fuerat, dicens: 'Hae sunt certae reliquiae, quas martyr paradisiacis virtutibus illustravit.'"

40

About his relics, which the priest Aredius took

When the priest Aredius, a truly religious man whom I commemorated in the second book of the miracles of the blessed Martin, came to me from Limoges, I asked him most attentively about his life and deeds, and also what miracles the most blessed Julian had brought about there; for he had built a basilica in honor of the blessed martyr, which he enhanced with his relics.

2 Since he is an extremely modest man, he hesitated a long time, but at last, and most unwillingly, explained: "When I first came to the blessed Julian's basilica, I took a bit of wax from his tomb. Going from there to the spring in which the blessed martyr's blood was shed, and having washed my face with its water, I filled a small flask with it as a blessing. And I call the almighty God to witness that before I reached home, it had been transformed into balsam in color, density, and odor.

3 "When the bishop of the city came to dedicate the building and I had showed it to him, he wished to place on the altar as a relic the very flask whose water had been transformed into balsam, saying: 'These are proven relics which the martyr has endowed with the powers of Paradise.'"

41

De paralytico sanato

Multa quidem et alia sunt, de quibus plurima praetermittens, aliqua pando.

2 Infirmus quidam omnibus membris debilis, plaustro impositus, ad eius monasterium est adductus. Qui cum ante ipsam basilicam in hoc vehiculo nocte iaceret, videt eam subito magno splendore fulgentem, vocesque in ea psallen-
3 tium tamquam multorum hominum audiebat. Dum haec agerentur et ille orationem funderet, quasi stupens factus nec memor dolorum eo appropinquante, splendor quem videret praeteriit ante oculos eius. At ille, fulgore demoto, in se reversus, sensit se pristinae saluti recuperatum.

42

De caeco illuminato

Caecus quoque adminiculo deducente ad sacrosanctum altare eius accedens, dum de opertorio sanctarum reliquia-
2 rum oculos attigit, lumen recepit. Sed et inergumeni, ab hac

41

How a paralytic was healed

There are, indeed, many additional miracles which I pass over to tell about a select few.

A certain ill man, who was unable to use his limbs, was 2
carried on a cart to Aredius's monastery. As he lay on this cart during the night right in front of the basilica, he suddenly saw it light up with great splendor and heard voices in
it as of many men singing psalms. While this was happening 3
and he was pouring forth a prayer, he became stunned, as it were, and no longer felt his pain; then the brightness which he had seen disappeared from his eyes. When the light had been removed, he returned to his senses and felt that he had been restored to his original health.

42

How a blind man was given light

A blind man who approached the basilica's holy altar with a guide received light when he touched his eyes with
the cloth covering the holy relics. But possessed persons too 2

palla cooperti, saepe mundati sunt. Et potestas iudicum, quotienscumque in eo loco superflue egit, confusa discessit.

43

De cruce altaris furata

Pendebat autem super ipsum altare crux holocrysa, eleganti opere facta, et erat tam praeclara visu, ut eam putares
2 ex auro esse mundissimo. Adventientibus vero barbaris, a quodam esse aurea aestimata, direpta est et sinu recondita. At is qui eam sustulerat tanto subito pondere praegravatur ut eam penitus sustinere non posset; statimque compunctus virtute martyris ac paenitentia motus, de itinere transmissam loco sancto restituit.

have often been cleansed by this cloth. And every time judges have tried to overstep the bounds of their power in this place they have left confounded.

43

About the cross stolen from the altar

Above the altar hung a gold cross, elegantly made, and so bright to the eye that one might think it made of the purest
gold. When the barbarians came, one of them assumed that 2
it was entirely made of gold, took it, and hid it in his bosom. But the thief suddenly became burdened with so great a weight that he could hardly carry it; struck by the power of the martyr as well as moved by remorse, he sent it back from where he was on his journey, restoring it to the holy place.

44

Qualiter expetita sunt eius pignora

Quae postquam gesta sunt, misit supradictus Aredius clericum suum, dicens: "Vade," inquit, "ad beati Iuliani basilicam et, fundens orationem, supplica ut tibi aliquid cerae vel pulveris de sepulcro iacentis largiri dignentur aeditui, ut delatum a<d> me cum benedictione suscipiatur."

2 Ille vero veniens, quae sibi fuerant imperata flagitat ac suscipit. Et, cum suscepta ferre vellet, tanto gravatur pondere ut vix cervicem posset erigere. Unde tremore magno concussus pavimento prosternitur; et iterum cum lacrimis orationem fundens, surrexit incolumis et acceptam sensit abeundi habere se libertatem.

3 Igitur arrepto itinere, incandescente nimium sole, siti corripitur. Veniens autem ad villam viae proximam, unam casulam adit, aquam deposcens. De qua egrediens iuvenis dare responsum, ut eos vidit, in terram corruit factusque est
4 sicut mortuus. Concurrentes autem parentes eius calumniabantur hominibus, asserentes parentem suum eorum magicis artibus fuisse peremptum, et, apprehensum puerum, elevaverunt eum semivivum. At ille de manibus eorum elapsus, percussis palmis, coepit debacchando clamare vel dicere quod martyris Iuliani virtute exureretur.

44

How his relics were sought

After these events, the aforementioned Aredius sent his cleric off, saying to him: "Go to the basilica of the blessed Julian and, after pouring forth a prayer, beg the custodian that some wax or dust lying around the tomb be given to you, so that it may be brought to me and received with a blessing."

The cleric went, asked for that which he had been or- 2
dered to request, and received it. But when he wished to take it with him, its weight increased so greatly that he could hardly straighten his neck. Overcome by a great shudder, he prostrated himself on the pavement; and when he had once more poured forth a prayer with tears, he arose unhurt and felt that he had received permission to leave.

He set out on his journey, therefore, and as the sun had 3
become very hot, was overcome with thirst. When he came to a country house close to the road, he approached one of the cottages and asked for water. A young man came out of it to give him an answer, but when he saw the company, he
fell to the ground and lay as though dead. His relatives came 4
running and blamed the men, asserting that their relative had been killed by their magic arts, and taking hold of the boy, lifted him up half-alive. But he escaped from their hands, pounded himself with his palms, and began to twist his body and shout that he was being burned by the martyr Julian's power.

5 Clericus vero haec audiens, posita super caput eius capsula cum pignoribus sanctis, fide plenus orare coepit attentius. Ipse quoque cum vomitu sanguinem daemoniumque proiciens, purgatus abscessit. Dehinc firmatus in fide portitor, iter totum cum psalmis et gratiarum actionibus carpens ad locum praeoptatum, martyre ducente, pervenit.

6 Iam exinde, tempore procedente, quanti energumeni, frigoritici, vel diversis morbis oppressi martyris virtute sanati sunt, nec nomina retineri, nec numerus potuit colligi.

45

De puero ad ariolos ducto, et alio per virtutem sancti sanato

Inter reliqua vero insignia suscipiendorum miraculorum ponimus et istud, quod insipientes corrigat et roboret sapientes.

2 Igitur Cautini episcopi tempore, quo, ingruentibus peccatis populi, Arverna regio ab excidio lues quam inguinariam vocant devastabatur, ego Brivatensem vicum expetii, scilicet ut qui meritis tutari nequibam, beati martyris

When the cleric heard these words, he placed the casket 5 with the holy relics on the boy's head and full of faith began to pray. The boy thereupon vomited out both blood and the demon, and left cleansed. This confirmed his faith, and the carrier accomplished the whole journey to his desired destination with psalms and thanksgiving, under the guidance of the martyr.

As to how many possessed persons, the fever-stricken, 6 and people oppressed by various diseases were healed by the martyr's power in the course of time after this, their names could not be recalled nor their number counted.

45

About a servant who was presented to wizards, and another one who was healed by the power of the holy man

Among the remaining extraordinary miracles that were experienced, we report this one, so that it may correct the foolish and strengthen the wise.

At the time of Cautinus's episcopate, when the devastat- 2 ing slaughter of the disease which they call "inguinal" assaulted the region of Clermont, I went to the village of Brioude so that, not deserving to be protected by my own merits, I might be saved by the protection of the blessed

Iuliani salvarer praesidio. In quo dum commorarer vico, unus puer ex nostris ab hoc morbo corripitur, reclinatoque
3 ad lectulum capite, graviter aegrotare coepit. Erat autem febris assidua cum stomachi pituita, ita ut, si aliquid acciperet, confestim reiceret; nec erat ei cibus confortatio, sed magis exitus putabatur. Denique mei, cum viderent eum in extrema vexari, ariolum quendam invocant. Ille vero venire non differens accessit ad aegrotum, et artem suam exercere conatur. Incantationes immurmurat, sortes iactat, ligaturas collo suspendit, promittit vivere quem ipse mancipaverat morti.

4 Haec autem me nescio agebantur; quae cum mihi delata fuissent, amarissimus reddor, et cum gravi suspirio illud commemoro quod Dominus per Eliam prophetam Oziae regi pronuntiat, dicens: "Quia dereliquisti dominum Deum Israel et consuluisti deum Acharon, ideo de lectulo in quo ascendisti non consurges, sed morte morieris" [2 Kings 1:16]. Nam iste, post adventum arioli validius febre succensus, spiritum exhalavit.

5 Cuius post obitum interpositis paucis diebus, puer alius simili laborare coepit incommodo. Tum ego eis inquio: "Accedite ad martyris tumulum et aliquid exinde ad aegrotum deportate, et videbitis magnalia Dei atque cognoscetis quid sit inter iustum et iniustum et inter timentem Deum et non servientem illi." Accedentes autem, parumper pulveris circa sepulcrum iacentis sustulerunt. De quo ut hausit infirmus cum aqua, protinus assecutus est medicinam, recuperatisque viribus ac restincta febre, convaluit.

martyr Julian. While we were staying in this village, one of our servants was seized by this disease, and having laid his
head down in bed, began to become very ill. He ran a con- 3
stant fever, accompanied by vomiting, and if he ingested anything, he immediately threw it up; food was no comfort to him, but seemed to lead to his end. At last, when my servants saw him to be in death's throes, they called in a wizard. He did not need to be asked twice, came to the sick man, and tried to practice his arts. Murmuring incantations, casting lots, and hanging amulets around the patient's neck, he promised life to the one whom he himself was chaining to death.

These things were done without my knowledge, however. 4
When they were reported to me, I became extremely bitter and with a deep sigh remembered what the Lord had said to King Ahaziah through his prophet Elijah: "Because you have forsaken the Lord God of Israel and consulted the god of Ekron, therefore you will not arise from the bed into which you climbed, but will die." For this servant burned with a more severe fever after the arrival of the soothsayer, and breathed out his spirit.

A few days after his death, another one of my servants be- 5
gan to suffer from a similar ailment. Then I said to them: "Go to the martyr's tomb and take something from there to the sick man, and you will see the great works of God and know the difference between the just and the unjust, and between the man who fears God and the man who does not serve Him." They went there and took away a tiny bit of the dust lying around the tomb. When the sick man had drunk this with water, the cure followed instantly, and when he had regained his strength, and the fever's fire had been put out, he recovered.

6 Intelligite ergo nunc, O omnes qui insipientes estis in populo, et, postquam ista discusseritis, scitote quia nihil sunt quae ad seducendum humanum genus diabolus operatur. Ideo moneo ut si quis vexillo crucis signatus, si quis baptismi ablutione mundatus, si quis vetustate deposita in novo nunc homine viget, talia postponat ac negligat. Quaerat autem patrocinia martyrum, per quos sanitatum miracula celebrantur, postulet adiutoria confessorum, qui merito amici sunt dominici nuncupati, et quae voluerit, obtinebit.

46

De rosis ad sepulcrum eius divinitus ostensis

Eo tempore, cum post obitum Proserii martyrarii, Urbanus diaconus huius basilicae ordinatur aedituus, mira res ad sepulcrum sancti apparuit. Nam vigilante diacono in lectulo suo, auditus est sonitus quasi ostium basilicae panderetur. Post multarum vero horarum spatium audivit eum iterum claudi. Post haec surgens de stratu, praecedente lumine accedit ad tumulum sancti.

Understand this now, therefore, all you foolish ones among the people and, after you have considered these facts, know that what the devil does to seduce the human race is worthless. Therefore I warn anyone who has been signed with the cross, anyone cleansed by the water of baptism, anyone who has put off the old Adam and lives in the new one, to avoid and reject such things. Let him rather seek the patronage of the martyrs through whom miracles of healing are celebrated, let him ask for the help of the confessors who are deservedly called the friends of God, and he will obtain what he wishes. 6

46

About the roses divinely shown at his tomb

After the death of Proserius, the guardian of the martyr's shrine, when the deacon Urbanus was ordained as the guardian of the basilica, a marvelous thing was manifested at the tomb of the holy man. For while the deacon lay awake in his bed, a sound was heard as though the door of the basilica were being opened. After many hours he heard it being closed again. After this he got up from his bed, took a light, and went to the holy man's tomb.

2 Mirum dictu, vidit pavimentum rosis rutilantibus esse respersum. Erant autem magnae valde cum flagrantia odoris immensi. In ipsas quoque cancelli celaturas mirabatur rosas intus (nonus enim erat mensis), et hae ita erant virides ac si easdem ipsius putares horae momento ramis virentibus esse decerptas.

3 Tunc cum grandi reverentia collectas secretius deposuit, multis exinde infirmis medicamenta distribuens. Nam energumenus quidam ex Turonico veniens, ut exinde delibutum potum sumpsit, eiecto daemone, purgatus abscessit.

47

De muliere inluminata

Mulier erat a nativitate caeca, quae se exhiberi a parentibus ad beati Martini tumulum deprecata est. Ubi cum venisset, prostrata per triduum ad cancellos qui ante sepulcrum sancti antistitis habentur extrinsecus, responsum accepit per somnium, dicente sibi sancto viro: "Si lumen recipere desideras, require basilicam sancti Iuliani, in qua, dum praesidium martyris expetes, ille coniunctus Martino visum tibi necessarium, simul orationum suarum suffragiis, revocabunt."

Astonishing to say, he saw the pavement strewn with glowing red roses. They were very large with a powerful fragrance. Through the openings in the balustrade he admiringly saw roses inside it too, and although it was September, they were so fresh that one would think that they had that very moment been cut from their living stems. 2

He gathered them with great reverence and put them in a secret place, subsequently giving them as remedies to many ill people. For when a possessed person who had come from Tours drank a potion made from them, the demon was expelled, and he departed cleansed. 3

47

How a woman was given light

A woman who had been blind from birth asked her relatives to bring her to the tomb of the blessed Martin. When she had come there and prostrated herself for three days at the balustrade in front of the holy bishop's tomb, she received an answer in a dream. In it, the holy man said to her: "If you wish to receive light, go to a basilica of the holy Julian. If you ask for the martyr's help in this, he and Martin will together restore the sight you need through their joint intercessions."

2 Exsurgens autem mulier, et ignorans quod in Turonico huius martyris reliquiae tenerentur, ad Santonicam urbem dirigit. Victorina etenim materfamilias, ex nobili stirpe progenita, in villae suae territorio basilicam construxerat reliquiasque beati martyris condiderat. Ad hanc ergo aedem mulier accedens, orat per triduum.

3 Die autem tertia advenit natalis baptistae domini. Stante autem populo et lectionem dogmata auscultante, subito murmur magnum oritur. Presbyter vero qui solemnia celebrabat, comprimere voces cupiens, interrogat quid hoc esset. Cui unus ex astantibus ait: "Murmur mitescere non potest, quia virtus Domini miraculum prodidit. Ecce enim mulier illa quae se caecam testabatur ortam, erumpente ab oculis sanguine, visum recepit!" Tunc omnes benedixerunt Deum, cognoscentes pariter quae fuerant gesta.

48

De reliquiis quas Nanninus presbyter detulit

Nanninus igitur, presbyter domus Vibriacensis, martyris huius gloriosi reliquias expetivit. Quas ex iussu beati Aviti pontificis assumptas, cum psallentio tulit usque ad basilicam sancti Ferreoli, quae procul ab ipso vico sita est.

The woman arose and, not knowing that some relics of this martyr were kept in Tours, went to the city of Saintes. For there the matron Victorina, of noble birth, had built a basilica in the territory of her country house in which she had placed relics of the blessed martyr. To this building the woman went and prayed for three days. 2

The third day was that of the birth of John, the Lord's Baptist. While the people were standing, listening to the biblical readings, suddenly a great murmuring arose. The priest who celebrated the solemnity, wishing to suppress the voices, asked what this was. One of those present said to him: "The murmuring cannot be quieted down because the Lord's power has produced a miracle. For here is a woman who says she has been blind from birth, and she received her sight when blood flowed from her eyes!" Then everyone, learning what had happened, blessed God. 3

48

About the relics which the priest Nanninus took

Nanninus, a priest of a shrine in the estate of Vibriacum, asked for relics of this glorious martyr. Having received them by the order of the blessed bishop Avitus, he carried them with psalm singing to the basilica of the holy Ferreolus, situated at some distance from the village of Brioude.

Et cum ad eam pervenisset, unus ex energumenis est mun-
2 datus. Procedens autem psallendo, cum ad medianam pervenisset horam, coram hoste improbo virtute sancti depulso, puella alia purgata discessit.

49

Quod de eiusdem reliquiis multi infirmi sanati sunt

Accedens autem ad locum ubi oratorium quod in honore sancti construxerat, posuit haec pignora in altari sancto.
2 Accedens autem ad eum unus cum amissis oculis, alius manu debilis, impleta oratione, hic lumen recepit post tenebras,
3 manus ille usum post otia diuturna. Mulier etiam nomine Aeterna cum filia ab hoste iniquo vexata, ad hoc altare curata, cum prole sospes abscessit. Frigoritici etiam in illo loco nonnulli salvati sunt.

And when he arrived there, one of the possessed was
cleansed. He continued his journey with psalm singing, and 2
when it was noon, the wicked Enemy was again expelled
by the power of the holy man, and another girl departed
cleansed.

49

How many sick people were healed by his relics

Having reached the place where he had built the chapel
in honor of the holy man, Nanninus placed the relics on the
holy altar. Then someone came to it who had lost his eye- 2
sight, and another with a paralyzed hand. After he had finished his prayer, the former received light after darkness,
and the latter recovered the use of his hand after long dis-
use. A woman named Aeterna came with her daughter who 3
was vexed by the wicked Enemy, and when Aeterna had been
cured at the altar, she departed healthy along with her
healed child. A number of fever-stricken men too were made
healthy in this place.

50

De alio caeco inluminato

Sed quoniam non est absurdum si beatus Iulianus cum Ioanne aut Martino dona sanitatum impertiat, cum quibus victor saeculi in caelo tripudiat, referam adhuc qualiter cum Nicetio Lugdunensi simili virtute floruerit.

2 Igitur infra terminum territorii Turonici, Litomeris quidam in honore sancti martyris basilicam aedificavit, in qua nos ex more ad benedicendum evocati, sancti Iuliani marty-
3 ris cum Nicetii Lugdunensis reliquias collocavimus. Sed non multo post tempore caecus adveniens, dum fideliter orationem fudit, visum recipere meruit. Memini huius caeci in libro vitae sancti Nicetii, quia dignum est ut communis virtus utriusque sancti scripta connectat.

4 Ergo his miraculis lector intendens intelligat non aliter nisi martyrum reliquorumque amicorum Dei adiutoriis se posse salvari. Ego autem Domini misericordiam per beati martyris Iuliani patrocinia deprecor, ut advocatus in causis alumni proprii, coram Domino assistens, obtineat ut absque impedimento maculae ullius huius vitae cursum peragam, atque illa quae confessus sum in baptismo irreprehensibiliter teneam, fideliter exerceam, ac viriliter usque ad consummationem huius vitae custodiam. Amen.

50

How another blind man was given light

But because it is not surprising for the blessed Julian to share the gift of healing with John or Martin, with whom he dances for joy in heaven as a victor over the world, I shall now relate how he flourished in a similar act of power with Nicetius of Lyons.

In the territory of Tours, a certain Litomer built a basilica 2
in honor of the holy martyr; when, according to custom, he called upon us to bless it, we installed relics of the holy martyr Julian in it together with some of Nicetius of Lyons. Not 3
long afterward, a blind man came, and while praying with faith, deservedly regained his sight. We commemorated this blind man in the book on the life of the holy Nicetius, because it is proper that a shared act of power connect the writings about each saint.

Let the attentive reader understand therefore that he can 4
be saved only by the help of the martyrs and other friends of God. I, however, pray for the Lord's compassion through the patronage of the blessed martyr Julian, so that standing before the Lord as an advocate in the cases of his foster sons, he may obtain from Christ that I may accomplish the course of this life without the impediment of any blemish, and that I may blamelessly maintain, faithfully exercise, and manfully guard until the end of this life that which I confessed at baptism. Amen.

THE MIRACLES OF BISHOP MARTIN

LIBER PRIMUS

Prologus

Dominis sanctis, et in Christi amore dulcissimis fratribus ac filiis ecclesiae Turonicae mihi a Deo commissae, Gregorius peccator.

Miracula illa quae dominus Deus noster per beatum Martinum antistitem suum in corpore positum operari dignatus est, quotidie ad corroborandam fidem credentium confirmare dignatur. Ille nunc exornans virtutibus eius tumulum, qui in eo operatus est cum esset in mundo, et ille praebet per eum beneficia christianis, qui misit tunc praesulem gentibus perituris. Nemo ergo de anteactis virtutibus dubitet cum praesentium signorum cernit munera dispensari: cum videat claudos erigi, caecos illuminari, daemones effugari, et alia quaeque morborum genera, ipsum medificante, curari.

2 Ego vero fidem ingerens libri illius qui de eius vita ab anterioribus est scriptus, praesentes virtutes de quanto ad memoriam recolo, memoriae in posterum, Domino iubente, mandabo. Quod non praesumerem nisi bis et tertio admoni-
3 tus fuissem per visum. Tamen omnipotentem Deum testem invoco quia vidi quadam vice per somnium, media die, in basilica domni Martini debiles multos ac diversis morbis

BOOK I

Prologue

To the holy lords and dearest brothers and sons in the love of Christ of the church of Tours entrusted to me by the Lord, Gregory, a sinner.

The miracles which the Lord our God deigned to perform through the blessed Martin, his priest, while he was situated in the body, he now deigns to confirm every day in order to strengthen the faith of believers. The same Lord who now illuminates his tomb with powerful deeds worked in him when he was in the world, and he now presents benefits to Christians through him, who then sent him as a leader to people who were about to perish. Let no one, therefore, have any doubt about the powerful deeds done earlier when he sees the gifts of the signs being given in the present: when he sees the lame raised up, the blind receiving their sight, demons being put to flight, and all other kinds of illnesses being cured by his healing.

As for me, trusting that book about his life written by 2
earlier authors, I shall set down for the record for those who come after me, at the command of God, as many of the present powerful deeds as I can remember. This I would not presume to do if I had not been admonished two or three times
through a vision. For I call almighty God to witness that 3
I once saw in a dream vision, in the middle of the day, that many ill people who were oppressed by various diseases were being healed in the church of the lord Martin, and

oppressos sanari, et videbam eos, spectante matre mea, quae ait mihi: "Quare segnis es ad haec scribenda quae prospicis?" Cui aio: "Non tibi latet quod sim inops litteris et tam admirandas virtutes, stultus et idiota, non audeam promulgare? Utinam Severus aut Paulinus viverent, aut certe Fortunatus adesset, qui ista describerent! Nam ego ad haec iners notam
4 incurro, si haec adnotare temptavero." Et ait mihi: "Et nescis quia nobiscum propter intelligentiam populorum si quis loquitur, sicut loqui potens es, eo habetur magis praeclarum? Itaque ne dubites, et haec agere non desistas, quia crimen tibi erit si ea tacueris."

5 Ego autem, haec agere cupiens, duplicis taedii adfligor cruciatu, maeroris pariter et terroris: maeroris, cur tantae virtutes, quae sub antecessoribus nostris factae sunt, non sunt scriptae; terroris, ut adgrediar opus egregrium rusticanus. Sed spe divinae pietatis illectus, aggrediar quod mone-
6 tur. Potest enim, ut credo, per meae linguae sterilitatem proferre ista qui ex arida cote in eremo producens aquas, populi sitientis exstinxit ardorem; aut certe constabit eum rursum os asinae reserare, si, labia mea aperiens, per me indoctum ista dignetur expandere.

7 Sed quid timeo rusticitatem meam, cum dominus Redemptor et Deus noster, ad destruendam mundanae sapientiae vanitatem, non oratores sed piscatores, nec philosophos sed rusticos, praelegit? Confido ergo orantibus vobis, quia,

while I was beholding them, my mother, watching me, said to me: "Why are you slow to write about what you see?" I said to her: "Are you not well aware that I am uneducated in letters and that, ignorant and untrained, I do not dare to publicize such admirable deeds of power? If only Severus or Paulinus were alive, or indeed Fortunatus were here, to describe these things! For I would incur the blame of awkwardness if I were to attempt to comment on these." And 4
she said to me: "And do you not know that if someone speaks to us in a way the people can understand, as you do so well, he will therefore be regarded as more brilliant? Therefore don't hesitate, and don't delay doing this, because you will be faulted if you are silent."

Wishing to do this, however, I am afflicted by the tor- 5
ment of a double anguish, grief as well as dread: grief, that such great deeds of power enacted in the days of our predecessors have not been recorded in writing; dread, of taking on this eminent task as an uneducated peasant. Inspired by the hope of God's goodness, however, I shall begin to carry out what I have been admonished to do. For I believe that 6
he is able to bring forth these things through the barrenness of my language since he once brought forth water in the desert from a barren rock to extinguish the fire of the people's thirst; and he will certainly once again have opened the mouth of an ass if, opening my lips, he sees fit to publish these things through my uneducated self.

But why am I anxious about my rusticity when the Lord, 7
our Redeemer and our God, to destroy the emptiness of the world's wisdom, chose not orators but fishermen, not philosophers but country folk? Because of your prayers,

etsi non potest paginam sermo incultus ornare, faciet eam tamen gloriosus antistes praeclaris virtutibus elucere.

I

Quod Severus vitam sancti Martini conscripsit

Multi enim sunt, qui virtutes sancti Martini vel stante versu vel stylo prosaico conscripserunt. Quibus primus ille Severus Sulpicius, cui tantus fervor amoris fuit in sanctum Dei, ut eo adhuc degente saeculo, unum librum de mirabilibus vitae eius scriberet, exinde post transitum beati viri duos libros scripsit, quos *Dialogos* voluit vocitari. In quibus nonnulla de virtutibus eremitarum, anachoretarumve, refe-
2 rente Posthumiano, inseruit. Sed in nullo inferiorem nostrum potuit reperire Martinum, quem apostolis sanctisque prioribus exaequavit, ita ut etiam diceret: "Felicem quidem Graeciam, quae meruit audire apostolum praedicantem; sed nec Gallias a Christo derelictas, quibus donavit habere Martinum."

therefore, I am confident that even if my unpolished speech cannot decorate these pages, the glorious bishop will nevertheless make them shine with his splendid deeds of power.

I

That Severus wrote a *Life* of the holy Martin

Certainly, there are many who have written about Martin's deeds of power, either in standing verse or in a prose style. Of these, Severus Sulpicius is the first, and his love of the holy man of God was so fervent that he wrote a book about the wonders of his life while the saint was still in this world, and then, after the blessed man had passed away, he wrote two books which he wished to call *Dialogues.* In these, with Postumianus as narrator, he inserted several of the
powerful deeds of hermits and anchorites. But he was un- 2
able to find our Martin in any way inferior to them because he considered him to be the equal of the apostles and earlier saints, so that he even said: "Greece was certainly happy, since it was worthy to hear the apostle preaching; but neither were the Gauls abandoned by Christ, for he gave Martin to them to have and to hold."

2

Quod eandem vitam beatus Paulinus versu composuit

Paulinus quoque beatus, Nolanus urbis episcopus, post scriptos versus de virtutibus eius quas Severus prosa complexus est, quinque libros, illa comprehendit miracula quae post eius gesta sunt transitum, id est, in sexto operis sui libro.

2 Ait enim: "Cum inergumini per cancellos basilicae aereo veherentur volatu, et saepe in puteum qui in ipsa habetur basilica impulsu daemonis iactarentur, abstracti exinde illaesi, populis spectantibus, sunt resumpti." Idque in eodem puteo, et nostris temporibus vidimus gestum.

3 Alius quoque daemon acquisitum vasculum praecipitem duxit ad amnem, quasi praedam quam ceperat dimersurus. Sed non defuit perituro beati confessoris auxilium. Nam ingressus in flumen et ulteriorem ripam petens nihil nocumenti accepit, sed siccis est etiam vestimentis egressus. Cumque ad cellulam Maioris monasterii pervenisset, mun-
4 datus apparuit. Hunc etiam testatur multas voces emittere solitum ac linguam gentium incognitarum saepissime loqui venturaque fateri et crimina confiteri. Sed, ut diximus, ut limen sanctum attigit, sanus abscessit.

2

That the blessed Paulinus rendered the same *Life* into verse

The blessed Paulinus, bishop of the city of Nola, after he had written five books in verse about the holy Martin's powerful deeds which Severus had treated in prose, gathered the miracles that occurred after his demise in the sixth book of his work.

For he said: "When the possessed were being lifted in 2
flight through the air over the chancel in the basilica, and often thrown by a demon into a well in that same church, they were pulled up from there unhurt and taken up while the people watched." I have seen this happen in the same well also in our own time.

Paulinus also tells us that another demon hurried the ves- 3
sel it had captured to the river, intending to drown the prey it had seized. But the blessed confessor's help was on hand for the one about to die. For having entered the river and sought the other shore, he was not hurt, and even came out with his clothes dry. And when he arrived at the saint's cell
in Marmoutier, he was seen to be cleansed. This man was 4
even said to have been in the habit of emitting frequent cries in different voices, and speaking the language of unknown peoples, and very often to have spoken of things to come and confessed crimes. But, as we said, as soon as he had touched the holy threshold, he became healthy and went home.

5 Egidius quoque cum obsederetur ab hostibus et, excluso a se solatio, turbatus impugnaretur, per invocationem beati viri, fugatis hostibus, liberatus est. Idque daemoniacus in medio basilicae, ipsa hora qua gestum fuerat, est professus sancti Martini obtentu hoc fuisse concessum.

6 Puella quaedam paralysis umore gravata et, quod peius est, errore cultus fanatici involuta, beati sepulcrum expetiit, vigiliisque celebratis, sanitati est reddita. Rursumque ad idolatriae vomitum revocata, languorem, quem obtentu pontificis caruerat, iterato incurrit.

7 Chunus quidam, rabidus instinctu daemonis actus, coronam sepulcri, quae sancti meritum declarabat, violenter arripuit. Mox lumine privatus, praedam cogente dolore restituit lumenque quod perdiderat recepit.

8 Quidam vero a Temptatore commotus, prolato gladio, cum quendam ferire conaretur in atrio confessoris, protinus ira in se retorta, veloci iudicio Dei prosequente, ipso se mucrone perfodit.

9 Denique cum populus ad beati templi ornatum columnas deferre cuperet gaudens, quidam vir, qui operi huic invidus et contrarius fuit, in alveum exclusum multa minabatur, pro eo quod solatium aliquod ad plaustra petentibus non praeberet. Cumque superbus equum feriret et in parvulo fluviolo

5 Aegidius too, when he was besieged by enemies and, because help was lacking, was distressed by the attack, called upon the blessed man and was liberated by the flight of the enemy. A possessed person in the middle of the church, at the very hour that this took place, declared that this had been granted through the intercession of the holy Martin.

6 A girl burdened with the humor of paralysis and, what is worse, involved in the error of pagan cult, came to the tomb of the blessed man, and after she had celebrated vigils there, was given back her health. After she had been called back to the vomit of her idolatry, however, she again incurred the illness of which she had been freed by the intercession of the bishop.

7 A Hun, acting rabidly under the compulsion of a demon, violently seized the crown above the tomb which declared the merit of the saint. At once deprived of his sight, he was forced by his pain to give back his booty and received the sight which he had lost.

8 A man was actually instigated by the Tempter to draw his sword, and when he attempted to strike someone in the confessor's forecourt, his anger immediately turned upon himself: God's swift judgment pursued him as he ran himself through with his sharp-edged weapon.

9 Then, when the people joyfully wished to transport columns for the decoration of the blessed temple, a man who was envious of this work and opposed to it barred access to the bed of a stream with many threats, so as not to offer help to those requesting passage through it for their carts. When the haughty man struck his horse, he was thrown into the shallow stream, and died in the bosom of the eddy

praecipitatus, in sinu aquarum gurgitis ictibus suis suffocatus interiit. Tunc, iuvene praecedente, columnae usque ad beatum templum delatae sunt.

10 Quotiens etiam ad beatum sepulcrum oleum fuisset positum, referunt illud vidisse adauctum. Sanctus vero Perpetuus episcopus, merito beati discipulus praeconandus, ampullam cum oleo ad sanctum tumulum detulit, ut eum virtus iusti infusa sanctificaret. Et eraso a marmore, quo sancta membra teguntur, pulvere, ac liquori permixto, ex quo in tantum oleum redundavit ut vestimentum sacerdotis nectareo effragrans odore oleagina unda perfunderetur. Multique ex hoc infirmi experti sunt salutem. Sed et procellae ab agris hoc liquore purificatis saepe prohibitae sunt.

11 Cum autem ad templum sanctum quidam devotus fide plenus accessisset et, gratiam sancti sitiens, cogitaret quid de beata aede raperet ad salutem, prope sepulcrum accedens, aedituum supplicat ut sibi parumper benedictae cerae largiretur e tumulo. Quam accipiens laetus abscessit, et agro, cui frugem severat, confisus imposuit. Adveniens autem tempestas saevissima, quae viciniam in annis praecedentibus saepe vastaverat, ab hac prohibita benedictione, nec ibidem ultra, ut consueverat, nocuit.

12 Magnifica vero atque desiderabili paschali festivitate adveniente, populus ad beati cellulam, in qua commoratus saepe frequentaverat cum angelis, devotus advenit. Et

of waters, suffocated by his own thrashing. Thereupon a young man led the people bringing the columns to the blessed temple.

Also, whenever oil was placed on the blessed tomb, it 10
is said to have been seen to increase in volume. The holy bishop Perpetuus, who was deservedly praised as a disciple of the blessed man, brought a flask of oil to the holy tomb so that an infusion of the power of the just man might sanctify it. When he had scraped some dust from the marble that covers the holy body and mixed it with the fluid, the oil overflowed so abundantly that an oily wave, exuding a fragrance of nectar, ran over the bishop's vestment. Many ill persons regained their health through this. But storms were often also kept away from fields which had been purified by this liquid.

Once a devout man, full of faith, came to the holy temple 11
and, thirsting for the grace of the saint, turned over in his mind what he might take with him from the blessed building for his health; approaching the tomb, he begged the custodian to grant him some blessed candle wax from the tomb. When he had received this, he departed with joy and full of faith placed it on a field where he had sowed a harvest. When a dangerous storm came that had often devastated the region in the preceding years, it was kept away by this benediction and never again ravaged that field as it used to do.

When the magnificent and longed-for feast of Easter had 12
come, the people devoutly went to the blessed man's cell, where he had often spoken with angels when he lived there.

singula loca allambens osculis vel irrigans lacrimis, in qua vir beatus ante sederat aut oraverat, sive ubi cibum sumpserat vel corpori quietem post multos labores indulserat, classe navium praeparata, amnem transire parat, ut beatum sepulcrum adeat, et cum fletu veniam deprecans coram confes-
13 sore se prosternat. Navigantibus autem illis, Temptatoris impulsu commoto vento, classis in profundo demergitur et sexus uterque ab amne diripitur. Cumque inter procellas fluctuum rotarentur et spes omnis evadendi deperisset, una omnium vox in clamore profertur, dicens: "Miserator Martine, eripe a praesenti interitu famulos famulasque tuas!" His dictis, ecce afflatus aurae placidus, omnes litori quod desiderabant, unda famulante, restituit: nec ullus deperiit, sed cuncti salvati paschalia festa summa cum exsultatione perfuncti sunt.

14 Non enim defuit illa virtus quae, Iordanem scindens, populum sub aquarum molibus margine arente traduxit, cum de fundo fluvii duodecim lapides ablatos, signa apostolica gestientes, Iosue litori, cui advenerat, consecravit; vel illa quae Petrum pereuntem pia amplectens dextera, ne periret, eripuit; vel quae nautam submersurum, Martini Dominum invocantem, de profundo pelagi ad litus, quod optabat, elicuit.

15 Quidam, pro benedictione aliquid cerae de sancta aede assumere flagitans, aliquid cerae de sepulcro sancti accepit,

When they had kissed and moistened with tears every single place where the blessed man had once sat or prayed, or where he had eaten or allowed his body to rest after many labors, they went to cross the river with a convoy of boats that had been made ready, to go to his blessed tomb and prostrate themselves in front of the confessor, begging his
forgiveness with tears. As they crossed the river, however, 13
the wind began to blow hard, impelled by the Tempter, and the convoy sank into the water, causing both men and women to be carried away by the river. While they were rolled about by the tempestuous waves, and all hope of escape had gone, everyone shouted forth in one voice: "Compassionate Martin, snatch the men and women who are your servants away from this present death!" As soon as these words had been said, behold, a gentle breeze and an obedient wave returned everyone to the shore to which they were headed: no one perished, and all, saved, performed the Easter festivities with the greatest rejoicing.

Thus that same power was present that, dividing the Jor- 14
dan, had led the people on its dry bottom between mountains of water, when Joshua, after he had taken up twelve stones from the bottom of the river, manifesting the sign of the apostles, consecrated them at the shore where they arrived; or that power which caught up Peter, about to die, with his compassionate right hand, lest he drown; or what drew the sailor, in danger of drowning and calling upon the Lord of Martin, from the depths of the sea to the shore he wished to reach.

Someone who had begged to be given some candle wax 15
from the holy building as a benediction, accepted some wax

et infra penetralia domus tamquam thesaurum caeleste reposuit. Factum est autem ut invidia Temptatoris immissum incendium domus voraci flamma circumureretur, et spar-
16 sum per aridas tabulas cuncta vastaret. Interea clamor ad caelum tollitur, et beati Martini auxilium imploratur. Meminetur etiam cerae particulam a sancti templo delatam. Quae reperta et igni iniecta, protinus cunctum restinxit incendium, novoque miraculo cera, quae ignem alere erat solita, violentiam ignis vi sanctitatis oppressit.

17 Haec Paulinus in sexto operis sui libro versu conscripsit, accepto a sancto Perpetuo episcopo de his indiculo. Verum cum ad eum huius indiculi charta venisset, nepos eius gravi tenebatur incommodo. At ille confisus in virtute sancti: “Si tibi,” inquit, “placet, beate Martine, ut aliqua in tua laude conscribam, appareat super hunc infirmum.” Imposita charta pectori eius, extemplo recedente febre sanatus est qui erat aegrotus.

18 Sed et Fortunatus presbyter omne opus vitae eius in quattuor libris versu conscripsit. His nos exemplis illecti, etsi imperiti temptabimus tamen aliqua de virtutibus sancti et beatissimi Martini, quae post eius obitum actae sunt, quantum invenire possumus, memoriae replicare: quia hoc erit scribendi studium, quod in illo Severi aut Paulini opere non invenitur insertum.

from the tomb of the saint and put it in an inner room of his house as a heavenly treasure. It happened, however, that a fire sent by the envy of the Tempter burned all around his home with voracious flames, spread among the dry beams and destroyed everything. Meanwhile, a cry went up to 16
heaven, imploring the blessed Martin's help. Then they remembered the particle of wax that had been brought from the temple of the saint. When it had been found and thrown into the flames, the whole fire went out at once, and, in a new kind of miracle, wax, which normally feeds fire, stifled the violence of the flames by the force of its holiness.

All this Paulinus wrote down in verse in the sixth book of 17
his work after he had received the information about these things in a summary from the holy bishop Perpetuus. At the time that the papyrus roll containing the summary had come to him, Paulinus's grandson had been afflicted with a serious illness. Trusting in the power of the holy man, however, Paulinus said: "If it pleases you, blessed Martin, that I write something in your praise, let it be shown upon this ill boy." When the document had been placed on the boy's chest, the fever disappeared at once, and he who had been ill was healed.

The priest Fortunatus too, however, wrote a whole poem 18
about Martin's life in four books. Encouraged by these examples albeit inexperienced, we shall nevertheless attempt to recount some of the powerful deeds of the holy and most blessed Martin which happened after his death, as many as we can find: for it shall be my intention to write about what cannot be found in the works of Severus and Paulinus.

3

De ordinatione et transitu beati Martini

Lucidus et toto orbe renitens gloriosus domnus Martinus, decedente iam mundo sol novus oriens, sicut anterior narrat historia, apud Sabariam Pannoniae ortus, ad salvationem Galliarum, opitulante Deo, dirigitur. Quas virtutibus ac signis illustrans, in urbe Toronica episcopatus honorem invitus, populo cogente, suscepit; in quo gloriosam et pene inimitabilem agens vitam, per quinquennia quinque bis insuper geminis mensibus cum decem diebus, octogesimo primo aetatis suae, Caesario et Attico consulibus, nocte media quievit in pace.

2 Gloriosum ergo, et toti mundo laudabilem eius transitum in die dominica fuisse manifestissimum est, idque in sequenti certis testimoniis comprobabimus. Quod non parvi meriti fuisse censetur, ut illa die eum Dominus in paradiso susciperet, qua idem dominus et redemptor victor ab inferis surrexisset et, ut qui dominica solemnia semper celebraverat impollute, post mundi pressuras dominica die locaretur in requie.

3

About the ordination and the passing of the blessed Martin

Resplendent and shining throughout the world, the glorious lord Martin, rising as a new sun in a world already declining, was born in Sabaria in the province of Pannonia according to the earlier history of his life, but was guided by God to accomplish the salvation of the Gauls. Illuminating these regions with his deeds of power and signs, he unwillingly accepted the honor of the episcopate in the city of Tours because its people compelled him to do so; having led a glorious and almost inimitable life there for twenty-five years, four months, and ten days, he died in peace in the middle of the night in the eighty-first year of his life, when Caesarius and Atticus were consuls.

His glorious passing, praised by the whole world, mani- 2
festly took place on a Sunday, as we will prove with unambiguous testimonies in what follows. And it was no small indication of his merit that the Lord received him into Paradise on the day that the Lord and Redeemer rose as victor from the netherworld, and that, after the tribulations of the world, he who had always celebrated Sunday services unpolluted, would rest in eternal peace on the Lord's day.

4

Qualiter sancto Severino episcopo psallentium de eius transitu revelatum est

Beatus autem Severinus Coloniensis civitatis episcopus, vir honestae vitae, et per cuncta laudabilis, dum die dominica loca sancta ex consuetudine post matutinos hymnos cum suis clericis circumiret, illa hora qua beatus obiit, audi-
2 vit chorum canentium in sublimi. Vocatoque archidiacono, interrogat si aures eius percuterent voces quas ille attentus audiret. Respondit: "Nequaquam." Tunc ille: "Diligentius," inquit, "ausculta." Archidiaconus autem coepit sursum collum extendere, aures erigere, et super summis articulis, baculo sustentante, stare. Sed credo, eum non fuisse aequalis meriti, a quo haec non merebantur audiri.

3 Tunc prostrati terrae, ipse pariter et beatus episcopus Dominum deprecantur, ut hoc ei divina pietas audire permitteret. Erectis autem, rursum interrogat senex: "Quid audis?" Qui ait: "Voces psallentium tanquam in caelo audio, sed quid sit prorsus ignoro." Cui ille: "Ego tibi quid sit narrabo. Dominus meus Martinus Episcopus migravit ex hoc

4

How the chanting of psalms at his passing away was revealed to the holy bishop Severinus

Now the blessed bishop Severinus of the city of Cologne, a man of honorable life and praiseworthy in every respect, on that day of the Lord, while he was visiting the tombs of the saints with his clergy as usual after the morning hymns, heard a choir singing on high at the hour of the holy man's
death. Calling the archdeacon, he asked him whether the 2
voices which he heard, listening intently, were also striking his ears. He answered: "Not at all." Then Severinus said: "Listen more carefully." The archdeacon then began to stretch his neck upward, prick up his ears, and lean on his walking stick to stand on tiptoe. But I believe that he did not equal the bishop in merit, so did not deserve to hear them.

Thereupon prostrating themselves on the ground, he and 3
the blessed bishop prayed to the Lord that the divine goodness would allow him to hear the chanting. After they had stood up the old bishop again asked: "What do you hear?" And he said: "I hear voices as it were chanting in heaven, but have no idea what this is." The bishop replied: "I shall tell you what it is. My lord bishop Martin has left this world, and

mundo, et nunc angeli canendo eum deferunt in excelsum. Et ut parumper morae esset, ut haec audirentur, diabolus eum cum iniquis angelis retinere temptavit, nihilque suum in eodem reperiens, confusus abscessit. Quid ergo de nobis peccatoribus erit, si tanto sacerdoti voluit pars iniqua nocere?"

4 Haec sacerdote loquente notavit tempus archidiaconus, et Turonos misit velociter qui haec diligenter inquireret. Qui veniens, eo die et hora manifestissime cognovit transisse beatum Martinum, quo sanctus Severinus audivit psallentium chorum. Sed et, si ad Severi recurramus historiam, ipsa hora eum sibi, scripsit, cum libro vitae suae fuisse revelatum.

5

Qualiter beato Ambrosio idem transitus est ostensus

Eo namque tempore beatus Ambrosius, cuius hodie flores eloquii per totam ecclesiam redolent, Mediolanensi civitati praeerat episcopus. Cui celebranda festa dominicae diei ista

now angels carry him up to heaven with singing. And when there was a short pause in our hearing this, the devil with his evil angels tried to hold him back, but finding nothing of his own in him, went away confounded. What, therefore, will happen to us sinners if the Evil One wanted to hurt even so great a bishop?"

As the bishop spoke about these things, the archdeacon 4
noted the time, and he quickly sent someone to Tours to make a careful inquiry about these events. When he arrived there, he learned that the blessed Martin had most certainly passed away on the very day and at the very hour that the holy Severinus heard the choir chanting. But if we return to Severus's history, he wrote that the saint was revealed to him too at that same hour, holding the book about his life.

5

How the same passing was shown to the blessed Ambrose

At this same time, the blessed Ambrose, whose blossoms of eloquence today spread their fragrance throughout the church, was bishop in charge of the city of Milan. It was his custom when he celebrated the feast of the Lord's day that

erat consuetudo, ut veniens lector cum libro suo non antea
2 legere praesumeret quam sanctus nutu iussisset. Factum est autem ut illa die dominica, prophetica lectione recitata, iam lectore ante altare stante, qui lectione beati Pauli proferret, beatissimus antistes Ambrosius super sanctum altare obdormiret. Quod videntes multi, cum nullus eum penitus excitare praesumeret, transactis fere duarum aut trium horarum spatiis, excitaverunt eum, dicentes: "Iam hora praeterit. Iubeat domnus lectori lectionem legere; exspectat enim populus valde iam lassus."

3 Respondens autem beatus Ambrosius: "Nolite," inquit, "turbari. Multum enim mihi valet sic obdormisse, cui tale miraculum Dominus ostendere dignatus est. Nam noveritis fratrem meum Martinum sacerdotem egressum fuisse de corpore, me autem eius funeri obsequium praebuisse, peractoque ex more servitio, capitellum tantum, vobis excitanti-
4 bus, non explevi." Tunc illi stupefacti pariterque admirantes, diem et tempus notant, sollicite requirentes. Qui ipsam diem tempusque transitus sancti repererunt, quod beatus confessor dixerat se eius exsequiis deservisse.

5 O beatum virum, in cuius transitu sanctorum canit numerus, angelorum exsultat chorus, omniumque caelestium virtutum occurrit exercitus: diabolus praesumptione confunditur, ecclesia virtute roboratur, sacerdotes revelatione glorificantur quem Michael assumpsit cum angelis, Maria

the lector, having come with his book, not presume to begin reading until the holy man had commanded him to do so
with a gesture. It happened that on that particular Sunday, 2
when the lesson from the prophets had been read and the lector was already standing before the altar to read from the blessed Paul, the most blessed bishop Ambrose fell asleep upon the holy altar. Of the many who saw this no one had the least thought of awakening him, but after a period of two or three hours had passed, they did wake him up, saying: "The hour has already passed. Let our lord command the lector to read the lesson, for the people are waiting, and now very tired."

The blessed Ambrose replied: "Don't be upset. Falling 3
asleep in this way was very worthwhile to me because the Lord deigned to show me the following miracle. For know that my brother Bishop Martin has left his body and I was participating in his funeral service, and that, after I had performed the service according to custom, there was only one verse of the psalm that I failed to finish because you woke
me." Stunned in admiration, the people then noted the day 4
and time and made a careful inquiry. And they found that Saint Martin's passing had taken place on the same day and at the same time that the blessed confessor had said he had participated in his funeral service.

O blessed man, during whose passing the community of 5
saints sang, the choir of angels danced, and the army of all the heavenly powers hastened to be present: the devil was confounded in his presumption, the Church was strengthened through spiritual power, the bishops were glorified by his revelation of him whom the archangel Michael took up

suscepit cum virginum choris, paradisus retinet laetum cum
6 sanctis! Sed quid nos in laudem eius temptamus, quod non sufficimus adimplere? Ipse est enim laus illius, cuius laus ab eius ore numquam recessit. Nam nos utinam vel simplicem possimus historiam explicare!

6

De translatione beati corporis sancti Martini

Operae pretium est enim illud inserere lectioni, qualiter sanctum eius corpusculum in locum ubi nunc adoratur fuerit, angelo annuente, translatum. Anno sexagesimo quarto post transitum gloriosi domni Martini, beatus Perpetuus
2 Turonicae sedis cathedram sortitus est dignitatis. Adeptusque hunc apicem, cum magno devotorum consensu, fundamenta templi, ampliora quam fuerant, super beata membra locare disposuit, quod sagaci insistens studio, mirifice mancipavit effectui. De qua fabrica multum quod loqueremur erat; sed quia praesens est, conticere exinde melius putavimus.

to heaven accompanied by the angels, whom Mary received with her choirs of virgins, and whom Paradise holds, happy, with the saints! But why do we attempt to praise him when 6
we cannot do this enough? He himself is the praise of Him whose praise never left his lips. Let me, therefore, at least be able to relate the unadorned history of his powerful deeds!

6

About the translation of the blessed body of the holy Martin

It is worth the trouble to include in this reading how his holy body was moved, with the help of an angel, to the place where it is now venerated. Sixty-four years after the passing of our glorious lord Martin, the blessed Perpetuus was elected to the episcopal dignity in the see of Tours. When he 2
had attained this high office, he decided, with much support from the devout, to lay the foundations of a church larger than the existing one over the blessed body, a project which he pursued with a wise zeal and completed wonderfully. There is much that might be said about its workmanship, but since it is still there, I have thought that it is better to be silent about this.

3 Adveniente ergo optato tempore sacerdoti ut templum dedicaretur, et sanctum corpusculum a loco ubi sepultum erat transferetur, convocavit beatus Perpetuus ad diem festum vicinos pontifices, sed et abbatum ac diversorum clericorum non minimam multitudinem. Et quia hoc in Kalendis Iuliis agere volebat, vigilata una nocte, facto mane, accepto sarculo, terram quae super sanctum erat tumulum coeperunt effodere. Quo detecto, manus, ut eum commoverent, iniciunt, ibique multitudo tota laborans, nihil prorsus per totam diem profecit.

4 Vigilata denique alia nocte, mane temptantes, nihil omnino agere potuerunt. Tunc conturbati atque exterriti quid
facerent nesciebant. Dicit eis unus ex clericis: "Scitis quia
post hoc triduum natalis episcopatus eius esse consueverat,
et forsitan in hac die se transferri vos admonet." Tunc ieiuniis ac orationibus et iugi psallentio die noctuque insis-
5 tentes, triduum illud continuatim duxerunt. Quarta autem
die accedentes, ponentesque manus, non valebant penitus
movere sepulcrum. Pavore omnes exterriti, iam in hoc stan-
tes, ut terra vasculum quod detexerant operirent, apparuit
eis veneranda canitie senex, ad instar nivis candorem efferens, dicens se abbatem, et ait eis: "Usquequo conturbamini,
et tardatis? Non videtis domnum Martinum stantem vos iuvare paratum, si manus apponitis?"

When the desired time came for the temple to be conse- 3
crated by the bishop, and for the holy body to be transferred from the place where it had been buried, the blessed Perpetuus invited the neighboring bishops, as well as a large multitude of abbots and various kinds of clerics to the day of the feast. And because he wished this to take place on July first, after they had spent the night in vigils and morning had come, they each took a pickax and began to dig up the earth above the holy tomb. When it had been uncovered, they thrust in their hands to lift it up, but although all of them worked at this the whole day, they accomplished nothing.

When they had thereafter kept vigils for another night, 4
they tried again in the morning, but could not effect anything at all. Then confused and severely frightened, they did not know what to do. One of the clerics said to them: "You know that the anniversary of his assumption of the episcopate used to be celebrated in three days' time, and perhaps he is telling you to transfer him on that day." Thereupon they applied themselves to fasting, praying, and singing psalms day and night, and kept this up continuously for
those three days. On the fourth day, they approached the 5
tomb and put their hands to it, but were still unable to move it in any way. All were stunned by fear, and on the verge of throwing earth on the casket which they had uncovered, when there appeared an old man with venerable white hair gleaming with a whiteness like that of snow, who told them that he was an abbot and said to them: "How long will you continue being confused and delaying? Don't you see the lord Martin standing ready to help you if you put your hands to it?"

6 Tunc, iactans pallium quo utebatur, posuit manum ad sarcophagum cum reliquis sacerdotibus, crucibus paratis ac cereis, imposita antiphona, dederunt cuncti voces psallentium in excelso. Tum ad senis conatum protinus sarcophagum cum summa levitate commotum, in loco ubi nunc adoratur,
7 Domino annuente, perducitur. Quo ad voluntatem sacerdotis composito, dictis etiam missis, ut ventum est ad convivium, requirentes sollicite senem, nequaquam reperiunt. Sed nec homo quidem exstitit, qui eum de basilica exire vidisset. Credo aliquam fuisse virtutem angelicam, quae et beatum virum se vidisse pronuntiavit et deinceps nulli comparuit.

8 In quo loco ex illa die multae virtutes factae sunt, quae per negligentiam non sunt scriptae. Nos vero quantum tempore nostro aut fieri vidimus, aut factum certe cognovimus, silere nequivimus.

7

De Theodemundo muto

Adveniens iuvenis quidam, Theodemundus nomine, audiendi loquendique obstructo aditu, quotidianis diebus ad sanctam basilicam recurrebat et, inclinans se ad orationem,

Then, throwing aside the mantle he had been wearing, 6
he put his hands to the sarcophagus with the other bishops, while crosses and candles were brought near, antiphons were sung, and all raised their voices to heaven in psalm singing. Then, upon the effort of the old man, the sarcophagus was immediately lifted with the utmost ease and, with the help of the Lord, moved to the place where it is now
venerated. When this had been done according to the 7
bishop's wishes, mass had been said, and it was time for the banquet, they searched diligently for the old man and could not find him. But no one had seen him go out of the church. I believe that it was some angelic power which said it saw the blessed man and thereafter never appeared to anyone.

From that day onward many powerful deeds were enacted 8
in this place which, through negligence, have not been written down. As for us, we cannot remain silent about how many we either ourselves have seen happen or know for certain to have happened in our times.

7

About Theodemund, a mute man

There came a young man named Theodemund, whose ways of hearing and speaking were obstructed and who came back to the basilica every day, bowing in prayer while

labia tantum movebat. Nam nullam poterat vocem emittere sensu integro, sed erat multatus vocis officio. Qui tam prompte videbatur orare, ut flere cerneretur inter ipsa tacita verba plerumque. Cui si quis pro mercedis respectu aliquid eleemosynae contulisset, continuo hoc similibus pauperibus erogabat, et stipem ab aliis nutu postulans, stipendia indigentibus porrigebat.

2 Cumque in loco illo sancto in hac devotione per trium annorum spatia commoratus fuisset, quadam die a divina pietate commonitus, venit ante sanctum altare, et stans oculis ad caelum elevatis et manibus, erupit ab ore illius rivus sanguinis cum putredine. Et conspuens in terram, coepit graviter gemere et excreare partes nescio quas cum sanguine, ita ut putaretur quod aliquis ferramento guttur eius incideret. Sed et tabes ex ore illius tanquam fila sanguinea
3 dependebat. Tunc disruptis aurium ac faucium ligaturis, elevans se et erigens iterum oculos et manus ad caelum, ore adhuc cruento in hanc primum vocem prorupit: "Gratias tibi magnas refero, beatissime domne Martine, quod aperiens os meum, fecisti me post longum tempus in tuas laudes verba laxare!" Admirante autem omni populo, et stupente de tali miraculo, interrogant si et auditum pariter recepisset. Qui libere omnia audire, populo testante, respondit.

4 Sanitati ergo hic redditus, a Chrodechilde regina pro virtute reverentiaque sancti Martini collectus est, et ad scholam positus omnem psalmorum seriem memoriae commendavit. Quem Deus perfectum efficiens clericum, per multos in posterum annos in servitio ecclesiae commorari permisit.

moving only his lips. For he was unable to utter any comprehensible word, deprived as he was of the ability to speak. He appeared to pray with such ardor that he was seen to weep a great deal between his silent words. If anyone gave him some alms out of compassion for his condition, he at once gave it to those who were poor like him, and when he begged, using gestures, for a gift from others, he gave the food to the needy.

When he had been practicing this devotion in the holy 2
place for three years, he was alerted by God's goodness one day and approached the holy altar; standing there with his eyes and hands raised to heaven, a river of blood and pus burst out of his mouth. Spitting on the ground, he began to moan loudly and to cough up globs of some bloody substance, so that one might think that an iron instrument was making incisions in his throat. And pus that looked like
bloody strings hung from his mouth. Then, what bound his 3
ears and jaws was broken, he rose up, again lifted his eyes and hands toward heaven, and burst forth, his mouth still bleeding, with these first words: "I give great thanks to you, most blessed lord Martin, because you opened my mouth and, after a long time, enabled me to utter words in your praise!" The people, all admiring this and stunned by such a miracle, asked him if he had received his hearing as well. He replied, with the people as his witness, that he heard everything freely.

After he had thus been given back his health, he was 4
taken up by Queen Chlotild because she revered the holy Martin's power and placed in a school, where he committed the whole sequence of the Psalms to memory. God made him a perfect cleric and allowed him to remain for many years thereafter in the service of the church.

8

De Chainemunda muliere caeca

Mulier quaedam, nomine Chainemunda, oculorum luce privata, nesciens visu tenere viam nisi alio ducente, devota valde et fide plena, venit ad venerabile templum beati Martini antistitis. Erat autem non solum, ut diximus, caeca, sed etiam toto corpore ulceribus plena. Obsederat enim omnia membra eius putredo cum pustulis, et erat miserabili facie, et horribilis ad videndum, ut tanquam leprosa putaretur a populo.

2 Cumque palpando diebus singulis ad aedem gloriosi praesulis cursitaret, post tres fere annos, stante ea ante sepulcrum, aperti sunt oculi eius ita ut cuncta clare prospiceret. Amotoque omni languore membrorum, atque siccato umore qui fluebat a corpore, nova cute superveniente, taliter est pristinae reddita sanitati, ut nec indicium quidem infirmita-
3 tis in eius corpore resedisset. Quae multos in posterum vivens annos, gratias omnipotenti Deo referebat assidue, quod eam per beatum confessorem suum sic instaurasset incolumem.

8

About Chainemunda, a blind woman

A woman named Chainemunda, who had lost the light of her eyes and was unable to see the road to travel except when guided by someone else, was very devout and full of faith and came to the venerable temple of the blessed bishop Martin. However, she was not only blind, as we said, but also ridden with sores on her whole body. For all her limbs were filled with pus and pustules, her face was hideous and horrible to look at, so that she was thought to be a leper by the people.

After almost three years, when she had been feeling her 2
way to the church of the glorious leader every day, as she was standing in front of the tomb, her eyes were opened so that she could see everything clearly. When all the illness in her limbs, too, had been taken away, and the fluid that used to flow from her body had dried up; a new skin came over it and she was restored in such a way to her earlier health that
not even a scar of her illness remained on her body. Living 3
for many years afterward, she assiduously gave thanks to almighty God because he had in this way renewed her health through his blessed confessor.

9

De beato Baudino episcopo

Quam praesens invocatio nominis eius mare procellosum compescuerit, non omittam. Cum beatus Baudinus episcopus Turonicae civitatis in villam navigio subvehente transiret, subito adveniente cum violentia venti nimbo taeterrimo, mare placidum commovetur impulsu flaminis, navisque undarum mole turbatur. Tollitur caput primum in fluctus, secundum declinatur inter undarum hiatus. Hi in scaena montis aquosi dependent, hi apertis undis in ima dehiscunt, sed nec antenna residet, quae beatae crucis signaculum praeferebat.

2 Tunc resolutis timore membris, et omnibus sine spe vitae iam mori paratis, prosternitur senior in oratione cum lacrimis, et geminas tendens palmas ad astra, beati Martini auxilium precabatur, et ut sibi dignaretur adesse velociter proclamat.

3 Unus autem ex perfidis dixit: "Martinus ille, quem invocas, iam te dereliquit, nec tibi in hac necessitate succurrit." Vere credo hanc vocem ab Insidiatore fuisse prolatam, ut beatum sacerdotem ab oratione turbaret. Sed ille hoc iaculum fidei lorica repellens, magis ac magis sancti viri praesidium flagitabat, simulque cohortabatur ut omnes orarent.

9

About the blessed bishop Baudinus

I shall not omit how the invocation of his name was immediately efficacious in calming down a stormy lake. When the blessed Baudinus, bishop of the city of Tours, traveled to an estate by boat, a hideous dark cloud suddenly came with a violent wind; the calm lake was churned up by the force of the blowing, and the boat was tossed about by the massive waves. The prow was first lifted up high above the waves, and then it was pulled down into the chasm between them. Some of the seamen hang on the side of a mountain of water, others are swallowed in the depths of the gaping waves, but the mast, bearing the sign of the blessed Cross, did not sink.

Then when everyone, their limbs powerless with fear, 2
had given up hope of living and was ready to die, the old bishop, prostrated himself in prayer with tears, held out both his hands to the stars and begged for the blessed Martin's help, crying for him to come quickly.

One of the unbelievers, however, said: "That Martin 3
whom you are invoking has already left you, and will not help you in this emergency." I truly believe that this remark was elicited by the Treacherous One so as to turn the bishop away from his prayer. But he repelled this javelin with the breastplate of faith, and entreated the help of the holy man more and more earnestly, at the same time urging all to pray.

4 Cumque haec agerentur, subito supervenit odor suavissimus quasi balsamum in navi, et tanquam si cum thuribulo aliquis circuiret, odor thimiamatis effragravit. Quo odore adveniente cessit violentia saeva ventorum, elisisque aquarum astantium molibus, redditur mare tranquillum.

5 Mirantur omnes morti iam dediti fluctuum pacem, et protinus data serenitate redduntur in litore. Quod nullus ambigat, beati viri adventu hanc tempestatem fuisse sedatam. Tunc omnes in commune Domino gratias referunt, quod eos per invocationem antistitis sui dignatus sit de hoc periculo liberare.

10

De eo, qui sancti reliquias Camaracum detulit

Huius tempore quidam de Camaracensi ecclesia reliquias beati Martini expetit. Quibus iam vespere acceptis, cum psallendo profisceretur, et dum Ligerem fluvium transit, sero factum est, et subito contenebratum est caelum, et ecce fulgura magna ac tonitrua magna descendebant.
2 Dum haec agerentur, duae puerorum lanceae, emissas flam-

And while this was happening, suddenly an extremely sweet 4
fragrance like balsam came over the boat, and as though someone walked around with a censer, the fragrance of incense spread about. With the arrival of this fragrance, the wild violence of the winds stopped, the mountains of water alongside the boat melted away, and the lake became tranquil.

All those already prepared for death were amazed by the 5
calmness of the waves, and when the sky had at once become clear, they were carried back to the shore. Let no one doubt that this storm was quieted by the arrival of the blessed man. Then everyone together gave thanks to the Lord because he had rescued them from this danger through the invocation of his bishop.

10

About the man who took relics of the holy man to Cambrai

At this same time, someone came from the church of Cambrai to request relics of the blessed Martin. He received them when it was already evening, and traveled while singing psalms; it had become late while he crossed the river Loire, and behold, suddenly, the sky darkened and great
bolts of lightning and loud thunder came down. While this 2

meas pharos, lumen euntibus praebuerunt. Ibantque fulgurantes hastae, non minus miraculi quam beneficii viatoribus praeferentes, virtutemque beati antistitis ostendentes.

II

De rege Galliciae populoque conversis

Deficit lingua sterilis tantas cupiens enarrare virtutes. Chararici cuiusdam regis Galliciensis filius graviter aegrotabat, qui tale taedium incurrerat, ut solo spiritu palpitaret. Pater autem eius foetidae se Arianae sectae una cum incolis loci illius subdiderat. Sed et regio illa plus solito quam aliae provinciae a lepra sordebat.

2 Cumque rex videret urgeri filium in extremis, dicit suis: "Martinus ille, quem in Galliis dicunt multis virtutibus effulgere, cuius, quaeso, religionis vir fuerit, enarrate?" Cui aiunt: "Catholicae fidei populum pastorali cura in corpore positus gubernavit, asserens Filium cum Patre et Spiritu sancto

was happening, two lances carried by the servants emitted beacons of fire, providing light for the travelers. The fiery lances in front of them represented as much a miracle as a benefit to the travelers, and manifested the power of the blessed bishop.

II

About the conversion of the king and the people of Galicia

My barren manner of speaking, that wishes to relate such great deeds of power, is unable to do them justice. The son of Chararic, a king of Galicia, was seriously ill and found himself in such a state of affliction that breathing was the only movement he could make. His father, however, had subjected himself, along with the inhabitants of that region, to the stinking Arian sect. That region was more befouled by leprosy, too, than was usual in other provinces.

When the king saw that his son was being driven to his 2
end, he said to those around him: "That man Martin who, they say, shines forth with many deeds of power in Gaul, tell me please, of what religion was this man?" They told him: "While in the body he governed his people of the catholic faith with pastoral care, asserting that the Son ought to be venerated as equal in substance and power with the Father

aequali substantia vel omnipotentia venerari debere, sed et
nunc caeli sede locatus, assiduis beneficiis non cessat plebi
3 propriae providere." Qui ait: "Si haec vera sunt quae profer-
tis, discurrant usque ad eius templum fideles amici mei,
multa munera deportantes; et si obtineant mei infantuli medicinam, inquisita fide catholica, quae ille credidit credam."
Pensato ergo auro argentoque ad filii sui pondus, transmisit
ad venerabilem locum sepulcri. Quo perlato, oblatis muneribus exorant ad beati tumulum pro aegroto.

4 Sed insidente adhuc in patris eius pectore secta, non continuo integram recipere meruit medicinam. Reversi autem
nuntii narraverunt regi se multas virtutes ad beati tumulum
vidisse, dicentes: "Cur non sanatus fuerit filius tuus, ignora-
5 mus." At ille intelligens non ante sanari posse filium suum
nisi aequalem cum Patre crederet Christum, in honorem
beati Martini fabricavit ecclesiam. Miroque opere ea expedita, proclamat: "Si suscipere mereor viri iusti reliquias,
quodcumque sacerdotes praedicaverint, credam." Et sic iterum suos dirigit maiori cum munere, qui venientes ad beatum locum reliquias postulabant.

6 Cumque eis offerrentur ex consuetudine, dixerunt: "Non
ita faciemus, sed nobis, quaesumus, licentia tribuatur po-
nendi quae exinde iterum assumamus." Tunc partem pallii
serici pensatam super beatum sepulcrum posuerunt, dicentes: "Si invenimus gratiam coram expetito patrono, quae
posuimus plus insequenti pensabunt, eruntque nobis in

and the Holy Spirit, but now too, placed in the heavenly
abode, he does not cease caring for his people through constant benefits." The king replied: "If the things you tell me 3
are true, let some of my faithful friends hasten to his temple bearing many gifts; and if they should obtain healing for
my little child, I shall acquire information about the catholic faith and will believe what he believed." After therefore
measuring a quantity of gold and silver equal to the weight
of his son, he sent it to the venerable place of the tomb. And
when this had been brought there, and the messengers had
given their gifts, they prayed at the blessed man's tomb for
the sick boy.

But because the teachings of the Arian sect still lived in 4
his father's heart, he did not deserve to receive a complete
cure immediately. For when they had returned, the messengers told the king that they had seen many deeds of power at
the tomb of the blessed man, and said: "Why your son has
not been cured, we do not know." And he, understanding 5
that his son could not be cured until he believed Christ to be
equal with the Father, built a church in honor of the blessed
Martin. When this marvelous work had been completed he
announced: "If I should deserve to receive relics of the just
man, I shall believe whatever the priests have preached."
And thus he again sent his men with greater gifts who requested relics when they had come to the blessed place.

When these were offered to them in the usual way, they 6
said: "This is not how we will do it; we request to be granted
permission to place something on the tomb which we will
then take up again." Then they laid part of a silk cloth which
they had weighed on the blessed tomb, saying: "If we find
favor with the patron we have entreated, what we have

7 benedictionem posita, quaesita per fidem." Vigilata ergo una nocte, facto mane, quae posuerunt pensitabant. In quibus tanta beati viri infusa est gratia, ut tamdiu elevarent in sublime aeneam libram, quantum habere poterat quo ascenderet momentana.

8 Cumque elevatae fuissent reliquiae cum magno triumpho, audierunt voces psallentium qui erant in civitate detrusi in carcerem, et admirantes suavitatem sonorum, interrogantes custodes quid hoc esset. Qui dixerunt: "Reliquiae domni Martini in Galliciam transmittuntur, et ideo sic psallitur." Tunc illi flentes invocabant sanctum Martinum, ut eos
9 sua visitatione de ergastulo carceris liberaret. Exterritis custodibus, et in fugam versis, disruptis obicibus retinaculorum, liber populus surgit a vinculo, et sic usque ad sancta pignora, populo expectante, venerunt, osculantes flendo beatas reliquias, simulque et gratias beato Martino pro sui absolutione reddentes, quod eos dignatus fuerit sua pietate salvare. Tunc obtentis per sacerdotem a iudice culpis, incolumes dimissi sunt.

10 Quod videntes gestatores reliquiarum, gavisi sunt valde, dicentes: "Nunc cognovimus quod dignatur beatus antistes nobis peccatoribus propitium se praebere." Et sic gratias agentes, navigio prospero, prosequente patroni praesidio, undis lenibus, temperatis flatibus, velo pendulo, mari tranquillo, velociter ad portum Galliciae pervenerunt.

placed on the tomb will weigh more afterward, and what we sought in faith will become a blessing for us." When they 7
had kept vigils for one night and morning had come, they weighed what they had put on the tomb. So much of the blessed man's grace had seeped into it that when they held up the balance's bronze weight, it went up at once as high as it could.

And when the relics were held up to great applause, those 8
who were confined in the city's jail heard the voices singing psalms, and admiring the sweetness of the sounds, asked the guards what the occasion was. These said: "Relics of the lord Martin are being sent to Galicia, and therefore psalms are being sung." Then the prisoners wept and called on the holy Martin to rescue them by his visit from the confinement of
prison. When the terrified guards turned to flee, the fasten- 9
ings of the prisoners' bonds broke, and these people rose free from their chains; thus, while the people watched, they came to the holy remains, kissed the blessed relics while weeping and at the same time thanked the blessed Martin for their release and for having saved them in his goodness. Through the bishop's intercession, the charges against them were thereupon dismissed by the judge, and they were let go as free men.

Seeing this, the bearers of the relics were overjoyed, say- 10
ing: "Now we know that the blessed bishop deigns to show favor to us sinners." And giving thanks in this manner, they sailed speedily under their patron's protection, with gentle waves, a moderate breeze, a billowing sail, and a calm sea, and quickly reached their harbor in Galicia.

11 Tunc commonitus a Deo quidam, nomine Martinus, de regione longinqua, qui ibidem nunc sacerdos habetur, advenit. Sed nec hoc credo sine divina fuisse providentia, quod eo die se commoveret de patria quo beatae reliquiae de loco levatae sunt, et sic simul cum ipsis pignoribus Galliciae portum ingressus sit. Quae pignora cum summa veneratione suscipientes, fidem miraculis firmant. Nam filius regis, amissa omni aegritudine, sanus properat ad occursum.

12 Beatus autem Martinus sacerdotalis gratiae accepit principatum, rex unitatem Patris et Filii et Spiritus sancti confessus, cum omni domo sua chrismatus est. Squalor leprae a populo pellitur, et omnes infirmi salvantur, nec umquam ibi postea usque nunc super aliquem leprae morbus apparuit.
13 Talemque gratiam ibi in adventu pignorum beati patroni Dominus tribuit, ut virtutes, quae ibidem illa die factae sunt, enarrare perlongum sit. Nam tantum in Christi amore nunc populus ille promptus est, ut omnes martyrium libentissime susciperent, si tempus persecutionis adesset.

Then, instructed by God, someone named Martin came 11
from a distant region and is now a bishop there. But I believe that it did not happen without divine providence that he left his country on the same day that the blessed relics were taken from their place, and that he thus entered the harbor in Galicia at the same time as they did. These relics were received with the greatest veneration and strengthened everyone's faith through their miracles. For the king's son, whose illness had disappeared completely, hastened as a healthy man to meet them.

The blessed Martin accepted the dignity of episcopal 12
grace, and the king, having confessed to the unity of Father, Son, and Holy Spirit, was anointed together with his whole household. The filth of leprosy was driven away from the people, all those who were ill were healed, and up to now the illness of leprosy has never subsequently appeared there on
anyone. The Lord bestowed such grace there upon the ar- 13
rival of the relics of the blessed patron that to relate the powerful deeds which happened there that day would take too long. For this people is now so fervent in their love of Christ that all would eagerly take on martyrdom if a time of persecution came.

12

De Ultrogotha Regina

Nam et Ultrogotha Regina, auditis miraculis quae ad locum fiunt quo sancta membra quiescunt, tanquam si sapientiam Salomonis veniret audire, expetiit ea corde devoto
2 prospicere. Abstinens ergo se a cibis et somno, praecurrentibus etiam largissimis eleemosynis, pervenit ad locum sanctum, ingressaque basilicam, timens et tremens, nequaquam audebat beatum adire sepulcrum, indignam se esse proclamans, nec ibidem posse, obsistentibus culpis, accedere.

3 Tamen, deducta in vigiliis et orationibus ac profluis lacrimis una nocte, mane oblatis muneribus multis, in honorem beati confessoris missas expetiit revocari. Quae dum celebrarentur, subito tres caeci, qui ad pedes beati antistitis longo tempore privati lumine residebant, fulgore nimio circumdati, lumen quod olim perdiderant receperunt.

4 Quo facto, clamor in caelum attolitur magnificantium Deum. Ad istud miraculum currit regina, concurrit et populus, mirantur omnes fidem mulieris, mirantur gloriam confessoris. Sed super omnia collaudatur Deus noster, qui tantam virtutem praestat sanctis suis, ut per eos talia operari dignetur, tale inter reliqua luminaria huic mundo beatum Martinum immensum sidus attribuens, per quem eius

12

About Queen Ultrogotha

Queen Ultrogotha too, when she heard about the miracles that happen in the place where the holy body lies, came to see them with a devout heart, as if she were coming to
listen to the wisdom of Solomon. Abstaining therefore from 2
food and sleep, and sending very generous alms ahead, she came to the holy place and entered the basilica in awe and trembling; she in no way dared to go to the blessed tomb because she professed herself to be unworthy to do so, and to be prevented by her sins from approaching it.

Nevertheless, having spent one night in vigils, prayers, 3
and copious tears, she brought many gifts in the morning and asked for a mass to be said in honor of the blessed confessor. While it was being celebrated, three blind men who had been sitting at the feet of the blessed bishop for a long time, lacking light, were suddenly surrounded by an intense fiery blaze and received the light which they had once lost.

At this a great cry, praising God, rose up to the sky. The 4
queen rushed to see this miracle, and the people too, and all admired the faith of the lady and the glory of the confessor. But above all our God was praised, who gives such power to his saints that he deigns to do such things through them, and who, among the other heavenly lights, gave to this world the blessed Martin as such a great star that through him

tenebrae refulgeant, qui vere sicut oliva fructifera, per singulos dies fructos exhibet Domino de conversionibus miserorum.

13

De eo qui a pustula in extremis positus laborabat

Sed nec hoc praeteribo, quod venerabilem conservum meum Fortunatum presbyterum retulisse commemoro. Quidam in Italia, dum veneno pustulae pervasus in discrimine sic ageretur, ut vivere desperaret, aliquos interrogat ad templum beati Martini quis fuerit. Tunc quidam ex astanti-
2 bus asserit se fuisse. Requirit aegrotus quid inde pro benedictione detulerit. Qui negat se aliquid praesumpsisse. Quem iterum interrogat qua tunc veste indutus sit, cum ad templum sancti occurrerit. Respondit, quod ea qua super se
3 ipso tempore utebatur. Tunc abscissam fideliter indumenti particulam imposuit super pustulam. Mox ut aegri membra tetigit, vulnus pustulae veneni vim perdidit; quae tali medicamine et virtutem sancti protulit, et infirmum refert incolumem.

darkness becomes bright, and who just like a fertile olive tree presents fruits to the Lord every day in the conversions of miserable persons.

13

About the man who suffered grievously from a pustule

I will not omit what I remember my venerable colleague, the priest Fortunatus, told me. Someone in Italy who was afflicted by a malign pustule found himself in such danger that he despaired of his life and inquired of others whether any of them had visited the temple of the blessed Martin.
Then one of the bystanders said that he had done so. The 2
sick man asked what he had taken from there as a blessing. The man denied having taken anything. The sick man then asked him what clothes he had been wearing when he went to the saint's temple. He replied that what he had on now
was what he had worn at that time. Then, in faith, he cut off 3
a small piece of this clothing and put it upon the pustule. As soon as it touched the sick man's limbs, the wound of the pustule lost the strength of its poison; this remedy made the saint's power manifest and rendered the ill man healthy.

4 Hanc apud Italos asserens specialem vigere medelam, ut si quis pustulae percutiatur vulnere, ad propinquum quod fuerit beati Martini oratorium habeatur perfugium, et aut ex velo ianuae, aut palliolis quae pendent de parietibus, quidquid primum raptum fuerit, si aegro superpositum adhaeserit, fit salubre. Haec medela genitorem suum carnalem ab interitu pustulae, ut ipse patris sui testis asserit, liberavit.

14

De castello Italiae, Tertio nomine

Idem his verbis retulit: "In cacumine castelli regionis Italiae quod dicitur Tertium, oratorium beati Martini fundatum est. Ibique turri vicinae, quotiens incursione barbarorum per fraudem hostis accederet nocturnis insidiis, quisquis de vigilantibus habuisset in turre lanceam, aut spatam, vel cultellum, seu grafium protulisset ex theca, fere per horae spatium tale lumen reddebatur ex universo gladio,

Fortunatus affirms that in Italy this particular remedy is in high repute, so that whoever is afflicted with a pustule rushes to the nearest chapel of the blessed Martin, and whatever is first taken, either from the curtain at the door or from the draperies that hang on the walls, if it is firmly placed on the ill man, makes him healthy. This remedy rescued his own father from a deadly pustule, as he, acting as witness for his father, affirms. 4

14

About the fortress in Italy called the Third

He also reported with these words that: "At the summit of a fortress in the region of Italy which is called the Third, a chapel for the blessed Martin was built. In a watchtower close by there, every time during a barbarian raid when an enemy treacherously approached during the night, for whichever of the watchmen in the tower had a spear, a sword, or a knife, or pulled a dagger from its sheath, its whole blade gave off such a light for almost an hour's time

2 tanquam si illud ferrum verteretur in cereum. Et mox et ipso signo custodes admoniti, magis intenti vigiliis, hostes latebrantes lapidibus exturbabant. Quod ope sancti Martini recto iudicio reputatur, qui vicinitate sua sibi devotis populis sedulam exhibuit praesentemque custodiam." Et hanc virtutem a supra dicto cognovimus.

15

De oleo cicendilis sub pictura beati

Sibi quoque in Ravenna atque in rhetorica socio suo Felici, ex oleo quod sub imagine picturae beati Martini in cicendili ardebat, dum tetigerunt oculos, lumen rediisse confessus est.

as though that iron had turned into a candle. The guards, 2
alerted at once by this signal, were more attentive during their watches and dislodged the concealed enemies with stones. Right judgment will attribute this to the aid of the holy Martin, who offers the people devoted to him in his vicinity constant and immediate protection." I learned about this powerful deed too from the aforementioned Fortunatus.

15

About the oil from the lamp beneath a picture of the blessed man

Fortunatus also declared that when they touched the eyes of Felix, his companion in the study of rhetoric at Ravenna, with the oil that burned in the lamp under a painting of the blessed Martin, light had returned to them.

16

De Placido procuratore

Similiter in praedicta urbe dum Placidus procurator, desperatus a medicis, ad aliud puellarum oratorium sibi vicinum confugeret et in atrio recubaret, venit noctu ad abbatissam beatus Martinus per somnium, quam requirens quid faceret, ait se requiescere. Dicit sanctus ad illam: "In Gallias habui iam redire, sed propter istum, qui foris iacet in atrio, me remoratum profiteor." Tunc surgens abbatissa, et referens visionem, fidem fecit homini quia de periculo liberaretur, quod certe meruit obtinere.

2 Sed ut praedictus presbyter asserit, multum desiderabilius in locis Italicis Martini gloriam venerari quam, si licet dici, quo propria membra recubant tumulata, in tantum ut frequentia miracula nec sparsa colligantur in verbis nec tam infinita recondantur in paginis.

16

About the procurator Placidus

Also in the aforementioned city of Ravenna, when the procurator Placidus had been abandoned by his doctors and fled to a chapel of nuns nearby, and was sleeping in its forecourt, the blessed Martin came to the abbess during the night in a dream and asked what she was doing; she replied that she was resting. The holy man said to her: "I should already have returned to Gaul, but I admit that I have stayed behind on account of that man who lies outside in the forecourt." The abbess then arose, told the man about her vision, and gave him the confidence that he would be rescued from his danger, which he indeed deserved to obtain.

In parts of Italy, as the aforesaid priest asserts, it is con- 2
sidered much more desirable to venerate Martin's glory than, if I may say so, where his body itself lies buried, so much so that because of their frequency, the widely scattered miracles there cannot be collected in words nor, being so infinitely numerous, stored in written pages.

17

De his quae Ambianis gesta sunt

In porta Ambianensi, in qua quondam vir beatus pauperem algentem chlamyde decisa contexit, oratorium a fidelibus est aedificatum, in quo nunc puellae religiosae deserviunt, sancti antistitis ob honorem parumper facultatis, nisi
2 quod eas devotorum alit saepe devotio. Erant tamen eis quodam tempore pauca apium alvearia, quae eis fuerant data, quae cum quidam invidus conspexisset, ait intra se: "Utinam aliquid de his vasis possem auferre!" Secuta autem nocte, instigatus a daemone, ablatis tribus vasis, navim onerat, ut scilicet transito amne sibi facilius quae abstulerat vindicaret.

3 Sed credo ei impedimentum fuisse hoc furtum, sicut postea manifeste probatum est. Igitur cum sole oriente ad portum fluminis causa transmeandi homines properarent, navim ad litus aspiciunt, apesque ex alveariis catervatim
4 emergere, hominemque seorsum iacere prostratum. Sed putantes eum a somno occupatum, sicut didicerant iam a puellis furtum factum, quantocius properant ad alligandum eum, sed accedentes mortuum reperiunt. Statimque puellis notum faciunt factum, et quod furatum fuerat cellulae restituunt, admirantes tam velociter in homine divinae ultionis accessisse sententiam.

17

About the events that happened at Amiens

At the city gate of Amiens, where the blessed man had once covered a freezing man with his cutoff cloak, a chapel was built by the faithful where religious virgins now serve, who, in honor of the holy bishop, hardly have any possessions, only those which the piety of the devout often provides. Once, however, they owned a few beehives which had 2
been given to them, and when an envious man had seen them, he said to himself: "If only I could take away some of these hives!" The following night, instigated by a demon, he took away three hives and loaded them on a boat, so as to more easily take possession of what he had stolen on the other side of the river.

But I believe that this theft was a stumbling block for 3
him, as was afterward clearly proven. Thus when the sun rose and men hastened to the dock to cross the river, they saw the boat on the other shore, the bees emerging in a swarm from their hives, and the man lying prostrate nearby.
But thinking him to be asleep and having already learned 4
of the theft from the virgins, they hurried as quickly as possible to bind him; when they reached him, however, they found him to be dead. At once they notified the virgins of this fact and restored what had been stolen to the chapel, admiring how quickly the sentence of divine vengeance had come upon the man.

18

De Siroialense oratorio

Sic et apud Siroialense oratorium, cuius altarium sancti confessoris manus alma sacravit; dum plerique beneficia expetita mererentur, quidam paralyticus adveniens, et cereum in status sui altitudinem nocte tota vigilans retinuisset; mane facto, ut lux reddita est mundo, ipse absolutis gressibus, populo teste, incolumis exsilivit.

19

De Bella caeca

Nec hoc silebo, quid caecitati contulerit, cum beati sepulcrum devota mulier expetisset. Quaedam de Turonica territorio femina, Bella nomine, amisso oculorum lumine graviter laborabat. Et cum die noctuque incessabilibus doloribus urgeretur, dicit suis: "Si ad basilicam domni Martini

18

About the chapel at Sireuil

Similar things happened, too, at the chapel of Sireuil, whose altar the gracious hand of the holy confessor consecrated; since many who sought blessings there had received them, a paralyzed man came and kept vigil the whole night holding a candle of his own height; when morning came, and light was restored to the world, his legs were freed from their bonds in the sight of the people, and he stood up healthy.

19

About Bella, a blind woman

I will not be silent either about how he dealt with blindness when a devout woman sought to come to the tomb of the blessed man. A woman from the territory of Tours named Bella suffered greatly from losing the light of her eyes. And since she was afflicted day and night with unceasing pain, she said to her relatives: "If I had been led to the basilica of the lord Martin, I would have received my health

ducta fuissem, continuo sanitatem recepissem. Confido etenim quod possit oculis meis lumen infundere, qui potuit pauperis lepram, osculo libante, sanare."

2 Deinde, adminiculo deducente, venit ad sanctum locum, ibique ieiuniis et orationibus crebris insistens, visum quem amiserat recipere meruit. Et ita sanata est ut quae caeca venerat alio perducente, caecis affatim dux futura regressa sit. Quae postea virum accipiens, et filios generans, recuperatori gratias rependit incolumis.

20

De Ammonio praecipitato

Et quia bis aut tertio de sola gloriosi nominis invocatione, et virtutes factas et pericula sedata narravimus, qualiter cuidam pereunti in ipso mortis praecipitio beatus pontifex
2 invocatus sustentaculum praebuisset, evolvam. Ammonius quidam, agens sanctae basilicae, dum de cena madefactus vino veniret, de rupe excelsa quae viae coniungitur, Inimico impingente, praecipitatur. Erat autem profundum loci illius fere ducentorum pedum.

at once. For I trust that he who could heal the leprosy of a poor man with the touch of a kiss can pour light into my eyes."

Thereupon she came to the holy place led by a guide, per- 2
sisted in fasting and frequent prayers there, and deservedly received the sight she had lost. And she was healed so completely that she who had come as a blind person led by another often returned in the future as a guide for other blind people. When she later married and had given birth to sons, she recompensed her healer by giving thanks as a healthy person.

20

About Ammonius's fall

Because we have two or three times related how deeds of power were done and dangers overcome by the sole invoking of his glorious name, I shall explain how the blessed bishop, having been called upon at the very precipice of
death, gave support to someone perishing. When one Am- 2
monius, a servant of the holy basilica, came back from his midday meal drunk with wine, he was pushed by the Enemy and fell off a high rock cliff alongside the road. The valley in that place lay about two hundred feet below.

3 Cumque per profunditatem praecipitii illius rotaretur, et deorsum sine alarum remigio volitaret, sancti Martini auxilium per singula descensionis suae momenta clamabat; tunc quasi manibus aliorum de iumento suo excussus, super arbores, quae valli inerant, deicitur. Et sic paulatim per singulos ramos descendens, sine mortis periculo ad terram usque
4 pervenit. Tamen ut opus Insidiatoris non usquequaque videretur cassatum, quod fuerat inchoatum, unum pedem eius leviter laedit. Sed veniens ad gloriosi domni Martini templum, orationi incumbens, omnem vim doloris amisit.

21

De alio appenso

Non credo haberi superfluum, si inseratur lectioni qualiter invocatio nominis eius vitam praestiterit morituro. Quodam loco unus propter furti scelera comprehensus, atque gravibus verberibus actus, ductus est ad patibulum ut
2 condemnaretur suspendio. Cumque in hunc exitum, morte iam appropinquante, venisset, orandi spatium petiit. Tunc sicut erat ligatis post tergum manibus, iactavit se pronus in

As he tumbled along the length of this precipice, and flew 3
down without the oarage of wings, he cried out for the help of the holy Martin at every single moment of his fall; then, as though he had been pushed off his horse by the hands of others, he was thrown on top of the trees in the valley. And in this way slowly descending from branch to branch he
came down to the ground without danger to his life. So that 4
the act begun by the Treacherous One might not seem to be completely in vain, however, Ammonius slightly injured one of his feet. But when he came to the temple of the glorious lord Martin and prayed steadfastly, he was relieved of all the force of his pain.

21

About another man, who was hanged

I do not think it will be regarded as superfluous if I insert in this reading how the invocation of his name granted life to one who was about to die. In a certain place, a man who had been arrested for theft and severely whipped was sent to the gallows so that he might be condemned to hanging.
When he had come to this extremity, and his death was al- 2
ready approaching, he asked for time to pray. Then, since his hands had been tied behind his back, he threw himself face down on the ground and began to invoke the name of the

terram, et coepit cum lacrimis invocare nomen beati Martini, ut etsi in hac necessitate ei non succurreret, vel a culpis eum in posterum excusaret.

3 Cumque completa oratione suspensus fuisset, recesserunt milites a loco illo; ipse autem ore semiaperto, parumper labia movens, sancti Martini semper nitebatur auxilium implorare. Discendentibus tamen illis, statim solutae sunt
4 manus et pedes eius. Et sic per biduum pendente eo, revelatum est cuidam religiosae ut eum tolleret. Quae veniens invenit eum adhuc viventem. Tunc adiutorio beati Martini de patibulo depositum, incolumem adduxit ad ecclesiam.
5 Ibique eum videntes stupescebant et admirabantur, dicentes: "Quomodo vivit?" Et interrogabant eum qualiter liberatus esset. Ille autem dicebat: "Beatus Martinus me de praesenti morte liberavit et hucusque perduxit."

6 Vere hanc ego virtutem in hoc homine ostensam, iuxta sensus mei intelligentiam non inferiorem censeo quam mortuum suscitatum: quem sic beatus confessor, confracto, ut ita dicam, mortis hiatu, et eius ab ore retractatum vitae restituit. Qui usque hodie ad testimonium virtutis beati viri vivus habetur in saeculo.

blessed Martin with tears, asking him, even if he did not rescue him in this hour of need, to forgive him his sins later.

After he had finished his prayer, he was hanged, and the 3
soldiers left the place; he, however, with his mouth half open and his lips barely moving, kept on trying to implore the help of the holy Martin. When the soldiers had left however, the bonds of his hands and feet were at once broken.
And in this manner he hung for two days, until it was re- 4
vealed to a religious woman that she should come to take him away. When she came she found him still alive. Having taken him down from the gallows with the blessed Martin's
help, she led him uninjured to the church. Those who saw 5
him there were stunned in amazement, asking: "How can he be alive?" And they questioned him as to how he had been liberated. And he said: "The blessed Martin rescued me from imminent death and brought me here."

Truly, I regard the deed of power exhibited in this man, as 6
my feelings understand it, to be nothing less than the resuscitation of a dead man: in this way the blessed confessor restored him to life, having, so to speak, broken open the jaws of death and pulled him out of its mouth. He lives in the world to this day as a witness to the power of the blessed man.

22

De Leomere contracto

Quid etiam in Condatensi diocesi actum sit, non praeteribo. Locus autem ille crebris virtutibus illustratur. Ab hoc enim vir beatus, sarcina carnis abiecta, migravit ad Domi-
2 num. Leomeris ergo quidam nomine, servus cuiusdam hominis Andecavini, a sanguine percussus, contracta manu, ligataque lingua rigebat; multoque tempore in hac debilitate detentus, neque sibi, neque domino aliquid operis exerce-
3 bat. Hic, fide commonitus, cum ad beati basilicam vigilasset, directa manu, deliberataque ab omni impedimento lingua, beati Martini miraculum populis testabatur, dicens: "Ecce quid in hac nocte sanctus Dei operatus est, me teste, probate!"

4 Reversus autem ad dominum suum narravit ei omnia quae acta fuerant. Sed ille minime virtutem gloriosi pontificis credens, ad solitum eum adaptat servitium. Qui cum
5 operari coepisset, sursum in debilitatem redigitur. Intelligens autem dominus eius Dei hoc esse mysterium, transmisit eum iterum ad locum sanctum, ad quem prius abierat, in quo ille cum maxima devotione pernoctans, dato die, sanitati quam prius meruerat instauratur.

22

About Leomer, who was paralyzed

I will not omit either what happened in the diocese of Candes. The place is indeed resplendent with frequent deeds of power. For it was from here that the blessed man threw off his burden of flesh and migrated to the Lord.
Someone named Leomer, the slave of a man from Angers, 2
had suffered a stroke and lay paralyzed with a cramped hand and a bound tongue; for a long time this debilitated state prevented him from doing any work for himself or his master.
After he, advised by his faith, had kept vigils at the 3
blessed basilica, his hand was straightened, and his tongue was released from every impediment; and he testified to the people about the miracle of the blessed Martin, saying: "Look and find out through my testimony what the holy man of God worked this night!"

When he returned to his lord he told him all that had 4
happened. But this man did not in the least believe in the power of the glorious bishop and assigned him to his usual service. When Leomer began to work, however, he was
again reduced to paralysis. His lord then, understanding this 5
to be a mystery of God, sent him again to the holy place where he had been earlier; there Leomer kept vigils with the greatest devotion, and when morning came, was restored to the health which he had previously deserved.

23

De Wiliachario soluto a catenis

Dignum existimavi et illud non omittere in relatu, quid Wiliacharium presbyterum referentem audivi. Tempore quo idem Wiliacharius per perfidiam Chramni Chlotharium Regem iratum incurrerat, ad basilicam sancti Martini confugit, atque ibidem in catenis positus custodiebatur, sed virtute beati praesulis comminutae catenae stare non potuerunt.

2 Nescio autem qua imminente negligentia foris atrium comprehensus est. Quem oneratum ferro, vinctisque post tergum manibus, ducebant ad regem. At ille voce magna clamare coepit, ut sibi beatus Martinus misereretur orare, nec eum sineret abire captivum, cuius devotus expetierat tem-
3 plum. Statimque in eius vocibus, orante beato Eufronio episcopo de muro civitatis contra basilicam, dissolutae sunt manus eius, et omnes baccae catenarum confractae ceciderunt. Perductus autem usque ad regem, ibi iterum in compedibus et catenis constrictus retinebatur.

23

About Wiliachar, who was released from his chains

I have considered it worthwhile not to omit in this account what I heard the priest Wiliachar tell. At the time that Wiliachar incurred the anger of King Chlothar through the perfidy of Chramn, he fled to the basilica of the holy Martin, and was chained and kept under guard there. But the chains could not withstand the power of the blessed bishop and broke.

Through some kind of mistake, he was apprehended out- 2
side the forecourt. Laden down with irons, his hands chained behind his back, they brought him to the king. He then began to shout loudly, praying that the blessed Martin have pity on him and not allow him to leave as a captive,
who had devoutly come to his temple. And immediately fol- 3
lowing his words, while the holy bishop Eufronius prayed from the walls opposite the basilica, his hands were freed, and all the links of the chains broke, letting them fall. When he was brought into the king's presence, however, he was there again restrained with foot fetters and chains.

4 Sed invocato nomine saepe dicti patroni, ita omne ferrum super eum comminutum est ut putares illud fuisse quasi lutum figuli. Hoc tantum erat in spatiis, ut non solveretur a vinculo quoadusque nomen illud sacratissimum invocasset; invocato autem, omnia solvebantur. Tunc rex alterioris ingenii, videns virtutem sancti Martini ibidem operari, et ab onere vinculorum absolvit eum, et pristinae restituit libertati.

5 Haec ab ipsius Wiliacharii presbyteri ore coram multis testibus factum esse cognovi. Utinam se mihi in tali virtute dignaretur manifestare beatus confessor, ut sic absolveret meorum ligamina peccaminum, sicut super eum contrivit vasta pondera catenarum!

24

De Alpino Comite debile

Alpinus quoque comes Turonicae civitatis cum per totum annum graviter ab unius pedis dolore consumeretur, et die noctuque requiem non haberet, atque inter ipsas torturae suae voces beati Martini iugiter auxilium imploraret,

But when he called upon the oft-mentioned patron, all the iron on him was so completely shattered that you would have thought it potter's clay. This happened only at intervals, so that he was not released from his chains until he had invoked the sacred name; at the very moment that he did invoke it, however, all of them fell apart. Then the king, who was an intelligent man, realizing that the power of the holy Martin was at work, released him from the burden of chains and restored to him his original liberty. 4

I learned about these events from Wiliachar's own mouth 5
and in the presence of many witnesses. If only the blessed confessor would manifest himself to me with such power that he would in the same way absolve me from the bonds of my sins just as he shattered the heavy weight of chains on Wiliachar!

24

About Count Alpinus, who was disabled

Alpinus too, who was count of the city of Tours, was consumed by pain in one of his feet for an entire year and had no rest day or night; between the cries elicited by his torture he continuously implored the help of the blessed Martin,

apparuit ei beatus confessor in visu nocte, hilari vultu arridens, et consueta deferens arma; ut beatum signaculum sanctae crucis super pedem infirmum imposuit, mox omni dolore fugato, sanus surrexit a lectulo.

25

De Charigisilo contracto

Haec experta, Charigisilus referendarius regis Chlotharii, cui manus et pedes ab umore contracti erant, venit ad sanctam basilicam, et orationi incumbens per duos aut tres menses, a beato antistite visitatus, membris debilibus sani-
2 tatem obtinere promeruit. Et postea antedicti regis domesticus fuit, multaque beneficia populo Turonico vel servientibus beatae basilicae ministravit.

until one night the blessed confessor appeared to him in a dream, smiling with a joyful face and carrying his usual arms; when he had made the sign of the Cross over the diseased foot, all pain fled at once, and the count arose healthy from his bed.

25

About Charigisil, who was paralyzed

Having heard what we have just related, Charigisil, King
Chlothar's referendary, whose hands and feet had been paralyzed, came to the holy basilica; after he had given himself
over to prayer for two or three months, he was visited by
the blessed bishop and deservedly obtained the health of his
sickened members. After this, he became the steward of the 2
above-mentioned king and procured many benefactions for
the people of Tours and the servants of the basilica.

26

De Aquilino amente

Narrabo et illud, qualiter diabolicae artis insaniae ad eius basilicam denudentur. Quidam, Aquilinus nomine, dum venationem cum patre suo in silvis Franciae exerceret, pavorem pessimum, Inimico insidiante, incurrit. Erat enim ei
2 tremor cordis, et interea videbatur exsensus. Parentes vero eius intelligentes eum diaboli immissione turbari, ut mos rusticorum habet, a sortilegis et ariolis ligamenta ei et potiones deferebant. Sed cum nihil valerent ex more, illi sancti Martini auxilia prompti, dolore cogente, requirunt, dicentes: "Potest hic insidiarum nudare malitiam, qui detexit umbram multam, ut audivimus, falso religionis nomine adora-
3 tam." Quem de regione commotum miserunt ad sanctam basilicam, ibique in oratione cum summa parcitate se continens, opem sancti poscebat assidue.

4 Cumque in hac fide diutius commoratus fuisset, omni pavore dempto, sensum ut habuerat ante, recepit, oblitisque parentibus, in eo loco usque hodie pro beneficio accepto deservit.

26

About Aquilinus, who lost his senses

I will also tell how the insanities crafted by the devil are exposed at his basilica. Someone named Aquilinus, while he was hunting with his father in the forests of Francia, incurred an overpowering fear through the treacheries of the Enemy. For he had a tremor in his heart and seemed to have
lost his senses. His parents, realizing that he was being dis- 2
turbed by an incursion of the devil, followed the custom of country people and brought him ligatures and potions from sorcerers and wizards. But when these, as usual, failed to help, compelled by their grief, they readily sought the help of the holy Martin, saying: "This man can expose the malice of these trickeries, since we heard that he unmasked many a
demon worshipped in the false name of religion." They took 3
him from the region and sent him to the holy basilica, and there he devoted himself to prayer, living very soberly, and assiduously asking for the holy man's help.

When he had stayed there for a long time in this faith, all 4
his fear having been checked, he recovered his senses, and, having forgotten his parents, serves in that place today in return for the benefit he received.

27

De Charivaldo debili

Sed et Charivaldus quidam per venationem similes incurrens insidias, latus unum, debilitata manu ac pede, perdiderat. Qui ad gloriosum templum famulorum manibus deportatus, ieiunis et orationibus se subdens assiduis per totum fere annum, quod cum fecisset, omnium membrorum sanitate recepta, gaudens remeavit at propria.

2 Et ideo monemus ut nullus sollicitetur ab ariolis, quia nihil umquam proderunt infirmis. Plus enim valet parumper de pulvere basilicae, quam illi cum medicamentis insaniae.

28

De fune absciso

De pulvere aut cera loci illius, vel quidquid rapere quis potuit de sepulcro, quantae virtutes aut assidue fiant, aut factae sint, quis umquam poterit investigare aut scire?

27

About Charivald, who was disabled

But one Charivaldus, too, incurred similar treacheries through the hunt, losing the use of one side of his body when his hand and foot were paralyzed. He was carried to the glorious temple by his servants and devoted himself to fasting and assiduous prayer for almost a whole year. When he had done this, he received the health of all his limbs and returned home joyfully.

And therefore I warn all not to be tempted by sorcer- 2
ers, because they never do anything useful for the sick. The slightest quantity of dust from the basilica is more powerful than these men with their foolish remedies.

28

About a rope that was cut

As for the dust and candle wax of this place, or whatever anyone could steal from the tomb, who will ever be able to investigate or know how many powerful deeds either happen constantly or have happened through them? To be

Unum tamen manifestum miraculum, quod a fidelibus comperi, putavi crimen ducere taceri.

2 Unus fide plenus expetiit ut aliquid pignoris de sancti basilica secretius deportaret, et multis conatus vicibus, numquam potuit, dum publice non praesumpsit. Reverti autem cupiens, nocte ad funem illum de quo signum commovetur advenit, ex quo fune decisam cultro particulam secum detu-
3 lit. Regressusque ad domum, multis exinde infirmis sanitatem accommodavit, ita ut non dubium esset aegrotum evadere, qui pignus illud meruisset fideliter osculari.

4 Ecce quid, sancte, praestas fidelibus qui tua moenia expetunt pie! Per te salvantur, qui pignora votive detulerint, et subsequente tuo auxilio, liberantur. Sed haec omnia fides strenua operatur, dicente Domino: "Fides tua te salvum fecit" [Luke 18:42].

29

De Chariberto rege, qui res ecclesiasticas pervasit

Videtur nec illud sileri, qualiter vir beatus praesidia famulis ad res suas defendendas quaqua iubet accommodet. Charibertus rex, cum, exosis clericis, ecclesias Dei negligeret,

silent, however, about one very well known miracle about which I learned from the faithful, I regard as tantamount to committing a crime.

One man, full of faith, attempted to take away secretly 2
some token of the holy man from the basilica, and having tried many times, was never able to do so because he did not dare to do it publicly. Wishing to return, he came at night to the rope with which the bells are rung, and having cut off a
piece with his knife, took it with him. After he had returned 3
home, it subsequently bestowed health on many ill people, so that there was no doubt that illness would be evaded by whoever deserved to kiss that token in faith.

Behold what you, holy man, grant to the faithful who de- 4
voutly seek your protection! By you are saved those who take away relics with a vow, and they are liberated by your subsequent help. But a strong faith makes all these things possible; as the Lord says: "Your faith has saved you."

29

About King Charibert, who seized church property

It seems best not to be silent either about how the blessed man, wherever he is in charge, gives his servants protection in defending their properties. King Charibert, who hated

despectisque sacerdotibus, magis in luxuriam declinasset, ingestum est eius auribus locum quendam, quem basilica sancti Martini diuturno tempore retinebat, fisci sui iuribus redhiberi.

2 Loco autem illi Navicellis nomen prisca vetustas indiderat. Qui accepto iniquo consilio, pueros velociter misit, qui reiculam illam in suo dominio subiugarent. Cumque haec recte non possidens videretur habere, iussit in locum illum stabularios cum equitibus dirigi, ibique sine aequitatis ordine praecepit equos ali.

3 Accedentes ergo pueri faenum quod coacervatum fuerat accipiunt in equorum expensas. Cumque iniunctum studiose ageretur servitium, atque equites appositum faenum coepissent expendere, corripiuntur a rabie. Et frementes ad invicem, disruptis loris, per plana prosiliunt, et in fugam vertuntur; et sic male dispersi, alii excaecantur, alii rupibus praecipitantur, alii se saepibus ingerentes, palorum acuminibus ultro transfodiuntur.

4 Tandem stabularii iram Dei intelligentes, paucos extra terminum loci, quos assequi potuerunt, expellunt, sanosque recipiunt, nuntiantes regi rem illam iniustissime retineri. Et ideo haec cum fuissent perpessi, dixerunt: "Dimitte eam, et erit pax tibi." Qui furore repletus sic dixisse fertur: "Sive iuste, sive iniuste, reddi debeat; regnante me haec basilica non habebit." Qui protinus divina iussione transitum

clerics, neglected churches, and despised bishops, lapsed further into vice when someone suggested to him that an estate which the church of the holy Martin had possessed for a very long time could be returned to him according to the laws of his royal treasury.

Ancient tradition had given the name of Nazelles to this estate. When he had taken this evil advice, he quickly sent servants to seize this small property by force as his possession. And to make it look as though he owned it, although by right he did not, he ordered stable-keepers with horses to be sent to the estate and, without any due process, for the horses to be fed there. 2

When the servants arrived they found hay that had been collected and took it for their horses' needs. While this task was being carried out as ordered, and the horses began to eat the hay placed near them, they were seized by madness. Neighing at one other and breaking their reins, they burst forth onto the fields and turned to flee; and thus unfortunately being dispersed, some were blinded, others fell off cliffs, still others ran into fences and were pierced through by sharp stakes. 3

At last the stable-keepers understood this to be the anger of God, took away the few horses which they could catch, brought them back in good health, and announced to the king that he was most unjustly holding onto the estate. And since they had suffered for this, they said: "Let it go, and you will have peace." Filled with rage, the king is reported to have said: "Justly or unjustly, let that estate be returned to me; as long as I am king, the basilica will not have it." Soon 4

5 accipiens requievit. Adveniente autem gloriosissimo Sigiberto rege in eius regnum, ad suggestionem beati Eufronii episcopi hoc in dominio sancti Martini restituit, quod usque hodie ab eius basilica possidetur.

6 Audite haec omnes potestatem habentes! Sic vestite alios, ut alios non spolietis; hoc adiungite vestris divitiis, unde damnum non inferatis ecclesiis. Vindex est enim Deus velociter servorum suorum. Et ideo monemus ut qui de potestatibus haec legerit, non irascatur. Nam si irascitur, de se confitebitur dictum.

30

De Eustochio Pictavensi

Simili conditione beatus confessor in rebus sibi iniuste ablatis apparuit. Eustochius quidam, cum plerumque contra iustitiam sanctum Eufronium episcopum de haereditate Baudulfi cognati sui pulsaret, qui heredem basilicam sancti Martini instituerat, commotus ab eo per assiduas iniurias
2 beatus pontifex aliquid ei de rebus illis reddidit. Portante autem illo hoc ad domum suam, protinus filius eius unicus in febrem corruit, unaque die et nocte graviter exaestuans,

after, he passed away by divine command and ceased his action. When the glorious king Sigebert took over his king- 5
dom, he restored this estate to the holy Martin's dominion
upon the advice of the blessed bishop Eufronius, and it belongs to the basilica up to today.

Hear this, all of you who have power! Clothe people in 6
such a way that you do not despoil others; add to your wealth
in such a way that you do not inflict a loss upon churches.
For God is the swift avenger of his servants. And we likewise
warn those of the powerful who read these things not to be
angered. For if one becomes angry, one admits that these
things are said about oneself.

30

About Eustochius of Poitiers

The blessed confessor appeared again in a similar situation, when things had unjustly been taken from him. One
Eustochius had often unjustly harassed the holy bishop Eufronius about the inheritance of his relative Baudulf, who
had designated the basilica of the holy Martin as his heir,
and had been disturbed by him because of his constant insults; therefore the blessed bishop returned one of those
possessions to him. When he had carried it home, however, 2
his only son immediately came down with a fever, and after

exspiravit. Cui tam praesens fuit mortis occursus, quam velociter pater eius de rebus sibi non debitis effectus est dominus.

3 Qui in exemplum Giezi possedit aurum et argentum, sed, quod illi erat pretiosius, acquisita animae lepra, amisit et filium, nec umquam meruit deinceps alium adipisci.

31

De eo qui in sancta porticu periuravit

Quam praesens et super alium ultio divina processerit, qui in sancta porticu periuraverat, ad comprimendam perfi-
2 dorum audaciam non silebo. Cum ad matriculam illam quam sanctus suo beneficio de devotorum eleemosynis pascit, quotidie a fidelibus necessaria tribuantur, consuetudinem benedicti pauperes habent, ut cum multi ex his per loca discesserint, custodem inibi derelinquant, qui quod fuerit oblatum accipiat.

sweltering for a day and a night, breathed his last. His encounter with death took place as soon as his father took possession of the things not owed to him.

Just as Gehazi had done, this man possessed gold and sil- 3
ver, but lost what was more precious to him, for in acquiring leprosy of the soul, he also lost his son, and never deserved to have another one.

31

About a man who committed perjury in the holy portal

In order to crush the audacity of unbelievers I shall not be silent about how divine vengeance immediately visited another man, who committed perjury in the holy portal. Daily 2
necessities are brought every day by the faithful to the poor roll, through which the holy man, in his kindness, nourishes the indigent with the alms of the devout; the blessed poor however, since many of them leave to go elsewhere, leave a custodian there to receive the offerings.

3 Quidam ergo devotus unum triantem mercedis intuitu
detulit, quem custos loci collectum fratribus occultare non
metuit. Convenientes autem pauperes ad sextam, sciscitati
sunt antedictum custodem quid sibi beatus pastor, solita
pietate respiciens, transmisisset. Audierant enim ibidem ali-
4 quid fuisse largitum. Qui ait cum sacramento: "Per hunc
sanctum locum et virtutes domni Martini, quia hic amplius
non venit quam unus argenteus." Necdum enim verba compleverat, sed adhuc in ore sermo pendebat, cum statim tremens corruit in terram, suoque lectulo aliorum manibus
redditus, coepit graviter singultare.

5 Interrogatus autem a circumstantibus quid sibi esset, respondit: "Triantem illum quem pauperes requirebant, periuravi, et ideo me praesens vindicta flagellat; sed rogo ut eum accipientes reddatis matriculae." Quo reddito, statim emisit spiritum.

6 O infelix, qui sic ab iniqua cupiditate praeventus periit,
ut et lucrum vitae perderet, nec damna adeptae pecuniae
possideret! Sed ad "quid non mortalia pectora cogit" ex-
secranda cupiditas? Quae invida quondam viduae duobus
minutis caeleste regnum mercanti fueras, modo hunc per
7 unum triantem ad ima praecipitas. Et quae Iudam appen-
disti laqueo in magistri pretio, hunc per parvum numisma
demergis in Tartara. Satis ergo haec ad comprimendam malorum temeritatem dicta sufficiant.

Once, a devout man brought a gold coin in order to gain a heavenly reward, but the custodian who received it was not afraid of hiding it from his brothers. When the poor came together at the sixth hour, they inquired of the custodian what the blessed shepherd Martin, tending them with his usual care, had sent to them, for they had heard that some- 3
thing had been donated there. The custodian replied with 4
an oath: "By this holy place and the lord Martin's deeds of power, no more came here than one silver coin." He had not quite finished saying these words, they were still issuing from his mouth, when he suddenly trembled and fell to the ground, and when he had been carried to his bed by others, began to sob violently.

Asked by those around him for the reason, he answered: 5
"I lied about that gold coin which the poor inquire after, and for that reason divine vengeance now scourges me; but I ask that you accept it now and return it to the poor roll." When it had been returned, he at once gave up his spirit.

O unhappy man, who perished overtaken by greed in 6
such a way that he lost the benefit of life and did not keep the guiltily acquired money! But "to what do you not compel the hearts of men," accursed greed? Once, you were envious of the widow who bought the kingdom of heaven with her two mites, now you hurl this man into the abyss for one
gold coin. After hanging Judas in a noose for accepting a 7
price for his master, you now plunge this man into the netherworld because of a small coin. Let what has been said suffice, therefore, to crush the temerity of the wicked.

32

Qualiter me virtus eius ab infirmitate restauravit incolumem

Ergo his exactis quae circa alios gesta sunt, aggrediar quae circa me indignum virtus praesentis est operata patroni.
2 Anno centesimo sexagesimo tertio post assumptionem sancti ac praedicabilis viri beati Martini antistitis, regente ecclesiam Turonicam sancto Eufronio episcopo anno septimo, anno secundo Sigiberthi gloriosissimi regis, irrui in valetudinem cum pustulis malis et febre; negatoque usu potus atque cibi, ita angebar, ut amissa omni spe vitae praesentis, de solis sepulturae necessariis cogitarem. Obsidebat enim me mors assidua cum ardore, animam cupiens expugnare de corpore.

3 Tunc iam valde exanimis, invocato nomine beati Martini antistitis, parumper convalui, et lento adhuc conamine iter incipio praeparare, insederat enim animo ut locum venerabilis sepulcri visitare deberem. Unde tanto desiderio affec-
4 tus sum, ut nec vivere me optarem si tardius direxissem. Et qui vix evaseram ex ardore incommodi, coepi iterum desiderii febre succendi. Nec mora, adhuc parum fortis iter cum

32

How his power restored me to health from an illness

Now that I have finished recounting things which happened to others, I shall undertake to relate what the ever-ready power of my patron has effected for my unworthy self.
In the one hundred and sixty-third year after the assump- 2
tion into heaven of that holy and praiseworthy man, the blessed bishop Martin, being also the seventh year that the holy Eufronius governed the church of Tours and the second year of the glorious king Sigebert, I lapsed into an illness with infected sores and fever; unable to drink or eat, I was so distressed that I lost all hope in the present life and thought only about the arrangements necessary for my funeral. For death insistently and ardently besieged me, wishing to force my soul from my body.

Then, already half-dead, having called upon the name of 3
the blessed bishop Martin, I felt slightly better, and from then on began a feeble attempt to make preparations for a journey, for the notion that I should visit his venerable tomb had fixed itself in my mind. From that time on, I was affected with such a longing to do this that I did not wish
to live if I did not set out there soon. And so I, who had 4
just escaped the burning heat of an illness, began in turn to be inflamed by the fever of longing. Without delay, and

meis arripio; actisque vel duabus vel tribus mansionibus ingressus silvas, corrui rursus in febrem, et tam graviter agere coepi, ut omnes me autumarent vitam amittere.

5 Tunc accedentes amici, et videntes me valde lassum, dicebant: "Revertamur ad propria; et si te Deus vocare voluit, in domo tua morere. Si autem evaseris, votivum iter facilius explicabis. Satius est enim reverti ad domum quam mori in eremo."

6 Ego vero haec audiens, vehementer lacrimabaret, plangens infelicitatem meam, locutus sum cum eis, dicens: "Adiuro vos per omnipotentem Deum, et reis omnibus metuendum iudicii diem, ut ad ea quae rogo consentiatis. De coepto itinere non desistite, et si mereor sancti Martini videre basilicam, gratias ago Deo meo. Sin aliud, vel exanime corpus deferentes ibidem sepelite, quia deliberatio mea est non reverti domum, si non eius sepulcro meruero praesentari."
7 Tunc una pariter flentes, iter quod coeperamus aggredimur. Praecedente ergo praesidio gloriosi domni, ad basilicam eius advenimus.

although still weak, I set out quickly on the journey with my companions; having traveled for two or three days and entered a forest, I again lapsed into the fever and began to suffer so greatly that everyone said I would die.

My friends came up to me and, seeing me utterly ex- 5
hausted, said: "Let us return home; if God wishes to call
you, you will die at home. If, however, you should escape this
predicament, you will more easily carry out the voyage you
promised. It is better to return home than to die in the
wilderness."

Hearing this, I wept vehemently and, bewailing my mis- 6
fortune, I addressed them, saying: "I adjure you by almighty
God and by all the accusations that are to be feared on the
day of judgment to consent to what I ask. Don't break off
this journey, and if I deserve to see the basilica of the holy
Martin, I shall give thanks to my God. If not, carry my dead
body and bury it there, because I am determined not to return home unless I have been presented at his tomb." There- 7
upon, all weeping as one, we continued the journey we had
begun. Led by the glorious lord Martin's protection, we arrived at his basilica.

33

De clerico nostro amente

Eo tempore unus ex clericis meis, Armentarius nomine, bene eruditus in spiritualibus scripturis, cui tam facile erat sonorum modulationes apprehendere, ut eum non putares hoc meditari, sed scribere; in servitio valde strenuus, et in commisso fidelis. Hic vero, inficiente veneno, a pustulis malis omnem sensum perdiderat, et ita redactus fuerat ut nihil penitus aut intelligere posset aut agere.

2 Tertia autem nocte postquam advenimus ad sanctam basilicam, vigilare disposuimus, quod et implevimus. Mane autem facto, signo ad matutinas commoto, reversi sumus ad metatum. Qui lectulis quiescentes, usque ad horam prope
3 secundam dormivimus. Expergefactus ergo, amota omni languoris et cordis amaritudine, sentio me pristinam recepisse sanitatem, et gaudens puerum familiarem, qui mihi serviret, evoco. Exsurgens autem Armentarius velociter coram me stetit, et ait: "Domine, ego parabo quod iusseris." At ego, existimans adhuc esse eum exsensum: "Vade," aio, "si potes, voca puerum." Et ait: "Ego quaecumque praeceperis adimplebo."

33

About our cleric, who lost his senses

At that time I had a cleric named Armentarius who was well trained in spiritual literature, and for whom it was so easy to apprehend the modulations of music that you would think he was writing them down without having to think about them; in service, he was very dedicated, and in his duties, reliable. This man, however, became infected with a poison and because of infected sores lost his senses completely, being reduced to such a state that he could understand or do hardly anything at all.

On the third night after we arrived at the holy basilica we 2
decided to keep vigils and did so. When dawn came and the
bell for matins sounded, we returned to our lodgings. We lay
down on our beds, and slept until almost the second hour.
When I woke up, all illness and bitterness of heart had gone, 3
I feel that I have received my former health, and joyfully call
my household servant to attend to me. Armentarius, however, quickly arose, stood before me, and says: "Lord, I am ready to do what you command." But I, thinking he was still out of his senses, say: "Go and, if you can, call my servant." And he says: "I shall carry out whatever you command."

4 Obstupefactus interrogo quid hoc esset. Qui ait: "Intel-
ligo me valde sanum, sed unus error est animo, quod nescio
de qua parte huc advenerim." Et incipiens, ita mihi impen-
5 dit servitium sicut erat solitus ante taedium. Tunc ego exsultans et flens prae gaudio, gratias omnipotenti Deo tam pro me quam pro ipso refero, quod intercedente patrono incolumem me corpore, illum mente reddiderit, et unus occursus ex fide etiam alteri amenti, qui nec petere noverat, salutem praestitisset. Sed nec praeteribo, quod post dies quadraginta eodem die primo vinum delectatus sum bibere, cum illud, faciente incommodo, usque tunc exosum habuerim.

34

Quod virtus eius ab agro nostro tempestatem prohibuit

Nos vero revertentes tres cereolos pro benedictione beati sepulcri portavimus. De qua cera quam multae virtutes factae sunt super frigoriticis et aliis infirmis, longum est enarrare. Sed unum e multis miraculum proferam. Agrum quendam possessionis nostrae grando annis singulis vastare consueverat, et tam graviter saeviebat, ut nihil ibidem cum venisset relinqueret.

Stunned, I ask what had happened. He says: "I feel com- 4
pletely healthy, but am confused about one thing: I don't
know how I came here." And he began to wait upon me
as he used to before his illness. Thereupon I, exulting and 5
weeping for joy, give thanks to the almighty God for myself
as well as for him, that the intercession of our patron rendered us healthy, me in the body and he in his mind, and that
one encounter out of faith had benefited another who had
lost his senses and not known how to ask for it. But I will
not forego saying that, after forty days without it, I for the
first time on that day delighted in drinking wine, whereas up
to that time, during my illness, it had been distasteful to me.

34

How his power kept a storm away from our field

When we returned home we took with us three small candles from the tomb as a blessing. How many deeds of power were done through these candles upon those with fevers and upon other ill people takes too long to tell. But I will report one miracle out of many. A field among our possessions used to be devastated every year by a hailstorm, and it raged so violently that when it had come it left nothing there.

2 Tunc ego in vineis illis arborem unam, quae erat excelsior ceteris, eligens, de sancta cera super eam posui. Post illam autem diem usque in praesens tempus numquam ibidem tempestas cecidit, sed veniens, locum illum tamquam timens praeteriit.

35

De ligno beati cancelli ad nos delato

Fide commonente, quidam ex nostris lignum venerabile de cancello lectuli, quod est ad monasterium sancti domini, me nesciente, detulerat, quod in hospitiolo suo pro salvatione retinebat. Sed, credo quia non sic honorabatur aut diligebatur ut sibi decuerat, coepit familia eius graviter ae-
2 grotare. Et cum penitus nesciretur quid hoc esset, nec emendaretur aliquid, sed quotidie ageretur deterius, vidit in visu noctis personam terribilem, dicentem sibi: "Cur sic tecum agitur?" Qui ait: "Ignoro prorsus unde hoc evenerit."
3 Dicit ei persona: "Lignum, quod de lectulo domni Martini tulisti, negligenter tecum hic retines, ideo haec incurristi. Sed vade nunc, et defer illud Gregorio diacono, et ipse

Then I chose one tree that was higher than the others in this vineyard and put a holy candle on it. After that day and up to the present time the storm never again came down there but, when it did come, it passed that place by as though afraid. 2

35

About the wood of the blessed railing which was brought to us

Acting out of faith, one of our company took away a small piece of the venerable wood of the railing around the bed in the monastery of the holy lord Martin , without my knowledge, and kept it as a blessing in his cottage. But, I believe, because it was not being honored and esteemed as it
deserved to be, the man's family became severely ill. And 2
since he had no idea why this was happening, and they were not getting any better, in fact getting worse every day, he saw in a dream at night a terrifying personage who said to him: "Why are you suffering in this way?" He replied: "I am completely at a loss as to how this has come about."

The personage said to him: "The wood which you took 3
from the lord Martin's bed and here keep with you in a careless manner is the reason this has happened to you. But go now and bring it to the deacon Gregory so that he may keep

illud secum retineat." At ille nihil moratus mihi exhibuit.
4 Quod ego cum summa veneratione collectum loco digno reposui. Et sic omnis familia in domo eius sanata est, ita ut nemo ibidem deinceps aliquid mali perferret.

36

Quod virtus eius nobis inimicos inhibuit

Factum est autem quodam tempore ut visitationis studio ad venerabilem matrem meam in Burgundiam ambularem. Cum autem silvas illas quae trans Berberem fluvium sitae sunt praeterirem, latrones incurrimus. Qui circumdantes
2 nos, volebant spoliare et interficere. Tunc ego ad auxilia consueta confugiens, sancti Martini praesidium flagitabam. Quod mihi protinus dignanter assistens, ita eos conterruit ut nihil contra nos agere possent. Sed versa vice qui venerant ut timerentur, timere coeperunt et cursu velocissimo fugere.

3 Sed ego non immemor apostoli dicentis, inimicos nostros potu ciboque debere satiari, potum eis offerre praecipio. Qui nequaquam exspectantes, quantum poterant, fugiebant; crederes eos fustibus agi, aut invitos contra possibilitatem

it with him." And the man brought it to me at once. Having 4
received it with the greatest veneration, I put it in a worthy place. And in this way the entire family in his house was cured so completely that from that time onward no one there suffered from any illness.

36

How his power kept enemies away from us

It happened once that I was traveling in Burgundy, wishing to visit my venerable mother. When we were passing through the forests on the other side of the Bèbre River, however, we ran into bandits. They surrounded us and
wanted to rob and kill us. Then resorting to my usual aid, I 2
implored the holy Martin's protection. Deigning to come to my assistance at once he so frightened them that they could do nothing against us. In fact, they who had come to frighten, began themselves to be afraid and to flee with the utmost speed.

But I, remembering the apostle's saying that our enemies 3
should be refreshed with drink and food, commanded that they be given a drink. They had no mind to wait for this and fled as quickly as they could; you might think that they were being beaten with sticks or that they were being forced,

caballorum suorum currere cogi. Et sic, tribuente Domino, et iuvante patrono, quo dirigibamus advenimus.

4 De quantis me tribulationibus et aerumnis eripuit, in quantis necessitatibus sua pietas astitit, vel quantas amaritudines sua virtute compescuit, non dicam ad scribendum, sed etiam ad referendum perlongum est.

37

De dysentericis

Quid de dysentericis dicam, ubi tam velociter invenitur medela, quam fideliter fuerit inquisita? Nam vidi mulierem a dysenteria per quinque menses graviter laborantem, ita ut cum necessitas commoveret, inter manus ad loca necessaria transferetur; quae simul et confortationem cibi, et virtutem
2 corpusculi superflue digerendo perdiderat. Me indice novi hanc ad basilicam vigilasse. Reddito autem post nocturnas tenebras die, abraso beati tumuli pulvere, et remedium haussisse simul et poculum. Eamque domi propriis gressibus fuisse redditam, quae veniens ab aliis fuerat sustentata.

unwilling, to outrun the capacity of their horses. And so, with the support of the Lord and the assistance of our patron, we arrived where we had intended to go.

From how many troubles and hardships he rescued me, in 4
how many emergencies his care was there looking after me, and how many bitter feelings he dissolved with his power, would take too long, not only to write, but even to relate.

37

About those suffering from dysentery

What shall I say about those suffering from dysentery, how quickly a remedy is found when it is sought in faith? For I saw a woman greatly suffering from dysentery for five months, in such a way that, when necessary, she was carried by the hands of others to the privies; at the same time, she lost the comfort of food as well as the strength of her poor
body through excessive diarrhea. Having seen her myself, I 2
know that she kept vigils at the basilica. When daylight returned after the darkness of night, she scraped dust from the blessed tomb and drank this remedy in a cup of water. And she who had come supported by others returned to her home by her own steps.

38

De energuminis et frigoriticis

Vel quid ego de energuminis et frigoriticis referam, quibus si vere fuerint parcitas et fides coniunctae, mox adminiculante patrono, cunctae submoventur insidiae? Sic multi ex frigoriticis, dum vi febris pessime quatiuntur, tota die inter altarium et sanctum tumulum decubantes, ad vesperum autem hausto ex beati sepulcri pulvere, continuo promerentur accipere sanitatem.

2 Nam Paulus energumenus, qui legionem daemoniorum dicebatur habere, insistente Inimico, machinam quae sanctae camerae erat propinqua conscendens, dixisse fertur: "Pereat vasculum quod, exustus, inhabito!" Et exaestuans, et praecipitans se deorsum, ita beati virtute leviter in pavimentum depositus est, ut nullum membrorum damnati corpusculi collideret.

38

About the possessed and those suffering from chills

And what shall I report about the possessed and those who suffer from chills, from whom, if abstinence and faith are truly combined, all treacheries are soon removed through the help of the patron? Thus many of those suffering from chills, while they are being violently shaken by the force of the fever, lying all day between the altar and the blessed tomb, at vespers, when they have drunk a potion of dust from the blessed tomb, deserve to receive their health instantly.

For the possessed man Paul, who was said to have a legion 2
of demons, climbed up the baldachin under the holy vault at the instigation of the Enemy, and is reported to have said: "Let the vessel perish which I, burned up, inhabit!" And when, burning hot, he threw himself down, he was deposited so gently on the pavement by the power of the blessed man that he bruised no part of his poor suffering body.

39

De Leomeria caeca

Leomeria quaedam caeca atque contracta, longo tempore miserabiliter vivens, dum iter illud per manus aliorum crebris occursibus utitur, quo ad beati basilicam itur, tandem ab eius pietate respecta, iacens ad sanctum ostium, lumen pariter gressumque recepit.

2 O si totum proderetur in publicum, quod singuli quique, dum fideliter poscunt, latenter recipiunt, et retinet occultum multorum conscientia, quod fideliter poscendo clam
3 quaesita sanitas est adepta! Quod si haec, ut diximus, cuncta publicarentur, non solum libros, sed nec ipsum mundum, ut ait evangelista de Domino, arbitror potuisse recipere!

40

De Securo contracto

Et quoniam sermo clausulam petit, unum vobis adhuc praeclarum miraculum, priusquam liber finem accipiat, enarrabo. Adolescens quidam, nomine Securus, ex utero

39

About Leomeria, a blind woman

A woman who was blind and paralyzed, having long lived a miserable life and frequently made the journey to the basilica of the blessed man supported by the hands of others, was at last healed by his care as she lay on the holy threshold, and received light as well as her ability to walk.

O if all were made public what each person, whoever he 2
is, receives secretly when he asks for it in faith, and if only many were aware of the hidden truth that health privately
sought by asking for it in faith is obtained! But, as we said, if 3
all these things were published, I think that not only books but, as the evangelist said about the Lord, even the world itself could scarcely contain them!

40

About Securus, a paralytic

And because this discourse needs a closing word before the book reaches its end, I shall relate one more brilliant miracle to you. A young man named Securus had come out

matris egrediens, manum aridam pedemque protulerat, et ita omnium membrorum siccata compage diriguerat, ut monstrum aliquod simularet. Erat autem et iugo servitutis
2 innexus. Quem cum viderent domini sui iam per septem annos nihil posse proficere, manibus deportantes posuerunt eum ante beatum sepulcrum, ut vel a praetereuntibus pasceretur, qui labore proprio ali non poterat.

3 Iacente autem eo in loco illo per multos dies, directus est pes eius qui fuerat debilis, manusque eius sicca, infectis sanguine venis, sanata est. Et ita omni corpore, accepta beati confessoris ope, formatus est ut putares eum denuo fuisse renatum. Qui puerulus a Iustino Comite redemptus, et ingenuus dimissus est. Et postea baptismum consecutus, usque hodie sub patrocinio sanctae ecclesiae persistit incolumis.

4 Quis umquam ista sic ex ordine inquirere aut referre poterit, ut ex aequo laudare sufficiat? Tamen nos, quantum investigare potuimus, scribere fideliter studuimus, hanc sperantes retributionem mercedis accipere, ut dum haec leguntur in laudem sanctissimi sacerdotis, nobis fortasse tribuatur refrigerium pro delictis, dicente poeta: “Forsan et haec olim meminisse iuvabit.”

of his mother's womb with a withered hand and foot, and his body was so stiffened by the atrophy of all his limbs that he looked like a monster. He was also bound by the yoke of
servitude. When his masters saw that he had not been able 2
to do anything useful for seven years, they carried him with their hands to the blessed tomb so that he who could not be nourished by his own work would be fed by passersby.

After he had lain in that place for many days, his lame 3
foot was straightened, and his withered hand was healed by blood flowing into his veins. And by receiving of the blessed confessor's aid he was so completely reshaped that you would think him reborn. The boy was ransomed by Count Justin and let go as a free man. Later, he received baptism and remains healthy up to this day under the patronage of the holy church.

Who will ever be able to investigate and relate these 4
things from beginning to end, so as to praise them enough? We, however, try to write faithfully about what we have been able to find out, hoping to receive the following reward, namely that, when these things are read in praise of the holy bishop, he may perhaps grant me relief from my sins; for as the poet says: "Perhaps even this it will someday be a joy to recall."

LIBER SECUNDUS

De virtutibus quae factae sunt postquam venimus nos

Prologus

Quoniam, perscriptis virtutibus sancti Martini, quod vidimus vel a fidelibus viris de anteacto tempore reperire potuimus, ardentes valde in hac siti ut non traderetur oblivioni quod Dominus exercere dignatus est in laudem antistitis sui, narrare etiam ea cupimus quae nostro tempore agi miramur, relinquentes non parvam materiam eloquentioribus, sumentes autem magnalia virtutum in nostris operibus, ut quod peritia non dilatat in paginis, numerositas virtutum extendat in cumulis.

I

Qualiter a febre et dysenteria erutus sum

Anno centesimo septuagesimo secundo post transitum beati Martini antistitis, Sigiberto gloriosissimo rege

BOOK 2

About the powerful deeds done after we came

Prologue

Having written about the holy Martin's powerful deeds which we saw or which we were able to find out about in earlier times through trustworthy men, and with the burning desire not to let those which the Lord deigned to perform in praise of his bishop fall into oblivion, we also wish to tell about those at which we marvel that are done in our time, thereby leaving no dearth of material for those who are more eloquent, but collecting the great works of his deeds of power in our writings so that what my lack of literary expertise cannot amplify in pages, the multitude itself of the powerful deeds will turn into a large heap.

1

How I was rescued from fever and dysentery

In the one hundred and seventy-second year after the passing of the blessed bishop Martin, while the glorious

duodecimo anno regnante, post excessum sancti Eufronii episcopi, non meo merito, cum sim conscientia taeterrimus et peccatis obvolutus, sed tribuente fideli Deo, qui vocat ea quae non sunt tamquam quae sunt, onus episcopatus indignus accepi.

2 Mense autem secundo ordinationis meae, cum essem in villa, incurri dysenteriam cum febre valida, et taliter agi coepi, ut imminente morte vivere omnimodis desperarem. Emittebant autem assidue digestionum officia quae accipere non poterant inexpensa, et erat horror cibi; cumque ab inedia deficeret virtus stomachi, febris tantum erat victus corpori. Nam nullatenus accedebat confortatio sumptuosa: erat autem et dolor gravis totam alvum penetrans et discendens ad ilia, non me minus consumens tortura sua quam febris exegerat.

3 Cumque sic ageretur mecum, ut non remansisset spes vitae sed cuncta deputarentur in funere, nec valeret penitus medici antidotum quem mors mancipaverat ad perdendum, ego ipse de me desperans, vocavi Armentarium archiatrum, et dico ei: "Omne ingenium artificii tui impendisti, pigmentorum omnium vim iam probasti, sed nihil proficit perituro res saeculi. Unum restat quod faciam; magnam tibi theriacam ostendam. Pulverem de sacratissimo domni Martini sepulcro exhibe, et exinde mihi facito potionem. Quod si hoc non valuerit, amissa sunt omnia evadendi perfugia."

king Sigebert was in the twelfth year of his reign, after the departure of the holy bishop Eufronius, I—not because of my merit, for I have a darkened conscience and am enveloped in sins, but by the act of a faithful God who calls upon qualities that are not there as though they were—received, although unworthy, the burden of the episcopate.

In the second month after my ordination, however, while I stayed in a country house, I incurred dysentery with a very high fever and began to be so ill that, death being near, I completely despaired of living any longer. For I continuously defecated undigested material and was repelled by food; since the strength my stomach could provide diminished through lack of sustenance, the fever was my body's only source of energy. For even an expensive medicine did not in any way help me: a severe pain penetrated my whole belly and, descending into my intestines, consumed me no less with its torture than the fever had distressed me. 2

While I was in this state, with no more hope of this life remaining and preparing everything for my funeral, the physician's antidote being not at all effective with the one whom death had seized for perdition, I myself, despairing about my state, called my physician Armentarius and I say to him: "You have applied all the resources of your art, you have already tried the strength of all your ointments, but no earthly thing is of any use to one who is about to perish. There remains one thing that I can do; I will show you a great remedy. Bring me dust from the most sacred tomb of the lord Martin, and make a drink with it for me. If this does not have an effect, all ways of evading death have been found wanting." 3

4 Tunc misso diacono ad antedictum beati praesulis tumulum, de sacrosancto pulvere exhibuit, dilutumque mihi porrigunt ad bibendum. Quo hausto, mox omni dolore sedato, sanitatem recepi de tumulo. In quo tam praesens fuit beneficium, ut cum id actum fuerit hora tertia, incolumis procederem ad convivium ipsa die ad sextam.

5 Visum est et hoc inserere lectioni qualiter me Deus arguerit, ne ante me permitterem stultos et faciles de beatis solemnibus obtrectare. In crastino autem postquam convalui, die dominico ad missam veniens, nolensque me fatigare, uni presbyterorum gloriosa solemnia celebrare praecepi. Sed cum presbyter ille nescio quid rustice festiva verba depromeret, multi eum de nostris irridere coeperunt, dicentes:
6 "Melius fuisset tacere quam sic inculte loqui." Nocte autem insecuta, vidi virum dicentem mihi: "De mysteriis Dei nequaquam disputandum." Testor enim Deum quia hoc a me non est compositum, sed ipsa verba quae audivi vobis exposui. Unde, dilectissimi, nullus de hoc mysterio, etiam si rustice videatur dici, disputare praesumat, quia apud Dei maiestatem magis simplicitas pura quam philosophorum valet argutia.

A deacon was then sent to the aforementioned blessed 4
lord's tomb to fetch dust from the most sacred place and, diluted, it was given to me to drink. When I had finished drinking it, at once, all pain went away and I received my health from the tomb. And this benefaction came so quickly that, while it took place at the third hour, I went to the meal healthy at the sixth hour that same day.

It has seemed good to me also to insert in this reading 5
how God reproved me so that I not permit stupid and frivolous people to disparage the blessed solemnities in my presence. For coming to mass on the day (a Sunday) after I had recovered and not wishing to tire myself, I ordered one of the priests to celebrate the glorious solemnity. But when this priest pronounced some of the celebratory words in a rustic way, many of our people began to laugh, saying: "It would have been better to be silent than to speak in so uneducated a manner." The following night, however, I saw in 6
a dream vision a man who said to me: "The mysteries of God should never be criticized." I call God to witness that this is not invented by me, but that I present to you the very words which I heard. Hence, most beloved, let no one presume to criticize this mystery, even if it appears to be pronounced in a rustic manner, because for God's majesty the simplicity of a pure heart is worth more than the cleverness of philosophers.

2

De infirmitate Iustini

Gratum arbitratus sum et illud non omittere quod mihi in libro anteriore excessit. Nam cum retulerim de cereolis illis quos de sepulcro beati antistitis sustuli, a quibus et tempestates sedatas et alias infirmitates prohibitas dixi, hos cum mecum detinerem, Iustinus, vir sororis meae, in valetudinem irruit et, invalescente febre cum doloribus membrorum omnium, valde ad extremum agi coepit.

2 Nuntius haec ad me delatus retulit, efflagitans, ut si quid medicamenti reperire possem, morituro transmitterem, ne obiret. At ego, in virtute antistitis beati confisus, unum ex cereolis transmitto per puerum, dicens: "Accendite illum coram eo, et in contemplatione luminis orationem fundat ad Dominum et deprecetur omnipotentiam antistitis ut ei succurrat." Missus autem puer quod dederam deportavit.

3 Quo accenso ante lectum aegroti, favillam scirpi, quem iam ignis consumpserat, cultro eradunt, dilutumque aqua, aegroto porrigunt ad bibendum. At ille, ut hausit, protinus sanitatem recepit, incolumisque redditus, nobis postea,
4 qualiter sibi virtus beati antistitis subvenit, exposuit. Nam referre erat solitus, quod ubi primum oculis eius iubar

2

About the illness of Justin

I have judged it pleasing not to omit what escaped my attention in the previous book. For when I was telling about the candle ends which I took from the tomb of the blessed bishop, by which I said that storms had been stilled and other evils had been averted, I forgot to say that I was keeping these with me when Justin, my sister's husband, fell ill and, due to an increasing fever and pains in all his limbs, began to be in great danger of ending his life.

A messenger sent to me told me about this and begged 2
that, if I could find any kind of remedy, to send it to the dying man, lest he depart from this world. And I, trusting in the holy power of the blessed bishop, sent him by a servant one of the candle ends, saying: "Light it in front of him and let him, while contemplating its light, send a prayer to the Lord and beg the omnipotence of the bishop to save him." The servant was then sent away, carrying what I had given him.

When the candle was lit before the ill man's bed, they cut 3
off a piece of the burned wick with a knife and, diluting it with water, gave it to the sick man to drink. And when he drank it, he at once received his health and was restored, as he later told us when describing how the holy power of
the blessed bishop had helped him. For he was accustomed 4
to relate that at the very moment that the ray of light

luminis progressum a cereo tenebras pepulit noctis, protinus in contemplatione flammae, febris recessit a corpore, ac stomachus qui diu languerat inedia, cibum consolationis efflagitat; et qui tantum aquam puram ad restinguendum febris ardorem haurire consueverat, nunc vinum desiderat.

5 Fecit haec virtus antistitis, quae saepe miseris opem proflua miseratione tribuit et infirmis medicamenta largitur.

3

De Maurusa chiragrica

Vereor ne, nimium progredi praesumens, obsoleat paginam sermo rusticior.

2 Maurusam quandam graviter chiragrici umoris dolor affecerat, ita ut retortis ad crura pedibus, nullatenus se erigere possit. Erat autem et oculorum luce multata, quae longo tempore graviter agens, tamquam mortua putabatur superstes; nec erat ei spes alimonii, nisi aliquis ei manum misericordiae porrexisset. Quotidie autem respectum intuens devotorum, victus necessaria deposcebat.

emanating from the candle drove away the darkness of night
from his eyes, immediately upon his contemplation of the
flame, the fever receded from his body, and his stomach, languishing for a long time in emptiness, asked for the consolation of food; and he who had been accustomed to drinking
only pure water to extinguish the burning of the fever, now
desired wine. This was done by the holy power of the bishop 5
who, in his overflowing compassion, often gives aid to the
suffering and grants remedies to the ill.

3

About Maurusa, who suffered from gout

I tremble with fear lest, through my presumption to continue, the page be demeaned by my somewhat rustic speech.

One Maurusa was so seriously afflicted by the humor of 2
gout that her feet were bent back under her shins and she could not stand up at all. Also deprived of the light of her eyes, she suffered greatly for a long time and was regarded as though she were a living corpse; nor had she any hope of nourishment unless someone compassionately handed her alms. Every day, therefore, she awaited the attention of the devout and begged for the food she needed.

3 Factum est autem ut quodam tempore extra solitum gravius ageret, nec poterat quemquem iudicare membrorum, nisi tantum in pectore flatus spiraminis discurrebat. Quae, iam valde exanimis, rogavit ut eam ad pedes sancti Martini deferrent. Ad quem locum cum manibus fidelium fuisset illata, dolore cogente, vociferans beati viri auxilium, ut sibi
4 miseretur orabat. Tandem pietas illa respiciens quae pauperes dimittere numquam consuevit inanes, in festivitate sua laxata sunt fila nervorum arentium; et sic de dextra, quam per sex annos non iudicaverat, signum beatae crucis ad os faciens, in pedibus restituta est, ita ut ad hospitiolum suum nullius usa adiutorio remearet, oculorum lumine non recepto.

5 Post annos autem duos iterum veniens ad beati patroni tumulum, coepit attentius, sicut erat opportunum, orare; mox, apertis oculis, in rediviva luce surrexit. Hanc virtutem ideo hic scripsimus, quia postquam huc advenimus illuminata est; nam antea a debilitate sanata fuerat.

Once it happened, however, that she was suffering more than usual, that she could not govern any of her limbs, and that only her breath went back and forth in her chest. Already almost lifeless, she asked to be carried to the holy Martin's feet. When she had been brought to this place by the hands of the devout, she cried out, in her pain, for the help of the blessed man, and prayed that he have pity on her. 3
At last his compassion, accustomed never to send the needy away empty-handed, attended to her, and during his feast the bonds constricting her withered tendons were loosened; and when she was thus able to make the sign of the blessed cross with her right hand, which she had not been able to use for six years, over her face, her feet were restored, so that she returned to her hut without any help, although she had not received the light of her eyes. 4

After two years, however, she again came to the tomb of the blessed patron and, as was appropriate for her, began to pray more diligently; very soon, her eyes were opened and she arose with revived light. We describe this powerful deed here since she was illumined after we came here; she had been cured of her illness earlier. 5

4

De servo Simonis presbyteri

Simonis fidelissimi compresbyteri nostri servus, Veranus nomine, qui erat ei in commissis promptuariis probatus, dum ad custodiam sibi dispositam resideret, superveniente umore podagrico, pedum gresso multatur. Qui cum per totum annum talibus doloribus vexaretur ut etiam viciniam in proximo positam commoveret, contractis subito nervis, ad plenum debilitatur.

2 Quod videns dominus eius, dolens exitum fidelis vernaculi, iussit eum ad pedes beati antistitis deportari, promittens votum et dicens: "Si eum reddideris sanitati, piissime domne Martine, in illa die absolutus a meis servitiis vinculo,
3 humiliatis capillis, tuo servitio delegetur." Positus ergo ad pedes pretiosissimi domni, cum per quinque dies ibidem iaceret immobilis, sexta die sopore comprimitur, et obdormiens visum est ei tamquam si in lectulo solitus sit homo pedem extendere. Expergefactus autem, sanus ab omni debilitate surrexit. Qui, tonsurato capite et accepta libertate, beati domini usibus nunc deservit.

4

About the slave of the priest Simon

Veranus, the slave of our most trusted fellow priest Simon, who had proved his value to him in caring for the storerooms, while sitting on the watch assigned to him, was deprived by an incursion of the humor of gout of his ability to walk. When he had been afflicted for a whole year by such pains that those in his proximity were also moved by it, he became totally debilitated when his tendons suddenly contracted.

When his master saw this, grieving for the loss of a faith- 2
ful servant, he ordered him to be carried to the feet of the blessed bishop and made a vow, saying: "If you restore him to health, most compassionate Martin, on that day he will be absolved from the bond of servitude to me and, tonsured,
assigned to your service." He was placed, therefore, at the 3
feet of the most precious lord Martin, and when he had lain there without moving for five days, he was overwhelmed by sleep on the sixth, and in his sleep it seemed to him, while lying in his bed as usual, that a man stretched out his foot. When he woke up, he arose healthy without any of his ailments. Having been tonsured and received his liberty, he is now employed in the service of the blessed lord Martin.

4 O admirabilem beati viri redemptionem! Quis umquam de mille talentis sic redemit sicut praesens nostrorum criminum suffragator, qui uno ictu, unoque momento, sine numismate auri, et corpus a debilitate et conditionem absolvit ab onere?

5

De paralytico Autisiodorensi

Quidam ex Autisiodorensi oppido, Mallulfus nomine, deferentibus manibus ad beati Martini sepulcrum iactatus est. Qui iugi oratione et ieiunio incumbens, pedes, quos intortos exhibuerat, subito, data sanitate, retulit in usu con-
2 sueto directos. Et ita sancti virtute quodammodo reformatus est, ut, qui aliorum manibus deportabatur, propriis firmatus vestigiis praesentibus nobis consurgeret sospes.

What a marvelous ransom by the blessed man! Who ever, with a thousand talents, thus redeemed someone as did the powerful intercessor for our crimes, who at one stroke, in one moment, without gold coins, absolved a body from illness and a condition from its burden? 4

5

About a paralyzed man from Auxerre

A man from the town of Auxerre, named Mallulf, was carried by others' hands to the tomb of the blessed Martin and put down there. Having devoted himself to prayer as well as fasting, his feet, which had been seen to be twisted, were suddenly cured, and he regained them, straightened, for
their customary use. And he was somehow so renewed by 2
the power of the holy man that, after being carried by the hands of others, his feet were strengthened in our presence and he stood up healthy.

6

De paralytico Aurelianensi

Alius autem paralyticus, ex Aurilianensi territorio carruca devectus, venit ad sanctam basilicam. Qui diebus multis iacens ad ostium illud, quod secus baptisterio ad mediam diem pandit egressum, beati antistitis implorabat auxilium. Factum est autem, ut una die iacens gravius extra solito torqueretur, ita ut vicini de proximo ad eius voces concurre-
2 runt. Dissolvebantur autem ligaturae nervorum eius et dirigebantur, propterea erat dolor intolerabilis; et sic, tribuente patrono, erectus super plantas, flens prae gaudio, populo teste surrexit. Qui continuo clericus factus et in sospitate firmatus, ad domum regressus est.

7

De paralytico ex Biturigo

Sed et alius gressu debilis, nomine Leuboveus, iam clericus, adveniens se per terra trahens, quia, paupertate faciente, non habebat qui eum ferret, de die in diem beati

6

About a paralyzed man from Orléans

Another paralyzed man, carried on a cart from the territory of Orléans, came to the holy basilica. Having lain for
many days at the entrance that is near the baptistery and
opens onto the south side, he implored the aid of the blessed
bishop. It happened, that as he lay there he was tortured
more than usual by pain, so that those nearby ran toward
him at his cries. It was, however, the confining bonds of his 2
tendons that were dissolving, and the tendons themselves
being straightened that was the cause of his intolerable pain;
and in this manner, with the help of the patron, the man was
raised to stand upon his feet, weeping with joy, in the presence of the people. He was made a cleric on the spot and,
strengthened in health, returned to his home.

7

About a paralyzed man from Bourges

But still another man unable to walk, named Leuboveus, already a cleric, who had come by dragging himself along on the ground because his poverty did not allow him to have

Martini limina requirebat. Qui dum quadam die a foris ad sancti pedes fleret, directis genibus atque pedibus, spectante populo, sanitatem recepit.

2 Tres virtutes istas ipsa die factas fuisse constat, quo Sigibertus gloriosissimus rex Sequanam transiens, sine collisione exercitus pacem cum fratribus fecit. Quod nullus ambigat hanc etiam beati antistitis fuisse victoriam.

8

De caeco illuminato

Eo quoque tempore caecus quidam stipem ab eleemosynariis postulans, cui non erat aliud in victu nisi qui manum porrexisset pietatis intuitu, nec erat domi praesidium nisi
2 miseratio devotorum. Die una, dum stante ante sanctum sepulcrum fixis staret vestigiis, subito corripuit eum dolor in oculis, et cum graviter ab hoc dolore consumeretur, coeperunt eius oculi spumam emittere. Et sic, erumpente a palpebris eius sanguine, in redivivam lucem renascens, lumen quod olim perdiderat videre promeruit.

someone carry him, went day after day to the threshold of the basilica of the blessed Martin. One day, while he wept at the holy man's feet from outside the church, his knees and feet were straightened and, as the people watched, he received his health.

These last three powerful deeds were done on the very 2
day that the most glorious king Sigebert crossed the river Seine and made peace with his brothers without their armies clashing. Let no one doubt that this was truly the victory of the blessed bishop.

8

About a blind man who received light

At this time too there was a blind man begging for a gift from almsgivers, who had no food other than what a pious hand extended to him, nor did he have the protection of a home except the compassion of the devout. One day, while 2
he was standing still before the holy tomb, a pain suddenly seized him in his eyes, and while he was being violently consumed by it, his eyes began to emit a froth. And in this manner, with blood bursting forth from his eyelids, he was reborn into a renewed light, deservedly seeing the light which he had once lost.

9

De alia caeca

Gunthedrudis quaedam de Viromandensi territorio, oculorum lumen perdiderat; quae relinquens domum et patriam, fide commonente, venit ad sanctam basilicam; ibique diebus multis deserviens, unius oculi meruit recipere visum. Qui mox oblita virum et filios, vesteque mutata, ad religionem ecclesiasticam, Domino inspirante, transivit.

10

De muliere a profluvio sanguinis liberata

Sed nec hoc silebo qualiter, velut ex veste Redemptoris nostri, ad beatum sepulcrum fluxus sanguinis sit siccatus. Mulier quaedam ex Arverno, veniens cum viro suo de pago Transaliensi, a profluvio sanguinis aegrotabat; secus autem atrium basilicae mansionem habebat. Quae diebus singulis ad sancti confessoris limina iacens, prostrata opem sanitatis poscebat.

9

About another blind woman

One Gundetrud from the territory of Vermandois, had lost the light of her eyes; advised by faith to leave her home and country, she came to the holy basilica; having served there for many days, she deservedly received her sight in one eye. Instantly forgetting her husband and children, she put aside her worldly dress and, inspired by the Lord, entered into the church's religious life.

10

About the woman delivered from a flow of blood

Neither will I be silent about how, just as once by the robe of our Redeemer, a flow of blood was dried up at the blessed tomb. A woman from the territory of Clermont, coming with her husband from the region of Trézelle, suffered from a flow of blood; she took lodgings near the atrium of the basilica. Lying prostrate at the threshold of the holy confessor every single day, she begged him to cure her.

2 Factum est autem ut quadam die accedens ad sanctum sepulcrum, orans et osculans, de palla quae super est posita aures et oculos sibi tangeret. Protinus, siccato rivo sanguinis, ita sanata est ut putaret se Redemptoris fimbriam conti-
3 gisse. Cuius vir in valetudinem irruens, ad ostium basilicae manibus depositus aliorum, fideliter exorans, restincta febre, convaluit. Et sic pariter, hic incommodo, haec a profluvio, sanati, magnificantes Deum ad propriam domum regressi sunt.

II

De muliere clauda

Coniux Animii tribuni, nomine Mummola, nocte conterrita a pavore, usum unius pedis perdiderat, et ita in debilitatem corruerat ut aliorum manibus sustentaretur evecta, sic
2 ubi disponeret progressura. Quae ad beati Martini pedes deposita, nocte tota cereum manu pro voto detinuit, nobis in basilica vigilantibus. Mane autem facto, moto matutinis signo, super pedem debilem constitit, ita ut, omni debilitate sedata, ad metatum suum propriis gressibus, nullo sustentante, libera remearet.

One day, when she had come to the holy tomb, and was 2
praying and kissing it, she touched her ears and eyes to the cloth lying over it. At once, the river of blood in her dried up and she was cured so thoroughly that she thought she
had touched the Redeemer's fringe. When her husband fell 3
ill, he was placed at the door of the basilica by the hands of others, and having prayed full of faith, the fever was extinguished, and he recovered. And having thus been healed in the same way, he from an illness and she from a flow of blood, they returned to their home praising God.

II

About a lame woman

The tribune Animius's wife, named Mummola, overcome with terror one night, lost the use of one foot, and lapsed into such debility that she was supported and carried by
others' hands when she wished to go somewhere. When she 2
had been placed at the blessed Martin's feet, she held a candle in her hand the whole night, as she had vowed, while we were keeping vigils in the basilica. When morning came, and the bell for matins had sounded, she stood up upon the lame foot in such a way that, all weakness extinguished, she returned to her lodgings on her own feet, no one supporting her.

12

De dysenterico sanato

Quodam vero tempore cum beatus Germanus Parisiacae urbis pontifex ad festivitatem antistitis gloriosi accederet, Ragnimodus, tunc diaconus, nunc episcopus, in servitium eius accessit, graviter a dysenteria laborans. Sed beatus Germanus prius ad villam ecclesiae suae, quae in hoc territorio sita est, venit.

2 Igitur cum ante noctem vigiliarum solemnitatis eius Turonis advenire coepisset, diaconem in villa residere iubet, dicens: "Ne forte fatigeris eundo, et aliquid deterius tibi contingat." At ille: "Potestas," inquit, "Dei est, quae nos iubeat iuxta meritum pati; nam ego non exeo aliter nisi ad basilicam beati antistitis eam. Confido enim quod si tumulum
3 eius attigero, salvus ero." Et statim, ascenso equite, ad basilicam venit. Mane autem, accepta potione de pulvere sepulcri, sedata protinus infirmitate, convaluit.

12

About a man who suffered from dysentery and was cured

Once, when the blessed Germanus, bishop of the Parisian city, came to the feast of the glorious bishop Martin, Ragnemod, then deacon, now bishop, came in his retinue, suffering severely from dysentery. But the blessed Germanus first went to a country house of his church which is situated in this territory of Tours.

Therefore, when he began to set out for the night of vig- 2
ils preceding Martin's celebration, he ordered his deacon to remain at the country house, saying: "Lest perhaps you tire yourself by going and something worse befall you." But Ragnemod said: "It is the power of God that commands us to suffer according to our merit; therefore I will not leave here in any other way than by going to the blessed bishop's basilica. For I am confident that if I touch his tomb, I shall
be made healthy." And, at once, he got up on his horse and 3
went to the basilica. The following morning, when he had ingested a potion made with dust from the tomb, his illness was immediately extinguished and he recovered his health.

13

De caeco illuminato

Ursulfus autem quidam, ex Turonica civitate de pago
trans Ligerem, caecus, beati Martini suffragia devotus expetiit. Qui duobus assidue mensibus ad eius templum deser-
2 viens, ieiuniis orationibusque perdurabat. Factum est autem
in una die resurrectionis dominicae, dum esset ad pedes
domni et cum reliquo populo missarum solemnia spectaret,
subito apertis oculis cuncta clare cernere coepit, ita ut ad
sanctum altare communicandi gratia, nemine ducente, veniret.

3 Quae autem fuerit causa caecitatis, edicam. Primo die
paschae iussus est a domino suo ut agrum circuiret, inventumque aditum unde pecora introibant, obseraret. Dum
4 eum claudere conatur, excaecatus est. Tunc, ut diximus, ad
beatum sepulcrum veniens, flens et eiulans, visum quem
perdiderat flagitabat. Die autem illa, dum populo gratia dominici corporis traderetur, et ei beatus antistes reddere lumen dignatus est ac, elucente sole, luminum suorum refulse-
runt stellae.

5 Quis umquam, rogo, talis medicus poterit inveniri, qui
in una infirmitate duas contulerit medicinas? Ecce in uno

13

About a blind man who received light

One Ursulf, from the city-state of Tours, in the region on the other side of the river Loire, was blind, and devoutly sought the blessed Martin's intercession. Assiduously coming to serve at his temple for two months, he persevered in
fasting and prayers. On one day of the Lord's resurrection, 2
while he was at the feet of the lord Martin and attended the solemnity of mass together with the rest of the people, suddenly his eyes opened and he began to see everything clearly, so much so that he came to the holy altar to receive the grace of communion without anyone guiding him.

I'll tell you the reason for his blindness. On the first day 3
of Easter he was ordered by his master to make a round of the field, and when he found an opening in the fence through which cattle were entering, he closed it. In trying to
do so, he was blinded. Then, as we said, having come to the 4
blessed tomb, and weeping and lamenting, he asked for the return of the sight which he had lost. On the day of his recovery, while the grace of the Lord's body was given to the people, the blessed bishop also deigned to give him back the light of his eyes, so that while the sun shone, the stars of his eyes reflected its light.

Who, I ask, could ever find such a physician, one who 5
gives two remedies for one illness? Behold, in one blind

caeco duae virtutes ostensae: cui corporales oculos ad contemplanda terrena prius aperuit, nunc cordis oculos, ne ea concupiscat, illuminavit; et ad suum dignatus est dicare servitium quem, ut ita dicam, renasci denuo fecit in mundum.

14

De puella paralytica

Sed nec hoc reticebo, quid in suam festivitatem operatus sit hic patronus. Palatina quaedam puella paralysi umore percussa, usum gressuum male redacta perdiderat, ita ut, contractis in poplitibus nervis, calcaneos ad crura coniungeret. Quam pater Turonis deferens, ante pedes beati Martini devotus exposuit; ibique tribus mensibus iacens, stipem a praetereuntibus postulabat.

2 Factum est autem in die insignis solemnitatis beati viri, ut illa, nobis missas dicentibus, in loco quem superius nominavimus fideliter exoraret. Cumque nos, rite sacrosancta solemnia celebrantes, contestationem de sancti domini virtutibus narraremus, subito illa vociferare coepit et flere,

man two powerful deeds were made manifest: in the one whose corporal eyes the blessed Martin first opened to contemplate earthly things, he now illumined the eyes of his heart so that he would not desire them; and he saw fit to dedicate to his service the one whom, so to speak, he caused to be reborn again in the world.

14

About a paralyzed girl

Neither will I keep silent about what this patron did during his feast. A girl at the royal court, afflicted by the humor of paralysis, had lost her ability to walk because of not having been taken care of properly, so that the tendons in her knees had contracted and her heels lay under her thighs. Her father brought her to Tours and devoutly placed her at the feet of the blessed Martin; lying there for three months, she begged passersby for alms.

It happened on the day of the blessed man's foremost so- 2
lemnity that, while we were saying mass, she was praying full of faith in the place mentioned above. And when we, celebrating the most sacred solemnity in the proper manner, were recounting the testimony of the powerful deeds of this holy lord Martin, she suddenly began to cry out and weep,

3 indicans se torqueri. At ubi, expeditam contestationem, omnis populus "Sanctus" in laudem Domini proclamavit, statim dissoluti sunt nervi qui ligati erant, et stetit super pedes suos, cuncto populo spectante; et sic, propitiante Domino, usque ad altare sanctum ad communicandum propriis gressibus, nullo sustenante, pervenit. Qui usque hodie incolumis perseverat.

15

De caeco illuminato

Merobaudis quidam ex pago Pictavensi, dum esset laborans in opere, caecitate pessima, Insidiatore immittente, percussus est. Qui cum per sex annos male agens in hac infirmitate duraret, advenit ad sanctum templum beati Mar-
2 tini, ibique assidue orationi incumbens. In crastina die de sancta festivitate, dum ad pedes beati Martini staret, subito visum est ei circa se tanquam coruscatio resplenderet; protinus apertis oculis, cuncta prospexit. Qui continuo clericus factus in eodem loco, sanus abscessit.

indicating that she was being tormented. And when this testimony was finished and all the people proclaimed "Holy" in praise of the Lord, suddenly her bound tendons were loosened and she stood on her own feet, all the people watching; and in this way, with the help of the Lord, she came on her own feet, no one supporting her, to the holy altar to receive communion. Up to this day she has remained healthy. 3

15

About a blind man who was given light

While he was working, one Merobaud from the region of Poitiers was struck totally blind at the instigation of the Treacherous One. When he had suffered this infirmity for six years, he came to the blessed Martin's holy temple and
devoted himself to assiduous prayer. On the day after the 2
holy feast, while he stood at the feet of the blessed Martin, it suddenly seemed to him that something like lightning flashed around him; at once, his eyes were opened, and he saw everything. He was at once made a cleric there and departed healthy.

16

De his quae nauta retulit

Fuit et illud insigne miraculum, cum Dominus in die Epiphaniorum obtentu beati antistitis ex aquis Falerna produxit, ac de alvei fundo vinum elicuit pauperi, qui quondam latices in vina mutavit.

2 Igitur cum quodam tempore iter agerem in pago Balbaciensi, ad Ligerem fluvium usque perveni. Cumque a nauta, qui nos ripae alteri transponere debebat, sollicite requirerem loca in quae piscaturi procederemus, locum indicat, dicens: "Sit vobis beatus Martinus in adiutorium." At nostri ingratae haec susceperunt, dicentes, quod in eius nomine
3 numquam captura visa est evenisse. Et ille: "Haud dubium sit, quia praestat haec virtus eius. Nam referam vobis, quae mihi hoc anno contigerit, vel qualiter per invocationem nominis eius, opitulante Domino, quod optavi promerui. Denique dies erat Epiphaniorum, et ingressus in promptuario, nihil potus quod haurirem inveni. Egressusque oravi, dicens: 'Sanctissime Martine, transmitte mihi in hac sacra solemnitate aliquid vini, ne epulantibus aliis, ego ieiunus remaneam.'

4 "Dum autem haec tacitus orarem, vocem in ulteriori ripa audivi me vocantem, ut navem homini qui iter agebat adducerem. Verum ubi, acceptis contis, tunsorum etiam

16

What a boatman reported

There was also that extraordinary miracle on Epiphany, when, at the request of the blessed bishop Martin, the Lord produced Falernian wine from water and made wine come forth from the riverbed for a poor man, just as he had once transformed water into wine.

Once when I was traveling in the region of Baugy, I came 2
to the shore of the river Loire. And when I carefully asked the boatman who was to take us to the other side about the places where we were going to go to fish, he pointed to one, saying: "Let the blessed Martin be your help." But our companions showed no gratitude for these words, saying that no
one had ever seen a fish caught in his name. He replied: "Let 3
there be no doubt that his power makes this happen. For I shall tell you what happened to me this year, how through the invocation of his name and with the Lord's help I deserved to get what I wished. In effect, it was the day of Epiphany and when I entered my storeroom I found nothing in it to drink. When I had left it I prayed, saying: 'Most holy Martin, send me some wine in this sacred solemnity lest, when the others are drinking, I remain deprived.'

"While I silently prayed these words, I heard a voice call- 4
ing from the opposite shore, asking me to bring a boat to a traveler. In truth, after I had taken up the oars, begun to

impetum fluctus secare coepi, et ut in medio amne perveni, subito excussus magnus ex gurgite piscis in navem cecidit. Quo confestim oppresso, transpositis hominibus, domum regressus sum, venditoque pisce uno vini modio, cum ceteris sum refectus. Ergo noveritis quam velociter in illud quod invocatus fuerit, si petatur fideliter, apparebit." Testor autem Deum quia haec ab ipsius nautae ore cognovi.

17

De Guntchramno Duce

Quodam die, dum Guntchramnus Boso contra vicum Ambiacensem Ligerem fluvium transmearet et, irruentibus iam tenebris, mundum nox horribilis retineret, subito adversante vento nautae turbantur in pelago; separatisque navibus quae pontem illum sustinebant, et aqua usque ad summum repletis, discendunt cuncti usque ad cingulum cum ipsis navibus in profundo, nequaquam tamen navibus subductis a pedibus.

2 Exterritus autem omnibus, Boso non rauce vociferans beati Martini auxilium proclamabat, et ut eis ad liberandum festinus occurreret, precabatur, dicens fidenter suis: "Nolite

cleave the pounding violence of the waves, and reached the
middle of the river, suddenly a huge fish sprang from the water and fell into the boat. Having immediately killed it and
ferried the men, I returned home, sold the fish for a cou-
ple of gallons of wine, and dined along with the others. You 5
will therefore know how quickly, if he is asked in faith, Martin will appear to help in situations in which he is invoked."
I call God to witness that I learned these things from the
mouth of the boatman himself.

17

About Duke Guntram

One day, while Guntram Boso was crossing the river Loire opposite the village of Amboise, as the shadows of dusk were already falling, and a dreadful night was enveloping the world, suddenly, the wind blew from the opposite direction and the boatmen were thrown into confusion in the water; the boats which sustained the bridge had been separated and completely filled with water, all went down with their boats up to their waists in the deep, without, however, losing the boats under their feet.

Everyone was terrified, but Boso called out in a loud 2
voice for Martin's help, praying that he rush to liberate them quickly, and saying full of faith to his company: "Don't be

timere! Scio enim quod dextera sancti viri ad auxilia por-
3 rigendum maxime in necessitatibus sit parata." Haec eo dicente, directis a Deo navibus, mutatoque vento contrario in secundum, nullo pereunte, pervenerunt litore, ubi tam praesens occurrit beati confessoris suffragium, ut etiam argentum, quod rapiente fluvio perdiderant, ipso denique fluvio in litus restituente, reciperent.

18

De Landulfo lunatico

Quidam ex Viennensi territorio, Landulfus nomine, graviter a lunatici daemonii infestatione vexabatur, ita ut plerumque ab hoste se vallari putans in terram corrueret, cruentasque ex ore spumas emittens, tamquam mortuus habebatur. Quod genus morbi ephilenticum peritorum medicorum vocitavit auctoritas; rustici vero cadivum dixere, pro eo quod caderet. Cumque se antedictus in hoc exitu videret affligi, audita beati praesulis fama, sanctam eius adiit basilicam, ut sibi praesentia cunctis suffragia subvenirent.

2 Sed cum in eodem loco plenus fide venisset, ardentius eum saevi daemonis pulsat audacia; nec ei licebat atrium

afraid! For I know that the holy man's right hand is most
ready to offer aid in emergencies." While he was saying this, 3
the boats were steered by God, the contrary wind changed
into a favorable one, and they reached the shore without anyone dying; there the blessed confessor's aid was so clear that, when the river itself washed it up on the shore, they even recovered the silver which they had lost when the river had seized it.

18

About Landulf, a lunatic

Someone from the territory of Vienne, named Landulf, was so gravely tormented and possessed by the demon of lunacy that he often thought he was being attacked by an enemy and fell to the ground, spewing bloody foam from his mouth and appeared to be dead. Experienced medical authorities call this kind of illness epilepsy; country people call it the falling sickness, because one falls down. When the aforementioned man realized that he was being tormented to the point of death, and had heard of the fame of the blessed bishop, he came to his holy basilica so that the intercessions that had been effective for all might also help him.

But when he had come to this place, full of faith, the sav- 2
age demon's audacity struck him even more keenly; nor was

egredi propter publicam daemonum infestationem; in atrio tamen nihil nocebatur. Nam visibiliter cum magno armorum strepitu venientes, conabantur eum cassis telorum acuminibus perfodere. Quod si se subderet terrae, ranarum su-
3 per eum multitudo horribilis desilire videbatur. Sed et voces publice ab eo audiebantur exprobrantium et dicentium: "Martinus, quem expetisti, nihil poterit tibi subvenire, quia nostris es ditionibus mancipatus." Sed ille ad haec fidenter immobilis signum crucis opponens, terribiliter eos per aera effugabat.

4 Post has autem vacuas et inanes immissiones, cum videret Inimicus eum sibi vindicare non posse, dolis eum temptavit illudere. Componens autem se in speciem veterani, venit ad eum, dicens: "Ego sum Martinus, quem invocas. Surge et adora coram me, si vis recipere sanitatem." Cui ait ille: "Si tu es domnus Martinus, fac super me signum crucis, et credam." At ille, audito nomine signi sibi semper contrarii, tamquam fumus evanuit.

5 Post haec autem stans ad pedes gloriosi domni factus est in stupore mentis, et vidit beatam basilicam novo lumine effulgere. Ex qua egrediens, sanctus dixit ad eum: "Exaudita est oratio tua, et ecce eris sanus ab infirmitate qua pateris!" Et sic beatae crucis signum super caput eius faciens, abscessit. Ille vero in se reversus, amotis omnibus insidiis, sensit se

he allowed to leave the atrium because of his visible infestation by demons; in the atrium, however, he was in no way harmed. For they came visibly with a loud clatter of their weapons and tried to run him through with the insubstantial points of their daggers. And if he crouched on the ground, a horrible multitude of frogs seemed to leap down
upon him. But he also heard voices reproaching him openly, 3
saying: "The Martin for whom you have come will not be able to help you, for you are bound by our powers." But he was immobile and full of faith and opposed the sign of the Cross to these words, making the demons flee in terror through the air.

After these empty and insubstantial attacks, when the 4
Enemy saw that he could not claim the man for himself, he attempted to deceive and delude him. Assuming the form of an army veteran, he came to him and said: "I am Martin, whom you are invoking. Rise and worship me if you wish to receive your health." Landulf said to him: "If you are lord Martin, make the sign of the cross over me and I will believe you." But when the demon heard the name of the sign that was always opposed to him, he vanished like smoke.

After this, however, while Landulf stood at the feet of 5
the glorious lord, he went into a daze and saw the blessed basilica shining with a new light. Stepping out of the basilica, the holy man said to him: "Your prayer has been heard and, behold, you will be healed of the illness from which you suffer!" And after he had made the sign of the blessed Cross over Landulf's head he departed. When Landulf had returned to his senses, all the demons' treacheries had been removed, and he felt that he had received

6 salutem integram recepisse. Tamen post receptam sanitatem, cum coepisset vinum uti superflue, corpusque diu abstentum imbre maduisset, latus ei cum uno pede manuque contrahitur. Sed parsimoniae se iterum deputans, caputque tonsurans, rursum beati virtute redditur sanitati.

19

De Theodomere diacono caeco

Dum singula quaeque miracula beati viri succincte scribimus, nec ea in ampliorem sermonem expandimus, verendo valde ac timendo iter carpimus inchoatum, ne forte dicatur a prudentioribus: "Multum haec poterat peritus ex-
2 tendere." Sed nobis in ecclesiastico dogmate versantibus videtur ut historia quae ad aedificationem ecclesiae pertinet, postposita verbositate, brevi atque simplici sermone texatur, ut et virtutem beati antistitis prodat, et sapientibus fastidium non imponat. Quo facto et lector provocetur in lectione et sanctus prodatur in opere.

3 Theodomeris diaconus cum prae umore capitis, decidentibus cataractis, oculorum aditus haberet per quattuor annos graviter obseratos, venit ad cellulam Condatensem, in

complete health. After the recovery of his health, however, 6
when he began to drink too much wine and to drench his body, long used to abstinence, with this liquid, his side as well as a hand and a foot contracted. But after he dedicated himself again to abstinence and tonsured his head, he was again restored to health by the power of the blessed man.

19

About the blind deacon Theodomer

As we write succinctly about each of the miracles of the blessed man, without expanding the stories into a larger discourse, we continue the journey we began with trembling and fear, lest perhaps more knowledgeable persons might say: "An experienced writer could have greatly expanded
these stories." But to us, versed as we are in church dogma, 2
it seems that the stories that pertain to the church's edification should avoid wordiness and be woven into a brief and simple speech, that makes clear the power of the blessed bishop without causing disgust in those who are more learned. This has been done; let the reader be provoked to go on reading and let the saint be revealed in his deeds.

When a humor in his head had caused cataracts to de- 3
velop, and his eyes had thereby been gravely obstructed for four years, the deacon Theodomer came to the cell at

qua vir beatus transiit. Prostratusque ad eius lectulum, nocte tota lacrimis et orationibus deducta, immobilis madefecit terram fletibus, tepuitque suspiriis eius venerabile lignum cancelli. Lucescente autem die, reseratis cataractis luminum, lumen videre promeruit.

4 Quid umquam tale facere cum ferramentis medici, cum plus doloris negotium exserant quam medelae, cum, distentum transfixumque spiculis oculum, prius mortis tormenta figurant, quam lumen aperiant? In quo si cautela fefellerit, aeternam misero praeparat caecitatem. Huic autem beato confessori voluntas ferramentum est, et sola virtus unguentum.

20

De Desiderio energumeno

In qua cellula cum Desiderius energumenus, ex Arverno veniens, nocte integra debacchasset, mane facto, coepit declamare quod eum beatus Martinus incenderet. In his vocibus evomens purulentum nescio quid cum sanguine, daemone eiecto, purgatus est, infectumque sanie pulverem derelinquens, cellulam egressus est sanus.

Candes, in which the blessed man had passed away. He prostrated himself beside the holy man's bed, spent the whole night without moving in tears and prayers, moistening the earth with his weeping and warming the venerable wood of the balustrade with his sighs. When the skies began to lighten at the break of day, however, the cataracts closing his eyes were opened, and he deserved to see the light.

Have physicians ever effected such a cure with their iron 4
instruments, since what they bring about is more a pain than a remedy when they hold the eye open and pierce it with their lancets, and thereby anticipate the torments of death before opening it up? In this process, if he is not very careful, the physician causes permanent blindness in the unlucky person. For this particular man, however, the blessed confessor's will was the iron instrument and his power alone was the ointment.

20

About Desiderius, who was possessed

In this same cell, Desiderius, a possessed man who had come from Clermont, raved for a whole night; and when day came he began to cry out that the blessed Martin was burning him. With these words he vomited some sort of pus with blood and with it ejected the demon, and was cleansed; he left the dust stained with a bloody mess and departed from the cell healthy.

21

De homine manum contractam habente

Quidam in eodem loco manum debilem contractis digitis detulit, ita ut ungues in palma eius affixi, decurrente interdum sanguine, dolorem ei nimium generarent. Hic proiciens se ad antedictum gloriosi domni lectulum, flens et deprecans, tam dolore instigante quam fide, postera die, directis digitis, manum recepit incolumem.

22

De Remigia matrona

Similem infirmitatem Remigia matrona incurrens, ad beatam cellulam valde devota pervenit. Quae vigiliis et orationibus insistens, cum matriculam quae ibidem congregata esset, pasceret, aridum brachium cum contractis digitis sanum extulit ad miscendum. Et sic tota die benedictis pauperibus deserviens, sospes remeavit ad propria. Haec in posterum annis singulis antedictis fratribus alimentum sufficiens exhibebat.

21

About a man with a deformed hand

In this same place someone brought his diseased hand with its fingers so deformed that the nails were sticking into his palms and blood sometimes flowed, which caused him considerable pain. He threw himself down before the bed of the glorious lord, weeping and praying, as much because of his pain as because he was inspired by his faith; the next day his fingers were straightened and he received a healthy hand.

22

About the lady Remigia

The lady Remigia incurred a similar malady and came with great devotion to the blessed cell. She had dedicated herself to vigils and prayers, and while she was distributing food to those registered on the poor-roll who had assembled there, her withered arm with its deformed fingers became healthy to mix their drinks. When she had ministered to the blessed poor in this way for the whole day, she returned healthy to her home. After this, she came every year and gave the aforesaid brothers the food they needed.

2 Factum est autem ut quadam vice una puellarum suarum male a quartani typi febre quateretur. Dum autem secundum consuetudinem veniens, pauperibus illis exhibebat victum, sancti viri implorat auxilium. Et per quattuor dies ad beatam cellulam continuatione orationis atque ieiuniis decubans, ab omni febre sanata puella, cum familia magnificans Deum domum regressa est.

23

De Vinaste caeco

Talia exercens quidam, Vinastis nomine, lumen recepit dum scilicet pauperibus illis victus necessaria ministravit. Hic autem caecitate maxima per annos plurimos aggravatus, habebat in consuetudine ut, veniens de regione sua ad antedictam sancti cellulam, pauperibus illis amplissimum alimentum exhiberet, vigiliisque devotissime celebratis, eos in satietate reficeret, quibus ipse, iuxta possibilitatem, tamquam famulus serviebat.

2 Dum igitur haec per multos, ut diximus, annos impenderet, quadam vice impleto voto servitioque simul, prosternitur ad cancellum sancti lectuli, et orans ac vale dicens,

It happened, however, that one of her maidservants was 2
severely racked by the quartan fever. When the lady came according to her custom, and offered food to those same poor people, she implored the help of the holy man. And after she had lain prostrate in the blessed cell for four days in continuous prayer and fasting, the maidservant was completely cured of her fever and the lady returned home with her company, praising God.

23

About Vinast who was blind

While doing such things, that is to say, while he supplied those same poor people with the food they needed, a man named Vinast too recovered his sight. Although he had been afflicted by total blindness for many years, he used to come from his home region to the aforementioned cell and to provide abundant food for these same poor people; after celebrating the vigils devoutly, he fed them until they were satisfied, ministering to them himself as much as possible as though he were their servant.

When he had dedicated himself to these things, as we 2
said, for many years, one day, when he had fulfilled his vow and his service to the poor, he prostrated himself before the balustrade of the holy bed, prayed and said farewell, and

regredi cupiebat. Post completam autem orationem exsurgens, apertis parumper oculis, intuetur cortinam sericam de cancello pendere, et ait: "Video tamquam pallium sericum
3 hic appensum." Cui aiunt sui: "Veritatem te videre cognoscimus." Ipse autem coepit iterum flere atque orare, ut beatus confessor opus coeptum dignanter expleret. Qui dum orat attentius, obdormivit, apparuitque ei vir per visum, dicens: "Vade ad basilicam domni Martini, et ibi plenam obtenes sanitatem." Qui nihil moratus, famulorum manibus deductus, ut limina beati confessoris attigit, lumen integrum, opitulante fide, recepit.

24

De homine omnibus membris contracto

In Biturigo quoque fuit quaedam mulier, quae concipiens peperit filium cuius poplites ad stomachum, calcanei ad crura contraxerant, manus vero eius erant adhaerentes pectori, sed et oculi clausi erant. Qui magis monstrum aliquod
2 quam hominis speciem similabat. Qui cum non sine derisione multorum aspiceretur, et mater argueretur cur talis ex

prepared to go home. When he arose after completing his prayer, however, his eyes opened slightly so that he could see the silk curtain hanging from the balustrade, and he said: "I
see as it were a silk mantle hanging here." His companions 3
replied: "We know that what you are seeing is there." Therefore he began to weep and pray again, that the blessed confessor might complete the work he had begun. While praying earnestly, he fell asleep, and a man appeared to him in a vision, who said: "Go to the lord Martin's basilica, and there you will obtain complete health." Immediately, he was led by the hands of his servants so as to reach the threshold of the basilica of the blessed confessor; there, through his faith, he recovered his full sight.

24

About the man crippled in all his limbs

In Bourges a woman conceived and gave birth to a son whose knees were bent up against his stomach and his heels to his thighs, whose hands stuck to his chest, and whose eyes were closed. He resembled some kind of monster
rather than the human form. Since many people laughed 2
when they saw him, and asked his mother why such a son came forth from her, she confessed with tears that he had been conceived on a night preceding a Sunday. Not daring

illa processerit filius, confitebatur cum lacrimis, nocte illum dominica generatum. Quem interimere non audens, ut mos matrum est, tamquam sanum puerum nutriebat. Adultumque vero tradidit mendicis, qui accipientes posuerunt eum in carrucam et trahentes ostendebant populis, multum per eum stipendii accipientes.

3 Dum haec per longa tempora gererentur, anno aetatis suae undecimo advenit ad festivitatem beati Martini, proiectusque a foris ante sepulcrum miserabiliter decubabat. Transacta autem festivitate, visum auditumque recepit. Inde reductus ad solitam consuetudinem, postulabat stipem.
4 Post annum fere aut eo amplius venit iterum ad solemnitatem, positusque est in loco in quo prius iacuerat; decursisque solemnitatis festis, directis omnibus membris, plenissimam obtinuit sanitatem. Quae nec credibilia fortasse videantur, ego eum sospitem vidi, nec audita ab aliquo, sed ab eius ore narrata cognovi.

5 Sed quia dixi, parentibus eius ob peccatum evenisse per violentiam noctis dominicae: cavete, o viri, quibus sunt coniuncta coniugia! Satis est aliis diebus voluptati operam dare; hanc autem diem in laudibus Dei impolluti deducite. Quia qui in ea coniuges simul convenerint exinde aut contracti aut ephilentici aut leprosi filii nascuntur. Sitque hoc, quod diximus, documentum, ne malum, quod una nocte committitur, per multorum spatia annorum perferatur.

to kill him, she raised him as mothers do, as though he were a healthy boy. When he had reached adulthood, however, she gave him to beggars, and they, having taken him on, put him on a cart and hauled it around to show him to the people, receiving a lot of money because of him.

When this had been going on for a long time, he came to 3
the feast of the blessed Martin in the eleventh year of his life and, having been thrown down, he lay in misery outside, facing the tomb. When the feast was over, however, he received his eyesight and hearing. When he had been led back from
there to his customary way of life, he begged for a living. Af- 4
ter almost a year or more he came again to the solemnity, and was set down in the same place where he had lain before; when the feasts of the solemnity had run their course, all his limbs were straightened and he received complete health. Lest, perhaps, this seems unbelievable, I myself saw him healthy, and I did not hear his story from anyone else, but learned about what has been related here from his own mouth.

But because I said that this had happened to his parents 5
on account of their sin in violating the night before Sunday: be careful, you people who are united in marriage! It is enough to engage in lustful acts on other days; on this day, conduct yourselves without pollution in praise of the Lord. For to those married people who come together on the night preceding this day deformed, epileptic, or leprous children will be born out of it. Let this story, as we said, be an example, lest evil committed on one night be endured for many long years.

25

De paralytico sanato

Illud prae ceteris admirandum miraculum, vobis orantibus, explicabo, quod post immensum maeroris cumulum magnum nobis gaudium patefecit, dum et virtutem beati protulit et quod titubabat erexit, cordaque nutantia populorum larga stabilitatis firmitate munivit.

2 Nam cum, venerabilem dominicae nativitatis noctem sacrosanctis deducta excubiis, procedentes de ecclesia, ad basilicam sancti ire disponeremus, quidam ex energuminis, atrocio ceteris, coepit nimium debacchari, et discerpens se atque collidens, clamabat: "Frustra Martini limina petis! Casso eius aedem aditis, qui vos propter multis criminibus dereliquit! Et ecce, vos abhorrens, Romae mirabilia facit! Ibi caecorum oculis lumen infundit; ibi paralyticorum gressus dirigit; sed et aliis quoque morbis sua virtute finem imponit!"

3 Ad hanc diaboli vocem omnis populus exturbabatur, en non solum obruta minorum corda, sed etiam nos ipsi pavore concutimur. Ingredientibus autem nobis cum fletu magno basilicam, omnes pavimento prosternimur orantes, ut sancti

25

About a paralyzed man who was healed

Because of your entreaties, I will relate the story of the miracle which is more admirable than the others; it is the one that, after an immense burden of grief, revealed a great joy to us since it manifested the power of the blessed man as well as raised up what was faltering, fortifying the wavering hearts of the people with broad and firm stability.

For when the holy vigil for the venerable night preced- 2
ing the Lord's birth had been conducted, and we went forth from the cathedral intending to go to the basilica of the holy man, one of the possessed, who was more appalling than the others began to rave excessively, clawing and striking himself, and shouting: "You approach Martin's threshold for nothing! In vain do you come to his temple for he has left you because of your many crimes! And, realize this: because he is disgusted with you he now makes miracles happen at Rome! There, he pours light into the eyes of the blind; there, he restores paralytics' ability to walk; and his power puts an end to other illnesses as well!"

At this voice of the devil, all the people became agitated, 3
and not only were the coarse hearts of the humble overwhelmed, even we ourselves were struck by that same fear. We entered the basilica weeping loudly, and we all prostrated ourselves on the floor, praying that we might deserve

4 viri praesentiam mereamur. Et ecce unus, Bonulfus nomine,
cui ante tres annos per nimiam valitudinis febrem manus
ambae cum uno pede contraxerant, et ad festivitatem beati
viri manibus directis, pede adhuc debili claudicabat, ante
sanctum altare sternitur, orans ut qui sibi manus aridas resti-
tuerat, pedem quoque contractum simili virtute dirigeret.
In hac autem oratione a febre nimia circumdatur, et tam-
5 quam extensus in aculeum nervorum dolore torquetur. Interea de supplice dolor excitat contumacem, et qui venerat
inquirere medicinam, coepit inferre calumniam. Aiebat
enim: "O domne Martine, sanitatem a te, non tormenta,
quaesivi! Quam si non mereor, vel doloribus non affligar!"

6 Cumque nos cum fletibus circumstantes beati praestolaremur adventum, et inter haec sancta solemnia agerentur, oblatis super altare sacris muneribus mysteriumque corporis et sanguinis Christi palla ex more coopertum, molliuntur contracturae nervorum, et disrupto post infirmi poplitis corio, defluente sanguinis rivo, pedem extendit incolumem.

7 Quod videns ego, Deo omnipotenti gratias agens, lumina fletibus madéfacta, in hac ad populum voce prorupi: "Timor a cordibus vestris omnis abscedat, quia beatus confessor nobiscum inhabitat! Nec omnino credite diabolo, qui nihil umquam protulit verum. Ille 'ab initio mendax est, et in veritate non stetit.'" [John 8:44]. Me autem ista dicente, omnium luctus laxatur in gaudium. Ipse etiam infirmus coram

the holy man's aid. And behold! There was a man, named 4
Bonulf, both of whose hands and whose one foot had become deformed three years earlier during a severe fever; his hands had been healed by the blessed man during his feast, but he still limped on his weak foot; Bonulf prostrated himself in front of the holy altar and prayed that the one who had restored his withered hands might with a similar deed of power also straighten his deformed foot. During this prayer, he felt enveloped by a high fever and tormented by a pain in his tendons, as though he were being stretched on a
rack. While this was happening, the pain caused by the tor- 5
ture aroused the suppliant's defiance, and he who had come to seek a remedy began to utter slander. For he cried: "O Lord Martin, I asked you for health, not torments! If I don't deserve health, let me not be afflicted by these pains!"

And while we, standing around him, waited with tears for 6
the blessed man's arrival, and in the meantime the holy solemnities were being celebrated, the holy gifts had been offered on the altar, and the mystery of the body and blood of Christ had been covered with a cloth as customary, the bonds constricting his tendons softened, and when the skin of his debilitated hamstring had broken, a rivulet of blood flowed out and he stretched out his foot, healed.

Seeing this, I gave thanks to almighty God, my eyes wet 7
with tears, and called out to the people with these words: "Let all fear depart from your hearts, because the blessed confessor lives with us! Don't believe anything the devil says, for he has never spoken the truth. He has been 'deceitful from the beginning, and there is no truth in him.'" As I spoke these words, everyone's grief turned into joy. The sick

8 nobis assurgens, in pedes constetit absolutus. Videns autem haec omnis populus, in caelum clamore prolato, plaudebat, dicens: “Gloria in excelsis Deo, qui, sicut quondam pastores angelico lumine, ita nos hodie praesentia confessoris beati clarificavit et eum nobis adesse praesenti virtute monstravit!” Et sic a timore Inimici omnes erepti, Christi praesidio roborati sunt.

26

De Piolo muto

Nec dissimili in virtute per sanctum Epiphaniorum diem vir beatus apparuit, cum os muti cuiusdam obstrusum coram populo reseravit. Piolus quidam, Condatensis clericus, a nativitate procedens manus clausas laborioso mundo protulit, in usu laboris inertes. Et hoc cur accesserit, utrum hic aut parentes eius peccaverint, ut sic mancus nascere-
2 tur, non est nostrae discretionis exsolvere. Unum tantum scimus, quod in eo, sicut et in reliquis infirmis, est ostensa gratia sacerdotis. Nam cum factus esset decem annorum, accrescentibusque unguibus graves dolores manuum pateretur, eosdemque ferre non toleraret, limina beati confessoris

man arose in our presence and stood on his feet, delivered
from his affliction. When all the people had seen this, they 8
let forth a clamor unto heaven and clapped, saying: "Glory
to God in the highest, who, just as he once shone upon the
shepherds with an angelic light, today illuminated us with
the presence of his blessed confessor and showed him to
be with us through this deed of power!" And in this manner
all were delivered from fear of the Enemy and strengthened
through Christ's help.

26

About Piolus, a mute man

The blessed man appeared in a similar deed of power on
the holy day of Epiphany, when he opened the obstructed
throat of a mute man in the presence of the people. One
Piolus, a cleric from Condat, from his birth had brought to
the world of toil deformed hands that were of no use for any
work. And why this occurred, whether either he or his parents sinned, so that he was born crippled, is not for us to
decide. One thing we do know, however, is that in him, as 2
in other ill persons, the bishop's grace was made manifest.
For when he had reached ten years of age, and his hands
were suffering seriously as his nails grew, so that he could
no longer bear the pain, he came to the blessed confessor's

adivit. Ibique diebus multis cum summa parsimonia demoratus, digitos directos manusque retulit sanas.

3 Post annos autem fere quinque pessimum incurrit incommodum et, dum vi nimiae febris atteritur, vocis elocutione multatur, ereptusque a febre, sine loquelae officio permane-
4 bat. Sed taliter fuerat aditus oris eius obstructus, ut nec qualemcumque mugitum posset emittere, sed annectens cum corrigia tres tabulas manu ferebat, easdem inter se collidens, sonum quem ab ore non dabat tabulis proferebat. Hoc opus vinitoribus utile est, cum vineta ab infestantium avium catervis defensare conantur.

5 Cum autem venisset antedictus ad sancti basilicam in ea nocte in qua dominus noster Iesus Christus fluenta laticum hauriens Falerna porrexit, ad beati pedes vigilare disposuit.
6 Transacto autem tempore mediae noctis, obdormivit. Qui cum nescio quid per visum periculi cerneret, pavore conterritus, in hanc vocem primum obseratum aperuit os: "Domne Martine, libera me!" Et sic erumpens ab ore et faucibus eius sanguis, auditum pariter et eloquium recepit.

threshold. And when he had remained there for many days fasting extremely strictly, his fingers were straightened, and he went back with healthy hands.

After almost five years, however, he became afflicted with 3
a severe illness and, since he was worn down by a violent high fever, his capacity for speaking was destroyed, so that after he had been delivered from the fever, he lost the ability
to speak. The obstruction in his throat was such that he 4
could not produce even an inarticulate bellow. Thus he tied together three tablets with a string and carried them in his hand, and by letting them collide with each other he produced the sound he could not make with his mouth. This device is used by vinedressers when they try to protect the vines from flocks of predatory birds.

When this man had come to the basilica of the holy man 5
on the evening before the day that our Lord Jesus Christ turned water he had drawn into Falernian wine, he prepared to keep the vigil at the feet of the blessed man. After midnight, however, he fell asleep. And when he saw some un- 6
known danger in a dream vision, he was overwhelmed with fright and opened his hitherto obstructed mouth with this first cry: "Lord Martin, deliver me!" And in this way, while blood flowed from his mouth and throat, he received his hearing at the same time as his ability to speak.

27

De muliere paralytica

Cum vero interempto Sigibertho Rege, Chilpericus regnum, exemptus ab imminenti morte, cepisset, Ruccolenus cum Cenomanicis graviter civitatem Turonensem opprimebat, ita ut cuncta devastans, nullam spem alimoniae in do-
2 mibus ecclesiae vel pauperum hospitiolis relinqueret. Postera autem die legatos ad civitatem mittit, ut homines qui propter culpam minime nobis incognitam ad sancti basilicam residebant extraherentur a clericis; quod si differretur fieri, universa promittit incendio concremare. Et nos haec audientes, maesti valde basilicam sanctam adimus, et beati auxilium flagitamus. Statimque paralytica, quae per duodecim annos fuerat contracta, dirigitur.

3 Ipse vero Ruccolenus ulteriorem ripam aggressus, morbo confestim regio sauciatur, atque ab infirmitatibus Herodianis, quas enarrare longum videtur, allisus, et sicut cera a facie ignis guttatim defluens, quinquagesima die ab hydrope inflatus interiit.

4 Sed nec hoc silebo, quod illo tempore alveus fluvii nutu Dei vel virtute beati viri, absque pluviarum inundationibus repletus, hostem, ne civitatem laederet, transire prohibuit.

27

About a paralyzed woman

When King Sigebert had been killed, and Chilperic, after being rescued from imminent death, began to reign, Ruccolenus, with his men from Le Mans, savagely devastated the city-state of Tours, destroying everything so completely that he left neither the church's estates nor the huts
of the poor any hope of sustenance. The day after, he sent 2
envoys to the city to demand that the men who were staying in the holy man's basilica seeking sanctuary on account of a charge well known to us should be taken out of there by the clerics; and he promised that if they delayed in doing this he would burn the whole place down. Hearing this, and being most dejected, we go to the basilica and beseech the blessed man for help. At once, a paralyzed woman, who had been crippled for twelve years, was straightened.

Ruccolenus himself, however, having reached the other 3
side of the river, was immediately attacked by the royal malady and by the ailments of Herod: to describe them seems tedious; wasting away as a candle does in drops while it is burning, he died swollen by dropsy fifty days later.

But I will not be silent about how at that same time the 4
river bed, at the command of God or by the power of the blessed man, was filled without inundation by rain, prohibiting the enemy from crossing, lest they should harm the city.

28

De muliere caeca

In die autem illa recurrentis solemnitatis, qua Dominus pro salute mundi mox passurus, confuso proditore discipulo, epulum apostolis ministravit, cum omnes ad ecclesiam properarent desiderabilia Domino vota dissolvere, quaedam mulier diuturna caecitate gravata, cum esset in villa, flere coepit et dicere: "Vae mihi, quia caecata pro peccatis non mereor hanc festivitatem cum reliquo populo spectare!"
2 Tunc cum fletu magno solo prostrata, nomen beati invocat confessoris; completa autem oratione, luci pristinae restituitur. Porro, recepto lumine, ob reddendas Deo gratias ad beatam basilicam cum admirabili oculorum claritate pervenit. Sed et unus ex energumenis die illa sancti virtute curatus est.

28

About a blind woman

During the annual solemnity of that day on which the Lord, when about to suffer for the salvation of the world confounded his treacherous disciple and served a meal to his apostles, and everyone was hurrying to the church to fulfill vows pleasing to the Lord, a woman who had long been afflicted with blindness remained in her estate and began to weep, saying: "Woe is me, for I have been blinded for my sins and therefore don't deserve to see this festival with
the rest of the people!" Thereupon she prostrated herself on 2
the ground with much weeping and invoked the name of the blessed confessor; and when she had finished her prayer she was given back her former eyesight unimpaired. After this had happened, she went to the blessed basilica to give thanks to God with wonderfully clear eyes. One of the possessed, however, was also cured on that day by the power of the holy man.

29

De duobus caecis

Duo caeci ex Biturigo venientes, arefactis palpebris et glutino coniunctis, ad pedes beati Domini orantes decubabant. Factum est autem in die festivitatis suae, astante populo, dum virtutes de vita illius legerentur, factus est super illos splendor corusco similis, et confractis ligaturis quae palpebras obseraverant, defluente ex oculis sanguine, lateque visu patente, cuncta cernere meruerunt.

30

De muliere muta

Mulier quaedam, cuius os patulum umor nimius cum febre ligaverat, ut nec linguam regere posset, sed tantum mugitum ut animal, non vocem ut homo poterat emittere, fide instigante, cum magna animi confidentia, atria beati

29

About two blind men

Two blind men who had come from Bourges, their eyelids withered and stuck shut, lay praying at the feet of the blessed man of the Lord. It happened upon the day of his feast, while the people stood around them, and the deeds of power from the story of his life were being read aloud, that a blaze as though of lightning appeared above them: the bonds blocking their eyelids were broken, blood flowed from their eyes, and their sight ranged far and wide; deservedly, they saw everything.

30

About a mute woman

A woman's mouth had been stuck in an open position by a great swelling combined with fever, so that she could not move her tongue and could emit only animal-like bellows and not a human voice; she was inspired by faith to come to the forecourt of the basilica of the blessed confessor with great spiritual confidence. And having stayed

confessoris aggreditur. Ibique multis diebus residens, et stipem simul atque oris apertionem postulans, tandem a sancti
2 virtute respicitur. Nam quadam die dominica, dum missarum solemnia celebrarentur, haec in sancta basilica cum reliquo populo stabat. Factum est autem cum dominica oratio diceretur, haec aperto ore coepit sanctam orationem cum reliquis decantare. Ipsa autem cum iugo servitutis haberetur vincta, de rebus beati confessoris redempta est, et nunc cum vocis officio ingenua perseverat.

31

De alia muliere debili

Nec minori miraculo se beatus vir adesse invocatum ostendit. Apra, quaedam religiosa, vi febrium oppressa, omnem usum membrorum, sola tantum lingua famulante, perdiderat. Nam cum manibus simul ac pedibus contractis iaceret, et die noctuque beati flagitaret auxilium, visum est ei quadam nocte venisse ad se senem, qui molli tactu membra
2 eius cuncta attrectaret. Expergefacta mane, sentit pedes cum una manu redditos sanitati et, stupens, ignorabat qui casus haec fecerit. Alia vero die admonita per soporem, ad

there many days, begging for food as well as praying for her mouth to be opened, she was at last attended to by the
power of the holy man. For one Sunday, while the solemni- 2
ties of mass were being celebrated, this woman was standing in the holy basilica with the rest of the people. While the Lord's prayer was being recited, her mouth opened and she began to chant the holy prayer along with the others. Because she was bound by the yoke of servitude, she was redeemed by the holy man's resources, and now, able to speak, remains a free woman.

31

About another debilitated woman

The blessed man showed himself to be present when called upon through an equally remarkable miracle. Apra, a nun, was attacked by a violent fever and lost the use of all her limbs; only her tongue still obeyed her will. In effect, while she lay in the basilica with her crippled hands and feet, imploring the aid of the blessed man day and night, it seemed to her one night that an old man came to her who
stroked all her limbs with a gentle touch. When she woke up 2
the morning, she felt that her feet and one of her hands had been healed and, astounded, did not know who had done this. On another day, she was admonished in her sleep, and

beatam basilicam nihil retardans proficiscitur. Nox autem illa erat vigilia de transitu confessoris. Mediae autem noctis tempore iam transacto vigilans, nescio quod terrore concu-
3 titur, et subito manus eius contracta dirigitur. Stupente autem populo, cuncta quae prius pertulerat enarrabat, cognoscens ipsius eandem fuisse virtutem prius in illa erectione pedum, quae nunc in manus suae directione clarebat.

32

De oleo ad sepulcrum sancti crescente

Cum talia miracula, quae scripsimus, quotidie cernamus, quid illi miseri sunt dicturi, qui Severum in Vita sancti antistitis mentitum esse pronuntiant? Nam audivi quendam, nequam, ut credo, repletum spiritu, proloquentem non potuisse fieri ut oleum sub Martini benedictione crevisset, sed nec hoc, quod elapsa ampulla super stratum marmoris corruens, perstitisset illaesa.

2 Quod ergo nuper actum est, multos in testimonium exhibens, declarabo. Quidam de diaconibus nostris male a quartani typi febre cruciabatur, quem cum plerumque arguerem, cur segnis ad basilicam sancti non profisceretur,

immediately went to the blessed basilica. That night was the one of the vigil preceding the death of the confessor. After midnight had passed while she kept the vigil, she was convulsed by an unknown terror and, suddenly, her contracted hand was straightened. She told the astounded people ev- 3
erything that had previously happened, and recognized that the same power which had restored her feet, now shone forth in the straightening of her hand.

32

About the oil that increased at the holy man's tomb

When we see such miracles as we have described every day, what will those miserable people say who assert that Severus lied in his *Life* of the holy bishop? For I heard someone who, I believe, was filled with an evil spirit, proclaiming that the oil could not have been increased under Martin's blessing, nor that the flask that fell on the marble floor could have remained unbroken.

I shall make known something that has recently hap- 2
pened, giving to many a proof of these things. One of our deacons was cruelly tormented by a quartan fever, and I had often reprimanded him, asking him why he was so slow in going to the basilica of the holy man, and why he did not

nec ex corde oraret ut ei virtus pontificis subveniret, tandem a nobis compunctus, ad beatum tumulum provolvitur
3 tremens. Dehinc cum paulisper ignis febrium quievisset, rogat sibi exhiberi ampullam cum rosaceo oleo semiplenam; iam enim ad ipsam febrem, exinde licet parum profecisset, multum tamen expenderat, et erat valde media. Perunguens ab hoc liquore frontem et tempora, postulat ut vasculum secus beati tumulum poneretur.

4 Quarta vero die, cum eum febris urgueret, ad basilicam petiit, provolutusque diutissime oravit. Apprehensam autem ampullam, quam reliquerat mediam, invenit plenam, admiransque virtutem beati antistitis, eam domum cum timore et veneratione reportat. Ex qua rursum cum esset perunctus, protinus omnis ardor quievit incommodi, nec ab eodem ultra confractus est.

5 Quid etiam de eadem ampulla post haec actum sit, non sine gravi suspirio atque miraculo memoramus. Nam cum in antedicti diaconis hospitiolo de pariete penderet, incursantibus insidiis Inimici, percussa est, atque in frusta decidit comminuta, effusumque oleum velociter terra absorbuit.
6 Tamen puer qui aderat, cum vidisset factum, accepto vasculo, ipsam terram exprimens parumper olei elicuit, rosamque quae effusa fuerat cum effracto vitro colligens, nobis exhibuit. Quod ego accipiens, diligenter in vasculum alterum transmutavi. Erat enim mensura olei quasi dimidii calicis parvuli, et tamen in vasculo duorum digitorum tantum altitudinem fecit.

pray from the heart that the bishop's power come to his aid; at last he was pierced to the heart by us, and prostrated himself, trembling, at the blessed tomb. Thereupon the heat of 3
his fever abated a bit, and he asked to be given a flask half full of rose oil; he had already used much of it to alleviate this fever, although it had barely helped him, and was no more than half full. When he had anointed his forehead and temples with this liquid, he asked for the flask to be placed beside the tomb of the blessed man.

On the fourth day when the fever again oppressed him, 4
he went to the basilica, prostrated himself and prayed for a very long time. When he then picked up the flask which he had left half empty, he found it full and, marveling at the power of the blessed bishop, carried it to his house with awe and veneration. When he had been anointed from it again, all of the fever's heat abated at once, and he has not been afflicted by it subsequently.

What happened to that flask after this we mention with a 5
deep sigh and wonder. For as it hung from the wall in the aforesaid deacon's cottage, it was struck by treacherous incursions of the Enemy and fell, shattering into many pieces;
and the earth quickly absorbed the spilled oil. When a ser- 6
vant who was present saw what had happened, he took a container, collected in it a little oil squeezed from the earth as well as the spilled rose oil with the pieces of broken glass, and showed it to us. I received it and transferred its contents carefully into another container. The measure of the oil was about half of a small cup, and in the container it stood only two fingers high.

7 In crastino autem prospiciens, erat altitudo olei quasi quattuor digitorum. Obstupefactus ego ob virtutem sancti liquoris, hoc signaculo meo munitum atque coopertum reliqui. Post dies autem septem iterum prospiciens, plus ibi quam unum sextarium reperi. Advocans autem diaconem et hoc ei ostendens, affirmabat cum iuramento, tantum tunc in effracta periisse ampulla, quantum nunc in ista cerneretur.
8 Quae usque hodie in Dei nomine beneficium petentibus praestat. Ipse quoque postea ab hoc unguento similem infirmum perungens, oleo crescente, sanavit, et multos deinceps per illud sanitati restituit.

33

De Allomere contracto

Proferat et Andegava regio miraculum suum, de qua Allomeris quidam, procedens cum contractis pedibus ac manibus, lingua etiam debilis, beati confessoris templum expe-
2 tiit. Ubi cum tota quadragesima resedisset, assidue orans ac deprecans ut eum virtus sancti antistitis visitaret, advenit dies illa dominica ante sanctum pascha, in qua Dominus noster Iesus stratas ab arborum spoliis vias incedens, Hierosolymis venit, turba prosequente ac clamante: "Hosanna, benedictus qui venit in nomine Domini!" [John 12:13].

When I checked the following day, however, the oil stood 7
four fingers high. Stunned by the power of the holy liquid, I secured the container with my seal and left it covered. Looking again after seven days, I found more than one pint in it. When I had called the deacon and shown it to him, he affirmed with an oath that what was now seen in this container was as much as had been lost when the flask broke.
Up to today it brings healing in God's name to those who 8
seek it. When the deacon, after this, anointed someone with an ailment similar to his with this oil, it healed him and went on increasing, and thereafter he restored many to their health by means of it.

33

About Allomer, a crippled man

Let the region of Angers too make known its miracle, for from there a one Allomer, traveling with crippled feet and hands and also suffering from a debilitated tongue, came
to the temple of the blessed confessor. He stayed there for 2
the whole of Lent, assiduously praying and begging that the power of the holy bishop might come to help him; then the Sunday preceding that of holy Easter came, on which our Lord Jesus came to Jerusalem riding through streets covered with tree branches, followed by a crowd shouting "Hosanna, blessed is he who comes in the name of the Lord!"

3 Illa ergo die cum iam sero factum esset, et ipse solus a foris ante tumulum decubaret, subito factus est in extasi, et pavore perterritus iacebat ut mortuus. Qui cum, ut ipse refert, per duarum horarum spatium aut amplius fuisset oppressus, tamquam de somno evigilans, subito ad sensum suum revertitur, elevatusque sursum, sanum se esse miratur.
4 Ibique tota nocte vigilans, mane nobis quae acta sunt ore proprio reseravit; clericusque factus, incolumis ad hospitiolum suum rediit.

34

De clerico caeco

Denique eodem anno, cum festivitas, quae in aestivo celebratur, desiderabilis populis advenisset, clericus quidam, cuius oculum nubes taetra contexerat ac ne lumen videre posset arcebat, aedem beati confessoris adivit. Vigilata cum reliquis nocte, illucescente caelo, dum de basilica procedit, visum quem olim perdiderat recipere meruit.

2 In eadem vero festivitate tres energumini multum se collidentes ac beatum antistitem declamantes, fatentes crimina

On that day, when it had already become late, and he lay 3
alone outside, facing the tomb, he suddenly went into a state of ecstasy and, overcome by terrible fear, lay as though dead. As he himself tells it, when he had been struck down for two hours or more, he woke up as though from sleep and suddenly returned to his senses; lifting himself up, he marveled
to find himself healthy. When he had kept the vigil there the 4
whole night, he revealed to us the next morning with his own mouth what had happened; and after he had been ordained a cleric, he returned healthy to his cottage.

34

About the blind cleric

Indeed, in that same year, when the feast came which is celebrated in the summer and longed for by the people, a cleric, whose eye was covered by a dark cloud that blocked the light so that he could not see, came to the temple of the blessed confessor. He kept the vigil with the others during the night; when the sky began to lighten and he went forth from the basilica, he deservedly recovered the sight he had once lost.

During the same feast, three possessed persons who had 2
been beating themselves violently and crying out to the holy

et ut sibi sanctus parceret deprecantes, tandem purulentum nescio quid ex ore proiciunt, et sic virtute sancti mundati sunt.

35

De carcerariis dimissis

In proximo autem, id est post tertium de festivitate diem, erant quattuor vincti in carcere. Cumque eos saevitia iudicis ita constringeret, ut nec victus necessaria ulli praebere lice-
2 ret, antistitis beati praesidia corde puro precantur. Dum haec igitur devote agerent, medio die subito scinditur trabes qua pedes eorum conclusi coartabantur, confractisque catenis, liberatos se sentiunt. Nec mora ostium petunt, quo aperto, ecclesiam sanctam, nemine prohibente, ingressi sunt.

3 Custodes autem in tantum obstupefacti fuerunt, ut nec verbis eos quidem increpare praesumerent; qui etiam sequentes eos, cum eisdem in ecclesia se abdiderunt. Illi autem maximas gratias Deo referunt, quod eos obtentu pontificis dignatus fuerit liberare.

man, confessing their crimes, and imploring him to spare them, finally spat out some pus-like substance from their mouths, and were thus cleansed by the holy man's power.

35

About the prisoners who were released

Soon thereafter, however—that is, after the third day of this feast—, there were four men chained in the prison. And since the ferocious judge so confined them that no one was allowed to bring them the food they needed, they prayed
with a pure heart for the aid of the blessed bishop. While 2
they were devoutly doing this in the middle of the day, the stocks enclosing their feet suddenly split apart, their chains broke, and they realized that they had been freed. At once, they went to the door, found it open, and went into the holy church without anyone stopping them.

The prison guards were so stunned that they did not dare 3
even to rebuke them with words; instead they followed the prisoners and hid themselves with them in the church. The prisoners gave the greatest thanks to God for deigning to free them at the bishop's request.

36

De pignoribus quae Leodovaldus Episcopus detulit

Multi etiam fide pleni reliquias beati viri portantes, virtutes multas experiuntur. Nam Leovaldus, Abrincatinae episcopus, sancti domni reliquias per presbyterum suum devotus expetiit. Quibus acceptis, cum terminum antedictae civitatis ingressus fuisset, occurrit ei adhuc, inter deserta posito, paralyticus deferentium illatus manibus; osculatus autem fideliter velum quo capsa sanctorum pignorum cooperta erat, mox in pedes constitit, ac propriis gressibus domum regressus est.

2 Haec enim agis, beatissime confessor, nec tibi sat est propriam aedem exornare prodigiis, nisi etiam diversos saltus, quos pedibus non adiisti, virtutibus tremendis illustres. Sed et deinceps caecus quidam, adminiculo deducente, in occursum earum velociter properat. Adveniens autem quando beati pignora in sanctum locabantur altare, expedita solemnitate, visum recipere meruit oculorum. Sed et alia nihilominus mulier, quae diu muta fuerat, sermonis usum recepit.

36

About the relics which Bishop Leodovald took with him

Many who, full of faith, carry relics of the blessed man on them, experience multiple deeds of power. Thus Leodovald, bishop of Avranches, devoutly sought relics of the holy lord Martin through his priest. When the priest had received them and had entered the territory of the aforesaid city-state but was still in the wilderness, a paralyzed man carried on others' hands approached him; when this man had reverently kissed the cloth covering the box containing the holy relics, he at once rose to his feet, and returned home walking.

You do these things, most blessed confessor, and it is not 2
enough for you to adorn your own temple with wonders, you also illuminate various regions which you have never visited on foot with awe-inspiring deeds of power. For thereupon a blind man, who was finding his way with a cane, also quickly came to meet these relics. He approached the relics of the holy man while they were being placed in the holy altar, and when the installation ceremony had been completed, deservedly recovered his eyesight. Another person too, a woman who had been mute for a long time, recovered her ability to speak.

37

De energumeno sanato

His etenim diebus ad beati viri basilicam quidam ex energumenis, cum multis se cruciatibus daemonum perferre declamaret, et vi se eici de acquisito vasculo per beatum antistitem fateretur, devolutus terrae sanguinem foetidum per os coepit eicere. Qui duarum fere horarum spatio iacens, expulso daemone, purgatus erectus est.

38

De puella muta

Puella quaedam parvula, indigena Turonicae civitatis, ab utero matris suae muta processit. Cuius os in tantum obseratum fuit, ut nec illas quae cunabulorum tempus exigit voces posset emittere. Mater vero de tam tristi fetu anxia, cum lugeret assidue, commonetur per visum ut beati praesulis sepulcrum adiret.

37

About a possessed person who was healed

In those same days, one of the possessed in the basilica of the blessed man cried out that he was suffering many demonic torments, and said that he was being violently expelled by the bishop from the body he had captured; then he fell to the ground and began to spew putrid blood from his mouth. After he had lain there for almost two hours, the demon was expelled, and he rose up cleansed.

38

About a mute girl

A poor little girl who was a native of the city-state of Tours was born from her mother's womb mute. Her throat was so blocked that she could not even emit the cries of infancy. Her mother, so troubled about her unfortunate offspring that she wept continuously, was admonished in a vision to come to the tomb of the blessed prelate.

2 Quae, exhibita secum puella, pergit intrepida, exposita-
que ante sepulcrum sancti; cum diutissime orasset, iterum
eam secum assumit. Accenso vero thymiamate, cum eam desuper retineret, interrogat eam si bonum ei odorem faceret.
Illa respondit: "Bonum." Hanc primam vocem filiae mater
3 maesta cognovit. Imposita vero ori eius aqua, quam quondam de fontibus acceperat benedictis, interrogat iterum
qualem ei saporem praeberet. Illa respondit: "Bonum." Tunc
mater cum gaudio sospitem domum filiam refert, quam tristis ad beati tumulum fide fida detulerat.

39

De eo quod Aredius presbyter pro benedictione portavit

Aredius, vir religiosus ex Lemovicino, causa tantum devotionis Turonos advenit, et beatum sepulcrum orando deosculans, ad monasterium sanctum, amne transito, pervenit. Qui dum singula loca visitat, quae vir beatus aut orando depresserat, aut psallendo sanctificaverat, ubi vel fesso

Taking her daughter with her, she went there without 2
fear, and placed her in front of the tomb; when she had prayed for a very long time, she took the girl with her again. When she held the girl above some burning incense, she asked her if it smelled good to her. The girl answered: "Good." That was the first word which the sorrowful mother
heard her daughter utter. Then she put some water, which 3
she had once been given from the blessed springs, in her daughter's mouth, and asked her again how it tasted. She replied: "Good." Thereupon the mother joyfully took home her now healthy daughter whom she had brought, sorrowfully but trusting in her faith, to the tomb of the blessed man.

39

About what the priest Aredius carried with him as a blessing

Aredius, a monk from Limoges, came to Tours because of his great devotion; after he had kissed the blessed tomb during his prayers, he crossed the river and came to the holy monastery. There he visited every single place the blessed man had either touched while praying or sanctified by

corpori somnum, vel inedia deficienti cibum praebuerat.
2 Dumque cuncta circuit, cuncta peragrat, venit ad puteum, quem sanctus Dei proprio labore patefecit, fusaque oratione aquam haurit, impositaque in ampullula, domum regrediens deportavit.

3 Cumque exinde infirmis multis tribueret sanitates, quadam vice Renosindus, frater eius, vi febrium impulsus, decubuit lectulo. Octava vero die cum iam oculis clausis in hoc iaceret, ut spiritum exhalaret, atque omnis familia perstreperet, mortem condolens patroni, vel funeris necessaria praepararet, venit in mentem presbytero ut de aqua beati
4 putei in ore defuncturo guttam inferret. Qua illata, ubi primum os eius attigit, mox oculos aegrotus aperuit, absolutaque etiam lingua, rogat sibi adhuc exinde ministrari. Acceptoque calice, ut bibit statim omnis febris effugit, et sic, admirante familia, sanus a lectulo in quo iacebat erectus est.

singing psalms, or which had supported him either during sleep when he was tired, or provided him with food when he was weak from fasting. While he was walking all around and 2
examining everything, he came to the well which the holy man of God had opened up by his own labor, and after he had prayed there, he drew some water, put it in a small flask, and took this with him when he returned home.

Once thereafter, when it had given health to many ill per- 3
sons, his brother Renosindus lay in bed, shaken by a violent fever. On the eighth day, when he was lying there with his eyes already closed, about to breathe his last, and the whole household wailed, lamenting the imminent death of its patron and preparing for his funeral, it crossed the priest's mind to pour a drop of the water from the blessed well into the dying man's mouth. When it had been brought, as soon 4
as it touched his mouth, the sick man opened his eyes, his tongue was untied, and he asked to be given more of it. After he had received the cup, while he drank, all of his fever immediately fled, and thus, while his household marveled, he was raised up healthy from the bed in which he had been lying.

40

De Sisulfo manco

Quid autem de istis miraculis mea parvitas poterit enarrare, cum assumptus sanctus Dei de mundo adhuc praedicator habeatur in mundo et, cum se palam populis ostentare nequeat, iugiter se patefactis virtutibus manifestat, dum caecos illuminat, dum paralyticos sanat, dumque et reliquos
2 aegrotos pristinae sospitati reformat? Sed ego, ut saepe testatus sum, indignum me censeo tanti viri signa depromere. Tamen quia audax audeo, veniam peto legenti. Quia enim me impellit amor patroni, et quia esse adhuc eum denuntiavi praedicatorem, dicam quid contigerit nuper.

3 Sisulfus, ex Cenomanicis pauperculus, dum in hortulo suo meridie obdormisset, nescio quid nequitiae perpessus est. E somno autem exsiliens, contractis in volam digitis, cum magno dolore manus debiles elevavit, ipso quoque dolore premente. Rursum solvitur in soporem, et vidit per visum: et ecce vir stabat ante eum nigris vestibus, cano autem
4 capite. Qui conversus: "Quid sic," inquit, "tu fletibus commoveris?" Et ille: "Ecce, venerabilis domine, dum parumper obdormivi, cum dolore expergefactus opus manuum mearum perdidi, et nescio quid sceleris commisissem."

40

About Sisulf, a lame man

What can my Insignificance contribute by telling about these miracles when the holy man of God, although taken away from the world, is still acting as a preacher in the world as he, unable to show himself openly to the people, manifests himself continuously in visible deeds of power, giving light to the blind, healing the paralyzed, and restoring other
ill persons to their former health? As I have often testified, I 2
regard myself unworthy to make known the signs of so great a man. But since I am so bold as to dare to do it, I beg forgiveness from the reader. For it is the love for my patron that impels me, and because I have just pronounced him still to be a preacher, I shall say what happened recently.

Sisulf, a poor man from the territory of Le Mans, was 3
sleeping in his garden in the middle of the day when he suffered some sort of evil. For when he woke up from his sleep he found his fingers bent into his palm and could only raise his debilitated hands with great pain. Under the stress of the pain, he subsequently fell asleep again, and saw a vision: behold, a man in black clothes, but with white hair, stood before him. Turning to him, the man said: "Why are you so up- 4
set and why are you weeping?" And Sisulf replied: "Behold, venerable lord, when I had been sleeping for a while, I woke up in pain and found that I had lost the ability to use my hands, and I don't know what crime I have committed."

5 Tunc vir ille, tamquam discipulis Dominus de caeco nato,
quia neque ille peccaverat, neque parentes eius, sed ut mani-
festaretur opus Dei in illo, ait: "Debilitas tua tormentum indicat populi delinquentis. Vade ergo nunc per vicos et cas-
tella, et ad civitatem usque pertende, et praedica, ut se
omnis homo a rapinis, periuriis, et usuris abstineat, et in die
dominico nullum opus, absque solemnitatibus mysticis,
6 agat. Ecce enim coram Domino in lacrimis decumbemus
veniam pro populo deprecantes, et adhuc spes est obti-
nendi, si emendatio subsequatur in plebe. Nam hostilitates,
et infirmitates, et alia multa mala, quae perfert populus, in-
7 dignatio Domini commovet. Et ideo annuntia velociter, ut
emendent, ne crudeliter in scelere suo depereant. Tu vero,
his peractis quae imperavi, Turonos ad basilicam meam propera; ibique te visitans, obtinebo apud Dominum ut sane-
ris." Cui ille: "Dic mihi, quaeso, domine, quis es, vel quod est
nomen tuum?" Cui vir: "Ego sum," inquit, "Martinus Turonorum sacerdos."

8 In his sancti verbis pauper surrexit a somno, apprehen-
soque bacello, iter imperatum aggreditur, et quae sibi fuerant imperata populis nuntiavit. Mense autem septimo
postquam haec acta sunt, beatam basilicam adiit, ibique
prostratus per triduum, quarta die a sancti virtute visitatus
9 est. Iam enim computruerat caro palmarum eius, quae
clausa detinebatur, et cum digiti eius directi fuissent, sanguis ab eisdem erupit. Sed his omnibus medicatis, ore proprio quae retulimus enarravit.

Then, as the Lord said to his disciples about the man 5
born blind: that neither he nor his parents had sinned but
that the work of God was to be made manifest in him, the
man said: "Your ailment betrays the torment of a sinful people. Go now to the villages and fortified places, travel as far
as the city of Tours, and preach that all abstain from rob-
bery, perjury, and usury, and that on the day of the Lord no
work be done other than the celebration of the mystic solemnities. For behold, we prostrate ourselves with tears be- 6
fore the Lord, begging forgiveness for the people, and up to
now there is hope of obtaining it, if the people mend their
ways. For the wars, the illnesses, and the many other evils
which the people suffer are brought about by the Lord's
indignation. Therefore proclaim quickly that they should 7
mend their ways, lest they perish cruelly in their crime. As
for you, when you have done what I have commanded, hasten to my basilica in Tours; there I shall appear to you and
obtain from the Lord that you be healed." Sisulf said to him:
"Tell me lord, I beg you, who are you and what is your name?"
The man said to him: "I am Martin, bishop of the people of
Tours."

At these words of the holy man, the poor man awoke 8
from his sleep, and taking up his staff, began the journey
that had been commanded, and announced to the people
what he had been ordered to say. In the seventh month after
these things happened, he came to the blessed basilica, and
having prostrated himself there for three days, was visited
by the power of the holy man on the fourth. Already, the 9
skin of the palms of his hands, clamped shut, had been putrefying, and when his fingers were straightened, blood
flowed from them. But when all these afflictions had been
healed, he told us with his own mouth what we have related.

41

De caeco illuminato

Facis ergo, beatissime confessor, tuo more, propitiaris iniquitatibus populi, et sanas languores omnium, cunctosque te fideliter invocantes tuis medicamentis illustras; nec fraudas extraneos quod propriis libenter indulges.

2 Homo ergo incola territorii Turonici, annorum quasi quinque, cum a febre lippitudinis gravaretur, decidentibus cataractis, obstrictisque palpebris valde caecatus est. Super quod malum adiciebatur et illud, quod a fuste percussus, disrupto visu, unus ei crepuit oculus. Iam enim per viginti quinque annos in hac caecitate degebat.

3 Admonitus ergo per visum, ad beati tumulum venit, ubi orationi incumbens, die tertia unius oculi lumen recepit. Dehinc animatus hoc medicamine, attentius coepit orare. Quarta autem die oculus qui crepuerat, reformato visu, aperitur. Qui licet non tam clarus cernatur ut alter, luminis tamen beneficium praebet.

41

About a blind man who was given light

You act according to your custom therefore, most blessed confessor, when you forgive the people's iniquities and heal everyone's illnesses, empowering with your remedies all who call upon you with faith; nor do you withhold from strangers what you gladly grant to your own people.

Thus a man who lived in the territory of Tours was af- 2
flicted, at about five years of age, with an inflammation of the eyes; cataracts formed and his eyelids stuck shut, so that he became wholly blind. In addition to that evil, his sight had been compromised when he had been struck with a stick that burst one of his eyes. He had already been living in this blindness for twenty-five years.

Advised by a vision, he came to the blessed man's tomb, 3
where he prostrated himself in prayer and on the third day received the light of one eye. Encouraged by this remedy, he thereupon began to pray more fervently. And on the fourth day, indeed, the eye that had been burst opened, its ability to see reconstituted. Although it did not see as clearly as the other one, it nevertheless gave him the benefit of light.

42

De manu hominis contracta

Debilis quidam, cuius manu contracta diriguerat, dum in atrium, quod ante beati sepulcrum habetur, oraret attente, in sancta eius vigilia visitatus est, directisque digitis manus eius ad usum pristinum restituta convaluit.

43

De puerulo suscitato

O quotiens hic prophetarum et sublimium virtutes virorum, quas olim gestas legimus, renovari miramur! Sed quid inquam? Quod hi multi fecerunt viventes in saeculo, hic solus renovat quotidie, etiam post sepulcrum. Quid ergo agimus? Quid silemus? Quid occultamus pauci, quod populi declamant multi? Non diutius in hac statione moremur.

42

About a man whose hand was crippled

A sick man, whose withered hand had become paralyzed, while he was fervently praying in the forecourt in front of the blessed man's tomb, was visited by the holy man during his holy vigil, his fingers were straightened, and his healed hand was restored to its original function.

43

About a boy who was brought back to life

How often do we look with amazement at the renewal, here, of the powerful deeds we read were performed in earlier times by prophets and great men! But what am I saying? What these many men did in this world, this man Martin, by himself, renews every day even from beyond the tomb! What, therefore, are we doing? Why are we silent? Why should a few of us hide what many peoples proclaim? Let us not delay any longer in this digression.

2 Proferamus novum Elisaeum saeculo nostro, qui cadaver defuncti vivum remisit a monumento, idque beatus confessor nobis praesentibus operatus est. Quae enim causa fuerit, adiutorium individuae Trinitatis efflagitans, explicabo.

3 Puer genitus, lacte materno deficiente, nutrici ad alendum datur. Quae hoc liquore sterilis dum non copiose, ut illi aetatulae opportunum est, lactis alimentum ministrat, coepit qui proficere debuerat, die praetereunte, decrescere, et ita minui ut nihil in eo amplius quam pellis tenuis, quae eius ossula contegeret, remaneret.

4 Qui, matre mortua, unum prope in hoc exitu duxerat annum. Erat enim unicum patri de uxoria dilectione quoddam
memoriale. Cui, ut diximus, victu minuente, deficienti ex
inedia, febris accessit. Ut autem eum hic fervor attigit,
concurrit pater ad ecclesiam, ne proles absque baptismi
5 regeneratione moreretur. Qui baptizatus, nec confortatus
corpore praeter illud spiritale remedium, iam suffossis oculis, iam palpebris laxatis atque demissis, iam nullum flatum
spiraminis habens, super beatum sepulcrum, patre eiulante,
deponitur.

6 Nec defuit virtus illa caelestis, quae quondam parvulum inter manus confessoris beati vivificavit. At ubi primum eius vestimentum coopertorium tumuli attigit, illico parvulus respiravit. Mirum miraculum! Videres pallentes genas

Let us present to our age the new Elisha, the one who 2
raised the body of a dead man from his tomb alive: the blessed confessor did this in our presence. Imploring the assistance of the undivided Trinity, I shall describe how this took place.

When the boy was born, his mother had no milk and he 3
was given to a wet nurse to be fed. Because she, not being a mother, did not have much milk and did not give him as much nourishment as he needed at his tender age, the boy, who should have been growing, became thinner day by day, and shrank so much that nothing more remained of him than mere skin covering his tiny bones.

His mother died, and the boy lived for almost a year in a 4
state of imminent death. He was his father's only reminder of his wife's love. Languishing, as we said, through malnourishment for insufficient feeding, he was attacked by a fever. When its heat touched him, his father hurried to the church, lest his offspring die without being reborn in baptism. After he had been baptized and had received the spiri- 5
tual remedy, his body was not however fortified; with eyes already sunken, eyelids already slackened and closed, and no longer breathing, he was placed on the blessed tomb, while his father wailed for grief.

But the heavenly power that had once revived a little boy 6
in the arms of the blessed confessor was at hand. For at the very moment that his clothing came into contact with the cover of the tomb, the little boy began to breathe again. An astounding miracle! You could see his pale cheeks gradually

gradatim, virtute divina insistente, rubescere, et sopitos oculos in lumine redivivo laxari. Tunc a sancto vivificatus et a patre receptus, sospes usque hodie in testimonium virtutis habetur.

44

De alio caeco illuminato

Sed et de Pictavo quidam caecus, per sex annos lumine viduatus, triduana prostratione ad beatum tumulum orans, lumen quo diu caruerat, operante solita virtute, recepit. Actum est autem hoc per festivitatem sancti patroni in qua Maroveus Pictavis antistes aderat, non immerito Hilarii beatissimi discipulus praeconandus. Qui, solemnitate explicita, cum illuminato concive gaudens remeavit ad propriam urbem.

becoming rosy as divine power came to them, and his drooping eyelids opening with their sight restored. Having been brought back to life by the holy man and received by his father, he remains healthy till today as a witness to the deed of power.

44

About another blind man who was given light

But a blind man from Poitiers too, having been deprived of his eyesight for six years, after he had prostrated himself in prayer at the blessed tomb for three days, received the light which he had lacked for so long through the workings of the usual power. This happened during the holy patron's feast in the presence of Maroveus, the bishop of Poitiers, who is not undeservedly praised as a disciple of the most blessed Hilary. When the solemnities were over, he returned joyfully to his own city with his fellow citizen who had been granted the light of his eyes.

45

De duobus puerulis sanatis

Apud Vultaconnum, quoque vicum Pictavensem, dum duo pueruli nocte dominica in uno stratu quiescerent, visum est eis quasi signum quod matutinis commoveri solet sonantem audissent, et surgentes de cubili suo, direxerunt ad ecclesiam. Cumque in atrium ecclesiae pervenissent, inve-
2 nerunt ibidem choros mulierum canentium. Exterritique valde, cognoscentes catervam esse daemoniorum, dum ad terram corruunt, nec se, ut est aestatis infirmitas, signo salutari praemuniunt, unus lumine, alius et lumine et gressu multatur.

3 Cumque per multorum annorum curricula in his infirmitatibus gravarentur, unus, qui tantum lumine caruerat, ad beati Martini basilicam devote veniens, ut orationem explevit, statim visum recepit. Alius, in eodem sancto loco lumine recepto, ad propria rediens, adhuc debilis claudicabat.

4 Veniensque ad cellulam Condatensem, in qua lectum beati viri habetur, dum ibidem nocte dominica vigiliae celebrarentur, subito, orante populo, sensit divinam virtutem adesse. Et, spectante plebe, se per terram trahens, contra parietem se erexit in quo fenestra retinetur, quae fuit

45

About two boys who were healed

At Voultegon, also a village in the territory of Poitiers, two boys were sleeping in one bed on a night before a Sunday when they seemed to hear the sound of the bell that customarily calls to matins; arising from their bed, they went to the church. When they had come into the forecourt of the
church, they found choirs of women singing there. Terrified, 2
for they recognized them as a group of demons, they fell to the ground in their youthful ignorance without protecting themselves with the sign of salvation; and so one lost the light of his eyes, while the other lost not only his sight but also his ability to walk.

When they had suffered these disabilities for many years, 3
the one who lacked only his eyesight came devoutly to the blessed Martin's basilica, and when he had finished his prayer, at once recovered it. The other, when he had recovered his eyesight in the same holy place, went home debilitated, still limping.

And on the way, when he came to the cell at Candes 4
which contains the holy man's bed, while the Sunday vigil was being celebrated there, suddenly, while the people prayed, he felt the presence of divine power. While the people watched, he dragged himself across the ground and drew himself up against the wall in which there is a window that

quondam beati corporis porta. Et orans atque prae gaudio lacrimans, integrae sanitati restituitur, nec ulterius ullam pertulit de malis infirmitatibus gravitatem.

46

De claudo directo

Puerulus quidam, Leodulfus nomine, pede sinistro debilis, dum cum reliquis petentibus stipendia quaerendo circuiret, Turonis advenit. Et parumper moratus, iter quod agere coeperat conatur explere. Progressusque claudicando cum satellitibus, decimo ab urbe milliario vi doloris opprimitur.

2 Relictusque vero a sociis, solus super ripam alvei eiulabat, multis ad festivitatem concurrentibus proclamans, et dicens: "Vae mihi quia solemnitatem gloriosi viri spectare nolui, ideo me virtus eius allidit. Qua de re rogo vos, fidelissimi Christiani, qui Deum timetis, subvenite ignorantiae meae, subvenite oppresso et debili, et si timor Dei manet, me us-
3 que ad sanctum locum deportate!" Igitur cum haec a multis

once was the door through which the confessor's holy body passed. And there, praying and weeping for joy, he was restored to his full health, thereafter never experiencing any more suffering from these evil infirmities.

46

About a crippled man who was restored

A boy named Leodulf, whose left foot was crippled, was traveling around with other beggars seeking alms when he came to the territory of Tours. After he had rested for a while, he tried to continue the journey he had begun. But, as he limped along with his companions, ten miles from the city he was struck by a severe pain.

His companions left him behind, and he sat alone, wail- 2
ing, on the bank of the river, and cried out to the many who were hastening to the feast, saying: "Woe is me! Because I did not want to attend the solemnity of the glorious man, his power has struck me. Therefore I ask you, devout Christians who fear God: come to the aid of my ignorance, help one who is burdened and feeble, and if you fear God, carry
me to the holy place!" When he had tearfully asked this of 3

praetereuntibus imploraret, quidam plaustro suo superpositum usque ad sanctam basilicam duxit. Ubi triduana oratione continuans, redintegratis pedibus, incolumis abscessit.

47

De contracto, quem bos trahebat

Erat quidam contractus qui, in similitudinem eremitae cui bos quondam solatium fuit, bovem unum habebat. Quem plaustro coniunctum, per domos trahebatur, stipem postulans devotorum.

2 Igitur cum, imminente festivitate pontificis, Turonis advenisset, prostratus coram sepulcro, et orationi incumbens, devotissime beati antistitis auxilium flagitavit, deportatusque iterum a suis ante sanctam apsidam tumuli ponitur. Cumque expletis missis, populus coepisset sacrosanctum corpus Redemptoris accipere, illico dissolutis nodis qui ge-
3 nua nexa tenebant, in pedes erigitur. Admirantibus cunctis, gratias agens, proprio gressu usque beatum altare, nemine sustentante, processit, sanus deinceps degens.

many passersby, someone put him on his cart and brought him to the holy basilica. When he had prayed there continuously for three days, his feet were made whole and he left in good health.

47

About a crippled man who was drawn round by an ox

There was once a crippled man who, like the hermit of former times whose ox was his only consolation, owned just one ox. Yoked to a cart, it drew the man to the houses where he begged alms from the devout.

Thus, when the feast of Bishop Martin approached, this 2
man came to Tours, prostrated himself before the tomb, set himself to pray, and most devoutly implored the help of the blessed bishop; he was lifted up by his companions and placed before the holy apse of the tomb. When mass had been completed and the people began to receive the sacrosanct body of the Redeemer, suddenly, the knots that held his knees bent were undone, and he stood up on his feet.
While all marveled, he gave thanks and walked on his own 3
two feet to the altar without anyone's support; thereafter, he remained in good health.

48

De eo qui manus ac pedes contractos habebat

Ex pago autem Carnonensi, qui in Andegavo territorio habetur insitus, vir quidam, nomine Floridus, manibus pedibusque contractis, ad sanctam cellulam Condatensem, de
2 qua beatus confessor ad Christum migravit, allatus est. Ubi dum in vigiliis et oratione paucis diebus vacavit, omnis aegritudo a corpore eius fugata discessit. Sicque directis membris, incolumis ad propria remeavit.

49

De eo qui contractum brachium detulit

Venerat dies festus solemnitatis beatae, in qua catervae populorum multae convenerant, et ecce debilis quidam contracto brachio adfuit. Dumque beatum sepulcrum labiis

48

About a man who had paralyzed hands and feet

From the region of Craon, situated in the territory of Angers, a man named Floridus, whose hands and feet were paralyzed, was carried to the holy cell at Candes where the
blessed confessor ascended to Christ. There, when he had 2
devoted himself to keeping vigils and praying for a few days, all infirmity was put to flight and withdrew from his body. And with his limbs thus straightened, he returned safe and sound to his home.

49

About another man who had a paralyzed arm

The feast day of the blessed man's solemnity had come, and a large crowd had gathered when, behold, there came a sick man with a paralyzed arm. While he kissed the blessed tomb with his lips and moistened it with his tears, imploring

osculatur, lacrimis rigat, voce beati confessoris auxilium implorat, fide non diffisus solitum praestolabatur auxilium.
2 Denique sacerdotibus qui advenerant ad agenda solemnia procedentibus, cum lector, cui legendi erat officium, advenisset et, arrepto libro, Vitam sancti coepisset legere confessoris, protinus hic, directo brachio, sanus erigitur et, spectantibus cunctis, praesidia quae fideliter petiit, impetravit.

50

De caeco illuminato

Sic et caecus in eadem festivitate supplex implorans receptionem visionis, ut pallulam attigit, quae a foris ad pedes sancti de pariete dependet, mox, erumpente a palpebris sanguine, teste populo, visum recepit.

the blessed confessor's help with his voice, he waited full of faith for the usual aid. When the priests who had come to 2
celebrate the solemnities proceeded to do so, and the lector, whose task it was to read, was there and had picked up the book and begun to read the holy confessor's *Life,* suddenly the man's arm was straightened; he was raised up healthy, and while everyone watched, he obtained the help which he had sought through faith.

50

About a blind man who was given light

Likewise, and during the same festivity, when a blind man humbly praying to receive his sight touched the curtain that hangs on the outside wall at the feet of the saint, blood suddenly spurted from his eyelids and, while the people watched, he received his sight.

51

De dysentericis

Cum autem morbus ille dysentericus cum occultis pustulis multas attereret civitates, ac inter reliqua loca urbs Turonica gravius laboraret, multi, abraso a beato tumulo pulvere et hausto, sanabantur. Plerique, de oleo quod inibi habetur delibuti, liberabantur; fuitque nonnullis remedium aqua illa unde sepulcrum ablutum est ante Pascha.

2 Igitur, cum multis multa tribuerentur beneficia, vidi unum in desperatione a dysenteria iacentem, quem ad basilicam ductum, aliis vigilias celebrantibus, noctem inquietam duxisse; diluculo vero accedens ad tumulum, potato cum vino pulvere, sanus rediit e sepulcro.

52

De alio ab umore gravi sanato

Alter quoque arreptus a febre valida, deiciens ore venenum, et per inferiorem partem extra modum solutus, lectulo decubabat. Igitur grassante veneno, laboranti oritur vulnus

51

About those who suffered from dysentery

When dysentery with its hidden sores was afflicting many city-states, and the city of Tours, among others, suffered greatly, many who scraped dust off the tomb and drank it were cured. Many who had been anointed with the oil which was kept there were freed; and for some, the remedy was the water with which the tomb was washed before Easter.

While many, therefore, were being granted many bene- 2
fits, I saw one man lying in desperation, having been brought to the basilica because of his dysentery, spending a troubled night there while others celebrated vigils; at daybreak, he went up to the grave, drank some dust mixed with wine, and came back from the tomb in good health.

52

About another man, who was healed of a burdensome swelling

Another man who had been seized by a violent fever, had vomited poison from his mouth and whose bowels been extremely incontinent, was lying in his bed. As the poison

in inguine, et incredibili modo movet se visibiliter usque ad plantam. Erat enim in magnitudo ovi anserini. Deinde sursum repetens, cum nimio dolore discurrit per latera, per brachia, et usque ad cervicem progreditur; deinde per aliud latus ad plantam usque deducitur; exinde retrorsum rever-
2 tens, ad eum locum unde primo ortum fuerat venit. Cumque taliter per membra vagaretur aegroti, quo miser tenderet, quid ageret, nesciebat, nisi tantum voces cum fletibus dabat. Exigebat enim dolor gemitum, cum in uno corpusculo tanti dolores irruerent.

3 Tandem cum haec nobis nuntiata fuissent, indico solitam theriacam a vero requiri Medico, quo vitam moriturus haberet, assumi de tumulo. At satellites cum magna festinatione currentes, elevato pulvere monumenti, deferunt ad aegrotum, delibutumque cum vino bibendum porrigunt. Quo hausto, ita omnis dolor fugatus est, ut ipsa hora redderetur incolumis.

spread, a swelling arose in the patient's groin and in an unbelievable manner moved visibly down to his feet. It was about the size of a goose's egg. Thereafter heading upward, it ran causing extreme pain along one side of the body, along his arms, and came up to his neck; then it headed down the other side to the other foot; and thence it turned back again
and went to the place in which it had first arisen. While it 2
was wandering in this way around the sick man's body, the unhappy man did not know where to go or what to do, except just to cry out and weep. For his distress elicited groans of sympathy, since so many pains were rushing to converge in one poor little body.

When at last these events had been reported to us, I indi- 3
cated that the usual remedy was to be requested of the true Physician, so that a man about to die might return to life, and that it was to be taken from the tomb. His companions then ran in great haste to take dust from the tomb, brought it to the sick man, and, having mixed it with wine, gave it to him to drink. When he had drunk it, the pain was so effectively put to flight that he was restored to health that very hour.

53

De exsense redintegrato

Sine numero populi talia audientes, de longinquis regionibus beati expetunt praesidia confessoris. In quo illud est prae ceteris admirandum, qualiter sensus hominum diaboli arte fraudati restituantur.

2 Quidam ergo Baiocasensis civis, dum vino nimium hausto turbatus per viam incederet, subito diversis flantibus ventis pulvis campi commovetur, et mixtus, ut solet, cum stipulis, in sublime levatur; fitque totus aer una nubes pulveris, de qua hic opertus, amisso sensu, equo deicitur. Igitur post paululum a suis inventus, domum turbulentus adducitur.
3 Hinc effrenis factus conabatur fugere, nemine persequente. Quid plura? Artatur vinculis, constipatur catenis, et in custodia detinetur. Qui dentibus fremens ob negatam sibi fugae libertatem, propriis se morsibus lacerabat.

4 Dum haec agerentur, admoniti parentes ad beati eum basilicam perduxerunt; ibique oratione per longum tempus facta sanus abscessit, vovens, ut singulis annis veniens, vota sancto redderet confessori. Deinde ad monasterium sibi proximum, humiliatis capillis ac presbyter ordinatus, coepit

53

About a frenzied man who was restored to his senses

Innumerable people, hearing about such remarkable deeds, come from faraway regions to seek the help of the blessed confessor. Among these deeds, the most marvelous one of all is how men's senses that have been deceived by the devil's trickery are restored.

A citizen of Bayeux was traveling on the road drunk from 2
an excess of wine when, suddenly dust from the fields swept up by various winds and mixed, as happens, with straw, was lifted up in the air; the whole sky became one cloud of dust; the man was enveloped by it, lost his senses, and was thrown from his horse. After a short time, he was found by his servants and brought home in a state of frenzy. For, having lost 3
control of himself, he tried to flee although no one was pursuing him. Why say more? He was restrained with bonds, fettered with chains, and kept under guard. Gnashing his teeth because he was denied the freedom to flee, he kept tearing his flesh with his own teeth.

While this was happening, his relatives were advised to 4
bring him to the blessed man's basilica; and after he had prayed there for a long time he left in good health, pledging to return every year to fulfill his vow to the holy confessor. And, after he had been tonsured and ordained a priest,

Deo strenue deservire, non tamen reddens quae promiserat
5 beato pontifici. Quarto igitur anno data, ut credo, iterum Inimico potestate, rursum ruit in redivivam amentiam, et, constrictus, ut fuerat prius, catenis, ad sanctam reducitur aedem; ubi per sex menses aut eo amplius, degens in vigiliis et orationibus, reddens quae prius ignave fraudaverat, sanus domum regreditur. Sed, peccatis facientibus, iterum vino saepius madefactus, in eadem tribulatione obiit.

54

De puella Lixoviensi caeca

Si singula quaeque, vel quae aguntur vel quae acta sunt, prosequamur, magnum cumulum congeremus de mirabili-
2 bus confessoris. Puella vero ex Lexoensi iam adulta, lumen amiserat oculorum; quae sancti limina devote adiens, per omne tempus festivitatis orabat humo prostrata. Tertia autem die post sanctam festivitatem, cum sui eam redire urgerent, rogat se ad sepulcrum beati deduci.

he began to serve God actively in a monastery close to his
home, without, however, fulfilling what he had promised
the blessed bishop. In the course of the fourth year after 5
this, as I believe, power over him was again given to the Enemy, and he again lapsed into insanity and was brought
chained, as before, to the holy basilica; there he stayed for
six months or longer, devoting himself to vigils and prayer,
giving what he had previously defaulted on through his
sloth, and returned home in good health. But his sins caused
him frequently to souse himself again with wine, and he
died in the same distress.

54

About a blind girl from Lisieux

If we go on recording every single deed of power, those
that are happening now and those that happened earlier, we
will create a huge mound of the confessor's wonders. Thus a 2
girl from Lisieux who had already reached adolescence lost
the light of her eyes; when she had come devoutly to the
threshold of the holy man, she prayed there prostrated upon
the ground throughout the feast. On the third day after the
festivities, however, when her companions urged her to return home, she asked to be led to the tomb of the blessed
man.

3 Ibique iterum atque iterum prostrata, de palla, quae sanctum tegit tumulum, oculos abstergens, et vale dicens, discessit. Cumque iam in navi ascenderet, ait: "Gratias tibi ago, beate confessor, quod etsi videre non merui, tua sancta
4 limina vel tactu praesensi." Cum igitur haec cum lacrimis edidisset, dum detergit oculos, lumen recepit; et conversa ait: "Forsitan haec est beati basilica?" Cui, qui propinqui erant, ita esse aiunt. Tunc illa: "Non revertar," inquit, "nisi gratias pro accepta sanitate referam patrono." Redeuntem autem, et in laudem antistitis declamantem multi viderunt. Quae, completa oratione, gaudens discessit.

55

De puero manum contractam habente

In eadem vero festivitate alius de Senonico puer manum aridam detulit. Post quartam autem diem solemnitatis beatae, dum stans ad pedes oraret, spectante populo, directi sunt digiti eius; viditque omnis conventus plebis magnalia Dei: qualiter inficiebatur manus a sanguine, ascendebatque gradatim per arentes venas, et ita erat manus bibula, ut putares spongiam diu aridam lymphis iniectam, sitienter

After she had prostrated herself there again and again, 3
she wiped her eyes with the cloth that covers the holy tomb, said goodbye, and left. And when she stepped into the boat, she said: "I thank you, blessed confessor, for even though I did not deserve to see, I at least felt your holy threshold by
touch." While she was saying this tearfully and wiping her 4
eyes, she received her eyesight; and turning around, she said: "Is that perhaps the basilica of the blessed man?" Those around her said that indeed it was. Then she said: "I will not go home until I shall have rendered thanks to the patron for the healing I have received." Having gone back, she was seen by many shouting the praises of the bishop. When she had completed her prayers, she left rejoicing.

55

About a boy who had a withered hand

During that same feast someone else came from Sens who had a withered hand. On the fourth day after the blessed solemnity, while he stood praying at the feet of the holy man and the people watched, his fingers were straightened; and the whole gathering of the people saw God's great deeds: how the blood came into the hand, and how it gradually spread through the withered veins; the hand was so thirsty that you would have thought it a dried-out sponge

haurire liquorem. Repletis ergo venis, roboratisque nervis, ac rubescente cute, pallidam manum extulit sanatam.

56

De muliere quae contractis in palma digitis venit

Pari quodammodo ordine Pictavensis mulier meruit obtinere medelam. Nam haec, contractis in volam digitis, unguibusque defixis in ipsis, ut ita dicam, ossibus, tota iam manu putrefacta, venit ad sancti festivitatem devota, optabilem expetens medicinam.
2 Igitur, spectatis ex more solemnibus, dicit suis: "Integro quidem corde ad deposcendum beati praesidium venimus, sed obsistentibus peccatis, non meruimus quod petebamus accipere. Consummata ergo nunc oratione, revertamur ad patriam, fidentes de bonitate praesulis, quod corpore imbecillo prosit animae fidelis oratio." Haec et his similia aiens, et quasi sancto vale dicens, discessit.

thrown into liquid, thirstily drinking the fluid. When the veins were full and the sinews strengthened, the skin became rosy, and the boy stretched out his hand, once pale, now healed.

56

About a woman who came with her fingers stuck into her palm

In a somewhat similar way a woman from Poitiers deserved to receive a remedy. For her fingers were bent and stuck into the hollow of her hand, her nails being as it were fixed to her very bones, and her hand was wholly putrefied; she came devoutly to the feast of the holy man, seeking the
cure she had been hoping for. When she had attended the 2
solemnities according to custom, she said to her companions: "We came with a pure heart to seek the aid of the blessed man, but our sins prevent us from deserving to receive what we ask for. Now that we have completed our prayers, let us go back to our home region, trusting in the prelate's goodness, that the prayer of a devout soul will benefit an afflicted body." Saying this and similar things, and intending to say farewell to the holy man, she left.

3 Vergente quoque in vesperam die, prope amnis Caris ripam accepit mansionem. Ad medium fere noctis expergefacta, gratias Deo refert, quod esset, quod viveret, quod vi-
geret, vel quod beati pontificis tumulum attigisset; quae
4 cum maximo fletu proferret, iterum obdormivit. Et ecce vir
crine cycneo, indumento purpureo, crucem gestans manu,
stans ante eam, ait: "Nunc sana eris in nomine Christi, Redemptoris nostri." Et apprehensa manu eius, misit digitum
suum inter digitos illius, qui clauserant palmam, et parum-
5 per movens, direxit eos. Dum haec in visu videret, evigilans,
defluente adhuc sanguine, sanam elevavit manum in Dei
laudibus. Diluculo autem regressa ad basilicam, et impleta
gratiarum actione, laeta redivit.

57

De ea quae dum in festivitate sancti Iohannis operabatur, debilitata est

In festivitate vero beati Ioannis cum populo ad missarum solemnia conveniret, mulier quaedam, accepto sarculo, agrum adiit, ut scilicet evulsa mali seminis zizania, messem

As daylight was turning into dusk, she found lodging near 3
the river Cher. When she woke up around midnight, she
gave thanks to God that she existed, that she was still alive,
that she was otherwise flourishing, and that she had touched
the tomb of the blessed bishop; when she had done this with
many tears, she fell asleep again. And behold, a man with 4
white hair, clothed in purple and holding a cross in his hand,
stood before her and said: "Now you will be healed, in the
name of Christ, our Redeemer." And taking her hand, he put
his finger between her bent fingers which covered her palm,
lifted them a little and straightened them. While she was 5
seeing this in her dream vision, she woke up and, with blood
still flowing from it, raised her hand now healed in praise of
God. At dawn she went back to the basilica, gave thanks,
and returned home rejoicing.

57

About a woman who became disabled while working on the feast day of the holy John

On the feast of the blessed John the Baptist, while the people came together for the solemn mass, a certain woman took a hoe and, all by herself, went to her field to uproot the weeds that grew from bad seed so as to clean up her harvest;

sola purgaret; nec enim poterat esse vallata divina solatio ob
2 reverentiam dominici praecursoris. Cum operari coepisset, protinus manus eius divino igne sunt apprehensae, facies quoque eius quasi emittens flammas, tota vesicis ac pusulis ebullivit. Urebatur misera non minus pudoris dolore, quam corporis, quando ea quae clam gesserat, invita prodebat.

3 Dehinc vociferando atque eiulando beati Martini basilicam velociter expetivit. Ante cuius sepulcrum in hoc tormento per quattuor mensium spatia prostrata, restincto omni vapore, in integritatem corporis solidata est. Erat enim ancilla cuiusdam civis Turonici, qui medietate pretii concessa, aliam requisivit.

58

De caeco et contracto

Puer Parisiacus, cuius artis erat vestimenta componere, increscente melancholia, id est decocti sanguinis faece, quartanarius efficitur; atque effervescente umore, ita omne corpus eius minutis pustulis coartabatur, ut a quibusdam leprosus putaretur. Sed et per omnia membra dolores pessi-
2 mos sustinebat, amborum oculorum luce multatus. Igitur

but she could not be protected by divine aid on account of any reverence for the precursor of the Lord. As soon as 2
she began to work, her hands were at once seized by divine fire, and her face too, as it were, emitted flames, all of it swollen with blisters and sores. The unhappy woman burned as much from the anguish of her shame as from that of her body when she thus unwillingly exposed what she had done in secret.

Shouting and wailing, she quickly went from there to the 3
blessed Martin's basilica. When she had lain prostrate in front of his tomb in torment for four months, the burning was extinguished, and her body was restored to health. She was the slave of a citizen of Tours, and he agreed to accept half of her price. With it he bought another female slave.

58

About a blind and crippled man

A manservant from Paris, whose skill lay in making clothes, had become increasingly affected by black bile—that is, by the dregs of attenuated blood—, and developed quartan fever; and a seething humor so plagued his whole body that it broke out in small sores in such a way that some people thought him a leper. In all his other limbs too, however, he suffered the severest pains, and both his eyes
were struck with blindness. Having heard about the blessed 2

auditam beati antistitis famam, et virtutes ubique vulgatas, Turonicam expetivit civitatem; accedensque ad basilicam sancti, per dies multos ieiunans et orans, recepto lumine, pristinae restituitur sospitati.

3 Erat enim ingenuus genere. Audiens autem Leodastis, qui tum Turonicum gerebat comitatum, quod talis esset artifex, calumniari coepit, dicens: "Refuga es tu dominorum, nec tibi licebit ultra per diversa vagari." Et vinctum in domum suam custodiendum dirigit. Sed nec ibidem defuit virtus an-
4 gelici confessoris. Nam cum apprehensus fuisset, statim ab infirmitate quam caruerat coartatur; et cum pessime ageret, videns comes nihil se in eum praevalere posse, relaxatum a vinculi liberum abscedere iubet. Ille vero ad basilicam regressus, sanatus est denuo.

59

De alia muliere, quae post ingenuitatem est vendita

Simile est huic et illud, quod mulier post emeritam libertatem rursum a patroni filiis barbaris venundatur. Sed virtute sancti, quo facilius defensaretur, contractis ad plenum

bishop's fame and about his well-known deeds of power, he went to the city of Tours and came to the basilica of the holy man; and when he had fasted and prayed there for many days, he received light and was restored to his original health.

He was of free birth. When Leodast, at this time count of 3
Tours, heard that he was such a skilled worker, however, he began to slander him, saying: "You are a fugitive from your masters, you are no longer allowed to go to different places." And he ordered him to be chained and imprisoned in his house. But the power of the angelic confessor was not ab-
sent even there. For when the man had been apprehended 4
he was, at once attacked by the illness from which he had just recovered; and when he fared so badly that the count understood that he would be of no use to him, he had him released from his chains and sent away free. When the man returned to the basilica, however, he was healed anew.

59

About another woman, who was sold after having received her freedom

Similar to that story is the one of the woman who, after earning her freedom, was sold again by the sons of her owner to some barbarians. But through the power of the

debilitatur membris. Nam et poplitum nervi ita retorsi sunt,
2 ut surae crura contingerent. Tunc relicta a dominis, quibus fuerat inique distracta, patrocinia beati expetit confessoris. Ad cuius aedem non multo tempore commorata, libertati simul ac sospitati donatur.

60

De oculorum et capitis mei dolore

Et quia prior libellus ab eo tempore initiatus est quo Paulinus reliquit, et sub quadraginta capitulis constabat impletus, destinavi hunc incoeptum in sexaginta complere. Scilicet ut beatus Martinus, qui viduatus ab hoc mundo virginitatis custodivit integrum decus, martyrium etiam vel in occultis insidiis vel in publicis iniuriis triumphaliter adimplevit, cui etiam aderat corona trigesimi, sexagesimi, vel
2 centesimi fructus, in his centum virtutibus augeretur. Spes enim mihi erat me non frustrari a voto, quod in octo annis, Domino iubente, complevi, ipsumque a virtute super me facta coeptum, ad me iterum sum regressus. Quod non sine

holy man, and so that she might more easily be protected, her limbs became paralyzed and completely debilitated. For the tendons at the back of her knees became so twisted that
the calves touched her hamstrings. Having thereupon been 2
abandoned by the masters to whom she had been unjustly sold, she sought the protection of the confessor. When she had stayed a short time at his temple, she was given her freedom as well as her health.

60

About the pain in my eyes and my head

And because the first book began where Paulinus had left off and was completed with forty chapters, I decided to fill this present one with sixty chapters. This is so that the blessed Martin, who, widowed from this world, maintained intact the glory of virginity, and even triumphantly enacted a martyrdom through suffering hidden assaults and public injuries, thereby deserving the crown of the thirtyfold, sixtyfold, and hundredfold fruit, might be similarly honored in
these one hundred deeds of power. For it was my hope not 2
to be disappointed in my vow to finish what, at the Lord's command, I completed in eight years, and, having begun this book with a powerful deed done for me, to return once more to myself. I think that this happened through God's

providentia Divinitatis esse arbitror factum, ut ad eum finiretur, a quo legitur coeptus.

3 In quo cum quinquaginta novem virtutes descripsissem, et sexagesimam adhuc attentius praestolarer, subito mihi sinistrum capitis tempus artatur doloribus, et pulsantibus venis, defluentibus lacrimis, tantus imminebat cruciatus, ut oculum vi comprimerem, ne creparet. Quod dum per unam diem ac noctem graviter ferrem, mane adveniens ad basili-
4 cam sancti, orationi prosternor. Qua expleta, doloris locum velo, quod ante beatum dependebat sepulcrum, attigi. Quo tacto, protinus et pulsus venarum et lacrimarum fluxus stetit. Post triduum vero dextram capitis partem similis attigit dolor pulsabant venae, atque ubertim lacrimae defluebant. Iterum mane consurgens, pari ut prius modo contacto velo capite, sanus abscessi.

5 Transactis vero decem diebus, visum est mihi minuere sanguinem; tertia autem die post sanguinis diminutionem, subiit mihi cogitatio, ut credo, per insidiatorem iniecta, quod haec quae pertuleram a sanguine evenissent et, si vena
6 protinus fuisset incisa, confestim ista cessassent. Dum haec cogito ac revolvo, amborum temporum venae prosiliunt, renovatur dolor qui prius fuerat, et iam non unam partem capitis sed totum arripuit caput. Commotus ergo doloribus, ad basilicam propero, ac pro cogitatione prava deprecans veniam, palla, quae beatum operit sepulcrum, caput tetigi; mox, dolore sedato, sanus recessi de tumulo.

providence that the book will end with the one with whom its reading began.

As for this book, when I had described fifty-nine deeds of 3
power and was still attentively awaiting the sixtieth, suddenly, my left temple was cramped with pain, and as my veins pulsed and tears flowed, the torment was so great that I pressed hard on my eye to keep it from bursting. When I had suffered like this severely for a day and a night, and daybreak came, I went to the basilica of the holy man and prostrated myself in prayer. After I finished, I touched the pain- 4
ful spot to the curtain that hung in front of the blessed tomb. At its touch, at once the pulsing of the veins and the flowing tears stopped. After three days, however, a similar pain attacked the right side of my head: the veins pulsed, and abundant tears flowed. Again, after I had arisen at daybreak and touched my head to the curtain as I had done earlier, I left healed.

After ten days had passed, my blood pressure seemed to 5
be reduced; but on the third day after the diminishing of my blood pressure the thought came to me, as I believe insinuated by the tricks of the Deceiver, that what I had suffered was caused by my blood pressure itself, and that if a vein had been cut at the outset, these pains would immediately have
stopped. While I was thinking these thoughts and turning 6
them over in my mind, the veins in both my temples begin throbbing again, the pain that had been there before was renewed, and it now seized not just one side, but my whole head. Distressed by the pain, I hasten to the basilica, and while asking forgiveness for the perverse thought, touched my head to the cloth that covered the blessed tomb; at once, the pain was stilled, and I left the tomb healthy.

7 Multa quidem sunt et alia quae vir beatus quotidie operatur, quae insequi longum est. Tamen si adhuc meremur videre miracula, placet ea alteri coniungi libello. Nam, ut diximus, hi duo libelli in hoc numero teneantur. Ego quoque pietati dominicae maximas refero gratias, quod mihi per suffragium antistitis gloriosi concessum est, ut quod in initio tractavi, potuerim usque ad finem perducere.

8 Deprecans, ut quod saepe confessor tribuit populis, mihi
peccatori largius indulgeat: purgetque me ab erroribus, quos
saepe conspicit et intendit, restituatque mihi lumen veritatis, eruat me ab infidelitatis lapsu, mundet cor et mentem a
lurida lepra luxuriae, purget cogitationes a concupiscentiis
pravis, atque omnem a me facinorum molem diluat atque
prosternat, ut cum in iudicio in sinistra parte fuero locatus,
ille me de medio haedorum sacrosancta dextera eius dignetur extrahere, reservatumque me tenens post tergum, sen-
9 tentiam iudicis praestoletur. Cumque eo iudicante fuero
flammis infernalibus deputatus, sacrosancto pallio, quo ille
tegitur in gloria, me contectum excuset a poena, dicentibus
regi angelis, quod quondam de monacho resuscitato dixerunt: "Iste est pro quo Martinus rogat."

10 Fiatque, ut quia non mereor illa claritate vestiri, vel ab irruentibus Tartarorum ministris merear liberari, nec tantum mihi noxa praevaleat, ut separer ab eius regno quem fideliter sum confessus in saeculo.

There are many other deeds too which the blessed man does every day which it would take too long to relate. However, if we should still deserve to see miracles after this, it will be pleasing for these to be added in another book. For, as we said, the present two books are to be limited to this number of stories. I also give the greatest thanks to the Lord whose goodness granted to me, through the intercession of the glorious bishop, that I have been able to bring what I treated at the beginning all the way to its end. 7

And I implore the confessor to grant to me, a sinner, more generously what he has often granted to the people: that he may cleanse me of the errors which he often sees and notices, that he may restore in me the light of truth, prevent me from falling into disbelief, purge my heart and mind of the lurid leprosy of lust, purify my thoughts of perverse desires, and that he may wash and cast off the whole weight of my crimes from me, so that at the Judgment, when I have been placed on the left-hand side, he will deign to snatch me from the midst of the goats with his sacrosanct right hand and keep me safe behind his back while awaiting the Judge's verdict. And when, according to the Judge's decision, I have nevertheless been sentenced to the infernal flames, that he will wrap me in the sacrosanct mantle that covers him in his glory and rescue me from punishment, while the angels say to the Judge, as they once said about the monk who had been revived: "This is the man Martin is interceding for." 8

9

And let it happen that, although I do not deserve to be clothed in light, I may still deserve to be rescued from the servants of Tartarus when they attack, and that the weight of my sins alone may not prevail over me so that I be separated from the kingdom of the One whom I have faithfully confessed in this worldly life. 10

LIBER TERTIUS

Prologus

Tertium, ordinante Christo, libellum de virtutibus beati Martini scribere incipientes, gratias agimus omnipotenti Deo, qui nobis talem medicum tribuere dignatus est, qui infirmitates nostras purgaret, vulnera dilueret, ac salubria me-
2 dicamenta conferret. Nam si ad eius beatum tumulum humilietur animus, et oratio sublimetur, si defluant lacrimae et compunctio vera succedat, si ab imo corde emittantur suspiria et pectora facinorosa tundantur, invenit ploratus laetitiam, culpa veniam, dolor pectoris pervenit ad medelam.

3 Nam saepius tactus beati sepulcri profluviis imperavit sistere, caecis videre, paralyticis surgere, et ipsam quoque pectoris amaritudinem longe discedere. Quod ego plerumque expertus, indignum me iudico, ut inter tantorum miraculorum moles etiam illa hic inseram, quae super me operari dignatus est. Sed iterum timeo ne noxialis appaream, si ea tamquam fraudulentus abscondam.

4 Testor enim Deum et spem illam quam in eius virtute posui, credens me ab illius misericordia non frustrari, quia quotienscumque aut dolor capitis irruit, aut tempora pulsus impulit, aut aures auditus gravavit, aut oculorum aciem

BOOK 3

Prologue

As I begin, at Christ's command, to write a third book about the blessed Martin's deeds of power, I give thanks to almighty God who deigned to provide us with so skilled a physician to purge us of our illnesses, wash our wounds, and grant us health-giving remedies. For if the soul is humbled 2
at his blessed tomb, and a prayer is raised to heaven, if tears flow down and true compunction follows, if sighs are emitted from the depths of the heart, and the guilty breast is beaten, weeping finds joy, guilt forgiveness, and the grieving heart achieves healing.

For, very often, touching the blessed tomb has compelled 3
bleeding to stop, the blind to see, the crippled to stand up, and even bitterness of the heart to withdraw far away. What I have often had experienced myself I consider myself unworthy to insert here among such a mass of great miracles, namely those things that the blessed Martin deigned to work upon me. But then again I am afraid to appear culpable if I, as if I were a deceiver, conceal them.

For I call upon God and the hope I have placed in his 4
power to witness that I believe I am not deprived of his compassion: whenever a headache suddenly comes upon me, a throbbing strikes my temples, or my ears' hearing has worsened, or a mist has clouded the sharpness of my eyes, or

caligo suffudit, aut aliis membris dolor insedit—statim ut locum dolentem vel tumulo vel velo pendente attigi, protinus sanitatem recepi, mirans tacitus in ipso tactu dolorem recessisse cum cursu.

I

De dolore faucium mearum

Quid autem nuper pertulerim, primum inseram huic libello miraculum. Dum ad convivium residentes post ieiunium ederemus, piscis infertur in ferculo, quem dominica cruce signatum dum edimus, una mihi ex aristis ipsius piscis iniuriosissime adhaesit in gutture. Quae dolores commovens graves, incidebat fauces acumine, et ipsam gulam longitudine obserabat; impediebat vocis sonitum, at neque ipsum salivae liquorem, qui saepe a palato defluit, transire sinebat.

2 Tertia autem die, cum neque tussiens neque excreans eam valerem proicere, recurri ad nota praesidia. Accedo ad tumulum, provolvor in pavimento, profusisque cum gemitu lacrimis, auxilium deprecor confessoris. Dehinc erectus, velo, quod dependebat, gulam faucesque et reliquum capitis
3 attigi. Nec mora, sanitatem recepi, et priusquam limina

a pain has settled in other parts of my body—as soon as I brought the afflicted part in contact with the tomb or the cloth hanging over it, I at once recovered my health, in silent amazement that, with that very touch, the pain receded so quickly.

I

About the pain in my throat

As the first miracle I shall place in this book what I experienced recently. While we were sitting at a meal after a fast and eating, a fish was brought in on a dish, and when we ate it, after having made the sign of the cross of the Lord upon it, one of its bones got stuck most distressingly in my throat. It caused great pain, its point pricked my throat, and its length obstructed the passageway; impeding the sound of my voice, it also did not allow the passage of the saliva that often flows from the palate.

On the third day, when I had not been able to expel it by 2
coughing or spitting, I hurried to turn again to my well-known remedy. I go to the tomb, prostrate myself on the pavement, and with profuse tears accompanied by sighs, I implore the confessor's aid. Thereafter I stood up and touched my throat, my larynx, and the rest of my head to
the cloth that hung over the tomb. At once, I recovered my 3

sancta egrederer, nullam fatigationem sensi. Quid tamen aculeus malus devenerit, ignoro. Non eum reieci per vomitum, non discessisse sensi in alvum. Unum tantum scio, quod ita me in velocitate sensi sanatum ut putarem quod iniecta aliquis manu, illa quae iniuriam faucibus intulerant abstulisset.

2

De puella debili sanata

Puella vero annorum duodecim, omnibus membris debilis, per sex annos tamquam mortua in domo parentum lectulo decubabat, non gressum faciens, non opus manuum implens, non lucem cernens, non sermonem eloquens, non audiens elocutum. Ad beati tumulum fundunt parentes preces pro filia, offerunt munera et adhuc vota promittunt.

2 Convenit autem populus ad solemnia, celebratur cum gaudio sacra festivitas. Tertia vero die festivitatis, vocat patrem puella, dicens: "Sitio." Qui gaudens quod filiae vocem, quam numquam audierat, meruisset audire, cucurrit velocius et, assumptum paululum aquae, puellae detulit ad bibendum. Qua hausta, ait: "Porrige mihi manum." Adpre-
3 hensa quoque pater eius dextera, levavit eam. Quae stans super pedes suos, elevatis ad caelum manibus oculisque:

health, and before I went out across the holy threshold I felt no more discomfort. What became of the hurtful spike I don't know. I did not vomit it out, nor did I feel it going down into my stomach. One thing I do know is that I felt healed so quickly that it was as if someone had put in his hand and taken away what had injured my throat.

2

About a disabled girl who was cured

A twelve-year-old girl who was disabled in all her limbs lay in bed as though dead for six years in her parents' home, not walking, not using her hands, not seeing, not speaking, and not hearing what was said. Her parents pray at the blessed man's tomb for their daughter, give gifts, and keep making promises.

Then the people came to the solemnities and the sa- 2
cred feast was celebrated with joy. On the third day of the feast, the girl called to her father, saying: "I am thirsty." Overjoyed to have deserved to hear his daughter's voice, which he had never heard before, he quickly ran to her and brought her a little water to drink. After she had drunk it, she said: "Give me your hand." And when he had taken her
right hand, he helped her get up. Once she stood on her 3
feet she lifted her eyes and her hands to heaven and cried:

"Gratias," inquit, "tibi ago, omnipotens Deus, qui respiciens humilitatem meam, me per sanctum antistitem tuum salvare dignatus es." Et sic, redintegratis membris, visum auditumque recepit, ac domum laeta regressa est.

3

De homine in cuius manu fustis adhaesit

Ante duos autem annos quam haec agerentur, quidam non metuens neque honorans diem sanctum dominicae resurrectionis, accepta annona, ad molam vadit, impositoque tritico, molam manu vertere coepit. Expleto autem opere, non poterat volam aperire, sed cum gravi dolore fustem
2 quem apprehenderat tenebat invitus. Post haec videns se non laxari, inciso ab utraque parte fuste, ad sancti basilicam venit, factaque oratione et vigiliis celebratis, laxatis digitis, manus eius ad opus pristinum restituta est.

3 Alio vero anno, in hac die sancta, operam propter quam prius increpitus a Deo fuerat, apprehendit, rursumque ei lignum in manu eius adhaesit. Ille vero cum dolore plorans ad basilicam sancti confessoris repetiit, sed non protinus meruit exaudiri. Post duos vero annos, ad eandem

"I give thanks to you, almighty God, who have taken notice of my humble person and have deigned to save me through your holy bishop!" And thus her body was healed, she recovered her sight and her hearing, and she went home rejoicing.

3

About a man whose hand stuck to a lever

Two years before these things happened, someone who neither feared nor honored the sacred day of the Lord's resurrection, took his harvested grain, went to the mill, and, after putting the grain in it, began to turn the millstone by hand. When he had finished the task, he was unable to open his hand, and against his will continued, with great pain, to
hold the lever that he had handled. Finally, seeing that it was 2
not being released, he cut the lever on both sides and went to the basilica of the holy man; when he had prayed and celebrated vigils there, his fingers were released, and his hand was restored to its former use.

Another year however, on that same holy day, he took up 3
the task for which he had previously been chastised by God, and again the wooden lever stuck to his hand. Crying with pain, he returned to the basilica of the holy confessor, but did not immediately deserve to be heard. But after two years,

festivitatem quam puellam sanatam retulimus, et iste liberatus est ab onere ligni.

4

De contracto sanato

Ex Lemovicino autem adveniens contractus qui nec gressum facere poterat nec lumen oculorum habebat, deportatus manibus devotorum ante sanctum sepulcrum deponitur; deprecatusque misericordiam beati antistitis, directis membris debilibus, sanitati donatur.

5

De caeco illuminato

Quidam caecus, qui longo tempore lumen caruerat oculorum, ad eandem festivitatem venit. Et facta oratione, dum ante sanctum sepulchrum staret, subito apertis oculis, recepto lumine, iucundatur.

indeed during the same feast in which we reported that the girl was healed, this man too was freed from the burden of the wooden lever.

4

About a crippled man who was healed

A crippled man coming from Limoges, who could not walk and did not have the sight of his eyes, was carried by the hands of devout people and placed before the holy tomb; and when he had prayed for the compassion of the blessed bishop, his crippled limbs were straightened, and he was given his health.

5

About a blind man who received light

A blind man who had been deprived of the sight of his eyes for a long time came to the same feast. When he had prayed and was standing before the holy tomb, suddenly his eyes opened and to his great joy he recovered his sight.

6

De debili sanato

Puer autem incola civitatis Turonicae, dum valetudine nimia ac diuturna consumitur, omnibus membris debilitatur et sine spe gressum a febre relinquitur, cui tibiae ceu funes intortae separari non poterant. Post discessum vero febris, expetiit a parentibus ut eum ad sanctam basilicam depor-
2 tarent. Quem exhibitum deponentes ad pedes sancti, orationem faciunt ut ei virtus solita subveniret. Tertia vero die cum ille vel parentes eius in oratione ac ieiunio perdurarent, exorto misericordiae lumine, distortis tibiis, a parentibus incolumis est receptus.

7

De eo qui clavem die dominico faciebat

Sic et alius, Senator nomine, de Cracatonno, Andegavensi vico, dum die dominico clavem facit, digiti ei ambarum manuum eius contraxerunt, unguibus in palmam defixis. Sic qui

6

About a disabled boy who was restored to health

A boy from the city of Tours, consumed by a severe and prolonged illness, became disabled in all his limbs and without hope of walking, for his shinbones were twisted like ropes and could not be separated. After the fever had left him, he asked his parents to carry him to the holy basilica.
When they had brought him, they placed him at the feet of 2
the holy man, and prayed that his usual power might come to the boy's aid. On the third day, while he and his parents persisted in prayer and fasting, the light of compassion arose, his legs were disentangled and he was received by his parents in good health.

7

About a man who made a key on a Sunday

Similarly, while another man named Senator, from Craon, a village in the territory of Angers, was making a key on a Sunday, the fingers of both his hands went into spasms,

2 ostium pandere voluit, manus reserare non poterat. Dehinc per quattuor mensibus iam unguibus in carne defixis, computrescente palma, auxilia expetiit confessoris; et per quattuor dies orationi ac ieiunio vacans, manus sanas elevans, incolumis est regressus, collaudans virtutem antistitis, et ut nullus aggrederetur quod ipse praesumpserat praedicabat.

8

De mortuo suscitato

Eo tempore, quo talia apud urbem Turonicam gerebantur, legati de Hispaniis, id est Florentius et Exsuperius, ad Chilpericum Regem veniebant. Quos cum ad convivium ecclesiae recepissem, epulantibus nobis, eo quod se assererent esse catholicos, Florentius, qui erat aetate senior, sollicite flagitat aliqua de beati viri virtute cognoscere. At ego, Deo gratias agens, interrogo si vel nomen eius in illis regionibus audiretur, vel vita illius legeretur ab aliquo.

2 Haec me interrogante, ait in illis locis magnifice honorari nomen eius, sed et se peculiarem alumnum antistitis narrat, dicens super se magnam eius virtutem ostensam fuisse.

fixing his nails in his palms. Thus the one who wished to open a door could not open his own hands. After this, when 2
his nails had been stuck in his flesh for four months and his palms were putrefying, he went to ask the help of the confessor; and after devoting himself for four days to prayer and fasting, he raised his hands, healed, and went home in good health, praising the power of the bishop, and warning that no one should undertake what he himself had dared to do.

8

About a dead boy who was revived

At the time when events like these were taking place in the city of Tours, legates from Spain, named Florentius and Exsuperius, came to King Chilperic. When I had received them at the church's meal and we were eating together, because they claimed to be catholics, Florentius, the elder one, asked earnestly to learn something about the power of the blessed man. And I, giving thanks to God, inquired whether his name was heard in those regions and whether his *Life* was being read by anyone.

In answer to my question he replied that his name was 2
magnificently honored in those regions, and he also told us that he himself was a special foster son of the bishop, saying that a great act of his power had been manifested upon

"Avus," inquit, "meus ante multorum curricula annorum basilicam construxit in honore beati Martini antistitis. Perfec-
taque ac eleganti opere exornata, Turonis clericos religiosos
destinavit, expetens pontificis reliquias, ut scilicet locum
quem in eius nomine aedificaverat, eius reliquiis consecra-
3 ret. Quod cum fecisset, per singulos dies veniebat, et prostratus cum coniuge, sancti pontificis auxilium implorabat.
Post multum vero tempus infans his nascitur. Cum autem
trium mensuum esset a febre pulsatus, in tantum exinanitur
ut neque papillam sugere, neque ullum alimentum valeret
accipere. Interea, perdurante morbo, cibo abnegato, palpi-
tante tantum spiritu, solus transitus praestolabatur. Nec
mora, ipse quoque exhalatur spiritus.

4 "Tum mater maesta vel avia de unicae ac primogenitae
sobolis morte, apprehensum inter brachia ante altare beati
Martini iam exanime corpusculum spe non incerti deposuerunt; et tamquam si sanctum visibilibus cernerent oculis,
avus alloquitur, dicens: 'Spes nobis erat maxima, beatissime
confessor, tua huc pignora deportare, per quae morbi depel-
lerentur, febres exstinguerentur, fugarentur caecitatis tenebrae, et aliae quoque infirmitates emendarentur, pro eo
quod de te legantur plurima, quae vel vivens feceris, vel post
5 transitum operaris. Nam audivimus te oratione mortuos
suscitasse, lepram osculo depulisse, energuminos curasse
verbo, venenum digito compressisse, et alia multa fecisse.
Hic apparebit virtus tua si et nunc iuxta fidem nostram hunc
resuscitaveris parvulum. Quod si non feceris, non hic ultra

him. "My grandfather," he said, "built a basilica in honor of
the blessed bishop Martin many years ago. When it was finished and decorated with elegant craftsmanship, he sent pious clerics to Tours to ask for relics of the bishop so that he
might consecrate the structure he had built in his name with
his relics. When he had done this, he used to come every day 3
and lie prostrate, with his wife, to implore the holy bishop's
help. After a long time, indeed, a child was born to them.
But when the boy was three months old he was stricken by a
fever and became so weak that he could not suckle or take in
any kind of nourishment. While the illness continued and
he rejected nourishment, breathing only feebly, his passing
was the only thing that was expected. Soon, he breathed out
his spirit too.

"Then the child's sorrowing mother, that is, my grand- 4
mother, and my grandfather, grieving for the death of their
only and firstborn child, took the now lifeless little body
into their arms, and they put it with no uncertain hope in
front of the blessed Martin's altar; and as though they were
seeing the holy man with their eyes, my grandfather said: 'It
was our greatest hope, most blessed confessor, that after we
brought your relics here illnesses would be repelled, fevers
extinguished, the darkness of blindness chased away, and
other infirmities also cured, because we read many things
about you which you did during your life and work now after
your passing. For we have heard that you revived the dead 5
with prayer, expelled leprosy with a kiss, cured the possessed with a word, drove out poison with your finger, and
did many other things. Your power will be manifested here
now too if, in accordance with our faith, you bring this little boy back to life. But if you do not do this, we will no

colla curvabimus, luminaria accendemus, aut alicuius honoris gratiam exhibebimus.’ Et haec dicens, relicto ante altare infantulo, abierunt.

6 “Mane autem facto venientes, invenerunt eum ad altare conversum, et dum admirarentur, suscepit eum mater in ulnis; et cognoscens eum resumpsisse flatum, applicat ad papillam, qui protinus, hausto lacte, confortatus est. Tunc mater cum patre vel omni domo, elevata in caelo voce, benedixerunt Deum, dicentes: ‘Nunc cognovimus quia magnus Deus es, et facis mirabilia solus, qui nobis parvulum confessoris tui oratione restituisti.’ Loco autem illi maiorem deinceps, quam prius fecerant, reverentiam exhibebant.” Haec ab ipsius Florentii ore ita gesta cognovi.

9

De eo qui pedem debilem habuit

Clericus erat ab urbe Pictava, in agro illius regionis qui ad sanctam basilicam pertinebat, unius usu pedis debilis, quem, ut ipse asserebat, per incursum daemonii meridiani perdiderat. Qui, inciso fuste ad mensuram geniculi, pelle

longer bend our necks to you, light lamps, or show you the grace of any honor.' After saying this, they left the infant in front of the altar and went away.

"When they came back the next morning, they found 6
him turned toward the altar and, while they marveled at what had happened, his mother took him into her arms; seeing that he had started breathing again, she put him to her breast, and soon, after he had taken some milk, he was became stronger. Thereupon his mother and father, along with their whole household, lifted their voices to heaven and blessed God, saying: 'Now we know that you are a great God and that you alone work miracles, who restored our little boy to us according to the prayer of your confessor!' And from that time on they showed that place greater reverence than they had previously." It was from Florentius's own mouth that I learned about these events.

9

About a man who had a disabled foot

A cleric from the city of Poitiers, from an estate in the region that belonged to the holy basilica, had become lame in one foot. He had lost the ability to use it, he said, through an attack of the noonday demon. He cut a stick up to the height of his knee, covered it with a piece of leather and,

superposita, ad ipsum geniculum extenso retrorsum vestigio, gressum quem pede nitebatur agere, fuste adminicu-
2 lante perficiebat. Ad antedictam basilicam novem post annos advenit, fusaque oratione per triduum, ante tertium festivitatis diem poplite directo surrexit. Adveniente autem ad sancti solemnia populo, qualiter per virtutem eius sanatus esset, edocuit.

10

De tibia matris meae

Matri vero meae hoc ordine virtus sancti subvenit. Tempore quo transactis parturitionis doloribus me edidit, dolorem in uno tibiae musculo incurrit. Erat autem subitaneus, tamquam si clavus affigens, atque ita fictam gravissimam dabat ut plerumque eclipsim generaret, nec erat quod eum mitigare posset, nisi cum diutissime contra ignem tentus a vapore foci obstupesceret; sed et, si unguentum aliquod parumper fuisset infusum, quiescebat.

2 Quid plura? Post ordinationem meam advenit Turonus vel ad occursum antistitis sancti, vel causa desiderii mei. Cum hic igitur per duos aut tres menses commorata fuisset,

bending his foot as far as the back of his knee, attached it to the stick, thereby managing with the stick the walking he
had been attempting with his foot. After nine years he came 2
to the aforementioned basilica, prayed there for three days, and on the third day before the feast arose with a straightened knee. And when the people came to the solemnities of the holy man, he explained to them how he had been healed by the confessor's power.

10

About my mother's leg

The holy man's power helped my mother in this manner. At the time when after undergoing the pains of childbirth she bore me, she incurred a pain in the muscle of one of her legs. It used to come suddenly, as though a nail was being driven into it, and gave such an severe shock that it often caused her to faint, and there was nothing that could alleviate the pain except its being stretched out for a very long time in front of a fire, so that it was dulled by the heat; but it also calmed down if some ointment was rubbed upon it for a short while.

What more needs to be said? After my ordination she 2
came to Tours both to visit the holy bishop Martin and because she missed me. When she had stayed here for two

et assidue beati pontificis auxilium precaretur, tandem respiciente miseratione consueta, discessit dolor a tibia quae per triginta quattuor annos feminam fatigaverat.

11

De mulieris manu sanata

Sed et alia mulier de Andegavo territorio, digitis in palma defixis, ut ad locum sanctum preces effudit, digitis directis, sanata manu discessit.

12

De puero a valetudine sanato

Puer familiaris noster, correptus a febre, graviter urebatur. Ardebant enim extrinsecus membra, intrinsecus vero sitis valida erat, et si potum aliquod recipiebat, mox reiciebat a

or three months, and gone on praying assiduously to the blessed bishop for help, his customary compassion at last looked favorably upon her, and the pain in her leg that had worn down the woman for thirty-four years went away.

11

About a woman whose hand was healed

When another woman too, from the territory of Angers, whose fingers were stuck in her palm, came to the holy place and prayed; her fingers were straightened and she went home with a healed hand.

12

About a boy who was cured of an illness

A boy belonging to our household was seized by a fever and started burning with intense heat. On the outside, his body burned, while inside he was extremely thirsty, and if he drank anything, it was at once rejected by his stomach,

stomacho, nihil tamen capiens cibi. Cumque in hoc labore quarto aut quinto die fatigaretur, petiit ut ei parumper exhiberent pulveris de sepulcro ad bibendum. Quo exhibito, vinoque diluto, ut hausit fideliter, recepta sanitate, convaluit.

13

De Theodae pede sanato

Theoda vero, Wiliacharii quondam presbyteri filia, dum ab umore pedum frequentius laboraret, unius pedis usum, qui in debilitatem redactus fuerat, perdidit. Post haec ad beatam advenit basilicam, in qua dum crebras effunderet preces, amota debilitate, incolumitati donatur.

14

De homine inclinato

Erat tunc temporis in villa quae sub tuitione sanctae matris ecclesiae habebatur, homo quidam qui, tamquam effractis renibus, inclinatus ambulabat. Hic iuxta illam evangelicae

which did not accept any food either. When he had been afflicted by this suffering for four or five days, he asked to be given a bit of dust from the tomb to drink. It was brought and diluted in wine, and when he drank it full of faith, he was given back his health and recovered.

13

How Theoda's foot was healed

Theoda, a daughter of the late priest Wiliachar, often suffered from a swelling in her feet and lost the use of one of them, which became lame. After this, when she came to the blessed basilica and poured out frequent prayers there, her lameness was removed and she was granted her health.

14

About a stooped man

There was at that time, on an estate managed by the holy mother Church, a man who walked with a stoop, as though his lower back was broken. Just like the woman mentioned

seriei mulierem deorsum proclinus nequaquam sursum poterat erigi, sed duobus in ascellis fustibus additis, incurvus
2 agebat gressum. Ad festivitatem autem adveniens, tertia die post acta solemnia erectus, ab omni incursione diabolica mundatus, sanus abscessit.

15

De Gundulfo debili

Gundulfus vero quidam, ipsius urbis civis, ab infantia sua cum Gunthario, Chlotarii Regis filio, habitavit. In cuius dum haberetur servitio et, ordinante rege, ascenderet in arborem, ut matura decerperet poma, effracto ramo, corruit,
2 collisoque ad lapidem pede, debilitatus est. Post multos vero annos dum in hac debilitate persisteret, et ascenso equite velociter eum impelleret ad eundum, lapsante gressu, praecipitatur, compressumque pedem alium, qui sanus erat, graviter laesit. Dehinc portari se ad sanctam basilicam postulat, proiectusque ad pavimentum, orationem fideliter fundit.

3 Nec morata est pietas, quae semper tribulantibus subvenire consuevit, sed protinus, ablato omni dolore, incolumis a pavimento surrexit. Igitur per triginta circiter annos, de alio pede, sicut superius diximus, iugiter claudicabat.

in the gospel, he was bent downward and could in no way raise himself upright, but leaning on two sticks placed under
his armpits, he walked leaning over. After coming to the 2
feast, however, he was straightened on the third day after the solemnities and, cleansed of every diabolical incursion, went away healthy.

15

About Gundulf, a disabled man

A certain Gundulf, a citizen of this city, lived from the time of his infancy with Gunthar, the son of King Clothar. While he was in his service, he climbed a tree on the king's orders to pick ripe apples; the branch broke and he fell. He
struck his foot on a rock, and became disabled. After endur- 2
ing this disability for many years, he mounted a horse and spurred it on to go faster; it stumbled and fell upon his other good foot, gravely injuring it. He then asked to be carried to the holy basilica, and throwing himself upon the pavement, poured out a prayer with faith.

3 Without delay, the compassion that is accustomed always to come to the aid of those in trouble immediately removed all his pain, and he arose healthy from the pavement. For about thirty years, however, as we said above, he had been constantly limping with the other foot. Finally, having

Tandem inspectis propriae conscientiae noxis, converti decrevit, scilicet, ut humiliatis capillis ipsi sancto deserviret antistiti.

4 Sed prius a rege praeceptum elicuit, ut res suas omnes basilicae traderet vivens. Quo facto, capite tonsurato, impletoque bonae deliberationis voto, pes eius, qui effractis ossibus fuerat breviatus, est elongatus. Et qui ante a duobus pueris sustentatus ibat, nunc sine ullius hominis adminiculo, quo voluerit, absque aliquo debilitatis impedimento discurrit.

16

De caeco illuminato

Post haec puerulus quidam ex Lemovicino caecus adveniens, lumen recepit oculorum hoc modo. Anno tertio nativitatis suae, cum iam gressum incipiens figere, erumpenteque lingua in verbis labra laxaret, dum matri alludit blande, dum oscula libat, dum collo eius appenditur, dum in ulnis defertur, commota per immissionem diabolicam, vi venti pulvis a terra cum paleis elevatur, et super puerum ac ma-
2 trem eius cum magno turbine fertur. Sed rustica mulier et

recognized the sins of his conscience, he decided to convert, that is, to serve that same holy bishop with his hair shorn.

But first he obtained a decree from the king that ordered 4
him to transfer all his possessions to the basilica while he was still alive. After this had been done, his head had been tonsured, and his generous vow fulfilled, his foot, which had become shorter because the bones had been broken, was lengthened. He used to walk supported by two servants, but now, without anyone's help, he runs about where he wants without any disability to impede him.

16

About a blind boy who received light

After these events, a blind boy coming from Limoges recovered the sight of his eyes in the following way. In the third year after his birth, when he was just beginning to learn to walk and to open his lips to let his tongue produce words, while playing sweetly with his mother, giving her kisses, hanging from her neck and being carried in her arms, dust and chaff was lifted from the ground by a violent gust of wind, swept up by a diabolic intervention, and was dropped on the boy and his mother in a huge whirlwind. The simpleminded and careless woman, however, 2

incauta non tractat se filiumque Salvatoris vexillo munire, ideoque praevalentibus insidiis oculi adolescentis repleti pulvere obserantur.

3 Qui diu vociferans, tandem mitigatus a matre permansit caecus. Adultus autem datus est mendicis, ut vel cum eisdem ambulans stipendii quiddam acciperet. Erant autem parentes eius valde pauperes. Igitur duodecimo caecitatis suae anno advenit Turonus ante diem solemnitatis qua Deus Pater, Verbum carni glutinans, mundo salutem invexit.

4 Decursa autem festivitatis vigilia, dum recedentibus aliis hic ad pedes sancti decubaret immobilis, tunc sensit quasi pupugisset aliquis oculos eius a spiculo, et statim sanguis ab his erumpens coepit defluere per genas eius. Aversaque sursum facie, vidit super se cereum elucere et, exclamans voce magna, ait: "Gratias tibi ago, sancte confessor Dei, quia virtute tua lumen recipere merui!"

5 O admirabilis gratia! O virtus immensa! Multimodis enim affectibus dona tua spargis in populis! Nam qui stipem petierat, lumen recepit, et diu extera luce, virtutis tuae lumine vultus ornatur. O si te multorum criminum tenebrae a nostris visibus non arcerent, nempe venires visibiliter, et infirmis voce Petri clamares: "Aurum et argentum non habeo, sed quod habeo do vobis: in nomine Christi Iesu abite incolumes!" [Acts 3:6]

did not think of protecting herself and her son with the sign of the Savior, and therefore the devil's trickeries prevailed: the young child's eyes were filled with dust and became blocked up.

After crying for a long time, he was at last calmed by his 3
mother, but he remained blind. When he had grown up, he was handed over to beggars so that, traveling around with them, he might receive some money for food. For his parents were very poor. In the twelfth year of his blindness he came to Tours before the celebration of the day on which God the Father, uniting the Word with flesh, sent his salvation into the world.

When the vigils before the feast were over, the others 4
had gone away, and he was lying motionless at the feet of the holy man, when he felt as though someone had pricked his eyes with a sharp point; and immediately blood began to flow from them over his cheeks. Lifting up his head, he saw a candle burning above him and cried out with a loud voice, shouting: "I thank you, holy confessor of God, that I have deserved to receive sight by your power!"

O marvelous grace! O immeasurable power! In many 5
ways do you scatter your gifts among the peoples! For he who had asked for a penny received light and, long deprived of external light, his face was adorned with the light of your power. O if the darkness of our many sins did not hide you from our sight, you would surely come visibly and cry out to the sick with Peter's words: "Gold and silver I do not have, but what I do have, I give to you: in the name of Christ Jesus, depart in good health!"

17

De Siggonis referendarii aure

Fuerat causa quaedam ut Remense oppidum peteremus, cumque ab Aegidio Episcopo, qui tunc ecclesiam regebat, benigne fuissemus excepti, illucescente in crastinum dominica die, ad ecclesiam accessimus, residentesque in sacrario adventum praestolabamur antistitis. Eo tempore sancti Martini reliquias, licet temerario ordine, super me habe-
2 bam. Igitur Siggo, referendarius quondam Sigiberti, ad occursum nostrum accedit, osculatumque iuxta me sedere deposco. Sed ille unam habens oppilatam aurem, vix de alia poterat quae loquebamur advertere.

3 Verum ubi sufficienter colloquio usi sumus, ille in domum vocatur ecclesiae. Protinus igitur ut a me discessit, disrupta auris surdae claustra, et quasi magnum exinde ventum exire sentiens, auditum recepit. Reversusque continuo mihi gratias agere coepit, dicens: "Tertia iam dies erat quod de hac aure auditum amiseram, sed cum tecum loquerer, sensi velo-
4 citer reseratam." Tunc ego confusus, ne mihi haec ascriberentur, aio: "Noli, dulcissime fili, mihi aliquid gratiarum referre, sed ei, cuius tibi virtus auditum restituit. Nam scias beati Martini mecum haberi pignora, cuius tibi potentia auditus gravitas est depulsa."

17

About Referendary Siggo's ear

We had reason to go to the town of Reims, and when we had been kindly welcomed by Bishop Aegidius who then governed the city's cathedral, and the next morning, a Sunday, was already dawning, we went to the cathedral and sat in the sacristy, awaiting the bishop's arrival. At that time, even though it was a bold thing to do, I had relics of the holy
Martin on me. Siggo, formerly referendary of King Sigebert, 2
came to meet us, and after we had kissed I asked him to sit beside me. He, however, had one obstructed ear and with the other could scarcely hear what we were saying.

When we had talked sufficiently, he was called into the 3
cathedral residence. At the very moment that he left me the obstruction in his deaf ear was shattered and, feeling as it were a great gust of wind blowing out of it, he recovered his hearing. Turning around immediately, he began to thank me, saying: "It has been three days since I lost the hearing of this ear, but while I was talking to you I felt it opening quickly."
Thereupon, embarrassed lest this should be ascribed to me, 4
I said: "Don't thank me in any way, dearest son, but him whose power restored your hearing. For know that I have relics of the blessed Martin with me, by whose power the obstruction to your hearing was expelled."

18

De infirmitate pecorum

Quodam vero tempore dum saeva lues taliter desaeviret in pecora, ut nec ad recuperandum genus putaretur aliquod remanere, quidam de nostris basilicam sanctam adiit, oleumque lychnorum qui camerae dependebant, suscepit cum ipsis aquis in vasculo.

2 Deportatumque in domum, pecora quae adhuc hic morbus non attigerat, intinctoque digito in liquore, per frontes et dorsa cruce dominica signat, ipsisque animalibus terrae deiectis ac resupinatis ex hoc unguine fide plenus infudit in ore. Mox dicto citius, clandestina peste propulsa, pecora liberata sunt.

19

De caeco illuminato

Abrincatinus quoque incola, cui per sex annos videndi usus fuerat denegatus, beati confessoris expetiit salvari praesidio. Ad cuius basilicam accedens, multoque tempore

18

About the cattle disease

Once, when a savage pestilence raged among the cattle so that it was feared that none would remain to reproduce the species, one of our people came to the holy basilica and put oil and water from the lamps that hung from the ceiling in a flask.

After he had carried home, he dipped his finger in the liquid and made the sign of the Lord's cross on the foreheads and backs of the cattle which had not yet been stricken by the disease; and as for the animals which had fallen down and were lying on their backs, he poured some of the ointment into their mouths with the fullest faith. At once, faster than words can say, the insidious plague was driven away and the cattle were freed of it. 2

19

About a blind man who received light

An inhabitant of Avranches, who had been denied the use of his eyes for six years, sought to be healed by the aid of the blessed confessor. After he had come to his basilica, he

ieiuniis et orationibus vacans, auxilium beati implorat antis-
2 titis. Denique adveniente sacrosancta festivitate, populis missarum solemnia spectantibus, huic visus est redditus; rediitque in patriam videns, qui ad sanctam basilicam alio deducente pervenerat. Ipse autem pro tantae pietatis gaudio vovit se ibidem tonsurari, quod postea devotus rediens implevit.

20

De alio caeco illuminato

Nam et quidam de transmarinis partibus veniens, dum operam exerceret in agro, subito orta super se violentia venti cum pulvere, lumine caruit oculorum; et qui diu caecis via fuerat, ipse domum alio regente deducitur. In hac enim
2 caecitate per trium annorum curriculum detinetur. Post haec basilicam beati confessoris expetiit, ad quam per quattuor annos orationi incumbens, visitatus virtute divina, patefactis luminibus, lucem videre promeruit.

devoted himself for a long time to fasts and prayers and implored the blessed bishop's help. When, at last, the most 2
holy feast came, and the people were watching the solemnities of the mass, he was given back his sight; and he who had come to the basilica guided by someone else returned to his home territory seeing. In return for the joys granted his great piety, he vowed to have himself tonsured there, a promise that he later fulfilled when he devoutly returned.

20

About another blind man who received light

Someone else, who had come from overseas, was working in a field when suddenly a violent wind full of dust arose all around him and he lost the light of his eyes; and thus one who had long been a guide for the blind was himself guided to his home by someone else. Over the course of three years
he was held fast in this blindness. After this he went to the 2
basilica of the blessed confessor, and after devoting himself to prayer there for four years, was visited by the power of God, his eyes were opened, and he was found deserving to see the light.

21

De Iuliano contracto

Sed haec fama, ut saepe diximus, non solum ad propriam urbem, verum etiam in aliis urbibus et paene in toto mundo vulgata perpatuit. Iulianus quidam ab Hispaniis veniens, manus et pedes habens debiles, ad hunc medicum devotus ingressus est, dicens: "Credo enim indubitanter, sanctissime praesul, quod poteris mihi ea medelae adiuvamenta praebere, quae ceteris in te sperantibus non es solitus denegare."
2 In hac credulitate orationi assidue insistens, et de Domini miseratione non dubitans, directis pedibus manibusque incolumis est redditus.

22

De muliere ad sancti lectulum illuminata

Verum quia in superioribus libellis saepius diximus et in loco illo de quo migravit ad caelos plerumque miracula celebrari, quid nuper gestum sit, pandam. Mulier indigena urbis Turonicae, visus claritate multata, cellulam Condatensem in

21

About Julian, a paralyzed man

But the holy Martin's reputation, as I have often said, was publicized and made known not only in his own city but also in other cities, and almost the whole world. A certain Julian, who had come from Spain with crippled hands and feet, devoutly approached this physician, saying: "I believe without doubt, most holy bishop, that you will be able to help me with the cure which you have not been accustomed to deny
to others who trust in you." In this belief he prayed assidu- 2
ously, not doubting the Lord's compassion; his feet and hands were straightened and he was restored to health.

22

About a woman who was given light at the holy man's bed

But, because in earlier books I have often said that miracles are often celebrated in the place from which he went to heaven too, I will make known what happened recently. A woman born in the city of Tours whose eyesight had been

qua lectulum beati antistitis habetur expetiit, putans sibi
2 praesidium fore si cancellos ipsius lectuli tetigisset. Lectulum autem non aliud dicitur, nisi quod in pavimentum illud, substrato cinere et apposito capiti lapide, Israel nostri temporis flexa cervice recubuit. Ergo ad hoc oraculum mulier viro adminiculante deducitur, in quo per multos dies orationem compuncta fundebat.

3 Tandem pietas saepe ad miserandum profusa eam respiciens, visum mulieri amissum restituit. Tantaque deinceps feminam fides accendit, ut usque ad diem sui obitus numquam a loco illo discederet.

23

De muto cui fratres abstulerant facultatem

Incola vero Andecavensis urbis, turbatis membris morbo, caput convertit ad lectulum; dehinc per dies singulos invalescente febre, cunctis artubus destitutus, auditu et locu-
2 tione pariter privatur. Post paucos vero dies cum de febre convaluisset, et sine voce maneret, ablata sibi ab fratribus facultatis parte, de domo paterna proicitur, dicentibus

compromised went to the cell at Candes that contains the bed of the blessed bishop, thinking that it would help her if
she touched the balustrade around it. This bed, though, is 2
only a place in the pavement with a layer of cinders and a stone placed at its head, where the Israel of our time slept with bent neck. Therefore the woman was conducted by her husband to this sanctuary, and for many days prayed there with a contrite heart.

Finally, the compassion that is often lavished upon those 3
who deserve pity looked upon her and restored to the woman her lost vision. From that time onward so great a faith was kindled in her that until the day of her death she never left that place.

23

About a mute man whose brothers had stolen his livelihood

An inhabitant of the city of Angers, when his body was racked by an illness, he took to his bed; from then on his fever increased every single day and he lost the use of all his limbs, his hearing, and his faculty of speech, all simulta-
neously. After a few days, when he had recovered from the 2
fever but was left mute, his share of the family possessions was taken from him by his brothers, and he was thrown out

fratribus: "Hic amens effectus est. Non patiatur Deus quod aut facultati nostrae inhaereat, aut partem hereditatis acquirat." Erant enim ingenui et possessionem propriam incolentes; sed nihil cogitantes de his quae Dei erant, eiecerunt mutum et surdum quem potius fovere debuerant.

3 Ille vero quamquam sine his usibus esset, sensum tamen in corde retinebat. Porro autem, adprehensis manu tabulis, inter se collisis, vocem quaerentis imitabatur. Cum hoc enim artificio ad supradictum vicum advenit ibique aliis stipem flagitantibus adiungitur. Sextus igitur iam defluxerat annus, quod pauper iste a divitiis sanctae cellulae vescebatur.

4 Factum est autem ut in una dominicarum nocte, dum in domo hospitis sui decumberet, subito locus ille immenso repleretur lumine, et ecce hic pavore perterritus solo prosternitur. Et statim visus est ei vir quidam sacerdotali habitu comptus, qui tangens eum et crucem Christi fronti eius imponens, ait: "Dominus te sanum fecit. Surge et propera ad ecclesiam, et age gratias Deo tuo."

5 Ipse autem, elevatam cum gratiarum actione vocem, clamoribus vicinia complet. Illico concurrunt omnes ad spectaculum et mirantur loquentem quem pridie viderant mutum. Interea signum movetur horis matutinis: aggregatur et populus, vigiliasque celebratas, virtus sancti clarificata perpatuit. His diebus duo energumini in hoc loco, eiecto daemone, sunt mundati.

of the paternal home. His brothers said: "This man has become insane. Let not God allow him either to cling to what belongs to us or to acquire his share of the inheritance." For they were free men, cultivating their own lands, but they did not think of the things that are God's and threw out the mute and deaf man whom they should instead have cared for.

The man, although he lacked these faculties, retained his intelligence. For he thereupon picked up two tablets and, banging them together, imitated the voice of one begging. With this artifice he came to the above-mentioned village [of Candes] and there joined others begging for money. Six years had already passed during which that poor man had been sustained from the wealth of the holy cell. 3

It happened, however, that on a night before a Sunday, while he slept in the house of his host [the holy man], the place was suddenly filled with an immense brightness, and overcome by terror, he prostrated himself on the floor. At once he seemed to see a man dressed in a priest's vestment who touched him and made the sign of the cross of Christ on his forehead, saying: "The Lord has made you healthy. Get up, hurry to the church, and give thanks to your God." 4

He shouted his thanks and filled the neighborhood with his cries. At once all ran toward this spectacle and were amazed to find the one whom they had seen mute the day before now speaking. Meanwhile, the bell sounded for matins: the people gathered too, and after the vigils had been celebrated, the holy man's deed of power was glorified and made known to all. In these days, two possessed persons staying in this place were cleansed by the expulsion of their demons. 5

24

De oleo crescente

Sed revertamur ad Aredium nostrum, immo etiam peculiarem, ut ita dicam, beati confessoris alumnum, cui saepius de suis pignoribus cernere miracula praestat. Hic ad festivitatem sancti cum illa qua solitus est benignitate, humilitate
2 et caritate pervenit. Regrediens vero ampullam parvulam de oleo sancti sepulchri completam secum detulit, dicens: "Forsitan infirmus aliquis in via adest, qui a beati Martini aede benedictionem, corde compunctus, accipere desideret."

3 Denique in quodam loco mulier devota accessit ad eum, exhibens ampullam aliam cum oleo, dicens: "Rogo te, serve Christi, ut tua hoc oleum benedictione sanctifices." At ille, ne vanitati subiectus videretur, ait: "Parva est virtus mea, sed, si placet, oleum de sepulcro beati Martini habeo, ex quo hoc oleum perfundatur. Tu vero, si credis eius virtutem magnam, ex hoc salutem hauries."

4 At illa gaudens, petiit expleri quae presbyter loquebatur. Vas etenim illud medium erat. Cumque de hoc liquore qui a basilica sancti assumptus fuerat, perfunderetur, protinus ebulliens oleum ampullam usque ad summitatem implevit. Quod matrona cernens, admirans virtutem confessoris beati, domum regressa est gaudens.

24

About the oil that increased

But let us return to our Aredius, the special foster son, so to speak, of the blessed confessor, to whom he, through his relics, often grants the seeing of miracles. He came to the feast of the holy man with his usual kindness, humility, and
affection. On his return he took with him a small flask full 2
of oil from the holy tomb, saying: "Perhaps there is some sick person on the road, who, with a contrite heart, wishes to receive a blessing from the blessed Martin's church."

In fact, a devout woman approached him in a certain 3
place, showed him another flask of oil, and said: "I beg you, servant of Christ, to sanctify this oil with your blessing." But he, to avoid seeming to be subject to vanity, said: "My power is small, but, if it pleases you, I have with me oil from the blessed Martin's tomb, from which a bit can be poured into this oil. If you believe in his great power, you will obtain health from this."

And she, rejoicing, asked the priest to do what he had 4
said. Her flask, however, was half full. And when some of the fluid that had been taken from the basilica was poured upon it, the oil immediately bubbled and filled the flask right up to the top. When she saw this, the lady was amazed at the blessed confessor's power and returned home rejoicing.

25

De digitis cuiusdam mulieris directis

Alia vero mulier, cuius digiti in ipsam palmam contracti defixi erant, basilicam beati Martini antistitis expetiit. Paucis quoque interpositis diebus, orationem fundens et sancti auxilium implorans, directis digitis, manum recepit incolumem.

26

De muliere contracta

Ante hos annos puella in infirmitatem pessimam ruens, membris omnibus debilitata contrahitur. Haec, auditis miraculis quae antistes gloriosus in singulis operabatur, nomen
2 eius invocabat devote. Post dies autem paucos rogat se ad eius basilicam deportari, in cuius atrio diebus multis iacens, fusa saepius oratione cum lacrimis, a virtute pontificis visitatur, sicque subveniente divina misericordia, sanata discessit.

25

About a woman whose fingers were straightened

Another woman, whose fingers had contracted and become stuck into her palm, came to the blessed bishop Martin's basilica. A few days later, while she was pouring out her prayers and imploring the holy man's help, her fingers were straightened and she received back her hand fully sound.

26

About a paralyzed woman

Years earlier, a girl lapsed into a most serious illness and became debilitated by the contraction of all her limbs. Because she had heard about the miracles which the glorious bishop was working in particular persons, she began to invoke his name devoutly. After a few days, she asked to be 2
carried to his basilica, in whose forecourt she lay for many days. After pouring out many tearful prayers, she was visited by the bishop's power and, saved in this way by divine compassion, she left cured.

27

De puero contracto

Puer vero ex Andegavo territorio, dum in domo parentum resideret, per immissionem, ut ipse asserebat, artis diabolicae, manuum pedumque perdidit usum, ita ut contractis intrinsecus digitis, ungulae in palmam defigerentur, nervique
2 poplitum arefacti calcaneos ad crura diverterent. Sicque per sex annos a parentibus male baiulatus, ad templum sancti antistitis deportatur. Sed in oratione perdurans, restitutis membris, iuxta nominis sui proprietatem quasi novus effloruit Floridus.

28

De caeco illuminato

Clericus ex nativitate servus ipsius sanctae basilicae, per incursum Insidiatoris lumine multatus, in hospitiolo pro-
2 prio, nihil ibi laborare potens, residebat aegrotus. Tribus fere annis hanc sustinens caecitatem, aedem beati sacerdotis

27

About a paralyzed boy

A boy from the territory of Angers who was living in the house of his parents lost the use of his hands and feet through what he said was an intrusion of devilish treachery, so that his fingers bent inward and his nails stuck into his palms, and the withered nerves of his knees turned his heels
toward the back of his legs. After he had thus been carried 2
about with difficulty by his parents for six years, he was taken to the holy bishop's temple. When he had persisted in prayer his limbs were restored and, according to the nature of his name, Floridus as it were flourished anew.

28

About a blind man who received light

A cleric who from birth been a slave of this same holy basilica was deprived of light by an incursion of the Treacherous One and lay ill in his poor lodgings, unable to do any
work there. After suffering this blindness for almost three 2
years, he went to the church of the blessed bishop, and when

expetiit, ibique deprecatus consuetam misericordiam, illuminatus rediit ad propria.

29

De homine, cui fustis in manu adhaesit

Ex Turonico vero territorio servus cuiusdam, dum die dominico saepem componeret, manus eius ad lignum ipsum haerere coeperunt. At ille velociter extracta dextera, dum factum admiratur attonitus, manus ipsa cum dolore magno contrahitur, defixae sunt quoque ungulae in palmam, contractisque totis digitis dexterae, ad diversorium regreditur cum maerore.

2 Post quattuor vero annos ad basilicam sancti advenit, orationeque facta sanatus est, praedicans populis ne factum eius quis imitaretur, ne tanti diei solemnia avarus agricola macularet, ne resurrectionis sacrae ac redemptionis nostrae caeleste mysterium humanitas infirma, terrena exercens opera, dissolveret.

he had prayed there for the holy man's customary compassion, he returned home having been given light.

29

About a man whose mallet stuck in his hand

When someone's slave from the territory of Tours repaired a fence on the day of the Lord, his hands began to stick to the wooden mallet. He quickly withdrew his right hand, and while he wondered at what had happened in amazement, that hand contracted with great pain, sticking his nails into his palm; after all the fingers of his right hand had contracted, he returned grieving to his lodging.

After four years he came to the basilica of the holy man, 2
and when he had performed his prayers he was healed; after this, he preached to the people that no one should imitate what he had done, lest a greedy farmer defile the solemnities of so great a day, and lest our weak humanity, by performing worldly works, should destroy the heavenly mystery of the sacred resurrection and of our redemption.

30

De puero, cui stomachus infirmabatur

Puerulus quidam ex Albigensi, tabescente diversis morbis stomacho, cibum potumque exhorrebat; ipsum quoque quod accipere videbatur cum gravi reiciebat amaritudine. Cumque per multos dies in hoc labore cruciaretur, fide plenus desiderium habuit veniendi ad basilicam beati confes-
2 soris. In qua per triduum ieiunans et orans, die quarta accipiendi cibi desiderium capit, vinumque ore delibans, confortatus est. Dehinc gratias agens, sanus discessit.

31

De dextera mulieris arida

Mulier quaedam, et ipsa, ut aiunt, ex Andegavo veniens, quae omnibus quidem membris arida erat, sed praecipue dexteram cum digitis aridiorem ceteris artubus deferebat, ad sepulcrum sancti prosternitur. Exinde regressa, per

30

About a boy whose stomach was afflicted

A certain small boy from the region of Albi whose stomach had stopped functioning because of various illnesses felt a loathing for all food and drink, and whatever he seemed to ingest he vomited out again with great bitterness. When he had been tortured by this affliction for many days he desired, full of faith, to go to the basilica of the blessed confessor. Having fasted and prayed there for three days, he felt 2
the desire to take food on the fourth and, after moistening his lips with wine, grew stronger. Thereupon he gave thanks and left in good health.

31

About a woman's withered right hand

A certain woman who, they say, came from Angers, all of whose limbs were withered, especially her right hand whose fingers were more withered than the other limbs, prostrated herself at the tomb of the holy man. When she had returned

2 paucum tempus in atrio commorata est. Succurrente vero interventu antistitis gloriosi, vena sanguinem, cutis ruborem, corpus reliquum fortitudinem recipiens, solidatum est. Cui haec fuit causa, ut ista referret, quia die sabbati post solis occasum, qui nocti dominicae adiacebat, panem voluit conformare.

32

De muliere cuius manus in se adhaeserunt

Simile huic alia mulier fecit, cuius manus introrsum contractae et ad se invicem coniunctae adhaeserunt. Cumque doloribus maximis vexaretur, viam ingreditur, dicens: "Si ad basilicam sancti Martini abiero, protinus haec abscedet infirmitas. Confido enim quod et mihi subveniet, qui saepe talia perferentibus est misertus."

2 Haec cum ita aieret, et inceptum, ut poterat, carperet iter, manus eius illico separatae sunt, non tamen directis digitis. At vero ubi ad locum sanctum accessit et orationem fudit, protinus ablato omni dolore, solidatis digitis, manus liberas cum gratiarum extulit actione.

from there, she stayed for a short time in the forecourt. There she was restored by the intervention of the glorious 2
bishop, her veins receiving blood, her skin a rosy glow, and the rest of her body its strength. The cause of her ailment, as she said, was that she had wished to knead bread on a Sabbath day after sunset, when the night before Sunday had begun.

32

About a woman whose hands stuck together

Something similar was done by another woman whose hands were contracted inward and became stuck to each other. And because she was afflicted by severe pain she went upon the road, saying: "If I go to the basilica of the holy Martin this illness will disappear at once. For I trust that he who has often shown compassion to others suffering such illnesses will help me too."

While she was saying these things and continuing her 2
journey as well as she could, her hands were at once separated, although her fingers were not yet straightened. But when she reached the holy place and poured forth her prayer, all her pain was at once taken away, her fingers were strengthened, and she raised her freed hands in thanks.

33

De morbo caballorum

In Burdigalensi autem regione hoc anno gravis caballorum exstitit morbus. Apud villam vero Marciacensem, quae in hoc termino continetur, subdita ditionibus beati Martini, oratorium est ipsius et nomine et virtutibus consecratum.

2 Denique adveniente supradicta clade, accedebant ad oratorium, vota facientes pro equis, ut scilicet si evaderent ex ipsis decimas loco conferrent. Cumque his haec causa commodum exhiberet, addiderunt ut de clave ferrea, quae ostium oratorii recludebat, characteres caballis imponerent.
3 Quo facto, ita virtus sancti praevaluit, ut et sanarentur qui aegrotaverant, et qui non incurrerant nihil ultra perferrent.

33

About a disease of the horses

In the region of Bordeaux there was in that year a severe illness of horses. In the estate of Marsas, which is located in this territory and is under the dominion of the blessed Martin, there is a chapel consecrated by his name and deeds of power.

When this disaster came, people went to the chapel and 2
made vows on behalf of the horses, that is, if they escaped the illness, to pay tithes for them to the place. And if and when this produced good results, they added that they would brand their horses with the shape of the iron key that
locked the door of the chapel. When this had been done, 3
the power of the holy man was so strong that those horses who had been ill recovered and those who had not been afflicted suffered nothing subsequently.

34

De lue quae cum vesicis fuit

Superiore quoque anno gravissime populus Turonorum a lue valetudinaria vastabatur. Erat enim talis languor, ut apprehensus homo a febre valida, totus vesicis ac minutis pus-
2 tulis scateret. Erant autem vesicae albae cum duritia, nullam habentem mollitiem, nisi tantum dolorem nimium inferentes. Iam si data maturitate crepitantes coepissent defluere, tunc adhaerentibus corpori vestimentis, dolor validius augebatur; in qua aegritudine nihil medicorum poterat ars valere, nisi cum dominicum adfuisset auxilium.

3 Multi enim de basilica sancta benedictionem petentes, opem merebantur. Sed quid de plurimis memorare necesse est, cum id meruerint ceteri, quod unam vidimus meruisse?

4 Uxor igitur Eborini Comitis, cum ab hac lue detinetur, ita his operta vesicis est, ut neque manus, neque planta, neque ulla pars corporis eius remaneret vacua, sed et ipsi quoque oculi ab his continebantur obtecti. Cum iam in discrimine mortis haberetur, sancti sepulcri benedictionem expetiit.
5 Tunc transmissum est ei de aqua, qua beati tumulus est in Pascha Domini ablutus. Denique delibutis ex ea vulneribus, ipsa exinde potum sumpsit. Mox igitur restincta febre, decurrentibus sine dolore vesicis, sanata est.

34

About an epidemic of boils

A year earlier, too, the people of Tours were ravaged by a debilitating epidemic. For it was a kind of illness that, when a man had been seized by a violent fever, his whole body
burst out with boils and small pustules. They were hard 2
white boils, without any softness, but causing severe pain. Once they ripened, they burst and began to leak; clothes stuck to the body, and the pain increased greatly; in this illness, the art of physicians could not achieve anything, except when the Lord's help was present.

For many who sought a blessing from the holy basilica in- 3
deed deserved to be helped. Is it necessary to record the experience of the many others who merited this when we ourselves saw one woman who did so?

The wife of Count Eborinus, then, was taken by this dis- 4
ease and was so covered with these boils that neither her hand, nor her foot, nor any part of her body was clear of them, and even her eyes too were covered over by them. When already near death, she sought the blessing of the
holy tomb. She was then sent some of the water with which 5
the tomb of the blessed man had been washed at the Lord's Easter. When her wounds were sprinkled with it, she took a drink from it. Soon her fever was extinguished, her boils began to disappear without pain, and she was healed.

35

De duobus paralyticis, et uno caeco sanato

Sed quoniam multae virtutes sunt, quas orbis totus experitur, de quibus ad nos nec minima, ut opinor, pars attingit, vel illa quae vicinitas experitur indicemus.

2 Invitatus itaque Badegisilus Cenomannorum Episcopus, ad quendam locum diocesis suae venit, ad basilicam beati viri et nomine et reliquiis consecrandam. Celebrata solemnia, invocantes nomen sancti Martini, duo paralytici gressum, caecusque unus visum recepit.

36

De Augusto contracto

Augustus autem, quidam civis urbis Turonicae, dum nimio renum dolore laborat, contractis pedibus et prope ad ipsos renes redactis, pessime debilitatur; in qua infirmitate
2 per duorum annorum curricula laboravit. Deinde a suis

35

About two paralyzed men, and one healed blind man

As there are many deeds of power which the whole world experiences, of which not even a tiny part, I think, come to our knowledge, let us at least report those which are experienced in this neighborhood.

Thus Bishop Badegisil of Le Mans went to a place in his 2
diocese in which he had been asked to consecrate a basilica with the name and the relics of the blessed man. After the solemnities had been celebrated, when they had invoked the name of the holy Martin, two paralyzed men recovered their mobility and one blind man his sight.

36

About Augustus, who was paralyzed

Augustus, a citizen of the city of Tours, suffered from a severe pain in his kidneys that bent his feet toward them, gravely weakening him; he suffered from this condition for
the course of two years. Finally, on the advice of those 2

commonitus, basilicam sancti expetiit, ibique per septem dies ieiunans et orans, dempto dolore, directisque pedibus, sanus abscessit.

37

De puella muta

Hoc tempore et mulier quaedam, dum discedentibus paribus, sola tantum remansit ad telam, apparuit ei sedenti umbra taeterrima, quae arripiens illam puellulam trahere coepit. At illa vociferans et plangens, cum nullum aspiceret
2 auxilium, viriliter tamen resistere conabatur. Post decursa vero duarum aut trium horarum spatia, regressae mulieres reliquae, invenerunt eam semivivam humo iacentem, nihil penitus loqui posse. Innuebat quidem illa manu, sed nihil intelligentibus, haec muta permansit.

3 Umbra vero, quae ei apparuerat, in tantum hominibus domus illius insidiata est, ut relinquentes locum alibi commigrarent. Postea vero, duorum aut trium mensuum diebus decursis, ad basilicam puella veniens, eloquium meruit recipere. Sicque cuncta quae pertulerat ore proprio enarravit.

around him, he went to the basilica of the holy man, and when he had stayed there for seven days fasting and praying, his pain was taken away, his feet were straightened, and he left healthy.

37

About a mute maidservant

In this time too a woman, when her companions had gone away and she was left sitting alone at the weaving loom, saw a horrid shade who grabbed her and began to drag her away. She cried out and wept, for she saw no help in sight, but
tried manfully to resist. After two or three hours had passed, 2
the other women returned and found her lying half-dead on the ground, quite unable to speak. She made a sign to them with her hand, but they did not understand, and she remained mute.

The shade which had appeared to her then made so many 3
insidious assaults on the people in her home that they left the place and went to live elsewhere. Later, when two or three months had passed, the girl came to the basilica and deservedly received back her ability to speak. Thus she related all that she had suffered with her own mouth.

38

De diacono Catalaunensi caeco

Interea Catalaunensis diaconus, ut mos illi genti est, aliis matutinales gratias celebrantibus, cum potum hauriret, oculorum amissione multatur; recognoscensque reatum suum, et se non dignam proposito suo rem gessisse, suspenditur a cibo potuque, pernoctans in vigiliis, orationibusque insis-
2 tens. Interea dum haec ageret, fama, quae totum late compleverat orbem, ad eius aures usque pervenit, esse scilicet apud Turonis Martinum antistitem, ad cuius sepulcrum saepe talium infirmitatum clades depulsa quiesceret. Nec moratur diaconus, sed illico iter institui iubens, ad basilicam sanctam non dubius de virtute beati viri pervenit, ibique prostratus solo, orationi subnixus, die tertia apertis oculis lumen recepit.

3 Ego vero dum cautius nitor extorquere veritatem, cur ei haec evenissent, haec ab eo didici: "Ante hos," inquit, "septem menses, dum, commoto matutinis signo, ecclesiam peterem, obviam habui unum amicorum meorum, in cuius amplexus et oscula ruens, sciscitari coepi, si cuncta
4 domui prospera reliquisset. Tunc revocatus a via, potum cum eodem haurire coepi. Postquam autem caritatem per

38

About the blind deacon from Châlons

Meanwhile, a deacon in Châlons, as is the custom of the people there, took a drink while others celebrated the thanksgiving of matins, and was punished by the loss of the sight of his eyes; recognizing his guilt, and the fact that he had done something not worthy of his vows, he deprived himself of food and drink, spent the nights in vigils, and
prayed constantly. While he was doing this, the report that 2
had filled the whole world far and wide reached his ears, namely: that at Tours there was Bishop Martin, at whose tomb the misfortune of such illnesses was often driven away and calmed. The deacon did not hesitate but at once ordered the journey there to be set afoot; he came to the holy basilica not doubting the power of the blessed man, prostrated himself there on the floor and dedicated himself to prayer. On the third day his eyes were opened and he received light.

When I cautiously tried to extract the truth about why 3
these things had happened to him, I learned the following from him: "Six months ago," he said, "when the bell for matins had sounded and I was on my way to the church, I met one of my friends. I rushed to embrace and kiss him, and then inquired whether he had left everything going well
at home. Then, distracted from the journey, I began to have 4
a drink with him. After the demands of friendship had

pocula explevisse visum est, vale dicto abscessit. Quo abeunte, tanto oculi mei glutino coniunctis palpebris adhaeserunt, ut eos nullatenus aperire possem.

5 "Denique cum in hac infirmitate tristis abirem, desiderium habui sepulcrum beati antistitis visitare. Die autem tertio postquam veni, cum eius sepulcro assisterem, subito febris magna oculos meos arripuit. At ego ingemere vehementer coepi, et sancti auxilium fortiter deprecari; illico autem erumpens ex oculis meis sanguis noctem pepulit, diemque reduxit." Haec nobis diaconus effatus, incolumis remeavit ad propria.

39

De muliere contracta et caeca

Erat etiam mulier quaedam caeca, quae contractis retrorsum manibus ac pedibus, cum parentum solatio celebrare beatam festivitatem gloriosi antistitis expetivit.

2 Quae cum die tertia post decursam festivitatem ad domum redire cuperet, prostrata in sancta basilica orare coepit, ut ei Dominus solitam misericordiae suae opem dignaretur ostendere. Quod dum cum lacrimis peteret, illico directis manibus ac pedibus stabilitis, ad sanctum adducta sepulcrum, gratias pro accepta sospitate peregit.

seemed to be fulfilled by sharing a drink, he said goodbye and left. As he did so, my eyelids joined up and my eyes were glued so tightly shut that I could not open them at all.

"When I thereafter left in this condition and was very 5
sad, I wanted to visit the tomb of the blessed bishop. On the third day after I had come, while I was standing near his tomb, suddenly a great fever seized my eyes. And I began to groan violently and pray urgently for the holy man's aid; at once, blood burst forth from my eyes, expelled the night, and brought back the light of day." When the deacon had told this to us, he returned to his home in good health.

39

About a woman who was contracted and blind

A blind woman whose hands and feet were contracted backward came, with the help of her parents, to celebrate the blessed feast of the glorious bishop.

On the third day after the feast, when she wished to re- 2
turn home, she prostrated herself in the basilica and began to pray that the Lord might deign to grant her the aid of his customary compassion. And while she was asking this with tears, suddenly her hands were straightened and her feet were made firm; then taken to the holy tomb, she gave thanks for the health she had received.

3 Post haec rogat se deduci ad ostium, ubi prostrata iterum dicit suis: "Non hinc consurgam, nisi prius mihi oculorum lumen reddat, qui pedum manuumque restituit usum." Haec ea dicente, subito energumini torqueri se proclamant, et
4 Martini adesse praesentiam confitentur. Sed cum diabolus, qui ab initio mendax est, ad credendum minime admittatur, rebus tamen ipsis beati viri praesentia declaratur. Nam femina haec, quae paulo ante directa fuerat, nunc illuminata, adesse beatum antistitem approbavit.

40

De paralytico sanato

Modico autem succedente spatio, iacebat paralyticus unus in grabato, qui ex Biturigo plaustro devectus advene-
2 rat. Ipse etiam pari modo virtute beati antistitis visitatus surrexit incolumis; suisque redditus gressibus, parentum spectante caterva, sanus excipitur.

After this she asked to be led to the door, where she prostrated herself again and said to her companions: "I shall not arise from here before the one who restored the use of my hands and feet gives me back the light of my eyes." As she was saying this, suddenly the possessed persons shouted that they were being tortured and confessed that Martin 3
was present. Although the devil, who was a liar from the be- 4
ginning, should in no way be believed, the events themselves declared the presence of the blessed man. For this woman, who had been straightened a little earlier, was now given light, proving that the blessed bishop was present.

40

About a paralyzed man who was healed

A short while after this, there was a paralyzed man lying on a stretcher, who had come carried on a cart from Bourges.
He was visited in the same way by the power of the blessed 2
bishop and arose healthy; when he had recovered his ability to walk while a crowd of his relatives were watching, he was received by them in good health.

41

De catenis super puellam confractis

His diebus puella quaedam, iam ex libertis parentibus procreata, a filiis patroni, confracta libertate, ad iugum servitutis addicitur; unde factum est ut, illa non acquiescente iniustis dominis quidquam operis exercere, catenis et compedibus vinceretur.

2 In qua custodia dum, aliis beatam festivitatem expetentibus, resideret flens et eiulans cur non interesset beatae festivitati, subito trabs in qua pedes eius artati erant scinditur; et haec quasi iam libera, nexa quidem catenis, elapsa beatam
3 basilicam expetivit. Verum ubi primum pedes eius sacra limina contigerunt, statim confractae catenae ceciderunt a collo eius, et sic incolumitate pariter libertateque donata est.

41

About the chains on a girl that were broken

During these days a girl, whose parents had already been freed, had her liberty violated and was subjected to the yoke of servitude by the sons of her former owner; thus it happened that because she was unwilling to carry out some work for her unjust masters, she was bound with chains and shackles.

When others were on their way to the blessed feast and 2
she was sitting in this imprisoned state, weeping and lamenting because she could not attend the blessed feast, suddenly the two-part beam in which her feet were enclosed came apart; and, as though already free although still enclosed in chains, she escaped and went to the blessed basilica. But the moment her feet first touched the sacred 3
threshold, the chains broke at once and fell from her neck, and in this way she was given her freedom to move at the same time as her liberty.

42

De libro *Vitae* eius inter flammas salvato

Quid si ad ipsa beatae vitae scripta recurram? Numquid non erit admirabile, quod sacer ille huius historiae liber, circumdatus flammis, nec adustus est nec consumptus?

2 Monachus igitur Maioris monasterii ex iussu abbatis ad cellulam aliam, quasi aliquid operaturus, accessit, ac pro salute animae ac vitae correctione, librum vitae beati antistitis detulit secum. Adveniente vero nocte, in lectulo se diuturno
3 oppleto stramine collocat, librum ad caput locans. Cui dormienti apparuit vir per somnum, dicens: "Noli dormire in his paleis, sanguine enim aspersae sunt." Credo ego, ut mortalitas habet, aliquod in his facinus perpetratum, et ob hoc non pateretur vir beatus verba laudis suae inibi volutari. Facilis autem prima visio viro fuit, nec secunda commonitio valuit; tertia autem terribiliter monachum quatit.

4 At ille surgens, et ad operam diluculo progrediens, puero iubet ut paleas a lectulo detractas igne consumeret, nihil de libro commemorans. Puer vero ignarus inter paleas

42

About the book of his *Life* saved from the flames

Why should I not return to the written version of his blessed *Life*? Will it not be found amazing if that sacred book of his history, when surrounded by flames, was neither scorched nor consumed?

At the command of the abbot, a monk of Marmoutier 2
went to another cell to do something there and took with him, for the health of his soul and the correction of his life, the book of the *Life* of the blessed bishop. When night came, he lay down on a bed that had been covered long before with straw, and put the book next to his head. While he 3
was sleeping, a man appeared to him in a dream saying: "Don't sleep in this straw, for it is sprinkled with blood." I believe that, as happens with humankind, some crime had been committed upon it, and the blessed man therefore did not allow the words of his praise to lie there in it. The first vision, however, did not impress the man, nor did the second admonition fare better; the third one, however, shook him terribly.

When he arose at daybreak and went to his work, he or- 4
dered a servant to remove the straw from the bed and consume it with fire, forgetting about the book. Unknowingly, the servant took the book along with the straw, threw it all

apprehensum librum foras eiecit, et ignem accendit. Quibus in favillam redactis, cum nihil aliud nisi cineres remansissent, apparuit liber illaesus, de quo non littera, non unum, ut veritas habet, folium est consumptum. Ita virtus divina custodire dignata est alumni quodammodo proprii laudes, ut librum eius flamma non ureret, quem aculeus concupiscentiae in hoc saeculo non adussit. Sed ne cui incredibile videatur, codex ipse apud nos usque hodie retinetur.

43

De duobus pueris sanatis

Denique dum quadam vice iter ageremus, duo pueri de
custodibus equorum aegrotare coeperunt, et unus quidem
eorum valetudine, alter dysenteria laborabat. Utrumque tamen febris valida retinebat, lassatique taliter erant, ut nec
2 super dorsa caballorum possent impositi sustineri. Extrac-
tum autem pulverem, quem de sepulcro sancti abstuleram
capsella, delutumque aqua ipsis haurire praecipio. Mox
compressa febre, restinctoque dolore, uterque convaluit.

out, and lit a fire. When the straw was reduced to ashes and
nothing was left of it except ashes, the book was seen to be
undamaged, not one letter nor, in truth, one page had been
consumed. Thus the divine power deigned to protect the 5
praises of one who was in a way his own foster son, so that
the flame would not burn the book of the one whom the fiery dart of lust had not set alight in this world. But lest this
seem unbelievable to anyone, the book itself is preserved
with us up to today.

43

About two menservants who were healed

Next, once while we were traveling, two menservants of
the keepers of the horses became ill, and one of them suffered from some sickness, the other from dysentery. A severe fever, however, held both of them in its grip, and they
were so exhausted that they could not stay upright when
placed upon horseback. I took out of its little box the dust 2
that I had taken from the holy man's tomb, and ordered it to
be diluted with water and given to them to drink. Quickly,
the fever was subdued, the pain was extinguished, and they
both recovered.

44

De Mallulfo contracto

Inclita sunt enim miracula quae quotidie Dominus ad laudem antistitis sui operari dignatur, et, ut saepe testatus sum, haec a me imperito narrari non possunt; tamen, ut ipsa imperitia praestat, elucubrabuntur, ne occuli videantur.

2 Mallulfus quidam Toronici territorii civis, aegritudine saeva compressus, lectulo in suo anhelus occubuit, ex quo tabescens incommodo, manibus pedibusque contrahitur. Quinque vero annorum curricula in hac debilitate sustinuit.
3 Sexto denique anno ad sancti basilicam se efferri deposcit, in qua orationi decumbens, perdita debilitate, sospitatem meruit adipisci.

44

About Mallulf who was paralyzed

The miracles which the Lord deigns to work every day in praise of his bishop are famous and, as I have often confessed, cannot be adequately related by me, an inexperienced writer; nevertheless, inasmuch as that inexperience allows, they will be brought into the light, lest they seem to be kept concealed.

A certain Mallulf, a citizen of the territory of Tours, was 2
struck by a fierce illness; as he lay panting in his bed, wasting away from this disease, his hands and feet contracted. He
suffered this disability for the course of five years. Finally, in 3
the sixth, he asked to be carried to the basilica of the holy man, and after devoting himself to prayer there he lost his disability and deserved to recover his health.

45

De alterius manibus directis

Et ne ob hoc cuiquam quae referuntur videantur incredibilia, quia singulorum nomina non sunt in paginis praenotata, facit hoc haec causa, quia cum a sancto Dei incolumitati fuerint redditi statim recedunt, et aliquotiens ita clam
2 redeunt, ut, si dici fas est, a nemine videantur. Cumque rumor surrexit beati antistitis apparuisse virtutem, vocatis ad nos custodibus aedis, quae sunt acta cognoscimus; nomina tamen non semper ab his discimus. Illos vero plerumque nominatim scribimus, quos videre potuimus, aut quos ipsi discutimus.

3 Venit ad festivitatem vir quidam ex Biturigo manibus debilis, cuius digiti in palma erant defixi in tantum, ut putaretur vermibus scatere. Sed celebrata solemnitate, directis ambarum manuum digitis, incolumitati donatus est; viditque eum omnis populus sospitem redeuntem.

4 Cui causa debilitatis ex hoc contigit, quod saepem segetis die dominico componere voluisset.

45

About someone else whose hands were straightened

And lest the things that are related seem unbelievable to anyone because the names of individuals are not mentioned in these pages, the reason for this is that when they are rendered healthy by the holy man of God they leave immediately, and sometimes go home so secretively that, if one may
say so, they are seen by no one. When a report arises that a 2
deed of power by the blessed bishop has occurred, we call the custodians of the building to us and learn from them what has happened; but we do not always learn the names from them. Often, however, we do write down the names of those whom we ourselves were able to see or whom we questioned.

A man from Bourges came to the feast with disabled 3
hands; his fingers were stuck in the palms so deeply that one would think they crawled with worms. But when the solemnity had been celebrated, the fingers in both of his hands were straightened and he was granted his health; all the people saw him going home healthy.

The cause of his disability came from the fact that he had 4
wished to mend a fence of a field on a Sunday.

46

De muliere cuius brachium contraxerat

Mulier ex Pictavo territorio erat cuius brachium contractis nervis emarcuerat. Ad sepulcrum autem beati viri veniens, ac in oratione vigiliisque pernoctans, brachium sanum retulit; sed illico a dominis in servitio mancipata,
2 eadem incurrit. Revertitur iterum, et sanatur. Tunc venientes domini eius et eam abducere nitentes, accepto de rebus sancti pretio, quieverunt, et ita haec libertati donatur.

47

De eo qui pro debito tenebatur

Hisce diebus cum quidam pro dissolvendo debito, quod in necessitatibus suis contraxerat, interpellaretur, nec esset virtus atque facultas ad reddendum quae mutuaverat, in

46

About a woman whose arm had been paralyzed

There was a woman from the territory of Poitiers whose arm had withered through contracted nerves. When she had come to the tomb of the blessed man and spent nights in prayer and vigils, she returned with a healthy arm; but as soon as she was chained in servitude by her masters, she incurred the same affliction. She came back a second time and 2
was healed. Then her masters came and tried to abduct her; but after having received money for her from the holy man's treasury, they released her. And in this way the woman was given her liberty.

47

About a man who was imprisoned for a debt

In these days, someone was ordered to repay a debt which he had incurred in a time of hardship, and since he did not have the capacity or means to repay what he had borrowed,

2 carcere coartatur. Denique, cum videret creditor, quod ei nihil extorqueri possit, quia nihil habebat, nec esset qui ei manum misericordiae porregeret, artius eum in vincula constringit, negatoque cibo ac potu, dicebat: "Ego te faciam ad omnium documentum fame tabescere, donec omnia reddas."

3 Haec autem cum agerentur, sancti antistitis reliquiae, quae in Suessionicum pagum ferebantur, per plateam praeteribant. Auditis itaque vinctus psallentium vocibus, oravit ut eum virtus antistitis sancti visitaret, statimque dissolutis ligaminibus, nullo retinente, basilicam sanctam ingreditur. Dehinc a devotis redemptus, a nexu debiti absolutus est.

48

De caeca illuminata

Factum est etiam in una festivitatum ut mulier quae, perdito lumine, in caecitate durabat, auditis sancti viri miraculis, alacri devotione basilicam eius expeteret. Prostrata autem super aridam humum ante sepulcrum, mox ut orationem fudit, lumen recipere meruit.

he was locked up in prison. At last, when the creditor realized that he would not be able to extort anything from the man because he had nothing, and that there was no one to extend a compassionate hand to him, he bound him more tightly in chains, denied him food and drink, and said: "I shall make you waste away from hunger as an example to all, until you repay me everything." 2

While these things were happening, however, the relics of the holy man which were being brought to the region of Soissons passed by in the street. When the chained man heard the voices singing the psalms, he prayed that the power of the holy bishop might visit him. At once his chains fell apart, and he entered the holy basilica with no one holding him back. Thereafter he was redeemed by the devout and released from the obligation of his debt. 3

48

About a blind woman who was given light

It also happened during one of the feasts that a woman, who had lost her sight and been blind for some time, heard about the miracles of the holy man and went with an eager devotion to his basilica. She prostrated herself on the dry ground in front of his tomb, and as soon as she poured forth her prayer, she deserved to recover her sight.

49

De paralytico omni corpore debile

In hac solemnitate advenit puerulus oculorum obtutibus clausis, aurium aditibus oppilatis, oris officiis obstructis, manuum usibus perditis, pedum gressibus condemnatis.
2 Quid plura? Ita erat omnium membrorum usu praemortuus, ut solo spiritu palpitaret. Ut autem locum sanctum attigit, omni prorsus debilitate submota, cum gratiarum actione sanus abscessit.

50

De presbytero a frigoribus sanato

Lupus Burdigalensis urbis presbyter quodam tempore graviter a quartano typo vexabatur, ita ut accedente febre, neque cibum neque potum sumere posset. Interea advenit festivitas sancti Martini antistitis. At ille, celebratis cum reliquo clero vigiliis, mane praecedit omnes et ad basilicam sancti festinat.

49

About a crippled boy whose whole body was disabled

During this solemnity, a boy came with his eyesight obstructed, his ears blocked, his mouth hampered from speaking, his hands unusable, and his feet unfit for walking. Need
I say more? He was so near death in the use of all his limbs 2
that he could do no more than breathe. As soon as he arrived at the holy place, however, every disability was at once removed and he left healthy, giving thanks.

50

About a priest who was cured of the chills

Lupus, a priest of the city of Bordeaux, was at a certain time greatly afflicted by the quartan fever, so much so that when it came he could not take food or drink. Meanwhile the feast of the holy bishop Martin arrived. And he, after having celebrated the vigils with the other clerics, went ahead of everyone the following morning, hastening to the basilica of the holy man.

2 Dum autem properat, obvium habuit Iudaeum, et eo inquirente quo pergeret, respondit: "Typum quartanum incurri, et nunc ad basilicam sancti propero, ut me virtus eius
3 ab hac infirmitate discutiat." Qui ait: "Martinus tibi nihil proderit, quem terra opprimens terreum fecit, et tu incassum eius aedem expetis. Non enim poterit mortuus viventibus tribuere medicinam."

4 At ille despiciens verba Serpentis antiqui, abiit quo coeperat, et prostratus coram sanctis pignoribus orationem fudit, reperitque ibi duas candelulas ex cera et papyro formatas. Quibus assumptis, ad domum exhibet, illuminatisque eis, favillam papyri cum aqua munda hausit, moxque sanitatem recepit.

5 Iudaeus vero ab hac infirmitate correptus, per anni spatium ventilatus est, sed mens iniqua nec tormentis mutari potuit umquam.

While he was hurrying there, he encountered a Jew, and when this man asked him where he was going, Lupus replied: "I've come down with the quartan fever and now I'm rushing to the basilica of the holy man so that his power 2
may expel this illness from me." The Jew said: "Martin will not be of any use to you because, covered with earth, he is made into earth, and you are going to his temple for nothing. For a dead man will not be able to give a remedy to the living." 3
But Lupus, ignoring the words of the ancient Serpent, continued to where he had set out for; prostrated near the holy relics, he poured forth his prayer, and found there two candles made of wax and papyrus. He took them and brought them home; he lit them, and when he had drunk the ashes of the papyrus with clean water, he soon recovered his health. 4
The Jew, however, was seized by this same illness and agitated by it for a year, but his wicked mind could never be changed even by these torments. 5

51

De infantulo Chardegisili filio sanato

Chardegisilus vero Santonicae urbis civis, cognomento Gyso, susceptis nobis ad domum suam, invitat ad oratorium quod mater eius aedificatum beati Martini reliquiis consecravit.

2 Denique cum expleta oratione solliciti essemus si ibidem virtus sancti antistitis ostensa fuisset, respondit: "Ante annum tertium puerulus iste, filius meus quem coram cernitis, cum adhuc penderet ad matris papillam, incommode agere coepit, ac per triginta dies aut eo amplius, inter manus non sine labore deportabatur, donec ita addictus est, ut nec ma-
3 millam valeret sugere, nec alium capere cibum. Deficiente autem eo, iam die sexto postquam gravius agere coepit, deposuimus eum ante altare flentes atque eius obitum praestolantes. Ego autem dolorem non ferens, discessi a domo, mandans mulieri ut cum obiisset statim sepulturae eum locaret.

4 "Flente autem genetrice, iacuit infans usque ad vesperum. Cadente autem sole elevat vocem suam, dicens: 'Dulcissima soror, ubi es?' Sic enim genetricem, ut blanditia in-
5 fantum habet, vocitare solitus erat. At illa accurrit, dicens: 'Adsum, fili dulcissime.' Susceptoque eo in ulnis, et mox porrecta papilla, hausto lacte, protinus convaluit."

51

About the healing of Chardegisil's infant son

Chardegisilus, surnamed Gyso, a citizen of the city of Saintes, received us in his home and invited us into the chapel which his mother had built and consecrated with relics of the blessed Martin.

After we had finished our prayers, we were anxious to 2
learn if the power of the holy bishop had been manifested there. He replied: "Two years ago, that little boy whom you see here, my son, who was then still at his mother's breast, began to fall ill; for thirty days or more he was carried around with some difficulty until he was so exhausted that that he
could not suck the breast or take in any other food. When 3
he became unconscious on the sixth day after his illness had worsened, we put him in front of the altar, weeping and expecting him to die. I, however, not being able to bear the grief, left the house and commanded my wife to bury him as soon as he died.

"While his mother wept, the infant lay there until the 4
evening. When the sun went down however, he raised his voice and said: 'Dearest sister, where are you?' For, in his charming childish manner, he was accustomed to address
his mother in this way. Running toward him, she said: 'Here 5
I am, dearest son.' She took him into her arms and after he had been given the breast and drunk milk, he soon recovered."

52

De clerico dysenterico

His diebus quando nobis haec relata sunt, unus clericorum nostrorum ventris fluxum incurrit cum febre, ac nimiam defectionem stomachi; et quae proiciebat per infe-
2 riorem partem, pars maxima cruor erat. Et ea causa eum magis affecerat, quia cibum quem accipiebat, invalescente nausea, statim reiciebat. Sed protinus, ut de sepulcri pulvere bibit, omni infirmitate dempta, firmatus est.

53

De appenso absoluto. Item de alio

Sed nec hoc silendum putavi, quod saepius in mortem praecipites, extensa pietatis dextera, sublevavit. Denique Genitoris civis nostri servus, a iudice pro furti scelere comprehensus, patibulo adiudicatur. Qui cum duceretur, nomen

52

About a cleric who had dysentery

In the days that these things were related to us, one of our
clerics began to suffer from diarrhea with fever and a most
serious malfunctioning of the stomach; and what he dis-
charged from his lower parts was mostly blood. What af- 2
flicted him the most was that when he did take food he
threw it up immediately through the onset of nausea. But as
soon as he drank some <diluted> dust from the tomb, his illness was completely taken away, and he was restored.

53

About a hanged man who was released. And another one as well

But I thought I should not be silent either about how the holy confessor has often come to the aid of those condemned to death by extending his compassionate right hand. Thus a slave of our fellow-citizen Genitor was arrested by the judge for theft and condemned to the gallows. While he was being led there he kept invoking the name

beati antistitis invocabat, dicens: "Libera me, sancte confes-
2 sor Martine, ab imminente periculo!" Appensus igitur ac so-
lus relictus, commoto subito vento, audivit vocem dicentem: "Liberemus eum." Et ecce a quattuor partibus caeli concussus stipes qui hominem sustentabat, cum immense caespite in modum arboris eradicatae a terra divellitur, et sic homo morti deditus redivivus erigitur.

3 Alius quoque qui multa fecerat scelera et, compunctus a Deo, paenitentiam pro malis quae gesserat agebat, apprehensus sine causa, simili nece damnatur, invocans semper sancti confessoris auxilium. Qui cum appensus fuisset, disruptis vinculis illaesus ad terram ruit. Sed mala mens homi-
4 num iterum appendit quem Deus eripuit. Quod audiens
abba monasterii a loco proximi, currit ad comitem, rogaturus pro eo, erat enim longe exinde quasi tribus milibus, obtentaque cum eo rei huius vita, rediit vivumque repperit. Quo a suspendio deposito, adduxit ad monasterium profitentem atque dicentem: "Quia sensi virtutem sancti Martini qui me eripuit."

of the blessed bishop, saying: "Rescue me, holy confessor
Martin, from the danger that hangs over me!" When he had 2
been hanged and left alone, therefore, a wind suddenly arose and he heard a voice saying: "Let us free him." And, behold, the stake from which the man hung was struck by wind from the four quarters of the sky and torn from the earth with a large clump of turf like an uprooted tree; in this manner the man who had been delivered to death was raised to life again.

Another man who had committed many crimes and, con- 3
science-stricken by God, was doing penance for the evils which he had caused, was seized without reason; condemned to a similar death, he kept invoking the aid of the holy confessor. When this man had been hanged, the ropes broke and he fell unhurt to the ground. But the wickedness of the human mind again hanged the one whom God rescued. When the abbot of the nearby monastery heard this, 4
he rushed to the count to request mercy for him (it was about three miles), and when he had obtained the life of the guilty man from him, returned to find him alive. When he had taken him off the gallows, he led the man to the monastery, who kept proclaiming and saying: "I felt the power of the holy Martin who rescued me."

54

De muto sanato

Erat enim homo infra terminum ipsius Turonicae urbis, ex vico montis Laudiacensis, et homo ille erat natura simplex, nexus vinculo coniugali. Cui cum coniuge quiescenti nocte media pavor exoritur, exterritusque ac de lectulo exsiliens, dum per hospitiolum suum vagatur trepidus, vocis
2 perdidit famulatum. Nec moratus, indicat nutu coniugi ut eum ad sancti basilicam exhiberet. Qui adveniens, dum ante beatum sepulcrum per sex assidue decubat menses in oratione, absoluta lingua, eloquium sicut antea habuerat, recipere meruit virtute beati antistitis.

55

De muliere cuius manus contraxerat

Mulier Transligeritana die dominico cum operam exerceret, quam in die illo fieri Patrum inhibet auctoritas, manus eius contracta diriguit, digitique in palmam defixi sunt.

54

About a mute man who was healed

There was a man from the village of Montlouis in the territory of this city of Tours, who was of a simple nature and bound by the laws of marriage. While sleeping alongside his wife, a fright came over him in the middle of the night; he jumped out of his bed terrified, wandered around his hut, trembling with fear, and lost the use of his voice. Immedi- 2
ately, he indicated to his wife by nodding that she should bring him to the basilica of the holy man. When he had come there and devoted himself assiduously for six months to prayer in front of the blessed tomb, his tongue was released and through the power of the blessed bishop he deserved to receive the speech he had previously had.

55

About a woman whose hand had been paralyzed

When a woman from Across-the-Loire worked on the day of the Lord, which the authority of the Church Fathers prohibits, her hand contracted and stiffened and her fingers

2 Quae dum doloribus cruciaretur, ad sanctam aedem confessoris accessit, vovitque ut, si ab hac sanaretur infirmitate, nullum opus deinceps in hac dominicae resurrectionis ageret die quod illi diei esset incongruum, statimque amotis digitis a palma, manu directa discessit.

56

De muliere contracta et caeca

Magna est enim pietas confessoris, quae sic arguit insipientes, ut ponens vitium ante oculos, reddat in posterum emendatos.

2 Pro hac causa mulier alia debilitatur. Nam cum die Sabbati post solis occasum, quod adiacet resurrectionis dominicae nocti, panem furno collocaret, brachium eius dolore quatitur. Post iniectum alium et tertium panem, manus invita lignum quod tenebat coepit astringere. Intelligensque mulier divinae se virtutis iudicio condemnari, velociter palam quam tenebat abiecit; nihilominus non effu-
3 gere potuit poenam. Nam ita manus eius cum gravi dolore contractae sunt, ut ungulae in ipsa defigerentur palma.

became stuck in its palm. Because she was tormented by pain, she came to the holy church of the confessor, and vowed that if she were cured of this infirmity, she would thereafter not do any work on this day of the Lord's resurrection that would be inappropriate to it; at once her fingers were loosened from her palm and she departed with a straightened hand. 2

56

About a paralyzed and blind woman

Great is the confessor's compassion, censuring the foolish in such a way that by putting their vices before their eyes, it makes them better persons thereafter.

For the same reason, another woman too became dis- 2
abled. For when she put a loaf of bread in the oven after sunset on the Sabbath day, when the night of the Lord's resurrection begins, her arm was struck with pain. After having put in another loaf and a third one, her hand began to clench, against her will, around the wooden spade she was holding. Understanding that she was being condemned by a judgment of divine power, the woman quickly threw away the spade she was holding; nevertheless, she could not escape her punishment. For her hands were so contracted 3
with the severe pain that her nails became fixed in the palm.

Ex hoc nullius medici se credens posse fomento sanari, beati basilicam expetivit, ibique fideliter orans, directis manibus, sanata discessit; vovitque ut per singulos menses, una hebdomada ad sanctum templum veniens, debeat Deo et beato antistiti deservire. Quod per unum annum eam observasse manifestissime cognitum est.

4 Post annum vero intermissa unius mensis hebdomada, non accessit ad sanctam basilicam. Sedenti vero in hospitiolo suo oculus ei a dolore transfigitur; illum autem comprimens perdidit, et alius quoque dolore coepit extemplo. In unius horae momento caeca ab oculis ambobus efficitur.
5 Nec mora, confessa culpam ad praesidia nota confugit, ibique orationem suppliciter fundens ac paenitentiam pro negligentia compuncte agens, die octava, sanguine ab oculis profluente, illuminata est.

57

De caeco illuminato

Hominis cuiusdam oculi crassa caliginis nube contecti, quodam glutino coniunctis palpebris fuerant obserati, et quod supererat viro, magnis doloribus tenebatur. Quid plura?

Believing that she could not be healed by any doctor's poultice, she went to the basilica of the blessed one, prayed there full of faith, and departed healed, with straightened hands; and she vowed that she would come to the holy temple one week each month to serve God and the blessed bishop. That she fulfilled this vow for a year is well known.

After a year, however, she missed a week in one month, 4
not coming to the holy basilica. But as she was sitting in her
hut her eye was pierced by pain; pressing it, she lost it, and
the other one at once also began to hurt. In the space of one
hour she was made blind in both eyes. At once confessing 5
her guilt, she turned to the help she knew and there, pouring forth a humble prayer and contritely doing penance for her negligence, she was given light on the eighth day, blood flowing from her eyes.

57

About a blind man who was given light

A man's eyes were covered with a thick cloud of darkness, his closed eyelids stuck together by some glutinous substance, and the rest of his body held fast by great pain. What more is there to say?

2 Festivitatem sancti cum reliquis devotus expetiit, attente exorans ut a virtute beati antistitis visitari mereretur in die solemnitatis. Sed sacra solemnia praevenit potentia confessoris, ostendens se adesse populis, cum tenebras pepulit lumenque refudit. Igitur ante diem tertium festivitatis, hoc in atrio quod apsidam corporis ambit, eo orante, subito aperti
3 sunt oculi eius, et aspiciens lucem videre meruit. Quod cum his qui aderant cum gratiarum actione narraret, dictum est ei ut silens potius orationem funderet, ut coeptam virtutem beatus antistes celerius adimpleret. Tunc prostratus terrae, cum in lacrimas prorupisset, firmatis oculis, a solo incolumis surrexit.

58

De paralytico et duobus caecis

Post diem vero tertium huius solemnitatis, erat quidam paralyticus hoc in loco exorans, cui debilitas hac de causa, ut ipse enarravit, evenerat, quia dum esset puer parvulus, et cum reliquis pastoribus pecorum in campo custodiam gereret, super fontem quendam obdormivit, aliis quoque ad

He came to the feast of the holy man devoutly with the 2
rest, praying earnestly that he might deserve to be visited by the power of the blessed confessor upon the day of the feast. But the power of the confessor preceded the sacred solemnities, showing its presence to the people when it expelled the darkness and infused light. Thus two days before the feast, while this man was praying in the courtyard surrounding the apse that contains the body, suddenly his eyes were
opened and, looking, he deserved to see some light. When 3
he made this known with thanksgiving to those around him, he was told that he should instead go on praying in silence so that the blessed bishop might quickly complete the deed of power he had begun. Then, after he had prostrated himself on the ground and had burst forth in tears, his eyes were restored and he got up from the floor healthy.

58

About a paralytic and two blind men

On the third day after this solemnity, a paralyzed man was praying in this place; the cause of his disability, he himself told us, was that when he was a small boy, looking after the cattle in the field with the other herdsmen, he had remained there alone when the others had departed at noon

2 meridiem recedentibus, hic solus remansit. Tandemque relictus a somno, dum consurgere nititur, doloribus coartatur. Mox membris omnibus contractus, ac retortis extrorsum brachiis, contractis in poplite nervis, calcanei ad crura deductis, cum nulla esset virtus eundi, immensae ab eo lacrimae cum magnis vocibus effluebant. Reversis autem sociis ad visenda pecora, hic eiulans invenitur.

3 Dehinc parentum ulnis ablatus, domui restituitur. Post dies vero paucos cum parumper a doloribus laxaretur, mendicis quibusdam deputatus est, cum quibus per decem aut eo amplius annos regiones urbesque circumiens, ad hanc quoque festivitatem adveniens, membris omnibus solidatus est. Duo eadem die illuminati caeci, duo energumeni ad sepulcrum antistitis emundati sunt.

59

De puero febricitante

Adolescens quidam ex nostris, nocturnis febribus vexabatur in tantum, ut ab hora diei octava usque in crastinum secunda diei hora, nullam aestuandi quietem posset accipere. Erat enim ei et horribilis omnis cibus, nec quidquam unde comfortaretur accipiebat. Dolor etiam saevus membra omnia quatiebat, sed et pallor genas obsederat.

and had fallen asleep at a certain spring. When he finally 2
awoke and tried to stand up, he was constricted by pain. Soon all his limbs contracted, his arms turned outward, the nerves in his knees contracted, and his feet were bent toward his calves; because he could not walk, he uttered great cries and shed many tears. When his companions returned to watch over the cattle, they found him wailing.

Carried away from there in the arms of his relatives, he 3
was brought home. After a few days, when the pains had eased a bit, he was given away to certain beggars with whom he traveled around the regions and cities for ten or more years, until he came to this feast and was restored in all his limbs. That same day, two blind men were given light and two possessed persons were cleansed at the bishop's tomb.

59

About a boy who had a fever

A young boy-servant of ours was so greatly afflicted by nightly fevers that from the eighth hour of the day until the second hour of the next day, he could not find relief from their raging heat. All food disgusted him and he could take in nothing that might nourish him. A savage pain, too, shook his whole body and pallor covered his cheeks.

2 Dumque sic inter manus ferretur parentum ut aeger, aegre obtinere potui ut ad sepulcrum beati antistitis deferretur. Tandem allatus, ut de sacrosancto tumuli pulvere diluto potum sumpsit, mox ab benedictione, fugato universo dolore, febris exstincta est. Nec mora, secreta digestionum loca puer expetit, deducitur in angulo ventris purgandi gratia.

3 Verum ubi voluntatem alvi flatu impellente profudit, statim duo vermes ab eo in modum serpentum processerunt, qui ita moveri oculis hominum videbantur, ut vivere putarentur. His igitur ab eo digestis, illico ad plenum sanatus est, et cibum, ut solitus erat, hausit et potum, ruborque genis, fugato pallore, redditur, membrisque omnibus solidatur.

60

De his quae in meo itinere gesta sunt

Opportunitatis causa nuper exstiterat ut ad visitandam genitricem meam in territorium Cavillonensis urbis adirem. Sed metuens superventuras infirmitates, de hoc pulvere, id

While he was being carried about as an ill person by his parents, I was, with some difficulty, able to arrange for him to be carried to the tomb of the blessed bishop. When he had at last been conveyed there and had taken a drink of diluted holy dust of the tomb, at once after this blessing, all pain was put to flight and the fever was extinguished. Immediately, the boy sought a privy to relieve his digestive system, and he was led to a corner to empty his bowels. 2

But when he had accomplished the wish of his bowels with a blast of air, at once two worms like serpents came forth from him, which to men's eyes seemed to move in such a way that they might be thought to be alive. When these had been expelled by him, he was at once fully cured, taking food and drink as he had been accustomed to do; his pallor was dispelled, rosiness returned to his cheeks, and his whole body was restored. 3

60

About the things that were done during my journey

Recently, there was an occasion for me to go to the city of Châlons-sur-Saône to visit my mother. Fearing that illnesses might come upon us, I ventured to remove and take with me some of this dust, that is, from the tomb of

est sepulcri beati antistitis, auferre et mecum deferre praesumpsi, scilicet ut cum quempiam nostrorum morbus aliquis invasisset, virtus sancti ope consuetudinaria subveni-
2 ret. Igitur, ubi ad matrem accessi, protinus unum puerum febris cum dysenteria arripit, atterit et consumit, ita ut negato usu vescendi, de solis febribus aleretur. Die tertia cum haec agerentur et ad me perlatum fuisset, delutum pulverem ad bibendum porrigo moribundo, statimque, fugata febre sedatoque dolore, convaluit.

3 His diebus a Verano Antistite audivi, quod quodam tempore dum typi quartani aestu ureretur, expetita beati Martini basilica, quae in loco illo erat, celebrata vigilia sanatus fuit. Nos vero ex hoc itinere Arvernum venientes, reperimus Avitum Episcopum a tertiano typo ita graviter concuti, ut etiam si aliquid cibi sumeret, statim reiceret; sed de hoc pignore potu sumpto, calcata febre roboratus est.

4 Duos ex pueris nostris valetudinaria febris invaserat, omnesque membrorum iuncturas, ut ex hoc contagio plerumque assolet, dolor saevus obsederat; sed ab hac benedictione potati, sanati sunt.

5 Ego ipse in hoc itinere cum dolorem dentium graviter sustinerem, et iam non solum ipsi dentes, sed omne caput venarum pulsibus, ac dolorum spiculis figeretur, ac tempora valide prosilirent; hoc praesidium expetii et mox, dolore depresso, convalui.

the blessed bishop, so that when some disease invaded any of our men, the power of the holy man would help with its usual protection. And indeed when I had reached my 2
mother, a fever with dysentery at once seized one of the servants and so weakened and consumed him that the use of food was denied to him and he was nourished solely by his fevers. On the third day of this illness, when he had been carried to me, I gave the boy, who on the verge of death, the diluted dust to drink, and at once the fever was put to flight, the pain eased, and he recovered.

In these days I heard from Bishop Veranus that once, 3
when he had suffered the heat of quartan fever, he had gone to the basilica of the blessed Martin in that place, celebrated vigils, and been cured. When we returned from this journey and came to Clermont we found Bishop Avitus being gravely shaken by the tertian fever, so much so that even if he did take some food he immediately vomited it up; but when he had taken some of the drink from this relic, the fever was suppressed, and he was restored.

A debilitating fever had invaded two of our servants and, 4
as this contagion usually does, had lodged a savage pain in all the joints of the limbs; but after they had drunk from this blessing, they were cured.

I myself suffered gravely from a toothache during this 5
journey, and then not only those teeth but my whole head was pierced by pulsing veins and sharp pains, and my temples throbbed heavily; when I sought this protection, the pain was subdued at once and I recovered.

6 O theriacam inenarrabilem! O pigmentum ineffabile! O
antidotum laudabile! O purgatorium, ut ita dicam, caeleste,
quod medicorum vincit argutias, aromatum suavitates supe-
7 rat, unguentorumque omnium robora supercrescit! Quod
mundat ventrem ut agridium, pulmonem ut hyssopus, ipsumque caput purgat ut pyretrum! Etiam non solum membra debilia solidat, sed, quod his omnibus maius est, ipsas illas conscientiarum maculas abstergit ac levigat!

8 Sufficiant ergo haec huic libello quae indita sunt. Tamen
si adhuc miracula cernere meremur, placet ea alteri libello
inseri, ut ea quae ostenduntur, non occuli sed magis vocibus
9 debeant propalari. De cetero vero virtutem eius deposcimus, ut qui talia praestat ex tumulo, nos, iam a peccatis Deo
mortuos, suscitare dignetur mortis istius de sepulcro, ut in
illo resurrectionis carnis nostrae tempore nobis obtineat in-
dulgentiam, cum ille provehetur ad coronam.

O indescribable remedy! O ineffable balm! O praisewor- 6
thy antidote! O heavenly purgative, so to speak, that beats
the skill of physicians, outdoes the fragrances of herbs, and
surpasses the strength of all ointments! It cleanses the stom- 7
ach like scammony, the lungs like hyssop, and purifies the
head itself like pyrethrum! Not only does it restore disabled
limbs but—what is greater than all these things—it wipes
away and eases the very stains of one's conscience!

Let the facts which have been included be enough for 8
this book. However, if we deserve to see miracles after this,
let them be inserted in another book, so that what is shown
can be not hidden but instead be disseminated by speech.
Finally, we ask for his power: that he who accomplishes such 9
things from his tomb, may deign to revive us, already dead
to God through our sins, from the tomb of that death, so
that at the time of the resurrection of our flesh he may obtain mercy for us when he is crowned.

LIBER QUARTUS

Prologus

Saluberrimo nos hortatu propheta admonet, dicens: "Honorandi sunt amici tui, Deus" [Psalms 139:17]. Nihilominus et in alio psalmo: "Qui timentes Dominum magnificat, beatitudine copulatur domus aeternae" [Psalms 15:4]. Ergo perspicue patet intellectui humano, quod admoneantur quique non solum immunes crimine, verumetiam noxialis criminis malo dediti, cultum reverenter reddere amicis Dei.

2 Quae res non solum in praesenti saeculo tribuit beneficium, verum etiam praestat et refrigerium in futuro. Nam cum saepe videamus virtutum insignia prodire de tumulis beatorum, non immerito commovemur debitam eis honoris reverentiam impendere, a quibus non desistimus infirmitatum remedia flagitare. Quorum precibus et ipsam peccaminum remissionem non dubitamus adipisci et non modo hanc mereri, verum ab infernalibus suppliciis eorum inter-
3 ventu salvari. Confidimus enim quod sicut hic morborum genera resecant, illic saevas tormentorum poenas avertant; et sicut hic mitigant febres corporeas, illic restingant aeternas; et quomodo hic luridae leprae ulcera sordentia mundant, illic delictorum maculas mederi suo interventu obtineant; ac sicut hic mortuorum cadavera ad vitam resuscitant,

BOOK 4

Prologue

The prophet admonishes us with most healthy advice when he says: "Your friends are to be honored, O God." Likewise in another psalm: "He who praises the men who fear the Lord is united with the blessed state of the eternal home." Hence it is abundantly clear to human understanding that not only those who are immune from crime, but also those given over to the evil of harmful crime, are being admonished to honor the friends of God reverently.

Doing this not only brings benefits in the present life, 2
but also grants solace in the future one. For since we often see the signs of the acts of power coming forth from the tombs of the blessed, we are rightfully inclined to show them the reverence of honor that is owed to those whom we do not cease to ask for remedies for our ills. By their prayers, we do not doubt that we will also obtain even the remission of our sins, and will not only deserve this, but even be saved
from the torments of hell by their intercession. For we are 3
confident that just as they remove all kinds of diseases here, they will avert the brutal punishment of tortures there; just as they diminish bodily fevers here, they will put out eternal ones there; just as they cleanse the filthy sores of pale leprosy here, there they will obtain the healing of the stains of sin by their intervention; and just as they revive the bodies of the dead to life here, there they will extend their hand

illic peccato sepultos ex Acherontis stagnis manu iniecta erutos vitae aeternae restituant.

4 Quocirca dum unusquisque laetificatur in gaudio proprio sub patrono, tunc impensius honorem reddit debitum, cum se senserit ab infirmitate qua detinebatur eius virtute mundatum, sicut nunc de beato ac toto orbi peculiare patrono Martino antistite et nos et innumeri populi sunt experti. Et utinam ignavia mentis nostrae permitteret eum sic venerari sicut decet amicum Dei qui tantis nos morborum oppressos generibus plerumque restituit sanitati.

I

De dolore ventris mei

Nuperrimo autem tempore ventris dolorem incurri. Et licet non usquequaque dabat solutionem, tamen doloris malum in illis intraneorum flexuosis recessibus vagabatur. Adhibui, fateor, saepius balneas atque res calidas super ipsas alvi torturas ligari faciebam, sed nihil mederi poterant infirmitati.

2 Sexta etenim dies illuxerat, quod magis ac magis dolor invalescebat, cum mihi venit in memoriam, ante paucos annos, sicut in libro secundo huius operis continetur scriptum,

and rescue from Acheron's swamps those buried by sin and restore them to eternal life.

4 Therefore, while each person enjoys delighting in his own patron saint, he more eagerly shows him due reverence when he feels himself cleansed by his power of an illness that had been afflicting him, as now we ourselves and countless people have experienced through the blessed bishop Martin, the special patron of the whole world. And let the weakness of our mind allow him to be venerated by us as befits a friend of God who often restores us to health after being oppressed by so many kinds of illnesses.

I

About my stomach ache

Very recently, I suffered a stomach ache. And although it did not cause constant diarrhea, a painful discomfort nevertheless kept ranging in the winding cavities of my intestines. I confess that I bathed many times and bound warm objects on top of those tortures in my stomach, but none of these could cure the illness.

It was when the sixth day had dawned, and the pain was 2
getting worse and worse, that I remembered that, as is written in the second book of this work, I had been cured of this ailment a few years ago by the power of the holy man. Boldly,

me ab hoc dolore sancti virtute fuisse sanatum. Accessi temerarius ad locum sepulcri, proiectusque solo orationem fudi, atque secretius a pendentibus velis unum sub vestimento iniectum filum, crucis ab hoc signaculum in alvo depinxi. Protinus dolore sedato, sanus abscessi.

2

De lingua et labiis meis

Quodam vero tempore lingua mihi graviter irriguerat, ita ut plerumque dum loqui vellem, balbutire me faceret, quod non mihi sine improperio erat. Accessi autem ad tumulum sancti ac per lignum cancelli linguam impeditam traxi. Protinus tumore compresso convalui. Intumuerat enim valde, et totum palati impleverat antrum.

2 Deinde post diem tertium labium mihi exsilire graviter coepit. Accessi iterum quaerere sospitatem ad tumulum: tactuque labio a dependentibus velis, protinus stetit venae pulsus. Et credo mihi haec ex abundantia sanguinis evenisse; non tamen sanguinem minuere studui, propter sancti virtutem. Nullam tamen mihi ultra molestiam fecit haec causa.

I approached the place of the tomb and poured forth a prayer while prostrated on the floor. Then I covertly took a thread from the cloths hanging over the tomb, put it under my clothes and made the sign of the cross with it over my stomach. At once, the pain stopped and I left healthy.

2

About my tongue and lips

Once my tongue became so gravely stiffened that often, when I wished to speak, it made me stammer, which I found embarrassing. I went to the tomb of the holy man, however, and ran the impeded tongue along the wood of the balustrade. At once, the swelling was subdued and I recovered. It had been greatly swollen and had filled the whole cavity of my palate.

Three days thereafter, my lip began to throb painfully. 2
Again I went to the tomb to seek health, and at once, when I touched my lip to the hanging cloths, the pulsing of the vein stopped. I believe this happened to me on account of a surfeit of blood; nevertheless I did not trouble to have myself bled, on account of my respect for the holy man's power. This ailment never bothered me again.

3

De puero a febre sanato

Denique puerulus parvulus gravabatur a febre et, exesis membris, cum nullum acciperet cibum, in hoc erat ut spiritum exhalaret.

2 Cucurrit ad me pater cum lacrimis, cui ego indicavi ut, delatum ad basilicam, nocte tota vigilaret. Quod cum fecisset, statim puerum sanum per virtutem antistitis sancti recepit.

4

De contracto, et caeca, et tribus energuminis

Ad festivitatem vero, quae mense quinto celebratur, adveniens quidam cuius digiti in palma contraxerant, oratione facta, digitis directis, abscessit.

2 Mulier vero caeca post octo annos, prostrata solo coram sancti sepulcro, illuminatis oculis, repedavit in locum suum.

3 Tres tunc inergumeni sancti virtute mundati sunt.

3

About a boy who was cured of a fever

A small boy was afflicted by a fever; his body was being eaten up, as he was not taking any nourishment, and he was about to breathe out his spirit.

His father came running to me in tears, and I told him to 2
carry the child to the basilica and to watch there all night long. When he had done this, he at once got his boy back, cured through the power of the holy bishop.

4

About a paralyzed man and a blind woman and three possessed persons

At the feast which is celebrated in the fifth month, someone came whose fingers had contracted into his palm; when he had prayed, his fingers were straightened and he left.

When a woman who had been blind for eight years had 2
prostrated herself on the floor near the tomb of the holy man, her eyes were given light and she returned to her own place.

Three possessed persons were then cleansed by the 3
power of the holy man.

5

De servo Theodulfi

Eo anno, id est Childeberthi Regis tertio decimo, ad festivitatem quae de beato eius transitu celebratur, venit servus Theodulfi civis Turonici, custos suillae; dum nocte circa gregem creditum excubaret, ne quiddam ex eo bestia raperet, aut fraus furis auferret, oculis subita caligine interfusis, lu-
2 men amisit. Qui per sex annos in caecitate durans ad hanc festivitatem advenit. Post tertium vero diem, sancti virtute illuminatus, a domino est dimissus ingenuus.

6

De multis infirmitatibus sanatis

Anno quoque quarto decimo regis supradicti, adveniente solemnitate sancti, duodecim paralytici directi, tres caeci illuminati, quinque inergumini emundati sunt.

5

About Theodulf's slave

That year, King Childebert's thirteenth, to the feast which celebrates the man's blessed passing came a slave who was a swineherd and belonged to Theodulf, a citizen of Tours; while he was on watch at night close to the herd assigned to him, to prevent a wild animal taking one of them or a thief from carrying one off covertly, a sudden darkness
came over his eyes and he lost his sight. After he had been 2
blind for six years, he came to this feast. Three days later, after he had been given light by the power of the holy man, he was let go by his master, a free man.

6

About many illnesses that were cured

In the fourteenth year of the above-mentioned King [Childebert], when the holy man's feast came, twelve paralytics were straightened, three blind men were given light, and five possessed persons were cleansed.

2 Adfuit huic festivitati et Aredius, Lemovicinae urbis abba, cuius in superioribus libellis meminimus, per quem Dominus paralyticam unam, quae per octo annos carrucae superposita in atrio beati confessoris decubuerat, directis vestigiis, restauravit. Nam adserebat ipse vir Dei sensisse se quasi beati Martini manum, cum infirma membra imposito signo crucis tactu salutari palparet.

3 Advenerat etiam in hac festivitate et Florentianus maior cum Romulfo palatii comite. Quibus non parva admiratio fuit de gloria confessoris, per quem Dominus talia tunc miracula dignatus est operari.

7

De uva apud Galliciam

Et quia Florentiani Maioris memoriam fecimus, quid ab eo didicerim nefas puto taceri. Tempore quodam causa legationis Galliciam adiit, atque ad Mironis Regis praesentiam accedens, negotia patefecit iniuncta. Erat enim eo tempore Miro Rex in civitate illa, qua decessor eius basilicam sancti Martini aedificaverat, sicut in libro primo huius operis ex-
2 posuimus. Ante huius aedis porticum vitium camera extensa

Also present at this feast was Aredius, abbot in the city of Limoges, whom we mentioned in earlier books; through him the Lord restored a paralyzed woman, who for eight years had been lying on a cart in the forecourt of the blessed confessor, by straightening her feet. The man of God himself claimed that he had felt as it were the blessed Martin's hand when, after making the sign of the cross, he stroked the diseased limbs with a healing touch. 2

Florentianus, mayor of the royal household, had also come to this feast, as well as Romulf, count of the palace. They were full of admiration for the glory of the confessor, through whom the Lord worked such great miracles at that time. 3

7

About a cluster of grapes in Galicia

And since we have mentioned Mayor Florentianus, I think it would be wrong to be silent about what I learned from him. He went one time as a legate to Galicia, and coming into the presence of King Miro, he made known the mission enjoined on him. At that time King Miro was in the city in which his predecessor had built a basilica for the holy Martin, as we have recounted in the first book of this work.
Along the arcade leading to this building was a long pergola 2

per traduces dependentibus uvis quasi picta vernabat. Sub hac enim erat semita quae ad sacrae aedis valvas peditem deducebat. Cumque rex sub hac praeteriens orationis gratia hoc templum adiret, dixit suis: "Cavete, ne contingatis unum ex his botrionibus, ne forsitan offensam sancti antistitis incurratis. Omnia enim quae in hoc habentur atrio ipsi sacrata sunt."

3 Hoc audiens unus puerorum, ait intra se: "Utrum sint haec huic sancto sacrata an non, ignoro. Unum scio, quod deliberatio animi mei est ab his vesci." Et statim, iniecta manu, caudam botrionis coepit incidere, protinusque dextera eius adhaerens camerae, arente lacerto, diriguit. Erat enim mimus regis, qui ei per verba iocularia laetitiam erat solitus excitare, sed non ei adiuvit cachinnus aliquis, neque
4 praestigium artis suae. Sed cogente dolore, voces dare coepit ac dicere: "Succurrite, viri, misero! Subvenite oppresso! Relevate appensum! Et sancti antistitis Martini virtutem pro me deprecamini, qui tali exitu crucior, tali plaga affligor, tali incisione disiungor!" Egressus quoque rex, cum rem quae acta fuerat didicisset, tanto furore contra puerum est accensus ut ei manus velit abscidere si a suis prohibitus non fuisset.

5 Dicentibus tamen praeterea famulis: "Noli, o rex, iudicio Dei tuam adiungere ultionem, ne forte iniuriam quam minaris puero, in te retorqueas." Tunc ille compunctus corde,

covered by a vine with grapes hanging on its branches, flourishing as though it were painted. Under this pergola was a path that led the pedestrian to the doors of the holy building. And as the king was passing under this while going to this temple to pray, he said to his companions: "Be careful that you do not touch any of these clusters of grapes lest perhaps you incur the displeasure of the holy bishop. For everything here in this courtyard is consecrated to him."

Hearing this, one of his servants said to himself: 3
"Whether or not these grapes are consecrated to this holy man or not I do not know. What I do know is that I definitely want to eat some of them." And he immediately put his hand into them and began to break the stem of a cluster; but his right hand at once stiffened up and stuck to the pergola, and the muscles of his upper arm withered. He was the king's jester, who was accustomed to entertain him with jokes, but he could not be helped by any laughter or by the
tricks of his art. In his pain, he began shouting and saying: 4
"Gentlemen! Hurry to come to the rescue of a poor wretch! Help one who is oppressed! Relieve me of my burden! And implore the power of the holy bishop Martin on my behalf to visit me, tormented as I am by such a catastrophe, afflicted with such a blow, and being dismembered!" When the king had come out and learned about what had happened, he became enflamed with so great a rage toward the servant that he would have cut off his hand if he had not been restrained by his retinue.

However, his servants also said: "Do not wish to add your 5
revenge to the judgment of God, O king, lest perhaps the injury with which you threaten the servant turn back upon you." The king's heart was pierced by this, and entering

ingressus basilicam, prostratus coram sancto altari, cum lacrimis preces fudit ad Dominum. Nec ante a pavimento surrexit quam flumen oculorum huius paginam delicti deleret.

6 Quo a vinculo quo nexus fuerat absoluto, ac in basilicam ingresso, rex elevatur a solo, et sic recipiens incolumem famulum palatium repetivit. Testabatur autem maior praefatus haec se ab ipsius regis relatione, sicut actum narravimus, cognovisse. Sic enim gloriosus pontifex suam illustrat urbem miraculis, ut deesse non sentiatur alienis.

8

De basilica sancti apud urbem Sanctonicam

Praesenti vero anno, Palladius Sanctonicae urbis episcopus, huius sancti confessoris reliquias petiit. Construxerat enim in eius honore basilicam, quam his pignoribus consecravit, meruitque ibi suscipere miracula quae saepius urbs
2 propria habet experta. Nam post duorum aut trium mensuum curricula, litteras eius accepi, in quibus indicavit tres paralyticos contractis pedibus advenisse, qui statim ut in

the church he prostrated himself in front of the holy altar and poured forth prayers to the Lord with tears. He did not arise from the pavement until the river from his eyes had deleted the record of this crime.

When the servant had been released from the invisible 6
chain with which he had been bound and had entered the church, the king arose from the floor; when he had in this way received his servant back in good health, he returned to the palace. The aforementioned mayor testified that he had learned about these things, just as we recounted them, by the king's own account. Thus the glorious bishop enhances his own city with miracles in such a way that he is not felt to be failing toward others.

8

About the basilica of the holy man in the city of Saintes

In this same year, Palladius, bishop of the city of Saintes, sought relics of this holy confessor. For he had built a basilica in his honor, which he consecrated with these relics, and he deservedly received the same kind of miracles there as
those which the saint's own city has often experienced. For 2
after two or three months, I received letters from him in which he said that three paralytics with crippled feet had

basilicam ingressi orationem fuderunt, directis vestigiis, sanitati sunt redditi. Duo caeci in eo loco lumen recipere, facta oratione, meruerunt, et amplius quam duodecim a febre frigoritica detenti, depulso tremore, convaluerunt.

9

De duobus dysentericis

Duo de pueris nostris, clericus scilicet Dagobaldus et laicus Theodorus, dysenteriam cum febre patiebantur; in tantumque lassati morbo erant, ut non aliter nisi manibus aliorum, cum digestionis necessitas advenisset, e strato sublevarentur. Sed de sepulcri pulvere hausto, statim convaluerunt.

come who, as soon as they had entered the basilica and had poured forth their prayers, had their feet straightened and were given back their health. Two blind men merited to receive light after they had prayed in this place, and more than twelve fever-stricken persons recovered when their attacks of chills were expelled.

9

About two men afflicted with dysentery

Two of our servants, that is, the cleric Dagobald and the layman Theodore, suffered from dysentery with fever; and they were so exhausted by the disease that when they needed to empty their bowels they could not get up out of their beds without assistance from the hands of others. But after they had drunk a potion of the dust of the tomb they recovered at once.

10

De patenis quas sanctus exhibuit

Est apud nos patena colore sapphirino, quam dicitur sanctus de Maximi Imperatoris thesauro detulisse, de qua super frigoriticos virtus saepe procedit. Nam in accessu febrium quis positus, qui cum tremore fieri solet, si advenerit et de ea aquam hauserit, mox sanatur. Est et apud Condatensem vicum alia quoque patena a sancto exhibita metallocrystallina, simile infirmis beneficium praebens, si fideliter expetatur.

2 Bodilo, unus de notariis nostris, cum stomachi lassitudine animo turbatus erat, ita ut nec scribere iuxta consuetudinem valeret nec excipere, et quae ei dictabantur vix poterat recensere. Tunc cum saepius verbis increparetur, super hanc beati viri patenam, quam nobiscum esse diximus, aquam fudit, ipsamque ore transponit. Mox sensui suo redditus, opus officii sagacius quam consueverat expediebat.

10

About the bowls which the holy man brought

There is in our possession a bowl the color of sapphire, which the holy man is said to have brought from the treasury of Emperor Maximus, and from which power often comes forth onto those suffering from fever. For when someone is placed in the heat of a fever which usually occurs with chills, if he comes and drinks water from it, he is soon healed. In the village of Candes, too, there is another metal-like crystal bowl, brought there by the holy man, that grants a similar benefit to the sick if this is requested with faith.

Bodilo, one of our scribes, was once so troubled in spirit 2
by a dysfunction of his stomach that he could not write as he was used to, nor take it down, and scarcely understood what was said to him. After he had often been scolded with words to do this, he poured water into this bowl of the blessed man which I said was in our possession, and brought it to his mouth. Soon, he was restored to his senses and carried out the duties of his office more capably than he had previously done.

II

De Bliderico, cui filii non erant dati

Sed quid mirum, si sensum adversitate turbatum reddat hominibus, qui saepius sterilitatem in fecunditate convertit? Blidericus quidam Carnoteni territorii civis, accepta uxore, ut dono Dei procreationis suae prole ditaretur orabat, sed nihil ex ea germinis merebatur accipere.

2 Tricesimus etenim annus curriculum expedierat, uxore sterili permanente, cum vir saluberrime pro animae commodo tractans, ait uxori: "Ecce saeculum quo utimur praeteriens est, et nulla inter nos suboles gignitur, quae, nobis deficientibus, congestum laboris nostri debeat possidere. Accedam," inquit, "ad basilicam sancti Martini, et eam faciam haeredem mihi, ut, liberis abnegatis, vel cum eadem quae habere potero possideam in futuro." Consensit mulier sapiens viri prudentis consilio.

3 Nec mora, proceditur ad basilicam sancti, fusaque oratione, invitat abbatem domi secum accedere. Quo accedente, tradidit ei omnem possessionem suam, dicens: "Sint haec omnia penes sancti Martini ditionem quae habere videor, et

II

About Blideric, to whom no sons had been given

But why be surprised if he who restores men who have been troubled by adversity to their right minds often turns sterility into fecundity? A certain Blideric, a citizen of the territory of Chartres had married a wife and was praying that he might be enriched by a gift from God, that is, by a child of his own begetting, but he did not deserve to receive any offspring from her.

When his wife had passed her thirtieth year and was still 2
sterile, the man took thought in a most healthy manner for the good of his soul, and said to his wife: "Look, our life in this world is going by and no child has been born to us, who, when we are grow frail, should possess the result of our work. I shall go," he said, "to the basilica of holy Martin and make it my heir, so that, if we are denied children, I may in the future possess together with the holy church whatever I am able to have." The woman wisely agreed with her prudent husband's decision.

At once, he went to the basilica of the holy man, poured 3
forth a prayer, and asked its abbot to come home with him. When he had come, he made all his possessions over to him, saying: "Let all these things which I seem to possess belong to the holy Martin, and from now on let my only claim on

hoc tantum exinde utar, ut de his dum vixero alar." Consignatisque rebus, coegit abbatem manere ibi.

4 Mirum dictu, post triginta, ut diximus, annorum curricula, in ipsa qua res suas basilicae tradidit nocte, cognovit uxorem suam, quae concipiens peperit filium! Sed et deinceps alios habuit, quod non ambigitur, hoc virtute sancti praestitum huic viro fuisse. Verumtamen non refragavit, acceptis filiis, promissionem homo ille, sed eis alia loca tribuens, quae primum sancto largitus fuerat confirmavit.

12

De caeca apud Turnacensem villam

Apud Turnacensem vero Cenomanici territorii villam, quae nunc in ipsius sanctae basilicae ditionibus retinetur, mulier quaedam diuturna caecitate detenta, et senio praegravata, ad oratorium villae ipsius residens, dum stipem quaereret ac assidue sancti Martini nomen invocaret, quadam nocte dominica coeperunt oculi eius a dolore compungi. Tunc illa prostrata coram sancto altari, erumpente sanguine, lumen recepit.

them be that I am supported from them while I am in this life." When the transaction of the properties had been signed and sealed, he insisted that the abbot stay there overnight.

Wonderful to recount is that although, as we said, she had 4
passed her thirtieth year, when he knew his wife in the very night after he had transferred his properties to the basilica, she conceived and bore a son! After that he had others too, which was undoubtedly brought about for him by the power of the holy man. However, when he had received sons, he did not break his promise but gave them other places and confirmed his previous gift to the holy man.

12

About a blind woman in the village of Ternay

In the village of Ternay in the territory of Le Mans, which is now under the authority of the holy basilica, there was a woman, long blind and now weakened by old age, who dwelt at the chapel of this village, begging for money and assiduously invoking holy Martin's name. One night before the day of the Lord, her eyes began to be pierced by pain. She thereupon prostrated herself before the holy altar; blood burst forth, and she was given her sight back.

2 Verumtamen reliquiae in ipso loco beatissimorum apostolorum, id est Petri et Pauli, habentur, sed haec asserebat virtute sancti antistitis se fuisse sanatam. Verumtamen fides nostra retinet in multorum sanctorum virtutibus unum Dominum operari, et nec illos disiunctos virtutibus, quos caelo pares, miraculis Dominus aequales reddit in terris.

13

De manu arida restituta

Ad festivitatem vero illam, cui Aunacharius Autissiodorensis urbis Pontifex adfuit, quidam manum aridam contractamque detulit, sed post diem tertium festivitatis, redintegratam domum reportavit.

The relics of the most blessed apostles Peter and Paul are kept in this place but, notwithstanding this, the woman claimed that she had been healed by the power of the holy bishop. Our faith believes, however, that one Lord is at work in the powerful acts of many saints, and that those whom the Lord makes equal in heaven and on earth are not separated in the great acts they perform. 2

13

About a withered hand that was restored

During the feast at which Bishop Aunachar of Auxerre was present, a certain man came with a withered and crippled hand, and on the third day after the feast he took it back home restored.

14

De Baudegisilo debili

Baudegisilus quidam ex Andegavensis urbis territorio, Baudulfi filius, vici Geinensis incola, dum umoris saevi iaculo sauciatur, debilitatus occubuit. Isque cum a patre paupere sine operis beneficio pasceretur, ut basilicae sancti Martini limina oscularetur, patrem lacrimis obortis efflagi-
2 tat. Qui nec mora in navi positum, quia vehi altera evectione non poterat, ante pedes sancti, id est foris sepulcrum, filium devotus exposuit. Qui per dies aliquot orationi vacans, et sancti auxilium poscens, amota debilitate sanitati restituitur, sicque cum genitore domi incolumis restitutus est.

15

De homine qui ceram transmisit

In Ausciensi quoque territorio erat homo, Caelestis nomine, cui multa erant apum alvearia. Ex quibus cum examen egressum alta conscendens longe conpeteret, et ille sequens,

14

About Baudegisil, a disabled man

A certain Baudegisil from the territory of the city of Angers, the son of Baudulf, an inhabitant of the village of Gennes, incurred his disability when he was struck by the lance of a savage humor. Since he was being supported by his father who was a pauper and had no way to earn a living, he implored his father with welling tears to let him kiss the
threshold of holy Martin's basilica. Having no other means 2
of transportation, he at once put his son in a boat and devoutly placed him at the holy man's feet, that is, at the entrance to the tomb. When Baudegisil had devoted himself to prayer for a few days, asking for the aid of the holy man, his disability was removed and his health was restored, and thus he returned home healthy with his father.

15

About the man who sent wax

In the territory of Auch there was a man named Caelestis who had many beehives. A swarm from one of these went out and flew up high and far away and, although he followed

nullum prorsus capiendi obtineret effectum, prostratus solo, sancti Martini invocat nomen, dicens: "Si virtus tua, beatissime confessor, hoc examen retinere voluerit, eumque ditioni meae reddiderit, quae in posterum ex eo procreata fuerint, mel usibus meis sumam, ceram vero ad luminaria basilicae tuae cum omni soliditate dirigam."

2 Haec effatus, cum adhuc terrae decumberet, statim examen apum super unam arbusculam, quae viro erat proxima, decidit et insedit, collectumque et in alveare reconditum domi detulit. De quo infra duos aut tres annos multa congregavit. Ex quibus cum iam amplius quam ducentas cerae libras aggregatas haberet, rumor hostilitatis obortus est. At ille, ne votum suum perire cerneret, ceram fossa humo operuit.

3 Pace quoque reddita, diaconum nostrum, ut eam peteret, arcersivit. Erat tunc cum eo puer, qui renum gravissimum perferebat dolorem. Qui accedens ad virum, et cognoscens ab ore eius quae gesta fuerant, ceram quae in terra latebat detegi iubet. Puer vero qui dolorem, quem diximus, patiebatur, accepto sarculo ut terram foderet, ait: "Si tu propitius es, sancte Martine, ad hoc munus hominis huius aspiciendum, contingat virtus tua renes meos, et sit mihi salus cum hanc detexero ceram." Et percutiens sarculo terram, sonuit ossiculum renum eius, et statim omnis dolor ablatus est. Et sic incolumis cum hac cera beatae basilicae praesentatus est.

it, he could not capture it by any means; so he prostrated himself on the ground and invoked the name of the holy Martin, saying: "Most blessed confessor, if your power would restrain this swarm and bring it back into my possession, from all that will be brought forth from this swarm in the future, I will keep the honey for my own use but send you all the wax for the candles of your basilica."

After he had said this, while he was still lying on the 2
ground, the swarm immediately alighted upon a bush near to the man, and settled there; he collected it, put it back in a hive, and carried it home. In two or three years, he gathered a great deal from it. When he had collected more than two hundred pounds of wax, a rumor arose that a hostile attack was imminent. Not wishing to see his vow be brought to naught, he hid the wax in a hole in the ground.

When peace had been restored, he invited our deacon to 3
come and fetch it. A servant was then with him who suffered a severe pain in his kidneys. When the deacon came to the man and heard from him what had happened, he ordered the wax lying in the earth to be dug up. The servant who, as we said, was in pain, took a hoe to dig in the ground and said: "If you look upon the gift of this man with favor, O holy Martin, let your power touch my kidneys, and let it be my healing as I uncover this wax." And as he struck the ground with the hoe, a small bone in his kidneys made a sound, and his pain was at once taken away. Healed in this manner, he was presented to the blessed basilica along with the wax.

16

De absolutione vincti

Homo quidam urbis Turonicae iudici culpabilis exstitit, quem in vincula compactum custodiri praecepit. Advenientibus autem diebus sanctis dominicae resurrectionis, iussit eum iudex in ulterius Ligeris fluvii litus in alia retrudi custodia. Ducebatur ergo non solum catenis colla revinctus, verum etiam post tergum manibus colligatis.

2 Cumque ad ripam nominati amnis advenissent, et navigium quo transire deberent praestolarentur, atque ille sancti Martini auxilium incessabiliter flagitaret, visum est repente custodibus, quasi ab aliquo capite verberati fuissent. Protinus in terram ruunt, ac catenae quae vinctum tenebant hominem confractae sunt, laxatae vero corrigiae de manibus solvuntur. Ipse autem liberum se sentiens, decumbentibus adhuc solo hominibus, secessit ab eis et sanctae ecclesiae limen ingressus est. Sicque a iudice relaxatur.

3 Ferebant enim nonnulli his diebus et apud Pictavensem urbem vinctos ab ergastulo carcerali fuisse resolutos. Quod ambigi non potest, quia unius confessoris virtus utramque urbem sacris potuit illustrare miraculis.

16

About a chained man who was released

A certain man from the city of Tours was pronounced guilty by the judge, who ordered him to be put in chains and guarded. When the holy days of the Lord's resurrection came, the judge commanded that he be confined in another prison on the other side of the Loire. He was conducted, therefore, bound not only with chains around his neck, but also with his hands tied behind his back.

When they had come to the shore of the above- 2
mentioned river and were waiting for the boat with which they were going to cross, and the bound man kept on imploring the holy Martin's help, suddenly it seemed to the guards that they had been struck on the head by someone. They fell to the ground at once, the chains which held the prisoner broke, and the manacles fell off, releasing his hands. Feeling himself free, the prisoner left the guards still lying on the ground, and crossed the threshold into the holy cathedral. And thus he was released by the judge.

Some say that in these days chained men in the slaves' 3
prison of the city of Poitiers too had been released. This cannot be doubted, for the power of one and the same confessor was able to illuminate both cities with sacred miracles.

17

De puero caeco

Puerulus parvulus, nomine Leudovaldus, servus cuiusdam Baudeleifi de vico Andegavensi, cui Crovio antiquitas nomen indidit, postquam renatus ex aqua et Spiritu sancto cum reliquis infantibus ludum in platea exercens, ut aetas illa patitur, huc illucque discurreret, subito commotus cum impetu ventus, et pulverem elevans, oculos infantis implevit.

2 Qui cum a caecitatis percussus doloribus cruciaretur, apparuit aviae eius vir quidam per somnium, taliter eam instruens: "Vade," inquit, "ad basilicam sancti Martini, et recipiet visum puer iste." Nec morata mulier, fide plena, venit ad festivitatem beati viri, recepitque illuminatum virtute pontificis nepotem suum.

17

About a blind boy

A small boy named Leudovald was the slave of a certain Baudeleif of a village in the territory of Angers that the ancients named Crovium; after his rebirth from water and the Holy Spirit, while he was playing in the street with other children and running here and there, as they do at that age, suddenly a gust of wind arose and lifted up dust that filled the child's eyes.

When he had been struck with blindness and was being 2
tormented by pains, a man appeared to his grandmother in a dream and instructed her in this manner: "Go to the basilica of holy Martin," he said, "and this boy will receive his sight." Wasting no time, the woman came full of faith to the feast of the holy man, and received back her grandson given light by the power of the bishop.

18

De puella caeca

Huius etenim urbis territorii puella, Viliogundis vocabulo, simili conditione caecatur. Dum enim cum reliquis puellulis per stratas villae ludum exercendo discurreret, venti violentia pulvis elevatus opplevit oculos eius. Quae statim, doloribus vexata, petiit parentes suos ut eam ad basilicam sancti Martini deducerent. Quo facto, protinus ut orationem pro ea fuderunt, illuminata est.

2 Nobis quoque egredientibus de sanctis missarum solemnibus occurrerunt simul praefatus puer atque puella, dicentes se ipsa hora lumen virtute beati antistitis recepisse. Quod nobis magnum praestitit gaudium, credentibus quod nos virtus beati confessoris visitare dignata sit.

19

De contracto et caeco

Litoveus autem quidam, ex infantia sua membris debilis, accedente febre, caecatus est; sed ad superiorem festivitatem veniens, directis membris, lumine tamen adhuc

18

About a blind girl

In the territory of the same city, a girl named Viliogund was blinded in a similar manner. For while she was running about in the village streets playing with the other children, dust lifted up by a violent wind filled her eyes. Afflicted with pain, she immediately asked her parents to bring her to the basilica of holy Martin. They did this, and at the moment that they poured forth a prayer for her, she was given light.

While we were coming out of the cathedral after the cel- 2
ebration of holy mass, the above-mentioned boy and girl met us and said that they had received light at that very hour through the power of the blessed bishop. It gave us great joy to believe that the blessed confessor's power had deigned to visit us.

19

About a crippled and blind man

A certain Litoveus, who had been disabled in his limbs since his childhood, was blinded by the onset of a fever; but when he came to the aforementioned feast, his limbs were

dempto, discessit. Sed cum ad hanc iterum regressus fuisset solemnitatem, exemptis tenebris, lumen ei clarum exoritur.

20

Item de alio caeco

In hac etiam festivitate et Leudardus, servus Eumerii Namneticae urbis diaconi, cum per sex annos caecitatis fuisset catena constrictus, ad basilicam accedens, virtute beati confessoris illuminatus est. Per visionem enim somnii admonitus fuerat ut huius sancti auxilia flagitaret antistitis.

straightened; he left still deprived of light, however. When he came back a second time to this solemnity, the darkness was taken away and a bright light arose in him.

20

About another blind man

Also during that same feast Leudard, the slave of Eumerius, a deacon of the city of Nantes who had been constrained by the chain of blindness for six years, came to the basilica and was given light by the power of the blessed confessor. For he had been advised in a dream vision to ask for the help of this holy bishop.

21

De eulogiis quas Motharius civis Turonicus sustulit

Quidam de civibus Turonicis, dum ad regis properaret occursum, vas cum vino, unumque panem ad sepulcrum una mansurum nocte deposuit, ut scilicet in itinere positus hoc haberet salutis praesidium. Quibus exinde assumptis, iter carpere coepit.

2 Factum est autem ut metatum requirens, hominis cuiusdam ingrederetur hospitium, depositisque sarcinis, mulier quae habebat spiritum immundum, beati Martini adventum vocibus immensis annuntiare coepit, et dicere: "Quid nos
3 persequeris, sancte? Quid nos crucias, serve Dei?" Tunc hospes ille qui venerat, accepto calice, paululumque vini de illo vase auferens, frustum benedicti panis effractum posuit in eo. Quod ubi mulier illa quae debacchabatur accepit, mox, cum sanguine eiecto daemonio, salvata est.

4 Alia in eodem loco mulier, quae diu a frigore febrium aegrotabat, accepto ab hac benedictione modico, mox ut sumpsit, sanata est.

21

About the consecrated food which Mothar, a citizen of Tours, took with him

One of the citizens of Tours, when about to go to a meeting with the king, placed a flask of wine and one loaf of bread at the tomb for the duration of one night so that he might have protection for his safety while traveling. After retrieving them from there, he began on his journey.

It happened that, needing a place to stay, he walked into 2
someone's inn, and when he had put down his luggage, a woman with an unclean spirit began to announce the arrival of the blessed Martin with loud cries, saying: "Why do you persecute us, holy man? Why do you torture us, servant of
God?" Then the guest who had just arrived was given a cup 3
and poured a bit of the wine into it from the flask; into it he put a piece broken off from the bread that had been blessed. When the raving woman had swallowed this, the demon was at once ejected with blood and she was saved.

Another woman in the same place, who had been ill for a 4
long time with the chills of fevers, also received a piece of this blessing, and was healed as soon as she had swallowed it.

22

De contracto directo

Silluvius, incola Baiocassinus, cum in rure positus operaretur quiddam, commoto vento, pavore perculsus, tremere coepit, ac membris omnibus destitui, vociferari etiam, et sibi mortem imminere testabatur. Interea concurrentibus vicinis ad spectaculum tale, ipse inter voces et ululatus, contractis nervis, debilitatur ad integrum; et non solum ei usus aurium denegatur, verumetiam et ipso lumine caruit oculorum.

2 Post quindecim vero annos dum in hac infelicitate degeret, ad festivitatem sancti Martini adveniens, solidatis membris, oculisque receptis, abscessit.

22

About a crippled man who was straightened

Silluvius, an inhabitant of Bayeux, was doing some work in the field when a wind got up. He was struck with terror, began to shake, lost the use of all of his limbs, and shouted, asserting that he was about to die. When his neighbors had gathered around such a spectacle, his tendons contracted and, all the while shouting and wailing, he became wholly disabled; not only was he denied the use of his ears, but the light even disappeared from his eyes.

After he had spent fifteen years in this unhappy condi- 2
tion, he came to the feast of holy Martin, his limbs were restored, and he left with his eyes restored.

23

De caeca ac debili sanatis

Nec dissimili virtute mulier Ermegundis, Andecavensis civis, vici incola Croviensis, contracta et caeca, in hac festivitate directa, illuminataque discessit. Sed et Charimundus, ex Bricilonno debilis veniens, virtute beati antistitis redintegratus est.

24

De plurimis caecis energuminisque sanatis

In huius etiam solemnitatis die virtutem nonnulli, cooperante Christi gratia, persenserunt. Nam Leodemundus caecus post septem annos, Domnitta post tres, et tres insuper alii caeci in hac festivitate visum per opem beati antistitis receperunt, energumeni plerique mundati sunt.

23

About a blind woman and a disabled man who were healed

By a similar act of power a crippled and blind woman, Ermegund, a citizen of Angers inhabiting the village of Crovium, was straightened during this feast, and she left having also been given back the light of her eyes. The disabled man Charimund, too, who had come from Brulon, was made whole by the power of the blessed bishop.

24

About many blind and possessed men who were healed

On the day of this solemnity, too, several people, with the help of Christ's grace, experienced the confessor's power. For Leodemund, blind for seven years, and Domnitta, blind for three and three other blind people as well, received their sight during this feast through the aid of the blessed bishop; many possessed people too were cleansed.

25

De puella a febre sanata

Leonis presbyteri nostri vernacula, cum ad villulam urbi proximam parentalibus ulnis deportata secessisset, vi febris opprimitur et, die ac nocte valde commota, in mortis discrimine cernitur. Quam videns presbyter exanimari violentia morbi, nocte ascenso equo, ad basilicam sancti confessoris accessit, pulsansque ostium cellulae in qua aedituus quiescebat, virum suscitare nequivit.

2 Cumque basilicam sanctam ingredi non valeret, coram apsida sepulcri fudit orationem, collegitque parumper de pulvere terreno, quod secum fide plenus evexit, eumque dilutum ut puellulae ad bibendum protulit, protinus febris abscessit.

26

De carcerariis absolutis

Fuerat nobis causa quaedam Childeberthi Regis adire praesentiam. Pergentibus quoque nobis, iter per pagum Remensem aggressi sumus, reperimusque hominem quendam,

25

About a girl who was cured of a fever

The maidservant of our priest Leo, when she had been carried to a small village near the city in her parents' arms, was oppressed by a violent fever and, agitated day and night, seemed to be on the point of dying. The priest, seeing her half-dead from the violence of the illness, mounted his horse in the night, went to the basilica of the holy confessor and knocked on the door of the cell in which the custodian was sleeping, but could not awaken him.

Since he was unable to enter the holy basilica, he poured 2
forth a prayer outside it, next to the apse in which the tomb is located; and then collected a bit of the earth there which he took with him full of faith; when he had diluted it and given it to the girl to drink, the fever immediately went away.

26

About prisoners who were released

There was a certain occasion that required us to go to meet King Childebert. As we were traveling and had entered the region of Reims, we came across a man who told

qui nobis relatu suo patefactum carcerem huius urbis, in quo inter reliquos vinctos huius famulus tenebatur, Martini virtute fuisse dicebat; vinctosque ab ergastulo absolutos, liberosque abscessisse narravit.

2 Erat enim huiusmodi carcer ita tectus, ut super struem tignorum axes validi superpositi pulpitarentur, ac desuper, qui eos opprimerent, insignes fuerant lapides collocati. Nihilominus et ostium carceris sera ferro munita, obducto clave pessulo obserabatur.

3 Sed virtus antistitis, ut ipse relator asseruit, lapides dimovit, disiecit pulpita, catenas confregit, et trabem quae vinctorum coartabat pedes, aperuit. Ac nec reserato ostio homines per aera sublevatos, foris tecto patente produxit, dicens: "Ego sum Martinus, miles Christi, absolutor vester. Abscedite cum pace et abite securi."

4 Sed cum nos ad regem accedentes, virtutis huius diffamaremus miraculum, affirmavit rex quosdam ex his qui absoluti fuerant ad se venisse, atque compositionem fisco debitam, quam illi fredum vocant, a se fuisse reis indultam. Hoc autem factum est ante quattuor festivitatis dies, in memorati regis anno sexto et decimo.

us his story of a prison of this city, holding among other chained men also this man's servant; he said that it had been opened by Martin's power and told us that the chained men had been released from the prison and had left as free men.

For the prison was roofed in such a way that heavy planks 2
were supported by a thick mass of beams, and on top of the planks large stones were placed to keep them down. Furthermore, the door of the prison was equipped with an iron bolt and fastened crosswise with another bolt secured with a key.

But the bishop's power, as this narrator claimed, re- 3
moved the stones, took apart the roof, broke the chains, and opened the stocks that confined the prisoners' feet. Without the door even being opened, he lifted the men up into the air and brought them outside through the open roof, while saying: "I am Martin, soldier of Christ, your liberator. Leave in peace and go in safety."

When we had come to the king and made the miracle of 4
this act of power known, he affirmed that some of those who had been released had come to him and that he had waived the fee which these accused men owed to the royal treasury, which they call *fredus.* This happened three days before the feast of Martin, in the sixteenth year of the aforementioned king.

27

De servo Nonnichii Episcopi a debilitate sanato

Adveniente autem festo beati Martini, Nonnichius, Namneticorum pontifex, ad basilicam sancti advenit, exhibens secum puerum membris dissolutum, nomine Baudegisilum. Celebratis igitur solemniis sancti, hunc, artubus restitutis, secum reduxit incolumem.

28

De Claudii regalis cancellarii febre

Nobis quoque cum rege morantibus, Claudius, quidam ex cancellariis regalibus, a febre corripitur. Cumque cibum potumque nimia oppressus febre exhorruisset, nobis quae patiebatur questus est, dilutumque pulverem, quem de sancti ac beati sepulcro pro salvatione levavimus, ut hausit, mox compressa febre, sanatus est.

27

About Bishop Nonnichius's servant, who was healed of his disability

When the feast of the blessed Martin was approaching, Bishop Nonnichius of Nantes came to the basilica of the holy man and brought with him a servant with disabled limbs, named Baudegisil. After the solemnities of the saint had been celebrated, the servant's limbs were restored and the bishop took this man back in good health.

28

About the fever of Claudius, a royal chancery clerk

During our stay with the king, Claudius, one of the royal chancery clerks, was seized by a fever. Rejecting all food and drink because of his oppression by this severe fever, he complained to us about what he was suffering, and when he had drunk a potion containing the dust which we had taken from the tomb of the holy and blessed man for our protection, the fever was soon subdued, and he was made healthy.

29

De eo quod Agnes Pictaviensis abbatissa de nauta quodam retulit

Venerabilis vero Agnes, Pictavarum sanctimonialium abbatissa, relatam sibi ab ipso cui contigit, Treverico scilicet negotiatore, rem miraculi provenisse, sic retulit: "Dum," inquit, "Mettis accessissem, interrogavit me quidam negotiator unde venirem. Dixi: 'De Pictavis.' Dixit mihi si aliquando ad basilicam beati Martini Turonis occurrissem. Dixi quod quando in Austria ambularem, sic ibi me praesentassem.

2 "Dixit mihi quale beneficium domni Martini senserat. Dum enim Mettis salem negotiasset, et ad pontem Mettis applicuisset, dixit: '"Domne Martine, me et puericellos quos habeo, et naviculam meam tibi commendo." Inter haec recubantes in navi, omnes obdormivimus.

3 'Mane excitans me cum puericellis, quos mecum habebam, invenimus nos ante portam Trevericam, nescientes quomodo venissemus, qui nos adhuc Mettis credebamus consistere, qua ratione aut navigatum est, aut volatum; sola commendatione beati Martini, nec fluvium sensissemus, et Mosellae tunc saevientis undas naufragas evitassemus. Et, quod satis est mirabile, quomodo inter saxa nocturno

29

About what Agnes, abbess of Poitiers, recounted of a certain boatman

The venerable Agnes, abbess of the nuns at Poitiers, recounted in this manner a story about a miracle that had been told to her by the one to whom it had happened, a merchant of Trier: "When I had reached Metz," she said, "a certain merchant asked me where I came from. I said: 'From Poitiers.' He asked me if I had been to the basilica of the blessed Martin of Tours. I said that when I had been on my way to Austrasia, I had presented myself there.

"Then he told me what kind of favor of the lord Martin 2
he had experienced. When he had been trading salt at Metz and had docked at the bridge of Metz, he had said: '"Lord Martin, I commend to you myself, the little boys I have with me, and my little boat." Having said this, we lay down in the boat and all fell asleep.

'Waking up the next morning with the boys I had with 3
me, we found ourselves in front of the gate at Trier, not knowing how we had got there, since up to then we had believed ourselves still to be in Metz, or how we had either sailed or flown there; through the commendation of the blessed Martin alone we had not felt the river and had avoided shipwreck on the waves of the Moselle, which was at that time very rough. And, a very remarkable thing, <we

tempore praeteriissemus incolumes, non nauta vigilante, non vento flante, non remo ducente.'"

30

De virtutibus Locodiacensis monasterii

Tempore post habito, cum usque Pictavam accessissemus urbem, libuit gratia tantum orationis monasterium Locociagense adire, quo congregatam monachorum catervam locaverat vir beatus. Ibi enim mortuum primum suscitasse
2 legitur, et ex illo ad episcopatum ductus scribitur. Ergo desideratum ego expetens locum, prosternor ad cancellos anguli, in quo dicitur defuncti spiritum reduxisse. Post effusas vero cum oratione lacrimas, ac celebratas solemniter missas, percunctor abbatem, si aliquod ibi Dominus miraculum ostendisset.

3 Asseruitque ille coram qui aderant fratribus, plerumque ibi illuminari caecos, ac debiles redintegrari. "Quid tamen nuper sit gestum," inquit, "tibi, domne, quia sollicite inquiris, evolvam. Mulier quaedam vicina loci huius, paralysi umore perculsa, officium membrorum omnium usquequaque

did not know> how we had passed unhurt between the rocks at night, no sailor keeping watch, no wind blowing, and no one rowing.'"

30

About the powerful deeds at the monastery of Ligugé

Some time after my return, when we had gone to the city
of Poitiers, we wished to go to the monastery of Ligugé
merely to pray; the blessed man had gathered and established a large group of monks there. One reads that he revived his first dead person there, and it is written that he
was conducted from there to become bishop. Therefore I 2
went to the place I longed for, and prostrated myself at the
railings in the corner in which he is said to have brought
back the dead man to life. After pouring forth a prayer with
tears and solemnly celebrating mass, I inquired of the abbot
if the Lord had manifested any miracle there.

And he asserted before the brothers who were present 3
there that blind men were often healed there and the disabled made whole. "But since you inquire with such interest, my lord," he said, "I shall tell you about what happened recently. A woman of this neighborhood had been struck with a crippling humor and completely lost the use

perdiderat. Quae carrucae imposita, a bobus trahentibus ferebatur, circuiens domos divitum, ut inopiae suae expleret necessitatem.

4 "Ergo dum delata ad hunc locum pavimento prosternitur, lento conamine accedens, velum quod sanctum tegebat cancellum devote osculatur, dicens: 'Hic te, beate confessor, adesse credo. Hic te mortuum suscitasse testificor. Confido enim quod si volueris, poteris me salvare ac sanitati restituere, sicut quondam, disruptis inferni faucibus, defuncti animam reduxisti!'

5 "Haec effata, genas lacrimis rigabat ubertim. Ac statim, impleta oratione, quidquid aridum, quidquid contractum, quidquid dissolutum fuit, redintegratum est mulieri in corpore a beati antistitis virtute.

6 "Simili sorte et alius paralyticus ad hoc accedens monasterium, ut velum ipsius cancelli attigit, amota omni debilitate, sanus abscessit." Distat autem ab urbe Pictava quasi stadiis quadraginta.

of all her limbs. Placed on a cart drawn by oxen she went round the homes of the wealthy in order to provide for the needs of her poverty.

4 "When she had been carried to this place, she prostrated herself on the floor and, approaching slowly and with effort, touched the cloth that covered the holy rail and devoutly kissed it, saying: 'I believe you to be present here, blessed confessor. Here I attest you to have revived a dead man. Therefore I believe that, just as you once broke through the jaws of the underworld and led back the soul of a dead man, if you wish to do so, you will be able to save me and restore me to health!'

5 "After saying this, she wetted her cheeks with abundant tears. And at once, when she had finished her prayer, whatever was withered, contracted, or powerless in her body was made whole by the power of the blessed bishop.

6 "In a similar manner another paralyzed man too who had come to this monastery, when he touched the cloth covering that same rail, had all of his disability removed, and he left in good health." The monastery of Ligugé is about four and a half miles from the city of Poitiers.

31

De fonte quem oratione sanctus ut oriretur obtinuit

Exinde regressi, Sanctonicum territorium ingressi sumus. Cumque in quodam convivio de beati Martini virtutibus fabularemur, haec mihi unus ex civibus, affirmantibus aliis vera esse, fideliter retulit.

2 Naiogialo villa est in hoc territorio sita, ad quam cum sanctus Martinus adhuc superstes in corpore adiret, obvium habuit virum exhibentem aquam cum vasculo. Erat enim puteus ille, de quo hanc exhibebat, situs in valle quasi mille passus a villa, et ex eo incolae haustam deferebant aquam.
3 Tunc ait vir Dei homini aquam ferenti: "Quaeso, dilectissime, contine manum tuam, et huic asello cui sedeo, paululum aquae ad bibendum indulge." Qui ait: "Si necessarium ducis animal tuum adaquare, accede ad puteum et, hauriens, dabis ei. Nam ego quod cum labore detuli non praebebo." Et haec dicens praeteriit.

4 Quo discedente, venit protinus mulier, et ipsa deferens aquam in urnam, dixitque ei similiter vir Dei. Quae, ac si Rebecca quondam, audiens nuntium Dei: "Et tibi praebebo," ait, "et asino tuo potum; nec mihi labor est ut iterum

31

About the spring whose appearance the holy man obtained during his life

Having left Poitiers, we entered the territory of Saintes. And at a certain meal, when we were speaking about the blessed Martin's acts of power, one of the citizens piously told me the following story, which the others present affirmed to be true.

There is a village called Nieuil in this territory to which 2
the holy Martin went when he was still alive in the body and where he met a man carrying a jar of water. The well from which he had taken this water was in a valley about a thousand paces from the village, and the villagers used to carry from it the water they drew. Then the man of God said to 3
the man carrying the water: "Dearly beloved, I ask you to extend your hand and give a little drink of water to the ass which I am riding." The man said: "If you think it is necessary to give water to your animal, go to the well, draw water, and give it to him. For I will not give you what I have taken the trouble of carrying." And with these words he went on his way.

Soon after he had left a woman approached, she too car- 4
rying water in a jar, and the man of God spoke to her in a similar manner. She, like Rebecca of old, listened to the messenger of God and said: "I will give you a drink too, as well as your ass; it is no trouble for me to draw water again.

hauriam. Tantum voluntas tua fiat, qui iter pergens necessitatem pateris." Et deposito de ulnis vasculo dedit asino illius bibere. Quo facto, iterum hausta aqua, impletoque vasculo, revertebatur ad villam.

Quam prosequens sanctus ait: "Reddam tibi pro mercede beneficium, quia adaquasti asinum meum." Et positis genibus in terra oravit ad Dominum, ut in loco illo fontis ostenderet venam. Ac statim consummata oratione, disrupta terra fontem immensum populis admirantibus patefecit, qui usque hodie beneficium praebet hominibus commanentibus in agro illo. In illius enim fontis ore est lapis in testimonium, qui vestigium retinet aselli huius super quem sanctus sedit antistes.

32

De incendio urbis Pictavae

Nec illud silendum puto, quod illo tempore cum Plato episcopatum Pictavae urbis adeptus est, virtus sancti fuit ostensa. Domus adiuncta ecclesiasticae domui incendio maximo cremabatur, ac scintillae cum carbonibus super

Let only your wish be done, whose journey exposes you to need." And she put down the jar she was carrying and let his ass drink. When she had done this, she went to draw water again, filled her jar, and returned to her village.

The holy man followed her and said: "I will give you a favor as a reward because you gave water to my ass." And, putting his knees on the ground, he prayed to the Lord that he might make a spring of water appear in that place. As soon as his prayer was finished, the earth split open and revealed to the astonished onlookers an enormous spring that today is still benefiting the people living in that region. At the mouth of the spring there is a stone as a testimony of the event: for it still shows the hoofprint of the ass upon which the holy bishop sat.

32

About the fire in the city of Poitiers

I think I should not pass over in silence either the fact that the power of the holy man was manifested at the time that Plato became bishop of the city of Poitiers. A house adjoining the cathedral residence was burning with a huge fire, and sparks and cinders, impelled by the wind, were

2 domum ecclesiae, impellente vento, cadebant. Sed ille de pulvere beati sepulcri secum habens, elevato chrismario contra ignem, exortus subito ventus vento illi contrarius, flammas a tecto ecclesiastico defendens, aliam pepulit in partem, et sic domus ecclesiae liberata est.

33

De puero a febre sanato

Cum autem puer eius in valetudine acerbissima febre exustus iaceret in lectulo et iam quasi exanimis haberetur, ut de hoc pulvere diluto porrexit infirmo, protinus, fugata febre, puer convaluit de labore. Sed ad basilicam sancti redeamus.

falling upon the church residence. But he had some dust from the holy tomb with him, and when he had lifted up the box containing it against the fire, a wind from the opposite quarter suddenly arose that pushed back the flames from the church roof in another direction, and in this way the church residence was saved. 2

33

About a servant who was healed of fever

When Bishop Plato's servant lay ill in bed, burned up by an extremely severe fever, and was thought to be almost dead, he gave the sick man some of this dust diluted with water; at once, the fever was put to flight and the servant recovered from his affliction. But let us return to the holy man's basilica.

34

De Leodulfo amente et debili

Cum autem ante hos annos terrae motus magnus terram concuteret, cunctaque valde moverentur quasi in uno momento casura, Leodulfus quidam ab eo vehementer excussus, non solum sensu multatur, sed etiam omnibus membris
2 debilis est effectus. Qui veniens ad basilicam sancti Turonis et orationi paucis diebus incumbens, et voci redditur et sensui, et membris omnibus quasi redivivus sospes est redditus.

35

De homine innocente per calumniam accusato, et liberato

Nec illud praetermittendum puto, quod innocenter homo accusatus per calumnias malorum, adducebatur ad
2 urbem vinctus loro, ut truderetur ergastulo. Cumque ante

34

About Leodulf, who had lost his mind and the use of his limbs

When a huge earthquake struck the earth before these years, and all things were so severely shaken that they seemed about to collapse in an instant, a certain Leodulf was struck so violently by it that he not only lost his mind but was also rendered disabled in all his limbs. When he had 2
come to the basilica of the holy man at Tours and had devoted himself to prayer for a few days, his voice and his mind were restored to him and, as it were brought back to life in all his limbs, he was made healthy.

35

About an innocent man who was accused through calumny and liberated

I think I should not pass over either how an innocent man accused by the calumny of evil men was brought to the city bound with a leather strap, to be thrust into prison. When 2

basilicam sancti Petri apostoli in publicum adductus aggerem devenisset, solutae sunt manus eius, dixitque custodibus: "In hoc apparet me a culpa quam dicitis esse immunem, cum meae manus divinitus sunt solutae." Tunc illi indignantes artius eum revinxerunt, et insuper adhuc alio loro ligamini adiecto, ut ita dicam, vincula ipsa vinxerunt.

3 Contigit autem eo tempore, ut nos de basilica sancti Martini per plateam veniremus. Hi autem cum nobis in obviam venientes appropinquarent, ut primum basilicam sancti homo vinctus aspexit, statim solutae sunt manus eius. Exsiliens de caballo in quo sedebat, pedes nostros arripuit, exponens se iniuste damnari. Sicque, nobis cum iudice colloquentibus, absque fatigatione discessit.

36

De muliere obmutescente sanata

Coniux Serenati hominis nostri, cum de cultura, viro praemisso, rediret, subito inter manus dilapsa comitantium terrae corruit, ligataque lingua, nullum verbum ex ore potens proferre, obmutuit. Interea accedentibus ariolis, ac

he had been led onto the public place in front of the basilica of the apostle Peter, his hands were freed, and he said to his guards: "This shows that I am innocent of the guilt with which you charge me, for my hands have been divinely released." Indignant at this, they thereupon tied him up him more tightly and adding another strap they, so to speak, bound the bonds.

It so happened however that, at that moment, we had 3
just left the basilica of the holy Martin and were walking in the street. These men were approaching and about to encounter us when, at the first moment that the bound man saw the basilica of the saint, his hands were immediately released. Jumping off the horse on which he was sitting, he seized our feet and explained to us that he had been unjustly condemned. And thus, after we had spoken to the judge, he departed without being harassed.

36

About a mute woman who was healed

When the wife of our servant Serenatus was returning from working in the fields, her husband having gone ahead, she suddenly collapsed into the hands of her companions; she fell on the ground, tongue-tied and unable to utter a word, and became mute. After this, wizards came saying

dicentibus eam meridiani daemonii incursum pati, ligamina herbarum atque incantationum verba proferebant, sed nihil medicaminis iuxta morem conferre poterant periturae.

2 Cumque familia mixto ululatu perstreperet, filius eius ad neptem nostram Eusteniam anhelus accurrit, nuntians matrem suam extremae vitae terminum attigisse. Quae adveniens ad aegrotam, eamque visitans, amotisque ligaminibus quae stulti indiderant, oleum beati sepulcri ori eius infudit, ceraque suffivit. Mox, sermone reddito, nequitiae dolo dirempto, aegra convaluit.

37

De frigoriticis sanatis

Tempore autem quo, post obitum gloriosissimi regis Guntchramni, Childebertus Rex Aurelianensem urbem adivit, puerorum unus aulicorum graviter a typo tertiano, accedentibus discedentibusque febribus, tremore superveniente, quatiebatur. Id cum nobis fuisset questus, de pulvere sancti sepulcri potum ei porreximus, quem hauriens, compresso tremore, convaluit.

that she was suffering an incursion from the noonday demon, and administered ligaments of herbs and words of incantations but, as usual, they were not able to give a cure to the dying woman.

While her household shouted and wailed, her son ran 2
breathlessly to our niece Eustenia to tell her that his mother was nearing the end of her life. She came to the sick woman and visited her, removing the ligaments which the foolish men had applied, poured oil of the blessed tomb into her mouth, and burned a candle. Soon, her faculty of speaking was given back, the deceit of the demon was broken through, and the sick woman recovered her health.

37

About fever-stricken people who were made healthy

After the death of the most glorious king Guntram, when King Childebert came to the city of Orléans, one of the court's servants was severely shaken by the tertian fever, with fevers coming and going, accompanied by chills. He complained to us about this and we gave him a drink with some dust from the holy tomb; when he had drunk it, the chills were subdued and he recovered his health.

2 In sequenti vero nocte, cum dies ille quo frangi consueverat advenisset, vidit per visum advenientem personam taeterrimam dicentemque sibi: "Ecce iam tempus tui tremo-
3 ris advenit. Quid dissimulas? Age quod consuevisti!" Haec eo dicente, advenit vir quidam vultu splendidus, caesarie niveus, aspectu decorus, dicens ei: "Ne tremueris, sed facito super frontem tuam signum venerandae crucis, statimque sanaberis." In hac visione expergefactus, munitusque hoc signaculo quo fuerat iussus, numquam ulterius quae pati soleret passus est.

4 Ab hoc typo reginae puella fatigata, potu huius sancti medicaminis sumpto, sanata est.

38

De caecis, energumenis et paralyticis

Non post multos dies, cum solemnitatis sanctae dies annuus recurrisset, nos a rege regressi, festivitati eius adfuimus, in qua quattuor caeci lumine recepto regressi sunt,

The following night, when the day approached on which 2
he was accustomed to being racked by the chills, he saw in a dream vision a hideous person coming toward him who said: "Look here, the time of your chills has come. Why pretend otherwise? Do what you have been accustomed to do!"
While he was saying this, there came another man with a 3
shining face, white hair, and an elegant demeanor, who said to the servant: "Don't shake, but make the sign of the venerable cross on your forehead, and you will be made healthy at once." Having woken up from this dream vision, he protected himself with this sign as he had been commanded, and never again suffered from what he had been accustomed to undergo.

A maidservant of the queen was also harassed by this 4
kind of fever, and after she had taken a drink of the <abovementioned> holy remedy, she too was made healthy.

38

About blind, possessed, and paralyzed men

A few days later, when the anniversary of the holy solemnity had come round and we, having returned from the king, were attending the saint's feast, four blind men, having

duo energumeni mundati, duo paralytici contracti, restitutis gressibus, incolumes redierunt.

39

De carceratis laxatis

Post paucos vero dies cum culpabiles quosdam urbis Turonicae iudicis sententia carcerali ergastulo conclusisset, lamentantibus vinctis, virtus beati confessoris apparuit, quae, diruptis vinculis compeditorum, liberos in basilicam abire permisit. Sicque et hi a iudice relaxati, ad propria recesserunt.

received light, went home, and two possessed persons, having been cleansed, as well as two contracted paralytics, whose ability to walk had been restored, returned home healthy.

39

About prisoners who were released

Several days after that, when certain guilty men of the city of Tours were shut up in prison by order of the judge, and these chained men were wailing, the power of the blessed confessor appeared, and by breaking the bonds of their fetters, it allowed them to go out to the basilica freely. Because of this, these men were released by the judge and went home.

40

De Maurano muto

Quidam in regione Cantabriae, Mauranus nomine, mane a lectulo consurgens, dum de domo egreditur, visum est ei quasi aliquo percussus fuerit in cervicem. Qui protinus ruens in terram, factus est tamquam mortuus, ac per triduum solo spiritu vivens, tamquam mortuus putabatur. Quarta autem die, apertis oculis, nihil poterat loqui, ablata enim ei fuerat fandi facultas.

2 Auditis enim beati Martini miraculis, unum triantem nautis porrexit, innuens cum supplicatione ut eum ad beati antistitis templum deferrent. Quibus abeuntibus, ille ad domum suam reversus, vidit ante pedes suos aureum in similitudinem triantis. Quo assumpto pensatoque, unius solidi appensus est pondere. Quod ille cernens, dixit intra se: "Reddidit mihi virtus beati Martini meritum pro faenore quod eius templo direxi."

3 Et accensus desiderio, voluit in unam atque aliam navim conscendere, sed a parentibus est retentus. Reperta autem tertia navi, retineri penitus non potuit. Qua accensa, cum impellente vento altum mare ingressi fuissent, os eius virtus sancti antistitis reseravit. Qui, extensis ad caelum manibus,

40

About Mauranus, a mute man

In the region of Cantabria someone named Mauranus had got out of bed one morning and was walking out of his house, when it seemed to him that he was struck on his neck by someone. Falling to the ground at once, he became as though dead and, living for three days only in his spirit, it seemed as though he were dead. When he opened his eyes on the fourth day, he could not talk, for his faculty of speaking had been taken away.

Having heard about the miracles of the blessed Martin, 2
however, he gave a coin with the value of a third of gold coin to some sailors, indicating and begging them to take it to the temple of the blessed bishop. When they had left and he returned to his home, he saw lying in front of his feet a gold coin that looked like a third. But when he had picked it up and weighed it, it had the weight of a whole gold coin. Seeing this, he said to himself: "The blessed Martin's power has rewarded me with interest for what I sent to his temple."

And burning with impatience to go there himself, he 3
wanted to board first one ship and then another, but was restrained by his parents. When he had found a third ship, however, he could no longer be held back. After he had boarded this, and they were blown by the wind to the high seas, the blessed bishop's power opened his mouth. Stretching out his hands to heaven, the man spoke and

locutus est, dicens: "Gratias tibi ago, omnipotens Deus, qui me hoc iter sulcare iussisti! Iam enim priusquam templum sancti tui videam, eius refertus sum beneficiis!"

4 Quibus navigantibus, Burdigalae urbi appulsi sunt, egressusque hinc de navi, ad basilicam sancti Dei accedens, ac votum suum exsolvens. Quae scripsimus ab ipsius ore relata cognovimus.

41

De contracto et vinculatis liberatis

Alia vero festivitate adveniente, quae in hieme celebratur, Maurellus quidam ex domo Ponticonensi, servus Agini Ducis, qui mense Martio per incursionem nescio quam unius poplitis perdiderat usum, et gressum figere non valens, adhibito sibi ad geniculum fuste, ut mos est claudorum, adfuit. Is cum per triduum orationem fudisset ad Dominum, quarta die, quae est in crastinum de festivitate, genu directo, sanus abscessit.

2 Post paucos autem dies homines qui carceris vinculis tenebantur, divinitus absoluti, sancti basilicam sunt ingressi et per iudicem immunes a damno laxati sunt.

shouted: "I give thanks to you, almighty God, who ordered me to sail on this journey! For already now, before seeing your saint's sacred building, I have been granted his favor!"

When, after sailing, they had reached Bordeaux, Maura- 4
nus left the ship, went to the basilica there of the holy man of God, and fulfilled his vow. What we have just written we learned as told from the man's own mouth.

41

About a paralyzed man and prisoners who were liberated

When the other feast came, which is celebrated in the winter, a certain Maurellus from the household of Ponthion came there who was a slave of Duke Aginus, and who had lost the use of one knee in March by some kind of attack; unable to walk, he had fastened a stick to his knee, as is the custom of the lame. When he had poured forth his prayer to the Lord for three days, on the fourth, which was the day after the feast, his knee was straightened and he left in good health.

A few days later, men who had been bound with prison 2
chains were divinely released; they walked into the basilica and were allowed to leave by the judge without punishment.

42

De alio contracto

Puer quidam pedibus manibusque contractus, de villa Themello in pago Turonicae urbis, vici Ambiacensis, adveniens ad basilicam sancti, dum inter reliquos petentes postularet victus stipem, visitatus a sancti virtute, directus abscessit.

43

De pueris febricitantibus sanatis

Alius quoque puerulus Euthymi presbyteri nostri, cum in valetudinem febris nimiae incidisset, ac exanimari ab eadem putaretur, de pulvere sancti sepulchri presbyter levans, ac fimbrias pallae superpositae disrumpens secum detulit, pulveremque puero hauriendum dedit, fimbrias vero collo eius alligavit. Mox, febre restincta, sanatus est.

42

About another crippled man

A servant of the estate of Thomeau, in the village of Amboise in the territory of the city of Tours, came with crippled feet and hands to the basilica of the holy man, and while he was begging for money for food among the other beggars he was visited by the power of the holy man, and left straightened.

43

About fever-stricken servants who were healed

Another servant too, this one belonging to our priest Euthymius, had fallen into the illness of a severe fever and was thought to have been almost killed by it; the priest took some dust from the holy tomb, tore out some threads from the cloth hanging over it, took them with him, and gave the servant the dust to drink, fastening the threads around his neck. Soon the fever was extinguished and he was made healthy.

2 Non dispari modo et Ulfaricus presbyter alteri puero febricitanti studium adhibens subvenit, et ille protinus per virtutem sancti febre carens, convaluit.

44

De Principio amente

Principius quidam vir bonus, Petrocoricae urbis civis, amentiam nescio quam incurrisse putabatur, et tam graviter
2 agebatur interdum, ut de sensu videretur excidere. Quod cum multis mensibus perferret, beati antistitis basilicam expetivit; ibique, ut arbitror, quattuor residens menses, abstinens se a cibo carnium ac vino, adiutus confessoris beati praesidio, incolumis domui suae restitutus est.

In a similar manner, the priest Ulfaric's care too helped 2
another servant stricken by fever; through the power of the holy man he lost the fever at once and recovered.

44

About Principius, who was mad

A certain Principius, a respectable man and a citizen of the city of Périgueux, was thought to have incurred madness in some way, and was being tormented so severely at that
time that he seemed to have lost his senses. When he had 2
suffered this for many months, he came to the basilica of the holy bishop; and after he had stayed there, I think, for four months, abstaining from meat and wine, he was helped by the protection of the blessed confessor and given back to his home in good health.

45

De caeco et contracto

Et quia rusticitas hominum, dum parum praedicationem sacerdotalem sequitur, ipsa se praeparat ad Dei offensam, quod nuper gestum fuit edicam.

2 Leodulfus quidam, Biturigae urbis homo, cum fenum se-
cuisset, metuens ne adventu pluviae venientis infunderetur
et laborem suum perderet, die dominico mane iunctis bobus, ad pratum direxit ac super plaustrum fenum agglome-
rare coepit, statimque pes eius unus quasi ardens ei visus est,
3 regressusque ad hospitium suum, quievit ab opere. Post missarum vero solemnia celebrata, iterum iunctis bobus opus
coeptum pergit explere, completumque cum esset plaustrum feno, statim oculi eius quasi a quibusdam aculeis
puncti, dolorem maximum intulerunt. Quibus conclusis
numquam deinceps eos aperire potuit.

4 Sicque per annum integrum in caecitate permanens, ad festivitatem sancti antistitis devotus advenit, cuius post diem tertiam, beneficio lucis quam perdiderat restauratus est.

5 Eo tempore et alius contractus adveniens, virtute sancti directus, propriis gressibus ad urbem suam regressus est.

45

About a blind man and a crippled man

And because human ignorance does little to obey priestly preaching and sets itself up for offending God, I will make known what happened recently.

A certain Leodulf, a man from the city of Bourges, having 2
mowed his hay and afraid that the imminent arrival of rain
would drench it and that he would lose the result of his labor, yoked his oxen at dawn on a Sunday, led them to the
field, and began to heap up the hay on top of a cart; when,
suddenly, one of his feet seemed to be on fire, he stopped
work and returned to his hut. After he had attended the cel- 3
ebration of the solemnities of mass, he yoked his oxen again
and went to finish the work he had begun; when the cart was
full with hay, it was as if his eyes were immediately punc-
tured with sharp points, which gave him acute pain. After
his eyes had closed, he was unable to open them again.

When he had remained in this blindness for a whole year, 4
he devoutly came to the feast of the holy bishop, and after its third day, he was restored to the benefit of the light which he had lost.

At that time, too, another crippled man came, was 5
straightened by the power of the holy man, and returned to his city on his own feet.

46

Advenerat quidam ex Brittannia, nomine Paternianus, qui caecus, mutus, ac surdus, et manibus contractus per quoddam contagium fuerat, et confectis omnibus membris a morbo; soli tantum pedes praebebant homini sustentacu-
2 lum. Patroni praepotentis hic expetiit basilicam, orationem fudit, apertis oculis lucem perditam aspexit, manus ad usum pristinum recepit; et se salvatum beati antistitis virtute demirans, sospitatis suae gratiam populis declaravit. Ob huius miraculi gratiam a multis munera capit, de quibus iam nonnullos a iugo captivitatis exemit.

47

Praesenti quoque tempore apud Burdegalensem urbem domus una ignibus comprehensa vehementer coepit exuri.
2 Cumque, flammis hinc et inde spatiantibus, aliae domus huic discrimini subiacerent, nec esset dubium easdem huius fomitis calore depasci, congregatus in circuitu populus nomen beati Martini coepit attentius invocare, et ne vicinas domos virtus eius exuri permitteret cum lacrimis deprecari.

46

Someone named Paternianus, who came from Brittany, was blind, mute, and deaf; his hands had become crippled through some evil disease, and all his limbs had been wasted
by the illness; only his feet supported the man. He came to 2
the basilica of the powerful patron, and after he had poured forth his prayer, his eyes opened and he saw the light he had lost and received the original use of his hands; full of wonder at his salvation by the power of the blessed bishop, he declared his gratitude for his health to the people. On account of the grace of this miracle, he received gifts from many people with which he ransomed several people from the yoke of captivity.

47

In the present time also, a house in the city of Bordeaux
caught fire and began to burn fiercely. When the flames, 2
traveling here and there, exposed other houses to this danger and no one doubted that they would be devoured by the heat of the blaze, people gathered round them and began to invoke the name of the blessed Martin fervently, begging with tears that his power should not allow the adjoining houses to be consumed.

3 Sicque ad elevatam vocem deflentium coepit crepitus flammae decidere, atque illis clamantibus ad caelum, advenit subito, antistite impartiente, praesidium. Collisumque supplici oratione incendium, restinxit plebs per lacrimas quod nequiverat superare per undas.

4 Eo tempore puer noster Laudovaldus cum graviter a dysenteria fatigaretur, ut de pulvere sepulcri accepit, protinus morbo caruit.

And thus while the shouts of the weeping people went in 3
this way up to heaven, the crackling of the flames began to
die down, and while they were still crying to heaven, suddenly, the help imparted by the bishop came. Thus the fire
was put out by humble prayer, and the people extinguished
with tears what they had not been able to overcome with
water.

At that time, our servant Laudovald was severely afflicted 4
by dysentery, but when he swallowed some of the dust from
the tomb, he immediately was free of sickness.

Abbreviations

AA = Auctores antiquissimi

App. = Krusch, *Appendix*

Bordier = *Les livres des miracles et autres opuscules de Georges Florent Grégoire, évêque de Tours,* ed. and trans. Henri L. Bordier. Société de l'Histoire de France, Publications 88 (De passione, virtutibus et gloria sancti Iuliani martyris, pp. 302–93), 103 (De virtutibus sancti Martini episcopi, pp. 2–335), 114 (Vitae patrum seu Liber de vita quorumdam feliciosorum, pp. 132–99) (Paris, 1857, 1860, 1862).

CCSL = Corpus Christianorum Series Latina

CSEL = Corpus Scriptorum Ecclesiasticorum Latinorum

DACL = *Dictionnaire d'Archéologie et de Liturgie chrétienne*

DS = *Dictionnaire de Spiritualité*

GC = *In gloria confessorum*

GM = *In gloria martyrum*

Historiae = *Historiae* [*Historiarum libri decem*], ed. Bruno Krusch and Wilhelm Levison. MGH SSrM 1.1, ed. altera (Hanover, 1951).

James = *Gregory of Tours: Life of the Fathers,* trans. Edward James. TTH 1 (Liverpool, 1985).

Krusch = Krusch, Bruno, ed. *Miracula et opera minora.* MGH SSrM 1.2 (Hanover, 1885).

MGH SSrM = Monumenta Germaniae Historica, Scriptores rerum Merovingicarum

PL = *Patrologia Latina*

RSV = Revised Standard Version

SC = Sources chrétiennes

SSrM = Scriptores rerum Merovingicarum

TTH = Translated Texts for Historians

Vita M = Paulinus Petricordiensis, *Vita sancti Martini*

VJ = *Virtutes sancti Iuliani*

VM = Sulpicius Severus, *Vita sancti Martini*

VP = *Vita patrum*

VPI = *Vitae patrum Iurensium*

VsM = Gregorius Turonensis, *Virtutes sancti Martini*

V-T = Vieillard-Troiekouroff, May. *Les Monuments religieux de la Gaule d'après les oeuvres de Grégoire de Tours* (Paris, 1976).

Note on the Texts

No autograph of Gregory's works survives, and the orthography of the earliest manuscripts of his *Histories* is distinctly Merovingian with frequent confusions of *e* and *i, o* and *u,* loss of final *–m,* as well as hyperurbanistic *–ae* for *e,* to name the main symptoms. Because Gregory pleaded his lack of education in the Roman classics, his orthography has been and still is disputed: are its many deviations from classical Latin usage his own, or, at least in part, those of Merovingian copyists? Editors must print something, and editorial choices have differed, with Krusch invariably preferring the most Merovingian variants.[1] The earliest manuscripts of Gregory's miracle books, however, date from the ninth century. Where their readings are more normative, they could, but do not have to, originate in corrections made during the eighth-century Carolingian spelling reform. Gregory's original spelling may be unrecoverable, but many orthographical variants have no effect on the meaning of the text. Seeing that scholars attribute a certain classical and Christian learning to their author,[2] this edition normalizes to the most classical orthography in the manuscripts. This choice may not satisfy Vulgar Latin or Romance philologists, but the focus here is on content, not on orthography. And in content there is no significant difference between the modern editions of the works here presented.

The Latin text is based on the more correctly spelled edition of Henri Bordier (1856–1862), based on that of Thierry Ruinart (1699), with occasional variants drawn from that of Bruno Krusch (1885) or his Appendix (1920). The full titles of the works, abbreviated in the text, are given in the Notes to the Texts. For reasons of reference, all the introductory passages to the chapters, whether so named in the original text or not, have been given the title "Prologus." In all of the texts, Bordier's spelling has been silently normalized, e.g., the substitution of *i* for *j, m(p)* for *n(p), e* for *ae,* and *ae* for *oe.* For easier reading, his punctuation too has regularly been modified.

Those who wish to explore the orthography of the surviving versions of Gregory's hagiographical works should examine Bordier's and, especially, Krusch's editions and the latter's Appendix. Bordier's and Krusch's different numbering of the chapter titles in the *VJ* has been indicated in the appropriate place in the Notes to the Texts.

Notes

1 In the Introduction to his edition of Gregory's works, Krusch outlines the spelling of the different manuscripts on pp. 27–31.

2 For instance, Zelzer, "Frage," 235–39; and Büchner, I, Einleitung xliv–xlv. Shanzer, "Gregory of Tours," agrees and discusses its various aspects.

Notes to the Texts

Vita Patrum

title Liber vitae patrum *Krusch*: Vitae patrum seu Liber de vita quorumdam feliciosorum *Bordier*

2.3.3 tantum sanctae reliquiae siccarentur *Krusch*: quo sanctae reliquiae ligarentur *Bordier*

Haec videns . . . ex lana *Krusch*: *om. Bordier*

2.4.6 Quos . . . linteis *Krusch*: *om. Bordier*

Oppletamque . . . collocavit *Krusch*: *om. Bordier*

4.1.7 Reddat *Krusch*: reddet *Bordier*

4.5.1 truclionem *Krusch, presumably from* trulleum *or* trulleus: truchione *Bordier*

5.prol.3 de infimis *Krusch*: de infirmis *Bordier*

5.1.1 Hic *Krusch*: Sic *Bordier*

6.6.1 confractus *Krusch*: contactus quidem *Bordier*

6.6.5 post octo vero annos time" *Krusch*: post octo vero annos expletos migrabis a saeculo" *Bordier*

Unde manifestum . . . discessisse *Krusch*: Quod postea manifestum fuit *Bordier*

7.4.3 in ora proiciens *Krusch*: in manu tenens *Bordier*

ecclesiam petit per quam *Krusch in brackets*: *om. Bordier*

10.3.4 sine radice radicibus *Krusch*: sine radice ramis *Bordier*

12.3.6 voce magna *Krusch*: *om. Bordier*

13.title reclauso *Krusch*: *om. Bordier*

14.2.3 erat enim magna patientia *Krusch*: erat autem magna patientia *Bordier*

15.prol.1 vanitantium *Krusch* and *Bordier:* vanitatum *Vulgate; Krusch sug-*

gests a parallel with Augustine's De moribus ecclesiae *c. 21, and with the older Itala translation of the Bible.*

15.1.1 genere Theifalus *Krusch*: gente Theifalus *Bordier*

16.prol.5 quia dexteram *Krusch*: quae dexteram *Bordier*

19.4.2 sanctificationemque *Krusch*: sanctimoniamque *Bordier*

De passione, virtutibus et gloria sancti Iuliani martyris

prol.2 innocuas *Krusch*: nocuas *Bordier*

5.1 congregationis nostrae *Krusch App.*: contagionis medelam *Bordier*

19.title periuravit *Krusch*: peieravit *Bordier*

21.1 qua *Krusch*: quia *Bordier*

25.3 decedentibus *Krusch*: decindentibus *Bordier*

31.2 Vidimus et nunc *Krusch*: Vidimus etiam *Bordier*

32.2 dum via cum psallendo *Krusch*: dum viatim psallendo *Bordier*

34.3 At ego *Krusch begins his chapter 35 here, and thereafter stays one digit ahead of Bordier until chapter 46, which he divides up into 46a and 46b. Bordier here continues his chapter 34, and his numbering has been followed.*

Bordier	*Krusch*
34	*34, 35*
35	*36*
36	*37*
37	*38*
38	*39*
39	*40*
40	*41*
41	*42*
42	*43*
43	*44*
44	*45*
45	*46a*
46	*46b*
47	*47*

35.title crevit *Krusch* note: creverit *Bordier*

35.6 Maius *Krusch*: magis *Bordier*

44.3 ut eos vidit *Krusch*: ut eum vidit *Bordier*

De virtutibus sancti Martini episcopi

Book 1

2.10 experti sunt *Krusch App.*: experiere *Bordier*

15.title sub *Krusch*: super *Bordier*

20.1 cuidam *Krusch*: quidam *Bordier*

Book 2

3.title Maurusa *Krusch*: Mauruza and Maurusa *Bordier*

24.3 aeatatis suae undecimo *Bordier and Krusch. The oldest manuscripts have* undecimo *(eleventh), which does not accord with the reference to the boy as* adultu[s] *(adult) in the previous sentence. Krusch notes that a later manuscript has* XLmo *(transcribed: fortieth), suggesting that earlier copyists may have misread* XLmo *as* XImo *(eleventh).*

Book 3

60.9 resurrectionis carnis nostrae tempore: resurrectionis carnis omni tempore *Krusch*

Book 4

6.3 talia tunc miracula *Krusch*: talia nunc miracula *Bordier; the reference here appears to be to the miracles just recounted, which is supported by the past perfect tense of the verb.*

15.1 nullum prorsus capiendi *Krusch*: nullum prorsus suscipiendi *Bordier*

30.1 Locociagense: Locotigiacensim *Krusch; still other spellings are mentioned by both Bordier and Krusch.*

45.title De caeco et contracto *Krusch*: De Leodulfo caeco sanato *Bordier. Bordier places this chapter's last sentence about a paralytic at the beginning of the next chapter, where it seems out of place.*

46.title *om. Krusch*: De duobus aliis contractis Bordier; *as indicated, in his edition the story begins with the last sentence of the preceding story.*

47.title *om. Krusch*: De incendio ope eius exstincto *Bordier*

Notes to the Translations

The Life of the Fathers

title Because it accords better with Gregory's intention as stated below, Krusch's title with "life," in the singular, has been chosen.

Prol.1 Mentioning listeners is evidence that the work was intended to be read aloud, perhaps to the clergy at mealtimes.

Prol.2 Aulus Gellius speaks of "lives" in his *Noctes Atticae* 1.3.1 and 13.2.1. Pliny's *Art of Grammar* does not survive; it is mentioned, however, in the preface to his *Natural History.* Pliny the Elder died in the Vesuvian eruption that buried Pompeii in 79 CE. As indicated in the Introduction, that Gregory here chooses to speak of "life" as that of the body alone seems to belie his intention to portray one holy "life" in its many variations.

Prol.3 In the manuscripts, *The Glory of the Confessors* [*GC*] follows the *VP.*

Krusch, 663, n. 1, notes that Gregory changes his mind about his titles.

Gregory says more about his lack of education in *VP* 2.prol, and in his *VsM* 1.prol.

Prol.4 Jesus heals a mute man in Mark 7:32–35.

1.prol.2 See the Introduction on the Levitical rules of purity and pollution with regard to the sacred (as in Leviticus 11:44 and James 1:21) then adopted by the Church.

1.prol.3 The Lamb is a symbol for Christ. Gregory appears to associate lust with fire in *VP* 15.prol.2.

1.prol.4 Romanus is thought to have lived from ca. 400 to ca. 460, and Lupicinus to have died in 480 (Heinzelmann, "Prosopographie," Romanus, p. 641, and Lupicinus 4, p. 682). An earlier and lengthier account of their life and deeds—*VPI*—is thought to have been written soon after the abbots' deaths around 515 CE. The many differences between this and Gregory's, much shorter, account may indicate that Gregory depended on another source and did not know the earlier Life, or only an unreliable summary of it (James, 3, n. 1). On the influence of the tradition of Saint Martin, the monastery of Lérins, and John Cassian's writings on these founders, see Prinz, *Frühes Mönchtum,* 66–69.

1.1.2 In the fifth century the Burgundians had occupied and settled the eastern part of what had been Roman Gaul; the Alemans remained in German territory.

1.1.3 Gregory uses different circumlocutions for the devil; when necessary they have been capitalized to avoid confusion with a human agent. As will be seen, and as indicated by Stancliffe, *St. Martin,* 194–95, actions could be attributed to the devil or a demon when the speaker was well aware that the agent was human. The angel Lucifer, identified with the devil, was expelled from heaven in Isaiah 14:12; similarly, Revelation 12:9.

demons: The earlier Life describes Romanus as living in a crevice in the rocks, roofed by an old pine tree (*VPI* [1.1] 7–8) but does not mention stones descending upon him as a reason for returning to the world.

1.1.4 Compare Virgil, *Aeneid* 3.56: *Quid non mortalia pectora cogis?*

The phrase "soldiers of Christ" is ironic: the men are being accused of weakness. The life of the saint was imagined, as that of the former martyr, as a battle against evil forces, as for instance in Ephesians 6:11. Gregory's monastic model, Cassian's *Institutes* (*VP* 20.2), calls monks *milites Christi* (1.1.1 and more often).

1.1.7 Being accused of weakness by a woman is a double insult, because, as in *VP* 19.prol.3, women were then regularly designated as the weaker sex.

1.2.1 The "banner of the Cross" is almost certainly a metaphor for its protection, perhaps alluding to the emperor Constantine's winning the battle of the Milvian bridge in 312 under the banner of the Cross (Lactantius, *De mortibus persecutorum* 44.5).

1.2.2 Condat is now Saint Claude, département Jura (V-T 241).

1.2.3 The monastery of *Lauconnum* is now Saint Lupicin, département Jura (Prinz, *Frühes Mönchtum,* 66).

The third monastery in Alemannia is now Romainmoutier, canton Vaud, district Orbe (V-T 230).

1.2.4 According to the *VPI* (1.8) 24, the brothers shared the position of abbot.

1.2.5 Rufinus's *Historia monachorum* (*HM*), which Gregory mentions as a monastic model in *VP* 20.3.2, transmits the Egyptian monks' counsel that drinking water increases the seminal fluid, which would increase the number of sinful erotic dreams, and also associates it with the presence of demons (*HM* 20.2.2, 27.7.3).

1.3.5 Compare Psalms 1:4, "the wicked are . . . like chaff."

1.3.6 Saint Martin, too, believed that every sinner could count on forgiveness, even the devil (Sulpicius Severus, *VM* 22.3–5); this was the controversial position of Origen.

1.3.7 Penance was an ecclesiastically supervised personal practice that consisted of fasting, praying, and exclusion from communion.

1.4.1 As in the Old Testament (Numbers 5:2), lepers were then separated from society. Whereas the Council of Orléans (549) had ordered bishops to feed and clothe lepers, the Council of Lyon (583) ordered their separation from society. Compare John 13:14–15, Jesus's command to wash each other's feet.

1.4.2 In Leviticus, leprosy is regarded as an impurity that prohibits contact with the sacred (13:8).

1.5.1 King Chilperic I ruled from ca. 460 to ca. 480.

1.5.2 In Gregory's writings, *quasi* can mean "as it were," indicating conscious imagination or unconscious illusion, but it has many other meanings, one of which is "to refer," as here, "to intention"; as will be seen, another important one is to refer to the perception of a true spiritual reality; see de Nie, "Gregory of Tours' Smile," 82–84.

1.5.3 Jacob stood before the Pharaoh in Genesis 47:7–10.

1.5.6 The Germanic kings had taken over the Roman state's treasury.

1.6.4 *VPI* 2.16 mentions this monastery as being Lauconnum.

Prinz, *Frühes Mönchtum,* 103–4, reports that Condat and Romainmoutier practiced the *laus perennis,* or continuous singing of praise, a custom followed by some monasteries in Constantinople.

2.prol.1 Luke 8:11 refers to the word of Christ's salvation as a "seed," and John 4:14 refers to Christ's teaching as water welling up to eternal life.

2.prol.3 In this prologue, Gregory makes it very clear that Christ's passion and death on the cross is the model to be imitated, not only in early Christian martyrdom but also in the late-antique Christian ascetic culture, itself sometimes referred to as a "bloodless martyrdom" (as in Sulpicius Severus, *Epistola* 2.12).

2.prol.6 Gregory here alludes to the gathering of the apostles in John 20:19.

"Lifted up into heaven," as in Luke 24:51, and Acts 1:9.

2.prol.7 Illidius was the fourth bishop of Clermont from ca. 370 to ca. 387; *Historiae* 1.45 gives a short version of this chapter.

Begging the readers' indulgences was a standard element in the literary introductions of the period and need not reflect any real lack of quality, as in Sulpicius Severus's preface to his *Vita sancti Martini.* Gregory, however, was serious about his lack of education.

2.prol.8 At that time, Avitus was archdeacon; he was bishop of Clermont from ca. 572 to ca. 594.

2.prol.9 The tradition of following the bridegroom derives from Isaiah 62:5, when God speaks to Jerusalem as his bride; Christ speaks of himself as a bridegroom in Matthew 9:15, and is understood to be the bridegroom mentioned in the story of the wise and foolish maidens in Matthew 25:1–13.

With his "crude rusticity," Gregory means not only the language of peasants but also the simpler, conversational, language of those not educated in classical literature and formal style.

2.1.1 Normally, the people's role was to acclaim the choice of the other bishops of the diocese and, sometimes, the higher clergy; a document of election was then sent to the king for his approval.

2.1.2 Maximus was Roman Emperor from 383 to 388.

Possession is described in the New Testament (for instance, in Mark 1:23–26) and continued into Gregory's time. Brown, *Cult,* 110, regards it as an articulation and resolution of tensions in a repressive situation.

2.1.3 Prostration was then the usual position of petitional prayer.

Saint Martin, too, had put his fingers in someone's mouth during an exorcism in Sulpicius Severus, *VM* 17.6. Rousselle, "Sanctuaire," 1098, regards this as a stimulus to induce vomiting, by which the evil spirit would exit the body, a well-known practice in Greek medicine; it would accord with this kind of cure usually being described as a "cleansing." The same technique is used below in chapter 4.4.2.

2.1.4 Illidius must have died in 384 or 385, for his successor, Nepotianus, was bishop of Clermont at a synod in 385.

2.2.2 An example of miracles "blemished" by their living agent's vainglory would be those of the deacon Secundellus in *VP* 10.2.

2.2.4 Gallus governed the church of Clermont from 525 to 551; his life is described below in *VP* 6.

Prayer with tears was regarded as the most perfect prayer, involving supreme contrition, that would be likely to reach its destination and its object; Gregory describes it at some length in his *VsM* 3 prologue.

2.2.5 This ostensibly casual reference to the pagan notion of "lot" (*sub sorte*) seems unintentional.

2.2.6 As will be seen, Gregory regards the speaking of words, especially holy names, as producing immediate spiritual effects.

2.2.7 As many other examples of fluid discharges at the moment of healing show, Gregory appears to have meant this literally; see for instance *VsM* 2.20.

2.2.8 Venerandus was Count of Clermont (Selle-Hosbach, *Prosopographie,* 163).

2.3.1 The first year of Illidius's episcopate was in 573–574.

Relics are here described as, literally, "sureties" of the saints' presence.

2.3.2 In this context, an "abbot" is the leader of the resident cathedral clergy.

2.4.1 Anointing was then part of the baptismal ritual.

2.4.2 The cock can be a symbol or manifestation of Christ, as in Gregory's favorite poet Prudentius, *Cathemerinon* 1.97–100.

2.4.3 The morning light is a symbol of Christ, as in John 1:9, and Prudentius, *Cathemerinon* 1.97–100.

It is unclear whether the dedication of her son was as the saint's lay client, or as a future priest.

The "bonds" of the illness may have been those inflicted by an evil spirit; as will be seen, Gregory often describes illness as caused by an almost personalized evil force.

2.4.4 Chunks of limestone are baked here, ostensibly to make cement.

A saint appearing to help during the building of a church is also described in *GM* 50.

2.4.6 On Avitus, see *Historiae* 1.45.

2.5.1 Emphasizing brevity was a literary cliché in this period.

2.24.3 "Eleventh" looks like a copyist's error for "fortieth": reading XL as XI (Krusch).

3.prol.2 *Temptationes* (Krusch) or *tentationes* (Bordier) can mean temptations, but also trials or tests, which here appears to be the case.

3.prol.3 Fashioned according to God in justice, sanctity, and truth paraphrases Ephesians 4:24.

3.1.1 On the Desert Fathers as models for hermits, see Brown, *Body and Society,* 213–40.

In the first quarter of the sixth century, the Persian empire persecuted Christians as possible allies of their enemy, the East Roman Empire.

Abraham rejoiced at his imprisonment, as a kind of holy martyrdom.

The apostles in Acts 5:18–19 were also freed by an angel.

3.1.2 Cyricus was abbot there in the period 475 to 484 CE. The church, now Saint Cirgues, was a bit more than half a mile outside the walls of Clermont (V-T 81).

3.1.3 An *amphora* can be a pointed vase with two ears, but also a liquid measure.

3.1.4 In 1 Kings 17:12–16 Elijah increases oil for a widow.

3.1.5 In the Old Testament, the Lord's word was expected to be invariably fulfilled (1 Samuel 1:23).

In Gregory's own experience, wine once also increased (*VJ* 35).

3.1.6 Sidonius Apollinaris was bishop of Clermont from 472 to 484/89. Gregory writes about him in his *Historiae* 2.21–23.

The seven cities were in southern France; at the time, it belonged to the Visigothic kingdom (see James, 19, n. 4). Victorius commits crimes and ends miserably in *Historiae* 2.20 and in *GM* 44.

3.1.7 The epitaph may be found in Sidonius Apollinaris, *Epistolae* 7.17.2.1–30.

As will be seen, malarial fevers were widespread in Gaul in this period.

4.prol.1 According to the apostle Paul in Galatians 5:19 and 5:22.

4.prol.2 Nobility of mind and generosity were aristocratic qualities, often praised by Gregory's friend, the poet Venantius Fortunatus, as in his *Carmina* 7.1.25 and 7.5.29–30.

4.prol.3 The (feminine) word "wisdom," along with "tabernacle," seems to point to Prudentius's *Psychomachia* 902–15 as the unexpressed context here.

4.1.1 Bishop Faustus could be the abbot of Lérins, later bishop of Riez (460–490) (Heinzelmann, "Prosopographie," 607).

Prudentius speaks of "gems of virtues" *(virtutum gemmae)* in his *Psychomachia* 911.

Quintianus attended the councils of Agde (505) and Orléans (511) as bishop of Rodez, meaning that he did not, as Gregory relates in his *Historiae* 2.36, leave the city before the Frankish victory over the Visigoths in the battle of Vouillé (507), which gave them southern France. Presumably Rodez thereafter temporarily reverted to Visigothic dominion, constituting the frontier between Visigothic and Frankish territory, and the bishop's presence at a Frankish church council could have aroused the Visigoths' suspicion (James, 22, n. 4).

4.1.2 On Bishop Amantius, see V-T 229.

4.1.3 In *Historiae* 2.36, Gregory says that it was the citizens who suspected him of favoring the Franks; see on this James, 22, n. 4.

4.1.4 Quintianus succeeded the former bishop Aprunculus in 514/15. Viventiolus is recorded as bishop of Lyons in 517.

4.1.5 Gregory hints that Apollinaris's quick death in 515 was a divine punishment for his improper manner of acceding to the episcopate (compare *Historiae* 3.2).

4.1.5 King Theodoric was a son of Clovis, ruling from 511 to 533.

4.1.6 On Proculus, see Proculus 6, Heinzelmann, "Prosopographie," 675.

4.1.7 As will also be seen below, the Christian precept of forgiveness (as in the Lord's Prayer in Matthew 6:14) was for Gregory, with a few exceptions, not applicable to disrespect for saints, whose holy power was that of God.

Compare 2 Timothy 4:14: *Alexander aerarius multa mala mihi ostendit, reddat ei Dominus secundum opera eius.* This, as applied to Proculus, and its being "chanted," looks very much like a curse. The notions of curse and revenge are prominent in the Old Testament, but as Gregory's stories in the *Historiae* show, revenge was also prominent in contemporary Germanic life.

4.2.1 King Theoderic probably besieged the city in 525 (James, 23, n. 9). Gregory writes about this in his *Historiae* 3.11–13, in *VJ* 13 and 23, and below in *VP* 5.2.

Singing psalms while visiting the saints' tombs here looks like a ritual invoking their divine protection, as also in *Historiae* 3.29; below, in *VP* 17.4, we see something similar in Trier.

4.2.3 Hilpingus is otherwise unknown.

As Avitus of Vienne's letters show, an elaborate system of honorifics was in place in the early sixth century; in these, *magnificentia vestra* is used for private persons, however (Shanzer and Wood, *Avitus,* 391–94, at 392). In the same period, Bishop Caesarius of Arles used *parvitas nostra* to refer to himself in his sermons (Caesarius Arelatensis, *Sermones* 236.2 and 5). Gregory refers to himself as *mea parvitas* in *VsM* 2.40.1, but his stories show that he was addressed as *dominus,* lord (*VsM* 4.30.3); in the formal dedication of his miracle stories of Saint Martin, he refers to himself as *peccator,* sinner (*VsM* 1.prol.1).

4.2.5 Vollore, département Puy-de-Dôme (V-T 346); the same events are narrated in *Historiae* 3.13.

Here Gregory does not object to violence perpetrated inside a church, as he usually does, there showing that divine punishment for such an act quickly follows, as in *VJ* 13.

4.3.1 The slaughter and destruction in Clermont is described in *VJ* 23.

Hortensius: see Heinzelmann, "Prosopographie," 627.

4.3.3 Shaking the dust off one's shoes before someone imitated the curse recommended by Jesus in Matthew 10:14–15 against those who do not receive, or wish to hear the words of, his disciples.

Quintianus here combines the imperative of a curse with a prayer for further vengeance. Below in *VP* 6.4 and in *Historiae* 4.35, this curse is adduced as the reason that Hortensius's son Evodius, and his grandson Eufrasius, later did not become bishop.

4.3.4 Quintianus's ritual act resulting in death at a distance looks like what late Roman law labeled sorcery *(maleficium)*. For Gregory, however, it resembles the power of the Old Testament prophets; in his view, only God's power can do this, sorcerers are ineffective (compare *Historiae* 5.39 and 6.35).

4.3.5 As will be seen, Gregory often uses "appear" and "is manifested" for what he believes to be divinely caused events.

4.4.1 In Matthew 25:40, Jesus declared that he himself would be fed when a poor man was fed.

4.4.2 Often, as in *VP* 8.4.3, evil spirits were forced to identify themselves by a process of spiritual torture that resembled Roman judicial torture to elicit confession (as Brown, *Cult,* 108).

The location of the monastery of Cambidobrum is unknown, and its name in nominal form unattested, but it is likely to be

Cambidobrum, apparently in the diocese of Clermont (V-T 464); also mentioned below in chapter 5.3.3.

4.4.3 The Rogations were three days of prayer, fasting, liturgical celebrations, and processions to demonstrate humility and ask for divine forgiveness for putative sins committed, instituted around 470 by Bishop Mamertus of Vienne after unusual natural phenomena—understood to be a divine punishment for sin—had caused fear in his city; other cities thereafter adopted them (*Historiae* 2.34).

4.4.4 A goat's hair shirt was the dress then adopted by ascetics, and in this case it was a sign of contrition.

The bishop's act resembles the prophet Elijah's prayer for rain in 1 Kings 18:42; Gregory seems to regard the bishop as a contemporary version of an Old Testament prophet.

4.5.1 Deuteronomy 26:17 also mentions the "ways" of God.

In Gaul, a "senator" was in theory an honorary member of the Roman Senate, but as Gregory often shows, a Gallo-Roman aristocrat by birth (*VP* 6.prol.3).

4.5.2 The basilica of Stephen was built by the wife of Quintianus's predecessor Namatius (*Historiae* 2.17).

Fever is here associated with the presence of a (probably demonic) "fire" that can be put out. Tertian and quartan fevers are malaria-like fevers with severe chills occurring every third or fourth day.

5.prol.1 Compare Matthew 5:12: "your reward is great in heaven."

5.prol.3 Galatians 4:6–7 also refers to coheirs with his Only Son.

Purple-colored robes were the prerogative of emperors.

5.prol.4 John 12:31, 14:30, and 16:11 also refer to the ruler of this world, the devil, whose dominion was restricted to this world.

5.1.1 Portianus was probably born in the period 450 to 470.

A "barbarian" is presumably a pagan of Germanic origin.

5.1.3 In this period, eyes were thought to emit a ray of light that "touched" its object and thereby became impressed with its pattern and transmitted this impression to the soul (Miles, "Vision," 127–28).

5.1.5 Monks were regarded as "clerics" in this period.

The monastery was later named after Portianus: Saint-Pourçain-sur-Sioule, département Allier (V-T 265).

Chewing salt was a self-mortification inspired by sayings such as Romans 8:13: "If you live according to the flesh, you will die, but if by the Spirit you put to death the deeds of the body, you will live."

5.2.1 Theoderic's destruction is described in *Historiae* 3.11–13.

The village of Artonne lies in the département Puy-de-Dôme (V-T 18).

5.2.2 According to *Historiae* 3.13, Sigivald was a relative of King Theoderic; his crimes are related in 3.16; he is also mentioned in *VJ* 13 and 23, and below in *VP* 12.2.

5.2.3 Singing the psalms was part of the canonical office of Matins.

5.2.4 The large snake was a manifestation of the devil (as in Genesis 3); it signifies the poison contained in the drink.

5.2.5 Touching the fringe of the robe of Jesus, in Matthew 14:36, resulted in healing.

5.2.6 In this period, prisoners of war were regarded as legitimate booty and if not redeemed by their families were put to work as slaves; redeeming captives, then, was an important work of charity, as also below in *VP* 15.4.2.

The resuscitation of Lazarus (John 11:43) is one of Gregory's prime models for saints' beneficial actions; he mentions it again below, in *VP* 7.7.14.

5.3.3 Nothing more is known about this Protasius.

Hermits could live alone in the wilderness or enclosed in a cell near a monastery, as here, and also in *Historiae* 6.29.

6.prol.1 Compare Prudentius, *Hamartigenia* 257: *auri namque fames parto fit maior ab auro.*

6.prol.3 Jesus commanded the leaving behind of worldly goods in Luke 18:22, 25.

6.prol.4 Gallus here applied Jesus's injunction in Matthew 10:37 to love him more than one's parents.

6.1.1 Gallus was born around 486.

Georgius and Leocadia were also the parents of Gregory's father (Florentius), Gallus's brother. Before our author took on the name Gregorius at his consecration to the episcopacy (perhaps as a tribute to his maternal great-grandfather Bishop Gregory of Langres; see *VP* 7), his name was Georgius Florentius (see *VJ* 23).

Vectius Epagatus is mentioned in Eusebius, *Ecclesiastical History* 5.1. Gregory mentions his forebear in *GM* 48 and *Historiae* 1.29.

6.1.2 Six Roman miles are the equivalent of a bit more than six English miles. Cournon: département Puy-de-Dôme (V-T 93).

Shaving the top of the head is part of the ritual of being ordained as a cleric.

6.2.1 In this period a very religious young saint was often characterized as a *puer senex,* a young old man (E. R. Curtius, *European Literature and the Latin Middle Ages* [New York, 1953], 98–101).

6.2.2 In this period young boys of notable families were frequently educated away from home in the household of a relative of high position; thus, as will be seen, Gregory himself was raised in his uncle Gallus's household (chapter 2.2.4).

6.2.3 According to *Historiae* 3.5, Theoderic's queen was a daughter of the Burgundian king Sigismund; her name may have been Suavegotho (Heinzelmann, "Prosopographie," 694, 697).

6.2.6 Saint Martin was known for setting fire to heathen temples (Sulpicius Severus, *VM* 14).

6.3.1 Bishop Quintianus died in 525.

Impetratus was the brother of Gallus's mother Leocadia (Heinzelmann, "Prosopographie," 629).

6.3.2 Gregory interprets as divine inspiration what to others may have appeared as his uncle's strategy of using his favorable position with the king as a means to acquire the episcopate.

6.3.5 Nicetius's biography is contained in *VP* 17.

6.3.6 In Gregory's view the document was foolish because the citizens' party would not recognize the will of God; Krusch notes that Marculf's *Formulae* 1.7 gives a *Consensus civium pro episcopatum* (ed. Zeumer, 47).

Selling or buying ecclesiastical offices was prohibited by Gallic church councils from 533 on, but the prohibition was evidently not successful (James, 36, n. 12).

6.3.7 A *triens,* or third of a golden *solidus,* was actually a generous gift; 4 golden *solidi* supported a soldier for a whole year (James, 36, n. 13).

6.3.8 A spiritual joke, perhaps hinting at either the Creation of Eve or the Crucifixion.

6.4.1 In this hierarchical society, goodwill was won through humility.

The Hebrews did not always listen to and obey Moses, as in Exodus 6:8.

6.4.3 Evodius was the son of Hortensius, who had insulted Bishop Quintianus (chapter 4.3).

Roman cemeteries were outside the city walls, and this is where the saints too were buried and given chapels or basilicas around their tombs. Going there to pray was here evidently understood to indicate that the bishop was asking these saints for help in punishing the wrongdoer.

6.4.5 Between 535 and 541 others signed acts of councils as bishop of Javols.

6.5.1 This bishops' gathering took place in 549.

Childebert I was king of Frankish Austrasia (511–558).

6.5.3 Presumably he left his seat with Gallus's clergy in the nave to sing with the other bishop's choir, in the apse.

6.5.4 The Church attempted to abolish the pagan names for the days of the week.

6.6.1 A *defensor* was a layman whose official task was to defend ecclesiastical interests in the secular sphere. Julianus is described in *Historiae* 4.32 as a miracle worker.

Severe shakings or chills were characteristic of these fevers.

6.6.2 The Bible's divine words seem to be understood as the presence of Christ, the Word.

6.6.3 Like Bishop Mamertus of Vienne (4.4.3), Gregory assumes a natural disaster is either a sign of divine displeasure or a sign of some imminent great event; see on this de Nie, *Views,* 27–69.

6.6.4 The same story about the plague is told in *Historiae* 4.5. The illness came from Crimea to the West in 543 CE and remained endemic there until the end of the seventh century.

6.6.6 On Rogations, see *VP* 4.4.3.

6.7.2 This revelation of the Lord probably took place in a dream.

6.7.3 Krusch (685, n. 1) notes that these allelujas would now be called Lauds; Psalms 146–50 were called *alleluiatici* from their first words (compare James, 40, n. 22).

6.7.4 Gallus probably died in 551. According to Gregory's description, he must have been born in 487 and made bishop in 525 (Krusch, 685, n. 2 and James, 40, n.23).

6.7.6 The basilica of Lawrence is mentioned in *Historiae* 2.20 (see V-T 247 and 83).

6.7.10 Gregory's *hauriunt* is not directly translatable into English (*haurire* means "to drink or draw into oneself"); it seems to indicate that he regarded this health as literally being absorbed or taken in through contact with the holy tomb.

6.7.11 Valentinianus is mentioned in chapter 6.5.2.

6.7.12 The holy man, as a "patron" or foster father, was said to have "foster sons." Gregory refers to himself as the martyr Julian's "foster son" in *VJ* 2.1.

6.7.13 "Breakings" were attacks of fever with its accompanying chills, as also in *VsM* 4.37.

7.prol.1 In Revelation 7:9 and Eucherius, *Formulae* 343–44, the palm is the reward and sign of perfection or victory over the things of the world.

7.prol.2 A body without stain would be one that had not experienced lust, which was regarded as pollution.

7.prol.3 The Lord's help could be thought of as "the shield of faith," *scutum fidei,* and "the helm of salvation," *galea salutis* (Ephesians 6:16–17).

7.1.2 Gregory was born ca. 450 and his sons were Tetricus, his successor as bishop of Langres, and one who fathered our author's mother, Armentaria (see Pietri, *Tours,* 792). Gregory of Langres, then, was our author's maternal great-grandfather.

7.2.1 Turning to the Lord meant embracing the religious life.

Gregory was bishop of Langres from 506/7 to 539; compare V-T numbers 97 and 98.

7.2.3 *Historiae* 3.19 gives a description of the fort of Dijon.

Praying during the night followed Psalms 119:62: "In the middle of the night I rose to praise you." It was the foundational text for the canonical night offices.

7.2.5 The "signal" was probably a bell.

7.2.8 Sulpicius Severus (*Gallus* [*Dialogi*] 2 [3].6) had reported that the possessed could hang in the air, even upside down, presumably bound with invisible demonic chains.

7.2.9 His granddaughter Armentaria was Gregory's mother.

7.3.1 "Manifesting the glory of the future resurrection" echoes Sulpicius Severus's, *Epistola* 3.17, description of the dead saint Martin.

7.3.2 The church inside the walls may be the one described in V-T 96.

The basilica of John the Baptist is mentioned in V-T 100. Gregory of Langres died in 539/40. The bishop's epitaph was written by Venantius Fortunatus (*Carmina* 4.2), probably at our author's request.

7.4.1 The heavens had also opened at Jesus's baptism (Matthew 3:16) and at Stephen's death through stoning (Acts 7:56).

Gregory sometimes (as in *Historiae* 4.37) says that angels played a role in miracles.

7.4.4 Tetricus was bishop from 539/40 to 572/73; Gregory mentions him in *Historiae* 5.5.

Altars faced east, away from the worshippers; from their point of view in the nave, this would be *behind* the altar.

7.4.6 *Apparuit* instead of *cerneretur* hints at divine agency.

Ostensum est (was shown) is a clearer indication of this.

7.5.1 Disrespecting Sunday was an infraction of the contemporary ecclesiastical law, based on the Jewish law of the Sabbath, to do no work on this day; see Matthew 12:2.

7.5.3 *Vidimus* seems to point to the author's personal observation but was perhaps conditioned by Severus's similar description of Martin's torture of the demons in the possessed (at which the author also was not present) in *Gallus (Dialogi)* 2 (3).6.

7.6.1 The thirty-third year of Nicetius's episcopate would have been in 539/40.

8.prol.1 Gregory regarded the bible's prophecies as "oracles."

8.prol.2 In Genesis 1:26 God says: "Let us make man in our image, after our likeness." In 2 Corinthians 4:4 it is said that Christ is the likeness (or image) of God. Patristic exegesis regarded Christ's deeds in the New Testament as announced in the prophecies of the Old.

8.prol.3 *Einfuli (infulae)* are woolen bands worn by pagan priests as a sign of their dignity; the term was later applied to Christian ecclesiastical headgear (Blaise, *Dictionnaire,* 444).

Krusch, 691 n. 1, has identified the unknown author of the Life as Nicetius's successor Aetherius (586–ca. 602); Heinzelmann, *Bischofsherrschaft,* 154 n. 373, and 155 n. 379, regards Aetherius as having commissioned the Life. Aetherius's *Life* of Nicetius was edited by Krusch in MGH SSrM 3, 518–24. Gregory complements his information with what probably were traditions in his family. In his *Historiae* 4.36 he gives a shorter version, with somewhat different accents.

8.1.1 Since Nicetius was the uncle of Gregory's mother, Armentaria (*Historiae* 5.5), his father, Florentinus, must have been her maternal grandfather (genealogical table: Pietri, *Tours,* 792, or Heinzelmann, *Gregor von Tours,* 12).

8.1.2 "Victor over the world" is here understood in the sense of overcoming its seductions to seek heaven; the Greek *Niketes* means victor. Nicetius was born ca. 513.

8.1.6 The conversation probably took place in a dream vision.

8.2.3 "Polluting contacts" would be sensual ones.

8.2.4 Gregory may then just have lost his father.

A *colobium* was a tunic with short sleeves.

8.3.1 This conversation took place in 552; Sacerdos had become bishop in 541 (Heinzelmann, "Prosopographie," 687: Sacerdos 2).

Childebert the Elder is Childebert I, king of Burgundy (511–558).

8.3.2 According to Gregory's genealogical table in Pietri, *Tours,* 792, Sacerdos was the brother either of Nicetius's father, Florentinus, or of Florentinus's wife, Artemia; Heinzelmann, *Gregor von Tours,* 12, decides for the latter.

8.3.3 Nicetius was consecrated bishop of Lyons presumably in the cathedral, built ca. 470 by Bishop Patiens (V-T 130). Sidonius Apollinaris described it in his *Epistola* 2.10.

A similar description of Nicetius is found in *Historiae* 4.36.

Count Armentarius's identity is unknown, but because of his name he was probably associated with Gregory's mother's family.

8.3.6 After his uncle Gallus died, Gregory probably went to Lyons to serve as a deacon with his maternal great-uncle Nicetius (Van Dam, *Saints,* 54–55).

8.4.1 The sanctuary was probably in the apse, where the choir would be.

A refrain is sung after each verse of a psalm.

8.5.1 Miracles are "signs" of the presence of the kingdom of God in John 2:11.

Nicetius would have been sixty in 573 (*Historiae* 4.36).

The story is also told, somewhat differently, in *GC* 60.

8.5.2 The basilica is that of the holy Apostles, later Saint Nizier (V-T 135).

8.5.3 Justus was bishop of Lyon from 374 to 381, and Eucherius ca. 435 to ca. 450 (Heinzelmann, "Prosopographie," 633 and 598, respectively).

8.5.6 In *Historiae* 4.36 Gregory tells us that Nicetius's successor Priscus persecuted the former bishop's friends, gives a different version of the story, and tells about more slander and heavenly vengeance after the bishop's death.

8.6.1 Gregory's deacon Agiulf was in Rome in 590, when Gregory I became pope (*Historiae* 10.1; *GM* 82).

8.6.4 We see a similar practice in *GC* 60.

8.6.5 Gregory mentions oil, and papyrus from Egypt, as important imports in *Historiae* 5.5. A papyrus roll containing the miracles of Nicetius is mentioned below in *VP* 7. 12.

8.7.1 The presence of the tomb, mentioned later in the story (5), appears to indicate that it was a certain place in Lyons.

8.7.3 Gregory recommends exerting pressure on a saint through incessant prayer, with a quotation from Luke 11:8 in *GM* 13.

8.7.5 To go to the saint's tomb in a church was to seek asylum there.

8.8.1 In *Historiae* 4.36 Gregory writes that the oil of the lamps near his tomb heals the sick.

Aetherius succeeded Priscus in 586.

8.8.3 Gallomagnus of Troyes was bishop from 562 to 582.

8.8.4 Pernay is located in the département Indre-et-Loire (V-T 204); it is not clear if it is the same one mentioned in *VJ* 50.

Gregory evidently has no qualms about using the pagan term "temple" for a Christian church.

8.8.8 Bishop Phronimius was an inhabitant of Bourges (*Historiae* 9.24) who served as bishop of Agde, then under Visigothic dominion, before 572/73, and fled to the Burgundian kingdom in 580; in 588 King Childebert made him bishop of Vence (James, 60, n. 24). The events related in this section must therefore have taken place before 580.

8.9.6 Touching the saint's signature, presumed to be linked to his holy power, here functions as an ordeal.

8.10.2 Guntram was king of Burgundy from 561 to 593.

Syagrius was bishop of Autun between 560 and 600.

8.11.1 This was perhaps the present Petit-Pressigny, département Indre-et-Loire (James, 62, n. 28). Relics were then always placed inside an altar.

8.11.3 The expedition to Comminges in 585 against the usurper Gundovald, who was defeated there, is described in *Historiae* 7.35–38.

8.11.6 Vigils were held during the evening and night before December 25.

8.11.9 Fire was sometimes used in Roman judicial torture, here metaphorically transferred to that by a saint (Brown, *Cult*, 108).

The man's dying without having done penance meant that he would go to (a fiery) hell (as in *Historiae* 2.23).

The third hour is about nine o'clock in the morning.

8.12.1 Even though it has never been in physical contact with the saint, the book's content is spiritually linked to its referent (words and names evoke the presence of their referents), and so the book itself becomes a source of holy power (on the "power" of words in Gregory's view, see de Nie, "'Power'").

8.12.3 The word "suddenly" points to an apparition.

9.prol.1 In Exodus 25 the Hebrews were exhorted in this manner to contribute to the building of the Lord's sanctuary.

9.1.1 In *Historiae* 5.10 Gregory says that Patroclus was eighty years old when he died in 576; if this is correct, he will therefore have been born in 496.

The territory of Bourges is now known as Berry.

9.1.4 Nunnio is otherwise unknown; see Heinzelmann, "Prosopographie," 658. He will have taught the boy martial skills and manners.

9.1.5 The Church was the "bride" of Christ, as in *Historiae* 1.1.

9.1.6 Compare Jesus's advice in Luke 14:26: "If anyone comes to me and does not hate his own father and mother . . . he cannot be my disciple."

Arcadius was bishop of Bourges from 535/38 to 541/49 (Heinzelmann, "Prosopographie," 559).

9.1.7 In *Historiae* 5.10 Gregory gives more details.

9.2.1 Néris is located in the département Allier (V-T 179 and 180).

9.2.2 The spirit confessed the saint's name presumably as the one who was "tormenting" him; sometimes demons also confess their own names and/or their crimes.

This is a variant of the practice of opening the Bible at random and reading the first verse seen as a divinely intended advice, as Augustine had done in the garden (*Confessiones* 8.12).

9.2.4 Mediocantus, Bordier; Moichant, Krusch and James. Later called Celle, département Allier, arrondissement Montluçon (V-T 58). Patroclus's retirement from the world took place in 558, since he lived there for eighteen years (paragraph 3), until his death in 576.

9.2.5 On exorcism by putting fingers in the mouth, see *VP* 2.1.3.

9.2.7 Presumably this was the plague that devastated central Gaul in 571, described in *Historiae* 4.31 (James, 68, n. 9).

These offerings were probably the bread and wine offered for the Eucharist, which was sometimes used as a prophylactic.

9.2.8 A description of the devil, also in 2 Corinthians 11:14.

The inclination to break his vow of solitude and service to God is here regarded as a spiritual poison.

9.2.11 As in ancient dream stories, the finding of a palpable object related to the dream's content was proof that the dream experience had been real.

10.1.1 Vindunitta is a former island in the river Brivet, north of Nantes, now the village of Besné, département Loire-Inférieure (V-T 32).

10.2.2 Sabaudus is not otherwise known.

10.2.4 The Book of Life is mentioned in Philippians 4:3.

10.2.6 In chapter 15.2 there is also a conflict between solitude and healing; there, Gregory does approve of healing at certain times, provided the hermit does not leave his cell. In chapter 11.3, a hermit heals through the window of his cell.

10.3.1 *Virtutes* can also be miracles; in this context, the term is ambiguous.

The story resembles that of Aaron's flowering rod in Numbers 17:8.

10.4.1 Brothers can be servants and/or other hermits.

10.4.4 Friardus died in 573, at the same time as Nicetius, according to *Historiae* 4.37. Gregory does not mention the fragrance there but says that the cell trembled when Bishop Felix entered, indicating the presence of an angel.

10.4.5 Here again *virtutes* can be virtues and/or miracles.

11.prol.1 The typical dance of saints in heaven is said to be a stately ceremonial, but very joyful, three-step (*tripudium* (*VJ* 50), which one is tempted to imagine as an ecstatic slow waltz.

11.1.1 *Historiae* 4.37 tells us that he died in his fiftieth year in 576; he was therefore born in 526 or 527.

Méallat is located in Arrondissement Cantal, département Mauriac (V-T 157).

11.1.13 The whole scene resembles Sulpicius Severus's description of Saint Martin's encounter with the devil in his *VM* 24.4–8.

11.2.3 Gregory here alludes to Moses's striking water from a rock in Exodus 17:6.

11.3.2 Rufinus's *HM* 6.1.2 also refers to a hermit, Theon, who blessed people through a window in his cell.

12.prol.1 Isaiah's words are closest to Gregory's quote here; in the *Vulgate,* however, *Proverbs, Ecclesiastes,* and *The Song of Solomon,* as well as *The Book of Wisdom [of Solomon]* are attributed to Solomon.

12.prol.2 On fear of the Lord, compare Psalms 111:10. Christ had said he was the true Vine and his disciples the branches, who should remain in him (John 15:4–5).

12.1.1 Pionsat is located in arrondissement Puy-de-Dôme, département Riom (V-T 206).

12.1.2 The Egyptian hermit Theon also socialized with wild animals (*HM* 6.2.9).

12.2.1 Sigivald was appointed by King Theoderic, his relative, to govern Clermont after its capture in 525; his crimes are described in *Historiae* 3.16, his miraculous repentance in *VJ* 14.

In his *Historiae* 5.12 Gregory says Bracchio was a Thuringian.

12.2.4 A *congius* was a Roman measure for liquids, each containing six *sextarii* (pints or half-liters).

12.2.6 On Christ's gentle yoke, see Matthew 11:30.

12.2.10 Sigivald was killed by King Theoderic, shortly before the latter's own death in 534 (*Historiae* 3.23).

12.3.1 Vensat was perhaps Saint Saturnin-de-Vensat, arrondissement Riom, département Puy-de-Dôme. But because it is a bit more than twenty-four miles from Pionsat, V-T 369 regards *domus Vindiciacensis* as unidentified.

12.3.2 A similar kind of ethereal fire is described in *GC* 38.

12.3.4 The monastery of Menat was located in the département Puy-de-Dôme, arrondissement Riom (V-T 158).

12.3.6 The cherubim and seraphim recall those in the vision of Isaiah 6:2.

12.3.8 Bracchio died in 576 (*Historiae* 5.12).

13.prol.1 In his *Institutes* 5.17.1, Cassian spoke of the monk as the true athlete of Christ fighting the battle according to the law *(veru*[*s*] *athleta Christi legitimo agonis iure certant*[*is*]*)*. The phrase *legitime certasset* occurs in Gregory's *VJ* 1.2 about Julian's martyrdom.

13.1.2 The location of the village of Bèbre is uncertain, perhaps it is Dompierre-sur-Bèbre, département Allier (V-T 373).

13.1.4 Senoch carried out a literal understanding of Psalm 1:2, about the just man who meditates on God's law "day and night"; Prudentius, *Cathemerinon* 6.139–44, speaks of sleep as the opportunity for an incursion of the devil, presumably in erotic dreams. As for the carrying of the stone on his neck, Cassian lets Abbot Serenus report that some monks took Jesus's command to "take up the Cross" (Matthew 10:38) literally (*Conlationes* 8.3.5).

13.3.1 The village of Trézelle is located in canton Jalligny, arrondissement Gannat, département Allier (V-T 331).

13.3.2 In Genesis 1:6–7 God is said to have separated the waters below the firmament from those above it.

13.3.4 Gregory's verbs clearly indicate that this was a seizure by force and a manipulation of the crowd by ritual acts; nevertheless, presumably because it was allowed to happen at all, he accepts it as God's will. In *VP* 9.3 there was a similar conflict over the body of the holy Patroclus.

13.3.6 The age of the priest Deodatus makes it likely that the events recounted occurred in the first half of the sixth century.

14.1.1 Martius was probably born around 435 (V-T 64).

14.1.2 Mars was the Roman god of war.

14.2.4 The description reminds of that in Virgil, *Georgics* 4.260.

14.3.1 John 1:9 speaks of Christ as "the true light."

14.4.1 Sweating in the good fight was a common athletic metaphor for a saint's exertions in serving God.

Abbot Martius died around 535 (V-T 64). If he was nearly ninety when he cured Gregory's father, he must have been born around 445.

A crown of righteousness is mentioned in 2 Timothy 4:8.

The chapel of the monastery now stands in Chamalières, département Puy-de-Dôme (V-T 64).

14.4.3 Jesus raised a dead man in John 11:43–44.

15.1.1 Senoch's death is mentioned in *Historiae* 5.7 as having occurred in 576; if he died at eighty (paragraph 4), he must have been born around 496.

James, 95, n.1, describes the Theifals (Taifals) as an Asiatic nomad people, like the Huns, who were probably settled near Poitiers as prisoners of war in the third or fourth century. *Historiae* 4.18 records their revolt against Duke Austrapius around 555, in which he was killed.

The place-name Tiffauges (département Deux-Sèvres) derives from Theifalia.

15.1.2 The chapel is now Saint-Senoch, canton Ligueil, arrondissement Tours, département Indre-et-Loire (V-T 269). It is also mentioned in *Historiae* 5.7 and *GC* 25.

Bishop Eufronius, Gregory's maternal great-uncle and predecessor, was bishop of Tours from 556 to 573.

15.2.1 Gregory arrived in Tours as bishop in 573.

15.2.3 The period indicated extends from November 11 to December 25.

15.2.4 This leniency is in sharp contrast to the condemnation of Secundellus's excursion in *VP* 10.2.

15.3.7 Saint Martin had once healed a snake bite by massaging out the venom (Sulpicius Severus, *Gallus* [*Dialogi*] 1 [2].2).

15.3.8 Similar punitive events occur in *VsM* 3.3, 7, and 9.

15.3.11 Bridge building had been a responsibility of the Roman state, now defunct.

15.4.1 Senoch died in 576 (*Historiae* 5.7).

15.4.2 A similar cry went up at Saint Martin's death (Sulpicius Severus, *Epistola* 3.10), and at that of Radegund (*GC* 104) and Monegunde (below, *VP* 19.4).

15.4.3 Gregory reports another miracle by Senoch, the cure of a blind slave, in *GM* 25.

16.1.1 Venantius probably lived in the second half of the fifth century, since his successor as abbot, Licinius, became bishop of Tours after 511 (*Historiae* 10.31).

T. Kerth, *King Rother and His Bride: Quest and Counter-quests* (Rochester, N.Y., 2010), 133, states that offering a shoe for the bride-to-be, for her to step into, was a twelfth-century Germanic custom symbolizing the transfer of his authority over her and mentions this custom in Gregory's *VP.*

Abbot Silvinus is not mentioned elsewhere. The monastery has been identified in V-T 320. Which rule it followed is not known. In *VP* 20.2 Gregory mentions the *Vitae patrum* of Rufinus and Cassianus's *Institutiones* as models for the monastic life, and in *Historiae* 10.29 he speaks of the rules of Cassianus, Basilius, "and the others who regulated the monastic life."

16.2.3 The implication is that this figure is the saint himself. The church is described in V-T 318.

16.3.7 In *VsM* 2.25 a possessed person cries that Martin has left Tours to perform miracles in Rome.

16.4.4 In *GC* 15 Gregory mentions other, similar cures of fever by Abbot Venantius and describes one of these.

17.prol.5 This protection is also mentioned in *Historiae* 10.29.

17.prol.7 Gregory presents the whole story as spoken by Aredius; quotation marks have been omitted.

17. 1.1 Nicetius's birth was presumably late in the fifth century, since he was made bishop in 525.

The clerical tonsure shaved the top half of the head.

17.1.2 This monastery is not otherwise known.

17.1.4 King Theoderic was king of Austrasia from 511 to 534.

Nicetius's consecration took place in 525. In *VP* 6.3, Gregory related that the citizens of Trier had first asked for his own uncle Gallus.

17.1.7 Nicetius was bishop from 525/26 to 566 (Gams, *Series,* 318).

17.2.2 Theodebert was a son of Clovis and ruled the kingdom of Austrasia from 534/35 to 547/48; on his accession and reign, see *Historiae* 3.22–27.

In *Historiae* 3.25, however, Gregory depicts Theodebert as virtuous, just, and generous to the poor.

17.2.4 The author of his crimes would have been the devil.

17.2.9 King Clothar was Theodebert's younger half brother; he had taken over the kingdom of Austrasia from Theodebert's son Theodebald in 555 and died in 561.

17.3.1 This deacon was almost certainly Abbot Aredius himself, then in lower orders.

17.3.3 King Sigebert was one of Clothar's five sons; he ruled Austrasia from 561 to 575.

17.4.2 Bishop Maximinus's church stood outside the south gate of Trier (V-T 330). Maximinus had been an influential bishop of Trier at the time of Emperor Constans, in the mid-fourth century (*Historiae* 1.37).

17.4.3 This plague probably occurred in 543, as in chapter 6.6.

17. 4.4 Bishop Eucharius was the first bishop of Trier in the third century (*Historiae* 1.37); his church, located outside the north gate, is now dedicated to Saint Matthias (V-T 329).

Nicetius would have stood on top of the cathedral, within the city walls (V-T 326).

17.5.2 The word "fulfill" is often used in the New Testament (as in Matthew 2:15) to refer to the effect of the sayings of the Old Testament prophets, to whose status Nicetius appears to be assimilated.

17.5.3 This story resembles that of the storm in Mark 4:37–39.

17.5.7 Queen Clothilde had used the same argument with her initially pagan husband Clovis, in *Historiae* 2.29.

17.6.1 Gregory assumes that everyone will understand that this was in a dream or vision.

17.6.2 Nicetius's death is not mentioned in the *Historiae;* it must have occurred after 561, because he then returned to his city after King Clothar's death (paragraph 3), and ca. 564 wrote a letter to Queen Chlodosinde, granddaughter of Clovis and wife of the Lombard king (James, 113, n. 14). Venantius Fortunatus praised Nicetius's character and his estate on the Moselle, respectively, in his *Carmina* 3.11 and 12.

The church of Saint Maximinus is described in V-T 330, its miracles in Gregory's *GC* 91, and the miracles at Nicetius's tomb in *GC* 92.

18.prol.1 Moses was regarded as the author of the first five books of the Old Testament, which include a great deal of legislation.

18.prol.2 Ambrose in his *Hexaemeron* 4.2 also refers to Christ and his Church as great lights.

18.prol.3 On biblical figures as "stars," compare Eucherius, *Formulae* 2.160.

18.1.1 Since King Alaric is mentioned as alive (18.2.2), Ursus will have been born in the last decade of the fifth century.

Toiselay (Indre, arrondissement Chateauroux; V-T 299); Heugnes, a forest in the canton of Ecueille, arrondissement Chateauroux (V-T 116); Ponçin, département Ain (Moreau, *Dictionnaire,* 352).

Sennevières, département Indre-et-Loire, in which there is now a Romanesque church dedicated to Leobatius: St Leubais (Moreau, *Dictionnaire,* 360; V-T 127).

18.1.2 Loches, département Indre-et-Loire, a bit more than four miles from Sennevières (V-T 128).

18.1.3 On "the sweat of his brow," compare Genesis 3:19.

18.1.4 Blowing a demon away was a form of exorcism; Martin had done it (*Gallus* [*Dialogi*] 2[3].8.2).

18.2.2 Alaric II was king of the Visigoths and ruled Spain and southwestern Gaul from 484 until his defeat by King Clovis and death in 507 (Heinzelmann, "Prosopographie," 549). The incident shows that at that time this territory was under his influence or in his kingdom.

19.title At least from the fourth century on women could live the "religious"—in fact, ascetic and penitential—life individually at home, supervised by the local clergy.

19.prol.2 As the good Samaritan had done in Luke 10:33–34.

19.prol.4 Gregory gives a brief summary of Monegund's life and relates some of her miracles in *GC* 24.

On the queen of Sheba, compare 1 Kings 10:1–3. Queen Ultrogotha, as the widow of King Childebert I (511–558) is also said to have come to Saint Martin's basilica as though to listen to Solomon's wisdom (*VsM* 1.12).

19.1.8 On manna, compare Exodus 16:13–15.

19.2.2 Esvres, canton Montbazon, arrondissement Tours, département Indre-et-Loire (V-T 108).

19.2.4 This small cell is described in V-T 325.

19.2.8 The *Benedictine Rule* 55.13 specifies that monks need a "mat" *(matta),* as well as a blanket, a light covering, and a pillow.

19.3.1 Jesus did this in John 9:1–6.

19.3.2 The terms used in this story, *maleficium, medificatus, nequitia,* as well as the mention of serpents, an appearance of the devil or his demons, point implicitly to magical practices, whose effectiveness, however limited, Gregory could not allow himself to recognize.

19.3.4 The deadly race is probably that of worms; the serpent was the symbol of evil and the devil (Genesis 3:14).

19.4.1 In *GC* 104, the nuns address the dying Radegund similarly on her deathbed.

19.4.2 To strive for peace and holiness was the apostle Paul's advice in Hebrews 12:14.

19.4.4 Monegund was buried in her own cell around 570 (V-T 325).

20.prol.1 Unfolding is an image that Gregory uses more often, meaning explication, explanation; the underlying image is that of a papyrus roll.

20.1.3 Parental authority is emphasized in Ephesians 6:1.

20.1.4 Compare *VP* 16.1.

20.2.2 The phrasing resembles that in *VM* 7.6.

20.2.3 The monastery of Marmoutier was founded by Saint Martin across the river from the city of Tours (V-T 144–47; Leobard's cell is V-T 146).

This Alaric is not otherwise known.

Sheepskins were prepared for parchment.

20.2.5 His hewing stone indicates that he lived in one of the caves.

20.3.2 Krusch identifies these as Rufinus's *Vitae patrum* (as it is titled in *PL* 73) and John Cassian's *De coenobiorum institutis.* The modern edition of Rufinus's work is entitled *Historia monachorum sive de vita sanctorum (patrum)* (ed. E. Schulz-Flugel, 1990). It is possible that Gregory saw this title and derived from it his emphatic use of the singular "life" (the *HM* also consistently speaks of the holy life in the singular), as well as his earlier title, *The Life of Holy Men.*

20.3.3 Saint Martin himself had neglected his appearance (*VM* 9).

20.3.6 Abbot Eustochius is not otherwise known.

20.4.3 Here, for Gregory, the tenth month was December and the twelfth was February; the year beginning in March. The year of Leobard's passing is not known but will have been after Gregory, arriving in Tours in 573, had been bishop for some time.

The Miracles of the Martyr Julian

Julian was martyred on August 28, 304 CE. A brief summary of the events and characteristics of his cult as presented by Gregory is given by Weidemann, *Kulturgeschichte* 2, 189–90. Van Dam, *Saints,* 41–48, surveys its historical development and gives a translation of Gregory's book about him based on Krusch's edition.

Prol.2 The biblical references here are, respectively, Genesis 4:4, 5:24, 6–8, 12:2–3, 26:24, 32:28–29, 41:39–40; Exodus 34:29; 2 Samuel 7:8–9; 1 Kings 3:11–14; and Daniel 3:25, 6:22. After "bedewing fire," Gregory here adds another oxymoron: harmless predatory beasts. Daniel's being "fed" refers to the prophet Habakkuk's being carried by an angel for six days from Judea to Babylon to give his bread to Daniel while he was in the lion's den (*Vulgate,* Daniel 14:30–38).

Prol.3 As is evident too in the description of David, Gregory believes in predestination; he evidently does not see a contradiction with his advice to everyone to follow examples of holy living, also in his *VP.*

1.1 Ferreolus's historicity is uncertain (Heinzelmann, "Prosopographie," 608).

Perhaps "the fragrance of martyrdom" is an allusion to the sweet fragrance said to have been perceived by the onlookers in *The*

Martyrdom of St. Polycarp 15, ed. and trans. Herbert Musurillo, *The Acts of the Christian Martyrs* (Oxford, 1972), 2–21, here p. 15.

1.2 Sulpicius Severus, *Epistola* 1.9–10, speaks of Martin's troubled and ascetic life as equivalent to martyrdom and of his victory as a palm branch, the usual reward of victorious athletes. The phrase *legitime certantem* resembles Cassian's description of the true monk as an athlete in his *Institutes* 5.17.1.

Sulpicius, *VM* 1.6, mentions belonging to "the heavenly army" *(caelestis militia)* as the aim of the Christian and elsewhere points to Martin's receiving "the crown of righteousness" *(corona iustitiae)* in heaven after his "having triumphed over the world" *(triumphatum*[. . .] *saeculum)* (*Epistola* 2.7).

The village of Brioude was about forty miles south of Clermont.

1.5 These deeds are the ones the holy man performed after his death, i.e. his miracles, as the following stories show. In contrast to the then current literary style, which as he himself testifies (*VsM* 2.19) expected decoration and amplification, Gregory—like his model Sulpicius Severus in a similar context (*VM* prol.3–5)—professes to want to tell the plain, unadorned truth. It will become evident that this did not preclude a certain amount of invention, as well as direct and indirect sermonizing.

2.1 Nicetius, bishop of Lyons from 553 to 573, was Gregory's maternal great-uncle; see *VP* 8.

2.2 There was a raised platform at the head of the church, on which the bishop's chair was located and from which the Bible passages were read by the lector (Blaise, *Dictionnaire,* 828).

2.3 Mamertus was bishop of Vienne from ca. 451/52 until after 474. The location of the new church is uncertain (V-T 343).

2.6 His head had not lost its hair: from *decido* (*de* and *cado,* fall down), as distinguished from *decido* (*de* and *caedo,* cut off).

2.8 "Our Sollius" is Sidonius Apollinaris, bishop of Clermont from ca. 470 into the 480s (*Historiae* 2.22–23). Gregory's own origins in Clermont probably account for the proprietary adjective. The quote is from Sidonius Apollinaris, *Epistola* 7.1.7.

3.2 The image of extinguishing a "funeral pyre" points to a notion of healing as resembling a resurrection from death, which occurs more often in Gregory's stories, as also, for instance, in chapter 44.3.

4.1 Compare *VP* 2, prol.7–9, on Gregory's education. His hesitation about writing is brought forward again in *VsM* prol.1; there it is overcome by a dream in which his mother admonishes him that his simpler style of speaking and writing is an advantage, because it is better understood by the people than the then current elaborate language of the well educated.

4.2 The emperor at Trier was Magnus Maximus, a general who had defeated the emperor Gratian in 383 and illegitimately established himself as a usurper at Trier; he was killed by the army of the legitimate emperor Theodosius in 388.

5.1 A chapel could be a small chamber, sometimes used as living quarters by monks (Blaise, *Dictionnaire,* 142); in this case, it is a small chapel protecting Julian's sarcophagus from the elements. On the notion and practice of asylum in Gregory's Gaul, see James, "*Pacifici,*" 36–44. *Contagio* can mean "widespread illness," but also "impurity, pollution" (Blaise, *Dictionnaire,* 212); that of inborn human sinfulness appears to be meant here. For as will be seen, for instance in *VsM* 3.60.7, Gregory believes that saints can effect forgiveness of sins.

5.2 This incident, and many that follow, indicates that the saint's holy power was believed to operate especially through the proximity of his relics, and to act as though his power permeated all the surrounding physical objects, including the building.

6.1 This vision and the event that followed it resemble a similar one in Saint Martin's life in Sulpicius Severus, *Gallus [Dialogi]* 3.8.4.

7.2 Hillidius is tentatively identified as a certain Helladius by Heinzelmann, "Prosopographie," 622. His present name in Clermont is "Allyre" (Bordier, 319, n. 1).

Gregory is thinking of Moses's leading the Hebrews across the Red Sea (Exodus 14:26–29).

7.4 Orosius, *Adversus paganos* 3.6.

8.1 Du Cange, *Glossarium*, 244, gives variants of "anax" elsewhere and surmises that it may have been of silver; Bonnet, *Latin*, 226–27, n. 5, speculates that this obscure word might be of Carthaginian origin.

Gundobad was king of the Burgundians from ca. 474 to 516, and an uncle of Clotild, who married the Frankish king Clovis; the queen is probably Caretena, who died in 506.

9.2 It is unclear why the notion of "humor"—usually referring to one of the four bodily fluids that were regarded as determining health and temperament—is used in connection with paralysis.

13.2 Clovis's son Theoderic punished Clermont's attempt to transfer its loyalty to his brother King Childebert, probably in 524 (*Historiae* 3.12 and 16).

13.3 John 10:1 thus qualifies a thief.

14.1 In *Historiae* 3.13 Gregory reports that Theoderic left his cousin Sigivald at Clermont as caretaker (*Historiae* 3.13 and 5.12; *VP* 12.2).

Bishop Tetradius of Bourges attended church councils in 506 and 511.

14.3 The paralyzed woman must be Fedamia, chapter 9.

16.1 Becco was count of Clermont while Sigivald was duke.

16.2 An *aureus* (golden coin) is the equivalent of a *solidus*.

16.4 Before the sun: compare Psalms 72:5.

18.2 Gregory attributes the thief's delusion not only to the power of the martyr protecting his clients but, curiously, also to the possessing agent, whose purpose would ostensibly have been a contrary one: to let the crime succeed. His point is that all possessed persons, as such, are deluded. On "wicked greed," compare Virgil, *Aeneid* 3.56–57.

19.1 A *triens* is one-third of a *solidus*, a gold coin.

On Gregory's evidence of the discovery and punishment of perjury through relics, see Weidemann, *Kulturgeschichte* 1, 311–12.

22.2 As will be seen, in this period *religiosus* could also mean living an ecclesiastically sanctioned and supervised individual religious life of abstention.

23.1 Gallus was bishop in Clermont from 525 to 551 (see *Historiae* 4.5–6, and *VP* 6).

Van Dam (*Saints,* 179, n. 17), speculates that this happened in 507, when King Clovis sent his son Theoderic to liberate Clermont from the Visigoths (*Historiae* 2.37). See above, chapter 13.

24.title Peter was Gregory's older brother (and bishop Gallus's nephew); he was killed in 574 (*Historiae* 5.5).

25.2 On Ferreolus's spring, see chapter 3.

A stadium is about one eighth of a Roman mile, which was slightly shorter than a modern mile; 10 stadia is a bit less than one and a half miles.

The story that the martyr's head was washed in this spring (chapter 3.1) may play a role in Gregory's hope for the healing of his head.

28.1 Gregory wrote a brief account of Aredius's life and deeds in *VsM* 3.24 and *Historiae* 10.29 and reported Aredius's account of the life and deeds of Bishop Nicetius of Trier in *VP* 17.

28.2 In *VP* 7.2.3–5 Gregory records that a church was regularly locked at night; the fact that it is open here may thus be part of the miracle.

29.1 Germanus was bishop of Auxerre during the first half of the fifth century. On his life, see *GC* 66, and Constantius of Lyons, *Vita sancti Germani;* the latter does not include the story told here.

29.3 The date is August 28. Gregory uses different systems of chronology, usually beginning the year in March (Weidemann, *Kulturgeschichte* 2, 386, cited in Van Dam, *Saints,* 187, n. 24); here he lets the year begin in March, as was the Frankish custom, and reckons September as the seventh month. In chapter 35.5 he appears to follow the Roman custom again, which began the year in January.

30.2 Saint Martin of Tours was born in Pannonia, in what is now Hungary; Privatus is thought to have been bishop of Javols or Mende during the fourth century and to have been killed by the Alemans (see *Historiae* 1.34).

30.3 For Ferreolus see above, chapter 1. Symphorianus of Autun is thought to have been a mid-third-century martyr; see *GM* 51.

Gregory regarded Saturninus as one of seven missionaries sent to Gaul in the middle of the third century and martyred at Toulouse (*Historiae* 1.30); see also *GM* 47.

32.4 This is the demon speaking; earlier, in the following story, and elsewhere, Gregory shows demons revealing hidden but true knowledge.

34.1 Gregory was consecrated at Reims in 573.

34.2 A condensed thought, presumably meaning consecrated with relics that would work miracles.

35.5 Since May is mentioned later in chapter 35.6, the fact that he calls it the fifth month would seem to mean that Gregory here follows the Roman custom and begins the year with January; but then the date of this event would be April 27, evidently counted as belonging to May. In chapter 29.3, however, he follows the Frankish custom of the year beginning in March. Van Dam, *Saints,* 187, n. 24, cites Pietri, *Tours,* 440–41, as arguing that Gregory here meant to write "the fifth day before the Kalends of the *third* month," which would be May in the Frankish system. She thus proposes to emend *quinti* to *tertii.*

35.6 Falernian wine was a well-known favorite wine from Campania, Italy.

35.8 "Nature" here means the substance of the four foundational "elements" that for Gregory constituted the world: earth, water, air, and fire—not what today is called the natural world. On the wine and the fishes, compare John 2:1–11 and Matthew 14:19–20.

39.2 Pagan Franks appear to be meant here.

40.1 Gregory spoke of Aredius in his *VsM* 2.39.

41.2 The reader's knowledge that these voices would be of saints and/or angels visiting from heaven, as in *VP* 7.2.4–5, is assumed.

42.2 A judge did not have the power to seize someone who had sought asylum in a church.

45.2 Cautinus was bishop from 553 to 571 (*Historiae* 4.7, 12, 13, 31).

This plague occurred in 571 (*Historiae* 4.31).

45.6 Signing the cross on the forehead is an element in the ritual of baptism.

The imagery of the "old" and the "new" man occurs in Ephesians 4:24.

46.2 November is the ninth month.

47.3 A saint's "birthday" was that of his passing and being born in heaven. In chapter 50.1 Gregory seems to indicate that John the Baptist may be understood to have participated in this healing.

48.1 The location of Vibriacum is unknown.

50.1 Nicetius of Lyons was Gregory's great-uncle on his mother's side (compare *VP* 8) and bishop of Lyons from 552 to 573.

50.3 Blind people are cured by Nicetius's relics in *VP* 8.5.1, 8.6.5, 8.8.3, 8.8.4–6, and 8.12.4–5; although *VP* 8.8.4–6 may be meant, Julian and Litomer are not mentioned there.

The Miracles of Bishop Martin

Book 1

prol.4 Dream visions in which an authority figure—here the author's mother—gives advice, a command, or a warning, were commonplace and regarded as veridical in this period; see on the dreams which Gregory reported, de Nie, *Views,* 213–93.

prol.5 Unlike those of his class, Gregory had not been educated in classical rhetoric and letters, but on the Bible and ecclesiastical writings; see *VP* 2.prol.

prol.6 Water in the desert: compare Exodus 17:6.

Opening the mouth of an ass: compare Numbers 22:28.

prol.7 Sulpicius Severus offers a similar apology in his *VM* ded.4.

1.1 Paulinus of Périgueux's poetic rendition of Martin's life was metrically scanned in cadences of long and short syllables called "feet."

Sulpicius Severus, *Gallus* [*Dialogi*], Book 1.

1.2 *Gallus* [*Dialogi*] 3.17.6.

2.1 Gregory here confuses Paulinus of Périgueux, the author of the *Vita sancti Martini* (*Vita M*), with his namesake of Nola, who wrote about the martyr Felix's life and deeds in verse.

2.2 This story is a condensed paraphrase of Paulinus of Périgueux, *Vita M* 6.54–70. Sulpicius Severus had also described the possessed as sometimes being suspended in the air (*Gallus* [*Dialogi*] 3.6.2).

2.3 See 2 Timothy 2:20–21 on man's body as a vessel.

Marmoutier was Martin's monastery on the north shore (V-T 147).

Paulinus, *Vita M* 6.82–90.

2.4 Paulinus, *Vita M* 6.97–100.

2.5 Aegidius was the commander of the Roman army in Gaul in the mid-fifth century; the reference is to the Visigoths' siege of Arles in 458.

Paulinus, *Vita M* 6.114–36.

2.6 Gregory sees a "humor" as a malign fluid agent in pustules, in gout (*Historiae* 5.42 and 10.15), and, as here, in paralysis.

Paulinus, *Vita M* 6.165–208.

2.7 After the battle of Châlons in 451, when the Roman general Aëtius and his allies defeated the invading Huns, some of these remained in Gaul; it is also possible, however, that this Hun had been a Roman mercenary.

Paulinus, *Vita M* 6.215–49.

2.8 Martin's church had two *atria* (colonnaded areas): one in the west at the entrance to the church, and one in the east around the apse containing the saint's tomb (V-T 318, pp. 312–13, 315)

Paulinus, *Vita M* 6.250–64.

2.9 Paulinus, *Vita M* 6.286, however, has *praecedis,* addressing the then dead man as having preceded the columns over the small stream, but (because of his mortal fall there) not stopping them. Krusch suggests that Gregory has misunderstood Paulinus, *Vita M* 6.265–89.

2.10 Paulinus, *Vita M* 6.298–319 and 6.322–25.

2.11 Paulinus, *Vita M* 6.325–34.

2.13 Paulinus, *Vita M* 6.351–403. Gregory has added details and invented the spoken words.

2.14 On Joshua and Peter, compare Joshua 3:12–17 and Matthew 14:29–31. The sailor may be the one referred to in Paulinus, *Vita M* 6.385.

2.16 Paulinus, *Vita M* 6.467–99.

2.17 The story is told in Paulinus, *Versus de visitatione nepotuli sui.* Gregory has invented Paulinus's spoken request.

2.18 As we saw above (prol.3), Gregory suggested that the contemporary miracles too might be better described by Fortunatus—who, in the dedication of his poetic version of Sulpicius's *Life of Saint Martin* to Gregory, had in fact offered to put his stories too into verse (*Epistola ad Gregorium* 2). As far as we know, it never came to this.

3.1 Sabaria in the province of Pannonia is now Szombathely, Hungary.

These were consuls in 397.

3.2 The notion that "pollution" by bodily fluids prohibits contact with the sacred, as in Leviticus 11–15, is prominent in Gregory's worldview; see the Introduction.

4.4 Sulpicius Severus, *Ep.* 2.1–6.

5.4 Ambrose, however, died on Easter Saturday 397 (McLynn, *Ambrose,* 367), and Martin on November 11, 397 (Stancliffe, *St. Martin,* 114–18); the story is therefore clearly a legend and the speeches invented by Gregory.

5.5 Sulpicius Severus, *VM* 27.1.

6.1 Perpetuus was bishop of Tours from 458 to 490.

6.2 This church is described in V-T 318.

6.5 The fourth day is July 4 (Van Dam, *Saints,* 208).

7.4 After her husband Clovis's death in 511, Queen Clotild retired to Tours and exerted influence there (*Historiae* 2.43, 3.28, 4.1, 10.31).

9.1 Baudinus was bishop of Tours from 546 to 552. The description of the ship in the storm resembles that in Virgil, *Aeneid* 1.106.

9.2 On powerless limbs, compare Virgil, *Aeneid* 1.92.

9.3 The breastplate of faith is mentioned in 1 Thessalonians 5:8.

11.1 Chararic is of uncertain historicity; Gregory is the only one to mention him. This Galicia is on the Atlantic coast of Spain.

The early fourth-century Alexandrian priest Arius's ideas were transmitted to the eastern Germanic tribes that later occupied Spain. Gregory evidently sees a spiritual connection between Arianism and the incurring of leprosy, mentioned in the next sentence.

11.11 Martin was bishop of Braga from 561/72 to 579. Gregory's friend Venantius Fortunatus corresponded with him (*Carmina* 5.1–2).

12.1 Ultrogotha was the wife of King Childebert I, who died in 558;

she was exiled from Paris by her husband's brother Clothar when he became king of the region (*Historiae* 4.20). After Clothar's death in 561, she was taken into protection by his son, King Charibert.

Monegund is here compared to the queen of Sheba in 1 Kings 10:1–2.

12.4 As will be seen, healings not infrequently changed lives.

15.1 The shrine was located in a church dedicated to the apostles John and Paul; after the Lombards had invaded Italy in 568, Felix became bishop of Treviso (Van Dam, *Saints,* 215, n. 30).

Fortunatus says this happened to himself in his *Vita Martini* 4.686–701.

18.1 Krusch locates Sireuil at Charente, arrondissement Angoulême, canton Hiersac. Bordier: Siran; either Siran-la-Late (Indre-et-Loire) or Saint-Ciran-du Sambot, near Angers.

19.1 Martin heals a leper in Sulpicius Severus, *VM* 18.3.

20.3 Virgil, *Aeneid* 1.301 speaks of "oarage of wings."

22.1 Candes is situated in the département Indre-et-Loire, arrondissement and canton Chinon.

23.title Wiliachar's daughter was married to King Clothar's son Chramn.

23.1 Clothar, son of Clovis, was sole king of Frankish Gaul from 558 to 561; Chramn, his son, plotted against him while married to Wiliachar's daughter (*Historiae* 4.16–17) and was killed by his father in 560 (*Historiae* 4.20). Wiliachar had fled to Tours, where he was responsible for a fire in the basilica of Saint Martin in 559 (*Historiae* 10.31). After his pardon, he became a priest (Van Dam, *Saints,* 219, n. 35; Pietri, *Tours,* 227, n. 225).

24.1 Alpinus was the first recorded count of Tours, apparently holding office during Clothar's reign in 561 (Pietri, *Tours,* 178, n. 28).

Martin had been a soldier before he became a monk and then bishop.

25.1 Charigisel was killed at the same time as King Sigebert in 575 (*Historiae* 4.51). A referendary was a court official in charge of producing and processing written documents.

26.2 Sulpicius Severus, *VM* 11.1–5 describes how Martin proved the "martyr" was a demon.

29.2 Nazelles is located in the département Indre-et-Loire, arrondissement Tours, canton Amboise.

29.5 Sigebert was the brother of Charibert; he ruled from 561 to 575. Charibert died in 567 (*Historiae* 4.26).

Eufronius was bishop of Tours from 555 to 573.

30.3 Gehazi was the servant of the prophet Elisha, who incurred leprosy as a punishment for his greediness (2 Kings 5:20–27).

31.1 V-T 318 does not mention a *porticus;* presumably it was a doorway on the outside (front?) of the church.

The poor roll was the register of those to be fed daily by the church.

31.3 The sixth hour was the hour after lunch; the Romans counted six daylight hours and six nighttime ones, their length thus varying with the seasons.

31.6 Compare Virgil, *Aeneid* 3.56 on greed. Mark 12:42 tells the story of the widow.

31.7 On Judas, compare Matthew 27:5.

32.2 Van Dam (*Saints,* 225, n. 44) suggests that this was in 563, ten years before his ordination.

36.1 The Bèbre River is a tributary of the Loire.

36.3 On feeding enemies, compare Romans 12:20.

38.1 Possession and fevers are often attributed to demonic agency.

38.2 Perhaps a wooden tower above the altar (Pietri, *Tours,* 389; V-T 317).

39.3 Similarly, John 21:25.

40.3 In 569 King Sigebert sent Count Justin to ask Bishop Eufronius to preside over the reception of the relic of the Holy Cross in Poitiers (Baudonivia, *Vita sanctae Radegundis* 16).

40.4 Similarly, Virgil, *Aeneid* 1.203.

Book 2

1 Justin was once healed by a relic of Saint Ferreolus (*GM* 70). His daughter Justina was prioress in the holy Queen Radegund's convent (*Historiae* 10.15); his other daughter, Eustenia, is mentioned in *VsM* 4.36.

1.1 The year of Gregory's ordination is 573.

1.4 The third hour is approximately 9 a.m., and the sixth hour noon.

1.6 This instance of direct address, resembling that in a sermon, coupled with Gregory's reference to his story as a "reading," seems to indicate that he intended his writings to be read aloud to a group of people, perhaps his clergy, perhaps (within a sermon) the whole church community.

3.3 Using the verb *iudicare* (to govern) for using one's limbs is unusual; it is also attested in Gregory's *Histories* 4.10 (Blaise, *Lexicon Latinitatis Medii Aevi,* s.v. 6).

"At the saint's feet" alludes to a supplicant's position before a living saint, and here means kneeling at the saint's tomb.

3.4 There were two annual feasts for Martin: the date of his consecration as bishop (July 4) and of his passing (November 11).

3.5 This probably took place on November 11, 573 (Weidemann, *Kulturgeschichte,* 1.207, n. 435; cited in Van Dam, *Saints,* 231, n. 52). The choice of "revived" and "arose" points to the cure as an implicit figure of resuscitation from the "death" suggested earlier.

5.2 With the term "renewed," spiritual rebirth or resuscitation from death again seems to be suggested.

6.1 She dared not enter the church building out of reverence or a sense of unworthiness.

6.2 Being ordained as a cleric is here an act of gratitude, or perhaps of intended service to the saint.

7.2 The implication of these three clustered stories is that the healed paralytics symbolize, and perhaps even make visible, what happened internally in the warring royal brothers Chilperic, Sigebert, and Guntram. The events referred to happened in 574, and Gregory describes them in his *Historiae* 4.49.

8.2 As often, Gregory describes pain as though it were itself a kind of evil power. "Renewed light" again points to spiritual rebirth as well as resurrection.

9.1 Being "advised" by "faith" appears to point to her having had a dream invitation from the saint.

In two following chapters, 22 and 23, *deserviens* and *servitio* consists of serving food to the poor who were registered with the church for daily feeding. Gundetrud probably took a vow and let herself be blessed or consecrated to the religious life as supervised and protected by the church; it is unclear how this was then more specifically organized in Tours.

10.1 A woman was healed by touching Jesus's robe in Matthew 9:20–22.

For Trézelle, Krusch (612, n.2) suggests once Trésail, now Allier, arrondissement Gannat, canton Jalligny.

11.1 As we have seen in similar incidents during the day, Gregory assumes the agency of an evil power as inducing what we today would designate as a stroke.

12.1 Germanus was bishop of Paris from ca. 555 to 576. *Historiae* 5.8 records his death and the miracles at his tomb, and mentions Venantius Fortunatus's *Life* of him. The feast is that of November 11, 574 (Van Dam, *Saints,* 233). Germanus was bishop of Paris from 576 to 591 (*Historiae* 10.26).

13.1 The Roman government had subdivided the country into smaller territories, based on the existing Gallic peoples, that were administered from an urban center known as a *civitas.* Tours was the city-state *civitas* of the Turones, as Paris was that of the Parisii.

13.2 Easter 575 (Van Dam, *Saints,* 234).

13.4 For the educated reader or listener, Christ as the Sun of righteousness (see Malachi 4:2) is intended; Gregory suggests that Christ's light also shines, or is reflected, in the man's eyes.

13.5 Instead of being a pleonasm, "reborn again" could point to baptism as the first rebirth.

14.2 July 4, 575 (Van Dam, *Saints,* 235).

16.1 Water is changed into wine in John 2.

16.2 Baugy is situated in département Saône et Loire, arrondissement Charolles, canton Marcigny.

16.4 A *modius* was about two gallons.

17.1 Guntram Boso, one of King Sigibert's dukes, had killed Theodebert, King Chilperic's son, in a battle in 575 (*Historiae* 4.50), and then taken refuge in Saint Martin's basilica. Chilperic later tried to have him captured (*VsM* 2.27; Van Dam, *Saints,* 237, n. 59).

Amboise is situated in département Indre-et-Loire, arrondissement Tours.

Gregory often associates darkness and night with increased activity of demons and here appears to imply that they are responsible for this sudden violent wind.

The phrasing appears to describe a bridge consisting of boats joined together.

18.4 Martin had been a soldier.

This story strongly resembles Martin's own encounter with the devil masquerading as an imperial Christ in *VM* 24.4–8.

19.3 On Candes, compare V-T 56; map p. 305.

There may be an implicit association here with Christ as light in many senses (as in John 1 and 9).

22.1 A *matrona* is a married woman of considerable social and economic status, here exhibited in her feeding the beggars congregating at Martin's monastery. Her ailment may have been connected with the fact that weaving, sewing, and embroidery were the usual occupations of women.

The "registered poor" were those on the poor roll.

It was then customary to drink wine mixed with water.

22.2 The context clearly shows that *puella* here means not a young girl in general but a maidservant; in the same context, as we have seen, *puer* (boy) means male servant.

24.1 Since the Roman day began at sundown, Saturday evening was regarded as Sunday, on which sexual activity was prohibited out of reverence for the Lord's day (Sunday) and in connection with attending church in a "pure" state.

24.4 November 11, 575 (Van Dam, *Saints,* 240).

25.2 Christmas 575 (Van Dam, *Saints,* 240).

26.1 January 6, 576 (Van Dam, *Saints,* 242).

On deformity as a punishment for sin, compare John 9:2.

26.5 The model here is John 2.

27.1 King Sigebert was killed in 575 (*Historiae* 4.51).

Chilperic was King Sigebert's brother; he seized the government over the territory of Tours and ordered Ruccolenus's mission against the city. Sigebert's young son Childebert, scurried into safety after his father's assassination (which, according to Gregory, had been carried out by order of Chilperic's devious wife, Fredegund (see *Historiae.* 4.51, 5.1 and 4), took over the rest of his father's kingdom.

27.2 Guntram Boso, no doubt accompanied by companions, had sought asylum in Martin's church at that time (*VsM* 2.17).

27.3 Jaundice was known as the royal malady.

In his *Historiae* 1.24, Gregory reports that, on account of his persecution of the apostles, Herod was struck by God with worms in his body and died while attempting to remove them with a knife.

In his *Historiae* 5.4, Gregory tells the story as taking place in 576.

28.1 The day before Easter 576 (Van Dam, *Saints,* 243).

29.1 July 4, 576 (Van Dam, *Saints,* 243).

31.2 Presumably she was told by Martin to come to his church to be healed.

November 11, 576 (Van Dam, *Saints,* 244).

31.3 As is also evident in *VsM* 2.29, among others, Gregory not infrequently associates Martin's healing power with the appearance and quality of light. A modern parallel is Agnes Sanford's book about her similar perceptions as a faith healer: *The Healing Light* (1948).

32.title Campania means countryside, but its use here seems to announce the later designation of this region as Champagne.

32.1 Compare Sulpicius Severus, *Gallus* [*Dialogi*] 3.3.1–4, 5–6.

33.2 Easter in the year 577 (Van Dam, *Saints,* 246).

34.1 The feast of Martin's ordination, on July 4, 577 (Van Dam, *Saints,* 246).

35.1 Apparently this happened on the fourth day after the feast.

36.1 Leodovald is recorded as bishop of Avranches from 576 to 578.

37.1 Here the demon and the human being appear to speak in alternation.

38.3 The "blessed springs" appear to be the baptismal font.

39.1 This must be the monastery of Marmoutier, founded by Martin himself at the beginning of his episcopate.

39.4 "Raised up" as if from death, for the man had been on the verge of dying.

40.2 In this context, a *signum* is a miracle that has the value of a sign, which points to an invisible reality—as in fact all miracles do. The fourth gospel uses this term consistently to indicate Jesus's miracles. Gregory here appears to use it as an equivalent for "deed of power" *(virtus)*.

This passage can be read to mean that Gregory believes his stories are, in essence, Martin himself preaching. At the same time, it points forward to Sisulf's being instructed by the saint to preach, as it were, in his stead.

40.5 Compare John 9:2 about the man born blind.

42.1 The vigil before Martin's feast on November 11, 577 (Van Dam, *Saints,* 250).

43.2 Gregory, as did many others in his period, thought in terms of "ages" of the world; in his *Historiae* 4.51, he counts the number of the world's years and divides them into unequal periods marked by significant events in biblical history, situating himself in a period after the crucifixion of Christ and implicitly expecting the world to end in the not too distant future.

2 Kings 13:21 tells us that the dead man hastily placed on top of Elisha's tomb unexpectedly came to life again. Christians regarded this incident as a support for their veneration of relics.

43.6 Sulpicius Severus, *Gallus* [*Dialogi*] 2.4.4–7 describes how Martin brought an infant back to life at Chartres.

44.1 July 4, 578 (Van Dam, *Saints,* 251).

Maroveus was bishop of Poitiers from ca. 568 to 591.

Hilary was bishop of Poitiers from ca. 315 to ca. 367 and the author of important theological writings, especially against the Arian heresy. Gregory means that Maroveus was steeped in the Hilarian tradition at Poitiers.

45.1 Voutegon, département Deux-Sèvres, arrondissement Bressuire, canton Argenton-Château.

46.2 November 11, 578 (Van Dam, *Saints,* 252).

47.2 July 4, 579 (Van Dam, *Saints,* 253).

49.1 November 11, 579 (Van Dam, *Saints,* 253).

51.1 The epidemic of dysentery took place in 580 (*Historiae* 5.34).

51.2 Gregory here points to the implicit inversion of receiving life through death, central in the theology of Christ's sacrifice for man's eternal life; it becomes explicit in the following story, 52.3.

52.title In this case, a swelling or tumor is clearly meant; perhaps Gregory imagined it to have been filled with a "humor" or evil fluid.

54.2 July 4, 580 (Van Dam, *Saints,* 255).

56.1 November 11, 580 (Van Dam, *Saints,* 256).

56.4 White hair is associated with the figure of the risen glorified Christ in Revelation 1:14; purple clothing indicated high dignity.

58.3 The mention of his free birth may be a revision or gloss added later to explain why Leodast "slandered" him by treating him as a runaway slave.

Leodast was replaced as count in 579 but still made great trouble for Gregory after that (*Historiae* 5.47–49).

60.1 "Widower of this world" is a metaphor for one who has rejected all worldly concerns.

The hidden assaults are those of evil forces.

The growth in faith through internalizing the divine word, as described in a parable in Matthew 13:23.

60.2 Assuming that Gregory began writing it in the year of his ordination, in 573, he must have finished writing this book in 581.

60.6 Gregory means the "perverse thought" of seeking a cure other than through the saint.

60.8 The metaphors of sheep and goats were part of the then current visualization of Judgment.

60.9 The reference is to the revived catechumen in the monastery of Marmoutier (Sulpicius Severus, *VM* 7).

60.10 Tartarus was the pagan name for the netherworld of the dead, here used of the Christian hell.

Book 3

2.2 November 11, 581 (Van Dam, *Saints,* 261).

3.1 Although Gregory sometimes refers to Sunday as the day of the Lord's resurrection (as in *VJ* 11, *VsM* 3.55.2 and 3.56.2), he was in this case (considering its mention in paragraph 3) probably referring to the annual Gallic festival on March 27 (Van Dam, *Saints,* 261, n. 74, citing Pietri, *Tours,* 453).

7.1 Craon, département Mayenne, arrondissement Château-Gontier.

8.1 In his *Historiae* 6.18, Gregory gives this date as in the year 582. The Visigothic kingdom of Spain had officially adhered to Arian Christianity until the conversion of King Reccared in 586.

8.2 Both Krusch and Bordier have *super se,* but the phrasing below seems to suggest that the infant was the speaker's father and that he here means himself as a member of his family.

8.3 Gregory hints that it is this child for whom the parents had been praying, and it would have to be the speaker's father.

8.4 All manuscripts have *avia,* which appears to be a designation of her relation to the teller of the story; the plural verbs thereafter and the mention of the *avus* speaking indicate that the grandfather was present, almost certainly as the father of the child.

8.5 Referring to Sulpicius Severus's *VM.*

9.1 The noonday demon appears in Psalm 90:6. It was called "Diana" by the country people and mentioned in the *Vita sancti Caesarii* 2.14.

9.2 November 11, 582 (Van Dam, *Saints,* 264).

10.1 Krusch notes here that Gregory elsewhere (*Historiae* 5. 5 and *GC* 9) uses *ficta* as the past participle of *figere.*

13.1 Wiliachar is mentioned earlier, in *VsM* 1.23. Someone could father a family and thereafter embrace celibacy in becoming a priest or even a bishop, as Gregory reports of his maternal great-uncle Gregory of Langres (*VP* 7.1–2).

14.1 The cure of the hunched woman is mentioned in Luke 13:11–13.

14.2 July 4, 583 (Van Dam, *Saints,* 264).

15.1 King Clothar I, one of Clovis's sons, reigned from 511 to 561. Gregory reports (*Historiae* 4.3) that Gunthar died before his father.

16.3 Christmas 582 (Van Dam, *Saints,* 266).

17.1 Aegidius was bishop of Reims from 565 to 590; he consecrated Gregory as bishop in 573 and was deposed by a church council for treason (*Historiae* 10.19).

17.2 Siggo is mentioned in *Historiae* 5.3. Sigebert I ruled the Austrasian part of the Frankish kingdom from 561 to 575.

18.1 The lamps had water under the oil at the bottom, perhaps so that the vessel itself would not become too hot or burn; see *VsM* 3.18.1, and Venantius Fortunatus, *Carmina* 6.5.280: Galswintha's lamp fell on the ground unbroken and continued burning, not put out by the water.

18.2 The adjective *clandestina* means "hidden" or "secret"; applied to the disease, it seems to imply that it is a covert diabolic attack. In *Historiae* 6.31, Gregory reports that this cattle plague followed upon the devastation of the territory of Tours by the armies of King Chilperic's dukes Desiderius and Bladast in 583.

19.2 July 4, 583 (Van Dam, *Saints,* 268).

22.2 The patriarch Jacob, also called Israel, slept with his head on a stone (Genesis 28:11).

23.3 This "wealth" provided for or consisted of the daily stipends given by the shrine keepers to the poor registered there on the poor roll.

24.1 November 11, 583 (Van Dam, *Saints,* 270).

24.2 Since a lamp there is not mentioned, it is probably oil that has been allowed to stand near or upon the tomb overnight so as to absorb the saint's holy power, as in *VsM* 2.32.

33.1 Marsas, département Gironde, arrondissement Blaye, canton Saint-Savin.

34.1 If this is the plague, it appeared in Gaul in 582 (*Historiae* 6.14–15) and 584 (*Historiae* 6.33).

34.4 Eborinus appears to have been count of Tours at that time.

35.2 Badegisil was a former *maior domo,* one of the palace's highest officials, of King Clothar, and bishop of Le Mans from 581 to 586; he is mentioned in *Historiae* 6.9 and 8.39.

37.1 Shade is another word for a demon.

39.1 July 4, 584 (Van Dam, *Saints,* 275).

39.4 The devil qualified in this way in John 8:44.

41.2 November 11, 584 (Van Dam, *Saints,* 275).

42.1 Sulpicius Severus's biography.

42.3 The adverb "terribly" may indicate that this shaking had a physical component, as sometimes occurred with a visionary warning, as in *VP* 8.5.4.

45.3 July 4, 585 (Van Dam, *Saints,* 277).

48.1 November 11, 585 (Van Dam, *Saints,* 278).

50.1 July 4, 586 (Van Dam, *Saints,* 278). These vigils were held in the main church of the city; Martin's basilica was outside the walls (map in Pietri, *Tours,* 305).

53.3 Gregory considered the man seized without reason, presumably because he was already paying for his crime by doing penance.

54.1 Montlouis, département Indre-et-Loire, canton Tours.

57.2 According to Van Dam, *Saints,* 281, this feast was in 587; other scholars are said to prefer different dates.

58.1 The implication here may be that the spring was inhabited by an evil power, perhaps by the noonday demon (as in *VsM* 3.9.1). Roman religion too tended to see nature as animated by spiritual beings.

60.3 Veranus was Bishop of Cavaillon, département Vaucluse, arrondissement Avignon; he is recorded in 585 in *Historiae* 9.4 as becoming the godfather of King Childebert's second son, Theoderic, and Gregory also mentions that he had the gift of healing.

Book 4

prol.3 Prudentius, *Cathemerinon* 5.127–28 describes a rescue from the Acheron River.

1.2 *VsM* 2.1.

2.2 A similar incident occurs in *VsM* 2.60.5–6.

4.1 July 4, 588 (Van Dam, *Saints,* 286); March is here the first month of the year.

5.1 November 11, 588 (Van Dam, *Saints,* 286).

6.1 July 4, 589 (Van Dam, *Saints,* 286).

6.2 Aredius is mentioned in *VsM* 2.39.1–4 and 3.24.1–4.

6.3 Florentianus and Romulf came to Tours as tax assessors in 589; Gregory then obtained from the king that all taxes were canceled, as they had been in previous times (*Historiae* 9.30). In *Historiae* 9.30 Gregory refers to Florentianus as the *maior domo* of Childebert's queen (or, if *regiae* instead of *reginae* should be read, of King Childebert II himself) (Selle-Hosbach, *Prosopographie,* 96, p. 94).

7.1 King Miro was king of the Sueves from 570 to 583 (*Historiae* 5.41, 6.43).

The basilica is mentioned in *VsM* 1.11.

7.5 Presumably this is a record kept in heaven, and the king has done vicarious penance for his servant.

8.1 From a distinguished family, Palladius was bishop of Saintes from 573 to 597. Through undiplomatic choices, however, he got into all kinds of trouble with the kings and with the clergy (*Historiae* 7.31; 8.2, 7; 8.22 and 43; *GM* 55).

10.1 Maximus was a Roman usurper emperor in Gaul (383–388). The gift of the bowl is evidently an oral tradition; there is no mention of it in Sulpicius Severus's writings about the saint.

*N*s and *s*s are often interchangeable; *accessus* comes from *accendere* (Bonnet, *Latin,* 268).

11.2 Blideric's gift with usufruct implicitly placed his property under the basilica's protection.

11.3 Presumably this was intended as a gesture of hospitality, but Gregory seems to suggest that the abbot's presence is the reason for the man's wife finally being able to conceive that night.

11.4 In the early sixth century, Bishop Caesarius of Arles was in the habit of returning gifts made to the church under such circumstances. The difference between the two practices may be that, as Gregory's stories show, he believed that the saint's power would punish any perceived disrespect severely.

12.1 Ternay, département Loire-et-cher, arrondissement Vendôme, canton Montoire.

13.1 November 11, 589 (Van Dam, *Saints,* 290).

Bishop Aunachar of Auxerre is mentioned in 573 and 589 (*Historiae* 9.32).

14.1 Gennes, département Maine-et-Loire, arrondissement Saumur.

15.3 The story seems to point to a dislocation in the back that resolved itself during this particular physical effort.

It is unclear if this "presentation" meant that, as the recipient of a miracle, his status (servitude?) was thereafter changed, as sometimes happened (as in *VsM* 2.4 and 57).

16.1 Easter 590 (Van Dam, *Saints,* 292).

17.1 The name Crovium is otherwise unknown; perhaps Cru, département Maine-et-Loire, arrondissement Saumur, canton Doué).

17.2 July 4, 590 (Van Dam, *Saints,* 292).

18.2 Gregory here seems to associate the simultaneous celebration of mass with these healings, as he also does in *VsM* 2.14.

22.2 November 11, 590 (Van Dam, *Saints,* 294).

23.1 Brulon, département Sarthe, arrondissement Flêche.

26.3 "The bishop's power" may be an abstract indication for a personal action by someone presenting himself as the saint. See also below, chapter 39, in which the saint's "power" works invisibly.

26.4 *Fredus* is a Germanic word for the fee paid to the king or his representative for his release of prisoners, as in *Historiae* 6.23 (Van Dam, *Saints,* 295, n. 106).

July 4, 591 (Van Dam, *Saints,* 295).

27.1 Nonnichius of Nantes had succeeded his relative Felix as bishop of Nantes in 582 (*Historiae* 6.15).

29.1 Agnes was abbess of the monastery of Sainte-Croix in Poitiers (*Historiae* 9.42).

Austria, later known as Austrasia, was the name of the northern Frankish subkingdom with its capital at Reims (see *Historiae*

5.14, 18). The city of Tours was located in the subkingdom known as Neustria, centered in Paris. Therefore Gregory must mean that Agnes says she is "on her way to" Austr(as)ia.

29.2 The surviving Latin text first has the third person singular but from here until the end of the story uses the first person singular or plural, as though the boatman himself were telling the story.

30.1 The revival of the catechumen and Martin's leaving there are described in Sulpicius Severus, *VM* 7.1–4 and 9.1–2.

31.4 On Rebecca, compare Genesis 24:45–46.

32.1 Plato had been Gregory's archdeacon at Tours; he served as bishop of Poitiers from 591 to ca. 599.

32.2 The cathedral itself has not been spoken of, therefore the episcopal residence must be meant; a certain inherent sacred quality is implied here.

35.2 The basilica of the apostle Peter had been built in the late fifth century (*Historiae* 2.14; V-T 319).

36.2 Eustenia was the daughter of Gregory's sister and Count Justin (about whom see *GM* 70; *VsM* 2.2).

She appears to imitate Gregory's advice to her father in *VsM* 2.2.

37.1 King Guntram had been king of the eastern part of Gaul; he died in 592.

38.1 July 4, 592 (Van Dam, *Saints,* 300).

40.1 Cantabria was located on the north coast of Spain.

41.1 November 11, 592 (Van Dam, *Saints,* 301).

Ponthion, département Marne.

Duke Aginus is mentioned in *Historiae* 10.8.

45.4 July 4, 593 (Van Dam, *Saints,* 302).

46.1 Pollution or invasion by an evil spirit is intended here.

Bibliography

Works of Gregory of Tours

Sancti Georgii Florentii Gregorii Turonensis Opera omnia, necnon Fredegarii scholastici Epitome et chronicum, cum suis continuatoribus et allis antiquis monumentis, ad codices manuscriptos et veteres editiones collata, emendata et aucta, atque notis et observationibus illustrata, cura et studio Theodori Ruinart. Paris, 1699. *De virtutibus sancti Juliani* liber I, col. 847–86; *De virtutibus sancti Martini* libri IV, col. 993–1140; *Vitae patrum* col. 1141–1256.

Les livres des miracles et autres opuscules de Georges Florent Grégoire, évêque de Tours. Edited and translated by Henri L. Bordier. Société de l'Histoire de France, Publications 88 (*De passione, virtutibus et gloria sancti Iuliani martyris,* pp. 302–93), 103 (*De virtutibus sancti Martini episcopi,* pp. 2–335), 114 (*Vitae patrum seu Liber de vita quorumdam feliciosorum,* pp. 132–99). Paris, 1857, 1860, 1862.

Miracula et opera minora. Edited by Bruno Krusch. MGH SSrM. 1.2. Hanover, 1885. Contains *De cursu stellarum ratio, qualiter ad officium implendum debeat observari* (pp. 854–72), *De passione et virtutibus sancti Iuliani* (pp. 562–84), *De virtutibus sancti Martini* (pp. 585–661), *De vita patrum* (pp. 661–744), *In gloria confessorum* (pp. 744–820), *In gloria martyrum* (pp. 484–561), and *In psalterii tractatum commentarius* (pp. 873–77).

Historiae [*Historiarum libri decem*]. Edited by Bruno Krusch and Wilhelmus Levison. MGH SSrM 1.1, ed. altera. Hanover, 1951.

Historiarum libri decem. Edited and translated by Rudolf Büchner. 2 vols. Augewählte Quellen zur deutchen Geschichte des Mittelalters. Freiherr vom Stein-Gedächtnisausgabe 2 and 3. Darmstadt, 1967.

Gregory of Tours: Life of the Fathers. Translated by Edward James. TTH 1. Liverpool, 1985.

The Miracles of the Bishop St. Martin. Translated by Raymond Van Dam. In Raymond Van Dam, *Saints and Their Miracles in Late Antique Gaul,* 199–303. Princeton, N.J., 1993.

The Suffering and Miracles of the Martyr St. Julian. Translated by Raymond Van Dam. In Raymond Van Dam, *Saints and Their Miracles in Late Antique Gaul,* 162–95. Princeton, N.J., 1993.

Primary Sources

Aetherius Lugdunensis. *Vita sancti Nicetii.* Edited by Bruno Krusch. MGH SSrM 3: 518–24. Hanover, 1896.

Ambrose of Milan. *Epistolae.* Edited by Otto Faller. CSEL 82.1. Vienna, 1968.

——. *Epistolae.* Edited by Otto Faller and Michaela Zelzer. CSEL 82.2. Vienna, 1990.

——. *Epistolae.* Edited by Michaela Zelzer. CSEL 82.3. Vienna, 1982.

——. *Hexaemeron.* Edited by Carl Schenkl. CSEL 32.1. Vienna, 1897.

The Apocrypha. Revised Standard Version of the Old Testament. New York, 1957.

Augustine. *Confessiones,* pt. 1. Edited and translated by William Watts. LCL 26. Cambridge, Mass., 1912. Reprint 1989.

——. *De civitate Dei.* Edited by Bernhard Dombart and Alfons Kalb. CCSL 47–48. Turnhout, 1955.

——. *Sermones. PL* 38.

Aulus Gellius. *Noctes Atticae* [*The Attic Nights*]. Edited and translated by John C. Rolfe. LCL 195, 200, 212. Cambridge, Mass., 1967–1970.

Avitus of Vienne. *Letters and Selected Prose.* Translated by Danuta Shanzer and Ian N. Wood. TTH 38. Liverpool, 2002.

Baudonivia. *Vita sanctae Radegundis.* Edited by Bruno Krusch. MGH AA 4.2: 377–95. Berlin, 1885.

The Holy Bible. Revised Standard Version. New York, 1952.

Biblia sacra iuxta Vulgata versionem. Deutsche Bibelgesellschaft. Stuttgart, 1983.

Cassian, John. *Institutiones.* Edited and translated by Jean-Claude Guy. SC 109. Paris, 1965.

Constance of Lyon. *Vie de Saint Germain d'Auxerre [Vita sancti Germani Autissiodorensis]*. Edited and translated by René Borius. Paris, 1965.

Eucherius of Lyon. *Formulae spiritalis intellegentiae.* Edited by Carmela Mandolfo. CCSL 66. Turnhout, 2004.

Eusebius of Caesarea. *The Ecclesiastical History [Historia ecclesiastica]*. Edited and translated by Kirsopp Lake and John E. L. Oulton. LCL 153 and 265. Cambridge, Mass. 1957–1959.

Fortunatus, Venantius Honorius Clementianus. *Carmina.* Edited and translated by Marc Reydellet. *Venance Fortunat, Oeuvres.* 2 vols. Collection des Universités de France. Paris, 1994–1998.

———. *Vita sancti Germani.* Edited by Bruno Krusch. MGH AA 4.2: 11–27. Berlin, 1885.

———. *Vita sancti Martini.* Edited and translated by Solange Quesnel. *Venance Fortunat, Oeuvres,* vol. 4. Collection des Universités de France. Paris, 1996.

Ignatius of Antioch. *Lettres. Martyre de Polycarpe,* Edited by Pierre Thomas Camelot. SC 10. Paris, 1951.

Lactantius, Lucius Caelius Firmianus. *De mortibus persecutorum.* Edited and translated by J. L. Creed. Oxford Early Christian Texts. Oxford, 1984.

Miracula sancti Stephani. Edited by J. Meyers et al. In *Les Miracles de saint Étienne: recherches sur le recueil pseudo-Augustinien (BHL 7860–7861). Études du Groupe de Recherches sur l'Afrique Antique,* edited by J. Meyers, 266–368. Hagiologia 5. Turnhout, 2006.

Orosius, Paulus. *Historiae adversus paganos [Histoires Contre les Paiens]*. Edited and translated by Marie-Pierre Arnaud-Lindet. Collection des Universités de France, vols. 296–97. Paris, 1990–1991.

Passio sancti Iuliani martyris. Edited by Bruno Krusch. MGH SSrM 3: 879–81. Hanover, 1896.

Plinius Secundus, Gaius. *Natural History.* Edited and translated by Harris Rackham et al. LCL 330, 352–53, 370–71, 392–93, 418–19. Cambridge, Mass., 1967–1971.

Prudentius, Aurelius [Clemens]. *Works.* Edited and translated by H. J. Thomson. LCL 387, 398. Cambridge, Mass., 1949–1953.

Rufinus, Tyrannius. *Historia monachorum in Aegypto sive de vita sanctorum patrum.* Edited by Eva Schulz-Flügel. Patristische Texte und Studien 34. Berlin, 1990.

Sidonius, Gaius Sollius Apollinaris. *Poems and Letters.* Edited and translated by William Blair Anderson. LCL 296, 420. Cambridge, Mass., 1963–1965.

Sulpicius Severus. *Dialogi* [*Gallus. Dialogues sur les "vertus" de saint Martin*]. Edited by Jacques Fontaine, with Nicole Dupré. SC 510. Paris, 2006.

———. *Vita sancti Martini* and *Epistolae* [*Vie de saint Martin*]. Edited by Jacques Fontaine. SC 133. Paris, 1967.

Virgil. *Aeneid.* Translated by Henry Rushton Fairclough. LCL 63–64. Cambridge, Mass., 1986.

Vita patrum Iurensium [*Vie des Pères du Jura*]. Edited and translated by François Martine. SC 142. Paris, 1968.

Vita sancti Caesarii episcopi Arelatensis [*Vie de Césaire d'Arles*]. Edited by G. Morin, revised and translated by Marie-José Delage, with Marc Heijmans. SC 536. Paris, 2010.

Zeumer, Karl, ed. *Formulae Merowingici et Karolini aevi.* Monumenta Germaniae Historica, Legum sectio 5.1. Hanover, (1886) 1963.

Secondary Sources

Achterberg, Jeanne. *Imagery in Healing. Shamanism and Modern Medicine.* Boston, 1985.

Blaise, Albert. *Dictionnaire latin-français des auteurs chrétiens.* Turnhout, 1954.

———. *Lexicon Latinitatis Medii Aevi.* Corpus Christianorum Series Latina, Continuatio Mediaevalis (outside series). Turnhout, 1975 .

Bonnet, Max. *Le Latin de Grégoire de Tours.* Paris, 1890. Reprint, Hildesheim, 1968.

Brown, Peter R. L. *The Body and Society: Men, Women and Sexual Renunciation in Early Christianity.* New York, 1988.

———. *The Cult of the Saints. Its Rise and Function in Latin Christianity.* Haskell Lectures on History of Religions, n.s. 2. Chicago, 1981.

———. "Relics and Social Status in the age of Gregory of Tours." In Brown, *Society and the Holy in Late Antiquity,* 222–50. Berkeley, Calif., 1982.

Du Cange, Charles. *Glossarium mediae et infimae Latinitatis.* Paris, 1678.

Gams, Pius Bonifatius. *Series episcoporum ecclesiae catholicae.* Regensburg, 1873–1886.

Heinzelmann, Martin. *Bischofsherrschaft in Gallien.* Beihefte der Francia 5. Zürich, 1976.

——. "Gallische Prosopographie, 260–527." *Francia* 10 (1982): 531–718.

——. *Gregor von Tours (538–594), Zehn Bücher Geschichte. Historiographie und Gesellschaftskonzept im 6. Jahrhundert.* Darmstadt, 1994.

James, Edward. "'*Beati pacifici*': Bishops and the Law in Sixth-Century Gaul." In *Disputes and Settlements: Law and Human Relations in the West,* edited by John A. Bossy, 25–46. Cambridge, 1983.

Klingshirn, William E. *Caesarius of Arles. The Making of a Christian Community in Late Antique Gaul.* Cambridge Studies in Medieval Life and Thought. Cambridge, 1994.

Le Blant, Edmond. *Inscriptions chrétiennes de la Gaule antérieures au VIII*[e] *siècle.* 2 vols. Paris, 1856–1865.

McLynn, Neil. *Ambrose of Milan. Church and Court in a Christian Capital.* The Transformation of the Classical Heritage 22. Berkeley, Calif., 1994.

Miles, Margaret. "Vision: The Eye of the Body and the Eye of the Mind in Saint Augustine's *De trinitate* and *Confessiones.*" *Journal of Religion* 63 (1983): 125–42.

Moreau, Jean. *Dictionnaire de géographie historique de la Gaule et de la France.* Paris, 1972.

Nie, Giselle de. "Gregory of Tours' Smile." In De Nie, *Word, Image and Experience. Dynamics of Miracle and Self-Perception in Sixth-Century Gaul,* VIII, 68–95. Variorum Collected Studies Series 771. Aldershot, 2003.

——. "The Language in Miracle—the Miracle in Language: Words and the Word according to Gregory of Tours." In De Nie, *Word, Image and Experience. Dynamics of Miracle and Self-Perception in Sixth-Century Gaul,* XVII, 1–29. Variorum Collected Studies Series 771. Aldershot, 2003.

——. *Poetics of Wonder. Testimonies of the New Christian Miracles in the Late Antique Latin World.* Studies in the Early Middle Ages 31. Turnhout, 2012.

——. "'The "Power" of What Is Said in the Book': Word, Script and Sign in Gregory of Tours." In De Nie, *Word, Image and Experience. Dynamics of Miracle and Self-Perception in Sixth-Century Gaul,* XV, 1–27. Variorum Collected Studies Series 771. Aldershot, 2003.

——. *Views from a Many-Windowed Tower. Studies of Imagination in the Works of Gregory of Tours.* Studies in Classical Antiquity 7. Amsterdam, 1987.

Pépin, Jean. *La tradition de l'allégorie de Philon d'Alexandrie à Dante.* Paris, 1988.

Pietri, Luce. *La Ville de Tours du IVe au VIe siècle: naissance d'une cité chrétienne.* Collection de l'École Française de Rome 69. Rome, 1983.

Prinz, Friedrich. *Frühes Mönchtum im Frankenreich.* Munich, 1988.

Rousselle, Aline. "Du sanctuaire au thaumaturge: la guérison en Gaule au IVe siècle." *Annales* 31 (1976): 1085–1107.

Selle-Hosbach, Karin. *Prosopographie merowingischer Amtsträger in der Zeit von 511 bis 613.* Bonn, 1974.

Shanzer, Danuta R. "Gregory of Tours and Poetry: Prose into Verse and Verse into Prose." *Proceedings of the British Academy* 129 (2005): 303–19.

——. "So Many Saints, So Little Time . . . the *Libri Miraculorum* of Gregory of Tours." *Journal of Medieval Latin* 13 (2003): 19–60.

Stancliffe, Clare. *St. Martin and His Hagiographer: History and Miracle in Sulpicius Severus.* Oxford, 1983.

Van Dam, Raymond. "Images of Saint Martin in Late Roman and Early Merovingian Gaul." *Viator* 19 (1988): 1–27.

——. *Saints and Their Miracles in Late Antique Gaul.* Princeton, 1993.

Vieillard-Troiekouroff, May. *Les Monuments religieux de la Gaule d'après les oeuvres de Grégoire de Tours.* Paris, 1976.

Weidemann, Margarete. *Kulturgeschichte der Merowingerzeit nach den Werken Gregors von Tours.* Römisch-Germanisches Zentralmuseum Monographien 3.1–3.2. Mainz, 1982.

Wood, Ian N. *Gregory of Tours.* Headstart History Papers. Bangor, Gwynedd, 1994.

Zelzer, K. "Zur Frage des Autors der Miracula B. Andreae Apostoli und zur Sprache des Gregor von Tours." *Grazer Beiträge* 6 (1977): 217–41.

General Index

Index of Illnesses

An asterisk (*) indicates that an affliction is divine punishment for disrespect of God or a saint; a dagger (†) indicates that an affliction is explicitly said to be caused by a demonic or diabolic incursion.